Painting the Web

D1522869

Other resources from O'Reilly

Related titles
Adding Ajax

CSS: The Definitive Guide

Head First HTML with CSS
  & XHTML™

JavaScript: The Good Parts

Photoshop Elements 6:
  The Missing Manual

SVG Essentials

oreilly.com
oreilly.com is more than a complete catalog of O'Reilly books. You'll also find links to news, events, articles, weblogs, sample chapters, and code examples.

oreillynet.com is the essential portal for developers interested in open and emerging technologies, including new platforms, programming languages, and operating systems.

Conferences
O'Reilly brings diverse innovators together to nurture the ideas that spark revolutionary industries. We specialize in documenting the latest tools and systems, translating the innovator's knowledge into useful skills for those in the trenches. Visit *conferences.oreilly.com* for our upcoming events.

Safari Bookshelf (*safari.oreilly.com*) is the premier online reference library for programmers and IT professionals. Conduct searches across more than 1,000 books. Subscribers can zero in on answers to time-critical questions in a matter of seconds. Read the books on your Bookshelf from cover to cover or simply flip to the page you need. Try it today for free.

Painting the Web

Shelley Powers

O'REILLY®

Beijing · Cambridge · Farnham · Köln · Paris · Sebastopol · Taipei · Tokyo

Painting the Web
by Shelley Powers

Copyright © 2008 Shelley Powers. All rights reserved.
Printed in Canada.

Published by O'Reilly Media, Inc., 1005 Gravenstein Highway North, Sebastopol, CA 95472.

O'Reilly books may be purchased for educational, business, or sales promotional use. Online editions are also available for most titles (*safari.oreilly.com*). For more information, contact our corporate/institutional sales department: (800) 998-9938 or *corporate@oreilly.com*.

Editor: Simon St.Laurent

Production Editor: Rachel Monaghan

Copyeditor: Genevieve d'Entremont

Proofreader: Rachel Monaghan

Indexer: Lucie Haskins

Cover Designer: Karen Montgomery

Interior Designer: Ron Bilodeau

Illustrator: Jessamyn Read

Printing History:

April 2008:   First Edition.

Nutshell Handbook, the Nutshell Handbook logo, and the O'Reilly logo are registered trademarks of O'Reilly Media, Inc. *Painting the Web*, the cover image, and related trade dress are trademarks of O'Reilly Media, Inc.

Many of the designations used by manufacturers and sellers to distinguish their products are claimed as trademarks. Where those designations appear in this book, and O'Reilly Media, Inc. was aware of a trademark claim, the designations have been printed in caps or initial caps.

While every precaution has been taken in the preparation of this book, the publisher and author assume no responsibility for errors or omissions, or for damages resulting from the use of the information contained herein.

 This book uses RepKover™, a durable and flexible lay-flat binding.

ISBN: 978-0-596-51509-6

[F]

Table of Contents

Preface

Ask 20 different people what the term "web graphics" means to them and you'll get 20 different answers: images, photos, illustrations, raster graphics, bitmaps, SVG, Photoshop, EXIF, CSS, web design, JPEG, Ajax, GIMP, GIF, developing with images, animations, buttons, icons—they all fall under this rather all-encompassing term.

When I think of web graphics, the one word that comes to me is "fun." From the very first time I programmed the layout of a house using FORTRAN, Photoshopped a photo, accessed metadata from an image, followed steps to create a "shiny" button, animated a display, created a CSS design—no matter how useful they are, these uses of graphics have been, and should be, fun. Contrary to expectations, one doesn't have to be a professional graphics artist or designer to have fun with web pages. I don't consider myself to be especially artistic, and I'm definitely not a designer by trade. However, I've enjoyed working with web graphics for years. Outside of free drawing, or originating graphical concepts or designs, most effects can be re-created just by following given steps or using well-designed and documented tools and technologies.

You don't have to spend thousands, either. Tools range from free to hundreds of dollars, with most of us able to get by with those tools toward the free end of the spectrum. Even those tools that have a price tag have trials, so you can give the tool a run before deciding to buy.

Regardless of your artistic ability, the state of your pocketbook, or your experience, one thing that you do need before working with web graphics is an interest in trying new things. You also need to be willing to dip your toes into various web technologies, because many web-based graphics are based on technologies such as CSS, JavaScript, or server-side functionalities such as ImageMagick or PHP.

I don't think it's possible to write a web graphics book that covers everything "but the kitchen sink," but I tried. Included are overviews of the specs and the concepts, such as JPEGs and lossy compression; how to ensure your photos look great online; how to create page objects, such as a shiny Web 2.0 button or reflections; PHP applications that create slideshows or generate images; camera to web page photo workflows; interesting CSS design effects; and fades and other effects created with JavaScript.

Many of the examples don't require any programming experience, but several do require some experience working with PHP or JavaScript. I've tried to keep the programming simple, easy to follow, and clean to read. Some exposure to both languages is needed, but you don't have to be an expert.

Several of the examples also use XML and CSS, but again, such use is kept as simple as possible. You don't have to be expert or pro, either at graphics or the Web, to work with any of the book examples.

How to Use This Book

The chapters in this book can be read in any order, but there is a method to the madness underlying its organization. First, the book moves from working with static graphics, using tools such as Photoshop and GIMP, to using programming languages (PHP and JavaScript) to generate or modify graphics. To complement this organization, the use of web-specific technology increases as you progress through the book.

Speaking of web technologies, there are several covered in this book. Tools, too. This is not the type of book that you'll want to gulp down in a couple of sittings. Instead, it is a book you should sip in small installments, reading through some chapter sections, trying out the examples, trying out the tools on your own, before moving on to a new topic.

Several applications are covered, but there are probably thousands of tools and utilities focused on web graphics, so what's covered here is nothing more than a sample. Several factors governed my choices of the technologies used in the book: the tool/utility/technology is significant or representative in the field, has unique or interesting properties, is relatively uncomplicated to install, and, most importantly, does not cost anything to use—at least, not while you're trying out the examples in this book.

All applications discussed in this book are either free to download or, if it's a commercial or shareware product, come with at least a 30-day free trial.

How This Book Is Organized

As I've mentioned, you can read the chapters in any order, though I would recommend reading Chapter 7 before progressing into the later sections of the book. Starting from the beginning, though....

Chapter 1, *You Must Have Fun*
> Includes an introduction to the book, as well as an overview of how the book defines "web graphics." Also included is the Web Graphics Hall of Shame, where former "luminaries" such as spacer GIFs and BLINK are covered.

Chapter 2, *Imagine*
> Provides an overview of the initial image types of GIF, JPEG, and PNG, including discussion on lossy versus lossless compression, color management, and optimization. Also included are issues of copyright, how to prevent hotlinking of images, and various online storage techniques.
>
> Adobe Photoshop, GIMP, and ImageMagick also are discussed in this chapter. Any of these tools could be used with the examples, but none of the tools are necessary.

Chapter 3, *Photographs: From Camera to Web Page*
> Covers the photo workflow. It includes a review of several photo editors, workflow tools, and RAW photo utilities, plus edits that can improve a photo specifically for web publication.
>
> Tools used in this chapter are:
>
> - UFRaw
> - Adobe Camera Raw*
> - Adobe DNG Converter
> - Adobe Photoshop CS3*
> - Adobe Photoshop Elements*
> - GIMP
> - NET.Paint
> - Paint Shop Pro*
> - Adobe Lightroom*
> - Apple's Aperture*
> - Fauxto
> - Picnik
>
> (Asterisks indicate software with a price tag.)

Chapter 4, *The Web As Frame*

Continues the work of taking a photograph from camera to the Web by examining the different ways a photo can be displayed online. The approaches explored include thumbnails embedded in the page, slideshows, and gallery software. This chapter also explores approaches to better presenting photos, from background colors to presentation effects.

Tools used in this chapter are:

- Gallery (online photo album software)
- Lightbox 2.0 (embedded photo expansion software)*
- Aperture* and Lightroom*
- Adobe Photoshop CS3*
- Postcard Viewer*
- Photoshop Elements for Window*
- The Java-based Gallery Constructor

Chapter 5, *Pop Graphics*

Focuses on the non-photographic raster images, including icons, logos, shiny buttons, and reflections. Some of the more popular Web 2.0 effects—reflection, shiny buttons, inlays, and shadows—are created using step-by-step tutorials. In addition, this chapter covers screenshot tools for posting screenshots online.

Tools used are:

- Adobe Photoshop*
- GIMP
- Skitch
- SnagIt*

Chapter 6, *Vector This: Early Days and Markup*

Introduces the concept of vector graphics and explores some earlier and current vector formats, including VRML and VML. This chapter then moves into a basic introduction to the Scalar Vector Graphic (SVG) format, including how to use SVG in a page, and some of the vector graphics editors.

Tools used are:

- Inkscape
- Sketsa (non-timed, fully functional demo)
- GIMP

Chapter 7, *SVG Bootcamp*

Provides a tutorial on working with SVG, including an overview and examples of all the major components. This chapter also covers the different ways that SVG can be incorporated into web pages, including how to work with embedded SVG. The basic shapes are covered, as are paths and curves. In addition, the use of gradients and text is included. In order to focus on the technology, I use only text editors and Inkscape to create the examples.

Chapter 8, *CSS Über Zone*

Focuses on tips and tricks related to CSS, rather than providing a general introduction. Included are instructions on how to reset global whitespace, how to better control your layout, and how to work with multiple classes. The CSS tool CSSEditor is explored in this chapter, as well as CSS validators and browser extensions, which are all freely available.

Chapter 9, *Design for the Non-Designer*

Covers some of the basics of design, including accessibility, validity, mobile-readiness, and especially readability. The use of color is explored, including its role in setting mood and enhancing the visual experience. Several web sites are visited, to explore what works—and what doesn't—with each.

Chapter 10, *Dynamic Web Page Graphics*

Gets into interactive effects created using the objects described previously in this book. This includes some of the more popular Ajax visual effects, such as Accordions and fades. This chapter doesn't use any specialized tools or editors.

Chapter 11, *Canvassing*

Covers the canvas object, as it's used with Safari and defined in HTML5. This chapter provides an overview of canvas, including an introduction to canvas objects and freeform paths, as well as the ability to work with images in canvas. Again, only a text editor is used for the examples.

Chapter 12, *Dynamic SVG and canvas*

Provides a more in-depth look at the dynamic capabilities of both SVG and canvas, including adding interaction with a script and creating dynamic effects. Also included is coverage of the SVG animation elements, as well as canvas bitmap manipulations.

Chapter 13, *Image Magic: Programming and Power Tools*

Covers various image development and generation applications that are accessible either at the command line, through applications, or via development with PHP and/or JavaScript. This chapter makes heavy use of ImageMagick and the operating system's built-in image libraries. The examples are created using relatively simple PHP and JavaScript, and require access to an ImageMagick installation and access to the command line. This chapter also provides examples of how to generate images.

Chapter 14, *The Geo Zone*

Covers many of the new geographical applications, including Google Maps and Yahoo! Maps. This chapter includes both non-programming and programming examples, and covers various geo-specific markups, as well as creating applications in PHP and JavaScript that are specific to the geoweb.

Chapter 15, *Like Peanut Butter and Jelly: Data and Graphics*

Focuses on visual effects related to traditional web applications, such as forms and data displays in tables or graphics. This chapter also looks at working with metadata, including metadata visualizations—demonstrated in SVG and the canvas element, and even generated using PHP and graphics libraries. No specialized tool is needed, but the chapter examples make use of several freely available PHP and JavaScript libraries and require some experience working with both programming languages.

Conventions Used in This Book

The following typographical conventions are used in this book:

Italic

Indicates new terms, URLs, filenames, and file extensions.

Constant width

Indicates computer coding in a broad sense. This includes commands, elements, options, variables, attributes, keys, requests, functions, methods, types, classes, modules, properties, parameters, values, objects, events, event handlers, XML and XHTML tags, macros, and keywords.

Constant width bold

Indicates commands or other text that should be typed literally by the user.

Constant width italics

Indicates text that should be replaced with user-supplied values or by values determined by context.

This icon signifies a tip, suggestion, or general note.

This icon indicates a warning or caution.

Using Code Examples

This book is here to help you get your job done. In general, you may use the code in this book in your programs and documentation. You do not need to contact us for permission unless you're reproducing a significant portion of the code. For example, writing a program that uses several chunks of code from this book does not require permission. Selling or distributing a CD-ROM of examples from O'Reilly books does require permission. Answering a question by citing this book and quoting example code does not require permission. Incorporating a significant amount of example code from this book into your product's documentation does require permission.

We appreciate, but do not require, attribution. An attribution usually includes the title, author, publisher, and ISBN. For example: "*Painting the Web* by Shelley Powers. Copyright 2008 Shelley Powers, 978-0-596-51509-6."

If you feel your use of code examples falls outside fair use or the permission given here, feel free to contact us at *permissions@oreilly.com*.

How to Contact Us

Please address comments and questions concerning this book to the publisher:

> O'Reilly Media, Inc.
> 1005 Gravenstein Highway North
> Sebastopol, CA 95472
> 800-998-9938 (in the United States or Canada)
> 707-829-0515 (international or local)
> 707-829-0104 (fax)

We have a web page for this book, where we list errata, examples, and any additional information. You can access this page at:

> *http://www.oreilly.com/catalog/9780596515096/*

To comment or ask technical questions about this book, send email to:

> *bookquestions@oreilly.com*

For more information about our books, conferences, Resource Centers, and the O'Reilly Network, see our web site at:

> *http://www.oreilly.com/*

Safari® Books Online

 When you see a Safari® Books Online icon on the cover of your favorite technology book, that means the book is available online through the O'Reilly Network Safari Bookshelf.

Safari offers a solution that's better than e-books. It's a virtual library that lets you easily search thousands of top tech books, cut and paste code samples, download chapters, and find quick answers when you need the most accurate, current information. Try it for free at *http://safari.oreilly.com*.

Acknowledgments

I want to thank the team that worked with me on creating this book, including my long-time editor, Simon St.Laurent, and my tech reviewers, Loren Webster, Elaine Nelson, and Chuq Von Rospach. In addition, I'd like to thank the production team: Ron Bilodeau, designer; Genevieve d'Entremont, copyeditor; Lucie Haskins, indexer; Rachel Monaghan, production editor; Karen Montgomery, cover designer; and Jessamyn Read, illustrator.

I'd also like to thank the developers and companies that provided the tools and technologies used in the book. I'd especially like to send a shout out to the creators of open and freely available tools—such as ImageMagick, GIMP, and others mentioned in these chapters—for all their hard work. Thanks to the generosity of these kind people, the world of web graphics is available to everyone.

CHAPTER 1

You Must Have Fun

Do you remember your very first web page? The first one you ever saw? I remember the first time I saw a web page. I'm not sure if such a memory is unusual, or if many people remember their first glance at what was to become ubiquitous in a very short time.

The time was late 1993 or early 1994. I was working at Intel as a contract software developer when one of the other developers asked me if I'd seen this application called Mosaic. I wasn't among the first to see this new type of application, but at that time the Web was still in its most primitive form. The first web page I saw had a white background, a larger, bolder header, and text formatted into several paragraphs. It wasn't anything special, and nothing to excite interest. However, in the page was a thing called a *hypertext link*, an underlined piece of text that, when clicked, opened another page—one on a completely different computer, connected to the first only by a domain-driven location.

The second site, like the first, was also incredibly simple. It featured the same black text on a white page, and the only typographical variation was the larger font for the titles. It was completely empty of any graphics. No CSS; no images or Flash; not even a `FONT` or `BLINK`. However, the two pages did demonstrate all that was critical about the Web: both pages were available to anyone with an Internet connection, each was at a specific location that could be called up again, and the pages were served through a coordination between server and client that was both unprecedented and mesmerizing.

What an odd way to begin a book about graphics: describing plain web pages completely devoid of any graphics. There is a purpose behind my madness. By describing this earliest glimpse of the Web, I hope to make an important point—that web graphics are not an essential component of the web experience. We can strip a page down to the most minimal markup without any use of Cascading Style Sheets (CSS), images, Scalar Vector Graphics (SVG), or Flash, and the page continues to be Weblike and useful.

Graphics are not necessary to the web experience. They can, however, add immeasurably to the richness of the Web, making the difference between a site that's lively, compelling, and exciting, and one that's merely functional. By looking at web graphics less as an essential component of the Web and more as an exhilarating companion and accessory, we can begin to free ourselves from the restrictions on, and requirements for, web graphics that have sprung up over the years, and to push against the "musts" that have constrained their use. Musts such as the following, for example:

- Web animation is good. On the other hand, web animation is bad. Same for Flash, Ajax, scripted effects, SVG, the canvas object, and so on.
- The creation and use of web graphics should be left to the professionals. One must have years of training and be hugely dedicated to work with web graphics.
- Sophisticated graphics require expensive software and equipment to produce.
- Web graphics are inaccessible bandwidth pigs that eat mobile devices for lunch.
- Web graphics are serious business because, as everyone knows, working with web graphics is *hard*.

So many musts, so little time.

I'm reminded of one of my favorite scenes from the Kevin Costner movie *Robin Hood*. In the movie, a Moor named Azeem (played by Morgan Freeman) is sitting at the edge of a village celebration, light shining on his dark skin. A cute little village girl approaches him shyly and asks, "Did God paint you?" Azeem responds in surprise with, "Did God paint me?" He then laughs gently and replies, "For certain." "Why?" she asks. "Because Allah loves wondrous variety."

All the various forms of web graphics—from CSS to images, Flash to SVG—can be many things, including useful, functional, and professional. Leaving aside all these practical considerations, though, I like to think that what graphics add to the Web is a wondrous variety. To support such a view, one can't be held down by all the musts; the only *real* "must" with web graphics is that they don't interfere with the functionality of the page. Once that's assured, anything goes.

In the rest of this chapter—the rest of this book, in fact—we'll look at the wondrous variety of web graphics. In the process, we'll also show we can bust every one of rules just described, and have a blast doing so.

What Was Good Enough for Grandpappy…

A functional world might be efficient, but it's not terribly interesting. It would be like living on a diet of bananas, nut and seed granola bars, and vitamin water—it might keep you alive, but it wouldn't be fun in the long run. In the end, when functionality is pushed up against individuality and choice, individuality triumphs. Black cars were good enough for Ford, but not the rest of us. Black and white TV was useful, but we wanted *In Living Color*. The whole premise behind the iPhone is that one can never have too many color buttons to touch. The push for variety has been the forerunner for the overall evolution of any invention in the past, and the Web is no exception.

If all web pages were simple text, we wouldn't need the enhancements we've achieved in serving up web applications. We added graphics, though, which pushed the color requirements, as well as the sizes of pages. Our monitors improved, both in size and number of colors supported.

Then we thought, how nice it would be to be able to add interaction and animation to pages. We created animated GIFs, Flash, and JavaScript-driven effects, which attracted more people to more applications, increasing the demand on the Web yet again, leading to yet more improvements in the underlying technology.

Music. Did someone mention music? Music to download, music to share, music to create and publish online, and music to sell. In just a few short years, the iTunes, eMusics, and Amazons have redefined not only how we use the Web, but how we find, purchase, and listen to music.

Of course, now we're faced with the ultimate media: video, including complete movies being streamed from sites. Let's see, tonight I think I'll watch *Core* through Netflix. Or perhaps I'll watch *Max Headroom* through Joost.

Pop! There went the Web! None of this is essential to the Web, but having access to such things has become essential to us. Some would say it was the economy of the Web that pushed improvements in web services. I put such improvements firmly on the graphical goodies.

Which of the items mentioned, though, are web graphics, the topic of this book? Most people think of image files with extensions of JPEG, GIF, or PNG when they hear the term "web graphics." However, I consider anything that impacts the visualization of a web page, above and beyond the components that provide the initial structure, part of the family of web graphics. This includes:

- Image files, as we would expect
- Visual attributes associated with the page elements, and the CSS that controls them
- Embedded or integrated graphics, such as VML, VRML, SVG, and the canvas element/object
- Scripted effects, such as those made popular with DHTML and now Ajax
- Packaged, interactive animations such as those provided by Flash
- Frameworks and libraries that generate graphical effects using any of the above

The one item missing is video, and that's primarily because video examples are a little hard to embed in book pages. Perhaps by the time this is ready for the second edition, we'll have a workaround for this particular challenge, and I'll add it to the list. For now, other than video and Flash, these items form the basis of this book.

Draw Me!

Back when matchbooks proliferated about as much as smokers welcome in restaurants, many of the matchbooks would have a picture of a clown or dog or some other character with the words, "Draw Me!" across the front. The matchbooks were put out by various art schools, and aspiring artists would do just that, sending in the result to get an evaluation of their skill. Evidently, to the schools, we all have a little artist in us because few people would be dissuaded from signing up for a course.

Figure 1-1. Matchbook cover with a picture of a dog and "Draw Me!"

One of the "musts" associated with web graphics is that we "must" be artists, or we "must" be designers, or even that we "must" have a degree or specialized training. Creating web graphics does require some artistic ability, but as the early matchbook art schools discovered, there's a little artist in all of us.

While a professional graphic artist may be necessary for many effects, it's not true for all. In fact, there are many effects that can be created with only a minimum of training, a little technology, and a willingness to give something new a shot.

For instance, later in the book I'll cover SVG, a way to create graphics using an XML vocabulary. The approach seems intimidating at first. How does one create a sophisticated graphic from simple primitive elements such as the following?

```
<circle r="6" cx="24" cy="16"/>
```

Yet there are by-the-number approaches one can take to make copies of an original design and then convert part or the whole to SVG, using a tool no more complex than a text editor.

Well-known computer technologist Sam Ruby uses SVG icons for each of the entries in his weblog. They're quite nice, and this surprised me a little because I never thought of Sam as a nascent artist. He wrote a post that described how he created the icons, using nothing more complex than vi, a popular Unix text editor.

The steps he followed are:

1. Embed the pattern to be copied or converted into an SVG document.
2. Resize it, if necessary.
3. Trace the areas on the original graphic using a sequence of SVG elements, such as circles and squares.
4. Use SVG paths to outline components of the graphic that don't fit within the existing pattern of other elements, such as circles.
5. Adjust width, color, and position as desired.
6. Remove the original image.

Though Sam didn't mention how he knew where to position the figures and their sizes, they wouldn't be too difficult to estimate from trial and error: change both position and size using the text editor until your copy fits as you want. Once you've captured the pattern in SVG, remove the original image, and voilà, you have your new design.

To simplify the approach, you can print out the original image, place it under graph paper, trace over the design, and use the lines in the paper to plot the outlines of the graphic elements you want to copy, as demonstrated in Figure 1-2. Then it's just a matter of transforming graph points to SVG polyline or path points.

Though having to map from a graph to an SVG document can be a bit tedious, the approach does demonstrate that you don't have to be an *artiste* to be creative. Of course, it would be nice if we could eliminate the tedious work with a handy tool or utility, but these all cost so much. Don't they?

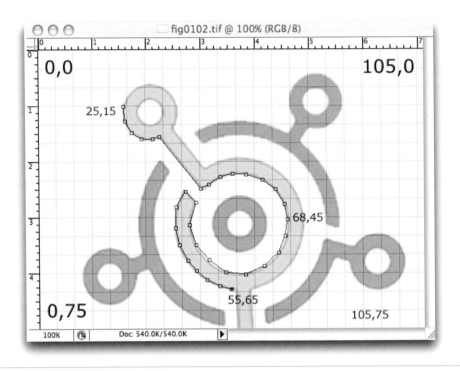

Figure 1-2. Demonstration of graph-based copying

 See Sam's original post on his SVG approach, with examples, at *http:// www.intertwingly.net/blog/2007/02/16/Recreational-SVG*.

$$$$$$$$$$$$$

If you want to do web graphics, be ready to put up the big bucks.

Or not!

Graphics work can require an initially heavy investment in more than just time. You could have to shell out thousands for a beginning setup: a high-end 12MP camera, possibly a scanner, definitely a modern computer maxed out with memory and space, expensive software, and so on.

You *could* have to shell out the bucks, and if you're a professional or have the money, all I can say is, happy spending! If you're not a professional, though, and don't necessarily have a lot of extra money, you can still do some pretty amazing things in web graphics for little or no cost. All it takes is a little ingenuity and a good understanding of what is or is not needed for working on the Web.

Pictures on the Cheap

Take that high-end camera I mentioned. If you're a serious photographer, you're going to want to invest as much as possible in a good digital camera and accompanying lens. The investment will pay off in the long run.

However, if you're mainly interested in photos for illustrative purposes, as a way of capturing events, or just for fun, most digital point-and-shoot cameras do an excellent job and provide enough resolution to print to the Web. In fact, you don't necessarily need a 12+MP camera unless you're considering publication to professional magazines, or expanding the images into larger wall art.

Consider the sizes of most images you find online. Very seldom are they over 600 pixels in width. Even the largest images are seldom beyond 800 to 1,000 pixels wide. Most of the point-and-shoot cameras I found online when writing this book can easily provide images up to 1,000 pixels wide and still provide plenty of detail, in a range of ISO speeds, and with built-in zooming lens, all for less than $250.00 US—and that's high end for a point and shoot.

Once you have your images, what kind of computer do you need? Well, the software you use tends to drive what you need for a computer, but nowadays computers are getting cheap. Even laptops are running less than $500, and one can get a desktop machine with a really nice monitor and plenty of memory and disk space for less than $700.

Again, depending on the software you use, you might not even need a more modern computer. I've used computers that were four and five years old to provide image processing and had little problem. The processes may be slower, but as long as the image file sizes are small enough (there's that point-and-shoot camera again), they're not so slow as to be painful.

Of course, if you're going to be using Adobe Photoshop, you'll need the newer machine, but you don't need Photoshop to process pictures or create graphics. The GNU Image Manipulation Program (GIMP) does an excellent job, works well with a variety of image types, and—with a little help from another free program, UFRaw—can even manage RAW files, which are image files where most or all sensor data is maintained with the image.

Another popular graphics program is Paint Shop Pro, and though not open source or free, it is most definitely affordable. In fact, there are many no-cost or low-cost software alternatives, a couple of which we'll look at (along with some of the more expensive varieties) in Chapter 3.

As for non-photographic work, the field gets even richer. In the last section I detailed a couple of approaches for incorporating other graphics into new SVG files. Instead of using a graph, you can use something like Inkscape to either trace over an image or create your own images and have the file saved as SVG.

Find more on images, image utilities, and programming with images in Chapter 2.

Programming for Pennies

How about if you're a software developer who wants to work with graphical front-end tool sets? After all, we've known for years about Microsoft's developer networks with their $2,500 price tag, and the tool sets from Adobe and other companies that cost in the hundreds, or even the thousands. Unless you're a professional using such tools for a living or a really dedicated hobbyist, such prices are beyond most of us. Even the professional can't afford most of the tools nowadays—they're priced for corporate access.

As with processing photos or creating graphical files, there are open source alternatives to most development environments. Anyone can use CSS and JavaScript to create a sophisticated application running in multiple browsers without paying a dime. Most paid tools provide either a lighter version for free or, at a minimum, a trial of the full feature version so you can play around with the technology for several days before making a decision to buy.

Between open, free, and trial versions of software and applications, we can easily explore the wondrous variety of web graphics without having a "wondrous" amount of cash.

 I can't guarantee that all applications will run on all computers, but I will guarantee that none of the examples and applications covered in this book will require you to buy anything. In some cases, you'll need to download trial software, but the trials will last long enough for you to get a feel for the software and definitely complete the exercises demonstrated in these pages.

Graphics: Taste Great, Less Filling

When considering the use of graphics on a site, people should ask themselves three questions:

1. How much bandwidth will the combined use of graphics cost?
2. What impact will the use of such graphics have on accessibility?
3. Will the graphics work on a smaller device?

The "fun" part of web graphics is that the site should be fun to everyone who accesses a web page or application—not just mouse-using, sighted people with high-end broadband connections and the latest computers and monitors.

There is no getting around the fact that many uses of graphics are not very accessible, but a surprising number are, or at least provide alternatives for those reading pages using screen readers or screen magnifiers. Something such as the `alt` attribute in an `img` element provides a way to textually describe an image. Providing a text link to go with an image's mouse-driven menu item allows access to site navigation regardless of whether a person is using a keyboard or a mouse.

As for bandwidth, image size can be optimized with little or no degradation in quality, and scripting can provide functionality to easily expand images from thumbnails. One of the simplest approaches to improving performance and speed of page downloads is to serve images from different subdomains.

Most browsers allow only two simultaneous HTTP requests to one domain. If you're serving up several images, only two can be accessed at any one time when this limitation applies. To enhance the page loading experience, especially if you're using a lot of images, you can create several virtual subdomains, such as the following:

```
img1.somedomain.com
img2.somedomain.com
img3.somedomain.com
```

Splitting the images across these subdomains will decrease the page load times without having to touch the image files themselves.

Another workaround to loading files is to embed graphics directly in the page. Newer graphical techniques, such as SVG and the `canvas` object, allow us to add sophisticated and dynamic graphics at the cost of a few bytes of bandwidth for the text to define the objects, plus a little CPU to create in the client. Newer versions of old favorites, such as CSS, provide new visual effects without any external object or files. JavaScript libraries, even the largest, can be both compressed and modularized so that only necessary objects are downloaded and bandwidth needs are minimized.

With the increasingly popular use of handheld devices, such as the new iPhone, sites have to play a virtual Gulliver, growing and shrinking gracefully to match their surroundings. At a minimum, sites can provide mobile CSS and programmatically strip images and Flash shows from a page. At a maximum, web applications using a variety of dynamic effects can provide sophisticated applications for devices with web access.

All three areas—accessibility, bandwidth, and mobile devices—can present challenges in the use of web graphics, but none are so insurmountable that the use of graphics has to be eliminated completely. There's no need to take web pages back to the version-one pages I described at the beginning of the chapter. How much of a challenge depends on how important the graphic is to the site.

It Hurts! Make It Stop!

Earlier I wrote that one of the "musts" associated with web graphics is that they're serious business because, as everyone knows, working with web graphics is hard.

Not a bit of it. As demonstrated in earlier sections, for almost every effect there are examples, samples, tutorials, and step-by-step instructions for how to create and re-create them. More than the documentation and other helpful material, the Web is rich nowadays with libraries and application programming interfaces (APIs) and frameworks in which to create sophisticated web applications that incorporate or are based on web graphics.

When creating static graphics, I've found that once you categorize an effect—"Web 2.0 reflection," say, for reflecting titles—there's invariably a tutorial, usually with figures, that leads you step by step in how to do it. Most of the tutorials are for use with Photoshop, but the steps can be mentally converted for use in other tools.

Embedded graphics such as SVG and the canvas object manage much of the tedious details of creativity, and all you have to do is pull together the pieces to create a more complex whole. Best of all, since both systems are based on open text in a web application, you can see how others have created effects and learn how to emulate such yourself. That's actually why I'm such a big believer in both SVG and the canvas object and have devoted so much space in the book to both.

Many rich web applications make use of Ajax graphical effects, such as hiding and showing page elements, moving or sizing, layering, fading, and responding to the application user's actions. The more common of these can be found already implemented as a single function call in a variety of libraries, such as Prototype, JQuery, moo tools, Dojo, Dean Edwards' base2, and so on. There are also server-side frameworks that allow one to code in Ruby, Python, or PHP, and have both the client and server-side functionality managed.

Though not covered in this book, even newer development tool sets and frameworks—such as Microsoft's Silverlight, Adobe's AIR/Flex, and the open source OpenLaszlo—can be used to create the graphics. It's rare when a person has to actually code a more complex visual effect from scratch.

Creating graphics does not have to be hard. Once you keep in mind the key element behind the use of graphics—that they aren't essential—you're then free to explore and innovate. Most importantly, you're free to have fun.

First, though, just when I've convinced you to flout conventional wisdom and break rules, we'll take a look at certain uses of web graphics in the past where convention and rules were basically blown out of the water, resulting in web sites that scare children and can physically harm small, furry animals. Seriously, these examples break that one, fundamental rule of web graphics: they must not interfere with the functionality of the web page. I call this list my Web Graphics Hall of Shame.

Web Graphics Hall of Shame

Of course, now that I've made a mockery of the rules of web graphics, I must back-track and state that there are times and places for some rules. In the world of web design and development, we're defined as much by our mistakes as our successes. In many ways, web design is perpetually living in the 1980s, so to speak, and surrounded by an excess of both the frivolous and the epitome of poor taste. We laugh at what we've done, even as we hold such in affection.

In light of this, I give you the Web Graphics Hall of Shame. Before beginning, though, note that I don't come here in disdain, but in celebration. Each of the web graphics listed in this section is a symbol of our growth, and as we all know, growth pains mark progress.

Using the technique made popular by the night-time comedian David Letterman and a generation of follow-up pundits, I give you the Hall of Shame, in descending order.

10. Under Construction

For a time the Web was littered with sites that were "under construction," many staying this way for months, or sometimes even years. Typically the page had some cute animated "Under Construction" graphic, a claim of wonderful things to come, and that was about it.

At times there would be some very decent use of graphics, so I don't want to necessarily pin the awfulness of these sites on the graphics. No, it was the overwhelming number of such sites that at one point left me with an idea that the Web was nothing more than the domicile for those with big ideas and little follow-through.

Today, you rarely see an "Under Construction" animation or image. It, like so many other uses of web graphics, was something that represented a specific era. Now most sites under development usually just have the site name, a description of what the site will be about, and perhaps links to additional information. Most sites don't even publish the URLs to search engines until they're ready for rollout, which is the better option.

9. Web Design and Graphics As Tail Wagging the Dog

This is a book on web graphics, not web design. However, it would be remiss of me not to touch on design where it pertains to the use of graphics and, in particular, to briefly discuss the sameness of use that defines entire generations of web design, and the part of graphics in such crimes against individuality.

In the beginning (and I don't mean that in a Biblical sense), pages had a sameness of look and feel, primarily because we didn't have a lot of choice. Until the first generation of Mosaic was released, we couldn't even add images to a web page.

Figure 1-3. Twofer: Under construction and wallpaper from hell

Now, even when we have considerable choice, web graphics advances and the availability of new techniques contribute heavily to whatever is the current look. Years ago, when the use of background images was new, everyone used a background image. Later, when the use of DHTML started to become more popular, script-driven drop-down menus were big. Then came Flash splash pages, rounded corners, and today's use of reflected mirror-image logos and the ubiquitous "beta" to describe services in a state ranging anywhere from bloody alpha to desiccated reliability.

Much of this sameness of design is based on excitement associated with "new toys" and our being enamored with their novelty, using whatever is new in web graphics capability as a driving force for design, rather than using the web graphics that work for our own individual tastes and needs.

It's a simpler matter, or perhaps hipper, to drive design from the latest advances in graphics, letting the bling take the blame when the design, inevitably, ages into obsolescence.

Figure 1-4. Example of web generation design, circa 2007—note the use of reflection on the name and the tacked-on "beta"; this is a design that will date quickly

Figure 1-5. Google's main search page: an example of web page design that's both classic and timeless

8. Hamster on a Color Wheel

Black text on white may be the most legible, but it soon paled on the generations of people used to color television and color photography, not to mention the flower power generation where everything was colorful even when black and white.

Luckily the W3C rescued us from a land of monochromatic pages by providing some attributes with the release of HTML 3.2. Included among these was the ability to change font color, background color, and, in a dizzying display of markup generosity, add a background image.

Suddenly, the Web was alive with color…and color…and color…and color. Where before we had sedate black and white, now we had bright and bold background images with pink, blue, red, and yellow text—sometimes all mixed up on the same page.

Not only that, but we could also change the background for individual table elements. Since most page layouts were managed with HTML tables, not only could we have an overall page color and pattern, we also could break the page into many different pieces and give each its own color or pattern, all in a blurry, headache-inducing visual extravaganza. It was like giving hamsters espresso made from the finest Colombian beans and turning them loose on color wheels, each with packets of paint attached.

Color is good, and I sometimes think we focus too much on what is tasteful and elegant, and not enough on individual expression. At the same time, though, putting text directly on a patterned background, or dark red print on black, or yellow ochre on pink, results in unreadable text. You can provide a subtle, transparent background image behind text, or use different colored fonts on different colored backgrounds, but you have to use caution. The first priority has to be readable text, not design.

(I was not immune to this colorful exuberance myself, experimenting with both color and pattern over the years. When I smile at the rodent with the wheel, I do so only in shared amusement.)

The caffeine hamster still lives, appearing from time to time. A good place to look for examples is at Tripod sites (*http://www.tripod.lycos.com/*). Just search for "rainbows" and "unicorns"—you'll find plenty of examples. Most sites returned are ones that haven't been updated for years, providing a history of web design embedded in really awful amber.

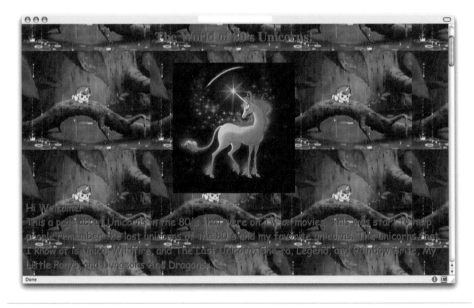

Figure 1-6. There's just something about unicorns that leads one to put colored text on a colored background, making the entire page virtually illegible

7. One Can Never Have Too Many Widgets

There are some sites that I read only reluctantly, not because of the writing or other content, but because the sites have so many widgets tied into external sites that it can take minutes for them to load all the data. I sit there, watching the status bar on my browser as one resource after another is loaded—too many from ad sites that have some serious performance problems.

Embedded access to external web sites has been a part of the web experience for years—mostly ads driven from some externally controlled process. In the last few years, though, we've seeing an explosion of externally linked material via the use of widgets.

Widgets add to the richness of the site: photos served off a Flickr widget; directions given via a Google map; a YouTube video or two; current *bon mots* from Twitter. However, widgets clamor for resources, not only in the web page, but also in your browser.

A minimal set of very useful widgets that are pertinent to the site's topic and focus can add to the uniqueness and novelty of a web site or application. If these are fronted by simple, lightweight, and attractive graphics, you'll be congratulated on your good taste.

However, indiscriminately slapping widgets in a helter-skelter display of clashing demands, solely because they're "cool," is gluttonous behavior that will, ultimately, cost you visitors.

6. The Browser Wars

It's hard to remember all the way back, but I vaguely recall that when the Netscape Navigator browser was first released, you had to license the product. Hard to imagine today, now that browsers are freely available, but Netscape's Navigator dominated the browser market until 1995. That was the year that Microsoft released its first browser, Internet Explorer.

The first version of IE wasn't anything interesting, but that all changed later, especially when both Microsoft and Netscape released version 4.0 of their products and introduced us to what became known as the Browser Wars.

Both companies released proprietary extensions into their browsers, especially with regard to the Document Object Model (DOM) they supported via JavaScript (or Jscript, for IE), providing interactive graphical effects. Both had large enough audiences that sites soon sprang up customized to one or the other. It's still not unusual to see sites developed specifically for IE, even today, when such single browser development is frowned on.

If you wisely decided to create sites that worked well with both browsers (and the others that started to appear), you then had to use cross-browser techniques and various tricks and gimmicks. JavaScript libraries that supported both browsers were full of conditional code, testing either the browser or whether an object existed, and then responding accordingly. As such, they were double or even triple what they'd be if all browsers supported the same object model.

As for CSS, the more famous IE-specific "bugs" were given names as solutions were found to work around the problems—names such as "Peekaboo bug" and solutions such as the box model hack.

The early browser wars were some of the worst times to develop web applications, but they were also important years in the growth of the Web. If companies had waited until organizations such as the World Wide Web Consortium (W3C) released specifications and then adhered directly to them, we most likely would not have the increasingly sophisticated technologies, specifications, and browsers that exist today. This includes advances in web graphics, many of which started life as a proprietary object or extension of one browser or another. Still, what a pain it was to be a web developer in the late 1990s. Tim Berners-Lee, proud papa of the Web, wrote the following in 1996, in the publication *Technology Review*:

> Anyone who slaps a "this page is best viewed with Browser X" label on a Web page appears to be yearning for the bad old days, before the Web, when you had very little chance of reading a document written on another computer, another word processor, or another network.

We don't have browser wars per se today, but we still face cross-browser disparities. Such disparities among browsers are now counterproductive to any future advances in web development, especially with regard to the use of more sophisticated JavaScript effects and the use of embedded web graphics (such as cross-browser support for SVG or the canvas object).

5. Mystery Meat Navigation

When Dynamic HTML (DHTML) was first introduced, what an incredibly exciting time in web development. With DHTML we could collapse and expand portions of the page, change colors, use transparency and clipping, and even create animated effects. Almost immediately, we started using DHTML for everything, and that included critical components of a web site, such as the navigation.

In the latter part of 1999, I was hired by a new dot-com in Boston to basically get the company's bread and butter applications back on their feet. The company had used an initial VC funding to hire a design group that burned through $1.2 million creating basically very pretty pages, none of which worked if scripting was turned off. None of the server-side functionality was created, but even if it had been, the site was completely dependent on image-based drop-down menus requiring mouse access. The irony of the situation was that one of the key testers of the system was blind.

What we did was ruthlessly rip out all script-based DHTML menus, simplified the site structure, and actually got to work building the backend application. Menus were images, true, but were given hypertext links, keyboard access, and alternate text.

It's easy to see mystery meat navigation today. If you use Firefox as a browser, install the NOSCRIPT Firefox extension, turn scripting off globally, and see which sites you can still navigate. Murmur to yourself, "Naughty, naughty" when you discover ones you can't.

 Dynamic, image-based menu navigation is also unfriendly to search engines. If you want your site to be included in search results, you need to provide a link-based, static menu system.

4. Animated GIFs

In the early days, the only active component of a web page was an animated GIF, and the world went insane with their use. There really isn't anything wrong with animated GIFs, and I use animated images such as *throbbers* (animated status indicators) myself, though sparingly.

It was the overuse of animated GIFs that became the problem. It seemed as if some sites had hundreds of these movable beasties, and not only did they slow down page access times, but also all that animation only served to distract, giving one a headache and a strong desire to flee for one's life.

 There's also another very real threat associated with any animated effect. People who suffer from photosensitive epilepsy can have seizures triggered by web page animations of a certain type. Any animation with a repeating pattern that can cause the monitor to flicker at a frequency between 2 Hz and 55 Hz (as noted in the U.S. government's Section 508 guidelines at *http://www.section508.gov/index.cfm?FuseAction=Content&ID=12#Web*) can cause such a seizure and should be located in a secondary page with a note warning the person entering such a page that the content is animated.

Animation is good as long as the web page reader controls the animation. We need the ability to turn on that movie, presentation, and so on. We need control, and animated GIFs deny us this control.

Ajax effects, such as the yellow fade that signals a change, are different. They're over quickly, and they serve a useful purpose: highlighting that a change has occurred. Animated GIFs, though, just sit there and move.

Animated annoyances are still around; however, most today are Flash, and most are ads. Why some people assume that if we're annoyed enough we'll click their ad or buy their product is beyond me. I think, though, that those who create animated ads are still mentally stuck back in a time of pages full of flying butterflies, gems that sparkled, cars that moved their little tires, and little choo-choo trains that puffed little-bitty clouds of smoke.

I suggest intervention, both for the creator of such ads and for those who host them. In the meantime, to see some interesting uses of annoying animated graphics (in addition to other murderous uses of graphics, not to mention horrid use of MIDI files), return to our friend Tripod (*http://www.tripod.com*) and this time search on "butterflies" and "rainbows."

 My intent is never to embarrass people by specifically pointing out egregious examples of challenging web design. By using the searching technique, I hope to point you to the sites in question without plastering their URL or name in these pages.

3. The Splash Page

Even today, it's not unusual for the front page of a site to be a splash page, playing some animated Flash sequence that, once finished, displays an "Enter Site" message.

The concept isn't bad, but it is counter to the Web, which implies that we never take control from the users. Splash pages do this by forcing people to wait through an animation in order to get to the "meat" of a web site.

 Web sites that resize your browser window also fit under the category of "taking control away from the user." There's a difference between opening a separate help window and mucking with the user's existing window. It's a bad practice, as bad or even worse than splash pages.

A comparable method for preventing access to content by the reader is the newer ads that use DHTML to position ads directly over articles or photos, which keeps you from viewing the item until you either view the ad in its entirety or find the small "Close" button that allows you to close the ad. Again, why a company would think we'd be disposed favorably to clicking through on a link or purchasing a product based on their annoying behavior boggles the mind.

There are times when you may be using technology that requires plug-ins or some other technological dependency, such as Flash or JavaScript. I'm assuming, then, that you're also providing an alternative of the site not dependent on such. Providing an entrance page that gives you alternatives, gives your users control, and still prevents pushing people into pages using technologies they don't have enabled.

Splash pages are effective only when the creators provide a "Skip Intro" or comparable link that lets a person jump beyond the page. It's still not the best approach, but at least it doesn't use graphics to disrupt the site visitor's web experience.

Like "mystery meat" navigation, splash pages are also unfriendly to search engines.

2. Don't BLINK

I imagine you would think the use of the BLINK element or the comparable MARQUEE would rate number one on this list. There is probably no more hated element in all of HTML than BLINK, with its irritating demand for attention. Just as with animated GIFs, the users of blink seem to believe that people have to be slapped for attention when viewing a web page. Or perhaps static text can't possibly be entertaining enough.

The MARQUEE element was never quite as bad as BLINK, and never had such wide usage. It provided the same level of annoyance, though, scrolling text too fast to read and distracting you from the material you're trying to understand.

The problem with both elements is that they, again, take control away from the application users or other site visitors. They distract without adding any meaningful content or service. They're a graphical device used to add an illusion of interaction when no real interactivity is supported. They're a cheap trick.

About the only places where both elements are in use today is in sites that have been long abandoned. Unfortunately, though, we now have modern variations of both, some of which are served via Ajax.

Many online newspaper sites provide headline or video sections where items are continuously scrolled, showing the top stories. Usually the scrolling occurs too fast to click the item you most want to see. A better approach is to present the top three most compelling headlines and a link to see additional items. At a minimum, providing a link to a secondary page that lists all items gives people an option.

A popular weblogging search engine did a major redesign fairly recently, and as part of the effort added a scrolling marquee-like effect to the top part of the page that was based on the use of tags (keywords used to classify web content) and refreshed using Ajax calls. Not only was it not useful, it caused performance problems with some browsers (such as my own Firefox on the Mac).

A popular Flickr badge used in page sidebars was based on an animated effect that would quickly expand and then contract images among the thumbnails presented, creating an effect that obscured most of the photos. Recently, people have started using a more static approach, which demonstrates that most uses of such animation is based more on a developer's wanting to "play" than a true customer interest.

Again, gentle uses of animation to highlight important information in an unobtrusive manner can provide useful information, while uncontrolled animated effects do little more than annoy. Now, if only we could get this point across to all of those animated ad creators.

Now that we've seen browser wars and animated "Best viewed by" messages competing with color madness and uncontrolled page overlays, what use of graphics could possibly be so awful that it beat out all of these and BLINK as the worst use of graphics in a web page? Oddly enough, it's an element that we can't see.

1. The Spacer

Before the adoption of CSS there were two main ways to control page layout. The first was HTML tables, and the second was a one-pixel transparent GIF commonly known as the spacer GIF.

When the IMG element was added to HTML, it was given attributes such as width and height, as well as padding through vspace and hspace. Typically the vspace and hspace attributes were used when controlling placement of content within table cells or other web page elements.

If you wanted to move content down the page or over to the side, you could use a spacer GIF and provide a width and height (or vspace or hspace) to create the effect. By using this technique, you could move text blocks, indent paragraphs, position elements where you wanted them, and so on.

 There's no universal agreement on who created the idea of the spacer GIF, though David Siegel, who wrote the book *Creating Killer Web Sites* (Hayden Books), is generally thought to be the first to make such tricks publicly known. For a real blast from the past, you can read his description of it at *http://www.killersites.com/killerSites/1-design/single_pixel.html*.

I still have my spacer GIF, a file called *blank.gif*, that I used in addition to tables to create various designs on my web sites. It was a clever idea, as was the use of HTML tables, for controlling layout in such a way that the layout would adapt as the browser was resized.

However, when the spacer GIF was used, people seldom set the alt attribute to an empty string (""), which would ensure the image wasn't picked up by screen readers. It must have been awful to access a page loaded with spacer GIFs, none of which had alternative text.

The spacer GIF, HTML table, FONT tag, and attributes like bgcolor and background all shared one thing in common: they provided ways of working around the lack of consistent CSS support and enabled not only a quick growth of web pages, but the first rudimentary controls on web page layout and appearance. Unfortunately, their use reduced the urgency to create and spread adoption of standards such as CSS, and even to this day, they are used in way too many sites, as people resist learning the newer technologies (since what they have still works).

I picked the spacer GIF as representative of the family of such old and outdated techniques to control the page's visual appearance. I placed it first in this list because no other single element has had such an adverse impact on the growth of standard, cross-browser web graphics.

On with the Wondrous Variety

As I wrote earlier, the only real rule for web graphics is that they shouldn't interfere with the functionality of the web page—in other words, they shouldn't interfere with the web experience. This means that:

- The use of color and pattern shouldn't be such that the content is hard to find and read.
- Animation should be useful, not distracting or harmful.
- The web page reader should be given control of any animated or advanced graphical techniques.
- The web page reader should not be kept from the content through use of abusive graphic techniques.
- Graphics should not be used to interfere with necessary functionality at a site, such as navigation.
- The use of web graphic techniques should serve a purpose, and should not be used just to be used (note, though, that enjoyment is a viable "purpose").

Other than these frankly common-sense approaches to using web graphics, there really are no other rules. Graphics do not have to be hard or expensive, or require that we all be a combination of Picasso and Norman Rockwell. All that's really required is a curiosity, an interest, and above all, a sense of fun. If this describes you, then you're ready for the rest of the book, and the wondrous variety of web graphics.

CHAPTER 2
Imagine

Nothing replaces text when it comes to providing information, but how dull our world would be without the imagery that has been a part of publications from the beginning. The very first book ever published, the Gutenberg Bible, contains exquisite illustrations, following a tradition of such ornamentation that extended to cultures all around the world and has lasted to today's new digital medium.

The graphics files we use on the Web have become so ubiquitous that it's difficult to imagine not having them. Computer graphics, though, are relatively new. They originated at MIT when a student named Ivan Sutherland used a light pen to draw objects to a computer in 1960. The type of image he created is known as a *vector graphic*. It's called this because the image is created through vectors or paths between mathematically derived computer points, and controlled by commands issued via an application of some form. Scalable Vector Graphics (SVG), featured in several chapters throughout this book, is an example of this type of graphic.

Another type of graphic is the *bitmap*, or *raster*, graphic. Unlike the vector, raster graphics consist of a set of points or dots, each containing color and other information. The commonly occurring Graphics Interchange Format (GIF), Joint Photographic Experts Group (JPEG), and Portable Network Graphics (PNG) are all examples of this type of graphic.

Incorporating graphics into web pages came about because of one simple HTML element: the IMG element, which was added to HTML 2.0 in 1995. Only one type of image format was allowed at the time: GIF. Not long after, support for JPEG was added. JPEG was (and still is) typically used for photographs, whereas GIF is primarily used for illustrations as well as for adding animation to web pages. Surprisingly enough, even with all the many innovations for graphics introduced in the years since, most web graphics in use today are still JPEG or GIF.

As much as both JPEG and GIF are used, they are not without their own unique challenges. JPEG is known as a "lossy" compression technique, which means data can be discarded as the image file is compressed, and the image can suffer as a consequence. GIF, although it's not lossy, is limited in the number of colors, making it a poor format for photos. On the other hand, GIF supports both transparent backgrounds and animations, which JPEG does not. The JPEG format has always been non-proprietary, but the GIF format utilized a patented compression technique.

Of course, it wouldn't be the Web if people didn't look at GIF on the one hand and JPEG on the other, and say to themselves, "There has to be something better." And work on the PNG format began.

Figure 2-1. Old meets new: a PNG file of an SVG graphic of the Lancaster rose, created in InkScape, found at Wikipedia

PNG supports rich colors, like JPEG does, but also supports transparency, like GIF. Because PNG also utilizes a lossless compression, it can handle sharp transitions used in icons and illustrations, just as with GIF, but it can also handle smooth transitions in photos, like JPEG. PNG files can be small if the number of colors is limited, though file sizes increase significantly when more colors are necessary. What was most important when work on the PNG format began was that compression not be based on a patented technique, as GIF was.

Despite all these benefits, PNG use is not widespread. The primary inhibitor to its adoption is that not all browsers provide full support for PNG, especially PNG transparency. However, lack of support is becoming less of an issue as time goes by.

Of course, regardless of what type of image you use in a web page, all images face the same constraints. Images in web pages are viewed in hundreds of different types of environments, from mobile phones to the older VGA monitors, which offer differing support for colors. In addition, images, especially larger ones, take considerable bandwidth to download and take a lot of space to store. Also, aside from these purely technical concerns, images posted to the Web can be copied, modified, and used by others—sometimes with permission, sometimes without.

Luckily, there are ways to improve the file size associated with using images, most without compromising quality. If we have limited access to our own server space, there are also other hosting options for our images and other media, though these can have their own unique challenges. In addition, there are certain things we can assume about the applications accessing the images, enough to ensure they look reasonably well in most devices.

Issues of copyright, unfortunately, are not as easily solved through technical innovation. Copyright and imagery is more a matter of learning options than anything else. However, there are technical solutions for a related problem: *hotlinking*.

Before we get into the more exotic flora of web graphics—the vector-based graphics such as SVG—first it's time to stop and smell the raster roses.

Raster Graphics and RGB Color 101

Raster graphics, sometimes called *bitmaps*, consist of a set of pixels organized in a shallow array, with each pixel containing location, its own array of color bits and, if supported, transparency. The more pixels added to a space, the higher the level of resolution and the better and more detailed the picture, even at greater levels of expansion.

You can see how these individual pixels form a more complex image in Figure 2-2, which shows a butterfly photo shown at actual size, and then a zoomed-in snapshot of the butterfly's head, greatly enlarged.

Figure 2-2. The pixel nature of raster graphics

The number of bits of color supported—the *color depth*—determines the number of overall colors supported for the image. The simplest raster graphic is one that supports only two colors: black and white. Of the others, the following are most common for web graphics:

- An image that supports 8 bits per pixel can support 256 colors overall ($2^8 = 256$).
- An image that supports 16 bits supports more than 65,000 colors (2^{16}) and is known as *realcolor*.
- One that supports 24 bits (2^{24}) supports more than 16.8 million colors, is photorealistic, and is known as *truecolor*.
- A 32 bit per pixel PNG image still supports only 24-bit color, with the additional 8 bits for the alpha channel to support transparency.

There are higher color depths for some image types, but 24 bit, or *truecolor*, is the maximum that humans can perceive.

The RGB Color Model

The color bits just described are from an RGB color model, and the colors formed are combinations of the three primary colors: red, green, and blue. Since all color is really light at a specific wavelength, the higher the intensity or luminosity for each "color," the brighter the color. There are a maximum of 256 possible intensity values for each color, ranging from 0 to 255, which is 100%.

The RGB color model is an additive model, which means the higher percentage of each color present, in combination with the percentage levels of the other colors, determines the resulting color. If the levels for all three colors are at 100%, the result is white; if all are at 0, the result is black. Figure 2-3 demonstrates the RGB model's additive nature.

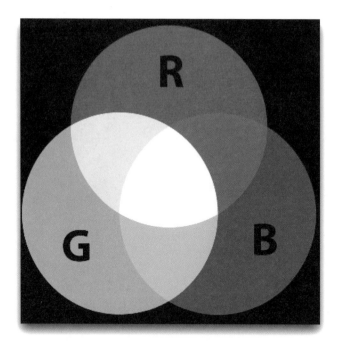

Figure 2-3. The RGB model's additive nature, via an SVG demonstration of such at Wikipedia

Additional colors are formed by combining these different color intensities: magenta is formed when blue and red are at their highest intensities (255) while green is at 0; yellow is created from red and green at 255, with blue kept at 0.

 There are other color models, including the CMYK (cyan, magenta, yellow, and key [black]) color model (used for print work), grayscale, HSV (hue, saturation, value), and so on. The only one covered in this book is RGB.

There are a couple of different ways to represent an RGB color. One is to just list the separate values, one after the other, in the red-green-blue order:

    255 127 0

Sometimes the values are included in parentheses, with the values separated by commas:

    (255,255,0)

For web page work, colors are usually specified as hexadecimal representations of the numbers. A decimal value of 255 is FF in hexadecimal. When the three values are concatenated and preceded by a pound sign, we have:

    #FFFF00

Or:

```
#ffff00
```

The hexadecimal value is typically used with web page design and Cascading Style Sheets (CSS), demonstrated later in the book. However, another approach is to pass the RGB values in a function-like syntax, such as the following (from the newer CSS3 Color Module currently under development):

```
rgb(255,255,0);
```

Or the following, which also includes alpha-transparency in the last parameter:

```
rgba(255,255,0,0);
```

Raster Graphics: A Text Example

When thinking of raster graphics, we usually think of photographs or drawings made with Paint or some other application and stored as BMPs, GIFs, JPEGs, or TIFFs (Tagged Image File Format). We also think of binary files, which display what looks like garbage when the image is opened in a plain-text editor.

There is nothing inherently binary about a raster image. We can represent a raster image in a text-based ASCII format, as long as we use a specific file structure. One text-based raster graphic format is the Pixel Portable Map (PPM), which we can create using nothing more than a text editor.

The format for a PPM file is like the following:

```
P3
# comment
350 500
255
0 0 255
...
```

The first line, P3, is a requirement when the data is given in ASCII format, and it's followed by an optional comments line. If you're specifying data in binary, you'll need to change the first line to P6.

The third line gives the width and height, which in this case is 350 × 500 pixels. The fourth line describes the maximum intensity of colors used in the image, which in this example is 255 (typical for GIF images). What follows, then, for the ASCII-formatted data, is a set of RGB values in RGB order, with each value separated by a space. In this example each color is separated by a carriage return, but they could all be on the same line.

In a PPM file, if the image is 500 pixels wide, the first 500 color definitions describe the topmost row of pixels, the second 500 color definitions the next row, and so on. Yeah, this could get a little tedious when building a PPM file manually, which is why they're usually created programmatically.

Example 2-1 builds a PPM file using PHP. The resultant file displays as four stripes, alternating white and green. The application contains an outer loop that controls the number of stripe pattern repetitions (two in this example), while the second loop controls the creation of the pixels along the horizontal axis (500 pixels in all). The final loop controls the repetition of the rows along the vertical axis (50 pixels in height for each).

Example 2-1. PHP program to create a PPM file with alternating green and white stripes

```php
<?php

// open or create PPM file
$ppmfile = fopen('colors.ppm','w') or die("can't open file");

// write out header
fwrite($ppmfile,"P3\n");
fwrite($ppmfile,"500 200\n");
fwrite($ppmfile,"255\n");

// create green and white color patterns
$green = "0 127 0";
$white = "255 255 255";

// outer loop, stripe pattern repetitions
for ($k = 0; $k < 2; $k++) {

    // secondary loop, writing out rows of pixels, 50 rows at a time
    for ($i = 0; $i < 50; $i++) {

        // inner, writing out the row of green pixels, 500 pixels wide
        for ($j = 0; $j < 500; $j++) {
            fwrite($ppmfile, "$green\n");
        }
    }

    // repeat the rows for the white now
    for ($i = 0; $i < 50; $i++) {

        // write out the white pixels horizontally
        for ($j = 0; $j < 500; $j++) {
            fwrite($ppmfile, "$white\n");
        }
    }
}

fclose($ppmfile);
?>
```

When the application is run from the command line, the *colors.ppm* file is created (or opened, erased, and rewritten if it already exists):

```
php ch02-01.php
```

The initial application and the generated PPM file are included with the examples, but you can re-create and run it yourself if you have access to PHP. If you can't run the PHP application from the command line, you'll need to have global write permissions for the directory to run through a browser.

To display the PPM file, use the following if you're using Mac OS X or Linux and you have ImageMagick installed:

```
display colors.ppm
```

You can also open it in several other drawing programs, such as Adobe Photoshop or GIMP. Figure 2-4 shows the generated PPM, opened in NeoOffice's Draw program.

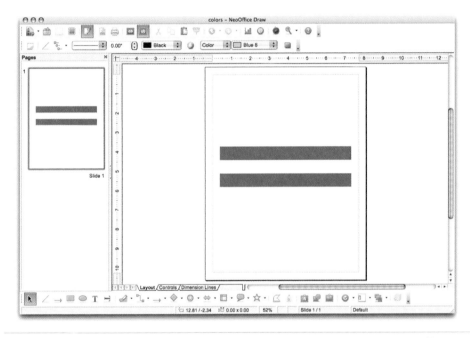

Figure 2-4. PPM file generated by the application from Example 2-1 and opened in NeoOffice

I provided this example for two reasons. First, I wanted to demonstrate the nature of a raster image, especially as it relates to a set of pixels, each with a given color. Nothing works better than to see the actual correspondence between color, pixel, and image. The second reason, as stated at the beginning of this example, is that there is some confusion about a raster graphics file being binary, while vector graphics are typically in ASCII. As you've seen, raster can just as easily be a nice text file, easy to open and edit.

 Whether a graphics file is binary or not doesn't seem important until you upload it to a site using FTP software. FTP software provides three types of uploads: binary, ASCII, and auto. The use of the latter is the default, and FTP software is smart enough know which format to use for each image.

A PPM file is more of a novelty than anything else, though. Most of the images we see on web pages are primarily GIFs, PNGs, and JPEGs, and I'll cover each type in detail next.

JPEG

Most photos online are JPEG, and this isn't likely to change anytime soon. Even with the introduction of PNG, the use of JPEG is so tightly ingrained in the human experience that it will take years before people start making the move to PNG.

The JPEG format is actually quite effective for photos. Even at moderately higher levels of compression, most photos look good in web pages, at least for relatively small photo sizes. It takes a lot of compression—and a larger image—before a photo will show degradation visible to most people. In addition, many digital cameras natively store images in JPEG format to save room on the disk. Even if a camera supports RAW format (where all image information is maintained with the image) or TIFF, chances are it will also support JPEG. Some cameras even allow the owners to specify the JPEG quality in order to control space use.

RAW or TIFF?

Speaking of cameras and capturing images as JPEG, given a choice between RAW and JPEG or TIFF and JPEG in your digital camera, I would recommend RAW or TIFF. You won't get as many pictures, but you're going to kick yourself when you get a really great shot and it's been saved on disk in a highly compressed, lossy JPEG.

The only time you might want to use JPEG is when you want to print images directly from the camera. JPEG images are both web and print ready, unlike RAW, which must be manipulated first. An alternative approach supported by several cameras (such as my own Nikon D200) is to pick both JPEG and RAW, which creates a copy of the image in both formats. Thus you'll have RAW for processing later in GIMP or Photoshop, but you'll also have JPEG for direct printing. Regardless, if your camera supports RAW, I recommend using it. I'm in good company with this recommendation. As a writer at the Nikonians web site writes (at *http://www.nikonians.org/html/resources/ guides/digital/jpeg_tiff_or_raw_3.html*), "Camera purists, large print aficionados, and weird website article writers prefer this mode above all others."

JPEG is web friendly because of the smaller file sizes that can be supported, typically without apparent impact on image quality. JPEG images may also be saved with progressive encoding, which means that when the image is first loaded, a low-quality version is displayed while the higher-quality image finishes loading and is prepped for display. This is just a nice way of ensuring the photo's space is filled quickly before the image is fully loaded.

The downside to the bandwidth friendliness of JPEGs is, as mentioned earlier, the fact that the format uses a lossy compression technique.

Lossy Compression

A lossy compression method is one that uses an algorithm derived, in part, from a basic understanding of human physiology in order to compress the size of a media file without seeming to lose quality. Using this approach, lossy compression can reduce the size of a file more than a file type that uses a lossless compression technique. From the JPEG image compression FAQ (at *http://www.faqs.org/faqs/jpeg-faq/ part1/*):

> JPEG is "lossy," meaning that the decompressed image isn't quite the same as the one you started with…. JPEG is designed to exploit known limitations of the human eye, notably the fact that small color changes are perceived less accurately than small changes in brightness. Thus, JPEG is intended for compressing images that will be looked at by humans. If you plan to machine-analyze your images, the small errors introduced by JPEG may be a problem for you, even if they are invisible to the eye.

For web work and smaller images, the errors introduced aren't a problem, but they make JPEG pretty useless for most publication purposes. For instance, the screenshots for this book are submitted for the publication process as either TIFF or PNG, but never, ever JPEG.

It isn't until an image is scaled larger that you see the degradation that comes with using a lot of compression. In Figure 2-5, two screenshots of the same image are shown, zoomed out to show detail and side by side, and each saved at different compression rates: 75% and 10%. This example demonstrates that a loss of image quality is considerable in the highly compressed image.

Figure 2-5. Differences between levels of compression in the same JPEG image

To add to the problems associated with using JPEG, a lossy compression technique is cumulative: if the image is opened, edited, and saved, the quality continues to degrade with each modification. Trying to salvage the image by saving at a higher compression rate won't do you a bit of good—the data is already lost.

The errors that affect the image quality—the boxy blurs that impact the nice, crisp edges—are known as compression *artifacts* (or artefacts). There have been attempts to reduce these, but they've focused on how to compensate for the artifacts when the image is viewed in an application, and use some form of interpolation to compensate for the quality. Regardless of the application, the overall apparent result differs little.

For most web use, a medium compression gives you a good image in a small file.

JPEG also has better color support than GIF, which leads to better image resolution with complex graphics such as photos. JPEG supports 24-bit color, which translates into support for millions of colors, as well as grayscale images. The larger number of colors means that the subtle transitions of color in photos can be reproduced realistically, without any dithering required.

 Dithering is the process where missing colors in an image are approximated using whatever colors are available. In the process, two colors from the existing color palette are placed next to each other in order to emulate a third.

Of course, just using JPEG as an image format doesn't mean that an image that looks great in your photo editor appears the same to everyone who accesses it on the Web. There are other factors at play, including how the image's colors are interpreted by each device that accesses it.

JPEG and Managed Color

With film, colors are managed by chemicals and processing. With digital photography, you, not chemistry, manage the colors.

It's rather amazing how many colors you can create when given the three primary colors in values ranging from 0 to 255 in any combination. Figure 2-6 shows a sampling of two such colors.

Or are these two different colors? Though the perception from the image is that they are two different colors, in actuality they are both the same. Both samples have an RGB value of (88,249,17): red = 88, green = 249, and blue = 17.

Where the two differ is the color profile used with each. A color profile is a table of colors that provides information about the color space. The first square in the figure has an embedded color profile of sRGB (more formally, sRGB IEC61966-2.1), which is the common profile for a PC monitor. The second uses the Adobe RGB, used primarily when the document is being prepared for printing. The differences reflect how the color space profiled interprets a color with a given RGB value of (88,249,17), and they can play havoc in how an image appears online.

Figure 2-6. Same color, two different color profiles

Let's say you've progressed beyond a direct upload from your camera to your web page. You've used an application such as Adobe's Photoshop to carefully crop, size, and prepare a photo until it looks just right. You then upload it to your web site, and when you open the image in your browser, it looks just awful. All the rich colors you loved in the original are gone, and you're left with a washed-out photo, with the color mysteriously leached out. You open it again in Photoshop, and there's the beautiful piece of work. Congratulations: you've just entered the world of *managed color*.

The color example in Figure 2-6 demonstrates that different agents handle color differently. To ensure that a photo created or modified in one color environment looks the same in another, colors are mapped between the two environments, so what is perceived as bright lime in one is perceived as the same bright lime in the other.

Color management isn't an issue when you map directly between one device and another, such as between one camera to one computer and one computer to one printer. In reality, though, there are many different kinds of cameras, as well as different scanners, monitors, and printers. More important to those reading this book, an image can be uploaded to the Web and accessed by any number of devices that run different operating systems and support different color spaces. It's infeasible to even consider mapping all of the possible configurations. What's needed, instead, is a standard set of color profiles that ensures some form of consistency.

An organization called the International Color Consortium (ICC) was formed to facilitate the creation and adoption of vendor-neutral, open color management systems. The ICC's focus is not on cases where a computer is mapped directly to a specific printer—what it calls a "closed loop" workflow. Instead, its interest is in the many devices mapped to many devices scenario, a process it terms an "open loop" workflow.

To support this, the ICC has created a set of profiles, each containing a predefined set of rules describing how color is managed. The data within these color profiles can be embedded within an image, ensuring that in a color-managed environment an image looks the same on my camera, PC, and printer. The device or application "reads" the embedded profile and adjusts the color accordingly.

When I created the two squares for the example shown in Figure 2-6, I used the same computer, a Mac OS X laptop. To me, they looked the same. The only difference is that I embedded a different color profile in each. How, then, can they end up differing so significantly?

With color management, there should be no difference. Surprise, though—most browsers don't support color management. Rather, they do, but like Henry Ford's idea of color, they support only one color profile: sRGB. When the image is opened in the browser, the embedded color profile is not used. Instead, the image is interpreted using the sRGB color profile, which can lead to significantly different perceived colors.

To demonstrate, Figure 2-7 shows a lotus flower with an embedded profile of Adobe RGB as it's displayed using Firefox 2, which doesn't support color management. Figure 2-8 is the same image displayed in Safari 3, which does support color management. Even in the pages of this book, there should be a noticeable difference between the two. In a web page, the difference would be even more apparent.

Figure 2-7. Image with embedded Adobe RGB color profile opened in Firefox 2

Figure 2-8. Image with embedded Adobe RGB color profile opened in Safari 3

At the time this book was published, only Safari 3.x and Firefox 3.x supported color profiles.

LCD for Color on the Web

Until the support for embedded color profiles is ubiquitous, or at least supported with most web browsers, you'll have to save images in such a way that they look good in most environments. In other words, find the lowest common denominator (LCD) to ensure the image looks decent, if not its absolute best, across the Web. For most images in a web environment, the LCD is more than sufficient.

Here are the steps:

1. Calibrate your monitor and make sure it displays colors accurately.
2. Set the gamma level to a value between that supported by a PC and that supported by a Mac.
3. Set your workspace for any photo editing tool to sRGB.
4. When opening an image with another embedded profile, convert to the working space (sRGB).

5. Edit the photo as you wish.

6. When saving the image, make sure you embed the sRGB color space, if this is supported.

In more detail, make sure your monitor is properly calibrated (search online for tips on doing this based on your operating system) and that you've picked a gamma level (brightness) midway between the default for PCs/Linux (2.2) and the default for the Mac (1.8). An image is always going to look a little dark for people using the default gamma on a PC and a little light for those using the default settings on a Mac, but not enough to distract from the overall appeal of the image.

If you're working with images for the Web, make sure you set the color profile for the application's working space to sRGB, which matches the color profile for most of the common monitors. If you produce for both the Web and for print, you'll need to remember to adjust your workspace color profile accordingly.

When you open an image in your photo editing tool, if the embedded color profile differs from the workspace (many cameras use Adobe's, which supports a wider gamut in the color space), discard the existing profile in favor of the workspace color profile.

When saving the image, either save without embedding a profile or save with that of the working space, the sRGB color profile. Using this approach, your images should display nicely on the Web.

> For more details on color profiles, see the ICC's web site, at the appropriately defined URL of *http://www.color.org*. Another nice tutorial with a web photo workflow can be found at *http://www.creativepro.com/story/howto/24697.html*.

GIF: Lossless and Paletted

CompuServe created the GIF format in the 1980s to provide a way of exchanging images at this early Internet service. The original version was 87a (GIF87a), and an improved version is 89a (GIF89a). If JPEG is optimized for continuous color images, GIF is optimized for what is known as "flat color" graphics, graphics that have sharp rather than continuous edges between changing colors.

GIF is an uncomplicated 8-bit format, supporting 256 colors. Additionally, to further save storage space, GIFs are based on an optimized palette, which maps each color in the palette to a specific RGB value.

> There actually is a way to support 24-bit truecolor GIFs, but such a practice is purely a hack, and with truecolor supported in JPEG and PNG, unnecessary for web graphics.

The 256 colors supported with GIFs is an optimal number of colors for using a color management technique known as *palettes*. With palettes, rather than each pixel having its own embedded RGB color, which takes 24 bits, it contains an 8-bit lookup value that is then used with a color lookup table to find the actual color. A version of PNG—8-bit PNG—also supports a palette.

The GIF format utilizes a lossless compression technique known as *LZW lossless data compression*. This type of compression works by finding a sequence of characters that form a pattern and then entering such in a table, where it's mapped to a given, shorter length code. Then, whenever the pattern repeats, the shorter code is used. As such, it works best when the same given pattern is repeated.

The simple color palette and lossless compression explains why GIF does well with solid colors rather than gradients, and with sharp, distinct edges between colors rather than gradual transitions. It is still better than JPEG for simple line drawings, illustrations, logos, and cartoon-like images.

Since the GIF format doesn't support the full range of colors that a 24-bit RGB space supports, dithering is used to compensate for those colors not represented. Although applications can do a decent job when saving an image as GIF, expanding the image's size beyond 100% can really show the dithering, as shown in Figure 2-9. Because of the limited color support, GIF is not the preferred format for photographs.

Figure 2-9. Photo saved as GIF, expanded to more clearly display the dithering used

GIF has two other capabilities that led to its early, and still continuing, popularity: animation and transparency.

GIF Animation and Throbbers

In Chapter 1, I mentioned in the Web Graphics Hall of Shame the use of spacer GIFs to control the layout of pages. Spacers are 1-pixel transparent GIFs that—when combined with the ability to add width and height attributes, as well as horizontal spacing (hspace) and vertical spacing (vspace) on an IMG element—can be used to push content to the side or down. Transparent GIFs can also be used to create logos and icons that are only partially colored, leading to effects that can work well with different background colors.

GIF is also the first image format to support animation, and it's still the only one that does. Animated GIFs were quite widespread years ago but lost favor, mostly because of the introduction of Flash, but also because the use of animated GIFs went beyond interesting to annoying rather quickly. The primary use for animated GIFs today is to provide *throbbers*, animated images that signal that some action is taking place. The throbber originated with the animated logos on earlier browsers, and has since made its way directly into the page. An animated image is still the best way to signal that some action is happening. Luckily, it's quite easy to create a throbber of your own using one of the free, online throbber generators. Figure 2-10 shows the web page for one throbber generator, ajaxload.info, as I create a throbber that's a dotted orange circle with "Load" in the center.

GIF Compression

Another aspect of the GIF format that led to its success, the compression technique, also led to work on a new format.

The LZW lossless data compression algorithm was created by Terry Welch in the early 1980s. Welch filed a patent on the technique in 1983, and the patent eventually ended up assigned to Unisys, seemingly unbeknownst to CompuServe.

Unisys required CompuServe and other commercial online services and applications to license the compression algorithm, but wasn't going to charge non-profit, non-commercial applications. In 1995, there was a fairly general uproar about the Unisys patent, enough that an effort was started to create a new format—one that combined the best of JPEG and GIF. That new format was called PNG, and other than not supporting animation, it can blow the doors off of GIF.

If you're more interested in the early years of GIF and the Unisys patent, see *http://lpf.ai.mit.edu/Patents/Gif/unisys.html*.

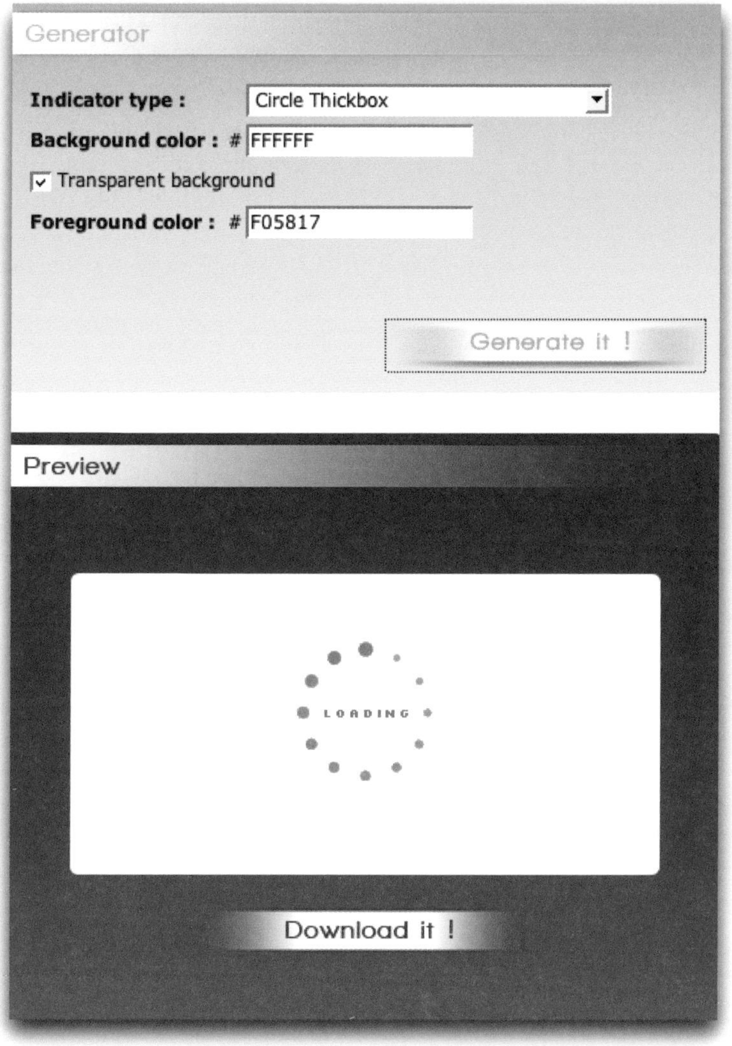

Figure 2-10. Generating a throbber using ajaxload.info

PNG

The PNG format has had a tough time of it because browser companies have been slow to support it. PNG was created as an alternative to GIF during the great days of the GIF patent war, but the GIF patent has expired, making one less reason for vendors to jump to its support.

The PNG format does well with both photos and illustrations, and though it doesn't compress files into as small a size as JPEG, at least it does so losslessly—without degradation of the initial image. The safe archival compression makes PNG a better format for photos that are going to be edited and re-edited.

In addition, the PNG compression technique is more accurate and efficient than that supported for GIFs, so PNGs can compress to a smaller file size than GIFs. File size can be reduced by saving PNG as 8-bit (PNG-8) rather than 32-bit (or PNG-24 in Photoshop, which saves 24 bits for color, 8 bits for alpha transparency), if the tool you are using provides this option. Note, though, that this reduces the color palette and can lead to dithering.

In fact, the only reason to keep either GIF or JPEG is that you can create animations with GIF, and JPEG compresses to a much smaller file than PNG. Oh, and if you want to use transparency and still support IE 6.x, you'll need to use GIF because IE 6.x does not have support for a specific type of transparency called *alpha transparency*.

PNG and Transparency

There are two forms of transparency: binary and alpha. Binary transparency only supports transparency that is all or nothing: the transparent pieces are either all transparent or completely opaque. Alpha transparency, on the other hand, supports degrees of transparency: a transparency can be partial, such as 50%, total (100%), or completely opaque. Of the web image formats, JPEG doesn't support transparency, GIF supports only binary transparency, and PNG supports both binary and alpha transparency.

There are always exceptions to every known fact in graphics. A new JPEG format was created, JPEG2000, which provides a compression technique that doesn't degrade, and also supports alpha transparency. However, as with GIF, there is a possibility of patent issues arising from the compression technique. I'm only aware of Safari having support for JPEG2000 through the underlying open source infrastructure for the browser, WebKit.

Binary transparency is based on one color being selected that then becomes transparent across an entire image. This color is completely transparent—there is no half way. A side effect of this color-based transparency is that GIF's transparency works well only when the color that's picked to be transparent is the same or similar color as the background that the image is placed against. If the background is significantly different or patterned, you'll get a rough halo effect that detracts from the quality of the image. This is even more apparent when you use anti-aliasing to create a smoother figure, especially when using curved graphics (such as letters or circles).

Transparency and Anti-Aliasing

Anti-aliasing is a trick used when a graphic differs from the clean lines of a rectangle. With a two-color image, the anti-aliasing is the same color as the graphic; with more than two colors, the tools examine the background color and the foreground color of an image, and then interpolate a color to use around the curve to "smooth" out the jaggedness of the curve. If you're using anti-aliasing and transparency with GIFs, it's especially important to make sure the background you're using to create the image is the same color you plan on placing the GIF against when added to a web page; otherwise the anti-aliasing will create odd bits of color that interfere with the smooth flow between image and background.

Figure 2-11 shows a GIF file of an abstract leaf, created using Photoshop and saved with a Matte color of white. The Matte setting tells Photoshop what background color the image will be used with, and Photoshop then uses this for the dithering to ensure the image looks good. Though it holds up somewhat against a darker gray color, it still looks much better against the white background.

Figure 2-11. Transparent GIF on white and dark gray backgrounds

A PNG image, on the other hand, with its 256 levels of opacity, stores information with each pixel about the level of opacity of that pixel. This controls how much of the background shows through with each, which eliminates that odd, ugly halo. PNG graphics with a transparent background look good against any background—solid or patterned, regardless of color, as shown in Figure 2-12.

Best of all, you can adjust the overall opacity of a PNG and have an image that has a completely transparent background while the color bits can be partially transparent, as demonstrated in Figure 2-13.

Figure 2-12. A PNG with a transparent background

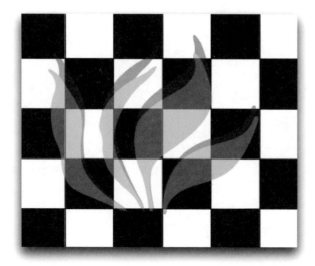

Figure 2-13. A partially opaque PNG

Images: Annotated, Embedded, and Optimized

You've added images to pages and you know how to use the img element. What more can you possibly learn?

Probably not a lot, but it doesn't hurt to have a little review just to make sure we're all on the same footing. Feel free to skip this section, though, if you're eager to get into issues of copyright and patent law. However, if you can hold off your anticipation for a little while, you might want to give this section a gander. Something about old dogs, new tricks.

Images. In Pages.

To add an image to a page, you'll use the `img` element, setting the `src` attribute to the URL for the image:

```
<img src="http://some.com/image.jpg" />
```

If you want your page to validate without errors or warnings, remember to "close" the element by adding the end slash, and make sure the element has an `alt` attribute:

```
<img src="http://some.com/image.jpg" alt="Photo of the boss at company picnic" />
```

The `alt` attribute supports accessibility. Screen readers, software that vocalizes what's happening on a computer screen, speak the text in this field. Providing meaningful text ensures that those dependent on such readers aren't locked out of the web page experience. Avoid repeating the name of the image file; use something meaningful, such as "Partially opened chocolate daylily." The text should be fewer than 100 characters and in whatever is the dominant language for the site. For decorative images that have no real meaning other than a visual context, use an empty string; screen readers should then just ignore the image.

Some browsers inaccurately display an info bubble known as a *tooltip* over the image that contains the alt text when the mouse cursor is over it; others don't. That's something we can't control.

Other allowable `img` attributes are `style`, to assign an element style or style class name, and `id` to identify the specific element. Older attributes such as `width`, `height`, `vspace`, `hspace`, and `align` are either deprecated in newer versions of HTML or not supported in XHTML—you should avoid using any of these older attributes.

Adding an IMG element to a page is only half the job of serving up an image through the Web. The other half is preparing the image for efficient loading. This includes optimizing the image.

I wrote in Chapter 1 that one optimization strategy for page performance is to use different domains or subdomains for different components of the page, in order to bypass the browser restrictions on multiple requests to a specific domain. Most restrict sites to two concurrent requests to the same domain. Using different subdomains, you can "encourage" the browser to make multiple concurrent requests, and the page loads more quickly.

There are other tricks to improve the page performance when using images. Some are format-specific, and some are not.

GIF Optimization

I covered the LZW compression technique for GIF images earlier in this chapter. An interesting aspect of this technique is that it compresses images horizontally. Consequently GIFs compress better, with smaller file sizes, when most of the imagery favors a horizontal placement.

When I first read of this, of course I had to try it out for myself. I created a banded two-color graphic, as shown in Figure 2-14. I saved it as a GIF, horizontally rotated it 90 degrees, and saved the image into a second GIF file.

Figure 2-14. Horizontally aligned two-color image for testing GIF sizes

The horizontally oriented image was 56 KB, while the one aligned vertically ended up being 76 KB. The sizing difference is minor, but if you're looking to squish out every byte, there you go.

There are also tools and utilities, online and for your computer, to optimize GIF files. Most of these utilities work by reducing the number of colors supported in the image, which reduces file size. This also reduces quality of image, unfortunately. Since most applications that create GIF files also optimize them when they're saved, though, it's unlikely you'll need any additional utilities.

Another optimization technique most tools support is choosing which row ordering to use with the image. A row ordering of `interlaced` is similar to choosing a progressive JPEG format: a poor-quality image shows first while the higher-quality image is being loaded into the browser.

JPEG Optimization

There is no greater impact on JPEG optimization than the compression level picked. This is the choice that most impacts file size and image quality. Some images can support higher levels of compression without perceptive degradation; others, less so. You'll want to experiment to find the levels that work best for you.

As with GIFs, there are utilities that optimize JPEGs, but whatever tools you use to create an image typically provide the functionality to change the compression levels, so it's unlikely you'll need such an optimizer.

Most image editing tools also support a standard baseline or progressive formats for JPEG. Again, the progressive format provides a "preview" copy of the image while the higher quality is being downloaded.

There are tools that allow one to make some types of modifications to a JPEG image, such as cropping and rotating, without any loss of quality at all. These take advantage of the fact that cropping can just shift things about without performing any compression. There are plug-ins for tools such as Photoshop that support this, as well as standalone tools, such as JPEGCrops. Of course, this doesn't change the fact that some compression may be desired in order to decrease file sizes.

 Access JPEGCrops at *http://ekot.dk/programmer/JPEGCrops/*.

PNG Optimization

PNG files can also be saved in an interlaced format, but the best approach to optimizing a PNG is choosing the palette-based PNG-8 over PNG-32 (PNG-24 for Photoshop) when saving the image. As stated earlier, you'll lose quality with this approach, but for web work the quality may not be impaired enough to be significantly visible.

There are PNG optimizers, including open source ones such as pngcrush and OptiPNG. The file size savings these can accomplish, though, again depends on how well the originating software does when saving the original image. Chances are, the savings won't be high.

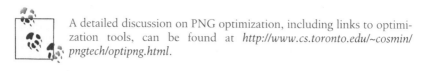
A detailed discussion on PNG optimization, including links to optimization tools, can be found at *http://www.cs.toronto.edu/~cosmin/pngtech/optipng.html*.

Steal This: Images, Copyright, and Hotlinking

The concept of copyright can fill books, and therefore my coverage here will be both light and high level. It must also, based on my personal experience, be focused on copyright in the United States.

You don't have to do anything special to obtain copyright on one of your images: it's yours as soon as you make it. However, anything on the Web is vulnerable, which means that just because you have the copyright on an image doesn't mean others can't take it for their own purposes.

If you find an image has been copied to another web site and you're unhappy about its use, there's not much you can do other than ask the person to stop using it. If he or she refuses, you can then check to see whether the company providing the server space for the pages containing the image has a term of use that prohibits using copyrighted material without permission. If it does, you can file a complaint with the company hosting the site. Be forewarned that people online can be pretty nasty about others who deny them their use of your image.

If the image takedown request fails, about all you can do at this point is get a lawyer and sue the individual. Even then, chances are that unless you can prove the person's use of your image has harmed your ability to make money from it, their use could fit under what is known as *fair use*.

Fair use states that copyrighted material can be used for criticism, commentary, reporting, teaching, and research, depending on whether the image is part of a body of work and how significant a part, as well as the economic impact to the copyright holder from making such a copy.

If you post a set of images, and the person copies just one in order to write on the topic covered by the images, or even on your own work, this probably falls within the fair use boundary. If they're not charging for the use of the image or otherwise benefiting financially from your work, and copying doesn't impact on your making money from the image, chances are that the use could fit within fair use. Unfortunately, there is no clear-cut way to determine exactly what is fair use and what is not. A resource to begin with, though, is Duke University's *Bound By Law*, a comic that explores copyright and fair use in a remarkably fun and clever manner.

Though *Bound By Law* focuses primarily on movie making, the topics covered can apply equally to images, including ones you create and ones you copy yourself—such as my use of the *Bound By Law* cover in this book.

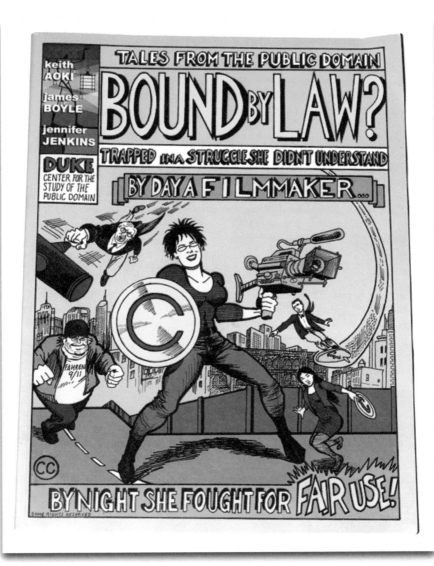

Figure 2-15. Front cover for the Bound By Law comic

Of course, you may not care about whether an image is copied. You can donate the image to what is known as the public domain. Copyrighted material where the copyright has expired also goes into the public domain, as does material that has been funded by a government agency (based on the principle that the people have already paid for the image through their tax dollars). When an item is in the public domain you can use it as you want.

Between full copyright and public domain is the Creative Commons. Creative Commons gives you the ability to formally give others permission to use your work under specific conditions. An example of such a license is Attribution Non-Commercial No Derivatives (by-nc-nd), which states that attribution must be given to the owner of the work, it can't be used for commercial purposes, and it must be used as is, without derivation. The Creative Commons doesn't legally impact your copyrights; it just gives you a tool to let others use your work without having to formally seek your permission.

 You can find out more about the Creative Commons at *http://creativecommons.org*.

If you do use the Creative Commons licenses, though, make sure you fully understand the impact of each license. When I was writing this book, several people who used the Flickr photo-sharing site discovered that their photos, which had been licensed as attribution only (cc-by) or attribution and shared alike (cc-by-sa), were being used by Virgin Mobile for a campaign in Australia. Images were displayed in ads at bus stops, in newspapers, and on the Web, many showing people with rather uncomplimentary text.

Figure 2-16. An image at the Virgin Mobile web site, at http://www.areyouwithusorwhat.com/

By allowing commercial use of the images, there was little the photographers could do about Virgin using the images for ads. The real issue became one of Virgin not getting model releases from the people who were recognizable in the ads—contra to laws in the U.S. and Australia.

Typically for non-commercial uses on the Web, you need not worry about getting signed releases of people (or of private buildings or property) if you use the images in an editorial context. You could run into problems, though, if you feature commercial logos or other trademarked images, especially at a site that generates income in some way (unrelated to the images).

OK to Copy, Not OK to Link

There are times when you don't care whether a person copies an image, but do care when she links directly to an image located on your site. This is known as *hot linking*, and can end up taking a lot of your bandwidth.

If your site is served by the Apache web server and you can create individual *.htaccess* files to manage traffic, you can add entries to this file to prevent hot linking.

The following entry, when added to the *.htaccess* file, will block all access to images from domains outside of your own, represented in this case by *some.com*:

```
RewriteEngine on
RewriteCond %{HTTP_REFERER} !^$
RewriteCond %{HTTP_REFERER} !^http://(www\.)?some.com/.*$ [NC]
RewriteRule \.(gif|jpg|png)$ - [F]
```

You can extend this rule to allow links from as many domains as you need or want. Just repeat the line with some.com, and replace with your domain or domains.

Instead of just blocking the image access, you can also redirect the access to another image. Some people do this and use a rather embarrassing image. I don't recommend this for two reasons. The first is that your bandwidth is still used to serve up this "message." The second is that most people who hot link really don't understand that it's "bad" to hot link. Blocking the image, without deliberately embarrassing anybody, is enough.

Of course, some people use this as an opportunity to advertise their services, by using an image that redirects people to a site or provides a "calling card." Another message could be a polite: "I don't care if you use this image, but please copy it to your own site." In that, case, modify the *.htaccess* entry to the following, which redirects the image linked to the "ad."

```
RewriteEngine on
RewriteCond %{HTTP_REFERER} !^$
RewriteCond %{HTTP_REFERER} !^http://(www\.)?some.com/.*$ [NC]
RewriteRule \.(gif|jpg)$ http://some.com/hireme.jpg [R,L]
```

After you've set up your *.htaccess* file to prevent hot linking, chances are that once your new image shows up in place of the hot-linked image, the link to the image will be removed, quickly.

Of course, another remedy for bandwidth and storage issues associated with images is to find a separate storage solution.

Image Storage

One thing that hasn't changed much in all these years of technological advancement is that serving images takes space on the disk and bandwidth. If anything, with the new space-guzzling cameras and multi-gigabyte storage cards, sometimes it takes a lot of space and considerable bandwidth.

You have a couple of different options for storing and serving up images. One is to store and serve them from your own server, either one you own, wholly, or one that you share with other people. The prices for these sites have gone down considerably, and you can pick up a couple of gigs of disk space and 30–50 GB of bandwidth for fifteen bucks a month, U.S.

Even with this generous allocation, though, you may find yourself pushing the envelope on space, bandwidth, or both. There are other alternatives to hosting images yourself, though most of these alternatives have constraints on usage attached.

Hosting on a Social Network Photo Site

Social networks are the big thing nowadays. These are sites where you use whatever service is provided, such as managing your photos for public access, but you also have access to several community features. The focus of these sites is not just to store photos, but to draw people into communities of like-minded folks.

One of the more popular sites is Yahoo!'s Flickr, found at *http://flickr.com* and shown in Figure 2-17. There are two different accounts, paid and free, and how many photos you can upload and whether you see ads or not depends on whether you've paid or not. The payment itself is quite small, and storage and bandwidth is unlimited.

There is a web application for uploading photos, shown in Figure 2-18, and several utilities to do the same on various clients. When you upload photos, Flickr creates variations based on size. You can also add information to the photo, such as title, description, annotations, and tags—keywords associated with the photos. If there is any accessible metadata associated with the photo, it's pulled out by Flickr for display when the photo is accessed.

Once the photo is uploaded, you can include it in sets, add it to a map, or send it to various Flickr groups, such as ones for B&W photos, butterflies, or photos in Missouri. If the photo is publicly accessible, anyone can come along and drop you a comment about the photo.

Flickr provides forums, the ability for its clients to create any number of groups, and also the ability to search on tags and other information. The service also provides slideshow software, lets you designate a Creative Commons license for any photo, if you wish, as well as providing ways of grouping photos based on clusters, and an "interestingness" factor.

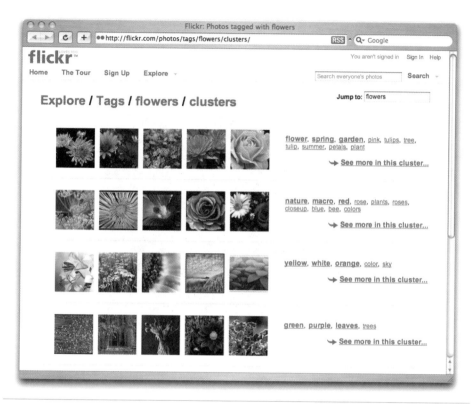

Figure 2-17. Flickr cluster page for flower photos

For the purposes of storage and bandwidth, you can store photos and other images at the site and then include links to any one of the sizes in your web page. All that's required by Flickr is to provide a link back to the main image page on Flickr. The service will create both the embedding and link HTML for you.

You can't store images used for web design at Flickr. The site is focused primarily on photos, but you can store other types of images—as long as you have the rights to the image and, as just stated, you don't use the site to store images that are part of your site's design.

Flickr is a very cost-effective approach, and the service is quite reliable. However, one of the downsides is that it is a centralized service and could change over time. For instance, when the site added a German language option, Yahoo! had to put restrictions on the German speaking accounts to put them in permanent "safe mode" because of the German government's restrictions on photo access for kids. This is something to be aware of for more "socialized" storage sites.

Flickr is nice, but sometimes you just want a place to put your photos without having "community" tagging along.

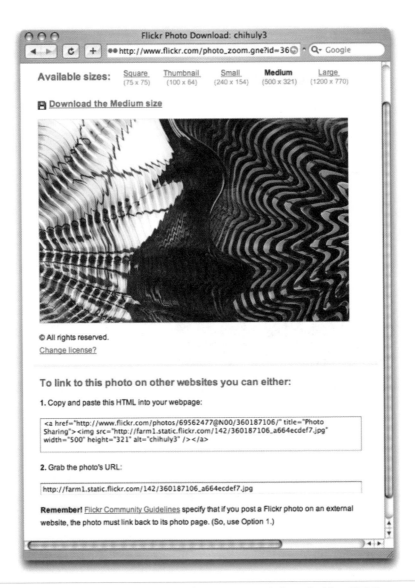

Figure 2-18. *The Flickr download page; note the text areas with the embedding HTML*

 Another thing to be wary of with Flickr is that publications and people now look for "free" photos to use in their sites or creations. If you're not comfortable with people using your photos, don't use a CC license. If you're really not comfortable with people using your photos, either keep the photos private or don't use Flickr.

Other hosts that provide the same or similar services are SmugMug (at *http://www.smugmug.com/*) and PhotoBucket (at *http://photobucket.com/*). Still more can be found by searching on the phrase "photo storage."

Other Hosting Solutions

A second option for storing photos and other media are sites that provide space for file storage and/or sharing that are not specifically related to photographs or other images.

One is a service such as Amazon's S3 (Simple Storage Service) at *http://aws.amazon.com/s3*. This is a site that provides storage facilities, including backup, as well as web services for uploading and downloading any kind of material, which includes photos.

A site like Amazon's S3 is not a particularly good one, though, for direct image access via the Web, because every access, including those that fail (i.e., return 404), counts when it comes to determining charges. Though it takes many thousands of such requests to trigger a few cents' charge, it would also be easy for malicious sites to trigger such requests automatically, and you may not know until many dollars worth of such charges later. This site can be made safer for access by using Amazon's other services, including hosted applications, and restricting image access to only these services.

Mashable, a popular site with info on the current web technologies, has a web page listing 80+ online storage options. The options are categorized by backup, for transmission only, or storage/sharing. Many are "free," though I would be careful about searching for any caveats associated with the "free" storage, and make sure you understand any bandwidth or other "incidental" charges that may exist.

One "free" site is DivShare, which was fairly young when I looked at it. The site has a free option, but also had ads associated with that use. With a subscription, though, you can store up to 5 GB of space and have 50 GB of bandwidth for image downloads for only a few bucks a month. Of course, the site states that it will store images "forever," but forever typically means something different in Internet terms.

 Access the Mashable page at *http://mashable.com/2007/07/28/online-storage/*. DivShare can be accessed at *http://divshare.com*.

External storage separate from a web site is actually more efficient than combining the two. The processes necessary to store and serve files require different resources than those necessary to perform computations, serve dynamic web pages, and run databases. In addition, servers focused purely on storage don't require all of the software for those running web sites, which means even more space freed up for image storage.

This brings up another issue: nothing really is "forever" online. Because of this, it's critical with any external storage that you have backups for all your externally stored images, that you understand completely the terms of service, and that, if all else fails, you have an exit plan.

Regardless of Choice, Have an Exit Plan

I've experimented with all variations of photo storage in the past. I've also had any number of web domains. I've found, through painful experience, that "hard editing" actual URLs to external sites, or even domains, can be a problem if you want to change the location at some point in the future. If you embed a link to an external site and then decide you don't want to use it anymore, you're stuck with a link to nowhere—or having to go through pages, manually or programmatically, to change the links.

There are two techniques to ensure you have an "exit plan" in place in regards to your image locations. The first is not to use full URLs when referencing images on your own site. A better choice is to use relative links when you're creating a link to an image source or within a hypertext link:

```
<img src="/images/botanical/flower.jpg" alt="Red rose at Botanical Garden" />
```

With this, it doesn't matter if you change your domain from *yourdomain.com* to *anotherdomain.com*, because the link will resolve based on the domain relative to the page, rather than hard edited into a page.

The second technique if you use multiple domains or external hosting is to use HTACCESS rules if you're hosted in an Apache environment, to redirect image requests from your site to the site where they're actually physically located. In this case, you'll probably want to use temporary redirecting, because the whole point of having the redirect is that you may end up moving the images at some point.

An example of a redirect is the following, which redirects all GIFs to another domain:

```
RedirectMatch (.*)\.gif$ http://www.anotherserver.com$1.gif
```

Variations of redirects based on keywords or rewrite rules can be found online.

Now, when a relative URL such as:

```
/image/rose.jpg
```

is accessed in a web page, and the directory "image" in your server has a redirect to a storage facility such as *ourspaceyourstuff.com/youraccount/image*, the image is loaded into the page regardless of how many times it's moved.

The only drawback to this method is that if you want to open the file in an application, as will be demonstrated later on in this book, you'll need to either have the image stored locally or first copy it to local storage.

Now, enough with the framework behind web images. Let's get to creating some pictures.

CHAPTER 3

Photographs: From Camera to Web Page

A few years back I was reading one photographer's discussion of his workflow using Photoshop, when he mentioned something about a default setting being "good enough" for the Web. Of course there was a time when print was synonymous with photography, but we can't assume that, today, the ultimate end for a photograph is on paper, with the Web being nothing more than a way to promote our paper-based end product. Nowadays, the Web has become *the* place for our photos, and realizing this changes the whole idea of default settings in tools as being "good enough" for the Web.

Digital photography and digital cameras have been around for years. In my opinion, it was the convergence of three components—affordable consumer digital cameras, personal computers, and a growing access and familiarity with the Web, as well as an increasing number of broadband users—that led to the explosion of digital photography and the huge number of photos and photo-specific sites we see today.

Before all of these components came together, most photography was film, printed out on paper, with copies made and sent to just a few close friends and family. Now the use of film is rapidly decreasing, and most photos are taken with a digital camera, uploaded into a computer, and either sent through email or posted online. The target audience has also changed: where before we published photos for close friends and family, now we're publishing photos literally to the world…and finding out that there is a fairly significant number of amateur photographers who do a rather nice job with their pictures, too. Even news sites have started making greater use of "amateur" material, a practice that is somewhat controversial.

Digital photography has become so prevalent now that it forms a major component of the web graphics genre, whereas 10 or even 5 years ago digital photography on the Web might rate only a footnote. Where the majority of "web graphics time" had previously been spent working on site design and creating graphical buttons and menus, more of that same time is now spent endlessly tweaking photos to publish to the Web. Even the most determinedly amateur photographer posts dozens, even hundreds, of photos to the Web yearly.

The *digiterati* among us are fortunate in our interest, too, because photography lends itself well to automated manipulation as well as step-by-step instruction, which means many techniques to improve photos can be replicated without having expensive equipment or years of training. You and I have an enormous number of editors, converters, libraries, and other applications we can use to manage the process of taking a photo from a camera to the web page. Frankly, you can't swing Texas roadkill without hitting tools and utilities for creating and/or manipulating photos. Far too many to cover in one chapter in a book.

What wondrous things we can do with these tools, too. Photography was never as fixed as most people assume. The picture didn't end at the close of the shutter, and amazing things have been accomplished in darkrooms. With digital photography and the associated editors, though, many a mediocre image can transcend its meager beginnings to become a good, if not great, work of art through simple manipulations of light.

More importantly, you don't have to be an Ansel Adams, Walker Evans, or Annie Leibovitz to publish photos online. Photos can be used to tell stories, highlight events, share experiences, and illustrate a concept or idea without being museum quality. In fact, the Web does less well with art show–quality photographs because of the varied, and limited, displays and small web spaces.

In this chapter, I'm going to cover the first stages of the photographer's workflow—the steps we take to bring a photo from camera to web page. I'm also going to survey some of the more popular, as well as interesting, photo editors and utilities. Most of the chapter, though, is focused on covering some of the ways photos can be manipulated to be at their best when published online.

 System requirements differ for all of the tools covered in this chapter, but the tools all have one thing in common: they are either free- or shareware, or have a fully functional trial for at least 30 days.

The Web Photographer's Workflow

Photographic workflow refers to the processes we follow to get a photo from our cameras all the way to publication. Different people use different approaches and tools—anything from a complete workflow tool, such as Aperture, to a variety of tools, such as a RAW image converter, photo editor, FTP tool to a site, and access through a slideshow program.

In his *The Digital Story* weblog, Derrick Story, O'Reilly's digital media evangelist, published a "Build Your Workflow" guide and accompanying podcast (audio post). In both, he describes these basic steps:

1. Acquire/capture (in camera)
2. Upload to computer

3. Organize (add metadata, rate, and sort)

4. Edit

5. Share (publish)

6. Save (archive)

The camera to web workflow follows these same steps, with the single variation being that the only sharing we're interested in is publishing the photos to the Web. How many tools you use to complete this process is dependent more on your interest, and perhaps budget, than on any other factor—including whether you're paid for your photographs or not.

 Derrick's workflow guide can be found at *http://www.thedigitalstory. com/blog/2007/08/build_your_workflow.html.*

Both amateurs and professionals alike make use of photo workflow tools, such as Adobe's Lightroom, Microsoft's Expression Media, Apple's Aperture, Camera One, or even the in-development open source blueMarine. These tools can simplify image organization, including adding bulk updates, such as metadata edits. They can also be used to edit photos, though most don't provide the sophisticated capability that even the simplest desktop editor provides.

Beyond the initial stages of photo management comes fine-tuning individual pictures. No matter how good the workflow tools, this typically requires the services of a photo editor. The better known of the photo editors is Adobe's Photoshop, and it is still the undisputed leader in its field. However, it's not the only option for photo manipulation. In fact, there are dozens of tools for editing photos, many of which are freely available for Windows, Mac OS X, and Linux. This is in addition to an increasing number of online photo editors, created with Flash or some other toolset.

The first step in the camera to web workflow, though, is downloading the photos from the camera. Camera manufacturers typically provide software to manage this for you, but many photo editors, RAW manipulation tools, and other utilities can do the same job.

In addition, most cameras also allow you direct access to the memory card from your computer, where you can find the folder with the images and copy it directly using whatever your file management tool is. This can actually be the fastest approach, and once copied, you can then use any photo management tool to import the photos or edit the files directly.

Which tools you can use with the photos direct from the memory card depends on the format in which they are saved. Many of the earlier inexpensive cameras store photos only in JPEG format, but most now provide several options: JPEG, TIFF, PNG, and some form of RAW image. I have two Nikon cameras, and the options I'm provided are RAW—which in this case is Nikon's NEF (Nikon Electronic Format)—or a variation of JPEG. One option does both: captures an image in NEF and then a JPEG file in basic, normal, or fine qualities. Since JPEG is a lossy format (as discussed in Chapter 2), I never use it and suggest that you don't either, unless you don't have any other option. Whether to use RAW, though, depends on how much you take advantage of its post-capturing capability.

Working with RAW Images

Unlike JPEG, GIF, or TIFF, RAW does not stand for anything other than an image that's stored in a "raw," unprocessed state. No compression routine is used, the data is not processed, and all camera sensor information possible is stored with the image.

The advantage to the RAW format is that you can modify certain characteristics of the image—exposure, color saturation, sharpness, white balance—after the image has been taken. About the only characteristics you can't change are ISO, aperture, and focal length of the picture—the characteristics of film, in fact.

The disadvantage of the RAW format is that the image files are quite large. However, with the multi-gigabyte memory cards nowadays, this isn't the issue it once was. My 4GB memory card can store over 200 photos, which is more than sufficient for my needs, and if it isn't I have additional memory cards on hand. Storing RAW data can also be slower, but not necessarily to the point where most of us would notice—especially with the increasing number of optimizations in today's digital cameras.

If all cameras supported the same RAW format, our lives would be so much simpler, but unfortunately they don't. As mentioned earlier, I have Nikon D200 and D70 cameras, and the RAW format Nikon supports is NEF. Canon supports CRW and CRW2 (Canon RAW); Sony's is SRF (Sony Raw Format). Rather than continue this proliferation of different formats, Adobe has proposed a RAW file standard: DNG, or Digital Negative. In addition to Adobe, other companies support DNG in their products, including Apple, Leica, Hasselblad, and so on, though not Nikon for my cameras. At least not yet.

Adobe has provided a DNG Converter for both the Mac and Windows that takes formats like my Nikon's NEF and turns them into DNG files. Once started, you input a folder, and the tool then converts the RAW images in the folder, as shown in Figure 3-1.

Regardless of format, some tools can work directly with RAW images, but others work through a secondary application that manipulates the RAW settings before sending the image on through to the application.

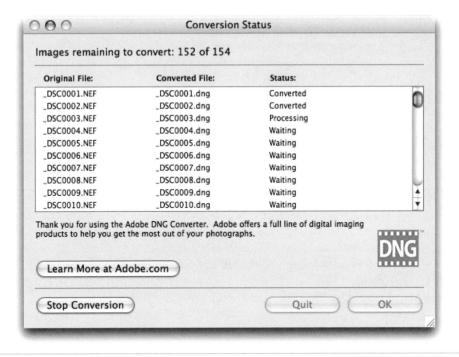

Original File:	Converted File:	Status:
_DSC0001.NEF	_DSC0001.dng	Converted
_DSC0002.NEF	_DSC0002.dng	Converted
_DSC0003.NEF	_DSC0003.dng	Processing
_DSC0004.NEF	_DSC0004.dng	Waiting
_DSC0005.NEF	_DSC0005.dng	Waiting
_DSC0006.NEF	_DSC0006.dng	Waiting
_DSC0007.NEF	_DSC0007.dng	Waiting
_DSC0008.NEF	_DSC0008.dng	Waiting
_DSC0009.NEF	_DSC0009.dng	Waiting
_DSC0010.NEF	_DSC0010.dng	Waiting

Thank you for using the Adobe DNG Converter. Adobe offers a full line of digital imaging products to help you get the most out of your photographs.

DNG

Learn More at Adobe.com

Stop Conversion   Quit   OK

Figure 3-1. Running the DNG Converter on NEF files

The DNG converters are free, available from the Adobe DNG site *http://www.adobe.com/products/dng/*.

Where the RAW pre-processor ends and the photo editor begins varies based on people's preferences and their own workflow. What I want from a RAW tool is a way of manipulating the camera settings, such as the white balance and exposure. I feel that sharpening and color balance, as well as contrast and brightness, are better set in the photo editor. Other photographers make wider use of the RAW utility functionality.

Some RAW tools also provide an "auto" feature to automatically adjust several settings for the image. This setting can be surprisingly accurate at times, but I've found that none of the tools is as good as I am at making the adjustments. I am forced to confess, though, that my belief in my own abilities may be more of conceit than an accurate assessment of capability.

There are a surprising number of RAW converters, editors, and utilities. I'll take a look at a few, just to give you an idea of how they work if you haven't used one previously.

Included with the examples for this book is a separate file consisting of images that you can use with the different tools and processes described in this chapter. This includes several RAW files in NEF format, used for most of the examples in this book.

UFRaw

One RAW editing tool is UFRaw, an open source RAW image utility that can be used either alone or with a tool like GIMP. As a RAW pre-processor, it's an accomplished application, but doesn't have all the functionality you'll need for most finished work, including sharpening and cropping. It does, however, provide options to change exposure, white balance, and color balance.

UFRaw can be downloaded from *http://ufraw.sourceforge.net/*. There are installations for Linux, Windows, and Mac OS X. Unless you want to build the application on Windows, use the "for dummies" installation. You'll also need to install the GIMP Toolkit (GTK+2) first, which is included with GIMP (covered later in this chapter). The Windows version of GIMP also has a Windows installer at *http://gimp-win.sourceforge.net/*. For the Mac, I recommend installing the application using Darwin/Mac ports.

Linux-Based Graphical Applications for the Mac

If you're a Mac user and interested in graphics, I strongly suggest you spend some time becoming familiar with the Terminal, X11 (X Windows), and the Mac package system, Macports (at *http://macports.com*), formerly known as Darwinports.

The Terminal is an application that provides command-line access to the Unix infrastructure on which Mac OS X is built; X11 is the windowing system used by many of the graphics applications; and the package system is a helper to ensure clean installations of Linux-based applications, including confirming that any prerequisites are installed.

There are a number of Linux-based graphics applications and utilities that can be easily installed on your Mac system through Macports, including several covered in this book.

To find out more on X11, check out the tutorial on X11 for the Mac at *http://developer.apple.com/opensource/tools/runningx11.html*. There are several good tutorials on Terminal at O'Reilly's MacDevCenter (at *http://www.macdevcenter.com/pub/ct/51*). Installation instructions for Macports can be found at *http://darwinports.com/install/*, and documentation can be found at *http://trac.macosforge.org/projects/macports/wiki/UsingMacPortsQuickStart* and *http://geeklair.net/new_macports_guide/*.

UFRaw has several options, including ones that highlight areas of the photo that are overexposed, underexposed, or both, as shown in Figure 3-2. One option can correct the exposure, and the highlighting reflects the corrections as they are made, as shown in Figure 3-3.

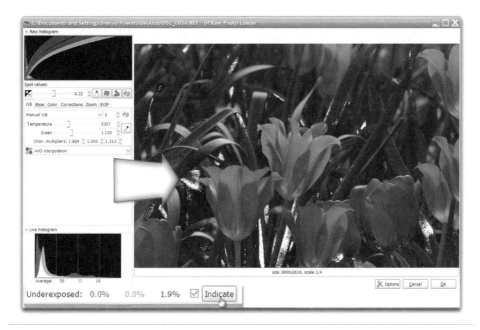

Figure 3-2. UFRaw with over- and underexposures highlighted

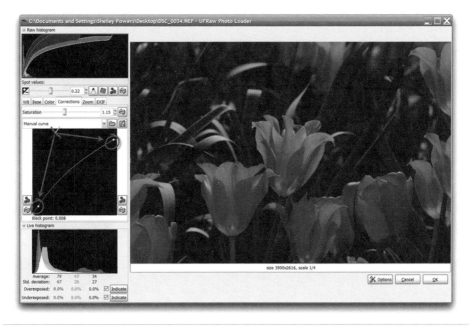

Figure 3-3. UFRaw with some correction for exposure applied

UFRaw also provides the option to change the white balance presets for the photo, based on what's supported by the individual cameras. The options I'm provided for my Nikons are:

- Manual WB
- Camera WB
- Auto WB
- Incandescent
- Fluorescent
- Direct Sunlight
- Flash
- Cloudy
- Shade

UFRaw can act as a plug-in for GIMP, or can be run as a separate application and the image saved in another format, such as TIFF or PNG.

What are the biggest advantages of UFRaw? It's open source, it's freely available, and it works in Linux, Mac OS X, and Windows. UFRaw also provides much of the functionality most people probably want from a RAW editor. However, as full of features as it is, it's not as featured as the superman of RAW tools: Adobe Camera Raw.

Adobe Camera Raw

The Adobe Camera Raw (ACR) utility is the heavyweight in the RAW world, especially when using version 4.1 and up, which is included with Adobe's Photoshop CS3 or Photoshop Elements. In fact, combined with Adobe Bridge for photo organization and Photoshop for editing, you have a complete photo workflow in these three tools.

One of the interesting components of ACR is the filmstrip. If you open more than one RAW file in ACR, they display as a filmstrip from which you can then either select individual photos for working or apply modifications to the entire batch at once. If you do apply a change to all photos, an exclamation point in a yellow triangle appears as the change is being made to each photo, in turn, as shown in Figure 3-4. Applying a global change to all photos is especially helpful if you know that the same RAW adjustments need to be made to all of the photos, not just one.

ACR also excels in what you can do to photos once they're opened in the tool. Not only can you change the camera RAW settings, such as exposure, color balance, saturation, sharpness, and white balance presets, you can also apply other modifications such as adding fill lighting and clarity.

Figure 3-4. Adobe Camera RAW filmstrip and applying a change globally

Fill lighting does just as it sounds—illuminates features cast into shadow by stronger background or side lighting. Using it in combination with exposure can provide a higher level of control over overall illumination and for fixing over- or underexposure problems.

The Clarity function, though, is something quite new. According to an excellent overview of ACR by Jeff Schewe at *PhotoshopNews*, Clarity is a variation of using Photoshop's Unsharp Mask with specific settings—an implementation of a technique known as Local Contrast Enhancement (LCE). I'll get into image sharpening techniques later in this chapter, but right from the start, I found that Clarity threatened to be my new best friend in the world of digital photography.

The *PhotoshopNews* Clarity article can be found online at *http://photoshopnews.com/2007/05/31/about-camera-raw-41*. The description of Local Contrast Enhancement can be found at *http://www.luminous-landscape.com/tutorials/contrast-enhancement.shtml*.

ACR doesn't just stop at camera RAW edits, fill lighting, and clarity—you can do a wide variety of photo adjustments, ranging from managing color to handling metadata. The issue then becomes one of just because we can make modifications in RAW tools, do we want to? Or are we better waiting to make such modifications in an editor?

If you're using a tool based on a family of products, such as ACR, then you're more or less using the same processes in all products; which tool you use to make the change is somewhat moot in these circumstances.

If, however, you're using a RAW tool that is separate from your editing tool, such as UFRaw and GIMP, then you're really going to want to pay attention to the results of each tool and adjust your usage accordingly.

 Most, if not all, digital camera makers provide software in some form to take photos from the camera and provide initial manipulation. Canon provides Digital Photo Professional, Nikon provides Nikon Capture, and other camera makers provide their own variations. These are good tools, and the only reason I'm not covering them is they all assume a specific type of camera, and I wanted to cover software that worked with most camera types.

Once a photo is beyond the RAW stage (whenever that is), you're then onto the next step in the photo workflow, which is editing the photo directly in a photo editor.

Editing Photos: Bending Light

Photography is about bending light. No matter the subject or the skill of the photographer, whether the image is captured on film or digitally, photography is really about working with light.

Picture too dark? Modifying overall illumination, enhancing contrast, even altering saturation and color values are all about changing the light present in the image. Shadows too dark or light areas too bright? Alter the exposure, before or after the photo is captured. Photo a little too soft or not soft enough? Sharpening an image is really finding the edges between areas in a photo with light differences and altering the transition between the areas so that it happens more quickly. Even when we resize a photo, algorithms base this process on light levels and repetition of patterns in the image.

All photo editors provide light manipulation routines of varying degrees of sophistication. Many provide enough primitive photo editing functionality that they can be combined to emulate the more sophisticated photo editing capabilities of the higher-cost tools. That's important if you're on a budget but you also want to publish the best quality photo.

Each person has different needs for a photo editor, but my list of requirements consists of the following (subject to change, of course, based on recent photo editing experiences):

- Primitive level support, such as the ability to resize/resample and crop
- Support for RAW images, either directly or through some form of plug-in or third-party tool
- Support for color profiles and color space
- The capability to export or save in any number of formats, including TIFF, PNG, JPEG, and GIF, as well as the ability to save in-process work
- The capability to back out any number of edits for those times when my experimentation really goes wrong
- The capability to remove an abstraction, flaw, or dust—especially dust—from the photo, using some form of cloning
- Some support for effects and filters, especially blur and sharpening
- Color and light manipulation, including levels, curves, and channel mixing
- The capability to select specific components of an image
- Layers
- Lens and other photographic distortion corrections
- Extensibility with plug-ins and add-ons

As for the goodies and gadgets present in the high-cost tools, rather than look at photo editors for what they provide, it's important to know what operations you perform routinely on photos, and then look for the editors that provide the best tools to accomplish these operations; or at a minimum, provide the necessary primitives that can be used to re-create the functionality.

If a photo editing software program provides essentials, such as curves, then many higher-level functions—Photoshop's Color Match, for example—can be emulated with no loss of functionality. The key is to understand what's happening with the higher-level function and then use more primitive operations to re-create the effect. Luckily, there are thousands of tutorials that provide step-by-step instruction in how to perform the higher-level functions of a tool such as Photoshop with less expensive tools, such as Paint Shop Pro, Photoshop Elements, or GIMP.

The next section focuses on typical photo editing tasks, particularly as each applies to photos published on the Web. Following that section is a list of photo editors and a look at how each compares on these tasks. By trying out the different examples, I want to demonstrate that when I say a tool "must" have Curves, there's actually a reason for my madness, not just that it's hip among photographers to say their photo editor must support Curves. The same applies to my other list of needs.

 For consistency, all of the examples in this section are implemented with Adobe Photoshop CS3. Later, we'll look at implementing the same functionality in different editors.

Color Match That Group: Optimization in Numbers

When we prepare a photo for printing, we optimize the photo for individual presentation. Publishing photos to the Web, though, can be a different experience because the photo may not be the only image displayed within the same visual space. In fact, the photo may be closely grouped with other related photos, and it's important to make both the individual photo and the group as a whole look good.

Case in point is a group of photos I took at the Apollo/Saturn V Center at the Kennedy Space Center. The subjects differ but are related: rockets, moon rovers, and other space-related equipment of historical interest. The venue was the same: a hangar-like atmosphere with the equipment either hanging from the roof or resting directly on the concrete floor. The lighting, though, differed drastically. Some items were lit with fluorescent, some with incandescent light, and natural light entered the building from hangar doors. Fill lighting usually was not an option because of the size of the displays.

Figure 3-5 shows the four images as they were first opened in the editor, each with its own unique lighting and color challenges. The photos used in this example perfectly demonstrate the concept of "optimization in numbers" with photographs. None of the photos is very strong by itself; all would most likely be rejected as individual pictures because of their flaws. However, as a group, pulled together for editorial purposes and tweaked to complement one another, four weak photos can make one strong illustrative statement.

The top-left photo of the moon rover has a yellow cast because of incandescent lighting. Viewing the histogram for the photo (Window → Histogram) shows that it's also a very *low key* photograph, largely underexposed and dark. The opposite of a low key photo would be one that's *high key*: too bright and overexposed. There's nothing wrong with either low or high key photos if the subject supports the effect. Low key photos tend to be dark-tempered and moody, neither of which we associate with a moon rover.

The bottom-left photo is also underexposed, though unlike the moon rover, at least there's no unusual color cast to the picture. The lighting and color is acceptable for the remaining two photos of the group, both of rockets, but not ideal. More importantly, none of the photos agree enough on either color or light with each other to create a nicely cohesive grouped display. The goal of the exercise, then, is to optimize and synchronize the color and brightness levels for the group, while not sacrificing either for the individual pictures.

Before I start, though, a brief word on photo histograms would be helpful. In Figure 3-5, histograms are shown to the right of the four grouped photos. These histograms show the overall luminance of the selected photo—the moon rover photo—followed by color channel histograms: Red, Green, and Blue.

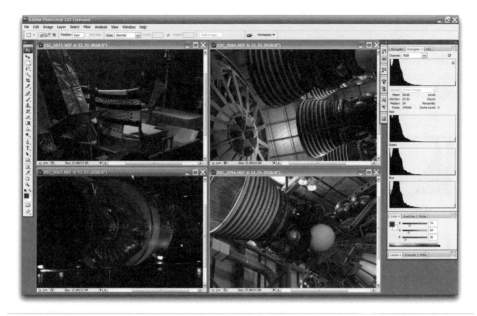

Figure 3-5. Grouped Kennedy photos before color or brightness adjustments

Photo histograms are used frequently in the examples in this chapter. Photo histograms display the frequency that pixels in the picture occur at each level of brightness, on a scale of 0 (black) to 255 (white). They're used to represent a photo's overall exposure.

For this chapter, I'm using an RGB histogram, which measures the exposure of light along the red, green, and blue channels and then computes an average. In addition, I'll also be working directly with the individual color histograms. For more on histograms, I recommend the Cambridge in Colour tutorials, specifically "Understanding Histograms" parts 1 and 2 (at *http://www.cambridgeincolour.com/tutorials/histograms1.htm* and *http://www.cambridgeincolour.com/tutorials/histograms2.htm*).

Classic Color Matching with Adobe's Color Match

There is one utility in one photo editor designed specifically to manage luminance and color matching between two images: the Color Match utility within Adobe Photoshop (Image → Adjustments → Match Color). Using the tool you can open two photos and use one as the template for color matching the other.

Without an inside look into the workings of the tool, we don't know how Color Match works, but we can use histograms of the matching image, as well as the before and after versions of the matched image, to tell us a story. Checking out the color channels between the post-processed image and the image acting as template shows that the white, black, and gray points between the images matches relatively closely—much more closely than before the color matching. The histogram patterns don't change as much as the overall tonal values of the picture matched. Figure 3-6 shows before and after color channel histograms for one color-matching operation. The first slide in each row is the before picture histogram for that color channel, the second picture is the one to be matched, and the third is the post-matched histogram values.

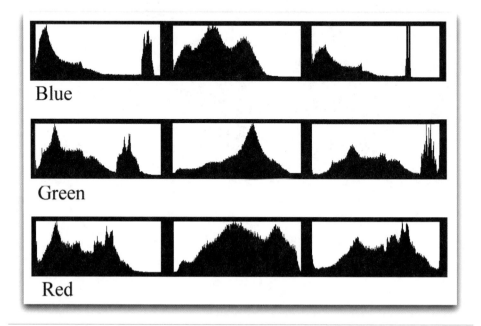

Figure 3-6. Before and after, and matching image color channel histograms

How rude of me, showing you histograms before showing you images. That's like posting an x-ray as the photo in a dating service. It might be accurate and informative, but it's not visually compelling. In this example, the photo to be matched was of the house I grew up in in Washington state. The other was a copy of Vincent van Gogh's *The White House at Night*.

An interesting and fun use of photo color matching, including Adobe's Color Match utility, is to use a classic painting as the template photo. The idea originated with James Daley, who used a set of classic old paintings as a way to spice up some very modern photographs. The result is dependent on how well the subjects match, as well as whether overall tone of the images is similar, but it can add a unique look to a rather dull photo.

 James Daley writes on his technique at *http://www.unfocusedbrain.com/ projects/match_color/*.

Figure 3-7 shows the result of my own matching operation. The sky is a little too yellow, and the image has lost too much contrast, but it's an intriguing approach and as good a place to start with photo manipulation as any.

Figure 3-7. Before, after, and matching image for using the Classic Color Match technique

How does the Color Match work with the Kennedy photo group? The results are less than spectacular. Two of the images are close enough that Color Match's effort is acceptable, but the differences among all the photos are enough that no one image can be used as the matching image with the other photos.

I've found that Color Match works well when there is some agreement on light values on the images before the color matching. Even if the subjects differ, it matters more that the overall image tone is similar. I've found less than acceptable results when the images differ dramatically in light values, even if the subjects match or the photos were taken in the same general area. In these cases, it's better to adjust the photos manually, rather than use automatic settings.

Besides, why should an algorithm have all the fun? Preparing a photo for publication is the funnest part of the photographic process—photography doesn't end after you press the shutter.

 Included with the examples are copies of old masters' artwork that you can use to try out Color Match, either with the examples in this book or your own photos.

Home-Baked Color Matching: Cooking with Levels and Curves

Matching photos is really an exercise in matching color on the three red-green-blue channels, as well as matching against overall luminosity. You don't need a special tool, as long as the photo editor provides something else: Levels, Curves, and the all-essential Histogram. Levels (in Photoshop, Image → Adjust → Levels) and Curves (Image → Adjust → Curves) are tools for manipulating overall illumination and color for a photo. Levels is used more for overall illumination changes, whereas Curves is highly effective when fine-tuning both illumination and color.

 The Luminous Landscape has good overview tutorials on both Levels and Curves (starting at *http://www.luminous-landscape.com/*). Earthbound has a nice tutorial on moving beyond Levels to Curves (at *http://www.earthboundlight.com/phototips/photoshop-curves.html*).

It helps to open the group of photos to be matched at the same time, unless there are too many or the tool doesn't support opening more than one image at a time. Once opened, identify the photos that need gross overall modification before starting the color matching. For the four Kennedy photos, initial modifications are made to the two images that are underexposed, and in the case of the moon rover, the photo that has the strongest color cast.

Using Photoshop and starting with the rover photo, create a Levels adjustment layer for the photo (Layer → New Adjustment Layer → Levels). Since color cast (to the yellow) is the biggest problem, set the photo's white point, as shown in Figure 3-8, by using the white point eyedropper tool to pick out that part of the picture that should be white: the top section of the canvas for the rover's seat.

By default, the white point is set to be a value of 255 for red, green, and blue, which works for this picture. The value can be adjusted, though, for other pictures.

Figure 3-8. After setting a new white point in the photo using Levels

This one modification removes most of the yellow cast made by the incandescent lighting. The Histogram window is opened to the side (Window → Histogram) and set to `all channels` view. The Histogram source is set to the `Adjustment Composite`, reflecting both the original photo and the changes made with the adjustment layer. As the figure demonstrates, the green and red channels have only minor adjustments—the blue channel, outlined in blue, is the one most drastically altered.

The image isn't perfect, though: it's still too dark, with too many dark shadows and too much contrast in the image. With the open Levels window Channel selection set to RGB, move the gray point (middle slider) of the Levels tool toward the left until it reaches a value of about 1.21. This raises the overall tone of the image without flattening out the contrast too much. The moon rover photo has now been sufficiently adjusted that we can move on to the next picture.

The next photo, the Apollo Rocket, is badly underexposed with a couple of "hot" spots where light is coming in through the door and reflected off of metal in the picture.

As with the moon rover, I create a Levels adjustment layer and move the gray point (the middle slider) until I've effectively doubled the range of tones for the picture, as shown in Figure 3-9. It looks washed out, as most of the contrast was lost with this move, but it does get the picture to an overall level that can then be used as the basis for fine-tuning.

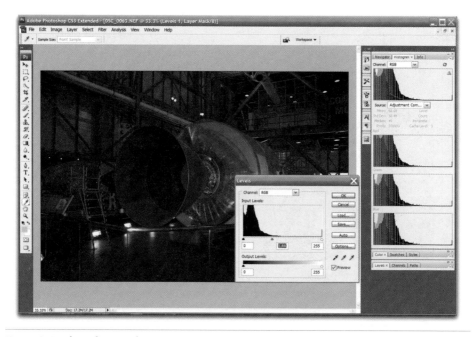

Figure 3-9. After adjusting the gray point to increase overall illumination for the Apollo rocket photo

The Curves tool is used for color matching tweaks from this point on. Curves gives us greater flexibility for making color adjustments beyond just increasing white, black, and gray points in a photo. Not only can we fix color casts, we can also more effectively match color across multiple images. Curves can either be applied directly to an image (Image → Adjustments → Curves) or via an adjustment layer (Layer → New Adjustment Layer → Curves).

When I'm matching images as a group, I look for common elements in all of the photos and then try to find where these common elements have about the same level of illumination. I use the green channel as illumination "control," and only modify the blue and red channels.

For instance, in the four pictures, the dull gold color of the wheel covers on the moon rover should be a relative match to the dull gold color in the one rocket photo. I use the Color Eyedropper tool from the Photoshop toolset (Window → Tools) to find a point in the gold in the rocket, and then look for a match in the green channels between this point and a point in the wheel cover. By match, I mean where the eyedropper values for green are the same in both. When I find the point where the greens match, I record the red, blue, and green values for that point, as well as the red, green, and blue values from the point in the source.

I use the same procedure to find color match points with other elements, such as the wall tiles, the aqua/turquoise of the building framework, the brighter yellow enamel on some of the metal work, and the sea green of some of the walls. This is in addition to grays, which are always the best testing points. Figure 3-10 shows some of these "match" points between two of the photos.

Figure 3-10. Test points in target photos

An interesting thing I've found with photographs is that when you look at an image, you might think it has too red a cast. However, when you test colors all around the picture, you may find it's saturated more to the cyan. So much for visual acuity, which is why I use the Color eyedropper and actual measurements rather than "eyeballing" the adjustment. Some sample measurements are, from source to target:

```
rgb(0,76,116) -> rgb(0,76,104)
rgb(163,150,93) ->  rgb(166,153,92)
```

Once I have my control points, so to speak, I pick out the best candidates for adjusting the colors on the target photo, and then use the Curves tool to make the change. The green channel curve isn't modified, being the illumination control; only the blue and red channels are changed in the target picture.

In this approach, I map out the blue values in the source and their mapped values in the target. For instance, if the source is a value of 114 and the equivalent target is 104, I know that the resulting blue curve will reflect an adjustment of moving the value of 104 to 114, as shown in Figure 3-11.

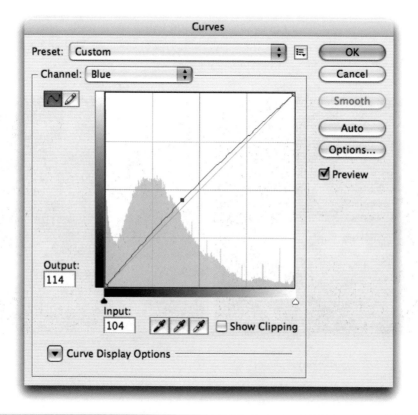

Figure 3-11. Mapping the target color point to the source color point in the blue channel

Typically I'll find three color points for matching: one in the darker color range, one mid-tone, and one lighter, as shown in Figure 3-12.

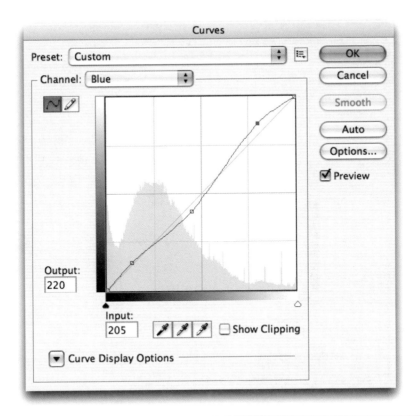

Figure 3-12. Mapping three control points in the source to the target in the blue channel

Figure 3-13 shows the Curves tool after making changes based on three control points for both the red and blue channels. Notice how neither the blue nor the red channels are changed that drastically? Remember that we're adjusting color points that reflect the same types of objects in each picture, but with differing color casts and illumination values. The adjustment should not be overly drastic or the result will be disappointing.

Typically I'll adjust for the red curves first, followed by the blue.

Here's a recap of the steps taken:

1. Open all the photos in the group at once, if possible.
2. Make any gross changes first, such as changing the overall illumination for a photo that is too obviously dark.
3. Pick one photo out as the control to make adjustments to the other pictures.

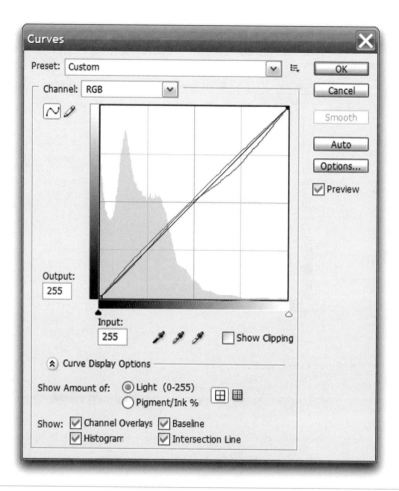

Figure 3-13. Curves, after adjusting the red and blue channels

4. Pick as many control points in the photo to match with the same elements in the other photos, as needed.

5. For each control point, match it against the points in the other photos that it should match with, and record the red, blue, and green RGB values for each: the control point and the match point in the other photo(s).

6. Create a new Curves adjustment layer in the photo that needs matching.

7. Keeping the green channel the same, adjust the red and blue channels to match the control point.

8. Repeat this process as often as necessary to adjust the photo more closely to the control picture. You may need to do some manual adjustment, or even pick a different control point if any adjustment ends up being too drastic.

Included in the examples are before and after web pages with the four images used in this example. The before picture web page is shown in Figure 3-14, and the after web page is shown in Figure 3-15.

Figure 3-14. Page with images fresh from the RAW shots

This same approach of testing color points with the Color eyedropper and then tweaking the curves can be used for correcting color casts within a single photo, when creating a panorama stitched together from many photos, or even when combining new figures into another picture. Adjusting color with the Curves tool can even be applied to selected sections of a photo, rather than the overall image, if the tool supports this (many do).

This approach is not using replacement color functionality, because I'm less interesting in "replacing" a specific color than in altering the light/shadow color casts between different pictures. Other approaches I've read about online include using colorizers, blurring, and blending. However, it's another approach (discussed in the next section) that has intriguing possibilities and is dependent on nothing more complex than blending layers.

Figure 3-15. Page with images after color/curves tweaking

Overlay Color Match Workaround

Months back I stumbled on to an alternative color matching capability that should work with any photo editor that supports layers. It's also a fun approach to experiment with, and works unexpectedly well.

To try out the technique, use the eyedropper to pick out what you perceive to be the main color from the image that's serving as a template. In the photo to be modified, create a transparent layer and set the blending mode to Overlay. Select the Paint Bucket tool and use it to fill the transparent layer. That's it, three simple steps:

1. Use the eyedropper to select a color.
2. Create a transparent layer using the Overlay blending mode for the photo to be modified.
3. Fill this layer with the Paint Bucket tool, with its color set to the previously selected color.

Using the open source tool GIMP this time, I used this technique with two of the Kennedy Space Center pictures. I first picked a neutral gray color from the more evenly toned picture, and used this gray in the overlay color matching technique in the other photo—in this case, the moon rover photo. I followed by adding more layers filled with colors matching secondary points in the template photo, as shown in Figure 3-16. To the left of the two photos is the layers view of the moon rover photo, showing the two new layers filled with the new overlapping colors.

Figure 3-16. Using the Overlay Color Matching technique with two Kennedy photos

This approach could also be used with the classic color matching technique discussed earlier (and shown in Figure 3-7). To refresh your memory after all that point-picking in the last section, instead of using another photo as the source image, a picture of a painting is used to provide the coloring template.

With this new classic color overlay matching technique, I can take a fabricated "ruin" and give it an antiqued patina, as shown in Figure 3-17.

In both of the figures, notice from the Layers panel (middle window) that I've used multiple layers filled with multiple colors to get to the final image. After considerable experimentation, I found that starting with lighter, more neutral colors first and then following with bolder, darker colors provides better results.

Figure 3-17. Using the overlay color matching approach with classic paintings

Of course, our jobs would be a lot simpler if we just dropped support for color altogether and went black and white. Except for the fact that black and white photography is dependent, first and foremost, on color.

It's Black and White and Not Red All Over

Sometimes when I look at photos online, I think the first control most people use to modify their photos is the saturation control. First, middle, and last tool used, really.

Skies are so blue they look made of crushed sapphires, along with ruby red lips, painfully bright yellow sunflowers, and green so rich it makes your teeth hurt. I didn't know that nature supported such brilliant colors. I hope to someday visit the planet that spawns such images.

I love color, as do most people. However, there is such a thing as too much color, and thanks to digital photography, we're pushing the limit of what is too much color all the time. Even without the "help" of the saturation controls, photographs embedded into web pages are fighting for eyeballs with garish ads, overly cute sidebar icons, and whatever other graphic the page owners have decided the page must have.

Converting color photographs to black and white (B&W) isn't just for the artistic elite or those wanting to create their own *noir* effect. B&W photos can enhance structure and shape—helpful if the photo is used to illustrate a story related to the subject of the photo. A B&W photo can also stand out more than a photo with weak or uninteresting coloring.

Converting a photo to B&W is easy: just use whatever saturation control the tool has and turn off all the color. You'll end up with a B&W photo, true, but you won't end up with the best B&W photo. To do that, you have to work with the B&W photo's colors.

In film photography, color filters were used with B&W film to control both contrast and detail. A color filter allows its associated color through, while blocking other colors. In other words, a green filter allows green light, a red filter allows red light, and so on. The filters can be used to create effects that can make a B&W photo doubly interesting and effective.

One example of what a filter can do is to increase contrast; to do so, use a filter color that is complementary to the dominant color where you want the enhancement. Complementary colors are:

- Green and magenta
- Yellow and blue
- Red and cyan

Getting these filter effects in Photoshop CS3 is a piece of cake with the new Black and White process. This control provides sliders for color adjustments, as well as several presets designed to emulate filters.

I built a Custom color filter, with heavy tinkering in both the red and green channels. Figure 3-18 shows the Black and White control panel, which has a drop-down for presets, as well as color sliders.

Figure 3-19 is a photo sampler showing the original color photo and several variations of presets from the Black and White utility, including the custom filter I designed. Beautiful, aren't they? Gives B&W a whole new perspective.

Other techniques provide effective approaches to control black and white conversion if you don't have access to such specialized controls—including the use of the Channel Mixer, probably one of the most popular techniques.

The Channel Mixer is an uncomplicated control, with three sliders for the red, blue, and green channels. The key to the Channel Mixer is that the initial luminance isn't affected as long as the sum of the values in all three channels is maintained at 100%. Creating an effect more than 100% brightens the picture; less than 100% darkens it.

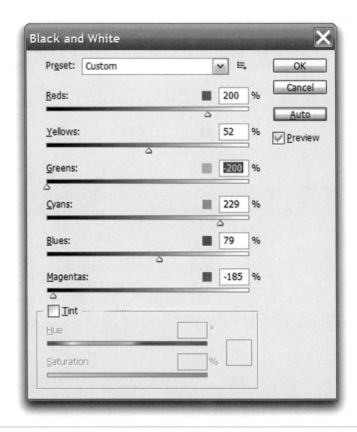

Figure 3-18. Black and White Photoshop control and target image

Some tools provide presets in their Channel Mixer tools to emulate filters, such as red and yellow filters. However, the filter effects also can be created manually. Much of this process is hit or miss, but there really isn't a "wrong" or "right" way to create any of the B&W effects—rightness is in the eye of the beholder.

Take an infrared effect. I say "effect" because a color photo captures visible light, and infrared is not from the visible light spectrum. A true infrared photo captures the infrared light at the time the photo is taken, using specialized equipment. However, an infrared-like effect can be faked using a variety of techniques.

One faux infrared technique is to create a Channel Mixer adjustment layer, convert it to monochrome, set the green channel to 200%, and adjust the red and blue channels so they equal –100%. This can lose details in the highlights in the photo, which can be corrected by creating a Curves adjustment layer and modifying the light levels as needed.

Figure 3-19. Same photo modified with Black and White control presets and custom filter

Once the new Curves layer is created, don't make any modifications yet—just save it, and then move it between the background image and the Channel Mixer layer. Then reopen the Curves layer, select the green channel, and adjust the brightness. I've found this works with some photos but less well with others.

A second technique still uses the Channel Mixer, only in this approach the image is not converted to monochrome. The red output channel is picked, but the red source channel is set to 0, with the blue source channel set to 100%. The blue output channel is picked next, and the opposite actions are taken: set the blue source to 0 and the red to 100%. Once this flip-flopping of colors is complete, create a new adjustment layer, but pick Hue/Saturation this time and set to the saturation levels to 0.

A third approach is to use a plug-in. I tried two, IR Film from ChromaSoftware (at *http://www.chromasoftware.com/ir_film.htm*) and Pseudo-IR from Cybia (at *http://www.cybia.co.uk/pseudoir.htm*). Plug-ins are always fun to play with.

Figure 3-20 features the same color photo used earlier, a monarch butterfly, but this time with the various faux infrared (IR) effects. From left to right, top to bottom, they are: the original; the infrared preset in the Black and White utility; the green filter effect with red set to –10 and blue to –90; swapping the blue and red channels; using the File IR plug-in; using the Pseudo-IR plug-in.

Going B&W isn't the only illustrative effect you can perform on your photos. We're just getting started.

Figure 3-20. Variations on a theme: faux IR effects

The Illustrative Effect

Chances are that if you're posting a photo because you think it's a good one, you're not going to do much more than make sure it's properly cropped and optimized. It's always fun to post a great photo.

However, if you're using a photo for illustration—to tell a story, to make a point, to annotate text—taking the photo is just the beginning. There's an amazing number of things you can do to a picture in order to convey mood or interest, to highlight a subject, or to convey a message. The photo becomes clay, and we become the sculptor.

Sharpen Me Up, Blur Me Down

Years ago when I was going to college, I worked for a photographer as a photo retoucher. In those days, photo retouching was actually done on the printed photograph using a variety of paints, chalk, and colored pencil.

When I was being trained in retouching, one of the first lessons I learned is that a slightly soft portrait could be blown up to a larger size, as long as the highlights in the eyes were sharp. We would use paintbrush and paint to "clarify" the highlight, which worked quite well. There were other approaches to sharpen a photo, using darkroom techniques. One was known as the Unsharp Mask—yeah, the one that most photo editors feature for digital sharpening.

In ancient pre-digital times, a positive transparency was made of a negative by exposing the negative on film rather than on paper. This new transparency was slightly blurred, and was sandwiched back with the original negative. The blurring on the positive transparency formed a halo effect around the objects in the negative and, since the effect is from a positive image, it's a contrasting color to the surrounded object. This haloing enhances the transition between elements in the picture, making the photo seem sharper. Hence, the name *unsharp* mask.

The same effect applies to digital photographs, except that we don't have to muck around with transparencies. It's the great irony of photography that sharpening is dependent on blurring: to be more precise, the Gaussian Blur.

The Gaussian Blur and "Mood"

The Gaussian Blur is the workhorse of photo and graphic editors. It's used to eliminate noise, and also is used in many popular filters, such as embossing, glow, and neon. In later chapters, it's used to create realistic object reflections. We've already heard how it's used to sharpen pictures. The Gaussian Blur can also be used to add "mood" to an otherwise moodless photo.

Figure 3-21 shows a mill spillway gate at Alley Spring Mill in Missouri. It's a picture with potential, not the least of which is the grain of the wood of the gate, the water and trees in the background, and the dark, shaded corner that counter-balances the brighter light of the opposite corner. It comes across a bit flat, though, and too detailed—there is such a thing as giving the eye too many places to look. What the photo needs is something to soften the image without losing that lovely wood grain. It needs atmosphere.

To generate both softness and mood, create a duplicate layer using Layer → Duplicate Layer. Once the duplicate layer is created, blend it with the original using the Overlay blending mode, available as a drop-down in the Layers window. Figure 3-22 shows the result of the initial blending. As you can see, the effect is garish, with the cumulative effect of the blending.

Now comes the mood. To soften the picture, apply a Gaussian Blur, accessed via the Filter → Blur → Gaussian Blur menu options. The filter control has a slider that sets the radius of the blur, as well as controls that determine the side of the image in the control, as shown in Figure 3-23. What's interesting is that the blur that shows up in the small preview window is much more extreme than that showing in the larger image with Preview selected. The reason is that the blur is being applied only to the top layer.

Figure 3-21. Original mill spillway gate before adjustments

Figure 3-22. Mill spillway gate with duplicate layer blended in as Overlay

Figure 3-23. Applying Gaussian Blur to the duplicate layer

What's also interesting is that the more the radius is increased for the blur effect, the clearer and sharper the initial picture. This is because the impact of the overlay is muted as the blur is increased, allowing more of the underlying image detail to show through. However, the detail that shows through now is softer, with a misty, other-worldly look, when compared to the previous entry. The overall luminance can be adjusted using the Levels tool. The adjusted image is much softer, without losing the detail. More importantly, the spillway gate blends into the picture without losing its character.

After the mood setting, it would be nice to reclaim some of the contrast in the gate, as well as the contrast among the trees and water plants in the background, but without losing that misty look we worked so hard to create and without making the picture muddy-looking with excessive contrast. What we need at this point is the Clarity sharpening effect (mentioned earlier), but Adobe doesn't make this available directly in Photoshop CS3. Or does it?

As stated earlier, the Clarity sharpening effect is based on a concept called the Local Contrast Enhancement (LCE) effect. The idea is to improve the local contrast—the small-scale contrast—in the picture rather than the overall contrast. Think of looking at a photo with squinted eyes: the detail you lose is the detail that could be aided by using the Local Contrast Enhancement technique.

To apply homegrown clarity, open the Unsharp Mask filter, and set the percentage small (start at 10%) and the radius quite large (begin at 50). Keep the threshold at 0.

The LCE effect is subtle, but it can really bring out the detail in the picture without losing the overall moody effect, as shown in Figure 3-24. This is especially important for web photos, when the size of the smaller images washes out much of the detail but you don't want to put this detail back at the expense of the overall picture.

Figure 3-24. After applying Local Contrast Enhancement to the mill spillway gate photo

You can use layers when varying the blending modes and making other adjustments, in order to experiment with new effects while leaving previous efforts untouched. You can also mask portions of any layer so that new effects apply only to the unmasked portions of the photo.

This technique applied a mood to an entire photograph. Sometimes, though, you don't want the entire picture, just one piece of it.

Knockouts and Extractions

I called them cut-outs, but other people refer to them as knockouts—extracting a subject or group of subjects from the rest of a photograph. The reasons to create knockouts are as varied as their uses. Maybe the background is too distracting or you want to add an overlap effect. Perhaps you want to create a knockout for humor, or to create an odd image to catch your web page viewer's attention. I have a friend who uses flower knockouts, deliberately sizing the photo so that the flower overlaps a given frame.

Isolating a subject from the rest of a photograph can be easy if the subject is all smooth curves and the background is a solid color. All you need to do then is tap the subject with the Magic Wand tool (or equivalent) and cut. Anything else, though, is going to take more work.

One approach to free-form selections of an image based on color is to use Photoshop's built-in Color Range tool, which can be accessed via Select → Color Range. The tool provides eyedroppers for removing or adding colors to the final selection, as shown in Figure 3-25 with several colors added to the selection.

Figure 3-25. Using the Color Range to select the subject

After selecting all of the colors to be masked, either you can cut away the background or, by right-clicking the selected area and choosing Select Inverse from the menu, you can select the subject, which can then be copied and pasted in a separate image. The result can be quite good, especially if the subject and the background colors don't have a lot of overlap. However, in most cases, there will almost always be some leftover background trash, as well as detail going missing, as shown in Figure 3-26.

Figure 3-26. After using Color Range to select colors and then deleting the selected regions

Another approach is to use the Extract Filter, which involves using a configurable brush to "paint" the outside of the area to select. When the area is outlined, it's filled, and it's this area that forms the selection, as shown in Figure 3-27.

Photoshop CS3 has a new Quick Selection that builds a selection based on colors picked out with an eyedropper. It provides more control over what is or is not selected than the Magic Wand. Other options include using layer masking, or even color channels to select the subject to be extracted or the background to be discarded. However, for most approaches, at some point you'll need to refine your selection.

Figure 3-27. Using the Extract Filter to select the subject

I use the Eraser tool to erase unwanted material and the History Brush to recover subject material I want to keep. When I do copy and paste the subject into another background, I also use the color matching routine (described earlier) to make sure the coloring of the pasted object matches the new background. Finally, if there's any extraneous background that needs to be eliminated, I use the Clone Stamp tool to cover the old background with the new.

To recap:

1. Select the subject using Color Range, the Extract Filter, one of the Select tools, or via channels or layer masking.

2. Clean up the selection if necessary, using the Eraser tool to remove extraneous material and the History Brush to recover accidentally deleted material.

3. Once the subject is attached to the new background (in a separate layer), use the color matching approach outlined earlier to match the luminance, light source, and coloring between the subject and its new background.

4. Use the Clone Stamp tool to fine-tune the edge of the selection.

There are hundreds of modifications you can make to a photograph to get it ready for the Web. First, though, you have to have an editor that provides the functionality necessary to re-create them.

Figure 3-28. Pasting the mill spillway gate into the inlet picture

Figure 3-29. You don't have to paste the subject into another photograph—let your imagination go wild

A Survey of Desktop Photo Editors

There are so many photo editors, it was hard to focus on which ones I wanted to survey for this book. There were some that obviously needed to be included, for their market share if no other reason. Others I included because of their quality in comparison to their relatively low (or no) cost.

Some tools work only in Windows, and others in multiple operating systems, including Linux, though this operating system had the fewest offerings. I even extended the survey to explore a few of the new online photo editing tools—a new and interesting breed of software that bypasses the whole operating system requirement.

The key item for me with all of the applications I examined was whether each provided the minimum set of operations I deemed critical for publishing photos to the Web. Let's revisit that list:

- Primitive-level support, such as being able to resize/resample and crop
- Support for RAW images, either directly or through some form of plug-in or third-party tool
- Support for color profiles and color space
- The capability to export or save in any number of formats, including TIFF, PNG, JPEG, and GIF, as well as save in-process work
- The capability to back out any number of edits for those times when my experimentation really goes wrong
- The capability to remove an abstraction, flaw, or dust—especially dust—from the photo, using some form of cloning
- Some support for effects and filters, especially blur and sharpening
- Color and light manipulation, including levels, curves, and channel mixing
- The capability to select specific components of an image
- Layers
- Lens and other photographic distortion corrections
- Extensibility with plug-ins and add-ons

Time to see how the various editors stack up.

Adobe Photoshop CS3

Adobe stresses that Photoshop is for the high-end graphics professional and that the average amateur photographer won't need its functionality. However, after years of following the community groups at sites such as Flickr, I've found that interest levels and passion follow lines other than whether you get paid for your photos or not. Photography has always generated intense interest, and with the newer digital cameras and the many avenues for public publication, the concept of *amateur* just doesn't mean the same anymore.

I use Photoshop and have for years. I first purchased it back when Photoshop was, more or less, a separate and unique product. Purchased it at a time, too, when it didn't seem to be as costly, though Photoshop has never been especially cheap. I love the product, though I'll be the first to admit I don't use all the functionality. Photoshop CS3 is chock-full of nooks and crannies, both for the graphics artist and for photographers.

What are some of the unique aspects of Photoshop that make it stand out? One is the assorted sharpening filters built into the tool, including Smart Sharpening, which works especially well if a photo is suffering from a mild case of hand shake. It has exceptional support for both layers and channels, as well as some of the best information displays, such as a multi-channel Histogram.

The tool also features a lot of software sugar, including tools to export for the Web, in addition to tools to generate photo galleries and shows. I'll cover this in more detail in the next chapter.

Included within the new release, CS3, is a new utility called the Adobe Device Central. This is a tool that gives us the ability to take whatever image we're currently editing and see how it looks in various mobile cell phones and other devices. When the Adobe Device Central opens, you're given a set of cell phone manufacturers and specific devices. Picking a device uploads the photo into a snapshop of the device. You can then further modify the image to match real-life circumstances, such as looking at the viewport with indoor reflections or stretching the image to fit the viewport, as shown in Figure 3-30.

It's a real eye opener to see what happens to a photo when it's viewed in a cell phone.

Included with Photoshop CS3 is Adobe Bridge, a wonderful photo management tool that provides some simple batch processing capabilities, such as adding metadata to a group of photos. It's also terrific for exploring your images in a lightbox-like setting so that you can quickly see which ones you want to open in Photoshop for additional editing. You also have access to various Photoshop services, including online backup and photo sharing, which are integrated as part of the product. In addition, as previously mentioned, Photoshop comes with Adobe Camera Raw for RAW image manipulation. The three products combine to cover the entire photo workflow, from camera to the Web.

How does it stack up to my needs?

All photo editors support resizing and cropping, and most desktop editors support saving the images in different formats—I won't cover the primitive operations from this point on. Through Camera Raw, Photoshop has excellent support for RAW images, along with historical support and the ability to back out of past edits. Abstractions can be removed through the Clone Stamp tool, and Photoshop's Filters are some of the best in the industry. In addition, Photoshop has multiple color and

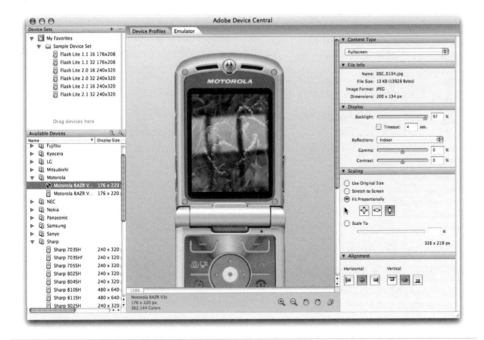

Figure 3-30. Screenshot of Adobe Device Central in action

luminance controls, such as Levels, Curves, Channel Mixer, and the new Black and White process.

There are several different ways to select an object, as was demonstrated earlier. Layers are an essential element for many photo modifications, and Photoshop defined the implementation that other products now follow.

Photoshop is the leader in the field of photo editing, and the number of Photoshop plug-ins, actions, and various other extensions is seemingly without limit. It was the tool I used to demonstrate the photo editing techniques, so we know it's capable of any and all photographic modifications.

Photoshop also provides a full library of distortion and other defect-fixing filters and tools, including fixes for lens correction and transform tools to manage skewing and custom rotation.

What are the negatives to Photoshop? One challenge is the confusing way in which Adobe groups Photoshop with other tools, and not being sure exactly what we need in order to upgrade the package of which Photoshop is a part. A second problem has to do with validating the software. Photoshop's keys validate an installation for one machine only, and if you need to move it, you have to uninstall it. A bit tough if your machine crashes and you lose the installation.

In addition, beta testers for Photoshop CS3 found that they had problems installing CS3 on the same machines the beta was installed in. Special scripts have been created to prepare a machine for installation of Photoshop, but the measures the scripts take are a little extensive.

Lastly, and probably most importantly, Photoshop is pricey. Too pricey for many, and too complicated for others. An alternative to the full installation of Photoshop is Photoshop Elements, which has most of the necessary photo editing tools without many of the extra features. Elements also includes many organizational capabilities, and support for the Adobe Camera Raw utility, all in a much more affordable package.

 The Adobe Photoshop page is at *http://www.adobe.com/products/ photoshop/index.html*. Downloads for trial access can be found along the top menu.

Photoshop Elements

Adobe provides Photoshop Elements for both the Mac and Windows. I tried out Photoshop Elements 5 for Windows for this book.

Photoshop Elements is an interesting tool to use, especially coming from a full Photoshop background. I kept expecting to find some tools that were not included in the product, but was surprised to find some nice functionality in Elements that doesn't exist in the parent product. In particular, the application has a wonderful tool called the Magic Extractor that easily selects a piece of a photo. If you're like me and can't hold a light pen or mouse steady to save your life, a tool that makes it easy to extract a flower or dog or house out of a photo is worth its weight in digital gold. With the Magic Extractor, just splash a little color on whatever you want to keep, click the button, and, Bob's your uncle, you have your object, as Figures 3-31 and 3-32 demonstrate.

Elements is easier to use than Photoshop right out of the box. Many of the operations are one-click, and are clearly labeled so their functionality is understandable for the newbie or moderately experienced photographer.

Photoshop Elements has built-in photo management capability, including the ability to capture photos directly from a camera, though it lacks the sophistication of Adobe Bridge. In addition, the product has more options for photo presentation, including an extensive selection of templates, though most of these seem to be focused on printing photos rather than publishing to the Web. For those interested in quicker fixes, such as slider controls for hue and saturation, red eye removal, and default sharpening, Elements has the Quick Fix tool, shown in Figure 3-33. It doesn't do a bad job, but I found that typically it didn't make the same corrections I would have made myself.

Figure 3-31. The Magic Extractor tool in action. Splash a bit of color…

Figure 3-32. Photoshop Elements after the flower has been magically extracted and the background filled in with color

Figure 3-33. Photoshop Elements' Quick Fix editing tool

Returning to my must-have list for photo editors, Elements automates many of the attributes that I manipulate manually. Doing so makes the tool easier to use, but which tools are included and which are not seems rather arbitrary. The tool has support for Levels but not Curves. What it does provide is a pseudo–curves tool that offers push-button choices with some brightness control. Transforms for correcting perspective are provided, but not a decent Channel Mixer.

One critical component Elements provides is support for Layers, and that includes being able to create a duplicate layer and control the blending mode, necessary for our "mood" alteration technique. The tool also supports a variety of filters, including Gaussian Blur, and the tool's support for sharpening is excellent, for both automatic and manual manipulation. Elements supports the Unsharp Mask, but also a variation of the parent Photoshop's Smart Sharpening capability. The latter is helpful if you have a photo with a lot of noise and want sharpening applied to edges rather than the noise.

Thankfully, many of the higher-level functions available in Photoshop can be emulated in Photoshop Elements by following clearly defined steps. In addition, the tool is extensible through the use of plug-ins, and people have provided extensions to add many of the more critical "missing" components. For instance, Photoshop plug-ins work in Elements.

One plug-in I believe is essential is the free SmartCurve, designed specifically for Elements, which provides the essential Curves editing (see Figure 3-34). This is essential for doing the color matching routine described earlier. In addition, another plug-in I tried out was a B&W conversion tool by theimagingfactory.

Figure 3-34. The SmartCurve plug-in available for Photoshop Elements

 The SmartCurve plug-in can be downloaded from *http://free.pages.at/ easyfilter/curves.html*. The trial for B&W conversion is available at *http://www.theimagingfactory.com/*.

The positives associated with Photoshop Elements is that it's inexpensive, there are numerous tutorials for using the application, and it makes use of Photoshop's plug-ins. The negatives are that support for the Mac lags behind that for Windows, and the hit-and-miss built-in support is a little frustrating once you move beyond push-button adjustment supports.

Returning to the photo editing examples, here's how to implement each in Photoshop Elements:

Color matching

Color matching can be implemented using the built-in Levels to adjust light levels, the eyedropper to sample color values, and then SmartCurve to adjust the overall color casts. Elements supports opening multiple documents at a time.

B&W conversion

B&W conversion can be managed either by the built-in Photoshop Elements black and white conversion tools or via one of the numerous Photoshop plug-ins.

Setting mood à la the Gaussian Blur

Photoshop Elements supports duplicate layers. Once the duplicate layer is created, it can be modified with the Gaussian Blur filter, and then blended using Overlay. Elements also supports levels to lighten the overall image if too dark. Elements also supports the Unsharp Mask in order to implement the Local Contrast Enhancement to add a clarity effect.

Knockouts and removing backgrounds

Selection can be made through a variety of lasso tools, including the magnetic lasso tool and the Magic Extractor. Once the item is cut out, it can be pasted into another photo or a separate file. Elements has an Eraser tool to delete extraneous material. Elements does not support the Photoshop History Brush, but the effect can be emulated by creating a new layer, making a merged copy of the photo on that new layer, and turning off visibility. To restore a portion of the image, turn on the visibility of the merged layer, and use the Eraser to "uncover" the portions of the image you want to recover.

Of course, Adobe isn't the only game in town when it comes to photo editors, and another quite powerful photo editor and graphics tool comparably priced to Elements is Paintshop Pro.

 Download the Photoshop Elements trial at *http://www.adobe.com/ downloads/*. Unfortunately, the only trial version of Elements is 5.0 for Windows. Surprising, because Adobe is good about providing trial copies of all its software.

Paint Shop Pro Photo XI

Paint Shop Pro has been around for years, and is currently at version 11. This full-featured photo and graphics editor is available at a very affordable price. That's the good news. The bad news is that it's only available for Windows.

Support for RAW images is built into Paint Shop Pro, though the tool does not provide any pre-edit manipulations, such as adjusting exposure and white balance presets.

It has many of the advanced photo editing tools—such as Curves, Levels, and Channel Mixing—but also has several push-button improvements. One is the Smart Photo fix, which works to correct all aspects of the photo: color, brightness, saturation, and sharpness. A variation of Smart Photo fix lets the photographer tweak the auto adjustments, providing a dual manual/auto fixing tool.

When using the advanced tools, Paint Shop Pro provides a preview function, like Elements and Photoshop. However, it goes a step further, providing a before and after image right in the tool. This gives you a nice comparison effect, which can help you quickly eyeball the impact of an effect.

Another rather fun aspect of Paint Shop Pro is the collection of special effects tools, such as the Time Machine and Lights, demonstrated in Figure 3-35. I'm not normally hot on the gimmicky effects with photos, but I found Lights to be an interesting effect to add to some pictures with darker corners. The Time Machine not only provides a nicely done aging effect, but also a fun trip through the history of photography. Education and effect in one tool. What a deal.

Figure 3-35. Paint Shop Pro Lights Tool

Effects is one thing that Paint Shop Pro has in abundance. As shown in Figure 3-36, additional toolbars provide Web-specific effects, primarily saving photo types and previewing in a browser. The tool also has an effects toolbar, including access to dozens (hundreds?) of effects through the Effects Browser. It has many specialized "fixes," such as ones for red eye and the purple fringing that can occur with photos where sunlight is reflected off of the top of waves. However, most of these can be fixed following simple steps available online, so I'm not sure having these prepackaged really buys us much.

Figure 3-36. Paint Shop Pro with menus and toolbars loaded and the Effects Browser opened

How does the tool do with the must-have list? It probably doesn't surprise you to hear that the tool supports every one of the items on the list, as well as the functionality demonstrated in the photo editing section. Some of the effects have to be emulated, such as an Unsharp Mask in order to implement the LCE effect, and Gaussian Blur, duplicate layers, and levels in order to implement the mood effect. Paint Shop Pro provides extensive support for selection and extraction via Smart Edge, Magic Wand, and a host of other approaches.

Still missing functionality? Paint Shop Pro also supports Photoshop plug-ins.

Paint Shop Pro is a tool loaded with features at a very affordable price. As mentioned previously, though, it is only available on Windows, and there's no indication that support will be extended to the Mac or Linux.

Another downside to the tool, and one that has cost it fans and loyal followers, is Paint Shop Pro's 8-bit limitation for most manipulations, filters, and plug-ins. When using the tool, you'll get used to a pop-up window stating that the effect requires that the picture be reduced to an 8-bit image first. Other tools support 16-bit image manipulation, including Elements.

Does it make a difference whether an image is edited as an 8-bit image as compared to a 16-bit image? Most modifications end up with some loss of data, but editing a photo as an 8-bit photo, which only supports 256 colors per channel, increases the loss of data as compared to 16 bit. For most photos for the Web, though, this difference may not be significant enough to be a problem.

Paint Shop Pro isn't alone in its lack of support for 16-bit images. Photoshop Elements can open an image as a 16 bit, but most of the tool's functionality that's impacted by color support—such as layers, levels, and so on—is disabled until the image is *downverted* to 8 bit. Photoshop CS3, on the other hand, provides extensive 16-bit support. In fact, opening a RAW image in CS3 automatically opens the image as 16 bit. You'll have to downvert it once in Photoshop to work with 8 bits.

Returning to the examples, the Paint Shop Pro alternatives are:

Color matching
> The same approach used to create the color matching in Photoshop CS3 can be used with Paint Shop Pro, but first you'll need to convert the image to 8 bits. Once converted, Levels Adjustment Layers can be used to manage overall light levels, the eyedropper used to sample colors, and Curves used to equalize the color casts of all the images.

B&W conversion
> Paint Shop Pro has direct B&W filter effects. It also supports grayscale conversion, as well as desaturation using the Hue/Saturation adjustment. In addition, Paint Shop pro has the Channel Mixer tool, which is highly effective for B&W conversion.

The Gaussian Blur effect
> Create a duplicate layer using the Overlay blending mode. Apply a Gaussian Blur effect to the duplicated layer, and once the effect you're interested in is achieved, flatten the two layers. To finish, create a Levels Adjustment Layer and adjust the overall light levels, and then apply the clarity effect using the Unsharp Mask.

Selection and extraction
> Paint Shop Pro supports a multitude of lassos for selection, including a Smart Edge Freehand lasso that's quite effective. Use it to outline the subject, clicking at short intervals in order to "anchor" the selection line to the outline. Once the selection is made and cut, use the Eraser tool to clean up any extraneous material.

As inexpensive as Paint Shop Pro is, nothing beats "free" when it comes to price. That leads to the next tool on my list, Paint.NET, a freely available application based on the .NET Framework.

Paint.NET

When I first started looking at photo editors to cover, Paint.NET came up several different times. Not only is it free, but it also has strong community support. Like Paint Shop Pro, it's only available on Windows.

Paint.NET has an open architecture, extensible with plug-ins. Unlike most other tools, though, Paint.NET does not support Photoshop plug-ins. Fortunately, there are a decent number of Paint.NET plug-ins available, and the number should increase over time.

 Paint.NET can be downloaded at *http://www.getpaint.net/index.html*. Like most open or free software, donations are appreciated. Tutorials are accessible from the community forum at *http://paintdotnet. forumer.com/viewforum.php?f=15*, and a list of plug-ins is at *http:// paintdotnet.forumer.com/viewforum.php?f=16*.

Paint.NET has a very simple interface, and for newbies wanting to learn how to edit photos, this application is probably a decent starting point. It also has some interesting effects, but is lacking functionality I would expect from a full-featured photo editor. As an example of this incompleteness, Paint.NET has support for layers, including the duplicate layer, but not adjustment layers or masking. From the roadmap at the application site, adjustment layers (and I'm assuming masking) should be included in version 4.0 of the tool.

The community has provided some interesting plug-ins, including support for 3D objects, shown in Figure 3-37.

How does it compare to my must-haves? I mentioned Paint.NET's layer support, and it also has support for Curves and Levels, but not a Channel Mixer. The Black and White conversion looks to be a straight desaturater, and Sharpen is relatively primitive, but Paint.NET supports the Gaussian Blur and other effects. It also provides an undo history, can read RAW images directly (albeit slowly), and has a clone stamp tool for removing flaws and aberrations. Objects can be selected using Magic Wand and various lasso selection tools.

If some functionality wasn't accessible through plug-ins, and if the community support were less, Paint.NET would have fallen from my list of covered tools. However, with both, enough of my must-haves are covered to make it acceptable. It's still a young tool and will only improve over time.

Following are the techniques to use with Paint.NET to implement the photo editing tasks.

Figure 3-37. The Paint.NET 3D effect

Color matching

Paint.NET does provide support for layers, Levels, and Curves, as well as an eye-dropper tool and the ability to open multiple images at a time. This is all sufficient in order to implement the color matching capability.

B&W conversion

With only primitive desaturation capability and no channel mixer, we're dependent on plug-ins. I used the Greyscale channel mixer in the WPF plug-in, which worked quite well.

The Gaussian Blur effect

Paint.NET supports duplicate layers, as well as the Gaussian Blur, and so half our work is done. The tool provides Levels and Curves for fine-tuned adjustment, but the only way to implement the Local Contrast Enhancement is to use another plug-in. The one I used was Sharpen+.

Selection and extraction

Paint.NET does provide multiple lasso tools and a Magic Wand to select objects. After selection, use the Eraser tool to clean up.

Paint.NET is only available for Windows. All the tools discussed so far only have versions for Windows or the Mac. What about Linux?

The most complete and sophisticated of the open source, free photo editing tools is the GNU Image Manipulation Program (GIMP). Unlike any other photo editor, GIMP is available on Windows, Mac OS X, and Linux. The built-in functionality is very complete but, like Photoshop, GIMP also has an open framework, which allows for the addition of plug-ins and extensions.

GIMP

The GNU Image Manipulation Program is one of the older and more sophisticated image editing programs. You can download the source, but there are also binaries (already compiled applications) for Windows, Unix/Linux, and Mac OS X. GIMP does require an installation of X11 to work on the Mac (X11 can be installed from the developer tools included with the Mac OS X CDs).

For this book, I used the stable GIMP 2.2.17 installer for Windows and the in-development as well as release version of 2.4 on my Mac, installed via Macports. The two are very different and since most documentation is for 2.2.17, I'll primarily reference its functionality. However, I'll provide screenshots of both.

GIMP is touted as a Photoshop replacement or "killer," a label that the developers of the tool would appreciate that we not use. They're not creating a Photoshop replacement as much as they are creating a complete and powerful photo editing tool.

GIMP doesn't have native support for RAW images, but support for RAW is provided through integration with UFRaw, covered earlier. UFRaw acts as a plug-in, and once installed, when you open a RAW image in GIMP, UFRaw intervenes to pre-process the RAW image.

GIMP does introduce color management into version 2.4, but it's limited to RGB and grayscale. This isn't a problem from the perspective of this book since our focus is on web graphics. GIMP also only supports 8-bit images, and as I mentioned in the section on Paint Shop Pro, 16-bit editing is preferred. The plan is to add 16 bit in the future.

There are several plug-ins that are developed specifically for GIMP, in addition to a plug-in called PSPI that allows us to use Photoshop plug-ins with GIMP. However, there is no version of the plug-in for Mac OS X, and the one I tried with Windows didn't seem to work.

 Download GIMP from *http://gimp.org* and find plug-ins from the GIMP Registry at *http://registry.gimp.org/*. PSPI is available at *http://www.gimp.org/~tml/gimp/win32/pspi.html*.

GIMP is a full-featured application, providing support for layers, a complete set of image editing tools, and a set of filters for everything from sharpening images to adding light effects (see Figure 3-38).

Figure 3-38. GIMP on the Mac

GIMP's power does not lie on the surface; you may not see all of its capability at first glance. The best way to learn how to work with GIMP is to search on GIMP with whatever functionality you're interested in, such as "GIMP convert black and white." There is a very nice set of tutorials at *http://www.gimp.org/tutorials/*. Most of the writing there is based on GIMP 2.2, but it should transfer to the newer version. You have to explore the menus, though, as the options have changed menu positions.

For instance, there are several methods for converting images to black and white. One is to use the Channel Mixer set to monochrome. (See Figure 3-39.) The Channel Mixer is under the Colors → Components → Channel Mixer in 2.4, but under Filters → Color → Channel Mixer in 2.2. Another approach is to use GIMP's Decompose process, which is under Image → Mode → Decompose in 2.2 and Colors → Components → Decompose in 2.4.

GIMP does support layers, including duplicate layers, but not adjustment layers. From my list of must-haves, as mentioned, GIMP supports all the color operations, including Curves, Levels, Channel Mixer, Hue/Saturation, Histograms, the ability to Decompose the image to a series of grayscale layers, each of which can be manipulated, and on and on. The tool has a very rich set of color functionality.

GIMP does not provide some key items, such as a free transform tool (allowing rotation, skewing, and so on), but it does have a set of discrete transform tools supporting scaling, shear, and perspective. GIMP has limited support for print color. However, it does support sRGB, which is what we're interested in for web graphics.

Figure 3-39. Using the Channel Mixer to convert the image to black and white

Since work on GIMP continues under an open source effort, expanded support for color, transforms, and other features are expected in the future.

In my opinion, beginning with GIMP 2.4, the Foreground Select tool, in addition to the Fuzzy Select tool, makes GIMP the superior product of all of the photo editors when it comes to selection tools. GIMP is also the only sophisticated graphics tool with native support for a Linux/Unix environment, though Photoshop has been ported to Linux using a Windows emulator (by the folks at Disney, no less). Unless you need specific components of Photoshop, GIMP really is an excellent option for most web graphics work.

To implement the photo editing tasks in GIMP:

Color matching
> GIMP supports Curves and Levels, as well as layers, which is what we need to create the Curves-based color matching. As was demonstrated in the overlay color matching section, GIMP supports this approach equally well.

B&W conversion
> GIMP provides numerous ways to convert color to black and white, including some seemingly unique to the tool, such as using Decompose RGB, in addition to the use of plug-ins. However, my favorite approach is to use the Channel Mixer.

The Gaussian Blur effect

This effect is as simple as creating a duplicate layer, setting the blending mode to Overlay, adding a Gaussian Blur effect (I suggest a setting of 70), and then merging the result. Once merged, the Local Contrast Enhancement technique can be applied via the Unsharp Mask.

Selection and extraction

GIMP supports numerous selection tools, including the Fuzzy Select, which does a remarkably good job with irregular objects. Version 2.4 also provides the Foreground Select Tool, which simplifies selecting an object: you create a selection region around the object and then brush over the object itself, being careful not to cross the region border. Between both, I'd say that GIMP has the best selection support of any of the photo editors, and that includes Photoshop.

Of course, the way to avoid installation issues is to use one of the web-based photo editors. The question with these, though, is do they have enough functionality to meet my minimum requirements? I checked out two: Fauxto and Picnik.

Online Editors: Fauxto and Picnik

There are numerous advantages to online photo editors. When you use online tools, you don't have to muck around with installations or upgrading. In addition, you can access the tool from all of your machines, regardless of what operating system the machine is running. Most of the time the tools are free, too, which is a powerful incentive to "go online" for all your photo needs.

Of course, there are always downsides to online photo editors. For instance, the company may go out of business, start charging unexpectedly, or limit access. Unless specifically designed for offline access, you'll only have access to the editor online, and it will be slow to upload images. In my opinion, the most significant downside to online photo editors is that most just don't provide the complete functionality of a desktop tool.

Considering the myriad functionalities that photo editors provide, it's not surprising to find that even the most sophisticated online photo editor is not as comprehensive as the simplest of the desktop tools. However, most people don't really need the sophistication—or the cost—of a tool like Adobe Photoshop. In fact, even Photoshop wizards don't always need all the sophistication of a tool like Photoshop.

Still, there are functionalities we *need*. A big one right from the start is that I haven't found any online tools that can process RAW formats. If you want to use RAW in an online photo editor, you'll need to convert your image to something like TIFF or PNG before editing. In addition, even if supported, RAW image files tend to be very large, which is impractical for file uploading. In the beginning of the chapter, I mentioned a couple of RAW converters; using either of these will work.

I wouldn't necessarily incorporate an online tool into your main photo processing work flows, but they might be a good secondary tool—especially if you're on the road and just want to process some photos for uploading to Flickr or SmugMug.

Fauxto

Fauxto is a Flash-based online photo editor that most closely resembles the more capable desktop tools. You can open multiple images from the Web, your computer, or those stored at Fauxto. The tool provides a minimal support for layers, a small set of somewhat generic filters, and tools to allow you to add text, lines, and graphics.

With Fauxto, you can compress or expand the image, move it relative to the canvas, rotate it, add geometric figures using solid and gradient color, add lines or freeform text, do smudging, erase parts of the image, and, as I mentioned in the last paragraph, apply filters. The filters can be used to sharpen or blur the image, convert to grayscale, adjust the hue and saturation, find edges, and add some effects, such as embossing.

You can add layers to an image, and there are several blend modes, similar to those supported in the desktop tools:

- Normal
- Multiply
- Screen
- Lighten
- Darken
- Difference
- Add
- Subtract
- Invert
- Alpha
- Erase
- Overlay
- Hardlight

Since Fauxto supports layers, an eyedropper, and some color control, can it also be used to implement the color matching or the Gaussian Blur effect? No, it cannot. The tools provided are primitive at best, with absolutely no control other than a button.

In addition, it can't really be used to select objects for background removal, nor does it provide the capability to clone sections of the photo for repair or removal of aberrations. Of the photo editing tasks I covered earlier, the only one that it can do is convert an image to black and white. Even then, it does a basic grayscale or desaturate conversion, but nothing more complex.

You can store images on Fauxto, though the interface is not intuitive. It's also overly dependent on the use of drag and drop, for purposes that just don't need it. Once the photos are uploaded, you can choose to make them available to public access, attaching tags (keywords) to aid searches.

Fauxto does provide basic photo manipulations, which are accessible anywhere you have Internet access (see Figure 3-40). For quick photo uploads requiring minimum editing, it can provide what you need, but be forewarned: keep your images small for uploading or you'll be waiting a considerable time.

Figure 3-40. Photo being edited in Fauxto, loaded in Firefox

Picnik Photo Editing: Less Is More

Picnik has what I consider to be one of the most intuitively obvious user interfaces of any of the tools I experimented with when writing this book. As soon as a photo is loaded, you notice a slider at the bottom right that allows you to instantly zoom in and out (something I really wish all other tools had).

Along the top, buttons are listed to auto-fix the image, crop, rotate, adjust exposure and color, sharpen, and fix red eye. Clicking on any of these replaces the top menu with a control bar specific to the option selected, as shown in Figure 3-41, which shows the crop option.

Figure 3-41. The crop option in the online photo editing tool Picnik

Clicking the Create option actually opens up an effects menu, with options to convert the image to grayscale, sepia, and so on. There are also other interesting effects you can apply, including Infrared Film Vignette (a 1960s look), and Night Vision. All of these options are available to all users, though if you want to edit full-screen and without the annoying ads, you'll have to purchase a premium membership.

Once you've adjusted the image, you can send it to your Flickr, Picasa, or Facebook account, email it, or save it back to your computer.

Picnik is a nice tool, nice enough to now be integrated with the Flickr photo web service. However, it doesn't handle most of my list of must have functionalities, and it remains more of a novelty for me than a true photo editor.

Photo Workflow Software

The tools we've looked at up to this point are primarily editors that manipulate individual items. Another type of photography software is a workflow tool that manages photos in bulk. Two of the best-known photo workflow applications are Apple's Aperture and Adobe's Lightroom. Neither is cheap, but both applications are available for a free 30-day trial. Aperture only runs on a Mac, whereas Lightroom works in a Windows and Mac environment.

 The trial for Aperture can be accessed at *http://www.apple.com/ aperture/*. The trial for Lightroom can be downloaded from *http:// www.adobe.com/products/photoshoplightroom/*. Aperture has fairly restrictive requirements for the application, and I could get it working on only one of my machines. Lightroom is more flexible in its machine requirements.

There is ongoing work on an open source, freely downloadable workflow application that goes by the name of blueMarine (found at *http://bluemarine.tidalwave.it/*). Like GIMP and UFRaw, it will be available on Windows, Mac OS X, and Linux and will make a nice companion to these other two pieces. However, the functionality for this tool is very much in an alpha state, and I'd recommend waiting for a more stable product before trying it.

The purpose of workflow software is to manage a group of photos, not specifically edit any individual picture. The software can take photos directly from your digital camera, provide a means with which to review and discard members, adjust the remaining, package them into a slideshow, and then publish them online.

In this chapter, I'm mainly interested in how the tools do from the perspective of a photo editor. In the next chapter, I look in more detail at their publication capabilities.

Apple's Aperture

Of all the tools tested in this chapter, Aperture had the most significant requirements. Much of this could be because of the application's touted "non-destructive" editing feature, which keeps snapshots of images in memory, as well as saves them to the disk.

Moving away from the tool's organizational capabilities, including the ability to rate photos, stack, group, and edit metadata, Aperture does provide individual photo editing capability. It's just really hard to find once you open the tool and after you've imported your test photos.

To get to what Apple calls the Adjustment Inspector, double-click any of the photos you want to edit. A side panel opens to the right listing several expandable sections that provide editing capabilities. Below is the Metadata Inspector to edit the metadata portion of the photo. Both panels can be resized to give the other panel room, or closed altogether. Another option is to turn on the Heads Up Display (HUD) via the Window menu, and then set the View to full screen. This provides much more space in which to work with the photo when editing.

In the Adjustments Inspector, we're given a Histogram and options to change exposure, saturation, and contrast, adjust shadows and highlights, and work with color and sharpness. The capabilities are controlled via sliders, and changes are immediately reflected in the photo and in the Histogram.

The Levels tool has a rather interesting interface, as shown in Figure 3-42. Two thumb tabs are provided for each white, gray, and black point, one for input, and one for output. A line connects the two, providing a visual representation of the changes made to the picture.

Figure 3-42. Examples loaded into Aperture, and Levels editing one of the photos

Aperture does a decent job with editing a single, individual photo. Doing preliminary edits in the tool is a quick way to process several photos at the same time. However, Aperture does not have the capabilities to create the photo editing tasks described earlier. There is no layers tool, nor true Curves or Levels. The desaturation capability is based on the Hue/Saturation slider, and though there is cropping, there is no selection tool.

Among the adjustments you can make are:

- RAW Fine Tuning, including a Boost option, Sharpening, and Color Blur correction
- Exposure, Brightness, Saturation, and Contrast sliders
- Levels and Shadow and Highlight controls
- White Balance correction
- Standard Hue, Saturation, and Luminance sliders
- Red eye and noise reduction
- Spot adjustment
- Monochrome color mixing

Note the following, which is not obvious: not all adjustment controls show when the Adjustments Inspector is first turned on. To add others, such as the Monochrome Mixer, you have to click the little plus sign at the top of the Inspector or HUD. As you turn these on, they will operate on your photo, but you can uncheck the option once you're finished adding adjustment items.

The Monochrome Mixer is more or less a Channel Mixer, providing the three color channel adjustments as sliders. The Sepia adjustment works as you would expect, and you can use a slider to control the intensity.

Aperture's Metadata editing is actually more interesting than the adjustments editing. Being able to quickly and simply add metadata to one or more pictures at the same time, to group them how we want, and quickly publish the results is very attractive. Whether it's attractive enough to warrant the price is up to the individual.

Adobe's Lightroom

I must confess that I find Lightroom's interface to be much more intuitive than Aperture's. Perhaps it's my exposure to Adobe's products over the years—I've developed Adobe Think.

Once you open the tool, though, you're given a list of panel tabs labeled with Library, Develop, Slideshow, Print, and Web, which makes it really easy to know where to go to create whatever you need.

In the Develop panel, there are some tools for batch processing photos, including an intriguing Auto Tone tool that attempts to equalize tone across the many photos. This, to me, is what all photo workflow tools should provide, because if a photo is going to be published as a batch, wouldn't it make sense that they have some visual cohesiveness?

I opened several of the Kennedy pictures in Lightroom and tried the Auto Tone across all of them (see Figure 3-43). Some photos ended up too light, others too dark, but the color casts were consistent. I'd say that this process is helpful if your photos have a fairly consistent exposure range right from the start and need final tweaking. Anything else, though, and you're still better off using the manual methods outlined earlier.

Figure 3-43. Using Lightroom's Auto Tone across several Kennedy Space Center photos

Lightroom provides a before and after view of the image being worked, as well as other options, including picking the white point for white balancing—available as a Develop menu option—and Presets.

Like Aperture, Lightroom provides several sliders, in addition to a Histogram that reflects changes over time. Among these are controls for contrast, levels, sharpening, lens correction, noise reduction, and even camera calibration. The options are:

- Basic manipulation, including white balance setting, exposure range, and color basics
- Tone Curve, which controls the shadows and highlights in the image
- The HSL/Color/Grayscale Mixer, similar to the separate panels in Aperture
- Split Toning, which provides separate control of hue and saturation for highlights and shadows
- Detail, which provides sharpening and noise control
- Lens correction
- The aforementioned camera calibration

Just as with Aperture, Lightroom does a good job of editing an image, but its strengths really rest in being able to process photos in bulk.

In addition, it seems to me that Lightroom also competes, somewhat, with the Photoshop trio of Bridge, Photoshop, and Camera Raw, as Bridge provides bulk metadata editing, Camera Raw offers bulk photo adjustment, and Photoshop covers, well, everything else. Perhaps it's my frugal nature, but I don't know that I would buy Lightroom if I already had Photoshop.

Regardless of how tight we are financially, what's important is that each tool we use fits how we want to process our photos. Which takes us back to the beginning of the chapter, and understanding how we take a photo from camera to the Web.

Photo Workflow: Camera to Web Redux

I have two Macs and a PC, and I managed to load all three with software when writing this book. It rather amazed me that it all worked together and I had a minimum of conflict or out-and-out battling for dominance. Other than each tool wanting to set itself as the default for opening certain types of files, they all behaved.

The point of this little anecdote is that you don't have to use only one tool, or one of each type of tool. If you want to have more than one photo editor installed on your machine—and you have the space and can afford it—load all editors if you wish and have a blast.

At the same time, I hope I demonstrated that you don't need several tools in order to prepare a photo for publishing on the Web. In most cases, a camera RAW processor and photo editor is all you need.

The type of tool is what's important, along with what it supports. Consider the groups of tools we looked at. First were the camera RAW tools. If you shoot in RAW you may or may not need a separate utility to process the RAW file, depending on whether your photo editing tool supports the format. Paint Shop Pro supports RAW directly; Photoshop does not, and provides a utility.

How much you process the photo in the RAW utility depends on how tightly integrated the tool is with the photo editor, and how much you like the results. If the utility is part of a set of products by the same company, you're probably better off performing the same processes in the editor until your RAW tool provides batch support, like Adobe's Camera RAW.

The next group of tools we explored were photo editors, after first looking at several different photo manipulation techniques primarily used by a web publisher. All of the photo editors provided the minimal functionality needed, though I had to go to plug-ins more than once. However, what's important is that I could do what I wanted to do with all of the desktop editors. Which one to use for most of my work then depends more on circumstances, finances, machine time, and preferences. For my work, I have the following configuration on my machines:

- My main Mac development machine has Photoshop CS3 installed (the simple installation, not the Extended edition). I also have GIMP 2.4 installed, Graphic-Converter (not covered), and ImageMagick (covered later in this book).

- My secondary Mac machine also has iPhoto installed as part of the iLife suite. I didn't cover iPhoto in this chapter, because Apple doesn't provide trials.

- My main media PC has Photoshop CS2 installed, GIMP for Windows, Paint Shop Pro XI, Paint.NET, Photoshop Elements 5.0, and Google's Picasso (not covered).

Note that my PC has an out-of-date version of Photoshop. It is OK to skip an upgrade from time to time.

Photoshop will probably always remain my main photo editor, but GIMP is quickly catching up to this tool, and Photoshop is no longer assured its prominent place in my heart.

Moving on to the other tool types, a final word on online photo editors. To me, Picnik is what an online photo editor should provide, instead of the pseudo-Photoshop-like interface of Fauxto. No online editor is ever going to have the features offered with the desktop tools I cover in this book. At a minimum, they're not going to be able to effectively deal with larger photo sizes, RAW files, or the more complex algorithms necessary for many of the more important photo modification processes.

 Of course, after I wrote this, Adobe came out with an announcement of its own effort to create an online photo editor, which will have most of the "essential" elements of Photoshop. Do look for this tool when you try out the various examples.

The workflow tools are interesting, and are wonders at organization. If you can afford one or the other and have massively huge libraries, consider getting one. If you're an Adobe fan, you'll probably want to stick with Lightroom because of application integration. Still, there's no reason you can't take your tools into new neighborhoods.

If you get a workflow tool for organization, don't depend on it as your sole photo editor. These tools provide a great deal of control, but not as much as we need to really make our pictures soar to new heights.

The same can be said for the online tools. Where the online photo editors fit into your photo workflow is for those times when you have a set of JPEG images you want to process for upload, and you either don't have a lot of time or don't have access to your primary photo software.

As an example, if you're on the road and you configure your camera to take both RAW and JPEG images, using an online editor to process the JPEGs for upload to your web site or online photo site until you get home is a really effective use of this type of tool.

To me, using such simple photo editors as your main photo editor takes away from the fun of processing photos. Ultimately, what tool or tools we use to get our pictures from the camera to being web-ready isn't a function of cost or coolness but of how much we enjoy the process.

We shouldn't consider tasks such as exploring different filter effects when converting a photo into black and white to be work—it's fun! I can't help thinking that anyone who would buy a book specifically on web graphics would feel the same. We're interested in web graphics not because we have to be, but because we want to be.

Now that we have our pretty pictures, nicely filtered, sharpened, and colorized, it's time to get them to the Web.

CHAPTER 4
The Web As Frame

Once your picture is just right, it's time to put it into a page and let it shine. Editing a photo is only half the fun when it comes to publishing photos on the Web. The other part is the presentation, and just as with the tools and technologies associated with photo editing, you have a lot of options for how you can display your photos.

If a photo is meant for story illustration, you can embed it directly into the text, and we'll look at clean approaches to do this. However, you can also add a photo "film-strip" at the bottom of the story, or to the side—even a link to a slideshow.

Speaking of slideshows, some of the same tools you use to edit the photo can also be used to generate either HTML or Flash slideshows; or you can use any number of freely available slideshow packages that are, more or less, drop and play. The functionality can also be implemented using JavaScript for a more modern "Ajaxy" feel.

Rather than a slideshow, you can also publish your photos in a more formal gallery. Again, some photo editors and workflow tools can generate galleries, or you can use server-side software that manages the gallery functionality for you. You can even embed a small piece of code into your web page and have it alter the photo that's displayed as part of a header, background, or sidebar item each time a person accesses a page.

Regardless of how you publish your photos online, one issue related to all the techniques is how large your published photo should be, which is indirectly related to the topic of thumbnails. Thumbnails are more than just miniaturizations of the larger photo—they can invite exploration or even provide their own unique presentation and statement.

The Art of Thumbnail Sizing

I would estimate that more than 90% of the thumbnails for photos online are generated automatically from whatever software is used to publish the photo online. The software does a good job, and the thumbnail looks OK, but we're not giving thumbnails the respect they deserve when we let the applications handle their creation.

A thumbnail is usually just a smaller, perhaps more optimized, version of a larger, better quality picture that is linked to the thumbnail. It's a way to provide a sample of the larger picture without burdening the person with big photos that may take longer to download, or that may take up too much page real estate.

Thumbnails, though, can provide a whole new way of looking at the photo, and even a way to create something new, interesting, and completely different from just the photo itself.

Consider another area of life where size matters: food and the presentation of such. Nothing better than sitting down to a turkey the size of a small bus or a big plate of lasagna (or a pot roast with golden roasted potatoes!), but I don't think there are any of us who don't appreciate the samplings of food we get at parties: pretty crackers with slivers of salmon or bite-sized hot mushroom tarts passed as hors d'oeuvres. There are restaurants that serve meals that are nothing more than a series of courses with smaller servings, one right after another, that mix taste and presentation. Between courses, wait persons pass out whatever the chef has created for *amuse-bouche* that day: tiny creations that explode the myth that food tastes the same no matter the dimensions. As Melissa Clark wrote in "Tiny Come-Ons, Plain and Fancy" for the *New York Times* in 2006, "The fact is that as long as it's small, tasty, and pleasing to the eye, almost anything can make an *amuse-bouche*."

The same concepts can be applied to photography, with thumbnails as the tasty tidbit, the *hors d'oeuvre*, the *amuse-bouche* that enlivens the page.

 The examples in this chapter use Photoshop CS3 or GIMP, but all the effects can be re-created using the desktop photo editors reviewed in Chapter 3. Whenever necessary, instructions are provided that show you how to manually create an effect.

Resizing, Resampling, and Retargeting

There is no area where the differences between a photo for the Web and one for printing are more apparent than that of photo resizing.

Photos published to the Web have one constraint on their size: the pixel dimensions. Printing, on the other hand, is heavily dependent on the resolution of the photo, because unlike monitors, TVs, and the like, printers can resize the pixels, and the higher the resolution, the better the print.

If you look at something like Photoshop's Image Size dialog, the top part has the pixel size, which is what we're interested in for web publication. The middle part, labeled as "Document," only matters to printing. The last part of the dialog, which has to do with constraining dimensions and resampling, affects both.

The Scale Styles setting is of interest if you've added layer styling, such as a drop shadow. Constrain Proportions, which is most likely replicated with other tools, allows you to set a new width or height and have the other dimension resize accordingly. Or not, if you want to adjust the image only on one dimension.

The last option, again supported in most photo and graphics applications, is resampling. Resampling uses an algorithm to interpolate between the image's current size and the size you want it to be. Some applications support one algorithm; others, including Photoshop, support several and allow you to pick the one you prefer. Most photo editors support the Bicubic algorithm because it provides the smoothest gradients. Other algorithms work better for hard-edged graphics, such as illustrations. You might want to spend some time exploring the resampling algorithms supported by your photo editor, to understand what works the best for you.

 Resampling is used when sizing a photo for the Web, but it should be turned off for printing.

Applications that work in batch to create thumbnails should use resampling. Some may even allow you to specify the algorithm. ImageMagick, which I cover later in this book, uses different methods based on the format of the file and whether the image is being increased or decreased.

Regardless of resampling algorithm, you don't want to "resize" your image by specifying smaller dimensions in the `img` tag in the web page, or use CSS to constrain image sizes. One reason is that you're not saving bandwidth, because the file sizes are the same. The other reason is that browsers do a lousy job of resizing photos. Plus, it takes longer for the image to display. Which leads us to the next issue: what size image?

iSizing

There is no right size for a published photo. The size of your pictures is determined by the tools you use, your web page layout, what you know of the people who visit your site and their connection type (and patience level), and the average monitor resolutions.

Years ago, we designed for pages 640 pixels or less. Nowadays that wouldn't hold the average photo. Today's conservative standard is to assume people are viewing your pages with 800×600 resolution. However, according to statistics at the W3 Schools (*http://www.w3schools.com*), 54% view pages with monitors set at 1,024×768, 26% at higher resolutions, 14% at 800×600, and 6% unknown. Of course, these statistics are based on the W3 School's visitor statistics—other sites may vary.

Regardless of what size layout you use for you web pages, you can use smaller images, or *thumbnails*, in your web pages, and then provide larger images for people capable of (and interested in) viewing them.

The thumbnail size can vary based of whether it's "standalone" or embedded into text. For my own sites, I use thumbnails ranging in size from 400 pixels to 600 pixels when the image doesn't have text wrapped around it. For photos embedded into text, I use thumbnails as small as 50 pixels. The size is dependent on how the thumbnail is being used and its subject.

Mobile Sizing

These sizes I mentioned in the last section should work with most computer monitors, but what about people accessing the pages, and images, with cell phones or other small handheld devices? In the section "Adobe Photoshop CS3," in Chapter 3, I demonstrated what a photo can look like on a cell phone, and the result wasn't very pretty. The average viewscreen for a mobile device is about 120 pixels wide. That's not a lot of space.

I've always admired people who can surf the Web on a device not much bigger than a dieter's chocolate bar, so much so that I create mobile stylesheets for all my sites. A mobile stylesheet is CSS that's linked in such a way that it's loaded only if the site is accessed by a mobile device. The link looks similar to the following:

```
<link rel="stylesheet" href="http://burningbird.net/wp/mobile.css" type="text/css"
media="handheld" />
```

In the stylesheet, I eliminate the problem of image sizes on mobile devices with the following CSS:

```
img { display: none }
```

For most of my sites, I just turn off image display for mobile devices, and then provide clean and simple access to my writing. This approach also helps conserve the device user's bandwidth, which can be quite limited.

In the last section, I mentioned not using CSS to size a photo. However, when dealing with mobiles, especially when embedding thumbnails into a page, resizing the image within a mobile stylesheet is an option. To manage varying sizes of thumbnails, the following just ensures the image is never wider than 50 pixels:

```
img { max-width: 50px }
```

The `max-width` attribute sets the maximum width of the image, and doesn't affect the size if the width is smaller than the amount specified. Most browsers, other than Internet Explorer 6.x, support `max-width`, and that includes many mobile devices. Or, you could just specify a fixed width, like the following:

```
img { width: 50px }
```

This doesn't eliminate the bandwidth issues, and using CSS to resize an image is not the best way to display your photos, but it will do for most handhelds. To test what the page looks like, I use the mobile device emulation built into the Opera browser to view the page in my laptop, as shown in Figure 4-1.

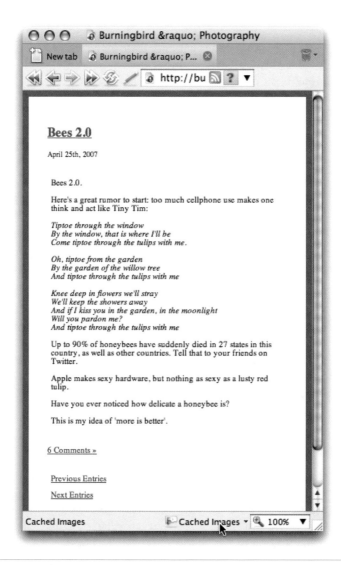

Figure 4-1. Viewing web pages using mobile CSS and Opera's mobile device emulation

The Opera emulator provides an option to turn images on or off, but this option doesn't impact the page in the figure, as my own CSS controls the image display.

Another approach is to use JavaScript to resize the images, but this is problematic on handheld devices. An advantage to using a script is that you can test the window dimensions and determine whether the page is accessed by a mobile or other small device. Again, though, this puts a scripting dependency on your site just for displaying images that may or may not display all that well on the device in the first place. In addition, many mobile devices don't support scripting when accessing web pages.

Instead of modifying the page or images using client-side script, you can also query for the user agent in your server-side application and use code to redirect image requests to mobile-sized images. However, not all mobile phones provide the correct user agent.

To make graphics on mobile devices even more challenging, Apple's new iPhone and Touch iPods with Internet access don't follow the same conventions as mobile devices and won't use a mobile stylesheet. The only setting that Apple supports in its devices is the size of the content area viewpoint, discarding spacing within the page:

```
<meta name="viewport" content="width=800" />
```

What the iPhone and Touch iPod do is shrink the page down, so it fits the display. To expand the material, the person uses a "pinching" motion or a built-in touch keyboard. To see what a page would look like in iPhone, a company called Marketcircle created an emulator called iPhoney that can display a page vertically or horizontally, just like in the device, as shown in Figure 4-2. The only difference is the emulator doesn't have touch control.

Figure 4-2. Web page with photograph displayed in the iPhoney emulator

 iPhoney is available at *http://www.marketcircle.com/iphoney/*.

Which leads us to our last "sizing" issue, one based on very new technology that will potentially have an impact on images served through the browser in the future.

Seam Carving

At the same time I was writing this book, the world of photography was all agog about a new algorithm for resizing photos that was making the rounds of the web sites. Called "seam carving" and invented by Dr. Ariel Shamir and Shai Avidan at the Efi Arazi School of Computer Science in Israel, this algorithm would examine a photo for vertical and horizontal paths through the photo that have the least "energy," and could then target these areas for either removal (for shrinkage) or expansion (for enlarging) without an overall negative effect on the photo.

 A video demonstration can be found at *http://www.faculty.idc.ac.il/ arik/IMRet-All.mov*, and the paper on the process can be downloaded at *http://www.faculty.idc.ac.il/arik/imret.pdf*.

It's a fascinating algorithm with interesting results, but most photographers had kittens when viewing it, especially when people began to shout out requests for this technology as browser extensions.

When we create a photograph, there is a reason for all that seemingly nonenergetic space within the photo. A field of white may seem to be extraneous material to the algorithm, but is an integral expanse of crystal white snow to the photographer. The algorithm creators used the text in a web page as an analogy of *re-targeting*, as they called their concept. In web pages, unless a column is a fixed size, as the page changes to a smaller size, the words wrap and are pushed down the page. Why not have the photos resize like the text?

The thing is, resizing a web page and causing the words to wrap doesn't impact the message of the text or result in dropped conjunctives—in other words, it doesn't say, hey, let's drop every other "and."

The Creative Art of Thumbnails

Most photo thumbnails are miniature versions of the parent photo, meant to be small enough to provide a low-bandwidth, space-friendly version of the picture that also piques enough interest for the user to click through to the larger image. Any of the applications that generate galleries (covered later in this chapter) create thumbnails just like this. For the most part, the result is satisfactory.

Still, for those times when you're embedding a photo into a web page or manually creating your own specialized gallery page, you might want to branch out and try something new.

Adding Drop Shadows

Rather than just create a plain, flat thumbnail, you might consider adding a shadow behind the image, to make the image pop out of the page. Most photo editors provide either plug-ins, specialized routines, or layer effects to create a shadow effect.

Photoshop provides layer styles that can create a beveled look, drop shadow, or other effect directed on the layer edges. It's quite simple to use, too. The first step is to convert your background image to a layer, if you haven't already done so. Double-clicking on the background in the Layers window and accepting the default name will do the trick. The next step is to increase the canvas size to make room for the *drop shadow*, the term for these shadows. The dialog to adjust the canvas can be accessed through the Image menu. The last step is to open the Layer Style dialog and select Drop Shadow or another effect.

In the Drop Shadow option window (Figure 4-3), adjust the angle representing the light source and the offset value (how much the shadow is "pushed" horizontally or vertically), as well as shadow color, opacity, and width. If your thumbnail is small, you'll want to keep your shadow small. In addition, if you plan on displaying several thumbnails in one web page, make sure the settings are the same for each for consistency.

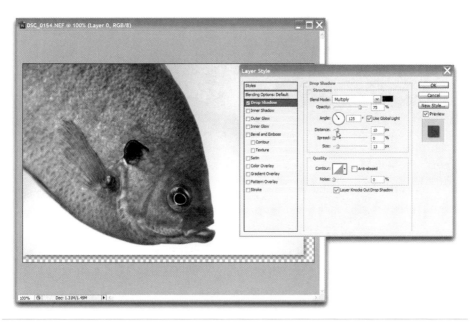

Figure 4-3. Photoshop's Drop Shadow option

Once finished, you could save the image as a PNG, which would preserve the transparency of the shadow. The problem with this is that IE 6.x does not respect alpha channels, and the image is going to look quite bad in this browser. If you have IE 6.x users (and 21% of my sites' viewers are still using IE 6.0), you'll probably want to flatten the image and then save it as a JPEG.

Figure 4-4. Thumbnail created in Photoshop using the Drop Shadow Layer Style

To recap the steps:

1. Convert the background to a layer.
2. Resize the canvas to allow for drop shadow.
3. Pick the Drop Shadow option from the Layer Styles.
4. Adjust the shadow.
5. Flatten the photo to save as JPEG.

Instead of layer modification, GIMP provides a Script-Fu process, shown in Figure 4-5, to generate a drop shadow on an image. You also don't need to provide canvas space; the tool automatically sizes the canvas.

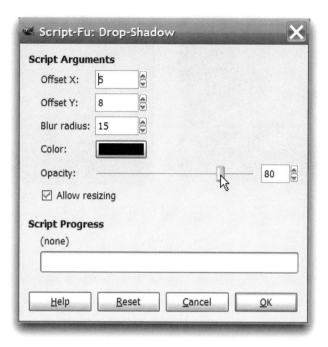

Figure 4-5. GIMP Script-Fu Drop Shadow process

GIMP's drop shadow process differs from Photoshop's in that there is no light source angle. Instead, you provide an X and Y offset value. Positive values put the shadow to the right, and negative values to the left.

Other applications either have built-in drop shadow support or can emulate it using well-published steps. Just search on the name of your tool and "drop shadow." You can also create your own drop shadow.

To create a home-baked drop shadow in a tool that supports layers (and we're all using tools that support layers), increase the size of the underlying canvas in order to have enough room for the shadow. Next, create a second transparent layer and add a rectangle the same size as the thumbnail. Fill it with the same color as your shadow, usually black.

Move the rectangle so that it matches the shadow location. A good place to start is 8 pixels below the thumbnail and 8 pixels to the right. Then, using the appropriate filter or effects setting in your editor, add a Gaussian Blur to the shape. Start with a blur setting of 15 and experiment from there until satisfied. Once you're finished, you have a shadow as good, or better, than the packaged products. Figure 4-6 shows the bird thumbnail with a shadow created by Script-Fu and a shadow created using the steps I just outlined.

Figure 4-6. Comparison of an automatically generated shadow and one created manually

To recap these steps:

1. Increase the size of the underlying canvas to hold the shadow.
2. Add a new transparent layer.
3. Create a rectangle the same size as the thumbnail.
4. Fill this rectangle with the color of the shadow (usually black).
5. Offset the shadow by moving it down or up or to the right or left, depending on where you want to place the shadow effect.
6. Apply a Gaussian Blur to the shadow layer.
7. Switch layer locations so the shadow is under the thumbnail.

Cut-Out Thumbnails

Rather than the typical rectangle, you might want to consider variations on the shape by using a *cut-out thumbnail*. In this type of thumbnail, rather than use the whole photo, you use a piece of it. The number of shapes you can use to create the cut-out are as varied as the leaves in the forest, but I'll look at two: ovals and slices.

Oval thumbnails seem to work nicely with the right subject. They don't work whenever the photo corners are important, because corners can't be captured with an oval. They are good, though, for a surprising number of subjects, including industrial photos, critter pictures, people, and flowers.

An oval thumbnail is simple to create—just cut out the shape. Unlike the rectangles, though, I've found that ovals work better with something to define a three-dimensional effect. A shadow works, but a bevel can work better. Another approach is a smooth, flat bubble effect, especially with industrial photos.

Figure 4-7 shows several thumbnails of birds, each cut into an oval and each given a beveled edge and drop shadow. With Photoshop, this is simple: just convert the background to a layer, select the oval (using fixed size to ensure the oval is the same for each thumbnail), invert the selection, and delete the background. Once the oval is cut out, then access Layer → Style, and select Drop Shadow, and Bevel and Emboss. This gives the images a nice three-dimensional feel without obscuring the image.

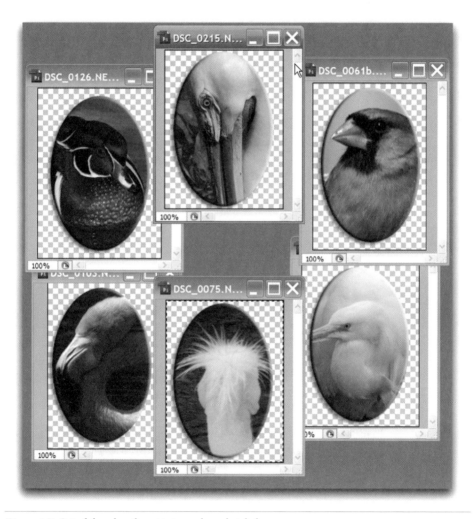

Figure 4-7. Set of thumbnails cut into ovals and styled

To recap the steps:

1. Convert the image background to a layer.
2. Using an elliptical selection (set to a fixed size to ensure that the oval is the same for all pictures), drag the selection using your keyboard, or mouse over the photo until positioned correctly.
3. Invert the selection, using Select → Inverse.
4. Delete the selection using the Delete key, or Edit → Cut.
5. Access Layer → Blending Options and select both Drop Shadow and Bevel and Emboss.
6. Adjust the settings for both until the thumbnail is styled as you like, and then duplicate the steps and style settings for all other grouped thumbnails.
7. Trim the excess background using Image → Trim and accept the defaults.
8. Save as PNG to preserve transparency, or flatten for JPEGs, setting the background color to the same color as your web page.

Once the thumbnails are cut, they can be embedded into a web page using the same technique given for a rectangle thumbnail. The rectangle enclosing the oval is no different than a rectangle enclosing a regular thumbnail. Later in this chapter, I'll demonstrate how these can be added to a web page for a manual gallery page. Figure 4-8 shows an example of a layout with the thumbnails to the left and the opened image to the right.

Figure 4-8. Oval thumbnails and displayed photo

Figure 4-8 demonstrates another aspect of thumbnail cutouts: what part of the original photo to capture in the thumbnail?

In the bottom row of the thumbnails, all the way to the left, is an odd-looking bird head with feathered tufts coming out. This bird actually isn't the primary bird in this photo, as shown in Figure 4-9. However, the fluffed head is eye catching, as well as curiosity inspiring—a better choice than the "real" subject of the photo.

Figure 4-9. Choosing a photo component to center in the cutout for a thumbnail

The best choice for a cutout thumbnail isn't always the main subject, or even the photo's center. A thumbnail should not only represent the original photo; it should form a creative statement in itself, and should also make the person want to click through on the image.

A cutout thumbnail is especially helpful if your photo doesn't make a good thumbnail by itself because the detail gets lost in the smaller size. Rather than shrink the entire photo, just cut out a portion that makes a good representation and use that. You can even use rectangles rather than ovals. But then, you can use triangles, polygons, puzzle piece or garden tool outlines, and so on.

Another thumbnail type is a slice—taking a stripe, either vertically or horizontally, from the photo. The slice can be any width and taken from any part of the photo. This type of thumbnail is easier to lay out in the page because they're usually aligned either in one column or one row, depending on the orientation of the images. The thumbnails also work best if the thumbnail is identifiable from the slice, and if the thumbnails in a group complement one another. Figure 4-10 shows five thumbnails, all from floral photos, each given a 90-degree (straight up and down) drop shadow.

Figure 4-10. Slice thumbnails from five floral photos

Expanding Thumbnails

The simplest thumbnail is linked using a hypertext link to the larger photo. Clicking the link opens the photo in a separate page. Simple, quick, and works regardless of the device or whether the person accessing the page is using a mouse or keyboard. For gallery presentations (we'll look at gallery software later), this isn't a bad approach.

It's also the best approach for linking directly to any of the expanded images. Here's a sample line of HTML for a hypertext link:

```
<a href="bigger.jpg"><img src="smallerimg.jpg" alt="smaller image" /></a>
```

However, it's irritating to have a new page open when you click a thumbnail that's embedded into a story, forcing you to return to the previous page once you've looked at the image. A workaround is to open the photo in a separate browser page or tab using the anchor element's `target` attribute. The following example uses this attribute:

```
<a href="bigger.jpg" target="separatewindow"><img src="smallerimg.jpg" alt="Smaller
image" /></a>
```

Again, though, you then have to switch between browser windows or tabs in order to enjoy both the photo and whatever else is associated with it. Another issue with using the `target` attribute is that it's not valid in XHTML. To work around the validation problem, JavaScript can be used to add a `target` attribute for each anchor so that the XHTML validates. Which means having to parse the page, find the anchors, ensure that scripting is turned on...OK, so it's not the best approach to take.

My favorite solution, and the one I use with all my sites, is to provide a hypertext link for a separate page if a person accesses my site without JavaScript enabled in his browser, or if he's not using a mouse. For everyone else, though, I use a JavaScript library to open the image directly in the page. I have my own software to manage this in-page display, the code for which I'll cover later in this book. However, there are excellent libraries that do the task for us, and are as easy as adding a few lines of script to a page's header.

One application is Lightbox2, created by Lokesh Dhaker. Everything required to use the application can be found in the download folders. To use it, upload the folders and add the following four lines to the HEAD section of the web page:

```
<script type="text/javascript" src="js/prototype.js"></script>
<script type="text/javascript" src="js/scriptaculous.js?load=effects"></script>
<script type="text/javascript" src="js/lightbox.js"></script>
<link rel="stylesheet" href="css/lightbox.css" type="text/css" media="screen" />
```

The application does make use of both the Prototype and Scriptaculous JavaScript libraries and if you're using either of these, or your own, you'll want to test for compatibility. Once the script is added, to enable the thumbnail-expanding functionality to any image, add the `rel="lightbox"` attribute to the anchor tag surrounding the `img` element, with an optional `title="Some title"` to provide a photo title:

```
<a href="heronsmall.jpg" rel="lightbox" title="Heron"><img src="herontiny.jpg"
style="border: none; float: left; margin: 0 5px 5px 0"/></a>
```

Clicking on the image overlays the page with a semi-opaque layer and expands the photo, as shown in Figure 4-11.

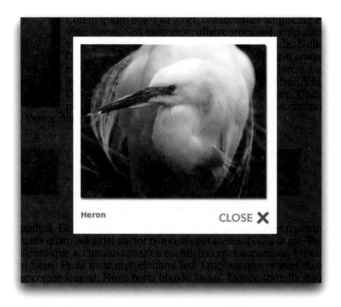

Figure 4-11. Thumbnail expanded using Lightbox2

Lightbox2 isn't the only thumbnail expansion software. Others, such as Highslide, provide a nice animated effect when opening the photo, as well as some photo scrolling capability. Searching on "JavaScript thumbnail" brings up dozens more.

> Lightbox2 is accessible at *http://www.huddletogether.com/projects/ lightbox2/*. Highslide is free for non-commercial sites, and is available at *http://vikjavev.no/highslide/*.

The effects that can be used for thumbnails can also be used for photos embedded into text or other content. In fact, the presentation of a photo can add as much meaningful context as the subject of the photo.

Embedding Photos: Condiment and Spice

Ever notice in magazines and newspaper articles that the editors will insert photos and other graphics, either of the subject or of something that complements the subject in some way? Using visual elements to accentuate text is a long established procedure, and is not just used to provide visual aids in how-tos or tutorials.

Photos accompanying news or stories of events set context, and also help frame the event in the user's mind. We are creatures who wrote with pictures at one time before we developed abstract languages and alphabets; we've not lost that need for visual reaffirmation of a story.

In other types of written works, the use of graphics draws the eye, can break up long passages of writing, and serves as a subtle accent to the core offering—like how the good use of spice makes all the difference between a good recipe and a really great one. Even the madly popular Harry Potter books had illustrations at the beginning of each chapter that helped frame the characters in our minds.

Prep

Adding a photo to a piece of writing is as simple as using an `img` element within the writing. A CSS style setting informs the browser how the image exists relative to the text, and adding an informative `alt` attribute ensures that those who visualize with senses other than sight have a chance to participate.

An `img` element is not a block element. In Figure 4-12, the text follows immediately after the image.

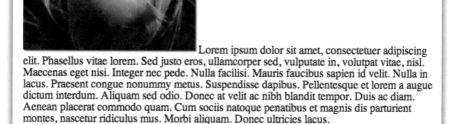

Figure 4-12. Inserting an image into a paragraph using default styling

To align the image with all of the text, we use CSS to "float" the element, either to the left or right, causing the text to flow around the object. If we float the image to the right, the text following the image flows to the left of the image; floating the image to the left forces the text to float to the right of the image. To show how this works, the following `img` tag with associated style setting is embedded directly into the document before the paragraph element containing the text:

```
<img src="heronsmall.jpg" alt="black and white photo of heron" style="float: left" />
<p>
<!-- paragraph text -->
</p>
```

This setting uses the default spacing for the `img` element. To add additional spacing, a margin is given around the object. Start with a 5-pixel margin, to the right and bottom, and then adjust accordingly:

```
<img src="heronsmall.jpg" alt="black and white photo of heron" style="float: left;
margin: 0 5px 5px" />
```

With a right float, use a margin set to 0 for the left and top, and 5 pixels to the right and bottom. Of course, we want to avoid using style settings as much as possible in elements, in order to make it simpler to modify in the future. What we can do is define left and right float classes in a stylesheet and then use these accordingly:

```
img.right
{
    float: right;
    margin: 0 0 5px 5px;
}
img.left
{
    float: left;
    margin: 0 5px 5px 0;
}
```

Figure 4-13 shows the same image styled with the float left setting.

 The figures in this section use the famous Lorem Ipsum, beloved text of layout designers and web page creators like you and me. I use the Lorem Ipsum generator available at *http://www.lipsum.com/* for all my layout testing, as well as for book examples such as the one in this chapter.

Aliquam erat volutpat. Donec tincidunt. Nulla commodo, arcu sit amet rhoncus eleifend, magna massa mattis quam, sit amet auctor risus est eget metus. Nulla at est. Proin vehicula fringilla dui. Pellentesque accumsan tortor eu est ullamcorper accumsan. Fusce sodales. Etiam tristique eleifend lacus. Proin nunc erat, eleifend sed, faucibus quis, varius et, orci. Etiam id elit vitae lectus ullamcorper feugiat. Nunc porta blandit lectus. Donec fringilla ipsum dictum ante. Ut semper vehicula quam. Integer nonummy semper massa. Etiam ornare, orci nec ullamcorper semper, lectus urna sodales leo, sed varius purus dui vitae lorem. Sed libero metus, congue nec, aliquam a, fermentum et, ipsum. Pellentesque volutpat ullamcorper magna. Mauris nibh risus, faucibus et, dignissim suscipit, blandit in, metus. Aliquam erat volutpat. Vestibulum ante ipsum primis in faucibus orci luctus et ultrices posuere cubilia Curae;

Figure 4-13. Page excerpt with the same image embedded using float left setting

By using CSS classes, we can alter the settings universally. This is handy if we set other attributes such as the border, background, and padding. We'll get into these and other CSS attributes in Chapter 9.

Of course, we don't have to embed images directly into text and instead can choose to use images about the same width as the paragraphs and forgo the float. Even using this approach, we can be creative with what we do with the image presentation in order to enhance the image's effect. I'll get into that in the next section, but first, there's another technique we can use that mixes embedded images with breaks and the use of CSS floating.

Float a Row of Images

The one thing that irritates me about tools that generate photo galleries and slide-shows is that they almost invariably use HTML tables in order to control the layout of the thumbnails or images. Why is the use of HTML tables such a pain? After all, tables are great for providing equal spacing that can adjust to the page size.

HTML tables are meant to display tabular data, such as data pulled in from a database. Screen readers treat the tables this way, as do many web robots that scan pages for content for search engines or other uses. It's semantically incorrect to use an HTML table for photo galleries, because automated processes accessing the page make an assumption that there's some meaningful reason behind grouping the data in the table. Meaningful in some way other than that it's an easy layout technique.

The use of an HTML table isn't necessary, either. The same technique we use to embed an image into a text block can be used to "align" images relative to each other. In Example 4-1, three small images are embedded into the test document, aligned one right after the other horizontally. The three images are contained within a div element to facilitate controlling the block of images within the main text body.

Example 4-1. Three images aligned horizontally using CSS

```
<div>
<img src="herontiny.jpg" alt="black and white heron" style="float: left; margin: 5px 10px"
/>
<img src="tinyduck.png" alt="male wood duck" style="float: left; margin: 5px 10px" />
<img src="tinycardinal.png" alt="curious male cardinal" style="margin: 5px 10px" />
<br style="clear:both" />
</div>
```

Notice that the images are all aligned to the left. The inline style settings used float each image to the left, pushing the rest of the content that follows to the right. The cardinal is now to the right of the wood duck photo, which is, in turn, to the right of the heron, though the order they're loaded into the page is opposite from the direction in which they appear.

Following the row is a break element, br, with a style setting of "clear:both". The clear property prohibits floating elements to the left or right based on the setting: left, right, both, or none (which is the default). This forces the content to move down to accommodate the images that have been floated. Since a float takes an element out of the natural page flow, if I didn't use the clear property, the rows of images would impact adversely on the HTML elements following the images. Now, the float is literally "cleared" before the next content item.

Rows of images can be made using this technique. To repeat the row just given, but this time putting the cardinal in the middle and switching the heron and wood duck, I would use the following, as shown in Figure 4-14:

```
<div>
<img src="herontiny.jpg" alt="black and white heron" style="float: left; margin: 5px
10px" />
<img src="tinyduck.png" alt="male wood duck" style="float: left; margin: 5px 10px" />
<img src="tinycardinal.png" alt="curious male cardinal" style="margin: 5px 10px" />
<br style="clear:both" />

<img src="tinyduck.png" alt="male wood duck" style="float: left; margin: 5px 10px" />
<img src="tinycardinal.png" alt="curious male cardinal" style="float: left; margin:
5px 10px" />
<img src="herontiny.jpg" alt="black and white heron" style=" margin: 5px 10px" />
<br style="clear:both" />
</div>
```

The key to using CSS to style rows of images is to use a container to set the overall width of the rows and using the float: left to flow images to the left. The row is followed by a br element using the clear property; otherwise, the rows will end up overlaying one another because there's nothing to "push" the content down the page.

I don't use float:right, because floating will push the image all the way over to the left or right, as far as possible. If the images don't fill the space, there will be a gap between the last non-floated image and the margin.

I use CSS with thumbnails, but also with graphics that I want to use as a visual break in a long block of text. This is in addition to other presentation effects that I add to the images while I'm creating them, detailed next.

Plating Photos

What's the difference between eating in and eating out, other than someone else does the cooking and clean up? One major difference is how the food is served. Even the simplest restaurant will add some garnish, such as an orange slice or parsley, to a dish. The fancier restaurants can take food presentation to an art form, a process known as *plating*. They don't do this to be froufrou or in order to charge you an additional 20 bucks. They do so for practical reasons: to heat plates for hot food or

Curabitur commodo, erat at rutrum facilisis, lorem velit commodo ligula, sit amet malesuada metus elit et ipsum. Morbi at lectus. Cras pulvinar justo sed felis. Sed imperdiet volutpat felis. Pellentesque vulputate enim eu est. Integer ac turpis. Nulla ornare, dolor eget ornare bibendum, justo lorem lobortis sem, id vulputate urna nibh at magna. Ut rhoncus laoreet mauris. Mauris interdum mattis ipsum. In quam.

Proin non dolor vitae felis faucibus feugiat. Etiam odio velit, mattis a, placerat vitae, cursus in, nisl. Nam sagittis nisl sed eros. Ut ornare. Proin sed felis quis eros ultrices ultricies. Vestibulum ante ipsum primis in faucibus orci luctus et ultrices posuere cubilia Curae; Pellentesque consequat sem eget enim. Ut facilisis nisl at mauris. Vivamus aliquam, orci nec lacinia consequat, felis lorem molestie neque, eu consequat ipsum augue nec dui. Nullam ligula nisi, aliquam et, mollis vitae, adipiscing sed, justo. Aenean convallis rhoncus sem. Suspendisse potenti. Morbi urna turpis, auctor ut, posuere quis, elementum vitae, est. Nunc condimentum lorem ac arcu. Nulla facilisi. Donec id sem convallis pede auctor sagittis. Sed sed mauris non augue suscipit volutpat. Integer consequat porttitor dui.

Figure 4-14. Layout with two rows of photos, with spacing and layout controlled by CSS

cool them for cold; to keep foods that should be separate apart; to add flavor in a controlled manner, such as placing raspberry sauce under a slice of fudge cake.

For the most part, though, the reason that good cooks plate their presentations is to enhance the experience—to ensure that the diner experiences the food with as many senses as possible.

This process of plating can also be applied to photographs. Too often we put a photo into a page and other than a border or drop shadow, we ignore everything else about it and around it. Adding a photo into a story is an opportunity to not only embellish the story, but also to indulge your creativity when preparing the photo.

Thanks to digital cameras and the advances made in technology to manage photos, publishing pictures online has become the new arms race: he or she with the most photos online wins. Sacrificed in that rush to get the pictures online is the enjoyment we can experience taking time with each individual picture.

Creating a Reusable Ladder Mask

I live for layers in a photo editor. They're probably the most helpful tool in our editing arsenals.

One use of layers is to create a template image that can be saved and reused multiple times. The template is copied each time it's used, and then pasted into a new layer in the target photo. Through the use of layers, I can then shift the template about until it's just right.

Figure 4-15 shows a series of beveled tiles, all created from one photo, embedded into a web page. The distance of the photos to each other is true to the original picture, because I use a template to "cut" out the individual items without impacting the layout of the items.

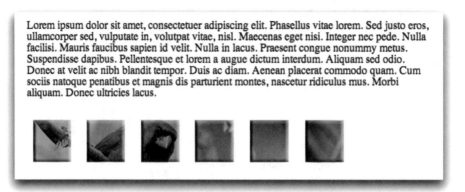

Figure 4-15. Beveled "tiles" from one photograph, used as a visual separator

The template is nothing more than a long rectangle with a series of same-sized squares, placed equidistant from one another, that are cut out, leaving a transparent background for each. To use such a template, first transform the background image into a layer. Then, copy the template and paste it into the photograph, first coloring the template in such a way that it doesn't match any nearby color, as shown in Figure 4-16.

At this point, use the Magic Wand (or whatever your photo editor supports) to "select" the template and delete it, leaving behind the isolated squares. You can crop out the rest of the picture, and use the Photoshop Bevel and Emboss layer style to add the beveled effect. The same challenges with alpha channels, PNGs, and IE 6.x relate to this type of effect, so you may want to flatten the image to a JPEG before saving.

Here are the steps to re-create this effect:

1. Create the template by cutting out the parts of the image that will remain in the final work.

2. Transform the photo into a layer if it isn't already.

3. Copy and paste the template into a new layer in the target photo.

Figure 4-16. Using the Beveled Tile template to cut out the tiles

4. Move the template around until the openings are aligned to your preference.

5. Color the template so that it doesn't match any color in the underlying photo, and then merge the two layers.

6. Select the template using whatever tool selects items based on color and proximity. I used Photoshop's Magic Wand for the work in this chapter.

7. Delete the selected item, and then crop the image down so that only the cut-out portions of the photo remain.

8. Apply an effect, such as the Photoshop Bevel and Emboss.

This makes a good "break" in text because the image is not so tall that the item is overly distracting. Depending on the topic of the text and the photo used, it should add color and a visual enhancement to the story. It can also be resized smaller to create an even subtler visual break.

 Novell provides a great tutorial in how to manually add a bevel effect in GIMP at *http://www.novell.com/coolsolutions/feature/17391.html*.

A variation using this pattern doesn't cut the template, but instead modifies it so that it becomes part of the picture. Figure 4-17 shows another example with the same template but a different underlying photo. In this version, a metal effect is added to the template by selecting the Drop Shadow, Bevel and Emboss, and Gradient layer styles, as shown in Figure 4-18. The underlying photo is trimmed down to fit within the frame, and then the two layers are merged into one.

Figure 4-17. Metallic row photo with "framed" seagull photo

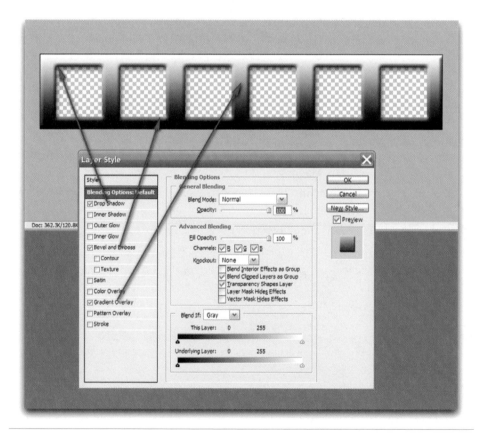

Figure 4-18. Creating the metallic frame using Photoshop Layer Styles

These examples provide alternatives to plain horizontal breaks, and are more for adding visual stops than focusing attention on the subject. The next few effects are used more for creating an editorial context with images.

Torn Edges

One popular effect for both photos and other graphics, such as screenshots, is a torn-edge effect. A torn edge can add a nice flourish to the image, but can also be used to add a more three-dimensional feel, as well as context, to the picture. There are numerous ways of accomplishing a torn edge, but the one I'm going to demonstrate is one of the simplest.

For this example, I'm taking a group seagull photo shot in Florida and giving it a torn edge, just below the beach line but without following the line exactly. The end result is shown in Figure 4-19.

Figure 4-19. Torn-edge effect created with Photoshop

For the effect, create a "tear" line along the sand using the Polygonal Lasso Tool, continuing around the bottom and back to select the entire bottom half of the picture. Delete the bottom part of the image.

Once the bottom part of the image is deleted, use the same Lasso tool to select along the torn edge, about 10 pixels in from the edge, and then follow the photo around the outside until the rest is selected. Invert the selection so that the edge is the only part of the image selected, as shown in Figure 4-20.

Figure 4-20. Using the Lasso Tool to "tear" a chunk off the bottom of the photo and then select the edge

Select the Filter → Distort → Ripple filter and use a medium distortion size, setting the amount to 100%. You might want to experiment with these values, or even use different filters, such as the Ocean Ripple.

Once the edge has been distorted, convert the photo to a layer, use the Magic Wand to select the bottom single-color portion of the picture, and delete it. This leaves a nice irregular edge to the picture. Accessing the Layer Style, add a Drop Shadow that is 5 pixels wide, with a light source set to 90 degrees, as shown in Figure 4-21. Flatten the image to convert to a JPEG, or you can leave the bottom transparent if you want to save the photo as a PNG.

To recap the steps:

1. Set the background color to white.
2. Use the Polygonal Lasso Tool, or any other tool, to create an irregular shape where you want the torn edge effect to be applied.
3. Select the edge about 10 pixels in or so.
4. Using the Filter → Distort → Ripple effect, distort the edge the amount you wish.
5. Convert the image to a layer, use the Magic Wand to select the bottom, white portion of the image, and delete it.

Figure 4-21. After the Ripple distortion has been applied, the bottom part of the photo deleted, and a drop shadow added

6. Add a Drop Shadow Layer Style set to 90 degrees, 5 pixels in size.

7. Flatten the image if you want to save as a JPEG.

Effects don't have to be restricted just to the edges of a photo. You can also create a broken effect directly through a photo, covered next.

Broken Photo

Another effect that's quite simple to create is a broken photo effect, with a jagged but clean-edged break through the photo itself. This could be used to visually enhance a picture or to make an editorial statement, such as creating a broken photo from a political rally or of an old building that was recently taken down.

This how-to uses a second seagull photo, this one of birds on the beach and birds just taking off. There's a nice, clear area of sand that marks the boundary between walking and flying birds, which forms a perfect break point for the picture, as can be seen in Figure 4-22.

To start, draw break lines using the Polygonal Lasso tool without making both sides completely parallel, because we want the effect to look not only like a break, but one that's pulled away a bit at one end, as shown in Figure 4-23.

Figure 4-22. A broken photo effect

Figure 4-23. Creating the break

Next, duplicate the layer, and in the top layer, use the Lasso tool to select the bottom part of the "broken" photo and delete it. You don't have to be too careful selecting around the break, because once you've deleted the bottom part of the tool, you use the Magic Wand to select the rest of the white area from the break and delete it, too.

The next step is to add a shadow to the top piece of the photo, again using a 90-degree light source, a shadow width of 10 pixels, and a distance setting of 10 pixels. Once that's finished, merge the two layers.

Group Effects

I don't modify pictures just for the sake of modifying them, though I enjoy trying out new effects. To return to the analogy of plating, I add the presentation effects to the photos so that they enhance the writings in which they're incorporated. This can be even more effective if you use a sequence of photos in the same page, each modified with a different but complementary effect.

The two seagull photos and a third are used to annotate a story on community. They're a natural subject, because seagulls are known to be both communal and competitive, and we have pictures that show gulls grouped tightly together, walking in lockstep, and then a picture with half the birds flown away and the rest either continuing to walk or thinking about flying away.

The pictures are color matched, first, using the techniques described in Chapter 3. Next, the first picture is modified with a Drop Shadow, the second with the broken photo effect, and the last with the torn edge. The torn edge picture is last because the diagonal of the tear leaves considerable white space below, which will look odd within text. However, at the bottom of an article, it creates an "arrowed" effect, which can be a nice finishing touch.

Consistency is key and goes beyond color matching when you're grouping photos using effects. If a light source is implied in the effect, such as the Drop Shadow, it needs to be in the same direction and intensity in all pictures—or, at a minimum, adjusted so that the position where the photo is in the page might account for light differences.

In the three grouped photos, shown in Figure 4-24, and without text, the Drop Shadow is applied to the bottom of all three pictures (set to the same light source angle and amount), and the photos are the same width as well as the same color, cast, and brightness, as mentioned earlier.

Any one of the photos can be fine by itself, but as a group they can be striking, and as annotation, very effective.

Another effect is to cut a picture into pieces, breaking the picture along natural lines—such as a horizon, or around an object—and then using each piece in sequence in the page. In fact, when you think outside the photo box and consider the concept of photo plating, there's a world of possibilities.

Figure 4-24. Grouping photos, each matched and given unique but complementary effects

Photo and effect grouping can also be applied to galleries, in order to create something out of the ordinary. Of course, the simplest galleries are those that are generated for us, which I'll cover next.

There are also any number of plug-ins and tutorials, as well as applications, to create effects within the photos themselves, such as adding a motion trail to a dog running in a picture, or distorting the eyes and head of a cat so that it appears to be coming out of the page and staring at you. All you have to do is search on "photo effects," and be prepared to spend the next several weeks exploring all the possibilities.

The only thing you'll want to be careful of is making sure the effect doesn't overshadow both the purpose and the page. Mad twirls and other distortions might be fun to create, but if they don't add to the message or to the page, we're back to the Hamster on the Color Wheel and animated unicorns that I discussed in Chapter 1.

Know why you're applying an effect, and what you hope to accomplish with it before you start playing.

Generated Galleries and Slideshows

The easiest way to get your photos in the face of your fans is to use a tool that automatically generates a photo presentation given a group of photos. You can pick a gallery type of show—where the items are presented in thumbnails that can be clicked to expand the photo—or a slideshow, with the photos displayed either through a navigation bar or in a timed sequence.

There are applications that do nothing more than generate slideshows or galleries. However, some of the photo editors and workflow tools we use for our other work also provide these shows, though you may have to poke around to find them.

Editor and Workflow Shows

Most workflow tools provide a gallery or slideshow capability, but not all provide tools to generate a web-based gallery or show. Two that I looked at in Chapter 3, Apple's Aperture and Adobe's Lightroom, both support the ability to generate an external photo display, though in this regard I found Lightroom to have the simpler and more intuitive interface.

Selecting a group of photos and clicking on the Web tab in Lightroom is all you need to do to create a web photo display using all default settings, shown in Figure 4-25. Once in the web page, you can change the template, including whether the show will be HTML or Flash. You can also define some characteristics of the photo layout, as well as modify the color palette.

Aperture's gallery option is fairly simple to use, but you have to find it. Figure 4-26 shows Aperture opened to the Web Gallery option, which is a small icon among the other tasks, as noted by the yellow arrow. Once found, though, it's a simple interface, though not as powerful as Lightroom's. You can select a specific theme, and once that's picked, choose the layout of the thumbnails, including the number of columns and rows per page. To finish, change the show's metadata, including title, subtitle, copyright, and description. You can also pick what kind of metadata to show for each photo, such as the caption, keywords, EXIF data, and so on. Note, though, that it can get a bit messy if you print everything out. Once you're done, you can export the gallery pages to your local computer, or you can export them to Apple's .Mac hosting system.

Figure 4-25. Defining a web display using Lightroom

Figure 4-26. Generating a web gallery using Aperture

Another feature about Aperture, whether good or not, is the tie-in between all of Apple's products, as demonstrated by the fact that you can export your gallery to .Mac. Aperture also ties into the AppleScript system within Mac OS X, which means you can add features such as a Publish to iPhone AppleScript (available at *http://automator.us/aperture/iphone.html*), which creates web pages fine-tuned specifically for iPhone. Of course, this begs the question of why you would want to generate a web gallery for only one device.

Returning to Lightroom, it's not surprising that Lightroom's web interface is so intuitive—Adobe shines when it comes to providing web gallery capabilities built into the company tools. Both Photoshop and Photoshop Elements have excellent and easy-to-use web gallery options.

In Photoshop, web galleries and slideshows can be generated via the File → Automate menu option. Among the options you'll be given are those to create High Definition Resolution images (HDRs), batch merge, PDF presentations, and Web Photo Galleries. Clicking on the latter opens a dialog that lets you pick the type of show to generate (HTML or Flash-based templates), as well as fine-tune some of the options, such as color and show name, as shown in Figure 4-27.

None of these tools provides what Photoshop Elements 5.0 provides, though. Photoshop Elements has more ways to generate just about every type of photo show you could ever want, both for the Web and your desktop, than any other photo tool I've looked at. One of my favorite options allows me to create a movie of my photos, with music, to play on my HD widescreen TV attached to my computer. I can really review the photos and make that keep-or-not decision in style.

All the options are available from the Elements Organizer, under the Create menu. The options are numerous, but the one I'm interested in for this book is Photo Galleries, which opens the Photo Galleries Wizard, shown in Figure 4-28.

The Photo Galleries Wizard provides several different layouts for the thumbnails, including filmstrips along the top, bottom, and sides. Other options include the size of the thumbnails. In the bottom of the page, the Wizard provides style options for controlling the appearance of the gallery. I'm learning how to hand-bind books as a hobby, so the Hand Made Paper template was my favorite.

Photos are added in the left, and you can add them individually or select a whole folder. Once the photos are added and the template is just right, clicking the Next button takes you to the finishing steps where you can name the Gallery and define characteristics such as background music, slideshow duration, and some color and font control. (See Figure 4-29.)

You can preview the show before exporting to make sure it doesn't need any further tweaking. Once you're happy, you can export the file locally and share it via several options, including uploading the show with FTP to your web site.

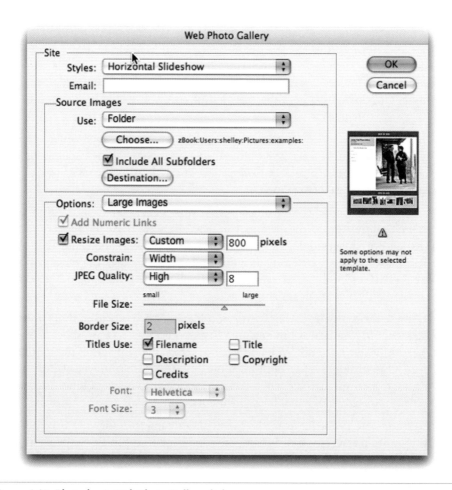

Figure 4-27. Photoshop's Web Photo Gallery dialog

Specialized Web Gallery Applications

There's a wealth of free or at least free-to-try tools that can create photo shows, with or without effects. Some of the generated shows are HTML-based, and some are Flash.

One popular platform-independent tool is the Java-based Gallery Constructor, available in installations for Windows, Linux, and Mac OS X. I tried the Mac product.

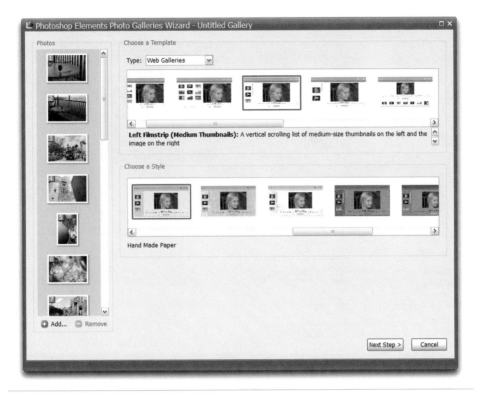

Figure 4-28. Photoshop Elements 5.0 Photo Galleries Wizard

Gallery Constructor can be downloaded at *http://www.through-the-lens.net/cms/index.php?page=Gallery_Constructor*. Installation instructions are provided for each environment.

One thing that sets Gallery Constructor apart from other gallery construction tools is support for RAW images. If you have a set of RAW images you want to quickly convert into a gallery without having to pre-process them first, this is the tool for you.

Once you open the tool for the first time, you can create a project just by accessing a specific folder. This triggers the tool to load thumbnails if any are provided for the images, as shown in Figure 4-30.

You'll then adjust the page template in the Gallery Template section, including providing a title and the number of thumbnails in the page. The Thumbnail Workflow tab provides options for controlling the appearance of the thumbnails, and the Image

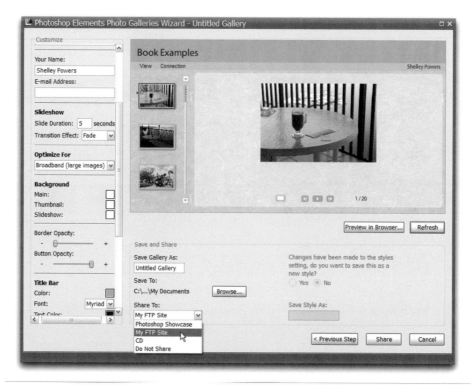

Figure 4-29. Finishing up the Photoshop Elements Web Gallery

Workflow controls the display of the single, enlarged photo pages. You can also preview the image, and when you do, you're given options to change the photo's gamma, contrast, brightness, and saturation options, as shown in Figure 4-31. You can also run a Slideshow immediately, without having to generate a hard copy of the show.

Once you've tweaked the gallery options, you're ready to generate the show. You can generate a hard copy to your local machine and also FTP the show immediately. You're given the option to tweak each photo in turn or accept the same settings for the entire show. The only issue you might have is memory errors, but the site provides a workaround for this. Note, though, that it's not a fast application, especially if you're working with RAW images.

There is another gallery generator that adds an effect to the images, and can also work cross-platform, as well as with most of the tools I've covered in this chapter and Chapter 3—PostcardViewer.

Figure 4-30. Loading a folder of images into Gallery Constructor

PostcardViewer is a Flash show that also has a standalone tool, in addition to a PHP-script-based alternative you just drop into a folder full of images. I tried the PHP-based application with some images I had already loaded with my server.

To use the PHP application, you'll need to download the viewer, unzip the *postcardviewer* folder, and upload it and its contents to your server. Copy or move the photos you want to include to the *images* subdirectory. You'll also need to download and unzip the *buildgallery.php* application. Upload this file to the same *postcardviewer* folder. There are options you can set within the file, and the Postcard-Viewer site has documentation on each of these.

 You can find the PostcardViewer application and instructions at *http://www.airtightinteractive.com/projects/postcardviewer/*.

Figure 4-31. Tweaking a photo in preparation for show generation

In the *postcardviewer* folder is a file, *imagedata.xml*, that you need to make writable by everyone via the FTP program you use. It's this file that provides the information the application needs. You could also edit it yourself; it's just a listing of image names and some dimension information. Figure 4-32 shows the PostcardViewer after the show is first opened, and Figure 4-33 shows it with one of the images expanded.

There's a world of other gallery creation tools that work in all environments, in addition to Windows, Mac, and Linux. Ultimately, though, if you're going to be publishing a lot of photos online, you'll probably want to use a more dynamically managed system, such as full-featured gallery software.

Figure 4-32. Photos loaded into PostcardViewer

One of the best places to get a listing of photo gallery generation applications is at About.com, at *http://graphicssoft.about.com/od/ webgallery/Web_Photo_Gallery_Creation_and_Automation_Tools.htm*.

Gallery Software on the Server

If you have your own hosted environment, you can use any number of server-side applications to display your photos. Two of the more popular photo gallery software applications are Gallery and Coppermine, both written in PHP, and both capable of working in most systems. In addition, several content management systems, such as WordPress and Drupal, also have photo uploading and management capability built in, either for adding photos to posts or for creating an entire gallery.

Figure 4-33. Focusing in on one photo within the Viewer

The grand poobah of server-side photo software, though, is Gallery. It's always been a powerful piece of software, but not always the easiest application to set up. Even now, with simple steps to follow, you still need to set up a database first and be able to modify directories and files. Most of the instructions are from the command line, but you can install Gallery using FTP.

At the time of this writing, there are three different versions of the Gallery application: Gallery 1, Gallery 2 (which I cover in this section), and Gallery Remote for client-side photo posting. For a brand-new installation, you're going to want to install Gallery 2.

Download Gallery at *http://gallery.menalto.com*. If you're not sure about the requirements for running Gallery, contact your hosting company and ask whether you can run Gallery on your site.

The application checks to make sure the required technology is present, but you'll need to create the database first. Most hosting sites provide database functionality, including database creation wizards, which handle all the tech required. The MySQL installation is the default install and doesn't require any additional modules.

What are the Gallery requirements?

- Unix or Windows
- A web server, such as Apache or IIS
- PHP (version 5 required after February 2008)
- Some image processing library (most sites have ImageMagick and/or GD installed)
- A database, such as the aforementioned MySQL, or PostgreSQL, Oracle, or SQL Server

Gallery runs well in both Windows and Unix environments, but most hosting companies run Linux (Unix). All but the cheapest hosting sites support all the other requirements.

 If your hosting company provides a site management package, there's a good chance Gallery is provided as a push-button installation. Check with the company before installing it manually.

During the installation process, you'll be given options as to which plug-ins to install. The list is lengthy, but many have to do with migration from Gallery 1, camera-specific options, integration with third-party tools, and so on. Go through the list carefully, and be conservative with what you install—you can activate or deactivate modules at a later time.

You can create multiple albums with Gallery, each with its own title, description, subdirectory, keywords, and other data. Each can be given its own layout and use a different predefined theme. Figure 4-34 shows part of the Theme configuration page in the Gallery Administration pages.

Gallery is one of the most configurable applications I know of, which is good and bad. Unless you're into development, you might want to start with design themes and get into the more advanced modification facilities only when you're familiar with the application.

You can access new themes at *http://codex.gallery2.org/Gallery2:Themes*. Browse through the many options, and once you've found the theme you like, install it via your own Gallery Site Admin pages through the Gallery → Plugins option. The installation is automatic, and once the new theme is installed you can activate it for any album. Also, once you become familiar with the tool and the templates, you can create your own design.

There's a variety of ways to add photos to a Gallery Album. The simplest is through the web browser directly to the site. You can upload one or more photos at the same time, and add both titles and descriptions. If the template includes the option, any metadata attached to the photo also gets parsed out when the photo is uploaded.

Figure 4-34. Gallery Site Administration pages

There are several client-based applications that can also be used to upload photos, including a Java application, a webcam connection, through Google's Picasa export file, via Windows XP functionality, and through an upload directory if photos are already uploaded to your site.

This latter option is nice if you've been uploading photos through a weblog or other content management tool. I used it when writing this book to add figures that I uploaded to a special directory for my tech reviewers. Once I specified the directory, it then listed each photo with a checkbox next to it. Clicking on any of the boxes uploaded the photo, as shown in Figure 4-35. You can use a symbolic link (symlink) to make it seem as if the photo is coming directly from the Gallery rather than the separate folder. This ended up being a nice way to peruse the figures from this book during the editing process.

One of the advantages of using the local server option is that it's faster to upload photos in batch using an FTP tool. The disadvantage, though, is that you can't give titles and descriptions for each item. You can, however, edit these for each item after they're loaded.

Figure 4-35. Using a local server to add photos to an album

A Bit of Code

A final way to integrate photos into your web pages is using a bit of code embedded into your web pages in such a way that photos are displayed randomly each time a person accesses the page. I've used this for years, both to create changeable sidebar photo displays and also to modify banners and backgrounds for my stylesheets.

Who knows who originated the first PHP-based sidebar photo randomizer. It's been around a long time, though, and is quite popular because so many weblogs and other tools are PHP-based.

If your web pages are PHP-based, all you need do to use a randomizer is organize the photos into one directory local to the site, and save the PHP in Example 4-2 to a file located wherever you want the photo to display.

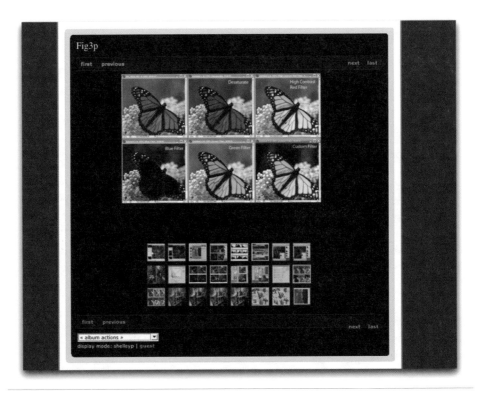

Figure 4-36. Gallery with the Ajaxian theme

Example 4-2. PHP script to randomly display photos

```php
<?php

$dir = "/home/someloc/www/images/";
$url = "http://somesite.com/images/";
$exts = array('jpg');

//collect list of images in current directory
$imgs = array();
if($handle = opendir($dir)) {
        while(false !== ($image = readdir($handle)))
                foreach($exts as $ext)
                        if(strstr($image, '.' . $ext))
                                $imgs[] = $image;
        closedir($handle);
}

//generate a random number
srand((double)microtime() * 1000000);
```

Example 4-2. PHP script to randomly display photos (continued)

```
//change the number after the % to the number of images
//you have
$ct = count($imgs);

$rn = (rand( )%$ct);

$imgname = trim($imgs[$rn]);

printf("<img src='$url%s' alt='' />", $imgname);

?>
```

The two items that need to be changed are the $dir and $url at the top of the script. These should point to the physical directory on the machine where the images are currently loaded and the web site address for the directory, respectively.

In addition, by default the application pulls in JPEG images only. If you want to add in PNG or GIF images, add them to the $exts array, separated by commas:

```
array('jpg','gif','png');
```

With this script embedded in the page, each time the page is loaded, a different image is loaded.

A variation on this is to incorporate this functionality into your stylesheet. I've used this to modify my CSS to change a banner image used in both my header and footer. To implement this in your space, create a PHP application page called photographs.php, shown in Example 4-3, and load into your template directory where the stylesheet and images are located.

Example 4-3. Modifying a stylesheet for a random image

```
<?php
// declare the output of the file as CSS
header('Content-type: text/css');
?>
#header {
<?php

$exts = array('jpeg');

//collect list of images in current (look) directory
$url = array( );
if($handle = opendir(dirname(__FILE__))) {
        while(false !== ($image = readdir($handle)))
                foreach($exts as $ext)
                        if(strstr($image, '.' . $ext))
                                $url[] = $image;
        closedir($handle);
}
```

Example 4-3. Modifying a stylesheet for a random image (continued)

```
//generate a random number
srand((double)microtime( ) * 1000000);

//change the number after the % to the number of images
//you have
$ct = count($url);

$rn = (rand( )%$ct);

$imgname = trim($url[$rn]);

printf("background-image: URL('%s');", $imgname);

?>
        background-repeat: repeat-x;
        background-position: top left;
}

#footer {
<?php

printf("background-image: URL('%s');", $imgname);
?>
        background-repeat: no-repeat;
}
```

The code is quite similar to that shown in Example 4-2, except it makes the assumption that the photos are in the local directory and returns a content type of CSS in the very first line of the application:

```
header('Content-type: text/css');
```

Returning the result of the application as CSS is critical in order to merge the results of this application into a stylesheet. The rest of the document in Example 4-3 is a mix of static CSS and PHP to generate CSS. To incorporate both the static and PHP-generated CSS into my stylesheet, I use the following as the first line (after documentation) in my main CSS file:

```
@import "photographs.php";
```

Now, any time the page is accessed, the background photo for both the header and footer banners are randomly drawn from a pool of photos. I've used this effect with my own photos, as shown with Figure 4-37, but I've also used public domain photos, such as the Hubble images, as well as images from NASA and NOAA. In fact, most photographs from agencies funded by the U.S. federal government are public domain.

I could go and on with photos, but it's time now to look at other forms of raster images, and then move on to the vectors.

Figure 4-37. Banner image rotated through dynamic alteration of stylesheet

CHAPTER 5

Pop Graphics

Photographs are only part of the raster graphics landscape. The other part consists of the buttons, borders, illustrations, and other graphics that originate in drawing tools rather than in cameras. In the beginning of the Web, these formed the heart and soul of web graphics, and though photographs and other newer forms of graphics are making inroads in web art, we'll always need our buttons and bows.

We all envy the graphical artists their ability to create wonderful art on the Web. Barring a miraculous, sudden infusion of artistic skills, though, most of us create the graphics we need by following one of the many tutorials crafted by those who have more talent than we do.

What are some of these graphics? Pretty, shiny buttons for the forms on our web pages; reflections for text and logos to create nice banner looks; border or background images; shine or shadows to add a three-dimensional look to objects; and even text graphic headers, though we should try to restrict use of these items.

But not all raster graphics are art, nor drawn from scratch. For illustration, we incorporate the use of screen captures, hopefully with graphics to highlight whatever functionality we're trying to point out. If the tools we use for screen capturing have the ability to add highlighting functionality directly, so much the better.

Before we get into the screen capturing and button drawing, though, let's take a quick look at the building blocks for raster graphics. At the end of this chapter, I'll revisit these tools and cover how we can "reverse engineer" the graphics we find, on the Web and elsewhere, in order to figure how to create our own versions.

The Graphic Toolbox: Shapes, Layers, Gradient, and Blur

The examples and demonstrations I cover in this chapter are not all-inclusive. In fact, they barely scratch the surface of available effects you can create. The reason I selected each is to demonstrate basic graphics tool functionalities from which you can build the same or other effects. After you've had a chance to go through all of the examples, plus other example tutorials that are plentiful online, you'll get to the point where you don't need to follow a tutorial—either you'll be able to create an effect from scratch, or you'll be able to look at an effect and "reverse engineer" how it was created just by eyeballing it.

What are these basic tool functionalities that form the basis of most online web graphics, and where can they be found in most tools?

Layers

Layers are essential in any graphics development. You can create different objects in each layer, and move them around independent of one another. Layers also allow us to add modifications to an image that we can then remove, independent of the other layers. We can use them to keep a selection active in one layer while we fill it with a gradient or solid color in another. By the time you're done with this section on raster graphics, you'll know deep in your heart that layers are your friends. Layers usually get their own top menu item in most tools.

The Gaussian Blur

The Gaussian Blur was used in the last two chapters, both to add a mood effect (Chapter 3) and to add a drop shadow to photos (Chapter 4). It continues to be an essential element in graphics creation in this chapter. Most tools provide a Gaussian Blur via whatever filter or effects top menu item the tool supports.

Rounded rectangles and other shapes

Rounded rectangles are used for buttons and badges and as building blocks for bigger works. They're usually created using the rectangular selection tool that all tools provide.

To create a rounded rectangle selection in Photoshop, draw the rectangle out using the Rectangular Marquee tool, then access Select → Modify → Smooth and set the radius to round the corners. Paint Shop Pro's Selection tool has a Rounded Rectangle option, but Paint.NET does not. A workaround I've used with Paint.NET is to create a rounded-corner rectangle object, then use the Magic Wand selection tool to select it.

In addition to rounded rectangles, most tools support ellipses, regular rectangles, and a variety of other shapes. You might find that different shapes are available via plug-ins rather than via the toolbar. For instance, in GIMP, to create a star or other geometrical figure, you'd select Filter → Render → GFig, and then create the shape in the dialog that opens.

The gradient

Most photo and graphics editing tools provide a gradient fill tool, and some provide gradient fills as attributes for objects, such as for a rectangle or an ellipse.

Layer styles

Most graphics tools provide some form of styling for the layer, including adding a drop shadow, inner glow, and so on. Photoshop's are accessible via the Layer menu (Layer → Layer Style), GIMP has a Layers Script-Fu extension, and Paint Shop Pro can emulate Photoshop's layer style. Most graphics tutorials assume you have access to Photoshop-like layer styles, so searching on the tool name and the effect (such as "Paint Shop Pro inner glow") should find you the information you need to convert the effect into the tool of your choice.

 There's a great Photoshop to Paint Shop Pro mapping page at *http:// paintshoppro.info/tutorials/photoshop_to_paintshoppro_dictionary.htm.* The GIMP Layer style extension is accessible via the GIMP plug-ins.

Masks

Masks are a way of hiding or showing all of a layer and then allowing parts to be exposed or hidden, based on the color with which you're "drawing" the change. Masks are a great way of protecting part of an image, so that any edits to the layer don't affect the hidden areas. This is especially important when you're creating reflection effects or adjusting exposure or tint for only a portion of the image. Adding a mask is usually an option available directly on the layer or through the Layer menu.

Transforms

Layer transformations provide the ability to scale an image vertically, horizontally, or both; rotate an independent selection; alter perspective; or skew a layer or selection. This is most important when we're working with reflections. How each tool supports transformations varies widely. It's a tool option in the Edit menu for Photoshop, but a control toolbar item in Paint Shop Pro if a vector image has been rasterized. Do check the documentation for whatever tool you decide to use when creating these examples.

 In this chapter, I decided to implement the examples using GIMP 2.4 or Photoshop. The techniques can also be used with Photoshop Elements and Paint Shop Pro, but you'll need to adapt for tool differences.

How the different functionalities get combined to form effects takes up the rest of the chapter. On with the graphics.

Shiny Buttons: Gel, Wet, and Glass

Shiny buttons—whether "gel," "wet," or "glass"—share similar characteristics. The buttons have a three-dimensional look and are given a hard- or soft-edged reflection. Most photo and graphics tools can create a shiny button: all you need is support for layers, gradients, masking, opacity support, and a little blurring help.

Creating a 3D Button in GIMP: Shiny

A popular form of button is one that has a highlight at the top, creating a three-dimensional "hard" shiny effect, as shown in Figure 5-1.

Figure 5-1. Final shiny button with white text

To create this type of button using GIMP, first create a new image, one that's big enough to provide sufficient space to work with the new image. You can always crop out the unneeded background later.

Once the image canvas is created, add a transparent layer and use the Rectangle Select tool to create a rectangle approximately 250 pixels wide and 200 pixels tall. Check the "Rounded corners" tool option, with a radius of 40, and make sure anti-aliasing is turned on. The initial rectangle can be somewhat larger than the final button, which will make it easier to manipulate. Scale it to finished size before adding text or other images, or you can zoom in on the image without affecting its actual size.

 For other editors, such as Photoshop, that support a rounded rectangle shape rather than a selection tool, you can always create the shape, select it, and then use the selection to implement the rest of this and the following button tutorials.

With the foreground color set to black, click the Edit → Fill with FG (foreground color) menu option to fill the rectangle with black, as shown in Figure 5-2.

Using the Rectangle Select tool with the same settings, create another rectangle about a third of the height of the first rectangle (approximately 33 pixels) and narrower (230 pixels wide), and place it just above the middle of the first rectangle, as shown in Figure 5-3.

Without deselecting the smaller rectangle, create a new transparent layer. Using the Gradient tool set to a linear pattern, with a black foreground, a white background, and opacity set to 50%, fill the smaller rectangle on the new layer—moving the gradient tool from the bottom of the smaller selected rectangle to the top. This adds the button's shiny highlight.

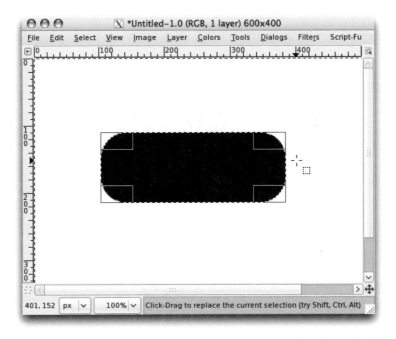

Figure 5-2. Creating the button base in GIMP 2.4

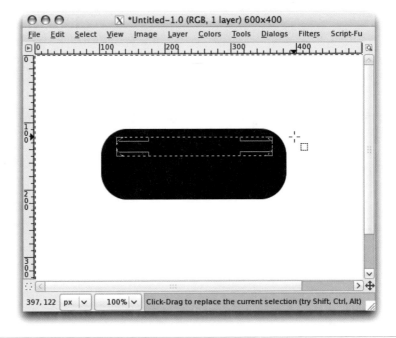

Figure 5-3. Adding highlight rectangle

All that's left now is to resize the button if you wish, and add the text and an optional shadow. In this example, I use a font family of Garamond Premr Pro Smdb Semi-Bold, 66 pixels tall, and colored white to create the button text, "Save Edits".

Finally, I activate the base button layer, select Filter → Light and Shadow → Drop Shadow from the menu, accepting the default of 8 pixels for X and Y Offset and a Blur radius of 15 pixels. If I wanted to get fancier, I could also select the text layer and add a Drop Shadow and Bevel effect to the text. For now, I'll stay with the flat text on the three-dimensional button, as shown earlier in Figure 5-1.

Delete the original background now that it's no longer needed, leaving the button on a transparent background. At this point you can save the image as a PNG, which would preserve the transparency of the shadow effect. However, as I mentioned in Chapter 4, IE 6.x doesn't respect alpha channel transparency, and the buttons would look nasty in this still-popular browser.

A better choice (at least for now until IE6.x has lost more of its audience share) is to convert the background color to fit the background where you're using the button and save the image as a JPEG, or save the image and the transparency using GIF. I've found that I get much better quality with a JPEG, so I flatten the image by making sure the background color is set to the background color of my web page where the button will be saved, and then flatten the layers using Image → Flatten Image. I also Autocrop the image.

Summarizing the steps:

1. Create a new image.
2. Create a rectangle the same shape as the final button. It doesn't have to be to scale.
3. Modify the rectangle to add rounded corners.
4. Fill the rectangle with your color of choice.
5. Create a second rectangle about one-third the height and narrower than the first.
6. Move this rectangle so that it's placed equidistant from the sides of the first, and just above the midpoint of the larger.
7. Create a second transparent layer.
8. Use the gradient tool, set to 50% opacity, to fill the smaller rectangle.
9. Add whatever text you want.
10. Trim the background to the button and shadow and either save as a PNG to preserve transparency, or flatten the image for a JPEG.

Creating a 3D Button, Two: The Dip

Most three-dimensional button effects are created in such a way that the depth of the image, or the "z" index of the image, protrudes out of the page toward the page reader, like a bump on paper.

If we're going to bump, though, shouldn't we also consider the concept of the dip, demonstrated in Figure 5-4? After all, if we're pushing against the flat boundaries of the web page, why limit ourselves to moving out of the page when we're perfectly capable of moving into the page?

Figure 5-4. The "dipped" button

To create a dip, start with a new image and replicate the black, rounded corner rectangle created in the last example. While the rectangle selection is still active, duplicate the newly created rectangle layer, and change the fill color for the rectangle in the new layer to a gray color (#dddddd). Using your mouse or keyboard, nudge the newly created rectangle down until its top is at the halfway mark on the original button base.

Select the Gaussian Blur, Filters → Blur → Gaussian Blur, and blur the new gray rectangle a significant amount—a blur radius of 75 pixels, as shown in Figure 5-5. Notice how only the portion of the gray button layer within the selection is blurred. (If you're using another tool, such as Photoshop, the blur amount will need adjusting.)

To remove the extraneous portions of the gray rectangle, invert the existing selection via the Select → Invert menu option. Make the blurred rectangle layer active, and then cut the area outside of the bottom-rounded rectangle using Edit → Cut. Figure 5-6 shows the image to this point.

Next, add the button text. Set the font to a font family of Garamond Premr Pro Smdb Semi-Bold, the color to white, and the size to 67 pixels. To match the example, set the text to "Edit This". Position the text block so that it isn't centered relative to the button base, but instead is centered a little high and a little to your left.

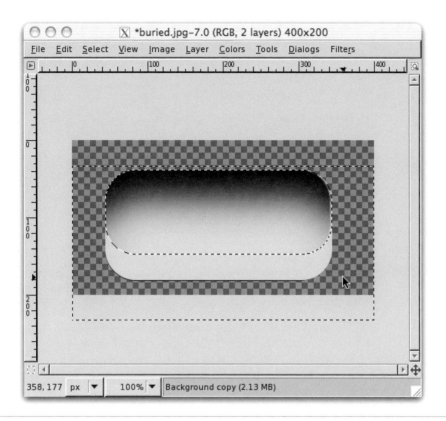

Figure 5-5. Creating the reverse shadow effect for the dip effect

Then, while the text layer is active, add a Drop Shadow (via Filter → Light and Shadow → Drop Shadow), setting the offsets and the radius to 15 pixels. This drop shadow helps create the dimensional effect.

The only task left is to save the image in any of the formats discussed previously, making sure to set the background color appropriately. Figure 5-4 showed the finished result, with a dark gray background. Note that the drop shadow behind the text combined with the lighter-colored shadow added earlier gives the image an inlay effect—that dip I mentioned earlier.

The "dip" can be used for page elements other than buttons. For instance, creating a very long squared-corner rectangle can be used to create an indented bar to "hold" a title, copyright notice, or any other text you want to highlight. You can also fill the indented button or bar with objects other than text, but they should be objects that show off the indented effect. Figure 5-7 shows such an embedded bar created in Photoshop, filled with images created using the Custom Shape tool. To make it look like the top of the embedded object is covered in hard plastic or glass, add a reflection

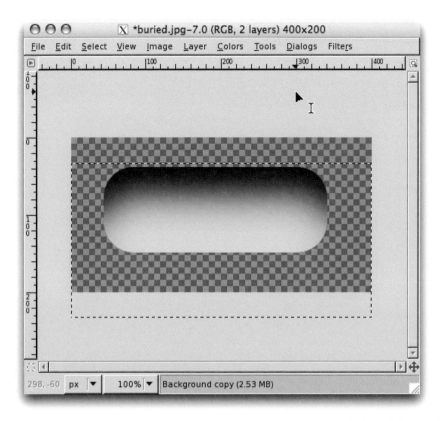

Figure 5-6. Clipping the background to the background layer shape

across the top, as shown in Figure 5-8. The reflection was made by creating a selection of only part of the graphic, and then filling that selection with a gradient fill that progresses from white to completely transparent. The overall fill transparency is then adjusted to about 50%. I'll cover more on reflections later in this chapter.

To summarize the steps to creating a "dip" button:

1. Create a new image.
2. Create a rectangle the same shape as the final button. It doesn't have to be to scale.
3. Modify the rectangle to add rounded corners.
4. Fill the rectangle with your color of choice.
5. Duplicate the rectangle, filling this new rectangle with the highlight color of your choice.

Figure 5-7. An embedded toolbar filled with shapes

Figure 5-8. Adding a hard shine to the embedded toolbar

6. Move this new rectangle down until the top third fills the bottom third of the original rectangle.

7. Blur the top rectangle, using a large blur pixel radius, starting out at 75 pixels.

8. Trim the top rectangle by activating the bottom layer, and use Layer → Transparency → Alpha to Selection, and then invert the selection. Reactivate the top layer, and cut the excess.

9. Add text, and while the text layer is active, add a Drop Shadow, with offsets and radius set to 15 pixels.

Creating a 3D Button, Three: The Wet Button

The "dip" is also the first part to creating a wet, aqua, or jelly button—a soft-looking, shiny button that appears filled with a transparent liquid. All that's required to complete the conversion from "dip" to "wet" is to add a shadow to the button base (set to an 8-pixel offset with a radius blur of 8 pixels) since we're now "raising" the button above the page, and use the technique described earlier with the first button to add a small, shiny reflection along the top of the button.

Figure 5-9 shows the button created in the last section, but modified with the "shine" rectangle at the top and the addition of a shadow.

Figure 5-9. Dipped button converted to an aqua button

Black is an elegant color and black buttons are quite handsome, but people like other colors, too. The main difference between creating the black button and other colors is that when you add the text shadow, it should reflect the darker color of the overall button instead of being black. This is because the shadow is virtually representing the light shining into the button being blocked by the button text. When the light is "blocked," the base color of the button is displayed. The color at the bottom of the button is lighter because the color is emulating an effect where the base color of the button is partially washed out by the light.

To see the wet effect in color, Figure 5-10 shows a blue aqua version of the "Edit this" button.

To make this new button variation, create the rectangle with rounded corners, but this time fill it with a dark blue (hexadecimal value of 0c27ef). While the selection is still active, duplicate the button layer, and then fill the button in the new layer with a brighter blue/aqua color (value of 00ffff). Move the top button layer straight down until the top of the button fills the bottom portion of the base button, as shown in Figure 5-11.

Figure 5-10. Bright blue aqua button

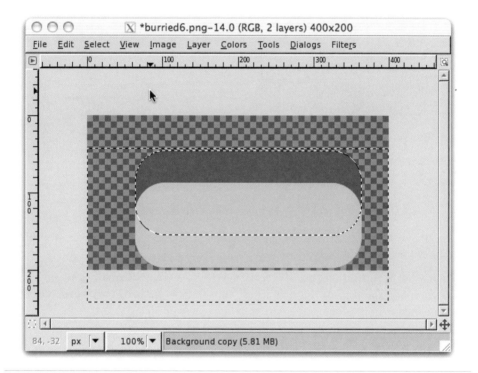

Figure 5-11. Creating the reflection in the blue button example

Apply the Gaussian Blur to the light-blue layer, but this time try a smaller radius amount. For this example, I used a value of 55 pixels.

Once the top button is blurred, make the background layer active, and then select the alpha channel using Layer → Transparency → Alpha to Selection. Invert the selection, make the top layer active, and select Edit → Cut to clip both layers to the button shape.

Using the same font as in the last section, create the text, offsetting it just slightly as in the last example, and then select the Drop Shadow filter. This time, though, change the shadow color to the same color as the darker color used in the base of the button (0c27ef), as shown in Figure 5-12. Keep the offset and pixel blur radius at 15 pixels.

Figure 5-12. Adding a text shadow with the same color as the button base

Merge the visible layers down, and apply a regular shadow with an offset of 8 pixels and the color reset back to black.

All that's left to do now is use the rectangle tool to create a small rounded-corner rectangle along the top. Add a new layer, and use the gradient tool to fill the small rectangle, using both blues as the dark and light ends of the gradient.

Because GIMP and Photoshop are quite different in how each implements its functionality, I've written out the steps to create something similar with Photoshop CS:

1. Create a new image.

2. Use the Rounded Rectangle tool to create a button of the desired size, shape, and base color. From the Layer menu, select the Rasterize option and rasterize the shape. This creates a new layer with the shape above the background.

3. Use the Magic Wand to select the rectangle.

4. Create a new layer.

5. Use the Paint Bucket tool to fill the selected rectangle shape in the new layer with the desired color, such as the bright aqua in the last example.

6. Use the mouse or keyboard to nudge the newly filled rectangle down until its top is about halfway down the darker-colored rectangle.

7. Deselect the selection, but keep focus on the newly created layer.

8. Select the Gaussian Blur filter and blur the new layer. I use a filter radius of about 27.

9. Activate the layer holding the button base.

10. Use the Magic Wand to select the button base. Using the Select menu, invert the selection.

11. Reactivate the top highlight layer. Press the Delete key, or otherwise cut the inverted selection, leaving just the highlight that's wholly contained within the base.

12. Choose the Horizontal Type tool and set the text to your preferred font, size, and color. I use Cooper Std, and in this case set the color to white.

13. Add the "Edit This" text to the button. This creates a new, fourth layer.

14. From the Layer menu, choose the Layer style and add a drop shadow. Set the shadow offset (Distance) to 25 and the size to 5, and change the color to the same color as the button base.

15. To create the reflection, create a new layer and use the Rounded Rectangle tool to create a small reflection rectangle at the top of the image. Once rasterized, use the Magic Wand to select the rectangle, and then delete the layer.

16. Create a new layer, and using the Gradient Fill tool set to white/transparent, fill the selection.

17. All that's left now is to set the background color and flatten the image, in addition to adding a button drop shadow. Figure 5-13 shows a squarish button in roses and pinks with a drop shadow, created in Photoshop CS3. The figure includes the Layers window, to better demonstrate the state of the button before it's flattened.

Experiment around with different colors, even dramatically different colors.

The examples to this point have been based on a button shape. There are times, though, when we'll want to create a 3D effect in other shapes, and I'll cover some techniques to do this in the next section.

Badges and Bows: Beyond the Buttons

Page badges and application icons are the two- or three-dimensional graphical shapes that are used to attract attention, convey simple messages, or visually represent an application. They can be used to note that an application is still beta, to indicate that a sale is ongoing, to highlight the date of an event, or even just to add a pretty effect to web pages.

Figure 5-13. Shiny, wet button created with Photoshop CS3

The main difference between a badge and an application icon is that the badge is not meant to look like something that can be clicked. An application icon, on the other hand, can look clickable.

Where the icon differs from a button is that the icon is usually graphical, with no text, whereas buttons have text describing what happens when you push the button. Buttons also have distinctive button-like shapes, whereas icons can be any shape, though square is the most popular. With icons, the graphics represent the action (open the application, save to file, and so on).

In this section, I focus on badges. Later, in the section on reverse-engineering designs, we'll look at some icons.

 In this section and the next, I'm switching to Photoshop for the examples. Note that when creating a shape such as a rectangle with Photoshop, you'll need to "rasterize" it before you can apply most of the modifications I'll cover. This is because the image is really a vector until you start treating it as a static image, such as when you apply transforms. You can rasterize the image by selecting the layer where the image resides, and then selecting Layer → Rasterize → Layer.

Simple, Shiny Irregular Shape

One popular badge is the multi-sided gradient-filled stubby star with blocky text off-set by 45 degrees, as shown in Figure 5-14. This is a very easy type of badge to make, especially when your tool supports layer blending modes.

Figure 5-14. A finished badge

When working with a rectangle or elliptical shape, it's relatively easy to add a "shiny" spot to the shape. However, when you're working with irregular shapes, it becomes more of a challenge.

One way to add both highlight and shadow to a shape is to outline part of the shape and use it to make the three-dimensional shading. I'm going to use that for the first badge I'll create, which is a 12-point stubby star.

The first time I saw this technique used to create a shiny badge was at the popular web site Scriptygoddess (*http://www.scriptygoddess.com/ archives/category/photoshop-tutorial/*).

To begin, create a new image, 600 pixels square, with a transparent background. You can resize the image later, but a larger image gives us room to work. Set the foreground color to a dark red (hex value of bb0000).

Next, create a star by selecting the Polygon tool and setting the number of sides to 12. (If you've not worked with the Polygon tool in Photoshop, it's one of the Geometry tools, which also includes Rectangle, Rounded Rectangle, Ellipse, and Custom.) Select the Polygon options from the Options toolbar, check the Star option, and indent the sides 25%. Make the star as big as you want.

Use the Gradient Fill tool to create a darker shadow at the bottom of the star. Select the star using the Magic Wand, and then create a new transparent layer. Set the background color to black, and draw down the selection with the Gradient tool to fill the star shape with a gradient, from dark red to black, as shown in Figure 5-15.

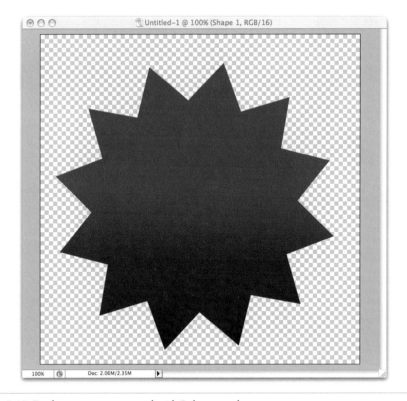

Figure 5-15. Dark maroon star created with Polygon tool

While the star is still selected, shrink the selection using the Select → Modify → Contract, creating a new selection that's 5 pixels in from the star edge, as shown in Figure 5-16.

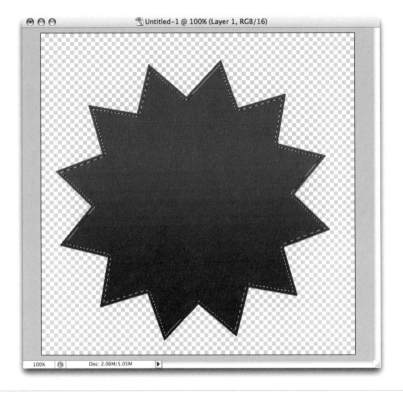

Figure 5-16. Area selected on the star

Using the Elliptical Marquee selection tool and holding down the Alt and Shift keys, create an oval selection that overlaps the star about halfway down. Holding the keys will return a selection area containing the overlap between the existing selection and the oval. Create a new transparent layer, reset the background color to white, and fill the selected area, from dark red to white, creating the highlight, as shown in Figure 5-17. Deselect the selection (Select → Deselect).

All that's left to finish the star is adding the drop shadow. Instead of using an offset with the shadow, create a uniform drop shadow all around the star by setting the Distance value to zero (0) and the shadow size to 9 pixels. The finished star is shown in Figure 5-18, and is ready to use as is or to have text or another figure added, as shown earlier.

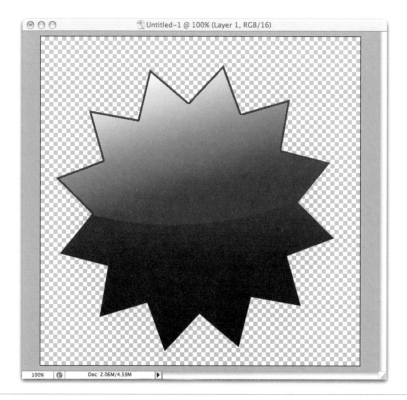

Figure 5-17. Highlight created using gradient fill

To summarize the steps just taken:

1. Create a new image.
2. Add a new figure, such as the 12-point star in this example.
3. Fill the image with a gradient, from base color to black, with the black at the bottom of the figure.
4. Select the geometric shape and contract it 5 pixels.
5. Using the elliptical selection tool and holding down the Shift and Alt keys, over-lay the figure until the bottom of the oval is as far down as you wish for the high-light. Only the top part of the figure, inset 5 pixels, will be selected.
6. Create a new transparent layer consisting of the base color to a white highlight, and fill in the selected area, from darker color to lighter at top.
7. Add a drop shadow with no offset, so the shadow completely surrounds the figure.

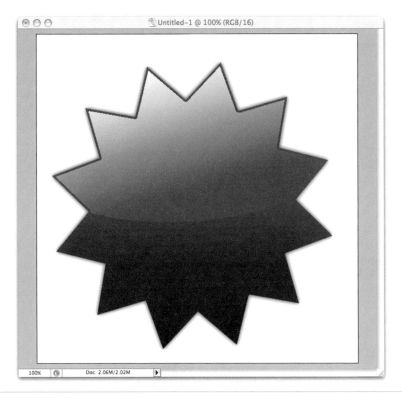

Figure 5-18. Finished shiny star, with drop shadow

Glowing Rather Than Shiny

A variation of the shiny badge approach described in the previous section is one that is less shiny and more polished. It makes for a nice variety, especially if there's a chance that the "shine" of the shiny button will detract from whatever is added to the badge face.

To implement the "soft glow" effect, create the same dark red (bb0000) 12-point star. Select the star using the Magic Wand or other selection technique.

Using the elliptical selection tool, create an oval selection while holding the Shift and Alt keys down to select the bottom part of the badge. Create a new transparent layer, and fill the selection area with black. Set the opacity of the layer to 40%, as shown in Figure 5-19.

Repeat the steps just described (including adding a new transparent layer) to create the badge highlight, except use white instead of black.

Figure 5-19. Creating the shadow layer

To soften the edges for both the highlight and the shadow, activate both the shadow and highlight layers in turn, and apply a Gaussian Blur in each, with the blur radius set to a high value, 50 pixels. Figure 5-20 shows the star at this point.

To clean up the background from blur that's overlapped the star, activate the original star layer, and then select the star using the Magic Wand. Invert the selection (using Select → Inverse), activate the shadow layer, and press the Delete key. Repeat the same steps to clean up the highlight layer.

At this point, you can create a drop shadow, like the previous example, or use an off-set drop shadow, as shown in Figure 5-21.

Do play around with layer or edge styles, depending on the tool you use. For instance, there's a Layers plug-in for GIMP that emulates Photoshop's layer style settings, including adding an inner and outer glow and an inner shadow, all of which can be used to add a more realistic 3D quality to a shape.

Figure 5-20. Gaussian Blur applied to shadow and highlight layers

Another variation is to use other colors for highlight and shadow, rather than white and black. The earlier finished badge in Figure 5-14 showed a variation on the softly glowing shape effect, this time using a gold highlight, and also adding an inner shadow, a dark-red edge preserved using Select → Modify → Contract to make the selection, and text added (the text is also given an offset drop shadow).

Recapping the steps:

1. Create a new image.
2. Add a new figure, such as the 12-point star, using whatever color you prefer.
3. Select the figure.
4. Use the elliptical selection tool, and—holding down the Shift and Alt key— select over the bottom part of the figure.
5. Create a new transparent layer, set the foreground and background colors to your base and shadow colors, and fill in the shadow selection area.

Figure 5-21. Glowing, rather than shiny, shape

6. Select Filter → Blur → Gaussian Blur and blur the shadow layer. Start with a blur radius of 25 pixels and adjust as necessary.

7. Repeat steps 3 through 6, but this time for the top of the figure and using the highlight colors.

8. Activate the original figure layer, select the figure, and invert the selection.

9. Activate the shadow layer and click Edit → Cut to clean up the background.

10. Repeat steps 8 and 9 to clean up the highlight area.

11. Add a drop shadow, edge effects, and text.

To summarize the glowing versus shiny effects, a glowing highlight is created using a solid color, which is then blurred considerably. A shiny effect is created by using a gradient fill and keeping the "hard" edges of the highlight. A glow effect is used to emulate a material that has a softer surface, such as a soft plastic or brushed aluminum or titanium. A shiny effect puts emphasis on the surface being very hard and very reflective, such as hard plastic, glass, or shiny metal.

Before moving on from badges and buttons, a final item to note from Figure 5-14 is the text. In this example, the font size for the first letter is much larger than for the rest of the word, and the text is rotated about 30 degrees.

You don't have to use the same size font for your badge text, and rotated text can add more of a splash to the image than text that's aligned horizontally.

> Of course, you can also use any number of plug-ins or even online graphics generators to create your badges, such as the generator at *http://www.web20badges.com/*, but there's nothing more satisfying than creating your own graphics from scratch.

Shiny buttons and badges are considered Web 2.0 items, but the techniques were used years before the term originated and never grow old. At least until we have alternatives through the use of SVG or other graphics specification (covered in Chapter 6).

Another popular Web 2.0 item that should have lasting power is reflection, which is covered next.

Reflecting on Reflection, and Shadowing Revisited

Reflections are a simple graphic technique with major visual impact, which explains their popularity. They also use a couple of editor functionalities I haven't covered yet in this book: the use of layer masking and transformations.

Reflections fall into two types. The first reflection type is used with simple objects, and really is nothing more than a sophisticated shadow technique. We'll look at a couple of variations of this type of "reflection."

> To emphasize shadow more than reflection, add a Gaussian Blur to the reflected text in the first couple of examples, and change the color to a neutral gray.

A true reflection, though, is more of a mirrored look, and it works best when we're using an object that either has a three-dimensional shape or, at a minimum, has detail that's reflected so that we know we're dealing with a reflection and not a "shadowy" effect.

There's no real "right" or "wrong" way to create a reflection: it's more dependent on the effect you're trying to create and your satisfaction with the finished product. You might even want to try a variety of techniques when applying a reflection, just to see what works best.

Reflection As Mirror Image

The simplest reflection is one where you create a duplicate of what you're reflecting, flip it vertically, and then adjust the layer's opacity to 50% or less.

In this example, I'm going to create a reflection of text on a blue/aqua background using Photoshop (see Figure 5-22).

Figure 5-22. Finished reflection

To start, create a new image, 500 pixels wide by 340 pixels with a white background. Using the font tool, set the font color to a deep blue (000066), the font family to Cooper Std Black, and the font size to 60 pt. Using this font, type "Hello World" in the new image.

Adding the text automatically creates a new layer. Activate this layer, and then duplicate it. Flip the duplicated layer by selecting Edit → Transform → Flip Vertical. Using the Move tool, move the item down so that the two image "bottoms" are almost touching, as shown in Figure 5-23.

Figure 5-23. Text duplicated in a separate layer and then flipped vertically, as well as moved

Next, adjust the opacity of the reflected text as much as you wish. To match the finished example in Figure 5-22, adjust it to 10%.

Reflected text using this approach is rather plain on a solid color background because there's no visual indication of light source. It's common to use a gradient to fill in the background of a reflected image. Another approach when you're using a straight "reflection" would be to use a solid light color for the top of the image and a deeper color for the bottom part of the image.

To demonstrate, set the foreground color to an aqua shade (hex of 13f4e1), and use the rectangle selection tool to select the top part of the image almost—but not quite—to the bottom of the first text layer. Use the Fill Bucket to fill the layer, as shown in Figure 5-24.

Next, invert the selection, set the foreground color to a lighter blue (hex value of 01b4dd), and fill the bottom. Experiment with different light and dark colors, and also try the colors in a gradient fill for comparison.

Another use for the reflection technique just described is to create a cast shadow, described next.

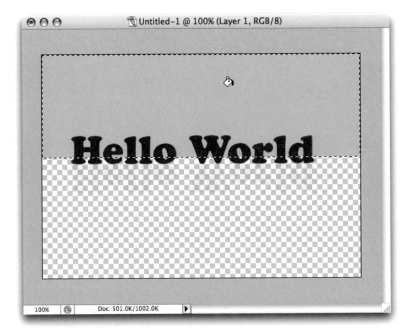

Figure 5-24. Filled top part of the reflected text image

Reflection As Cast Shadow

In earlier examples, the only shadows have been drop shadows. Another type of shadow is a cast shadow, which is a form of reflection. The difference between the two is that reflections are mirror-like because the object is resting directly on a reflective surface and ambient light impacts on both equally. The reflected object really is a reflection. Shadows differ because the reflected image is created by a light source behind the object, distorting the reflected image as it changes position.

 Another difference, of course, is that a shadow loses object detail. Right now, though, we're focusing on shape and perspective, not detail.

There are two adjustments we need to make in order to add the cast shadow distortion, especially with a light source closer to the horizontal plane of the object. One is that the end of the reflection closest to the subject should be the same width as the subject, but the end toward us will widen out.

The second adjustment is to scale the height of the object, either making the height longer or shorter, depending on where we exist relative to the object. In addition, if we're more interested in creating a shadow than a reflection, light that's closer to the horizontal plane of the object casts a longer, more diffuse "shadow"; light higher up casts a shorter, stronger shadow.

Returning to the example just created, we're going to add both perspective and scaling to the image to create more of a three-dimensional illusion. To make the transform easier to see, we'll also reset the background to white.

After the text has been rasterized, choosing Edit → Transform → Perspective from the menu gives us a transform box around the reflected layer, as shown in Figure 5-25. Pulling the bottom-left corner to the left widens the "bottom" part of the reflected image, giving us a wider perspective.

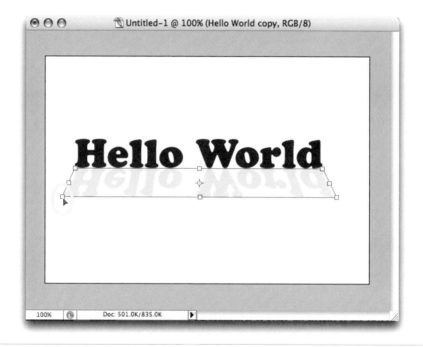

Figure 5-25. Adding Transform-Perspective to the shadow text

Choosing Edit → Transform → Scale, scale the reflection the desired amount. Longer reflection is used for a light source closer to the horizontal plane of the object, shorter for one higher up. To match the finished image, in Figure 5-26, scale the vertical a little longer than the original. Note that you'll want to experiment with both perspective and length to get the effect you're most interested in.

After applying the transformations and adding back in the two-tone background, we can add other image changes, such as a white half-sun on the horizon behind the words and then a Gaussian Blur to the reflected text to make it more shadowy looking, similar to that shown in Figure 5-26. Really, there's no limit to the tweaks and adjustments we can make using just a few of the tools we've worked with previously.

Figure 5-26. After applying transformations and Gaussian Blur to shadow and adding the two-tone background and a half-sun

The examples to this point have been more shadow than reflection. In the next several sections, we'll focus more on the reflecting component of reflections and less on the shadows.

A True Reflecting Reflection

When working with reflections, it's better to use a subject that has some variation in its face, so that we're not left with any confusion about whether we're dealing with a reflection or a shadow.

For instance, if we're working with solid color text, it helps to add an element that has a different color. To demonstrate, since we've done the ocean color scheme, in the next example we'll go to the forests, as shown in the finished reflection effect in Figure 5-27. The text is green, but it's accompanied by a tan-colored plant.

Using the same font family and size as the last example, create a new image that's 600 pixels wide and 400 pixels tall, with the background set to white in the beginning, but this time the font color is a deep green (11600e).

After typing "Hello World", create a new transparent layer and change the Shape tool to Custom. We're working with a "forest" theme, so from the Custom Shape drop-down, pick one of the tall grass shapes. Setting the color to a deep beige (d6bd8d), create the object, just a little taller than the font and centered between the two words, as shown in Figure 5-28.

Figure 5-27. Finished reflection with gray gradient as background

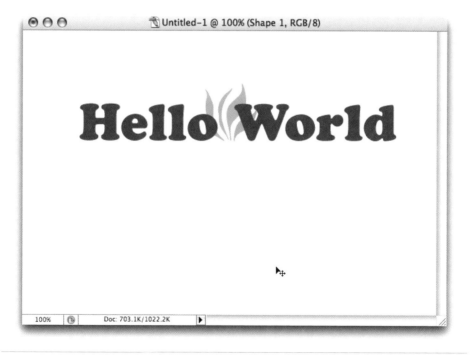

Figure 5-28. Creating a new Hello World…with friend

Using the Layers tool window, select all the layers but the background and merge the layers so there is only one layer to use for the reflection. Duplicate this layer using Layer → Duplicate Layer, flip it vertically using Edit → Transform → Flip Vertical, and move the new layer down to get the reflection, as shown in Figure 5-29.

Figure 5-29. Reflected text/pattern

A reflection, especially one observed at an angle or a distance, doesn't typically "show" all of the reflected image. However, the cutoff for the reflection must be gradual, or it won't look natural. One way to achieve this effect is through the use of the Layer Mask and the Gradient Fill.

Activate the reflected text layer, and then add a Layer Mask by selecting Layer → Layer Mask → Hide All. Photoshop creates a black-filled layer mask, hiding the layer contents, as shown in Figure 5-30.

Next, double-check that Photoshop set the foreground color to white and that the background color is black. Make sure the mask is active, and then use the Gradient Fill tool, choosing the Foreground to Background fill and linear options. Starting above the top text, draw down with the tool until about halfway through the reflected text. You should have a lighter image with the top fading away, as shown in Figure 5-31.

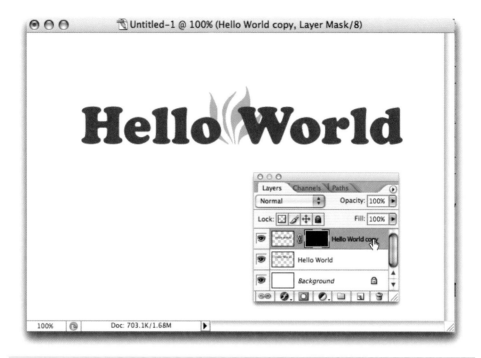

Figure 5-30. Adding a Hide All Layer Mask on the reflected image

To finish, add whatever background you want, such as another two-tone background, a gradient fill, or even a solid color. To match the finished result shown earlier in Figure 5-27, use a gradient to fill the background, with the foreground color set to neutral gray (cccccc) and the background to white. Fill the background from the bottom of the image to the top in a straight, linear fill. Try out alternatives. It's amazing what different choices can do to create a "feel" in the picture.

A couple of things to note about this example: first, you don't *have* to add another color element or three-dimensional effect. You can just use straight text and depend on the gradual fade to give more of a reflection than a shadow effect. Second, I didn't adjust either the perspective or scale of the reflected image in this example. In my opinion, these actions are for shadows, not reflections. However, you may find otherwise—one thing about web graphics is that we're encouraged to explore our own tastes.

The last example I'm going to demonstrate uses a reflection of an object that is itself skewed, to create the effect of looking at an object indirectly.

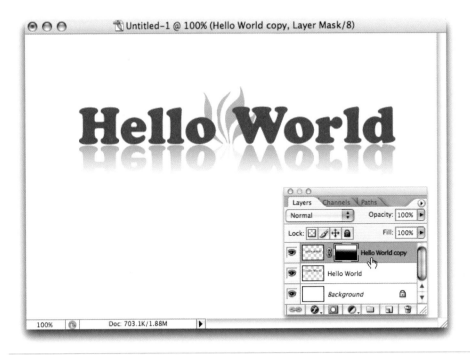

Figure 5-31. Using a layer mask and gradient to create a fading reflection

Reflecting Screenshots and Pictures

Reflections become a more interesting challenge when two new components are added. The first is if there's a lot of detail in the object to be reflected, such as creating a reflection of a book, with both images and text on the original object. The second challenge is when you want to add some perspective to the object you're reflecting and the reflection has to pick up that perspective.

Figure 5-32 shows just such a challenging reflection. In it, a screenshot of the O'Reilly web page is "stood" on end, giving it a solid three-dimensional feel. To create the effect, the web page is first skewed, in order to change the perspective of the viewer looking at the page: we're not looking at the page directly; we're looking slightly turned to the side, as if it's framed in plastic and set on a shiny desk. Before it fades into the bottom of the page, the reflection also echoes this skewing. To add to the feel that this is an object standing up perpendicular to the shiny desk, a diffuse shadow is added behind the screenshot.

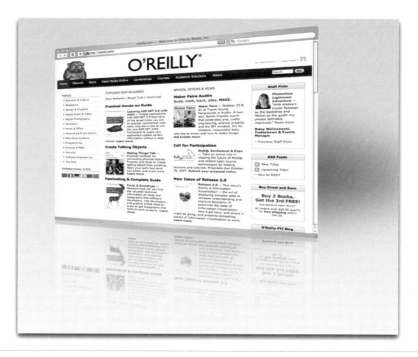

Figure 5-32. Stand-up screenshot, with reflection and shadow

I've seen this approach used for screenshots for web pages and applications, in addition to reflections of books, magazines, newspapers, and even photos. It's useful and can look very sharp; plus, it's an intriguing editing challenge.

To re-create Figure 5-32, first either open a photo or grab a screenshot of your favorite web page. To match the example exactly, grab a screenshot of O'Reilly's web site, though the contents will, of course, be different by the time you try this example.

Create a second new image, 1,200 pixels square—wide and tall enough to provide a good working surface—with a white background. Resize the screenshot or photo until it's about 800 pixels wide, select around it, and copy it into the new working image.

Making sure the copied image layer is active, select Edit → Transform → Skew. Create a side perspective of the image by pulling down on the copied image's top-left corner, and pulling up a little on the bottom-left corner. The right side is left alone. When you're finished, apply the transformation, leaving an image that looks similar to that in Figure 5-33.

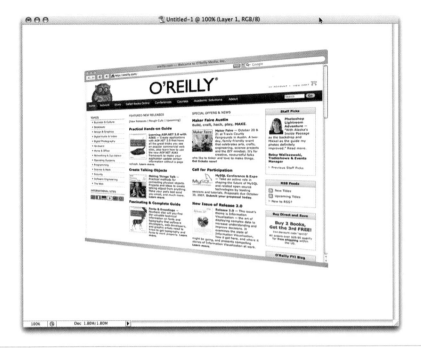

Figure 5-33. Skewed image

Paste a second copy of the original screenshot image again into the working document, flip it vertically, and move it down until the bottom-right edges of both images are just barely touching, as shown in Figure 5-34.

The original image and the reflected image have to align along the bottom, but the process isn't as straightforward as it might seem. Your first inclination might be to use the skew tool along the top edge of the reflected image, since you're trying to match up the two where they would touch. However, if you do, although the images might align where they touch, the actual reflection doesn't because the elements contained within seem to be compressed as compared to the original screenshot.

Even though the reflected image's top won't end up in the final product, you'll need to skew it, as you're also skewing the reflected image's bottom to align with the original image—checking to see that not only are the image "bottoms" aligning, but also that the contents of both the original image and the reflected image align. The reflected image is really a "mirror" of the top, which means you want to mirror the skewing as well as the image.

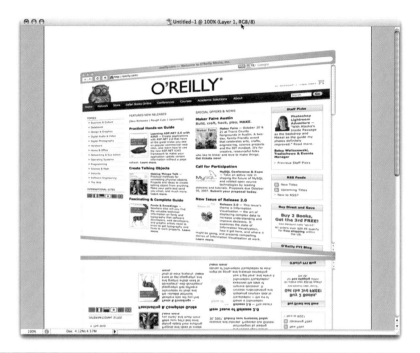

Figure 5-34. Reflecting image added to working copy

It might help to turn on the image grid (via View → Show → Grid) to ensure that all the columns within the screenshot line up, in addition to the edges, as shown in Figure 5-35.

The next part is the easy one. Create a layer mask on the reflected image layer, and, using the Gradient Fill tool set to white foreground/black background, fill in the bottom image until only the top part of the image shows.

To match the finished image shown earlier, select the background layer, and, setting the Gradient Fill tool to a lighter blue (cbd8e2) foreground and a white background, fill in the background layer, as shown in Figure 5-36.

The next step is optional. If you wish to add a cast shadow behind the screenshot, create a dark-gray rectangle about the same size as the screenshot and then rasterize it.

Using the Transform tools, both Skew and Rotate, manipulate the rectangle until it approximates where a shadow would be. It might help if you move the shadow layer to between the reflection and the upper layer, and move the front end of the rectangle to the "front" to provide a guide for the back part of the shadow, similar to what is shown in Figure 5-37.

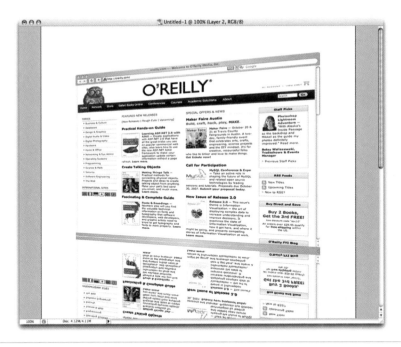

Figure 5-35. Original image and reflection, aligned along the bottom

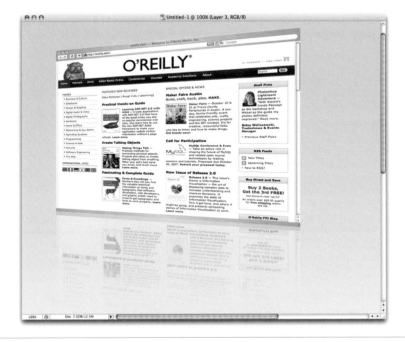

Figure 5-36. Image reflected and background filled in with blue gradient

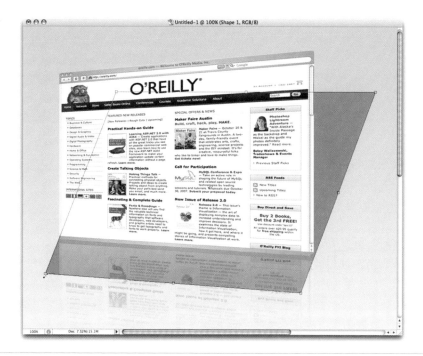

Figure 5-37. Creating a cast shadow for the stand-up screenshot

When the angle of the shadow is about right, move and scale the shadow until it's completely behind the screenshot. The shadow doesn't have to be perfect, because the next step is to apply a Gaussian Blur to it. The blur radius is quite large, because we really want only a hint of a shadow, not one that's strongly marked. Begin with a radius of 50 pixels and adjust from there.

Once the shadow is created, merge the layers and resize to the size you need or want, and you're ready with a screenshot that will impress your web page readers. This approach is also a great way of posting web design prototypes or showcasing an application, in addition to a photograph or any other "flat" material.

Reverse-Engineering Ideas

I found the idea for the "stand up" screenshot created in the last section—using perspective, reflection, and a shadow—from a dressed-up screenshot I saw at the Apple site for iTunes, shown in Figure 5-38. I get many ideas from sites online, or even in desktop applications or the operating system interface. My products may not be as polished as many that I find, but they don't send children running in fear or cause grown men to wet themselves in laughter either. That works for me, especially when I have fun trying out the various ideas. "Fun trying out" is the operative term here.

Figure 5-38. Apple iTunes page that served as inspiration for my own O'Reilly stand-up image

I mentioned earlier that after you've had a chance to work with different types of graphics, using all of the techniques covered in this chapter—including Gaussian Blur to create both shadow and highlight, Gradient Fill to add depth, the selection tool to create shadows and shine, and layers, layer masks, and the transformation tools—you'll find yourself eying every graphic you come across online, figuring out how to create the effect yourself.

Copying images directly is a violation of copyright unless the copyright owner gives you permission to use the image. In addition, re-creating an image exactly is also a violation of copyright, unless the original image is provided as both model and example. Learning from existing work, though, by studying the art you find online—seeing where a gradient is used, how a highlight is created, the nice border effects—is not only perfectly acceptable, it's encouraged.

Earlier in this chapter, in the section on creating a "dip" button, I showed a couple of embedded toolbar figures, the second with a light streak across the seemingly hard plastic interface. That idea came from Microsoft's Zune page, shown in Figure 5-39, where a light streak is drawn across the front of the Zune players, providing detail about the players—the visual interface is flat, hard, and plastic.

The example also uses a new way of showing a break between wall and surface, by using a gray blurred shadow behind the bottom of the Zune players, and continuing the gray (at least this is my guess) into the gradient used to create the Zune reflections.

Figure 5-39. Microsoft's Zune page, showing light streak across the hard plastic on the Zune players

If I have any problem with the image, it's the fact that the light streak is coming from an angle, but the shadows in the picture seem to be straight on.

Feel free to innovate with your use of reflection, shadow, light streaks, and highlights, but remember one thing: they all have to agree. Pick your image's light source location and make sure all the elements in the image are consistent.

Eventually, you may find yourself looking at everything with an eye for how it was created, in order to incorporate new techniques. The same can be said for looking at real-world objects, and thinking to yourself how they could be created in the two-dimensional world of the Web. It might help to take photos of the real-world items in order to put them into a two-dimensional format. Or even combine real-world photos with graphically created backgrounds.

In addition, as you are working through your own creations, jot down the steps you're taking with pencil and paper. Don't depend on the editor's history tool or the layers, or even naming layers. Don't use a computer note to track steps.

By using pencil and paper, you're forced to slow down and think about what's happening with each step. This can not only give you ideas of what to try next, but also makes the steps easier to re-create when you get an effect you like. Using pencil and paper also means not having to flip from editor to text editor and back in your computer.

There's one last raster graphic to take a look at in this chapter, and then we'll move on to the vectors. We're about due for a change of pace.

Instant in Time: Screenshots

This book is full of images, most of them screenshots of graphics in some form of creation or manipulation, or finished products. The screenshot tools I used for this book also create images for web pages. The only difference is that we typically save the screenshots in JPEG for the Web, which is not a format that works well in a print format.

Operating systems have a built-in capability to get a screenshot. In Windows, pressing the Print Screen key captures a screenshot of the screen, placing the image in the clipboard, which can then be pasted into an editor. Apple provides a utility called Grab that can be used to create screenshots. Grab supports a free format selection, as well as screenshots of windows and the entire screen. You can also do a timed screenshot of the screen if you want to capture the mouse.

These work, but none provide any level of sophistication in capturing screen images. In addition, none of the built-in approaches provide a way to annotate a screenshot once it's been made. Screenshot software can also be used to create screen casts, which are used to make tutorials or demonstrations.

While writing this book, I used three different products to take screenshots in addition to the operating system built-ins: the wildly popular Snag-It for Windows from TechSmith; Faststone's Fast Capture, also for Windows; and beta software for the Mac called Skitch, from Plasq. I liked all three, though they each had their foibles. Searching on "screenshot tool" returns others you can try.

 A Snag-It trial download can be grabbed at *http://www.techsmith.com/ screen-capture.asp*. The site also includes videos on how to use the product, and documentation. Fast Capture can be found at *http:// www.faststone.org/FSCaptureDetail.htm*. The company also provides a free 30-day trial. Skitch, at *http://skitch.com*, is freely available, and can be downloaded at *http://skitch.com/signup*.

Snag-It is probably one of the most popular screen capture tools. It's extremely simple to use: you start it up, and as you want to capture items, you can either use one of the built-in keyboard commands or access the tool directly—to take a snapshot of a window, a selection area, or even the whole screen, as shown in Figure 5-40.

Snag-It can be configured to use different keyword combinations, and also provides a timed option, so that you can put the cursor back into the capture. This is particularly important if you want to denote a specific action or show a drop-down.

Snag-It also has several annotation options. You can use arrows or text, or draw boxes around items. You can also add any number of "edge" effects, such as the popular—and perhaps overused—torn edge. In addition, the tool provides a way to add new graphics libraries, such as the larger arrows and cursor hand used in some of the screenshots shown throughout this book. Figure 5-41 shows a screen capture where I'm adding all sorts of annotations. You'll probably not want to do this at home.

Figure 5-40. Screen capture of the Snag-It main capture page

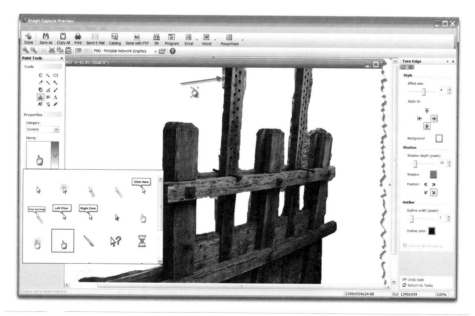

Figure 5-41. Snag-It's Editing interface

Once you're finished with an image, you can save it to the local drive, send it via email, or post to your site via FTP. You can even save versions of the image specific to a Microsoft Office application, but we're not interested in that in this book.

Faststone's Fast Capture supports the same type of screen captures that Snag-It does. It also provides customizable shortcut keys, as well as a small, out-of-the-way menu that can be accessed via mouse to activate the tool.

Like Snag-It, Fast Capture also supports after-capture editing. In the initial capture window, shown in Figure 5-42, you can covert the capture to grayscale or sepia, crop it, or send it out using IM, as well as save the document in Microsoft Office format. Clicking the Paint option pulls up Microsoft Paint, which causes me to shudder, so I didn't touch this option.

Figure 5-42. Fast Capture main edit screen

No offense intended to Microsoft's venerable Paint program, one of the very first Windows applications ever built. Though I find it extremely limited in functionality, it's sophisticated enough to re-create the Mona Lisa, as the video at YouTube demonstrates (*http://www.youtube.com/watch?v=uk2sPl_Z7ZU*).

You can also add edge effects in the main window, though Fast Capture's choices are limited compared to Snag-It.

Clicking on Draw opens the second editor page (Figure 5-43), where you can add text, figures, arrows, and even a highlight. It adds a nice shadow effect under both arrows and figures, as does Snag-It.

Figure 5-43. Fast Capture's Draw application

I like both tools, including the fact that both provide a true 30-day trial. Several other tools I looked at added "trial" or words to that effect for every saved image, which to me isn't a true trial of the software.

Fast Capture has a freeform capture tool, but on the other hand, Snag-It has a way of capturing a scrolled web page. Both support timed content, though I think that Fast Capture's approach is simpler to use. Snag-It provides the ability to add graphics libraries, but Fast Capture is about half the cost. However, neither is expensive.

Both tools also have one major drawback: they only work in Windows. In fact, most screen capture tools only work in Windows. That's why I was excited when a web page reader was kind enough to send me a beta invite to Skitch, the screen capture tool for the Mac.

Skitch is different in many ways from the other capture tools because the creators have embedded a Web 2.0 social aspect to the tool. You can save images to the hard drive, but you can also post them to your MySkitch online account. In addition, Skitch also maintains a history of images, so you can "flip" the tool over and see previous screen captures, and even open them. Figure 5-44 shows the main edit page for the tool, including the drawing tools that allow us to add arrows, boxes, and text labels. Figure 5-45 shows the screen capture history.

Figure 5-44. Capture of Skitch's main edit screen

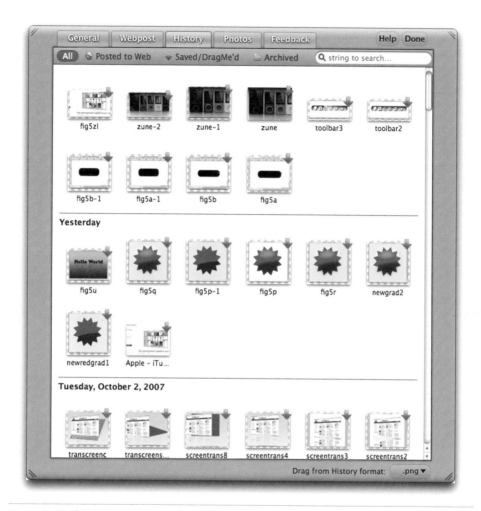

Figure 5-45. Skitch's screen capture history page

The screen capturing options in Skitch are not as broad as Fast Capture's or Snag-It's, but that's because the tool is focused more on social use than on screen capturing for documents. That's also the irritation with the tool, because the only way to save a JPEG or PNG of the capture is to drag and drop it to a folder. Still, Skitch is definitely a contender, and it's nice to start seeing options in the Mac world.

What we need from a tool and what we want are two different things. What we need is the ability to capture the cursor, in addition to capturing an application "in action," such as capturing a drop-down when it's opened. It would be nice to have different capturing options, such as window and freeform, but they aren't essential. Capturing the entire screen and then cropping to the selection or window works for most cases. The only time this fails is with rounded corners.

We also don't need edge effects or drop shadows on the image, because we can create these ourselves. Using a tool to annotate isn't required, either, because you can always open a screen capture in a photo or graphics editor and add the effects yourself. If you want a shadow for your arrows or boxes, create the annotation on a separate transparent layer and add a drop shadow. If you want to add text or another item, you've got a powerful editor's options to add anything you want.

Still, when you're putting together a show, it's nice to have the tool do most of the work of getting the screen captures.

OK, that's enough of that for the rasters, at least until we get into the dynamic use of imagery later in the book. Let's turn our attention to vectors.

CHAPTER 6

Vector This: Early Days and Markup

The strength of vector graphics is their ability to scale to any size, small or large, without affecting the quality of the image. This is because the image is based on object definitions, such as draw a line from point A to point B, and the only difference in sizing is the length of the drawn line. There is no "low, medium, high" quality to vector graphics: they're always the highest quality.

Another advantage to vector graphics from a web perspective is that we can create relatively complex, and large, graphics, and the bandwidth requirements can be a whole lot less than the requirements for a comparable raster image. Additionally, vector graphics lend themselves to manipulation, both at the server and in the page once it is loaded. We can dynamically generate a raster image, such as a JPEG, based on changing data, but the process isn't as simple as doing the same with a vector format, such as SVG.

A paper presented at XML Europe 2001 by Chris Lilley and Dieter Weidenbrück titled "WebCGM and SVG: A Comparison" lists the following requirements for a web-based vector graphics system:

- Scalable
- Efficient
- Revisable
- Object-addressable
- Integratable with other web content

What worked for 2001 still works today. Though the paper addressed two specific formats, WebCGM and Scalar Vector Graphics (SVG), the concept can also include Vector Markup Language (VML), in addition to the three-dimensional formats such as Virtual Reality Modeling Language (VRML) and X3D.

In this chapter I'm going to spend a brief time covering some of the formats just mentioned as well as proprietary forms of vector graphics. Then, the rest of the chapter is devoted to an introduction to one of my favorite web graphics formats: SVG.

WebCGM

Have you ever heard of WebCGM? Unless you follow all the specifications coming out of the W3C or are heavily into the world of web graphics, chances are you haven't. The CGM in the name stands for Computer Graphics Metafile, and the WebCGM 1.0 specification has been a W3C recommendation since 1999. There's also a WebCGM 2.0 specification that reached recommended status in 2007.

 The W3C URL for WebCGM is *http://www.w3.org/Graphics/WebCGM/*.

WebCGM is based on an earlier non-web-based specification, CGM, an ISO standard in use since 1987. With all this background, though, WebCGM has never reached popular support to the point where any browser I'm aware of provides native support for the format, though there are browser plug-ins and tools to create WebCGM content.

SVG, which I'll be covering later, is also a W3C vector graphics recommendation, leading to the question: why two formats? Oddly enough, at the XML Europe 2004 conference, another paper was presented by Lofton Henderson and Dieter Weidenbrüeck (see *http://idealliance.org/papers/dx_xmle04/papers/02-02-03/02-02-03.html*; I'm assuming this is the same Weidenbrüeck mentioned at the beginning of the chapter). In their abstract, they wrote:

> In 2003, the authors set out to provide an objective answer to the persistent question: why there are two W3C standards, WebCGM and SVG, for Web-based graphics? In a nutshell, the reason has been summarized as "WebCGM for Web-based technical graphics, SVG for graphic arts and creative graphics."

WebCGM is not a trivial format. Even attempting to find examples and a better understanding of how it works proved surprisingly difficult. Since it is a format geared more toward complex, technical specifications; used primarily by the automotive, aerospace, and oil industries; and not necessarily delivered in a browser, I'm not going to cover it beyond this brief introduction. If you have extra time—lots of extra time—and want to learn more, I suggest you start at the W3C site, and be sure to have plenty of coffee or another highly caffeinated beverage on hand.

The 3Ds

Before XML was big, while the Web was just a young pup, I was working with VRML. It still amazes me to this day that this three-dimensional language faded out into relative obscurity—especially considering how surprisingly sophisticated it was.

Today's popular 3D world consists of community forums such as Second Life. Yet the idea of something like a Second Life—where people could enter a three-dimensional world with avatars and interact with one another—was conceived well over 10 years ago, and VRML was going to give it to us. It was an exciting technology that generated intense early interest and then, suddenly, seemed to have fallen almost completely off the radar as a viable web graphics format. Why? Several reasons, really. Performance issues, browser support (or lack thereof), and the fact that at about that time Macromedia introduced its specification killer, Flash.

A major disconnect with VRML, though, had to do with the VRML specification itself. The VRML specification left a lot of implementation details up to the browser makers and, as we've seen over the years in regards to scripting, CSS, and HTML, this is never a good idea: where the makers can differ, they will differ. I remember how difficult it was at one point to try to get my little VRML 1.0 lava lamp to work for more than one VRML client.

I will say that unlike WebCGM, there is growing support for more mainstream access of the 3Ds, aided in part by a small but viable community of 3D enthusiasts. Their efforts are focused primarily on the original VRML, (version 1.0), the later release (VRML97), and today's replacement, X3D.

 A good place to start learning about the older VRML and the newer X3D is the Web3D Consortium, at *http://www.web3d.org/*.

Where X3D differs from VRML is greater precision in how the syntax is implemented. Additionally, VRML specifies object declarations using a curly brace syntax, whereas X3D can be specified in proper XML syntax in addition to the "VRML classic" encoding.

An example of the VRML encoding of X3D is shown in the following code snippet, which defines both a `transform`, which controls the overall lighting and orientation of the object, and the object (in this case, a cone):

```
Transform {
  rotation 0 0 1 3.14159
  translation 0 2.4 0
  children
    Shape {
      appearance Appearance {
        material Material {
          diffuseColor 1 1 1
          transparency 0.2
        }
      }
      geometry Cone {
        bottomRadius 0.4
        height 0.5
      }
    }
}
```

The XML syntax is shown in Example 6-1, taken from the Web3D web site examples. It describes a world consisting of a red sphere and a blue box against a black backdrop.

Example 6-1. X3D as XML describing a blue cube and red sphere

```
<?xml version="1.0" encoding="utf-8"?>
<!DOCTYPE X3D PUBLIC "ISO//Web3D//DTD X3D 3.0//EN"
  "http://www.web3d.org/specifications/x3d-3.0.dtd">

<X3D version='3.0' profile='Immersive'>
xmlns:xsd='http://www.w3.org/2001/XMLSchema-instance'
xsd:noNamespaceSchemaLocation='http://www.web3d.org/specifications/x3d-3.0.xsd'>
  <head>
    <meta name='title' content='RedSphereBlueBox.x3d'/>
    <meta name='description' content='X3D specification example: show simple shapes,
        including different materials and geometry'/>
    <meta name='editors' content='Don Brutzman and Joe Williams'/>
    <meta name='created' content='June 2002'/>
    <meta name='modified' content='8 June 2003'/>
    <meta name='reference' content='http://www.web3d.org/x3d/specifications/ISO-IEC-19776-
        X3DEncodings-XML-ClassicVRML/Part01/examples.html#'/>
    <meta name='identifier' content='http://www.web3d.org/x3d/content/examples/Basic/
        X3DSpecification/RedSphereBlueBox.x3d'/>
    <meta name='generator' content='X3D-Edit, http://www.web3d.org/content/README.X3D-
        Edit.html'/>
    <meta name='license' content='../../license.html'/>
  </head>
  <Scene>
    <Transform>
      <NavigationInfo headlight='false' type='EXAMINE' transitionType='"ANIMATE"'/>
      <DirectionalLight/>
      <Transform translation='3.0 0.0 1.0'>
        <Shape>
          <Sphere radius='2.3'/>
          <Appearance>
            <Material diffuseColor='1.0 0.0 0.0'/>
          </Appearance>
        </Shape>
      </Transform>
      <Transform translation='-2.4 0.2 1.0' rotation='0.0 0.707 0.707 0.9'>
        <Shape>
          <Box/>
          <Appearance>
            <Material diffuseColor='0.0 0.0 1.0'/>
          </Appearance>
        </Shape>
      </Transform>
    </Transform>
  </Scene>
</X3D>
```

The example, as rendered by the Media Machines Flux plug-in in Firefox, is shown in Figure 6-1.

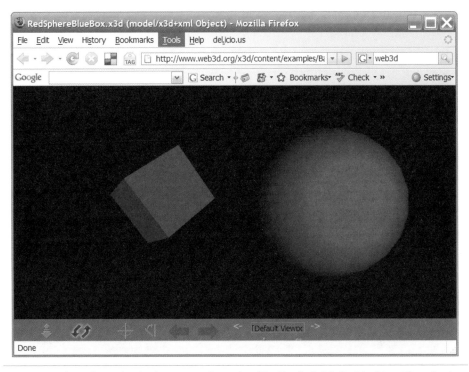

Figure 6-1. Blue cube and red sphere example rendered by Firefox's Media Machines Flux plug-in

What makes the XML encoding attractive is that X3D, unlike VRML, can be incorporated directly into XHTML. This ability to incorporate a completely new specification directly into a web page is a key usability item, and one that we'll look at more closely as it relates to SVG later in this chapter.

Though there is currently no built-in support for X3D or VRML in the main browsers, there is a VRML97 plug-in for Firefox, the Cortona VRML client for both the PC and the Mac. Another Windows-based browser plug-in for Internet Explorer and Mozilla is SwirlX3D. Access any of the examples at the site, and the control will be automatically installed. A third plug-in and associated gallery is Media Machines, with a Flux plug-in that works with both IE and Firefox on Windows.

 The Cortona VRML client is available at *http://www.parallelgraphics. com/products/cortona/*. SwirlX3D can be downloaded from *http://www. pinecoast.com/swvdownload.htm*. The Media Machines Flux plug-in can be accessed at *http://www.mediamachines.com/developer.php*.

There are also a decent number of examples online, as well as tutorials for both specifications. A good place to check for examples is the example page at the Web3D Consortium. Most of the examples are given in X3D, but there's usually a link for a VRML97 file in addition to examples showing X3D embedded in XHTML.

Figure 6-2 shows a Firefox browser with one such file loaded, this one of a fish. Notice the controls that allow for "fly," "walk," and "study." The first two allow us to change our viewpoint relative to the object, while the last item allows us to twist and turn the item about, as demonstrated in Figure 6-3.

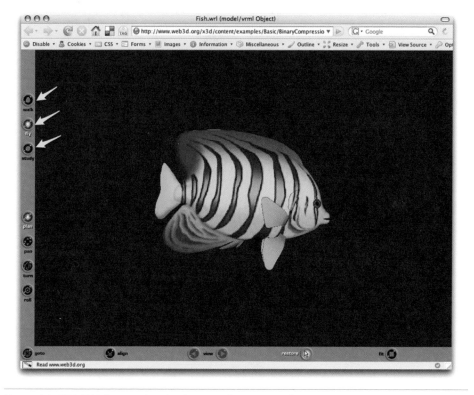

Figure 6-2. VRML Fish opened in the Cortona plug-in in Firefox

Due to the lack of built-in support for the 3D specifications in any of the main browsers, not to mention the complexity of working with the specifications and concepts, I won't be covering it in more detail in this book. I do suggest, though, that you consider trying out the Firefox plug-in and the examples at the sites I pointed out. It takes little time to get the browser set up, and it's a fun way to spend an hour or two. Then, if you continue to be interested, check out any of the tutorials available to try the technology for yourself (my suggested starting point is SwirlX3D, at *http://www.swirlx3d.com/*). No compiler is required, just a viewer capable of reading

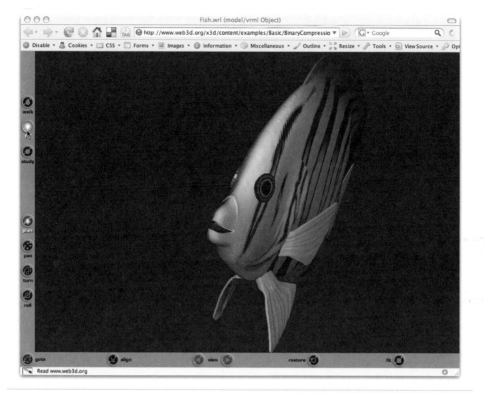

Figure 6-3. VRML Fish manipulated in a viewer to demonstrate the 3D nature of the object

VRML or X3D. At a minimum, you'll be able to play Rubik's Cube online, as shown in Figure 6-4.

Though there isn't native support for the 3D specifications in the browsers, there is built-in support for the XML-based vector graphics formats—sort of—which I'll cover next, starting with the Little Orphan Annie of XML vector graphics, VML.

VML

Vector graphics are dynamic in nature, which means they exist as text, instructions, and object definitions until an appropriate application interprets the instructions and objects and generates a viewable graphic. In the case of the markup, the graphics are defined via XML rather than through some programmed entity, though the end result is the same—pretty pictures.

The release of the first XML specification in 1998 spurred interest in its use to define vector graphics. Only problem was, different groups had different ideas of what would make the "perfect" vector graphics markup language.

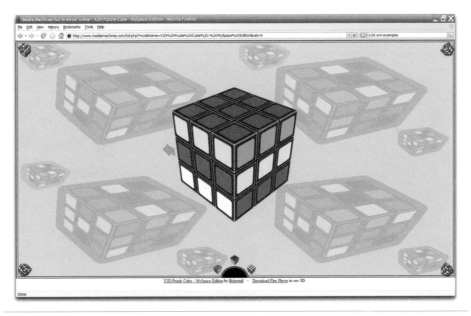

Figure 6-4. Playing Rubik's Cube at the Media Machines site using the Flux plug-in in Firefox

The OS Effect

The 3D specifications demonstrate another aspect of web graphics that really has nothing to do with the Web: the impact of the underlying graphics support systems within the different operating systems.

It's simpler to create a plug-in that will support three-dimensional effects working with IE and Firefox in Windows than it is to create a Firefox-only plug-in doing the same that works with Windows and the Mac, or even Windows, the Mac, and Linux. We touched on this in Chapter 2 when looking at the impact of operating systems on graphics. As we can see, the impact goes beyond just the rasters.

That's why it's important to not only configure which browser is being used but also on which operating system when you're making your graphics decisions, as well as creating the graphics.

Microsoft, Macromedia, and other companies joined together to create one of the first XML-based markups: Vector Markup Language, VML. Of the originators, only Microsoft still supports its use—in its Office products and in Internet Explorer.

The VML specification is at *http://www.w3.org/TR/NOTE-VML*. Microsoft's VML reference is at *http://msdn2.microsoft.com/en-us/library/bb264280.aspx*, but be forewarned that Microsoft does sometimes move its documentation around.

One of VML's strong points is that it was intended as an extension to HTML rather than a completely separate specification. Because of this, VML is actually quite simple to use in a web page.

VML Basics

To start, a `vml` namespace is added to the HTML opening tag:

```
<html xmlns:vml="urn:schemas-microsoft-com:vml">
```

A Microsoft-specific binary behavior for IE to recognize and process the VML is embedded into the `head` element of the web document:

```
<style> vml\:* { behavior: url(#default#VML); }</style>
```

Objects are defined as XML entities and their properties as attributes. The following creates an oval 100 pixels in height, 200 pixels wide, filled with red, and bordered by a 10-pixel green border:

```
<p>
  <vvml:oval style="width:200px; height:100px" fillcolor="red"
        strokecolor="green" strokeweight="10px" />
</p>
```

The element is an oval, and the border is defined by `strokecolor` for color and `strokeweight` for width of border. The `fillcolor` defines fill color, naturally; the `style` attribute is used to define the width and height of the element. Other settings in the `style` attribute could also position the element, but in this example, the element is relatively positioned. The oval is embedded in an HTML paragraph element, demonstrating how VML can be simply integrated into HTML.

Recapping the attributes just described:

`style`
  Regular CSS-style settings, such as width, height, and position

`fillcolor`
  Color used to fill a closed object

`strokecolor`
  Color of the border or line for a non-closed object

`strokeweight`
  Width of the border or line for a non-closed object

There are several other predefined shapes. The following is a rectangle, 400 pixels wide, 100 pixels tall, and yellow fill with a black border:

```
<p>
  <vml:rect style="width:400px; height: 100px" fillcolor="yellow"
        strokecolor="black" strokeweight="5px" />
</p>
```

A rectangle with rounded corners can be created using the roundrect element. The only new attribute is arcSize, a percentage that defines the size curve at the corners. A value of 1.0 actually creates a circle. Lesser values will just round the corners of the rectangle. If the value is not provided, a default of 0.2 (20%) is used:

```
<vml:roundrect style="width:200px; height:100px" fillcolor="blue"
        strokecolor="yellow" strokeweight="10px" arcSize="0.4" />
```

A line is specified by providing from and to values, giving the coordinates in x-y pairings (x being horizontal, y vertical):

```
<vml:line strokecolor="red"
    strokeweight="2pt"  from="100pt,100pt" to="200pt,150pt">
</vml:line>
```

Multiple, connected lines can be defined using a polyline:

```
<vml:polyline
        style="width: 200px; height: 200px"
        stroked="false"
        filled="true"
        fillcolor="blue"
        points="8, 65, 72, 65, 92, 11, 112, 65,
                174, 65, 122, 100, 142, 155, 92,
                121, 42, 155, 60, 100">
    </vml:polyline>
```

This code snippet creates a blue star shape with no border, 200 pixels tall and wide. The points are given in the points attribute, with each pair given as an "x," or horizontal, value first, then "y" for the vertical, with each individual point separated by a comma. A new attribute, stroke, is set to false for no border or line; another, filled, is set to true to mark a filled object.

Another predefined element, curve, acts like polyline, except the object has two attributes, control1 and control2, which control the two points of a Bézier curve created with this element:

```
<vml:curve style="width:100;height:100"
      from="0,100" to="120,100"
      control1="40,10" control2="80,10"
      strokecolor="yellow" strokeweight="3px"/>
```

The markup just given creates an upside-down yellow smile. The two control points act as *pull points* for the curve. Think of a piece of elastic string pulled between two poles. Grab it with your fingers on both hands and pull either up or down with each—that's how the control1 and control2 attributes work.

The last shape is arc, with two new attributes, startangle and endangle, both of which describe the arc:

```
<v:arc
  style="position:width:200;height:200"
  startangle="90" endangle="270" strokecolor="green" strokeweight="2px"
  fillcolor="cyan">
  </v:arc>
```

Example 6-2 has a web page with an example of all these shapes displayed. Absolute positioning is used to position the elements so they're all easily seen at a glance. Note that no DOCTYPE is used in the page. In addition, a namespace of v is used instead of vml in this example—it doesn't matter which you use, only that you are consistent with the namespace in the same document.

Example 6-2. Example page using different shapes supported in VML

```
<html xmlns:v="urn:schemas-microsoft-com:v">

<head>
  <title>VML Examples</title>
  <style>
    v\:* {behavior: url(#default#VML);}
  </style>
</head>

<body>

<v:oval style="position:absolute;left:50;top:20;width:200px; height:100px"
        fillcolor="red"
        strokecolor="green"
        strokeweight="10px" />

<v:polyline
        style="position:absolute;left:240;top:160;width: 300px; height: 200px"
        stroked="false"
        filled="true"
        fillcolor="blue"
        points="8, 65, 72, 65, 92, 11, 112, 65,
                174, 65, 122, 100, 142, 155, 92,
                121, 42, 155, 60, 100">
     </v:polyline>

<v:roundrect style="position:absolute;left:50; top: 155;width:200px; height:100px"
     fillcolor="blue"
     strokecolor="yellow"
     strokeweight="10px"
     arcSize="0.4" />

<v:arc
   style="position:absolute;left:50;top:190;z-index:2;width:200;height:200"
   startangle="90" endangle="270" strokecolor="green" strokeweight="2px"
   fillcolor="purple">
   </v:arc>
```

Example 6-2. Example page using different shapes supported in VML (continued)

```
<v:curve style="position:absolute;left:0;top:100;width:800;height:600"
    from="0,300"
    to="800,300"
    control1="200,600"
    control2="600,0"
    strokecolor="black"
    strokeweight="3px"/>

</body>

</html>
```

As can be seen from the page, VML isn't overly complicated to use, just a little verbose. The result of accessing this page in Internet Explorer can be seen in Figure 6-5.

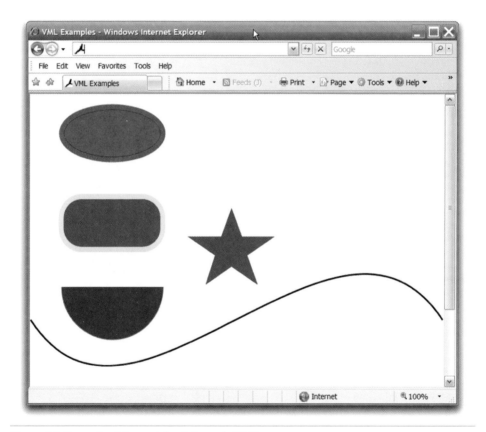

Figure 6-5. Example of the predefined shapes in VML

In the next section I'll touch briefly on some of the more advanced constructs of the
specification.

A Brief Trip into Advanced VML

If all we had to work with were predefined shapes, VML's history would be much shorter. Of course, this might be for the best, considering that only Microsoft seems to use it, but Microsoft's use is enough to keep life in the markup. Still, since VML is the only vector graphic supported natively in Internet Explorer, we might as well have some fun with it.

Another entity in VML is the shape. The shape element is a way to create a graphic of any shape, not just the predefined ones. An example of a shape is the following, which creates a yellow triangle:

```
<v:shape
  filled="true"
  fillcolor="yellow"
  style="height: 200px; width: 200px"
  path="M 0,200 L 100,0, 200,200 X E">
</v:shape>
```

The path attribute is used to define the shape; M is "move" and L is "line"; and the path from left to right is:

- Move to coordinate of x equals 0, y equals 200
- Draw line to coordinate of x equals 100, y equals 0
- Draw line to coordinate of x equals 200, y equals 200
- Close line (X)
- End line (E)

The line command applies to each coordinate until another command is given.

Of course, once you've done all the hard work of creating a complex shape, you then have to copy and paste the item to reuse it. A better approach would be to define a shape, and then use the defined shape whenever the pattern is needed. Enter the shapetype element.

A shapetype works just like shape, except that it's used to define a template rather than an actual object. The element can then be given an id attribute to identify it for later access. Whenever the design calls for the shape, the shape element references the template through the type attribute:

```
<v:shapetype
  id="triangle"
  filled="true"
  fillcolor="yellow"
  path="M 0,200 L 100,0, 200,200 X E">
</v:shapetype>

<v:shape type="#triangle" style="width:50px; height: 50px" />
<v:shape type="#triangle" style="width:200px; height:100px" />
```

This code snippet creates two yellow triangles, one 50 × 50 pixels, and the other 200 × 100.

Once you have a shape, you can do more than just fill it with plain color. Instead of adding attributes to an element, you add an element, which then modifies the parent element. The predefined triangle is modified to add a gradient fill that starts with blue and ends with red, at 50% opacity:

```
<v:shape
    style="position: relative; left: -60px; height: 200px; width: 200px"
    path="M 0,600 L 300,0, 600,600 X E">
<v:fill color="blue" color2="red" type="gradient" opacity="50%" />
</v:shape>
```

The element that modifies the triangle's fill is called, appropriately enough, fill.

We're not finished with our shapes. Sometimes you might want a more complex object made up of more than one element. In these cases, you can use the group element, giving us a container to which we can add any number of other elements and treat the whole as a single entity. The following code creates the yellow triangle shape, and then groups the paired triangles into one unit with group:

```
<v:group
   id="triangle"
   filled="true"
   fillcolor="yellow"
   path="M 0,200 L 100,0, 200,200 X E">
</v:shape>
<v:group id="triangles">
<v:shape type="#triangle" style="width:50px; height: 50px" />
<v:shape type="#triangle" style="width:200px; height:100px /">
</v:group>
```

Example 6-3 pulls together these advanced VML objects into another page, shown in Figure 6-6. It's just a simple page, more to demonstrate how the objects work than to create anything.

Example 6-3. VML sampler with more advanced VML objects

```
<html xmlns:v="urn:schemas-microsoft-com:v">
<head>
  <title>VML Example</title>
  <style>
    v\:* {behavior: url(#default#VML);}
  </style>
</head>

<body>
<v:shapetype
  id="triangle"
  filled="true"
  fillcolor="yellow"
  path="M 0,200 L 100,0, 200,200 X E">
</v:shapetype>
```

Example 6-3. VML sampler with more advanced VML objects (continued)

```
<v:shape type="#triangle" style="width:300px; height:500px" />
<v:shape type="#triangle" fillcolor="green" style="width: 400px; height: 600px" />
<v:shape type="#triangle" fillcolor="purple" style="width: 400px; height: 60px" />

<v:group style="width: 6cm; height: 6cm"
  coordorigin="0,0" coordsize="250,250">
  <v:oval style="position: absolute; top: 15; left: 15;
                 width: 200; height: 200"
    filled="true" fillcolor="red">
  </v:oval>

  <v:polyline style="position: absolute; top: 25; left: 25;
                     width: 200; height: 200"
    filled="true" fillcolor="blue"
    points="8, 65, 72, 65, 92, 11, 112, 65, 174, 65, 122,
            100, 142, 155, 92, 121, 42, 155, 60, 100">
  </v:polyline>
</v:group>

<v:shape
  style="position: relative; left: -60; height: 200px; width: 200px"
  path="M 0,600 L 300,0, 600,600 X E">
<v:fill color="blue" color2="red" type="gradient" opacity="50%" />
</v:shape>
</body>
</html>
```

This is a light introduction to VML, included primarily to give you a feel for how it looks. Of course, if you don't have a Windows machine with IE installed, it's hard to see how the example looks.

 If you're a Mac or Linux user, you might be wondering how you can see a static example working in Internet Explorer when you don't have a Windows machine. There are services that provide screenshots of a page in various browsers in various operating systems. One such is BrowserShots at *http://browsershots.org/*, which is free. Others are paid services. They won't work for dynamic examples, but they will work for the VML examples in IE, and for the SVG and canvas later in this chapter and the next two chapters.

In addition, many web page validators, such as Total Validator, provide screenshot capability. However, these sites are focused on validation rather than screenshots, and you won't want to abuse their generosity by requesting several screenshots in a day.

VML is a viable specification because of its use in Office and IE. However, no other company uses it, and even Microsoft has not said whether it will continue to support it in the future. So, though it is viable, it's also "dead" in that it has nowhere to go in the future. The place for vector graphics in the Web of the present and future is reserved for SVG, discussed next.

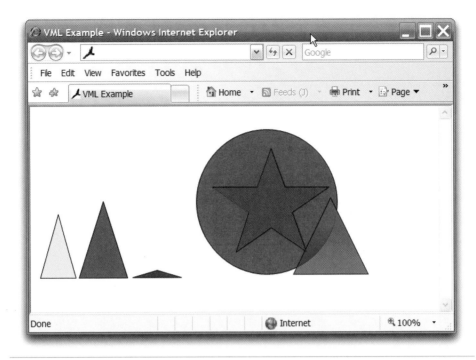

Figure 6-6. Advanced VML object sampler

Hello SVG

At the same time VML was submitted to the W3C, Adobe and Sun, in conjunction with other companies, created another specification, Precision Graphics Markup Language (PGML). When faced with conflicting specifications, W3C took a little of one, a smidgen of the other, and created an amalgamation of both: Scalar Vector Graphics, or SVG.

Many of the concepts introduced in the section covering VML—such as the use of XML, predefined objects, and being able to transform, manipulate, and group objects—were ported into SVG. The main architectural difference between the two is that SVG is a completely separate XML vocabulary, whereas VML was designed as an extension to HTML.

For all the similarities, though, SVG is a much more powerful vector graphics markup than VML. More importantly, it has become the de facto industry standard, and most of the main browsers now implement some form of native support for SVG—that is, most of the main browser makers at the time this was written except one, unfortunately: Internet Explorer.

The best way to get a feel for SVG is to jump in immediately with the ubiquitous Hello World example.

A First Application

In this first look at SVG, I've created a separate SVG XML document. In the next chapter I'll cover the different ways we can embed SVG in web documents, but for now, we'll work with SVG independent of an HTML or XHTML web page.

The first look at SVG is a variation of the traditional "Hello, World!" application that programmers create when working with a new technology. This version has a small image of the globe (courtesy of NASA), surrounded by three ellipses, forming a pseudo variation of the symbol used for an atom. Below the graphic are the words "Hello, World!" in Times New Roman.

The text to create this image can be found in Example 6-4. As you can see, SVG is not terribly complex, or verbose.

Example 6-4. Hello, World! SVG Page

```
<?xml version="1.0" standalone="no"?>
<svg width="600px" height="600px" version="1.1"
     baseProfile="full"
     xmlns="http://www.w3.org/2000/svg"
     xmlns:xlink="http://www.w3.org/1999/xlink">
<defs>
<ellipse id="ellipse1" rx="200" ry="80" fill="none"
stroke="rgb(0,0,0)" stroke-width="2px" />
</defs>
<use x="200" y="400" xlink:href="#ellipse1" transform="rotate(-30 100 100)
translate(90,-40)" />
<use xlink:href="#ellipse1" transform="rotate(30 100 100) translate(420,60)" />
<use xlink:href="#ellipse1" transform="rotate(-90 100 100) translate(-30,400)" />
<image x="360" y="185" width="80" height="80" xlink:href="helloworld.png" />
<text x="240" y="500" font-family="Times New Roman" font-size="3.5em" fill="darkblue">
Hello, World!
</text>
</svg>
```

Delving into the example, the document is a valid and well-formed XML document. However, unlike many XML documents you've probably seen in the past, this one doesn't have the usual DOCTYPE.

In the past, I did use a DOCTYPE like the following with SVG documents:

```
<!DOCTYPE svg PUBLIC "-//W3C//DTD SVG 1.1//EN"
  "http://www.w3.org/Graphics/SVG/1.1/DTD/svg11.dtd">
```

Through the Mozilla SVG project page I found a link to a helpful site with SVG authoring guidelines by Jonathan Watt. Among the helpful tips is a section on not using a DOCTYPE. The reason?

> The SVG DTDs are a source of so many issues that the SVG WG has decided not to write one for the upcoming SVG 1.2 standard. In fact SVG WG members are even telling people not to use a DOCTYPE declaration in SVG 1.0 and 1.1 documents. Instead always include the 'version' and 'baseProfile' attributes on the root <svg> tag, and assign them appropriate values….

The reasoning behind not using the DOCTYPE sounded good to me, and I've dropped use of one in SVG documents.

 The Mozilla SVG project page is at *http://www.mozilla.org/projects/svg/*. Jonathan Watt's SVG authoring guidelines are at *http://jwatt.org/svg/authoring/*.

Instead, following this advice, I added both the version="1.1" for SVG 1.1 and baseProfile="full" to the opening svg element tag. The baseProfile corresponds to the specific subset of SVG, and I'll get into more detail on this later in this chapter, in the section "SVG Full, Tiny, and Basic." The SVG document is enclosed within opening and closing svg tags, regardless of whether the SVG document is standalone or embedded in another XML document, such as XHMTL.

I also added the namespaces for the SVG and XLink vocabularies. If you've not worked much with XML, a namespace is nothing more than a way to identify a vocabulary in a document in cases where multiple vocabularies are used and each may have the same named elements. The namespace is assigned to an alias, such as xlink for the XLink vocabulary, which is then used with elements or element attributes:

```
xlink:href="helloworld.png"
```

One vocabulary can be the default, which means the element or attribute name is given without the alias. In this case, the SVG vocabulary is the default.

Within the SVG document, a definition section is created using the defs element, which contains the definition for a single ellipse element. Anything within a defs element isn't implemented; it's just a way of predefining content to be used later.

In the document, this predefined ellipse element is used three times to create the three "orbiting" ellipses around the center globe in the finished graphic. SVG transformations are used to rotate and move the ellipses so that they're positioned correctly.

The globe itself is a JPEG, included in the page using the SVG image element, and the "Hello World" message is defined with a text element. The attributes of both elements are described in more detail later in this chapter.

Example 6-4 is opened directly in an SVG-capable browser—in this case, Opera—as shown in Figure 6-7. SVG-enabled browsers include the following:

- Mozilla browsers Camino and Firefox
- Opera version 8 and up
- Konquerer with the use of a plug-in
- Internet Explorer with the use of a plug-in
- Safari 3.0 and up

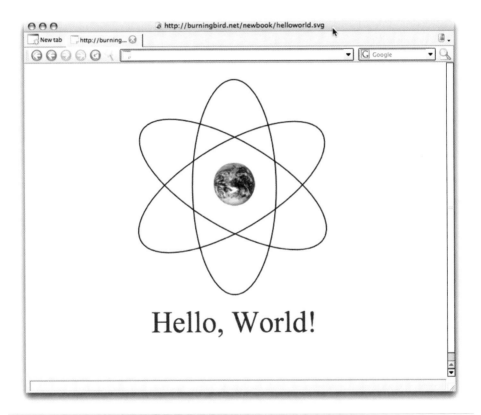

Figure 6-7. First SVG application: "Hello, World!"

Adobe has provided an SVG plug-in for use with Internet Explorer and other browsers, but it's being discontinued in January 2009. It's the only plug-in I'm aware of, and hopefully either it will still be available when this book comes out or some other plug-in developer will step up and provide a replacement. Microsoft has not made any commitments to supporting SVG, and unfortunately did not include support for the specification with the IE8 beta released at the time this book was published.

Other browsers implement most of the SVG functionality, except for the more advanced features, and this is dependent on whether the browser is committed to supporting SVG Full or SVG Tiny.

SVG Full, Tiny, and Basic

The Hello SVG example is based on the full implementation of version 1.1 of the SVG specification. SVG 1.1 became a W3C recommendation in 2003. Based on the growing interest and use of mobile devices, work began on two different mobile specifications: one for cell phones and one for more capable devices, such as PDAs. The former is SVG Tiny, and the latter SVG Basic. Both were recommended beginning in January 2007.

The mobile versions of SVG are based on an assumption that the devices will have limited CPU, memory, power, and bandwidth (according to the SVG specifications) and are constrained accordingly. The limitations aren't overly restrictive, as you can tell when looking at examples of SVG animations made with the Tiny specification.

One such example site is at *http://www.tinyline.com/svgt/samples/samples/index.html*, created with the TinyLine SVG toolkit, which is specialized for mobile SVG applications.

The primary differences between the specifications lie in their support for the Document Object Model (DOM) and scripting. For this chapter and the next, I'm focusing on static SVG, more or less equally implemented in all my target browsers.

This leads to the next question: how much of the SVG specifications do the web browsers support?

Browser Support

Earlier I listed browsers that support SVG. What I didn't list was that no one browser implements the SVG 1.1 recommendation in its entirety.

At the CodeDread site, the site's owner, Jeff Schiller, has a continuously updated diagram of SVG support in both browsers and plug-ins, based on the SVG 1.1 test suite at *http://www.w3.org/Graphics/SVG/Test/*—each of which you can access yourself, and each with a PNG image of how the test should look if it succeeds.

If you enjoy working with SVG, Jeff Schiller's CodeDread site, at *http://www.codedread.com/*, is essential reading. Jeff's SVG support graphic can be found at *http://www.codedread.com/svg-support.php*.

In his diagram, Schiller assigned a red line for a failed test and a green line for a test that succeeds. Figure 6-8 is a screenshot of the test graphic, and as can be seen by the preponderance of red, complete SVG support is still a work in progress.

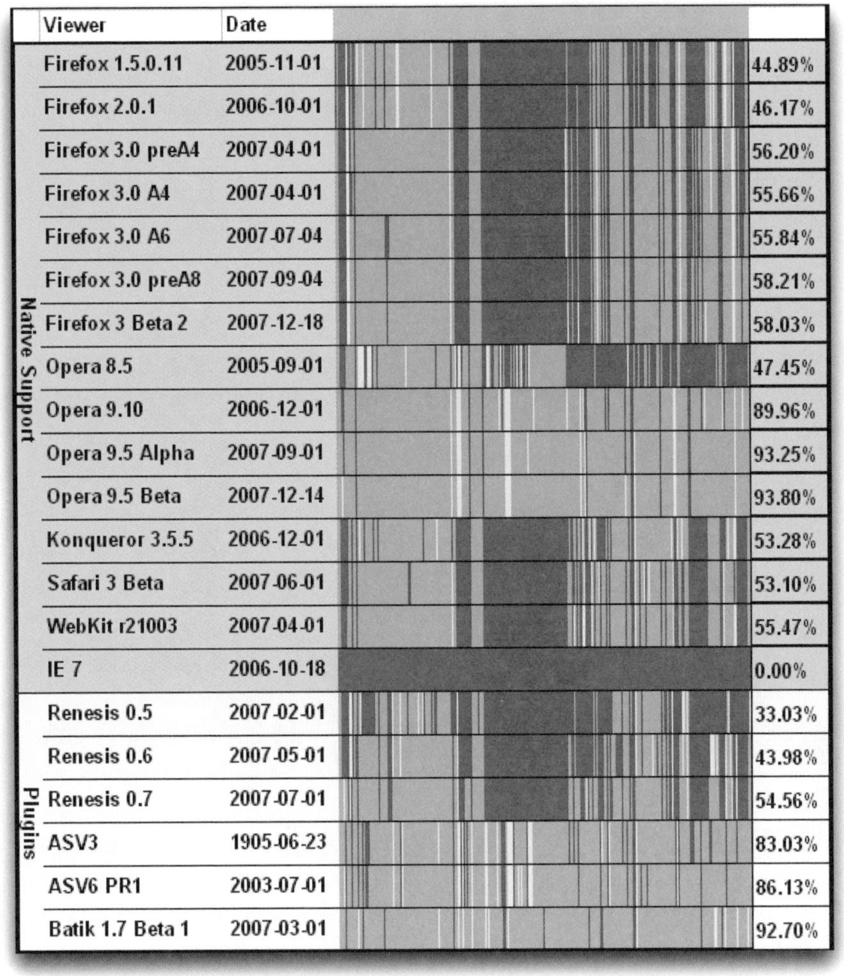

	Viewer	Date		
Native Support	Firefox 1.5.0.11	2005-11-01		44.89%
	Firefox 2.0.1	2006-10-01		46.17%
	Firefox 3.0 preA4	2007-04-01		56.20%
	Firefox 3.0 A4	2007-04-01		55.66%
	Firefox 3.0 A6	2007-07-04		55.84%
	Firefox 3.0 preA8	2007-09-04		58.21%
	Firefox 3 Beta 2	2007-12-18		58.03%
	Opera 8.5	2005-09-01		47.45%
	Opera 9.10	2006-12-01		89.96%
	Opera 9.5 Alpha	2007-09-01		93.25%
	Opera 9.5 Beta	2007-12-14		93.80%
	Konqueror 3.5.5	2006-12-01		53.28%
	Safari 3 Beta	2007-06-01		53.10%
	WebKit r21003	2007-04-01		55.47%
	IE 7	2006-10-18		0.00%
Plugins	Renesis 0.5	2007-02-01		33.03%
	Renesis 0.6	2007-05-01		43.98%
	Renesis 0.7	2007-07-01		54.56%
	ASV3	1905-06-23		83.03%
	ASV6 PR1	2003-07-01		86.13%
	Batik 1.7 Beta 1	2007-03-01		92.70%

Figure 6-8. Result of running SVG 1.1 Test Suite against several browsers and plug-ins

However, beginning in 2008, support for SVG has been aded to the new Acid3 standards test case at the Web Standards project, and this has spurred significant increases in SVG support in Firefox, Safari/WebKit, and Opera. (More on the Acid3 test at *http://www.webstandards.org/action/acid3/.*) Support for SVG is now far enough along that I use it extensively at my own web sites.

For most applications that support SVG in some form, such as browsers, the pre-defined objects are supported, as is grouping, text, the ability to define and reuse shapes, transformations (such as rotations), and many of the filters. Aside from some minor font differences, the Hello World example is exactly the same in Opera 9.5, Safari 3, and Firefox 3.

Still, there's always room for improvement, especially with more complex effects and the use of JavaScript to dynamically alter SVG, as we'll see in later chapters. First, though, a look at what does work.

The SVG Shapes

SVG has several predefined shapes, similar in nature to those we examined for VML: rect (rectangle), circle, ellipse, line, polyline, and polygon. Each of the shapes is a separate XML element, with several attributes that determine its appearance and behavior.

In Example 6-4, I used an ellipse to draw each of the elliptical circles around the globe:

```
<ellipse id="ellipse1" rx="200" ry="80" fill="none"
stroke="rgb(0,0,0)" stroke-width="2px" />
```

Note the attributes given the element: id, fill, rx, ry, stroke, and stroke-width. These are only a few of the attributes available to the ellipse and other shapes, and they affect the shape in the following ways:

id
> Provides a way to access the object later in the markup or via application code

rx
> The x-axis radius of the ellipse (the width of the ellipse)

ry
> The y-axis radius of the ellipse (the height of the ellipse)

fill
> One of the many paint attributes, fill paints the interior of the shape (black by default)

stroke
> Another paint attribute, stroke paints the outline of the shape (none by default)

stroke-width
> The size of the outline

Not specified are several other attributes, each of which has a default value, though the attribute isn't explicitly given. The cx attribute specifies the x-axis center of the ellipse, and cy specifies the y-axis center. If either or both are omitted, a default value of 0 (zero) is used.

URIs and Reuse Through defs and use

In the SVG 1.1 specification, the authors note the use of Uniform Resource Identifiers (URI) in order to access elements contained elsewhere. Two are used in Hello World: one to access the defined ellipse shape, and a second to access an external document.

Rather than replicate the ellipse for the three shown in the Hello World example, I created one as a template within a defs element. The defs element is a container element that allows us to add any content to the page that isn't meant to be drawn immediately. This allows us to create a simple or complex design using any number of SVG elements that isn't drawn out immediately, and which we can use in one or more places in the document.

To be able to access the pre-defined ellipse template later in the document, it's given a specific identifier via the id attribute. This identifier is then referenced via another element, use, which basically "uses" the defined template within the document. The XLink attribute, xlink:href, is how the use element accesses the identified template.

An advantage to creating template designs whenever a pattern is used more than once is that we can modify characteristics of the design in one place, and the alteration propagates across all objects. Because the ellipse is predefined, I can change it to a green color (green is "in" nowadays), broaden the stroke width, lengthen the ellipse along the x-axis, change the stroke color, and add a new opacity setting, and the changes reflect across all uses:

```
<ellipse id="ellipse1" rx="220" ry="80" fill="green" fill-opacity="0.1"
stroke="seagreen" stroke-width="4px"  />
```

Figure 6-9 shows this change reflected in this code. As you can see, the changes make a significant impact on the figure, but at least the change only had to occur in one place. For very complex images, where a pattern can be used dozens, even hundreds of times, defs is essential.

One change that is applied to each ellipse is their rotation within the coordinate system, discussed next.

Coordinate System, Grouping Objects, and Object Rotation

SVG is rendered within a space referred to as the *SVG canvas*. What controls what we see is a defined viewport, the size of which is given in the opening svg element in Hello World. All the elements used in the example either fit within this viewport or are clipped if their dimensions exceed these given boundaries.

The individual uses of ellipses have their own specific location within the coordinate system, given via the x and y attributes, for adjusting the x-axis and y-axis location of the left-top corner of the bounding box for the object.

Figure 6-9. Hello World with altered ellipses

Additionally, each ellipse is rotated using the SVG `transform` attribute. This transforms the object's coordinate system, not the object itself, which might be our first guess. In this case, the coordinate system for each ellipse is altered using rotation and then translation, which rotates the object and then moves it within the new coordinate system.

```
<use xlink:href="#ellipse1" transform="rotate(-90 100 100) translate(-30,400)" />
```

The `transform` is applied to the object before any other positional or scaling attribute, so in this case, the object is rotated counter-clockwise 90 degrees within a newly defined coordinate system equal to 100 pixels by 100 pixels (as compared to 0,0, the default `cx` and `cy` values). The object is then "moved" 30 units "up" along the x-axis and 400 units "left" on the y-axis. The use of "up" is relative and references the default coordinate system, which starts at the top-left at zero/zero (0,0), and positive values move "down" the x-axis and "right" along the y-axis.

I'll be spending a great deal of time on this topic in Chapter 7, but one side effect of the use of `transform` on an object is that you can quickly become confused about exactly what you are changing. For instance, to change the vertical position of the ellipse rotated 90 degrees, you might think to change the x value of the `translate` transform. However, in the newly adjusted coordinate system of the object, when the object was rotated 90 degrees the entire system was rotated 90 degrees, and moving the object "up" actually means moving the object to the right along the x-axis.

Yes, it is hard to twist your mind around this one. A better demonstration would be to show a diagram with the axis outlined and then see what happens when we apply this same transform. Example 6-5 contains the SVG for the demonstration of a transform.

To create this example, I'm introducing another new SVG element: the g, or grouping element. The g element contains other SVG elements, which are then treated as a whole unit rather than as individual elements. In Example 6-5, a group is created consisting of two lines and an ellipse. The lines are formed into a replica of the SVG coordinate system, with a blue line tracing the x-axis and a red line tracing the y-axis. A green ellipse is added to the image, similar to what was in Hello World. The grouped item is then included in a `defs` element.

Example 6-5. A transform's impact on the coordinate system

```
<?xml version="1.0" standalone="no"?>
<svg width="800px" height="600px" version="1.1"
    baseProfile="full"
    xmlns="http://www.w3.org/2000/svg"
    xmlns:xlink="http://www.w3.org/1999/xlink">
<defs>
<g id="grid">
<line x1="50" y1="50" x2="50" y2="400" style="stroke:red;stroke-width:2px" />
<line x1="50" y1="50" x2="400" y2="50" stroke="blue" stroke-width="2px" />
<ellipse rx="120" ry="50" cx="200" cy="200" fill="green" fill-opacity="0.1"
stroke="seagreen" stroke-width="4px"  />
</g>
</defs>
<use xlink:href="#grid" />
<use xlink:href="#grid" transform="rotate(-90) translate(-450,400)" />
</svg>
```

The first use of this new, more complex template is a straight drawing of the shapes, just as they are defined. The second, though, is transformed, first with a rotation and then moved through a translation. Figure 6-10 shows the template as it's first defined and then after it's been transformed. Note that the emulated coordinate lines actually reflect the new coordinate system for the object, after it's been transformed.

It's easier to see now that to move the vertical ellipses "up" or "down" in the Hello World example, the x-axis value would need to be modified, not the y-axis values.

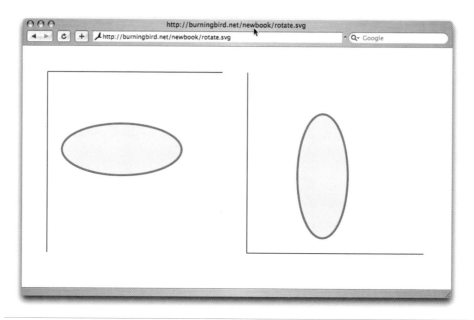

Figure 6-10. A pattern emulating an object in a coordinate system that then gets rotated and moved

Style, Units, and Color

SVG also supports the `style` attribute in its elements, in addition to many CSS settings. Instead of specifying the `fill` or `stroke-width` attributes in the previous example, they could have been added to the `style` attribute:

```
<line x1="50" y1="50" x2="400" y2="50" style="stroke:blue;stroke-width:2px" />
```

In his SVG guidelines, Jeff Schiller discourages the use of the `style` attribute, and he has valid points.

The origination of CSS was based on separating presentation from organization, which doesn't apply in the same way with SVG. In addition, we've long been discouraged from using the `style` attribute inline with elements, because it makes little sense to do so—if we're going to use a CSS style setting, we're going to use a stylesheet and then make an adjustment in one place, rather than repeat a change across several elements. The same reasoning applies with using the inline `style` with SVG.

We can use a stylesheet, and we'll look at this in the next chapter. However, the use of the inline style setting is best left for those times when we want to override an existing stylesheet setting.

One difference between using a `style` attribute and an SVG styling property (as the attributes are termed) is that units of measurement are required for style CSS but not for SVG attributes. In the Hello World example, some of the elements have attributes with units provided, and others don't. When units are not specified, the length is then assumed to be in *user units*, which is equivalent to the familiar px, or pixel.

If you wish to use another unit of measurement, such as em, pt, mm, in, or other allowed units, you will need to state the unit explicitly. Otherwise, you don't have to specify units if you use the styling properties valid for each SVG element.

That leads us to the last attribute I'll look at in this chapter, and that's color. Just as with CSS, there are specific named colors you can use with SVG elements, but you can also use hexadecimal format (#00ff00) as well as RGB format (rgb(0,0,0)). All elements that take a color can use any one of these three formats. The following three lines create the same red rectangle with a black outline:

```
<rect fill="red" stroke="black" stroke-width="2" width="100" height="100" />
<rect fill="rgb(255,0,0)" stroke="rgb(0,0,0)" stroke-width="2" width="100"
height="100" />
<rect fill="#ff0000" stroke="#000000" stroke-width="2" width="100" height="100" />
```

There were other objects introduced into Hello World, such as the use of an image and text, but I'll cover those in Chapter 7, where I dig more deeply into the SVG specification. Hopefully this introduction will be enough to whet your appetite for more.

CHAPTER 7

SVG Bootcamp

I have a special place in my heart for Scalable Vector Graphics (SVG). There's something satisfying about being able to put together a little XML and get a pretty picture. Better still, you can easily generate that picture on the server or modify it in the client.

The one missing piece from the Web is the ability to embed graphics directly into a page rather than link to them in a separate file, or to embed a graphic and then be able to modify it after the page is loaded. Without this ability we're dependent on third-party technology, such as Flash or Java applets.

SVG has been a long time coming, too. Work started on this in the last century, but it's only been in the last few years that mainstream browsers have started implementing at least some parts of SVG. Before, we were dependent on plug-ins, and unfortunately we're still dependent on a plug-in for Internet Explorer. We have made progress, though, because the other major players—Firefox, Opera, and Safari—have committed to SVG and made a decent start following through on that commitment.

I introduced you to SVG in the last chapter with a "Hello, World!" standalone SVG page. This chapter digs into the concepts introduced in the last chapter. Later in this book, we'll explore dynamic applications based on SVG.

 This chapter serves as a general introduction to the basic elements of SVG, including some SVG editors. Because of the breadth of topics covered in this book, I can't go into SVG in the depth it deserves. For a more in-depth look, I would recommend *SVG Essentials*, by J. Eisenberg (O'Reilly), or Kurt Cagle's *SVG Programming: The Graphical Web* (Apress).

SVG Full, Basic, and Tiny

SVG is an XML-based specification, which means that first and foremost all SVG applications must be valid XML. Being XML-based also means that whatever XML tools are provided on the server and within browsers are also available for use with SVG. This is important because there is a lot of tool support for XML documents, and it's nice not to have to reinvent parsers and other applications just to work with yet another format.

SVG is maintained and released by the W3C. The latest recommended version of the SVG specification is 1.1, but there is a candidate for a version 1.2 known as SVG Tiny.

SVG Tiny is a subset of the basic SVG specification, created specifically for the new generation of resource restricted mobile devices. When SVG 1.0 was first released, there was a great deal of concern about how "bloated" the specification was because it had to meet the needs of a lot of different customers. With the release of 1.1, the W3C provided different Document Type Definitions (DTDs) for SVG: the full specification, a Basic specification that's geared toward higher-end mobile devices, and SVG Tiny, which is for lower-resource mobile devices such as cell phones (Basic and Tiny originally released as SVG Mobile 1.1).

Beginning with work for SVG 1.2, SVG Tiny has been split out into its own specification, which will then be used as a baseline document for the full version of SVG 1.2—going from the restricted model to the fully featured, rather than the reverse direction as happened with 1.1.

 In this chapter and elsewhere in this book, assume that the SVG I use is based on SVG 1.1 full. For more on the SVG specifications and up-to-date news related to SVG, check out the W3Cs SVG site at *http://www.w3.org/Graphics/SVG/*.

Browser Support: Standoffish or Integrated

Not all browsers support SVG equally, and Internet Explorer doesn't support SVG at all. Of the other popular browsers, most will process standalone SVG files but differ in how SVG is integrated directly into web pages.

The Hello, World example in Chapter 7 was a standalone SVG document, saved with an *.svg* extension and served with a MIME type of image/svg+xml. These separate SVG files can be accessed directly or incorporated into a web page using either the embed or object element or via an iframe. Of the three, embed is a deprecated element, and iframe isn't XHTML Strict compliant, though it does validate with XHTML Transitional. The only element that's valid with XHTML 1.0 Strict is the object element. Since this element is supported by Firefox 2.x and 3, Safari 3.x, and Opera 9.x, that's the only element I'll use to demonstrate incorporating a separate SVG file into a web page.

SVG Through the object Element

Once you have a valid, working SVG file (tested by opening it directly into a browser that supports SVG), you can then incorporate it into a web page.

To get things started, Example 7-1 contains a web page with an SVG file incorporated into the page through an `object` element. The `object` is modified through a `style` attribute, which sets the width and height and adds a border. The external SVG file is the second Hello World example from Chapter 6.

Example 7-1. Using the object element to embed an external SVG file

```
<!DOCTYPE html PUBLIC "-//W3C//DTD XHTML 1.0 Strict//EN"
        "http://www.w3.org/TR/xhtml1/DTD/xhtml1-strict.dtd">
<html xmlns="http://www.w3.org/1999/xhtml" lang="en" xml:lang="en">
<head>
<meta http-equiv="Content-Type" content="text/html; charset=utf-8" />
<title>Embedded SVG</title>
</head>
<body>
<p>
<object data="helloworld2.svg"
style="width:800px; height: 510px; border: 1px solid #ff0000; padding: 20px; ">
<p>No SVG support</p>
</object>
</p>
</body>
</html>
```

Figure 7-1 shows this page opened in Safari 3 on the Mac. It's little different than the examples shown in the last chapter, except for the border around the object element. The example can be served as an HTML or XHTML document, depending on the file extension and DOCTYPE.

There are some limitations associated with embedding an SVG element into a page using the `object` element. First, if the SVG file doesn't have a background color—if, for instance, it's meant to be transparent—the version of Safari I used for this book automatically adds a default white background. This can cause some problems if you want to overlay the SVG over the page background.

Another issue with embedded SVG is that the size of the container for the SVG can affect the size of the displayed SVG, both of which can vary based on the browser or how the SVG view port is defined within the SVG document. In a later chapter we'll look at creating an animated analog clock with SVG, which is drawn to fill the page when opened as a file, but scales nicely when opened into an object in a page.

For HTML web pages, the object `element` (or the deprecated `embed` or `iframe`) has to be used to incorporate SVG, but it's not ideal. What's the point of a vector graphic based in XML if we can't add SVG directly into an XHTML document, incorporating it into both the flow of the layout and the document's object model for script access?

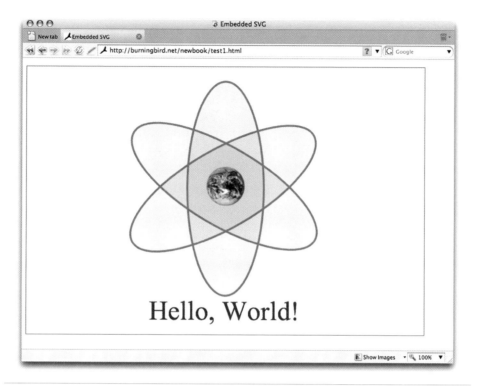

Figure 7-1. SVG embedded into an XHTML web page

Inline SVG

To embed an SVG document directly into a web page, the page must be defined as XHTML, and valid XHTML at that. Being able to utilize SVG in documents is the main reason why I converted all my sites to XHTML 1.1 Strict—a decision that didn't come without its challenges. Happily, all the major browsers support inline SVG, so the extra work does have its rewards.

 All browsers support inline SVG except IE, which doesn't yet support the XHTML MIME type of application/xhtml+xml, much less SVG.

Just like with SVG, not all browsers support XHTML documents equally. As an example of a browser quirk, we can serve XHMTL documents with an *.html* extension, but when you're using inline SVG, some browsers won't process the SVG XML if the browser believes it's processing HTML. If you use an *.xhtml* extension, though, or use an XHTML content type if the output is dynamically generated, other browsers will serve the XML up as XML instead of processing it as HTML elements formatted as XML. You're left with a challenge: how to serve up an XHTML document that's processed like HTML for those browsers that don't support XHTML, but treated like the XML-based syntax it is for those browsers that do? There is a solution to this XHTML-serving conundrum: asking the browser what it can deal with.

During the communication between the browser and server, both can learn a lot from each other. For one thing, the server can ask the browser or other user agent whether it can accept a certain content type. The server uses the HTTP_ACCEPT request to discover this information. An HTML web page has a content type of html/text, but an XHTML page has a content type of application/xhtml+xml. If the browser doesn't understand the XHTML content type, the page can then be served up as html/text; otherwise, the page is served up as XHTML.

Some web applications provide plug-ins that test whether a browser can support XHTML and then return the appropriate content type. I use one of these with my weblogs. A second option is to modify the *.htaccess* file if your hosting company supports these files, and most do.

The *.htaccess* file is a way of controlling how web pages are served up through the Apache web server directly within a site or subdirectory, rather than for all sites and subdirectories served by the same web server. This is how people who have shared hosting accounts (which is most of us) can add some web server control to our sites. We can use various rewrite rules and conditions in the *.htaccess* files, and then the web server uses this information to know how to serve pages up accordingly.

 To read more about inline SVG and XHTML, along with setting up a site to support them, check out the SVG Wiki page at *http://wiki.svg.org/ Inline_SVG#XHTML_.28XML.29_vs_HTML*.

The ins and outs of *.htaccess* and its rules and conditions are way outside the scope of this book. Any number of tutorials are online, though, easily found just by searching on "htaccess tutorial." For now, once you're comfortable with working *.htaccess*, add the following script to the file to ensure that SVG works inline with your XHTML web pages:

```
AddType text/html .xhtml
RewriteEngine on
RewriteBase /
RewriteCond %{HTTP_ACCEPT} application/xhtml\+xml
RewriteCond %{HTTP_ACCEPT} !application/xhtml\+xml\s*;\s*q=0
RewriteCond %{REQUEST_URI} \.xhtml$
RewriteCond %{THE_REQUEST} HTTP/1\.1
RewriteRule .* - [T=application/xhtml+xml]
```

First of all, this *.htaccess* entry adds the XHTML MIME (content) type for the extension if a page extension is used (dynamic applications don't always use file extensions). The entry then uses HTTP_ACCEPT to check whether the application that accesses the resource can process XHTML. If it can't, the page is returned as HTML;

if it can, the page is returned as XHTML. If the page isn't returned as XHTML, the inline SVG won't work, but at least the page *will* load.

In Chapter 6, I mentioned how DOCTYPEs aren't needed, either for an XHTML document or for SVG. The same applies with SVG embedded in XHTML, unless you're interested in validating the document. Since I do want to validate the document, I include a special DOCTYPE that enables both SVG and MathML:

```
<!DOCTYPE html PUBLIC
    "-//W3C//DTD XHTML 1.1 plus MathML 2.0 plus SVG 1.1//EN"
    "http://www.w3.org/2002/04/xhtml-math-svg/xhtml-math-svg.dtd">
```

You do need to include the namespaces for both the XHTML vocabulary and the SVG vocabulary, in addition to any others you use, but each can be included in its respective opening element: the html element for the XHTML document and the svg element for SVG. If you're using more than one svg element in your document, you'll probably want to include the SVG namespace in the opening html tag, along with the namespace declaration for XHTML and any other vocabulary you're using.

Following are the first few lines of the headers for documents at my site:

```
<!DOCTYPE html PUBLIC
    "-//W3C//DTD XHTML 1.1 plus MathML 2.0 plus SVG 1.1//EN"
    "http://www.w3.org/2002/04/xhtml-math-svg/xhtml-math-svg.dtd">
<html xmlns="http://www.w3.org/1999/xhtml"
      xmlns:svg="http://www.w3.org/2000/svg"
      xmlns:xlink="http://www.w3.org/1999/xlink" xml:lang="en">
```

The documents are XHTML documents with embedded SVG, which explains why I saved the default namespace for the XHTML document and assigned svg to the SVG namespace.

Adding an SVG block directly into an XHTML page isn't that much different from adding an SVG block into a standalone document. The svg element establishes the boundaries of the SVG canvas—the drawing area—and any SVG elements within the opening and closing svg tags are constrained to the area defined using attributes in the opening tag.

Example 7-2 has a web page formatted as XHTML 1.1 and includes two svg elements that are acting as "capstones" for the text block. The fill colors for the SVG match the default background color for the div element, which is white. All three primary page elements—the two svg capstones and the div element with the text—are bordered by a 1-pixel-wide black border.

Example 7-2. SVG embedded "inline" into an XHTML document

```
<!DOCTYPE html PUBLIC
    "-//W3C//DTD XHTML 1.1 plus MathML 2.0 plus SVG 1.1//EN"
    "http://www.w3.org/2002/04/xhtml-math-svg/xhtml-math-svg.dtd">
<html xmlns="http://www.w3.org/1999/xhtml" xmlns:svg="http://www.w3.org/2000/svg">
<head>
<title>Inline SVG</title>
```

Example 7-2. SVG embedded "inline" into an XHTML document (continued)

```
<style type="text/css">
body
{
        margin: 20px 50px;
}

svg
{
        display: block;
        margin: 0;
}
div.para
{
        background-color: #fff;
        width: 498px;
        margin: 0;
        border-left: 1px solid #000;
        border-right: 1px solid #000;
}
.para p
{
        margin: 0 10px;
}

rect
{
        fill: #fff;
        stroke: #000;
        stroke-width: 1;
}
</style>
</head>
<body>
<svg:svg version="1.1" width="500" height="25"  >
    <svg:rect  width="100%" height="50" rx="30" ry="30" />
</svg:svg>

<div class="para">
<p>Lorem ipsum dolor sit amet, consectetuer adipiscing elit. Curabitur tincidunt tempus
quam. Maecenas iaculis arcu eget lorem. Suspendisse fermentum tortor sed odio. Mauris ut
augue. Vestibulum ut metus. Proin ac diam ac justo tincidunt fermentum. Sed dictum
ultricies odio. Proin viverra vehicula ligula. Aliquam erat volutpat. Etiam consectetuer
pede eget tortor. Mauris id mi. Mauris dignissim pharetra massa. Donec sed erat sed tellus
mollis tempor. Nunc sodales porta magna. Donec commodo velit ac mi. Praesent ultricies,
libero a sagittis scelerisque, libero magna vulputate justo, et lacinia nulla ligula
egestas metus. Pellentesque ligula. Vivamus rhoncus congue tortor. Praesent rutrum
dignissim augue. </p>
</div>
```

Example 7-2. SVG embedded "inline" into an XHTML document (continued)

```
<svg:svg version="1.1" width="500" height="25"  >
    <svg:rect y="-25" width="100%" height="50" rx="30" ry="30" />
</svg:svg>
</body>
</html>
```

Figure 7-2 shows the page from Example 7-2, opened in Opera.

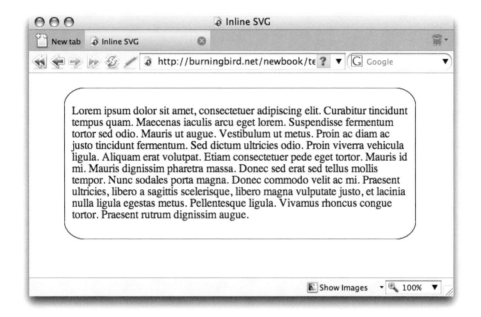

Figure 7-2. Two SVG elements embedded into an XHTML document

An important consideration for the example is the use of `display: block` in the CSS for the page. If the `svg` element isn't given a block display type, the browser renders the SVG inline. Since the element is wide enough to "wrap," it seems to be treated as a block. However, it also gives it extra whitespace following the element. This extra whitespace is the "text descender" area for the content—reserved for the portion of the text that would normally extend below the baseline (for letters such as *g*). This text descender reserved area prevents the clean alignment between the top `svg` element and the following `div` element (and also what follows the second `svg` element). Giving the element the block display means it will be treated in a manner similar to a `div` element, giving us better control over placement.

Also notice that unlike the `div` element, which incorporates the border into the element width, `svg` adds the stroke width external to the rectangle's width. This explains why the example sets the `div` element's width to 498 pixels, while each `svg` rectangle is given a full 500 pixels.

To be specific, the stroke width falls halfway into the element's space and halfway into the space outside of the element, with the center of the stroke exactly on the border of the element. In a web page with a stroke width of 1 pixel, there is no smaller unit of measurement, and the stroke width is pushed to the "outside" of the space. With wider stroke widths, though, the element area will get eaten up, just not as much as it would for XHTML elements with a border.

In addition to demonstrating how SVG is used within an XHTML document, Example 7-2 also provides a different way of looking at SVG: as integrated into the page design rather than as a cheap and dynamic replacement for raster images. This is a part of SVG that I don't think has been explored nearly enough, and later in this and other chapters I'll provide other examples of this type of SVG use.

The Structure of the SVG Space

Though svg elements are treated like a div element in Example 7-2, SVG is a complete specification, and there's a lot more to the svg element than is first apparent when looking at that example.

First of all is the coordinate system. You may have noticed that the svg elements had width and height but didn't specify the units, such as px for pixels. When a numeric value is given but no unit of measure, SVG assumes that the element is using the default client unit of measurement. With web pages, this is pixels. Giving a value of 500 to the width of a rectangle in SVG is equivalent to using 500px. You can specify the unit of measurement, but there's no requirement that you do so. You're not even going to lose style and best practice brownie points if you don't.

When the SVG elements are defined, each is given a width and a height. These form the boundaries of the SVG *viewport*, the area of the SVG document that is actually displayed to the web page reader. In addition to using specific values, you can also use percentages—for example, "100%" if you want the SVG element to take up all of the given area. Note, though, that using percentages could impact certain aspects of the SVG rendering in a given browser. For instance, using percentages for the width of the SVG element will prevent the rendering of gradients in the version of Safari 3 I was using when this book was written.

By default, in the coordinate system, the top-left corner of the viewport is set at an x value of zero (0) and a y value of zero (0). Increasing values of x move along a horizontal line to the right; increasing values of y move along a vertical line from top to bottom. Figure 7-3 shows three rectangles, all the same size but each given different starting (x,y) pairs. The first rectangle with the solid outline has an x,y pair of (10,10), the second with the dashed outline starts at (110,110), and the third, with a dot outline, at (210,210).

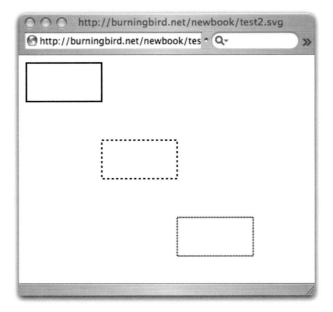

Figure 7-3. Demonstrating the coordinate system

Later we'll see how the coordinate system can be altered, as was demonstrated in Chapter 6 with the Hello World example.

> Another part of the coordinate system is the viewBox and preserving the aspect ratio of the SVG contents. I'll cover viewBox later in this chapter, in the section "Transformations."

SVG Elements

The power of SVG lies in the fact that it's relatively simple to use, can support large figures that don't require much bandwidth, and can scale from the tiny to the extremely large—without any decrease in quality. It is this last characteristic that sets the vector graphics like SVG apart from the rasters, such as JPEGs, covered earlier.

The SVG components I'll focus on are those currently supported in Mozilla-based browsers, which is most of SVG 1.1 and more than enough to get us started with this marvelous technology.

SVG objects fall into different categories:

- Common attributes shared by one or more SVG objects
- Visual objects, including shapes, such as rectangles or circles, images, freeform paths, and text

- Processing constructs, such as facilities to group objects, and including script for dynamic manipulation and performing conditional tests
- Informational elements, such as titles and metadata
- Visual attributes, such as fills, gradients, and filters
- SVG animation, which wasn't implemented in the version of Firefox I used when writing this book but is partially implemented with Safari and Opera. Examples are given in Chapter 8.

This isn't an official categorization—just a way of getting a handle on all the various elements that make up SVG, and as good a way of introducing the goodies as any.

 Many of the examples that follow are standalone SVG applications, which means they'll work in an `object` or `embed` element and thus in HTML. Some of the examples will be inline SVG, whenever it makes more sense because of how the SVG is used.

Rectangles and Paint Attributes

Most of the SVG elements share a similar set of attributes, each of which is grouped into major categories by the W3C. Rather than just talk about the attributes, we'll jump into trying each one out by using one of the more common visual elements: the rectangle.

Rectangles in SVG are created using the `rect` element. They have both a `width` and a `height`, and setting either of these to zero (0) disables the rendering of the rectangle. Rectangles also occupy a position within the viewport, with x marking the position of the rectangle's left side within the coordinate system, and y marking the rectangle's top position. The following text defines a rectangle 100 pixels square, located at a position 10 pixels down from the top of the SVG viewing area and 10 pixels to the right of the left side of the viewing area:

```
<rect width="100" height="100" x="10" y="10" />
```

Rectangles can also have rounded corners, with the rounding represented by an ellipse with a horizontal radius designated by rx and a vertical radius designated by ry. You can specify different values for each, but the result can be funny looking. For instance, Figure 7-4 shows two rectangles, resulting from the following two lines of SVG:

```
<rect width="100" height="100" x="10" y ="10" rx="5" ry="45" />
<rect width="100" height="100" x="110" y="10" rx="45" ry="45" />
```

Using equal values for the radius generates a smooth corner, and unequal values a jagged corner.

To recap the rectangle attributes:

x

Horizontal position of the rectangle's left side

y

Vertical position of the rectangle's top

Figure 7-4. Two rectangles, with equal and unequal corner ellipse radius values

`width`
> Width of the element

`height`
> Height of the element

`rx`
> Horizontal radius of the ellipse used to round the rectangle (if a rounded rectangle)

`ry`
> Vertical radius of the same rounded-corner ellipse

In Figure 7-4 both figures are black, the default color for filled objects. The color of the fill and the border are attributes from the *paint attribute* family. Included in this family are attributes such as `fill`, `stroke`, `stroke-width`, and so on. Unlike some of the attributes I'll look at later, most SVG implementations support all of the paint attributes.

The `fill` and `stroke` paint attributes act much like those in the paint and graphical editors we've looked at in previous chapters. The fill paints the interior of a closed object, up to the dimensions of the object. The stroke paints the edge of the object, overlapping the edge if the stroke width is wider than 1 pixel, the smallest unit in web pages. The actual size of an object that's colored using the fill attributes doesn't change, but the size can change based on stroke width. The stroke width will always fall both inside and outside of the object's edge. Strokes can also be altered to show a pattern, as well as modified at the edges where a stroke joins, such as the corners on the rectangle. In addition, the opacity of both the fill and the stroke can be altered.

All paint attributes can be defined either as attributes on the elements or as settings within a `style` attribute identical to that used with CSS. Colors can be expressed as RGB values, hexadecimals, or via one of the named allowed colors, following the same characteristics used with CSS2 colors.

> The W3C maintains a sample list of named colors and their RGB values at *http://www.w3.org/TR/SVG11/types.html#ColorKeywords*.

The best way to see how the paint attributes work is to look at a paint sampler showing various fill and stroke effects. Example 7-3 consists of a set of rectangles, each filled with a different color and given a different border through use of stroke and stroke-width. To simplify the example, the rectangle is predefined, and all other characteristics not pertinent to the example are preset. This defined rectangle is then reused throughout the example.

Example 7-3. The SVG paint sampler

```
<?xml version="1.0" standalone="no"?>
<!DOCTYPE svg PUBLIC "-//W3C//DTD SVG 1.1//EN"
  "http://www.w3.org/Graphics/SVG/1.1/DTD/svg11.dtd">
<svg width="800" height="500" version="1.1"
    xmlns="http://www.w3.org/2000/svg" xmlns:xlink="http://www.w3.org/1999/xlink">
  <title>Paint Sampler</title>
  <!-- Define rectangle used with most of the examples -->
  <defs>
    <rect id="rectfig" width="150" height="100" />
  </defs>

  <!-- Different color definition techniques -->
  <use xlink:href="#rectfig" x="10" y="10" fill="red" stroke="blue" stroke-width="3" />
  <use xlink:href="#rectfig" x="200" y="10" fill="rgb(255,255,0)" stroke="rgb(0,127,0)"
stroke-width="6" />
  <use xlink:href="#rectfig" x="390" y="10" fill="#ff00ff" stroke="#600"
stroke-width="8" />

  <!-- Different stroke techniques -->
  <use xlink:href="#rectfig" x="10" y="140" fill="darkturquoise"
      stroke="firebrick" stroke-width="3" stroke-dasharray="4,6,10"  />
  <use xlink:href="#rectfig" x="200" y="140" fill="oldlace"
      stroke="teal" stroke-width="8" stroke-linejoin="bevel" />
  <use xlink:href="#rectfig" x="390" y="140" fill="khaki"
      stroke="indigo" stroke-width="15" stroke-opacity=".5" />

  <!-- Opacity and use of style -->
  <rect x="80" y="330" width="400" height="80" fill="darkgreen" />
  <rect x="20" y="280" width="530" height="100"
      style="fill: gold; fill-opacity: .5; stroke: midnightblue;
            stroke-width: 15; stroke-dasharray: 2,2,5; stroke-linejoin: round" />
</svg>
```

In addition to the rectangles, the example also makes use of XML comments—each marked by the XML comment beginning and ending characters, <!-- and -->—and a title element similar to the HTML title. There should be only one title element per SVG document (or per block if the element is embedded into an XHTML page).

Figure 7-5 shows the SVG file opened in Firefox. I've added letters, post-screen capture, to make it easier to differentiate the examples as I describe each. From the top-left:

- Rectangle A is filled with the named color red, and the rectangle is given a blue stroke with its width set to 3 pixels.

- Rectangle B is filled with yellow, set using the RGB format of 255,255,0, with a dark-green stroke (also set using the RGB format) set to 6 pixels in width.

- Rectangle C is filled with purple, using the hexadecimal format, with a dark-red stroke that is 8 pixels wide.

- Rectangle D is filled with the named color darkturquoise, and the stroke is firebrick. The stroke is also modified by the use of the stroke-dasharray attribute, which establishes a pattern of color, no-color for drawing the stroke. In this example, the dasharray is defined as 4,6,10, which is 4 pixels colored, 6 pixels not colored, and 10 pixels colored. The pattern then repeats, except on the second repetition, 4 pixels are not colored, 6 pixels are, and 10 are not.

- Rectangle E is filled with the named color oldlace, and the stroke color is teal. The stroke width is 8 pixels wide, and the stroke corners are beveled through the use of the stroke-linejoin attribute.

- Rectangle F is filled with the named color khaki, the stroke color is indigo, and the stroke width is 15 pixels. The stroke's opacity is also altered through the stroke-opacity attribute, set to 50%. Note how the underlying filled area of the rectangle shows through the part of the stroke that overlaps the rectangle. Figure 7-6 shows this rectangle resized and with the rectangle outlined in black to show the stroke overlap.

- Rectangle G is filled with the named color gold, the stroke color is midnightblue, and the stroke width is 15 pixels. A stroke-dasharray pattern of 2,2,5 is used, and a round strike-linejoin, which only shows up on two corners. The fill's opacity is set to 50% (.5), which shows another rectangle underneath, filled with dark green.

One fill "color" I didn't demonstrate was setting the fill color to none, which is equivalent to creating an element with no background color at all. If a rectangle is set to no fill, you won't see it if a stroke isn't provided.

I want to spend a little more time on the stroke-dasharray attribute. The examples shown in Figure 7-5 show irregularly repeating patterns, where the color and non-color areas change widths in each iteration of the pattern. The line element, though, is a better SVG predefined object for demonstrating stroke patterns.

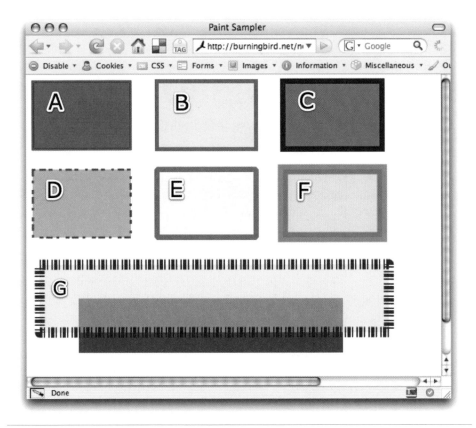

Figure 7-5. Rectangles created with Example 7-3

Lines, Stroke Patterns, and desc

An SVG line is probably one of the simplest objects to create. You give the x,y coordinates of the start of the line and the x,y coordinates of the end, and that's it. The following draws a diagonal line that starts at 10,20 and ends at coordinate point 100,150:

```
<line x1="10" y1="20" x2="100" y2="150" />
```

Actually, the SVG just given won't draw a thing—no stroke was defined for the line, and therefore there is no visual element to the object. Rectangles and circles have a default fill, but there is no such thing as a default stroke for any of the elements. Since lines are dependent on stroke, one has to be provided:

```
<line x1="10" y1="20" x2="100" y2="150" stroke="black" />
```

In the last section I demonstrated a couple of stroke dash patterns. Most were irregular, in that there was no attempt to have the patterns repeat evenly. To make a more

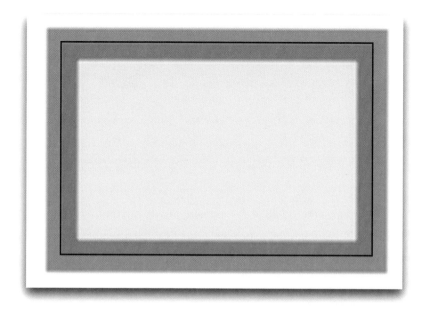

Figure 7-6. Focus on rectangle F, showing overlap of stroke

regular stroke dash pattern, you could provide a "double number," each the same length, which creates a traditional dotted border:

```
<line x1="10" y1="60" x2="600" y2="60" stroke="black" stroke-width="4"
        stroke-dasharray="2,2" />
```

To create a more regular pattern using stroke-dasharray, you need an even number of pattern members, and you have to repeat the pattern once. Think of using stroke-dasharray as climbing a mountain: the first pattern goes up the hill, and the repeated pattern brings you back down again.

Example 7-4 shows SVG that creates five lines, each using a black stroke, with the width set to 4 pixels to better display the dash patterns. Each line is given a different pattern, beginning with no dashes in the first and ending with a regularly repeating sequence of dots and dashes in the last. The example also makes use of the desc element, which provides a text description of what the SVG is doing for applications such as screenreaders.

Example 7-4. Demonstrating different stroke patterns

```
<?xml version="1.0" standalone="no"?>
<!DOCTYPE svg PUBLIC "-//W3C//DTD SVG 1.1//EN"
  "http://www.w3.org/Graphics/SVG/1.1/DTD/svg11.dtd">
<svg width="800" height="500" version="1.1"
    xmlns="http://www.w3.org/2000/svg" xmlns:xlink="http://www.w3.org/1999/xlink">
  <title>Stroke Sampler</title>
```

Example 7-4. Demonstrating different stroke patterns (continued)

```
<!-- Different stroke patterns with lines -->
<desc>Fives lines with different line patterns</desc>
<line x1="10" y1="20" x2="600" y2="20" stroke="black" stroke-width="4" />

<line x1="10" y1="60" x2="600" y2="60" stroke="black" stroke-width="4"
      stroke-dasharray="2,2" />

<line x1="10" y1="100" x2="600" y2="100" stroke="black" stroke-width="4"
      stroke-dasharray="8,2,8,2" />

<line x1="10" y1="140" x2="600" y2="140" stroke="black" stroke-width="4"
      stroke-dasharray="8,2,1,2,8,2,1,2" />

<line x1="10" y1="180" x2="600" y2="180" stroke="black" stroke-width="4"
      stroke-dasharray="2,2,2,2,2,2,5,2,5,2,5,2,2,2,2,2,2,2,5,2,5,2,5,2"/>
</svg>
```

Figure 7-7 shows the page opened in Firefox. Note that the stroke width changes the pattern height but not the pattern itself. Using a very wide stroke will give you a very "hairy" pattern. You might want to keep the wider stroke settings for solid lines.

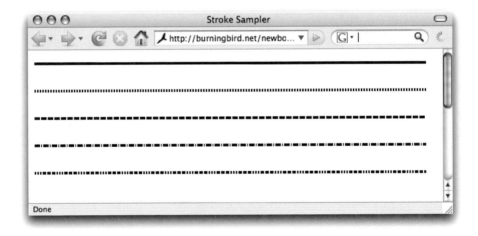

Figure 7-7. The stroke sampler from Example 7-4, with different stroke-dasharray patterns

Another visual element used with lines is the addition of arrows at the line's ends. However, these are usually dependent on the path element, which I'm covering later in this chapter.

Earlier, in Figure 7-5, I added text labels to the different rectangles using the screen capture tool. A better approach would be to add text labels directly into the SVG, which leads us to the next SVG element I'm covering: text.

Text

Text support in SVG is simple to manipulate, but also rich enough to meet a variety of needs, including different languages that read text from right to left or have characters that require a different orientation from English.

 This book focuses on text as it's used with the English language, and it won't cover aspects of the element such as writing mode.

An SVG text element, like the other SVG elements, has a position and can be colored using the same attributes used with lines and rectangles. This includes both color fill and stroke. One limitation with SVG 1.1 is that text doesn't "word wrap" like text in HTML does, which is annoying. Thankfully, word wrapping should be a part of SVG 1.2.

The simplest use of text requires a given position for the element, but everything else has a default value, including color and font. The following creates text at a position of 50,50:

```
<text x="50" y="50">
  Hello World
</text>
```

The positional attributes, x and y, mark the bottom-left baseline of the text (depending on orientation). The reason that the position needs to be provided, at least for the y attribute, is that the default is 0,0, which means that the text baseline starts at the very top of the page—where we can't see the text.

Of course, we shouldn't depend overmuch on default attributes. Providing a position in the page may show the text, but how the text is rendered differs among browsers when defaults are used. Figure 7-8 shows how this text would appear in Firefox, Safari, and Opera. The main variation among the browsers is the default font family.

An interesting twist on the x and y attributes for text is that both can hold a sequence of comma- or space-delimited values, not just a single value. If the sequence is provided, each value is then mapped to the appropriate character and the entire content is "spaced" according to these values. If a single value is given, then this is the given position of the first letter of the text, and default spacing is followed for the rest. If no value is given, the default of zero (0) is used. The following snippet of SVG converts the previous example to provide extra spacing for the letters along the horizontal:

```
<text x="50,70,90,110,130,150,170,190,210,230,250" y="50">
  Hello World
</text>
```

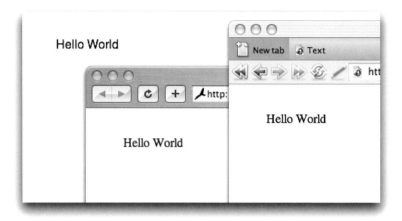

Figure 7-8. Default text handling in Firefox, Opera, and Safari

Providing a way of overriding the default spacing for text is an interesting idea. Unfortunately, implementation of this feature varies widely among browsers. The only browser that worked when I tested it was Opera, as shown in Figure 7-9.

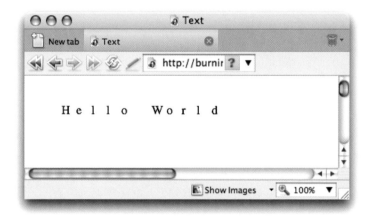

Figure 7-9. Opera's processing of an array of values for the x attribute

Rather than spacing out text by giving each character a position, we can also specify a text length with the textLength attribute, and the text is adjusted accordingly:

```
<text x="50" y="50" textLength="500">
hello world
</text>
```

Again, unfortunately, at the time I wrote this, `textLength` was implemented only by Opera. Another attribute, `rotate`, also had limited support. It works with Opera and somewhat with Safari, but currently not with Firefox. This attribute doesn't rotate the entire word, just the letters that map to the rotation values given. Figure 7-10 shows the text both with a long text length and with each character rotated, as it displays in Opera and Safari.

```
<text x="50" y="50" textLength="400" rotate="45 30 90 45 10 20 -180 0 30 120"
   font-size="18">
   hello world
</text>
```

As can be seen from the figure, consistent implementation has a ways to go for the `rotate` attribute.

 Support for SVG is changing so dramatically with Firefox, Safari/Web-Kit, and Opera that by the time you read this, all three will most likely render all of this book's SVG examples the same.

The snippet of SVG that creates Figure 7-10 uses one of the many other properties from the font and text attribute group that can alter text: `font-size`. If you've worked with CSS, you'll recognize many of these attributes.

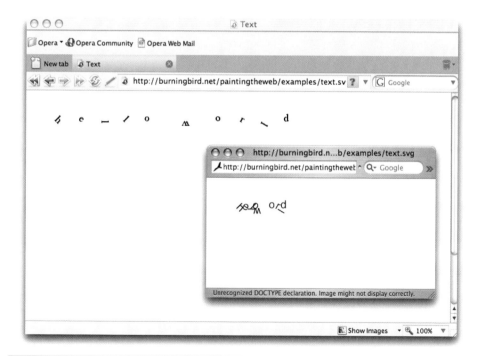

Figure 7-10. Opera's support for text rotate attribute

Of the font and text attributes, we'll use the following for the examples in this chapter and later:

font-family
>   States the font family, such as Arial or serif

font-size
>   Specifies the font size, including unit (unless in pixels)

font-style
>   Options are normal, italic, oblique, and inherit

font-weight
>   Among the options are numerical values, such as 300, and verbal specifications, such as bold

text-anchor
>   Options are start, middle, end, and inherit

To see how the different font attributes work on the same piece of text, Example 7-5 shows an old phrase we used in typing class. It's repeated several times with different combinations of font attributes, in order to view the differences in the text. I've also tossed in some of the previous paint attributes, just to break things up a bit.

Example 7-5. Applied text and font attributes

```
<?xml version="1.0" standalone="no"?>
<!DOCTYPE svg PUBLIC "-//W3C//DTD SVG 1.1//EN"
  "http://www.w3.org/Graphics/SVG/1.1/DTD/svg11.dtd">
<svg width="100%" height="600" version="1.1"
    xmlns="http://www.w3.org/2000/svg" xmlns:xlink="http://www.w3.org/1999/xlink">
  <title>Font Attributes</title>

  <desc>Light green letters with dark green border, italic, Arial, 2em in size</desc>
    <text x="20" y="40" font-size="2em" font-family="Arial" fill="#00ff00"
stroke="darkgreen" style="font-style: italic" >
    The quick brown fox jumped over the lazy dog
    </text>

  <desc>Blue, bold, and verdana</desc>
    <text x="20" y="80" font-size="16pt" font-family="Verdana" fill="blue" font-
weight="bold" >
    The quick brown fox jumped over the lazy dog
    </text>

  <desc>Orange, verdana, font size, and letter spacing</desc>
    <text x="20" y="120" font-size="24" font-family="Verdana" letter-spacing="10"
fill="orange">
    The quick brown fox jumped over the lazy dog
    </text>

  <desc>Text anchor set to middle</desc>
    <text x="20" y="160" font-size="16pt" font-family="Verdana" text-anchor="middle" >
    The quick brown fox jumped over the lazy dog
    </text>
```

Example 7-5. Applied text and font attributes (continued)

```
<desc>Patterned border</desc>
<text x="20" y="230" font-size="36pt" font-family="Times New Roman"
    fill="yellow" stroke="black" stroke-dasharray="2,2" >
The quick brown fox jumped over the lazy dog
</text>

<text x="100" y="350" font-size="72pt" font-family="Georgia" fill="red" stroke="black"
stroke-dasharray="1,2,1,2">
Fyn&#201;
</text>
</svg>
```

Figure 7-11 shows the page opened in Firefox 3.

Figure 7-11. Variations of font and text decoration with text elements

Notice in particular the last line, the "Eacute" character, with the accent on the capital "E" at the end. In the example, this character is represented by the sequence É. SVG is an XML format, and as such, supports internationalization through Unicode character encoding.

SVG supports, at a minimum, UTF-8 and UTF-16 encodings, which include Eacute and other characters supported in the ISO Latin Alphabet No. 1 character set. This includes the traditional ASCII characters many of us see on our keyboards, in addition to characters found in several Western Europe languages: French, Spanish, Finnish, German, and so on. It also includes characters such as trademark and copyright, as well as several mathematical symbols.

A listing of XML entities, like the one used for Eacute, can be found at *http://xml.coverpages.org/xml-ISOents.txt.*

That's enough to get us started with text. Back to the drawing.

Circles, Ellipses, and Gradient Fills

Rectangles and lines aren't the only "basic" shapes in SVG; where would we be without our circles and ellipses? Just as with rectangles, both object types—circle and ellipse—have their own attributes that define the characteristics of the shape, and can be painted, have their opacity altered, and be bordered by different colored and pattered strokes. In addition, like other closed shapes, circles and ellipses can be filled with gradients, which we'll also look at in this section.

Circles can be positioned with cx and cy attributes, which mark the circle's center point. In addition, an r, for radius, is provided to define the size of the circle. The following creates a circle with a radius of 20 pixels and located at a center point of 30,30:

```
<circle cx="30" cy="30" r="20" />
```

An ellipse also takes an x- and y-axis radius, rx and ry, in addition to the center x and y value, to mark the vertical and horizontal lengths of the shape. The following SVG creates an ellipse that is 250 pixels long and 100 pixels tall, located at a center point of 300,200:

```
<ellipse cx="300" cy="200" rx="250" ry="100" />
```

By default, both the circle and the ellipse just described are filled with black and have no border. Both accept a fill attribute, as well as all of the stroke attributes. For something different in this section, we'll look at using gradients to color the objects.

A gradient in SVG is different than a solid color fill in that gradients are a separate element, gradient. Gradients are usually constructed within an SVG defs element and are given a unique identifier through the id attribute. This identifier is assigned in the fill attribute, using a syntax of fill="url(#SomeId)" where *SomeId* is the identifier of the gradient.

Gradients in SVG provide more points of control than gradients in some other applications, but at their simplest require only a couple of points of information. To create a standard linear gradient, two stop elements are needed, to determine when the gradient starts and the colors used in the transition. The following creates a gradient starting at 0 and ending at 100% of the length of the ellipse. The colors are aqua and purple, and the gradient is used to fill the ellipse created earlier:

```
<defs>
  <linearGradient id="MyGradient">
    <stop offset="0%" stop-color="aqua" />
    <stop offset="100%" stop-color="purple" />
  </linearGradient>
</defs>
<ellipse cx="300" cy="200" rx="250" ry="100" fill="url(#MyGradient)" />
```

Multiple colors can be used, each given its own stop:

```
<linearGradient id="MyGradient">
  <stop offset="0" stop-color="aqua" />
  <stop offset="50%" stop-color="yellow" />
  <stop offset="100%" stop-color="purple" />
</linearGradient>
```

By default, gradients transition along a straight line, from beginning color to end. You can control the line on which a gradient flows by providing starting and stopping points for this new line with the x1,y1 and x2,y2 attributes.

The default transitioning direction is horizontal, which means that the starting and ending y values would be the same, and since the color transitions evenly from the top and bottom, would be set to 50% for both y1 and y2, with x1 and x2 set to 0 and 100%, respectively. To do the same vertically, you'd set the x1 and x2 values to 50%, and set y1 and y2 to 0 and 100%. Or, to reverse the flow both ways, set the first value to 100% and the second to 0.

You can even choose values between 0 and 100% if you want the transition to start or end later. For instance, with circles, the "corners" where the transition would normally start aren't included in the fill. To show a stronger transition, start and end the transition at values between 0 and 100%.

Example 7-6 shows a sequence of ellipses, each filled with a two-color (red and yellow) gradient. One main gradient pattern is created, which is then used to create secondary gradients, each with a different set of x1,y1,x2,y2 values. The secondary gradients use the XLINK href attribute to reference the first gradient. The original gradient and its variations are then used with the six ellipses.

Example 7-6. Controlling the linearity of the gradients

```
<?xml version="1.0" standalone="no"?>
<!DOCTYPE svg PUBLIC "-//W3C//DTD SVG 1.1//EN"
  "http://www.w3.org/Graphics/SVG/1.1/DTD/svg11.dtd">
<svg xmlns="http://www.w3.org/2000/svg"
  xmlns:xlink="http://www.w3.org/1999/xlink">
  <title>Gradients</title>

  <defs>
    <linearGradient id="gradient">
      <stop stop-color="rgb(255,255,0)" offset="0"/>
      <stop stop-color="red"   offset="100%"/>
    </linearGradient>
```

Example 7-6. Controlling the linearity of the gradients (continued)

```
    <linearGradient id="gradient1" xlink:href="#gradient"
      x1="0" y1="50%" x2="100%" y2="50%" />
    <linearGradient id="gradient2" xlink:href="#gradient"
      x1="50%" y1="0" x2="50%" y2="100%" />
    <linearGradient id="gradient3" xlink:href="#gradient"
      x1="50%" y1="100%" x2="50%" y2="0" />
    <linearGradient id="gradient4" xlink:href="#gradient"
      x1="0" y1="0" x2="100%" y2="100%" />
    <linearGradient id="gradient5" xlink:href="#gradient"
      x1="0" y1="25%" x2="75%" y2="100%" />
  </defs>

  <desc>Three ellipses with gradients with different transitions</desc>
  <ellipse cx="200" cy="150" rx="150" ry="100" fill="url(#gradient)" />
  <ellipse cx="500" cy="150" rx="150" ry="100" fill="url(#gradient1)" />

  <ellipse cx="200" cy="350" rx="150" ry="100" fill="url(#gradient2)" />
  <ellipse cx="500" cy="350" rx="150" ry="100" fill="url(#gradient3)" />

  <ellipse cx="200" cy="550" rx="150" ry="100" fill="url(#gradient4)" />
  <ellipse cx="500" cy="550" rx="150" ry="100" fill="url(#gradient5)" />
```

```
</svg>
```

Referring to Figure 7-12, the first ellipse uses the default transitioning, and the second emulates this by using a linear gradient in which the starting and ending y values are set to 50%. In the third and fourth ellipses, the x1 and x2 values are set to 50%, and the transition happens along the vertical axis: down on one, up on the other. Finally, in the last set of ellipses, the transition occurs along the diagonal, from top-left to bottom-right in both. The only difference is where the starting and ending points are on the transition. As the arrows added to the graphic illustrate, these starting points occur outside the object in the first ellipse, and more or less in the object fill in the second, creating a stronger transition effect. If the object had been a rectangle, where the corners aren't cut, using such stepped starts and stops wouldn't be necessary.

Another variation on gradients is the spreadMethod, which controls what happens in areas outside of the transitioning effect when stop values are set between 0% and 100%. The three options are:

reflect

    Reflects the pattern

pad

    Pads the non-covered area with the nearest color

repeat

    Repeats the pattern

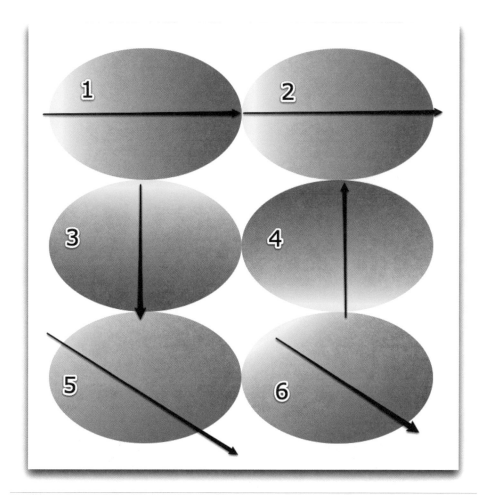

Figure 7-12. Adjusting the linearity of gradients in ellipses

Example 7-7 is another SVG page, this time showing three circles side by side, each colored with three colors instead of two. A dark midnight blue is used now for the center transition color, to better highlight the spreadMethod options. Each option is applied to each circle in this order: reflect, pad, and repeat.

Example 7-7. Using spreadMethod to alter gradient

```
<?xml version="1.0" standalone="no"?>
<svg xmlns="http://www.w3.org/2000/svg"
    xmlns:xlink="http://www.w3.org/1999/xlink">
  <title>Gradients</title>
```

Example 7-7. Using spreadMethod to alter gradient (continued)

```
<defs>
  <linearGradient id="gradient">
    <stop stop-color="rgb(255,255,0)" offset="0"/>
    <stop stop-color="midnightblue" offset="50%" />
    <stop stop-color="red"   offset="100%"/>
  </linearGradient>
  <linearGradient id="gradient1" xlink:href="#gradient"
      x1="30%" y1="30%" x2="70%" y2="70%" spreadMethod="reflect" />
  <linearGradient id="gradient2" xlink:href="#gradient"
      x1="30%" y1="30%" x2="70%" y2="70%" spreadMethod="pad" />
  <linearGradient id="gradient3" xlink:href="#gradient"
      x1="30%" y1="30%" x2="70%" y2="70%" spreadMethod="repeat" />

</defs>

<desc>Three circles, each with different spreadMethod option</desc>
<circle cx="150" cy="150" r="100" fill="url(#gradient1)" />
<circle cx="350" cy="150" r="100" fill="url(#gradient2)" />
<circle cx="550" cy="150" r="100" fill="url(#gradient3)" />
```

```
</svg>
```

Figure 7-13 shows the three circles, labeled with the respective spreadMethod value.

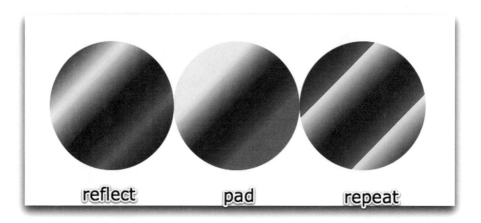

Figure 7-13. Demonstrating the three spreadMethod options

The last gradient we'll look at is radialGradient, which fills a space with a circular gradient. Color stops are given in the same way as with linearGradient, and the use of spreadMethod is also the same. Where the two differ is that the radialGradient's pattern is controlled by other attributes: cx and cy—which control both the bounding box and r, the radius—and fx and fy, which control the focal point of the gradient. The last two attributes are especially helpful if you're creating a gradient "shine" with another object.

Not all browsers support all attributes equally. Opera 9.x did a rather poor job with `spreadMethod` in radial gradients, Safari defaulted to `pad`, and Firefox managed just fine.

The last example for this section, Example 7-8, uses `radialGradient` to create four circles, each using different variations of the attributes. The first circle uses the defaults, and the second resets the circle's x and y values to 0 and sets the `spreadMethod` to repeat. The third circle gradient changes the focal point to 30% along both the horizontal and vertical axes, adjusts the gradient's x and y values to 20%, and sets the radius to 100%. This creates a light source glow, which provides a three-dimensional quality to the circle. This is further emphasized with the last circle, which uses the same attributes, but with monochrome colors of black, white, and gray.

Example 7-8. Using radial gradient with various different attribute settings

```
<?xml version="1.0" standalone="no"?>
<svg xmlns="http://www.w3.org/2000/svg"
   xmlns:xlink="http://www.w3.org/1999/xlink">
  <title>Gradients</title>

  <defs>
    <radialGradient id="gradient">
      <stop stop-color="rgb(255,255,0)" offset="0%"/>
      <stop stop-color="midnightblue" offset="50%" />
      <stop stop-color="red"  offset="100%"/>
    </radialGradient>
    <radialGradient id="gradient1" xlink:href="#gradient" />
    <radialGradient id="gradient2" xlink:href="#gradient"
        cx="0" cy="0" spreadMethod="repeat"/>
    <radialGradient id="gradient3" xlink:href="#gradient"
        cx="20%" cy="20%" fx="30%" fy="30%" r="100%" />
    <radialGradient id="gradient4" cx="20%" cy="20%" r="100%" fx="30%" fy="30%">
      <stop stop-color="white" offset="0%" />
      <stop stop-color="#666" offset="50%" />
      <stop stop-color="black" offset="100%" />
    </radialGradient>
  </defs>

  <desc>Demonstrating various radialGradient settings</desc>
  <circle cx="150" cy="150" r="100" fill="url(#gradient1)" />
  <circle cx="350" cy="150" r="100" fill="url(#gradient2)" />
  <circle cx="550" cy="150" r="100" fill="url(#gradient3)" />
  <circle cx="750" cy="150" r="100" fill="url(#gradient4)" />

</svg>
```

Figure 7-14 shows the page as it would be opened in Firefox 3. The example looks the same in Safari, but you'll want to remove the second circle if opening in Opera, as it has a great deal of problems with the given `radialGradient`.

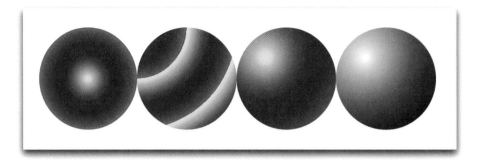

Figure 7-14. Variations of radialGradient

Gradient and solid colors aren't the only fills that can be used with solid objects. SVG also allows for the creation of repeating patterns, demonstrated in the next section, which also looks at the last two of the basic SVG elements: polylines and polygons.

The Polys: Polylines and Polygons

The "polys" are simple techniques for creating regular or irregular shapes that are either filled (polygon) or not (polyline). Both take a set of paired values assigned to a points attribute, with each pair in the format of x,y with spaces between the pairs (for example, 500,50 400,300). The polygon automatically closes the object, connecting the last point with the first; the polyline doesn't. Both take stroke attributes, but only the polygon can be filled.

The best way to demonstrate both elements is through an example. Example 7-9 contains both a polygon and a polyline: the polygon has a seagreen fill and an aqua stroke, and the polyline has a blue stroke. Both shapes are parallelograms.

Example 7-9. Using polygon and polyline to create parallelograms

```
<?xml version="1.0" standalone="no"?>
<svg xmlns="http://www.w3.org/2000/svg"
    xmlns:xlink="http://www.w3.org/1999/xlink">
  <title>Polys</title>

  <desc>parallelogram polygon and polyline</desc>
  <polygon points="150,50 500,50 400,300 50,300"
      fill="seagreen" stroke="aqua" stroke-width="5" />
  <polyline points="150,350, 500,350, 400,600 50,600"
      stroke="blue" stroke-width="5" fill="none" />
</svg>
```

Figure 7-15 shows both shapes. Notice that the shape is completed between the end point and the beginning with the polygon, but not with the polyline.

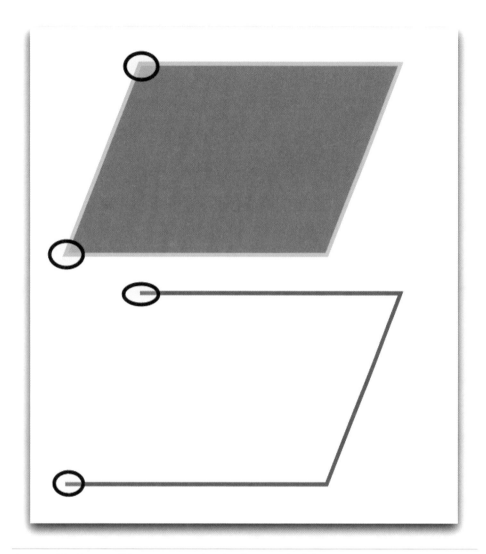

Figure 7-15. Two parallelograms created with polygon and polyline

In the example, the polyline has a fill of "none". This is set explicitly because the browser will attempt to fill the shape regardless of object type, which can lead to interesting but unwelcome results.

With the polygon, another option is to provide a fill-rule. If the polygon lines intersect in such a way that an area is completely contained within the polygon, that area is filled depending on whether the fill-rule is set to "nonzero" or "evenodd"—nonzero fills it, and evenodd doesn't. However, you can also get odd fill results when the polygon attempts to complete the object from the first and last point.

The browser will take the shortest, straightest route, and everywhere an intersection occurs, a possible fill can occur. Instead of a single object, you could end up with several little filled objects.

 Polylines will fill a shape unless fill is set to "none". Polygon completions may lead to unexpected results, and so it's best to "complete" the polygon yourself.

Polygons and polylines both take arrays of points, which can have spaces, line feeds, or commas separating the x,y value pairs, but a comma must be used to separate the points.

A more sophisticated way to draw complex images is path. The is the SVG element most used by graphics programs, and is covered a little later in this chapter.

The Image

Raster elements can be incorporated into SVG through the use of the SVG image element. Through image, you can add any number of JPEG or PNG elements to the SVG document. You can also include images defined using SVG, but support for this is limited at this time, so I'll focus on including JPEG or PNG images for now.

 Opera 9.x does support opening SVG files with the image element, so use this browser if you want to give this concept a try.

The Hello World example in the last chapter used an image of a globe in the application:

```
<image x="360" y="185" width="80" height="80" xlink:href="helloworld.png" />
```

I mentioned the image types in the last paragraph and specified JPEG or PNG. You can open GIF files, too, though the W3C doesn't mention these.

What happens with the images when opened depends on the image element settings. If the image container is larger or smaller than the image opened, it's correspondingly resized by default. However, you can control what happens with the image through the use of the preserveAspectRatio attribute. This is a fairly complex concept that is associated with viewports and the viewBox, and it gets its own section later in this book, following the description of paths.

Groups and SVG As Containers

SVG elements can be treated individually or as a group. The container element used to group one or more SVG elements together is known simply as g. Its use is just as simple: surround the elements to be grouped by the opening and closing g tags:

```
<g>
<rect x="10" y="10" width="100" height="100" fill="red" />
<rect x="5" y="5" width="50" height="50" fill="blue" />
</g>
```

Any number of attributes can be applied to the group defined by the g element, including style settings, animations, and transformations.

The group element isn't the only way to group a bunch of SVG elements; it also can be used to create nested SVG documents:

```
<svg xmlns="http://www.w3.org/2000/svg" version="1.1">
<svg x="0" y="0" width="400" height="400">
...
</svg>
</svg>
```

Two other attributes are used with the svg element in this example: x and y, to set the location of the new nested svg element in relation to the containing SVG canvas. In the viewBox section later, nested svg elements are used to demonstrate the concept of preserving aspect ratios.

Paths, Patterns, and Markers

A line is nice but limited, in that you can only use it to draw from here to there. Polylines and polygons can be used to create more complex images, but not images where the drawing "pen" is moved to a new location in the page without drawing any figure between. The SVG path removes these limitations by providing the ability to draw any number of connected or non-connected points, creating complex lines or even complete images once they're filled in and colored.

Unlike the polygon and polyline functionality discussed in the previous section, a path doesn't take a sequence of points and connect them. Instead, a path takes a sequence of commands and draws the image, or images, based on these commands. The commands are case sensitive, and the type of "lines" drawn change from straight line to curved. Complex drawings generated by drawing tools, like those described later, are invariably created as paths.

Basic Path Commands

Path commands either move the drawing "pen," draw straight lines, or draw curves. They're case sensitive, in that lowercase commands are relative and uppercase are absolute. The basic commands are:

M *or* m

The moveto command (relative or absolute) moves the digital pen to a new location, beginning a new subpath.

L *or* l

> The lineto command (relative or absolute) draws a line from the current location to the new.

Z *or* z

> Closes the current subpath by drawing a straight line from the current location to the initial starting point.

The path is specified in the d attribute (for path "data"), and all the previous stroke and fill options are available to the path. The essential component of paths is knowing when to use absolute and relative commands. You can use either, but you don't want to use one thinking you're using the other.

To demonstrate how the path works, Example 7-10 is an SVG document that creates a green house with two yellow windows and a yellow door. Two paths are used: one for the green house, and one for the windows and door. As stated earlier, unlike polygons, paths don't have to draw items that are connected. The example also uses absolute commands, M and L, to create the image. I find absolute imaging to be easier to control.

Example 7-10. Using SVG paths to create a house with features

```
<?xml version="1.0" standalone="no"?>
<svg xmlns="http://www.w3.org/2000/svg"
    xmlns:xlink="http://www.w3.org/1999/xlink">
  <title>Path</title>

<desc>green house with yellow windows and a door</desc>
<g transform="translate(200,100)">
<path d="M 0 150 L 100 0 L 200 150 L 200 300 L 0 300 L 0 150" fill="green" />

<path d="M 75 300 L 75  200 L 125 200 L 125 300 L 75 300
        M 25 250 L 25 200 L 50 200 L 50 250 L 25 250
        M 150 250 L 150 200 L 175 200 L 175 250 z" fill="yellow" />
</g>
</svg>
```

The three separate subpaths that draw the door and windows are featured on separate lines. With SVG, a quoted line can be continued across line breaks, since whitespace within the path's data string is not an issue. You can also use commas between the pairs of values if that makes it easier to track the pairs. The last subpath also features the close path (z) command, which closes the figure between the last point and the first. Figure 7-16 shows the simple house these two paths create.

There are also a couple of shortcut commands:

H *or* h *n*

> Draw a horizontal line to *n*

V *or* v *n*

> Draw a vertical line to *n*

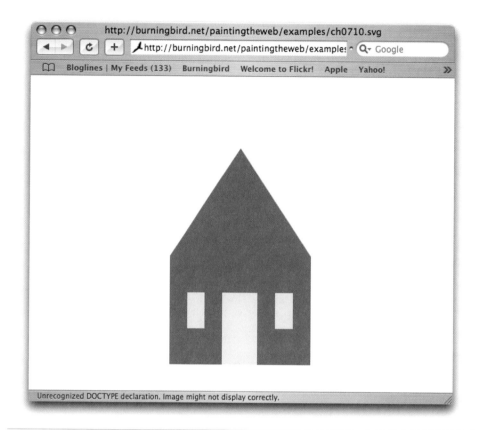

Figure 7-16. House created with SVG paths

Another shortcut technique is to provide a set of paired values for the move or line commands, and then you don't have to repeat the command. However, this can make the paths harder to read.

Of course, if our lives were all right angles and straight lines, we wouldn't have to worry about seams in our clothing. It would be a pain to have to draw out tiny little lines in order to create a convincing curve. Luckily, curves are built into paths.

Three types of curves are supported with SVG paths, as discussed in the next sections:

Elliptical arc commands
> Draw elliptical arcs between two points and given rx and ry radius and an x-axis rotation.

Cubic Bézier commands
> Draw cubic Bézier curves given an end point and two control points, one at the beginning of the curve and one at the end.

Quadratic Bézier commands
> Draw quadratic Bézier curves given an end and control points.

An Elliptical Arc Curve Path

An elliptical curve begins with the command A or, with the case denoting absolute and relative values, per previous commands. The elliptical arc curve is based on a defined ellipse, defined by a horizontal radius, rx, and vertical radius, ry. Other parameters that follow are x-axis-rotation, which controls how the ellipse is rotated compared to the existing coordinate system; large-arc-flag, set to 0 if the arc's measure is 180 degrees or fewer or 1 if it's more; sweep-flag, set to 0 if the arc is drawn in a negative angle direction, 1 if positive; and the ending x,y point.

To demonstrate how all of the different parameters work, Example 7-11 contains a circle, forming our "ellipse" for the arcs. Several different arc paths are drawn, as shown in Figure 7-17.

Example 7-11. The parameters for the elliptical arc

```
<?xml version="1.0" standalone="no"?>
<svg
      xmlns="http://www.w3.org/2000/svg" version="1.1">
  <title>Elliptical</title>
  <circle cx="300" cy="200" r="100" fill="yellow" />
  <path d="M300,200 V300 A100,100 0 0,1 200,200 z" stroke="blue" fill="blue" fill-
opacity=".2" />
  <path d="M300,300 A100,100 0 1, 1 200,200" stroke="red" stroke-width="2" stroke-
dasharray="4,3,4,3" fill="none" />
  <path d="M300,300 A100,100 0 0, 0 200,200" stroke="green" stroke-width="2" stroke-
dasharray="2,2" fill="none" />
  <path d="M300,300 A100,100 0 1, 0 200,200" stroke="purple" stroke-width="2" stroke-
dasharray="5,2,3,5,2,3" fill="none" />

</svg>
```

The first, in solid blue and filled, draws an arc from the bottom of the circle to the left side, and is joined by lines drawn from the center of the circle. The sweep-flag is set to 1, since the arc is being drawn in the negative, counter-clockwise direction.

The second arc, in a dashed red color, is the same arc, except the large-arc-flag is set to 1, signaling an arc greater than 180 degrees; the sweep-flag is still 1, drawing the arc in the counter-clockwise direction. The result of the attribute settings draws an arc that encompasses the circle outside of the initial arc, mirroring the circle.

The next arc, drawn with a dotted green line visible through the blue fill, is the same as the blue, except that the sweep-flag is set to 0 and the arc is drawn in the positive direction.

Finally, the last arc, in a dash-dot purple stroke, is given a sweep-flag of 0, for positive direction, and 1 for large-arc-flag, which then draws an arc around the original ellipse, excluding the first arc.

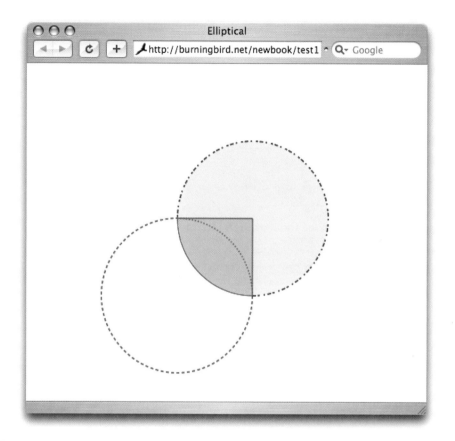

Figure 7-17. Circle with several arcs drawn on it

Quadratic Bézier Curves

Quadratic Bézier curves are the easiest of the curves. All you need to provide is the command (Q or q, depending on absolute or relative positioning), followed by an x,y pair representing the curve control and an x,y pair representing the end of the curve. Think of a flexible wire that you pick up somewhere between the two end points, and the sides falling down gracefully in a curved arc.

The following creates a petal-like shape, with a reflected curve along the horizontal:

```
<path d="M100,100 Q250,50 400,100 Q250,150 100,100" stroke="black" />
```

You don't have to "guess" what will happen with a quadratic Bézier curve. Imagine a straight line drawn with one end halfway between the first end point and the control of the curve, and the other end halfway between the control and the end of the curve, halfway between the height of the control and an imaginary straight line between the two curve end points. Find the midpoint on this line, and you'll have the midpoint of the top of the curve.

Example 7-12 creates four different curves, each different because of the curve control point given to the quadratic Bézier curve command.

Example 7-12. Four different curves created with the quadratic Bézier curve command

```
?xml version="1.0" standalone="no"?>
<svg  xmlns="http://www.w3.org/2000/svg" version="1.1">
  <title>Quadratic Bézier</title>

  <desc>Quadratic Bézier Curves with annotation</desc>
  <g transform="translate(-50,50)">

  <desc>Initial curve end points and straight line marked in dash-dash-dot</desc>
  <path d="M100,200 Q 300,100 500,200" fill="none" stroke="black" />
  <path d="M100,200 L 500,200" fill="none" stroke="gray" stroke-dasharray="5,5,2,5,5,2" />
  <desc>Representation between curve control point and end points, dashed red</desc>
  <path d="M100,200 L 300,100 L 500,200" fill="none" stroke-dasharray="5,5"
stroke="red" />
  <desc>Intersection between curve straight lines and curve top in dotted blue</desc>
  <path d="M200,150 L 400,150 M200,150 L200,200 M400,150 L400,200" fill="none"
stroke="blue" stroke-dasharray="3,3"/>
  <text x="180" y="140" font-size="8pt">
  200,150
  </text>
  <text x="380" y="140" font-size="8pt">
  400,150
  </text>
  <text x="280" y="90" font-size="8pt">
  300,100
  </text>
  <text x="80" y="220" font-size="8pt">
  100,200
  </text>
  <text x="480" y="220" font-size="8pt">
  500,200
  </text>
  <path d="M600,200 Q 800,0 1000,200" fill="none" stroke="black" />
  <path d="M600,200 L 1000,200" fill="none" stroke="gray" stroke-dasharray="5,5,2,
5,5,2" />
  <path d="M600,200 L 800,0 L 1000,200" fill="none" stroke-dasharray="5,5" stroke="red" />
  <path d="M700,100 L900,100 M700,100 L700,200 M900,100 L900,200" fill="none"
stroke="blue" stroke-dasharray="3,3" />
  <text x="680" y="90" font-size="8pt">
  700,100
  </text>
  <text x="880" y="90" font-size="8pt">
  900,100
  </text>
```

Example 7-12. Four different curves created with the quadratic Bézier curve command (continued)

```
<text x="780" y="-10" font-size="8pt">
800,0
</text>
<text x="580" y="220" font-size="8pt">
600,200
</text>
<text x="980" y="220" font-size="8pt">
1000,200
</text>

<path d="M100,400 Q200,300 500,400" fill="none" stroke="black" />
<path d="M100,400 L500,400" fill="none" stroke="gray" stroke-dasharray="5,5,2,5,5,2" />
<path d="M100,400 L200,300 L500,400" fill="none" stroke="red" stroke-dasharray="5,5" />
<path d="M150,350 L350,350 M150,350 L150,400 M350,350 L350,400" fill="none"
stroke="blue"
                    stroke-dasharray="3,3" />
<text x="180" y="290" font-size="8pt">
200,300
</text>
<text x="130" y="340" font-size="8pt">
150,350
</text>
<text x="330" y="340" font-size="8pt">
350,350
</text>
<text x="80" y="420" font-size="8pt">
100,400
</text>
<text x="480" y="420" font-size="8pt">
500,400
</text>

<path d="M600,400 Q960,200 1000,400" fill="none" stroke="black" />

</g>
</svg>
```

Figure 7-18 shows the four different curves. The first three curves are annotated with the points of interest associated with the curves. With the first three, the gray dash-dash-dot line is the straight line between the two curve end points; the dashed red line is the straight line from each end point to the given control point; and the blue dotted line is the most interesting of all of the annotations.

The blue line is formed by finding the midpoint between the end points and the control point on either end. When these two points are connected, the midpoint of the line that results is equivalent to the midpoint of the curve. As you can see from the three annotated curves, it doesn't matter where the control point is placed or how "high" the control point is—this same equation can be used to find the midpoint of the resulting curve. Which means the converse is true: given a desired curve in an existing drawing or plan, you can derive the values to be used in the quadratic Bézier curve command to create it.

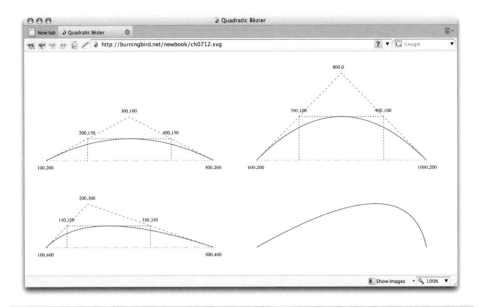

Figure 7-18. Annotated quadratic Bézier curves with different curve control points

In the example SVG, the last curve isn't annotated. I'm leaving that to you, so you can join in the fun.

In addition to the regular quadratic command, there's a shorthand notation, T or t (case, again, represents absolute or relative positioning), which can be used to repeat and mirror the previous curve value, so that you only have to specify the end point:

```
<path d="M100,100 Q200,0 300,100 T500,100 z" stroke="black" fill="orchid" />
```

Example 7-12, the earlier house example, and the example in the next chapter also use a transform, covered later in the section "Transformations."

Cubic Bézier Curves

The cubic Bézier curve command, C or c, is somewhat the same as the quadratic command, except that the cubic takes two control points: one toward one end of the curve and one toward the other end. The two control points can be close or far apart, and can even occur on different sides of the arc.

```
<path d="M100,100 C250,0 300,0 400,100" stroke="black" />
```

This curve has end points of (100,100) and (400,100), with the first control point at (250,0) and the second at (300,0).

Deriving the projected curve from the command or the command from the curve isn't quite as simple for the cubic as it is for the quadratic. You have to draw a line connecting the two ends and the control points. Then, you draw a line from the midpoint between the one end and its nearest control point, to the midpoint between the two control points, and on to the midpoint between the last end point and its control. Then, you draw a line from the midpoints of the two lines you just created, and the midpoint of this line becomes the midpoint of the derived curve.

Example 7-13 shows two cubic Bézier curves that are quite different. The first curve has control points at the same height and equidistant from the end points. The second, though, has a first control point that's actually to the left of the first end point, and the second end point is below the end point baseline.

Example 7-13. Two cubic Bézier curves, annotated

```
<?xml version="1.0" standalone="no"?>
<!DOCTYPE svg PUBLIC "-//W3C//DTD SVG 1.1//EN"
  "http://www.w3.org/Graphics/SVG/1.1/DTD/svg11.dtd">
<svg
    xmlns="http://www.w3.org/2000/svg" version="1.1">
  <title>Cubic Bézier</title>
<g transform="translate(-50,0)">
<path d="M100,300 C300,50 500,50 700,300" stroke="black" fill="none" />
<path d="M100,300 700,300"  stroke="gray" stroke-dasharray="5,5,2,5,5,2" />
<path d="M100,300 L300,50 500,50 700,300" stroke="red" stroke-dasharray="5,5" fill="none" />
<path d="M200,175 L400,50 600,175" stroke="blue" stroke-dasharray="3,3" fill="none" />
<path d="M300,112 500,112" stroke="orange" stroke-width="3" stroke-dasharray="3,3,5,3,3,5"
fill="none" />
</g>
<g transform="translate(-50,0)">
<path d="M700,200 C600,10 1000,400 900,200" stroke="black" fill="none" />
<path d="M700,200 900,200" stroke="gray" stroke-dasharray="5,5,2,5,5,2" fill="none" />
<path d="M700,200 L600,10 1000,400 900,200" stroke="red" fill="none" stroke-
dasharray="5,5" />
<path d="M650,105 L800,205 950,300" stroke="blue" stroke-dasharray="3,3" fill="none" />
<path d="M725,155 L875,252" stroke="orange" stroke-width="3" stroke-
dasharray="3,3,5,3,3,5" fill="none" />
</g>
</svg>
```

Shown in Figure 7-19, the dashed red line marks the line that connects the two ends and the control points, and the blue dotted line marks the connecting lines from the two midpoints of the dashed red line. Drawing a line between the two midpoints of these two lines, shown in an orange dash-dash-dot line, gives us the midpoint of the curve. It's hard to see this last line with the second figure, because the orange line actually mirrors the curve, and the curve midpoint is on the baseline.

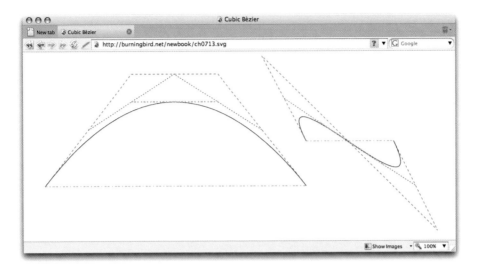

Figure 7-19. Two cubic Bézier curves with midpoint annotation

The shorthand technique for the cubic curve, S or s, repeats the curve from the second control point to the current location. We then provide the new second control point and the new end point:

```
<path d="M100,100 C200,0 300,0 400,100 S500,200 700,100" stroke="green"
fill="none" />
```

Paths, Markers, and Arrow Heads

Paths that mark a sequence of steps or outline a route on a map need some kind of indication of direction, and that's where the SVG marker comes into the picture. Markers are really patterns created with circles and paths that can be used to mark the beginning of a path (circle) and its steps and end (arrow heads). Once these patterns are defined, they can be used with the following attributes: marker-start, marker-middle, and marker-end. Markers can be used with paths, polylines, polygons, and lines.

A circle can be used to mark the beginning of a line. The following creates a circle marker to begin the line that follows in the SVG:

```
<defs>
<marker id="startCircle" markerWidth="14" markerHeight="14" refX="6" refY="6">
  <circle cx="6" cy="6" r="5" fill="none" stroke="black" />
</marker>
</defs>
<path d="M100,100 L300,100" marker-start="url(#startCircle)" stroke="black" />
```

The `markerWidth` and `markerHeight` set the width and height of the marker's viewport. If the circle's dimensions were beyond this viewport, nothing would show. The `refX` and `refY` are used to align the circle with the path, positioning the circle so that the beginning of the path is centered exactly within the circle.

Of course, a starting bubble is only part of the direction indication—we also need an arrow head at the other end. The following SVG snippet modifies the image just created, adding an arrow head at the other end of the line:

```
<defs>
<marker id="startCircle" markerWidth="14" markerHeight="14" refX="6" refY="6">
  <circle cx="6" cy="6" r="5" fill="none" stroke="black" />
</marker>
<marker id="endArrow" markerWidth="7" markerHeight="14"
        refX="7" refY="7">
        <path d="M0,0 L7,7 0,14" fill="none" stroke="black"/>
</marker>
</defs>
<path d="M100,100 L300,100"
      marker-start="url(#startCircle)"
      marker-end="url(#endArrow)" stroke="black" />
```

The circle is set using the `marker-start` attribute, and the arrow head set with the `marker-end`. This instructs the SVG agent into positioning the elements accordingly. For the arrow, the path is used to create the arrow head, and the `refX` and `refY` values are set to ensure that the arrow head fits snugly against the line. Figure 7-20 shows the completed arrow.

Figure 7-20. "Arrow" made from a path line with a circle arrow start and a path arrow head

Of course, if the path to which the direction indicators are added meanders rather than going in a straight line, you'll want to add indicators all along the path, and that's where `midMarker` enters. Since these arrows could be going in any direction, the marker `orient` attribute is set to `"auto"` so that the arrows are automatically aligned correctly with the line, regardless of orientation. Example 7-14 creates just such a meandering line with indicators.

Example 7-14. Meandering path with directional markers

```
<?xml version="1.0" standalone="no"?>
<!DOCTYPE svg PUBLIC "-//W3C//DTD SVG 1.1//EN"
  "http://www.w3.org/Graphics/SVG/1.1/DTD/svg11.dtd">
```

Example 7-14. Meandering path with directional markers (continued)

```
<svg
     xmlns="http://www.w3.org/2000/svg" version="1.1">
  <title>Directional Markers</title>

  <defs>
<marker id="startCircle" markerWidth="14" markerHeight="14" refX="6" refY="6"
orient="auto">
   <circle cx="6" cy="6" r="5" fill="none" stroke="black" />
</marker>
<marker id="midArrow" markerWidth="7" markerHeight="14"
        refX="7" refY="7" orient="auto">
        <path d="M0,0 L7,7 0,14" fill="none" stroke="black"/>
</marker>
<marker id="endArrow" markerWidth="15" markerHeight="20" refX="7" refY="7">
<path d="M0,7 0,0 14,7 0,14" stroke="black" fill="black" />
</marker>
</defs>

  <desc>Meandering path with arrow direction markers</desc>
  <path d="M50,50 200,50
          A20,30 0 0 1 220 80 L220,250
          A20,30 0 0 0 240 270 L350,270
          A20,30 0 0 0 370,240 L370,200
          A20,30 0 0 1 390 180 L450,180" stroke="black" fill="none"
          marker-start="url(#startCircle)"
          marker-mid="url(#midArrow)"
          marker-end="url(#endArrow)" />
</svg>
```

Elliptical arcs are used to create the "curves" in the path, and directional arrows are added to the line at the beginning and end of the curves. Figure 7-21 shows the resulting image.

There's one last aspect of paths to examine and then we'll get into the last major component of SVG: transformations and the all-important `viewBox`.

Paths As Patterns

Paths are such a handy beast. They can be pushed, molded, shaped, and shot like an arrow. Paths can also be used to create patterns, which can then be used as yet another kind of object "fill." Patterns are supported in Opera and Safari 3, as well as Firefox 3.

Patterns are defined like markers, in the `defs` section. Pattern attributes are `width` and `height`, which cover the bounding box for the pattern. The coordinates for the start of the pattern are also given with an x,y pair. Additionally, an attribute, `patternUnits`, can be given a value of `"objectBoundingBox"` and `"userSpaceOnUse"`. The latter sets the pattern measurements based on the current coordinate system, the former based on the bounding box of the element.

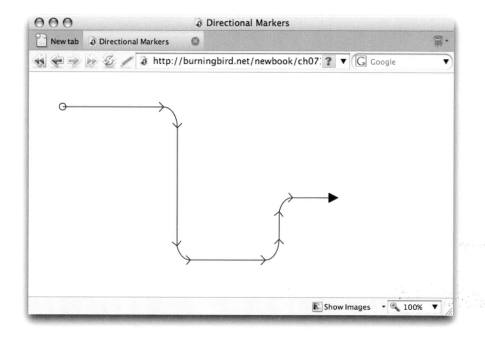

Figure 7-21. Meandering path with directional arrows

Example 7-15 shows two patterns consisting of the same two overlapping paths, with the only difference between them being the patternUnits setting. Each is used to fill a shape: a rectangle for the pattern where the patternUnits is set to objectBoundingBox, the circle to the pattern using userSpaceOnUse. Figure 7-22 shows the result.

Example 7-15. Two shapes filled with two user-defined patterns

```
<?xml version="1.0" standalone="no"?>
<!DOCTYPE svg PUBLIC "-//W3C//DTD SVG 1.1//EN"
  "http://www.w3.org/Graphics/SVG/1.1/DTD/svg11.dtd">
<svg
     xmlns="http://www.w3.org/2000/svg" version="1.1">
  <title>Pattern</title>
<defs>
  <pattern id="myPattern" x="0" y="0" width="10%" height="10%"
patternUnits="objectBoundingBox">
  <path d="M0,0 25,0 25,25 0,25 z" fill="yellow" stroke="red" />
  <path d="M0,25 25,0 50,0 z" fill="red"   />
  </pattern>
  <pattern id="myPattern2" x="0" y="0" width="10%" height="10%"
patternUnits="userSpaceOnUse">
  <path d="M0,0 25,0 25,25 0,25 z" fill="yellow" stroke="red" />
  <path d="M0,25 25,0 50,0 z" fill="red"   />
  </pattern>
</defs>
```

Example 7-15. Two shapes filled with two user-defined patterns (continued)

```
<desc>Rectangle and circle filled with user defined patterns</desc>
<rect x="20" y="20" width="300" height="300" fill="url(#myPattern)" stroke="black" />
<circle cx="500" cy="180" r="150" fill="url(#myPattern2)" stroke="black" />
</svg>
```

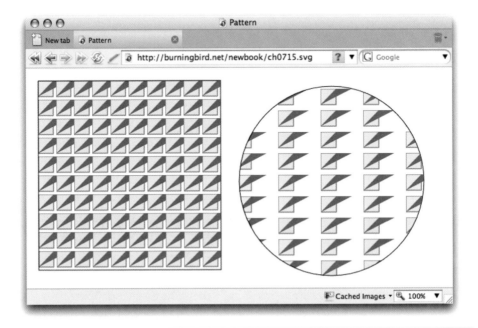

Figure 7-22. Using patterns to fill shapes

If you want to have a little fun with the example, resize the browser window and watch the pattern in the circle change as the "user coordinates" change. Since the application is using the default 100% width, changing the browser window changes the application width, which then changes the pattern and pattern spacing.

Revisiting the Viewport and the viewBox

For the most part, you won't need to make any modifications to the default coordinate system other than specifying the initial width and height of the canvas area supported:

```
<svg width="500" height="500">
```

In the end of the last section covering patterns, I also demonstrated one of the repercussions associated with the canvas size, particularly when using percentages. In that example, the pattern that was set to use the user coordinate system altered as the browser page sized, because the canvas was set to 100% of the browser page by default. When the page resized, so did the pattern.

The same holds with objects: if the objects are sized using explicit dimensions that exceed the canvas, they're truncated; otherwise, if they're sized using percentages, they'll resize with the canvas. The following tiny SVG application creates such an object, and if you load the page in a browser and resize it vertically and horizontally, the box will change size *and* shape:

```
<?xml version="1.0" standalone="no"?>
<!DOCTYPE svg PUBLIC "-//W3C//DTD SVG 1.1//EN"
  "http://www.w3.org/Graphics/SVG/1.1/DTD/svg11.dtd">
<svg
    xmlns="http://www.w3.org/2000/svg" version="1.1">
  <title>Resizing box</title>
  <rect x="20%" y="20%" width="20%" height="50%" fill="red" stroke="black" />
</svg>
```

If sizes are given in real units rather than in percentages, the resizing client space issue doesn't occur, but other issues could arise—including the aforementioned truncated image. There are multiple ways of controlling what is displayed within the canvas without having to abruptly cut off the image, even if the image supposedly seems to extend beyond the canvas borders. One way to do so is with the viewBox.

The viewBox

Note that the viewBox, like many other attributes in SVG, is case-sensitive, and it needs to be formatted exactly as it's spelled here in this book. It's defined with four values, each given in a string with commas or spaces between each value:

```
<svg width="500" height="500" viewBox="0 0 500 500" version 1.1>
```

In this SVG snippet, the first two values in the viewBox are the minimum x and y coordinate of the new user coordinate system, and the second two values specify the new width and height. In this example, the viewBox and the initial viewport are exactly the same, and what you see for the viewBox is what you would expect to see if no viewBox were given.

However, if the viewport changes size but the viewBox remains the same, whatever is contained within the viewBox could also change. For instance, if I cut the viewport in half along its vertical axis but leave the width the same, I would have the following:

```
<svg width="500" height="250" viewBox="0 0 500 500"
    xmlns="http://www.w3.org/2000/svg" version="1.1">
```

This viewBox has a 1:1 ratio with the viewport along the width, but the height now has a 2:1 ratio. What happens to any of the images contained within the document differs based on one other attribute: preserveAspectRatio.

preserveAspectRatio

There are several possible settings for preserveAspectRatio, impacting not only the size of the image but also its alignment.

If preserveAspectRatio is set to "none", then modifying the viewport will compress or expand the contents of the svg element accordingly. Example 7-16 contains an SVG page that creates a boxed triangle using the XML ENTITY notation, which allows us to define a block of XML that will then be used whenever the named entity is used within the document. It's then used in three nested svg elements, each given a different viewport in relation to the viewBox, which remains unchanged among the three. The first viewport is narrower than the viewBox, the second exactly the same size, and the third much longer.

Example 7-16. Exploring the results of using preserveAspectRatio and viewport size as a ratio of viewBox

```
<?xml version="1.0" encoding="UTF-8"?>
<!DOCTYPE svg PUBLIC "-//W3C//DTD SVG 1.1//EN"
  "http://www.w3.org/Graphics/SVG/1.1/DTD/svg11.dtd"
[ <!ENTITY TriangleBox "
<rect x='10' y='10' width='200' height='200' fill='yellow' stroke='red'/>
<path d='M20,190 L105,20 195,190 z' fill='green' stroke='white' />
">
]>
<svg  xmlns="http://www.w3.org/2000/svg" version="1.1">
    <desc>Decreasing width</desc>
   <!-- using nested SVG elements -->
    <svg width="100" height="500"
    viewBox="0 0 250 500"  preserveAspectRatio="none" >
    <title>viewBox</title>
    &TriangleBox;
    </svg>

    <desc>viewport and viewBox the same</desc>
    <svg x="110" width="250" height="500"
    viewBox="0 0 250 500"  preserveAspectRatio="none">
    <title>viewBox</title>
    &TriangleBox;
    </svg>

    <desc>now image is stretched vertically</desc>
    <svg x="350" width="250" height="800"
    viewBox="0 0 250 500"  preserveAspectRatio="none" >
    <title>viewBox</title>
    &TriangleBox;
    </svg>

</svg>
```

The preserveAspectRatio attribute is the same in all three nested svg elements: set to none. Figure 7-23 shows this SVG document opened in Safari 3.

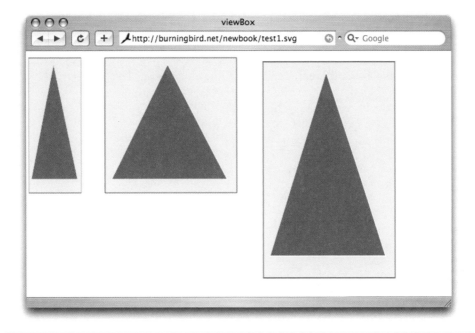

Figure 7-23. The same image opened with different viewports

What happens with other `preserveAspectRatios`? There are a variety of different options, but they're all based on a combination of the following:

xMin,YMin
> Align the `viewBox` element's minimum x or y coordinate with the smallest x, y value in the viewport.

xMid,YMid
> Align the x,y midpoint value for the `viewBox` element with the midpoint x,y value for the viewport.

xMax,YMax
> Align the minimum x plus width, minimum y plus height, with the maximum x and y value of the viewport, respectively.

These are combined in various options, such as xMinYMax, xMaxYMax, and so on, which explains why the Y is capitalized while the x is not: to follow the given camel case notation of the other SVG attributes (where the first letter is not capitalized, but each word in the name following is).

Two other options that affect how `preserveAspectRatio` works are `meet` and `slice`. If the `meet` option is given, the aspect ratio is maintained, the `viewBox` is visible in the viewport, and the `viewBox` is scaled however it needs to be to match the other options given.

A value of slice also means that the aspect ratio is maintained, but the viewBox is scaled to completely cover the viewport.

The only way to really get a handle on preserveAspectRatio is to look at the options in action. Example 7-17 shows several different nested svg elements, each given a matching rectangle to differentiate them in the document. The viewport for each SVG element is altered, as is the preserveAspectRatio setting.

Example 7-17. preserveAspectRatio's effects

```
<?xml version="1.0" encoding="UTF-8"?>
<!DOCTYPE svg PUBLIC "-//W3C//DTD SVG 1.1//EN"
  "http://www.w3.org/Graphics/SVG/1.1/DTD/svg11.dtd"
[ <!ENTITY TriangleBox "
<rect x='10' y='10' width='200' height='200' fill='yellow' stroke='red'/>
<path d='M20,190 L105,20 195,190 z' fill='green' stroke='white' />
">
]>
<svg  xmlns="http://www.w3.org/2000/svg" xmlns:xlink="http://www.w3.org/1999/xlink"
version="1.1">
    <title>viewBox and preserveAspectRatio</title>
    <defs>
      <text id="first">
        xMidYMid meet
      </text>
      <text id="second">
        xMaxYMax meet
      </text>
      <text id="third">
        xMinYMax slice
      </text>
      <text id="fourth">
        xMinYMin slice
      </text>
      <text id="fifth">
        xMaxYMax meet
      </text>
      <text id="sixth">
        xMaxYMax slice
      </text>
    </defs>
    <desc>Decreasing width</desc>
    <!-- using nested SVG elements -->

    <rect width="100" height="300" stroke="black" fill="none" />
    <svg width="100" height="300"
    viewBox="0 0 250 300"  preserveAspectRatio="xMidYMid meet" >
    &TriangleBox;
    </svg>
```

Example 7-17. preserveAspectRatio's effects (continued)

```
    <rect x="110" width="400" height="300" stroke="black" fill="none" />
    <svg x="110" width="400" height="300"
    viewBox="0 0 250 300"  preserveAspectRatio="xMaxYMax meet">
    &TriangleBox;
    </svg>

    <rect x="550" y="0" width="250" height="720" stroke="black" fill="none" />
    <svg x="550" y="0" width="250" height="720"
    viewBox="0 0 250 300"  preserveAspectRatio="xMinYMax slice" >
    &TriangleBox;
    </svg>

  <rect y="310" x="10" width="500" height="100"  stroke="black" fill="none" />
  <svg x="10" y="310" width="500" height="100"
   viewBox="0 0 250 300"  preserveAspectRatio="xMinYMid slice" >
   &TriangleBox;
   </svg>

  <rect y="420" x="10" height="200" width="250" stroke="black" fill="none" />
  <svg x="10" y="420" width="250" height="200"
   viewBox="0 0 250 300"  preserveAspectRatio="xMaxYMax meet" >
   &TriangleBox;
   </svg>

  <rect y="420" x="270" height="300" width="250" stroke="black" fill="none" />
  <svg x="270" y="420" width="250" height="300"
   viewBox="0 0 250 300"  preserveAspectRatio="xMaxYMax slice" >
   &TriangleBox;
   </svg>

  <!-- labeling diagrams -->
  <text x="20" y="280" fill="black" font-size="10">
    <tref xlink:href="#first" />
  </text>
  <text x="320" y="280" fill="black" font-size="10">
    <tref xlink:href="#second" />
  </text>
  <text x="720" y="680" fill="black" font-size="10">
    <tref xlink:href="#third" />
  </text>
  <text x="435" y="380" fill="black" font-size="10">
    <tref xlink:href="#fourth" />
  </text>
  <text x="20" y="600" fill="black" font-size="10">
    <tref xlink:href="#fifth" />
  </text>
  <text x="400" y="700" fill="black" font-size="10">
    <tref xlink:href="#sixth" />
  </text>

</svg>
```

To make it easier to identify each `preserveAspectRatio` effect, each is labeled in the image, using another text-based element not discussed in the earlier section on text: `tref`. The `tref` element isn't currently implemented in Firefox, but it is in Opera and Safari, as you can see in Figure 7-24.

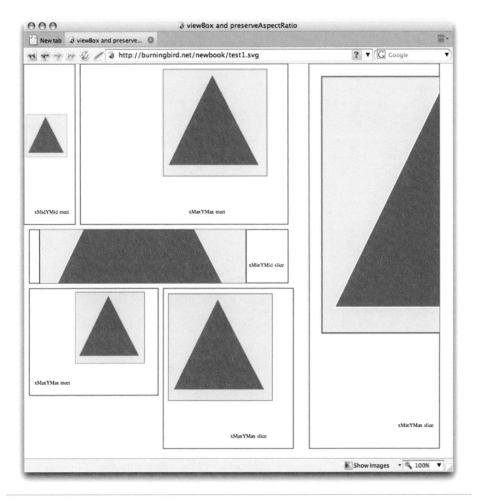

Figure 7-24. Several examples of differing preserveAspectRatio settings

In all the images, the aspect ratios are maintained. The long image with the ratio of `xMinYMax` slice is sliced once the image is resized so as to fill the viewport, and the minimum required aspect is met: in this case, the maximum Y value (setting of y plus height). To keep the aspect ratio, the image is sliced along the horizontal.

The same occurs with the image labeled `xMinYMid` slice, except this time the image is sliced along the vertical once the YMid midpoint constraint is met. In the other images where the `meet` option is given, the image is resized based on whether the other combinations of xMin/Max/Mid and YMin/Max/Mid are met. To see for yourself how these work, open the example in a browser (I recommend Opera, as this example seems to strain Safari to its maximum) and try changing the different `preserveAspectRatio` settings to see the result.

Changing the `viewBox` works fine when you're altering the user's view in relation to the viewport, but if you want to work on subsets of the image, you need to work with transformations.

Transformations

The Hello World example from the last chapter used two forms of transformation: `translate`, to change the coordinate origin, and `rotate`, to change the rotation of the coordinate system. Both were changed using the `transform` attribute, in this case applied to the ellipse that formed the orbits around the small planet image.

The important point to remember from that example is that it's the coordinate system that's changed; the image just reflects the modification. This applies to all transforms:

`translate (x, y)`
> Provides a translation (movement) of the x,y origin. If the y value is not provided, it's assumed to be 0.

`scale (x, y)`
> Scales the coordinate system. If the y value is not set, it's assumed to be 0.

`rotate (angle cx cy)`
> Rotates the coordinate system by the given angle about a point. If the optional cx and cy values are not given, it's assumed to be the origin of the current user coordinate system.

`skewX(angle)`
> Performs a skew transform along the x-axis.

`skewY(angle)`
> Performs a skew transform along the y-axis.

`matrix(a b c d e f)`
> Applies a transformation matrix.

I don't want to get into matrix mathematics, so I won't be covering the matrix transform. I do recommend that you read more about the transform associated with the SVG specification at the W3C site. In the meantime, the other transforms can be demonstrated without having to resort directly to the math.

In earlier examples in this chapter, I used the `translate` transform to move complete images in order to make room for other images. This is one of the simplest of the transforms, because all it really does is modify where "0,0" is within the newly transformed coordinate system. To move the grouping to the left, use a negative relative value for `translate`'s x value; to move it down, use a positive y value; and so on.

The rotate transform is a little trickier, primarily because it's a little more difficult for us to imagine what happens to the image after the transform. Figure 7-24 repeats the last figure from Chapter 6, which shows what happens when a group is rotated –90 degrees around the existing user coordinates and then moved to the right using a translate:

```
<?xml version="1.0" standalone="no"?>
<svg width="800px" height="600px" version="1.1"
    baseProfile="full"
    xmlns="http://www.w3.org/2000/svg"
    xmlns:xlink="http://www.w3.org/1999/xlink">
<defs>
<g id="grid">
<line x1="50" y1="50" x2="50" y2="400" stroke="red" stroke-width="2px" />
<line x1="50" y1="50" x2="400" y2="50" stroke="blue" stroke-width="2px" />
<ellipse rx="120" ry="50" cx="200" cy="200" fill="green" fill-opacity="0.1"
stroke="seagreen" stroke-width="4px"  />
</g>
</defs>
<use xlink:href="#grid" />
<use xlink:href="#grid" transform="rotate(-90) translate(-450,400)" />
</svg>
```

Though not used in the example, the rotate transform can also take a center point of the rotation, such as the following, which would rotate the element around an x,y point at 100,100:

```
transform="rotate(-45 100 100)"
```

The skew transforms perform in a manner similar to the skewing you might do with a paint editor like Photoshop. Think of grabbing a corner of an image and pulling it out or pushing it in, and the image compensates, but only along one axis, x or y. It's hard to describe the skewing, so it's best to demonstrate it.

Example 7-18 shows the same red square, 200 pixels on each side, that is then skewed 45 degrees horizontally and 15 degrees vertically.

Example 7-18. The skewX and skewY transforms

```
<svg width="800px" height="600px" version="1.1"
    baseProfile="full"
    xmlns="http://www.w3.org/2000/svg"
    xmlns:xlink="http://www.w3.org/1999/xlink">
<title>Skewing</title>
<defs>
  <rect id="myrect" width="200" height="200" fill="red" stroke="black" />
</defs>
<desc>Square, skewed horizontally 45 degrees</desc>
<use xlink:href="#myrect" transform="skewX(45)" />
<rect width="200" height="200" stroke="gray" stroke-dasharray="3,3" fill="none" />
```

Example 7-18. The skewX and skewY transforms (continued)

```
<desc>Same square, skewed vertically 15 degrees</desc>
<use xlink:href="#myrect" x="400" y="0" transform="skewY(15)" />
<rect x="400" width="200" height="200" y="0" fill="none" stroke="gray" stroke-
dasharray="3,3" />
</svg>
```

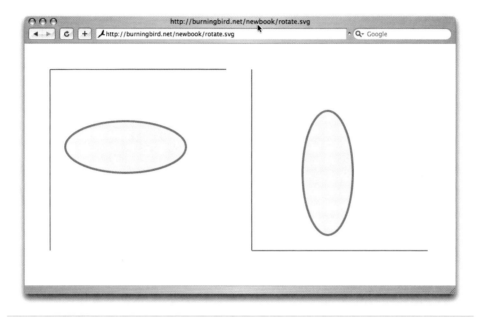

Figure 7-25. Different coordinate systems after a transform

Figure 7-26 shows the resulting page. The two dashed gray squares reflect the location of the red squares before they were skewed.

The scale transform concept is simpler to imagine, in that it scales the coordinate system, somewhat like viewBox did in the last section, except that it applies to only a particular element or group.

You can use multiple transforms in the same attribute. They are implemented in order, which means the order is important, and changing it will change the results. If you scale an image first and then perform a translate, the translate will operate within the new scaled coordinate system.

To demonstrate the importance of order when applying multiple transforms, Example 7-19 shows the same rectangle, starting from the same position and using the same types of transforms, but given in different orders.

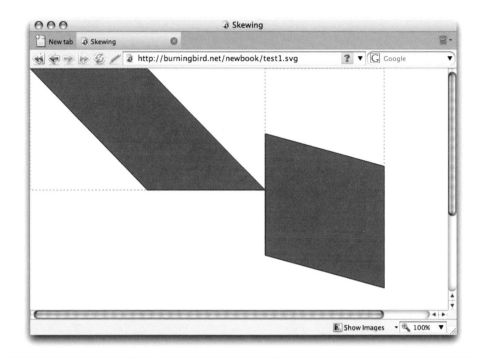

Figure 7-26. Results of applying x and y skewing to two similar rectangles

Example 7-19. Applying the same transforms in different orders

```
<?xml version="1.0" standalone="no"?>
<svg version="1.1"
    baseProfile="full"
    xmlns="http://www.w3.org/2000/svg"
    xmlns:xlink="http://www.w3.org/1999/xlink">
<title>Transform Order</title>
<defs>
  <rect id="myrect" width="100" x="400" y="100" height="100" stroke="black" />
</defs>
<g transform="translate(-50,-50)">
<use xlink:href="#myrect" fill="blue" transform="scale(1.5) translate(-300,-50)
skewX(15.0) rotate(15.0)" />
<use xlink:href="#myrect" fill="red" transform="translate(-300,-50) scale(1.5)
rotate(15.0) skewX(15.0)" />
<use xlink:href="#myrect" fill="lime" transform="skewX(15.0) rotate(15.0)
translate(-300,-50) scale(1.5)" />
<use xlink:href="#myrect" fill="yellow" transform="scale(1.5) skewX(15.0) rotate(15.0)
translate(-300,-50)" />
</g>
</svg>
```

Figure 7-27 shows the differences among the rectangles with the different transform order. The rectangles end up in different places, but the skew and rotate look pretty much as we would expect. If we used larger values for the rotate or scale, we wouldn't even see some of the rectangles—they would end up falling outside of the page canvas.

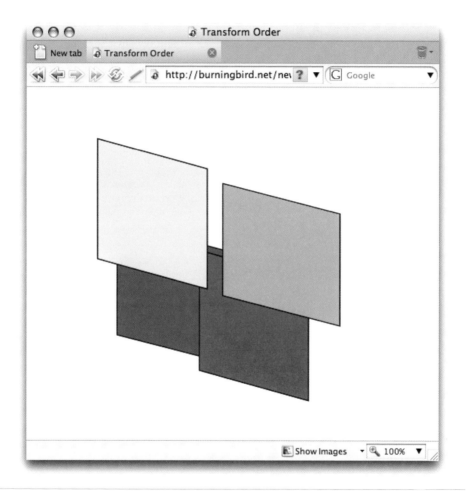

Figure 7-27. Applying the same transforms in different orders

The example just given grouped all of the rectangles within a group element, and moved the batch 50 pixels to the left and to the top. The use of the `transform` attribute is especially helpful when you're dealing with several elements that are grouped.

OK, though we really have only touched on the richness of SVG, it's time to look at a few tools and SVG in the wild, and then move on.

Two other major components of SVG, animations and filters, are demonstrated in later chapters.

SVG Tools

All you really need to create an SVG image is a text editor. However, creating more complex images may get a bit complicated to do manually. Instead, the majority of complex SVG images are created via some program or by using either a special-purpose SVG editor or an editor that supports the SVG vector type.

Many vector drawing tools generate SVG content: GIMP, GIMPShop, Adobe Illustrator, Corel's Xara Xtreme for Linux, as well as other Corel products. In addition, there are also some SVG-specific editors. Of these, one is the undisputed king of the hill: the open source Inkscape.

 Check your tool's documentation to see whether it supports SVG, either when a file is saved or through some form of export or conversion.

Inkscape

Inkscape is an open source SVG editor with versions for Windows, Linux, and Mac OS X. Once installed, opening the application shows a canvas area where new drawings can be created, a color palette along the bottom, and various tools along the left side. Among the tools are those to create circles and rectangles, a calligraphy pen effect, text, spirals, and a general polygon/star tool, as well as a freehand pencil and tool to create Bézier curves and straight lines.

 Download and read about Inkscape at *http://inkscape.org*. The site also includes links to multiple and single author galleries, as well as documentation.

Figure 7-28 shows the tool with several images drawn, including a spiral, a star, a calligraphic *S*, a gradient rectangle, a red circle, and a very crude attempt at a flower with leaves.

You might notice from Figure 7-28 that I'm not exactly a great freehand artist. Luckily, one of the features that Inkscape provides is the Trace Bitmap operation, which can trace a bitmap image to create an SVG path.

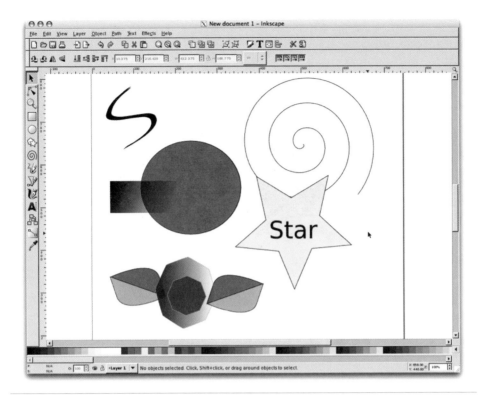

Figure 7-28. Playing around with various tools in Inkscape

There are multiple ways to discover the image to trace, including edge and brightness detection. I found that the trace functionality works best with images that have strong edges. To improve the results, you might want to run a Local Contrast Enhancement (LCE) on the original image (as described in Chapter 3) first. The trace also works extremely well with vector-based drawings, and is a good way to derive new drawings from pieces of existing artwork.

Figure 7-29 shows a bitmap trace on a bonsai tree against a light-colored background. Once you have the image, you can change the color fill of the edges and apply all sorts of transformations on the path. You can also open the SVG file in another SVG editor, such as Sketsa, discussed next.

Figure 7-29. Running a Bitmap Trace on an existing photograph

Sketsa

Unlike Inkscape, Sketsa is a commercial product, but it does have a 30-day trial. The trial can be downloaded at *http://www.kiyut.com/products/sketsa/index.html*, and requires the Java Runtime JRE 1.5 or above.

The toolset for Sketsa isn't overly rich. The tool does provide a nice real-time display of the actual SVG commands that are made to create each component in the image, as shown in Figure 7-30. It also matches the SVG elements and action more closely than Inkscape does.

The usual tools are supported, including a pen tool that will create curves when dragged, an image-embedding function, text, and shapes. What sets Sketsa apart is the very nice way of downloading plug-ins built into the tool (Figure 7-31), though there aren't as many plug-ins available as there are for Inkscape. It also is quite speedy, at least in the Windows version I tried. It has a ways to go before it's comparable to Inkscape, but it is nice to have a variety of options.

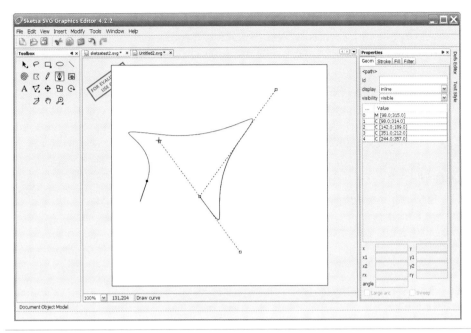

Figure 7-30. View of Sketsa with an image in process and SVG commands toward the right

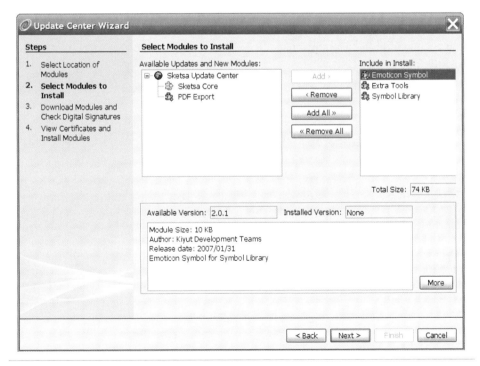

Figure 7-31. Sketsa's plug-in and module installer

SVG Converters and Other Tools

Because of the vector nature of SVG, it's actually pretty simple to create a PNG or JPEG from an existing SVG file. You can't right-click on the object and save it, but you can run a conversion tool.

One conversion tool is ImageMagick, which we'll look at later in this book. The W3C has a fun page, at *http://www.w3.org/2002/05/svg2stuff.html*, which uses XSLT to transform SVG into HTML or text. Instead of getting an image, you'll get a text representation of what's in the SVG—not a bad way to look at the image from an accessibility perspective, as the results focus on the textual description of the file objects (such as `title` and the `desc` elements).

One of the most useful SVG toolsets, Batik, is from the Apache organization and can be downloaded from *http://www.w3.org/2002/05/svg2stuff.html*. Batik is a Java application that requires a JRE 1.4+ runtime. You do need to make sure to follow the installation instructions for Batik, including using the Java JAR archive tool to extract and run the separate applications.

Batik can be used to convert Java applets or applications into SVG format, which is a great way to get the results onto the Web if you don't have a Java-enabled web site. If you are running a Java site, Batik also provides Java2D calls that can generate SVG.

You can also convert SVG files into raster format with the `batik-rasterizer` tool, using a command like the following:

```
java -jar batik-rasterizer.java someimage.svg
```

Batik also includes a "prettyprinter" for SVG files, converting them into nicely readable files:

```
java -jar batik-svgpp.jar someimage.svg
```

The installation also comes with a folder of sample SVG files, ready to learn from and play with. "Play with" is the operative term, too, because one of the advantages of SVG, as we'll see in the last section of this chapter, is the ability to learn from others' work and adapt it to our own use.

Another online tool is VectorMagic (at *http://vectormagic.com*). This tool takes a bitmap image that may or may not be a particularly great image, and creates a vector-based drawing in SVG of the image. The service isn't free, but you do get two free conversions to try out the tool.

Once you provide the image, the next step asks you to identify the type of image and provides its own guess. For instance, for a photo, it will ask, "We believe this image is a photograph," and you answer either yes or no, as shown in Figure 7-32.

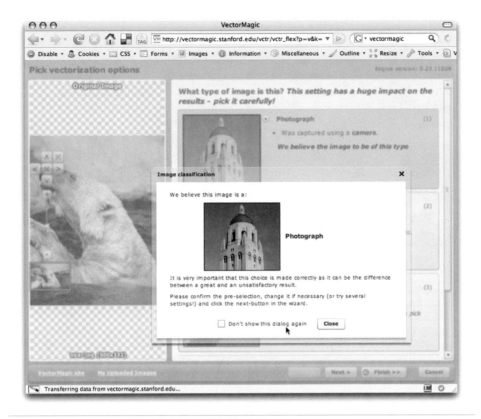

Figure 7-32. VectorMagic step confirming the type of image

The next step asks what quality we want for the result: high, medium, or low. The highest option will generate a larger file, but in this case I picked the high option. It took a couple of minutes, but Figure 7-33 shows the final result of vectorizing a photo of a bear playing in water.

At this point, I can save the file in PNG, SVG, or EPS format. I can also share it with others, reprocess it, or edit the result. It's a fascinating tool, and I definitely recommend you spend time with it.

> These are just a few of the SVG tools you can find online if you search on "SVG editors," "SVG convert," or "SVG tools." One place to start is SVG Implementations, at *http://www.w3.org/2002/05/svg2stuff.html*, and at the W3C's SVG site.

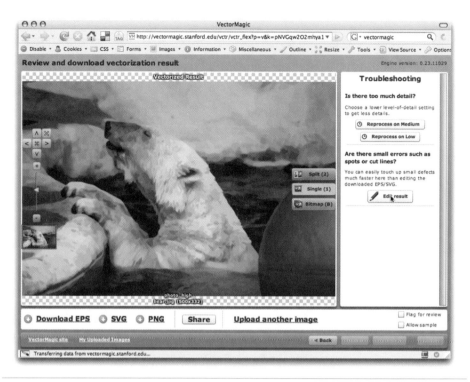

Figure 7-33. Finished result of converting a photo to a vector-based drawing

Static SVG Secrets

Now that you have a good idea of how to create an SVG image from scratch or with a tool, let's return to the concept of embedding SVG into web pages.

SVG has its greatest strengths in dynamic usage because it can be generated with any number of server-side technologies, becomes part of the web page, and can then be manipulated using client-side applications. SVG can also be used as illustrative images, or even as replacements for other PNG or JPEG images, though you have to be careful about browser support.

I've also used SVG as annotation directly in HTML text. For instance, I've used SVG to create tiny little musical notes, which I then used around a line of text to annotate the fact that the phrase that followed was from a song. I didn't even create the notes directly: I found copies of the SVG at Wikipedia and adapted them for my own use.

Finding and Adapting SVG

As more browsers support SVG, look for more instances of SVG to appear "in the wild." This is great because the more examples, the more we can learn from looking at the SVG used to create the individual files. Better yet: if the SVG is public domain or open for copying or reuse, we can start with a ready-made image and adapt.

 How does copyright apply to SVG? Just the same as it applies to photos and writing. Where SVG is different from a book or photo is that SVG (like the Web 2.0 graphics I covered in Chapter 5) can provide rich sources of learning, without our having to copy the exact SVG file or image.

For a weblog post, I wanted to provide a symbol to signify that a phrase I embedded was a line from a song. I could format it as italics and list the song and artist, but I wanted to add some form of musical notation.

I searched on SVG music notes and musical notation and found two pages at Wikipedia—a source of numerous such examples, and most are in the public domain or free to use under a Creative Commons license. The music notes SVG was found at *http://en.wikipedia.org/wiki/Image:Musical_notes.svg*, and the image is reproduced in Figure 7-34. The musical notation SVG is at *http://en.wikipedia.org/wiki/Image: Music_notation.svg*, and is reproduced in Figure 7-35.

 Another excellent source of SVG that you can use and adapt is the Open Clip Art Library, at *http://www.openclipart.org/*. Not only are the images available for use and adaptation, but also many of the artists provide the steps they took to create the images. I make extensive use of this library for my site designs.

Figure 7-34. Music notes SVG from Wikipedia

Figure 7-35. Music notation SVG from Wikipedia

Adapting the Image

All I needed from the two images was two different notes, one to use on either side of the phrase. Typically you can look at the coordinate information for the figures to determine the part of the image you want to use. Best of all, you don't have to worry about using some magic wand or color matching to separate the piece you want from the rest of the image.

Both images were made with Inkscape, so there was a lot of Inkscape-type data added into the image, which I didn't need. Once I had the image separated, I then needed to apply a group element around the existing image and a transform to size and position it just right. Example 7-20 shows the resulting file for one of the notes.

Example 7-20. Adapted SVG from a Wikipedia image

```
<?xml version="1.0" encoding="UTF-8" standalone="no"?>
<!-- Created with Inkscape (http://www.inkscape.org/) -->
<svg
   xmlns:svg="http://www.w3.org/2000/svg"
   xmlns="http://www.w3.org/2000/svg"
   xmlns:xlink="http://www.w3.org/1999/xlink"
   version="1.0"
   width="20"
   height="20">
  <g transform="scale(2.0) translate(-69,0)">
    <path
       id="text22657"
       d="M 71.664116,3.50414 L 71.664116,4.382789 L 71.727379,4.382789 L 71.790642,
4.382789 L 71.889051,4.488227 C 72.570882,5.205205 72.887197,5.739425 72.94343,6.238497 C
72.950459,6.336906 72.950459,6.540753 72.929372,6.681336 C 72.901255,6.983592 72.809875,
7.320994 72.690379,7.60919 C 72.641175,7.721657 72.641175,7.749774 72.662262,7.806008 C
72.704437,7.890358 72.802846,7.925504 72.887197,7.890358 C 72.908284,7.883329 72.929372,
7.862241 72.94343,7.848183 C 72.992634,7.791949 73.126189,7.370197 73.182423,7.082001 C
73.238656,6.814891 73.252715,6.64619 73.252715,6.38611 C 73.252715,6.161176 73.245685,
6.055738 73.196481,5.86595 C 73.105102,5.507461 72.950459,5.184117 72.598999,4.614753 C
72.275657,4.087564 72.205364,3.968067 72.092897,3.757191 C 71.917168,3.405732 71.825788,
3.103475 71.797671,2.794191 C 71.790642,2.752016 71.790642,2.695782 71.790642,2.667666 L
71.790642,2.62549 L 71.727379,2.62549 L 71.664116,2.62549 L 71.664116,3.50414"
       style="font-size:7.02919579px;font-family:Emmentaler" />
```

Example 7-20. Adapted SVG from a Wikipedia image (continued)

```
    <path
        id="rect22663"
        d="M 71.632479,2.555203 L 71.720344,2.555203 C 71.759286,2.555203 71.790636,2.
586553 71.790636,2.625495 L 71.790636,8.305412 C 71.790636,8.344354 71.759286,8.375704
71.720344,8.375704 L 71.632479,8.375704 C 71.593538,8.375704 71.562187,8.344354
71.562187,8.305412 L 71.562187,2.625495 C 71.562187,2.586553 71.593538,2.555203
71.632479,2.555203 z " />      <path
        id="text22667"
        d="M 70.890591,7.735721 C 70.588336,7.763837 70.293109,7.883334 70.033029,8.080151
C 69.751861,8.291027 69.562073,8.572195 69.491781,8.860392 C 69.477722,8.944742
69.477722,9.120472 69.49881,9.190764 C 69.519897,9.268085 69.555044,9.352436 69.597219,
9.408669 C 69.787007,9.654691 70.187672,9.746071 70.623481,9.633604 C 70.827328,9.57737
71.045233,9.471932 71.235021,9.331348 C 71.516189,9.120473 71.705977,8.839304 71.776269,
8.551107 C 71.790328,8.466757 71.790328,8.291027 71.76924,8.213706 C 71.698948,7.946597
71.474014,7.777896 71.143642,7.735721 C 71.080379,7.728692 70.946824,7.728692 70.890591,
7.735721"
        style="font-size:7.02919579px;font-family:Emmentaler" />
    </g>
</svg>
```

Notice the scale (2.0) value applied as a transform. If you look at the initial object paths, though they look large at first glance, they're really quite small. The grouped image elements also have to be moved to the left and top within the canvas area from their position to the right in the original image.

After the images have been isolated, the files cleaned up, and the objects transformed to the right size, next comes embedding them the page. I have two options: I can use an object to load the SVG file, or I can copy the SVG and embed it directly in the post. I chose to embed the SVG directly.

Embedding the Musical Notes

The SVG notes are going to be added directly into page text on either side of a phrase. Right off the bat, we know the container svg elements need to have a style setting applied to display the blocks inline, as compared to block in previous examples.

The block for the first note has the following SVG and g settings:

```
<svg:svg xmlns:svg="http://www.w3.org/2000/svg"
    width="13" height="14" style="display: inline;" >
    <svg:g  transform="scale(1.9) translate(-67,-3)" image-rendering='optimizeQuality'>
```

This SVG snippet introduces the last SVG attribute I'll be covering in this chapter: image-rendering. All image processing in browsers is based on a trade-off between speed of processing and quality. The image-rendering attribute provides a hint to the application that implements the SVG about how it should be processed. Following are the options for the attribute:

`auto`

Lets the agent determine the balance between speed and quality, but directs it to lean toward quality

`optimizeSpeed`

Use if speed is more important than quality

`optimizeQuality`

Use if quality is more important than speed

`inherit`

Inherit the settings from the parent element, if set

In the example, I wanted the best quality I could get considering how small the images were going to be:

```
<svg:svg style="display: inline;"
    version="1.0"
    width="15"
    height="15">
  <svg:g transform="scale(0.07) translate(-150,-50)" image-
rendering='optimizeQuality'>
```

The musical notes, in-page, are shown in Figure 7-35.

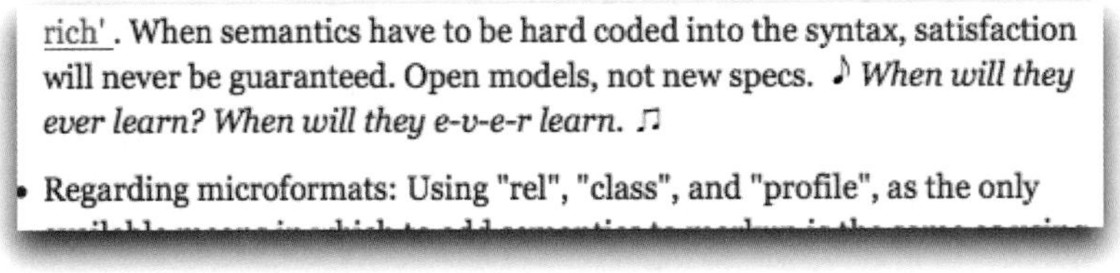

rich'. When semantics have to be hard coded into the syntax, satisfaction will never be guaranteed. Open models, not new specs. ♪ *When will they ever learn? When will they e-v-e-r learn.* ♫

• Regarding microformats: Using "rel", "class", and "profile", as the only

Figure 7-36. Musical notes embedded in the web page

I use SVG in other places in my web pages and add the SVG namespace in the first SVG block, in the header elements in my page. I had to repeat the SVG namespace because not only do my weblog posts get published to a web page, but they also get published to a syndication feed. This is just one of the many interesting challenges associated with incorporating SVG into our everyday work.

Issues with SVG Embedded into Pages

Aside from browser differences, there are some other issues with using SVG. For instance, when I've annotated text with my tiny musical notes in WordPress, all the SVG for the notes gets added into the post entry and stored into the database. This takes up more database file space than a link to a PNG file would. On the other hand, the PNG file also takes up space in the same system, so the SVG could be smaller, regardless of whether it's stored in the database.

In time, as more browsers implement the concept of linking to externally defined SVG elements (which are incorporated into the page with the use element, like the following), the less we'll have to repeat commonly recurring elements:

```
<use xlink:href="library.svg#musicnote1 />
```

The use element works with Opera, but not with Firefox. At least, not yet. However, this type of modularization will make the most significant change in the general use of SVG.

Another aspect of embedding SVG into something like a weblog post is the syndication feed created from the posts. By default, the post content is "escaped" and treated like HTML. If I want the SVG to show up as SVG, I would have to modify the feed program to treat all of the content like XHTML so that the SVG also works. Since support for both XHTML and SVG is still somewhat limited, it's best to just leave the feed as escaped HTML.

If I do leave the text as escaped HTML, I'll most likely want to run a filter on the output to remove the SVG, so it doesn't show up as long strings of text that aren't supposed to be published to the reader.

In addition, if I'm using objects or namespace declarations from elsewhere in the document, these may not be available in the feed or other publication and might have to be duplicated into the post.

Finally, it's important to ensure that the SVG degrades gracefully, by not providing essential information in SVG format. Not all browsers read SVG, and not all people who access your web pages appreciate purely visual images.

CHAPTER 8

CSS Über Zone

You've worked with CSS for a while, and feel pretty confident of what you're doing. Then you reach a site that has some slick design work and open up its stylesheet to see how the elements are styled. You read through the sheet, becoming increasingly mystified at all the weird and strange notation. Congratulations: you've just entered the CSS Über zone.

Probably the most revolutionary specification to come out of the W3C—after HTML, of course—is Cascading Style Sheets (CSS). With CSS, we finally had a way to define a stylesheet in one file and use it in hundreds of pages without having to litter font tags all throughout our web page content. Even though "style" is often about text, CSS can enhance your graphics or spare you from creating them.

The introduction of CSS hasn't been without problems, though. Even now, a decade after the first release of the specification, we still have to deal with browser differences. In addition, there are some aspects of CSS that aren't necessarily trivial. Using CSS to control multiple columns is always a bit of a challenge, especially when you get a site looking just right in one browser and it looks like garbage in another. Still, CSS has opened up a world of design possibilities and simplified web site maintenance at the same time. You're just not going to find many modern sites without at least some CSS.

CSS isn't complicated, but it is extensive. Entire books have been written about CSS that don't include all the many nuances of the specification and its uses. I'm not going to try to stuff an introduction to CSS into one chapter. Instead, I'm going to introduce you to some handy tips and how-tos I've discovered over the years that have simplified my use of CSS, as well as opened up new ideas and opportunities. You don't have to be an expert to appreciate or use anything from this chapter. Some basic exposure to the most common CSS style attributes is all you need.

This chapter focuses on CSS, level 2. The specification can be found at *http://www.w3.org/TR/REC-CSS2/*. Probably *the* book on CSS is Eric Meyer's *CSS: The Definitive Guide* (O'Reilly). If you need more of an introductory work, you might try *Head First HTML with CSS & XHTML*, also from O'Reilly.

Selector Magic

Most CSS in use is relatively straightforward, and the only notation you see in stylesheets is the pound sign denoting a class, a period for an id selector, curly brackets, semicolons, and maybe a colon for a pseudoclass. It's a shame, too, because most people probably do need more of CSS than they're using but don't know what's available—especially in regards to CSS selectors and the rules that govern which stylesheet rule gets applied to what object.

Using the Universal Selector to Globally Reset Whitespace

The common forms of selectors are the pound sign (#) for designating an id selector and a period (.) for a class. The king daddy of all selectors, though, is the universal selector, sometimes called the wildcard selector, designated by an asterisk (*).

What's the universal selector used for? It's not a commonly implemented selector, and shouldn't be used except where absolutely needed. Its use is necessary, though, if you want to globally reset the attributes of all elements.

As an example of where you might want to use the universal selector, one of the problems with positioning columns side by side is that there is default whitespace built into most HTML elements. For instance, an image is a block element with some padding, a header also has both padding and margin, and so on. The problem with these defaults is that if you're positioning columns side by side in a given element that's only so wide, and the two columns are sized to fit the space but the defaults kick it in, one column is going to end up being pushed down the page.

To eliminate *all* built-in margins and padding, use the following universal selector setting:

```
*   {
    margin: 0;
    padding: 0;
}
```

I've seen this trick called the "global whitespace reset," which is as good a name as any.

Curious to see how well you manage the CSS in your web site? Add this as the first line of your stylesheet. You'll quickly be able to find out whether your use of whitespace and your layout are based on CSS or on browser built-in values. First thing you'll notice, most likely, is that your paragraphs might seem off.

Want to remove even more default presentation settings? Set all elements to display: inline:

```
*   {
      margin: 0;
      padding: 0;
      display: inline;
}
```

Figure 8-1 shows the current front page from one of my sites with all style settings removed, and Figure 8-2 shows the same page but with a stylesheet that has only global whitespace reset, with the display: inline setting. Quite a difference.

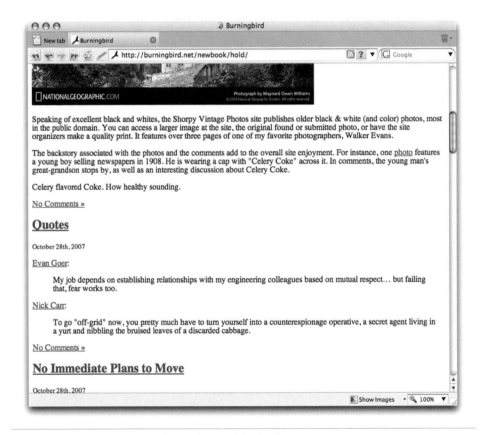

Figure 8-1. Page with no CSS styling and using default whitespace

Figure 8-2. Page with the global whitespace reset and all blocks set to display inline

Globally resetting whitespace can be an extreme measure, and might have unintended consequences. Another approach is to provide a more extensive set of "default" settings for your elements. Eric Meyer has provided just such a default stylesheet setting, at *http://meyerweb.com/eric/thoughts/2007/05/01/reset-reloaded/*.

What else can we do with selectors? Plenty.

Dropped Caps with Pseudoelements

You've most likely seen dropped caps in books or religious manuscripts. Dropped caps are the capitalized first letter in a paragraph or a section of paragraphs that is both increased in size and dropped down from the line of the rest of the sentence. All the other words in the sentence then flow around this dropped capital.

The CSS to create the dropped cap shown in Figure 8-3 is:

```
float: left;
font-family: Old English, Georgia,serif;
font-size: 2.0em;
font-style: italic;
margin-right: 0.06em;
margin-bottom:  -0.15em;
padding: 0 3px;
color: #006;
background-color: #fbfbfb;
```

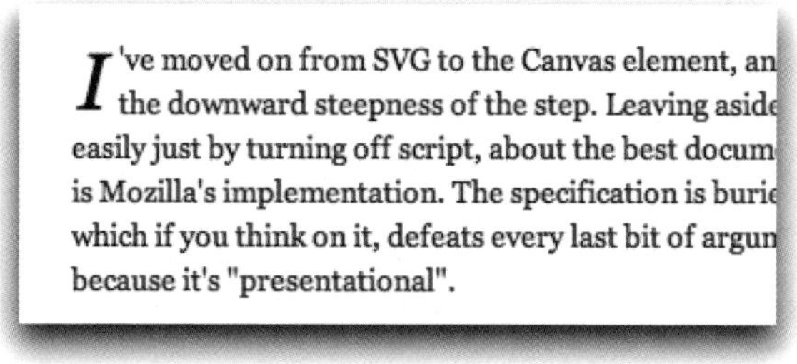

I've moved on from SVG to the Canvas element, an
the downward steepness of the step. Leaving aside
easily just by turning off script, about the best docum
is Mozilla's implementation. The specification is burie
which if you think on it, defeats every last bit of argun
because it's "presentational".

Figure 8-3. Example of CSS-styled dropped cap

This CSS floats the first letter to the left of the text, increases its size and line height, changes the font color, and adjusts the margin and padding. Nothing exciting, really. To use it, you can then include the letter to be dropped with a span element:

```
<span class="dropcap">T</span>he...
```

What a pain, though, having to manually include this everywhere it's needed. That's where the magic of selectors and *pseudoelements* come in. For the example shown in Figure 8-3, what's needed is a way to apply a style setting to the first letter of a paragraph, and only to the first paragraph within a given entry.

The first letter of the paragraph is handled easily enough with the first-letter pseudoelement:

```
p:first-letter {
...
```

When included in a stylesheet, every first letter starting a paragraph would begin with a dropped cap. To apply the dropped cap to just the first paragraph within some container element, such as a div, you can combine the first-letter pseudoattribute with the first-child pseudoelement, in combination with the descendant selector for the specifically identified div element:

```
div.entry p:first-child:first-letter{
...
```

The div element has a class selector of entry, and is a descendant selector by specifying the div element before the paragraph pseudoelements.

Now only the first paragraph gets the dropped letter. However, we're not done yet. If you include a blockquote with paragraphs within the same div element, such as:

```
<div class="entry">
<p>...</p>
<blockquote>
<p>...</p>
</blockquote>
</div>
```

both the first paragraph of the blockquote and the first paragraph in the div element container would have dropped caps. Setting the div element as a descendant selector means that style setting is inherited by contained elements, including the blockquote.

To ensure that only the first paragraph has a dropped cap, use the child selector (>) with the div element:

```
div.entry > p:first-child:first-letter
```

The child selector differs from the descendant in that the style setting is only applied on paragraphs that are direct children of the div element, and the setting is now inherited by other contained elements.

This combination of selectors and the style setting results in the dropped cap shown earlier in Figure 8-3:

```
div.entry > p:first-child:first-letter
{
    background-color: #fbfbfb;
    color: #006;
    float: left;
    font-family: Old English, Georgia,serif;
    font-size: 2.5em;
    font-style: italic;
    margin-bottom: -0.15em;
    margin-right: 0.06em;
    padding: 0 3px;
}
```

Elements inherit a variety of style settings, depending on what class or identifier they're given, the global element settings, and so on. Elements can also inherit style settings from more than one class, as described in the next section.

Specificity and Multiple Class Names

Aside from using the magic combinations of selectors, as just described, there are two ways to attach a specific CSS style setting from a stylesheet to an element: through the id attribute and through the class attribute. The id attribute is used to identify a specific style setting for one individual item; the class attribute is meant to be used with multiple elements:

```
<div class="content">
...
</div>
```

In recent years, the class attribute has been used for more than CSS styling—it's also used for microformats, for accessibility, even for dynamic Ajaxian effects. Outside of the div element, it's the hardest-working web page component:

```
<div class="content leftside address">
...
</div>
```

Leaving aside the non-visual uses of class, multiple stylesheet classes can be used for one or more elements, and the rendering agent will merge the effects based on certain rules and priorities.

One such rule is *specificity*, which states that a stylesheet setting assigned to a specific element tag has priority over a more general setting. As an example, consider the following style settings:

```
p.inner { color: #00ff00; }
div p { color: #ff0000; }
p { color: #0000ff; }
```

Normally, when more than one style setting can apply to an element, the last one listed is the one that's applied. However, in this example, the selector specifying a paragraph that is a descendant of the div element has a higher specificity than the more general paragraph (as long as the paragraph is contained within some div element). At the same time, if the paragraph is given a specific class name, inner, it has an even higher specificity. For the following then:

```
<div>
<p class="inner">
...
</p>
</div>
```

the font color would be green (#00ff00) because the class selector has a higher specificity than the descendant selector (div p) and a higher specificity than the general paragraph setting.

All of this could get confusing, except that the W3C provides a handy calculation algorithm that can be used to determine the specificity for a given element. Consider a three-digit number, with each decimal position calculated as follows:

- Count the number of ID attributes. This is assigned to the hundreds.
- Count the number of other attributes and classes. This is assigned to the tens.
- Count the number of element names, assigned to the ones.
- Ignore pseudoelements.

Given the following stylesheet setting, what would its specificity value be?

```
div > p:first-child:first-letter
```

No identifier is given, nor is a class; two HTML elements are specified, and pseudo-elements are ignored. The specificity is 0 (identifiers) + 0 (attributes and pseudoclasses) + 2 (HTML elements), for a total of 2.

Given the following:

```
img [alt]
```

one HTML element is specified, as well as one attribute (the square brackets denote that the setting applies only to images that have an `alt` attribute). The value is 0 (identifiers) + 1 (attributes and pseudoclasses) + 1 (HTML element), again for a specificity of 2. The following, though:

```
p#right
```

specifies an identifier, for a value of 100 for #right and 1 for the element—a whopping 101. As you can see, adding an identifier to an element more or less guarantees that the identifier stylesheet setting overrides all others.

The following:

```
div #reds .colors p
```

has a specificity of 112: 100 for the identifier (#reds), 10 for the class (.colors), and 2 for the two elements (div and p).

Calculating the specificity is a little tricky, especially when you add in the normal CSS inheritance, where descendant elements inherit style settings, following yet another set of CSS application rules. CSS inherited values, however, have no specificity.

For instance, if the font-family for the entire page is set using the body element, and paragraphs are given a different font family, even though paragraphs are descendants of the overall document, the body setting applies only to elements that don't have other, more specific settings. The paragraph stylesheet setting would override the body setting for paragraphs. Precise specification of both identifier and class help to protect against unintended inheritance effects.

What happens, then, if multiple classes are given for one attribute? Where there is no conflict, the style settings are combined. Where there is a conflict, the classes are applied in the order that they occur in the stylesheet, not in the order that they occur in the class attribute. The later classes in the stylesheet override the earlier classes.

As I said earlier, multiple classes are used for accessibility and semantics, but that doesn't mean that the class names couldn't serve multiple purposes: providing semantics, accessibility, and a visual design element. One use of classes on elements is for microformats, which are ways of using specific structures of HTML combined with classes to designate a specific type of information, such as hCard for addresses and organizations and hCalendar for event information:

```
<div id="content">
  <div class="vevent">
    <h3 class="summary">Fun Graphics</h3>
    <p class="description">Having fun with web graphics!</p>
    <p>To be held on <abbr class="dtstart" title="2008-03-12T08:30:00-05:00">12 March
2008 from 8:30am EST</abbr>
    until <abbr class="dtend" title="2008-03-12T09:30:00-05:00">9:30am EST</abbr></p>
    <p>Location: <span class="location">The St. Louis Arch</span></p>
  </div>
</div>
```

Attaching a visual element to the semantic markup is as simple as providing stylesheet information. Example 8-1 shows a page with a single hCalendar event and an embedded stylesheet providing visualization to the semantic information. Note the use of descendant selectors to add precision in case a specific class, such as "description," can be used in more than one context.

Example 8-1. Formatting the semantics of microformats

```
<!DOCTYPE html PUBLIC "-//W3C//DTD XHTML 1.0 Strict//EN"
        "http://www.w3.org/TR/xhtml1/DTD/xhtml1-strict.dtd">
<html xmlns="http://www.w3.org/1999/xhtml" lang="en" xml:lang="en">
<head>
<meta http-equiv="Content-Type" content="text/html; charset=utf-8" />
<title>hCalendar</title>
<style type="text/css">
#content
{
   margin: 40px;
}
.vevent
{
  margin: 10px 30px;
  padding: 10px;
}
.vevent .summary
{
 font-size: larger;
 padding: 5px;
 color: #00f;
}

.vevent .description
{
   margin-left: 20px;
   font-style: italic;
}
.dtstart,.dtend
{
   color: #f00;
}
```

Example 8-1. Formatting the semantics of microformats (continued)

```
.vevent .location
{
    color: #00f;
}
</style>
</head>
<body>
<div id="content">
  <div class="vevent">
    <h3 class="summary">Fun Graphics</h3>
    <p class="description">Having fun with web graphics!</p>
    <p>To be held on <abbr class="dtstart" title="2008-03-12T08:30:00-05:00">12 March 2008
from 8:30am EST</abbr>
    until <abbr class="dtend" title="2008-03-12T09:30:00-05:00">9:30am EST</abbr></p>
    <p>Location: <span class="location">The St. Louis Arch</span></p>
  </div>
</div>
</body>
</html>
```

The result, shown in Figure 8-4, has a nicer presentation than one using default formatting, and doesn't impact either the accessibility of the information or the semantics. Because the page is using an established microformat, newer browsers that support established microformats can also access the data, transferring it to your appointment or address book application.

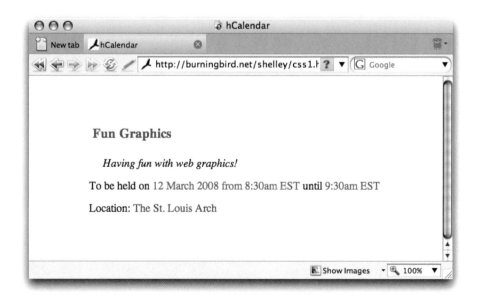

Figure 8-4. Visually formatted hCalendar page entry

As I just demonstrated, there is no reason not to attach a visual component to class names added primarily for semantics. Comes to that, there's no reason that multiple class names can't be used, each created in such a way that a different visualization is created with each combination of classes.

Example 8-2 has a simple page with three images and two different stylesheet settings to visually format the images. The first image is styled with the class thumb, the second with the class yellow, and the third with both classes.

Example 8-2. Multiple classes combined for visual effect

```
<!DOCTYPE html PUBLIC "-//W3C//DTD XHTML 1.0 Strict//EN"
        "http://www.w3.org/TR/xhtml1/DTD/xhtml1-strict.dtd">
<html xmlns="http://www.w3.org/1999/xhtml" lang="en" xml:lang="en">
<head>
<meta http-equiv="Content-Type" content="text/html; charset=utf-8" />
<title>hCalendar</title>
<style type="text/css">

# content { margin: 20px; padding: 20px }.thumb { border: 1px solid #000;  margin: 0px;
padding-bottom: 25px; background-image: url(magnify.gif); background-position: right
bottom; background-repeat: no-repeat; }

.yellow { background-color: #ff0; margin: 15px; padding: 15px }
</style>
</head>
<body>
<div id="content">
<img src="robin1thumb.jpg" class="thumb" alt="Robin" />
<img src="robin1thumb.jpg" class="yellow" alt="Robin" />
<img src="robin1thumb.jpg" class="thumb yellow" alt="Robin" />

</div>
</body>
</html>
```

Figure 8-5 shows the page with the three images. Notice in the third image how the style settings for thumb, such as the background image and border, are applied in addition to the settings for yellow, which specify a different padding amount, background color, and margin. Since the yellow style setting is positioned later in the embedded stylesheet than thumb, its attributes would override any overlapping values.

True class inheritance.

 For more on microformats, see *http://microformats.org*. For a fun look at CSS specificity, see the Specificity Wars, at *http://www. stuffandnonsense.co.uk/archives/css_specificity_wars.html*.

Figure 8-5. Demonstrating class "inheritance" in CSS

CSS Tips and Tricks

If you search on "CSS tricks," you'll find an assortment of handy CSS tips and tricks. Many of the tips are so popular and so important, they're repeated in most lists, and rightfully so. Several have to do with bypassing browser differences, others are for solving common problems, and still others are for adding fun effects.

Here are some of my favorite CSS effects I've discovered and applied over the years. Among them are old favorites, and hopefully there are some new ideas for you to try. It's not a comprehensive list by any means. I've tried to focus on effects that aren't duplicated in many of the other CSS lists found on the Web.

Same Length Sidebars

Multiple columns laid out side by side are fairly common. Sometimes all the columns have the same background color, and sometimes they don't. When different background colors are used and the layout is maintained using CSS, sometimes the color for one column comes up short for the shorter column. Some people don't mind, and others really hate the look. I'm one of the latter.

To ensure that the color extends all the way down to the bottom of the page for the shorter column of a two (or more) column layout, use a background image that has the same width and color of the columns as the background image for the multi-column container.

To start, create a new image in your favorite photo/paint program, as wide as you want your content area, but make it short—it's going to repeat, and you don't need to increase the image file size unnecessarily. You can vary the background image by adding borders, additional color stripes, even a repeating design. All that matters is that the image needs to gracefully repeat vertically, so make sure any patterned items are set up accordingly. Figure 8-6 shows an example of a background image.

Figure 8-6. Created background image

Add the new background image to the container that holds your columns, making sure that the background color for the columns is not set, so as not to override the pattern of the background. Use CSS to make the background repeat vertically.

Example 8-3 shows just such a page, with two columns and a footer, all wrapped in a `wrapper` element.

Example 8-3. The background image column trick

```
<!DOCTYPE html PUBLIC "-//W3C//DTD XHTML 1.0 Strict//EN"
  "http://www.w3.org/TR/xhtml1/DTD/xhtml1-strict.dtd">
<html xmlns="http://www.w3.org/1999/xhtml">
<head>
<title>Background Image Trick</title>
<meta http-equiv="Content-Type" content="text/html; charset=utf-8" />
<style type="text/css">
body
{
        margin: 0;
        padding: 0;
}
#wrapper
{
        background-color: #ff0;
        background-image: url(background.jpg);
        background-postion: top left;
        background-repeat: repeat-y;
        margin: 0 auto;
        width: 800px;
}
#sidebar
{
        float: right;
        width: 200px;
}

#sidebar ul
{
        background-color: #fff;
        margin-right: 35px;
}
#content
```

Example 8-3. The background image column trick (continued)

```
{
        float: left;
        padding: 15px;
        width: 500px;
}

#footer
{
        clear: both;
        padding: 20px;
}
</style>
</head>
<body>
<div id="wrapper">
<div id="content">
<!-- insert content here -->
</div>
<div id="sidebar">
   <ul>
     <li>Option 1</li>
     <li>Option 2</li>
   </ul>
</div>
<div id="footer">
<p>Footer brought to you by me</p>
</div>
</div>
</body>
</html>
```

The two columns are positioned using the CSS float attribute, which aligns them side by side. To ensure that the footer clears both columns, the CSS attribute setting clear: both is added to the footer element; this ensures the footer is pushed below both columns. Figure 8-7 shows the page opened in Opera, with some filler in the content column to better demonstrate the background image effect.

div Play Dough

We don't want to add to page complexity by dumping a bunch of div or other elements into the page design. At the same time, though, we don't want to shortchange ourselves by not trying out some new web design tricks just because they add more divs to an existing stack of page elements.

Ten years ago, I wrote, "The div element is the play dough of the Web." You can use it to group, contain, position, and frame. It has no semantics, so using it anywhere won't affect the meaning of the page. It has no accessibility constraints, so its use won't impact adversely on screen readers.

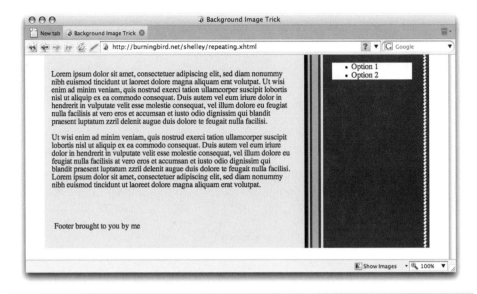

Figure 8-7. Using the background image column trick

The div is not a replacement for other HTML elements. For instance, it's not a header element, and shouldn't be used in place of any of the hi–h6 header elements. It's also not a list item, and shouldn't be used in place of ul/li or ol/li. Nor is it a quote (blockquote), citation, address, abbreviation, and so on, to be used in place of these other, more meaningful page elements.

The div is a way to define a section of the web page: nothing more, nothing less. However, for all the places where it shouldn't be used, it's the most important page element and, frankly, we'd still be back with layout-by-tables if it weren't for the div element.

Aside from its layout capability, there are other uses for the div element. Earlier in this book, I covered how you can add shadows, both internally in a picture and to a picture itself. You can also use CSS to create a shadow, using a combination of div elements and/or transparency.

Example 8-4 contains a web page, complete with CSS stylesheet, that contains a content section and an overlaying image block with associated shadow. The image block and shadow are both positioned absolutely, and the shadow is semitransparent and offset from the original block. To ensure that the shadow lies under the image block, the image block's z-index (position in the stack) is set to 2, which is a higher level than the default of 1.

Example 8-4. Web page demonstrating a "shadow" div element

```
<!DOCTYPE html PUBLIC "-//W3C//DTD XHTML 1.0 Strict//EN"
        "http://www.w3.org/TR/xhtml1/DTD/xhtml1-strict.dtd">
<html xmlns="http://www.w3.org/1999/xhtml" lang="en" xml:lang="en">
<head>
<meta http-equiv="Content-Type" content="text/html; charset=utf-8" />
<title>Shadowed Div</title>
<style type="text/css">
body
{
    background-color: #ccf;
}
#content
{
    width: 500px;
    margin: 20px auto;
    background-color: #fff;
    padding: 10px;
}
#container
{
    position: absolute;
    left: 200px; top: 170px;
    padding: 20px;
    border: 1px solid #000;
    background-color: #fff;
    z-index: 2;
}

#shadow
{
    position: absolute;
    left: 210px; top: 180px;
    width: 325px; height: 266px;
    background-color: #000;
    filter:alpha(opacity=40); -moz-opacity:0.4; opacity:0.4;
}
</style>
</head>
<body>
<div id="content">
<h1>Web Page Contents</h1>
<!-- enter some stuff here --></div><div id="container"><img src="robin1thumb.jpg"
alt="Robin" /></div><div id="shadow"></div></body></html>
```

The actual content is removed from the example to save book space, but Figure 8-8 shows the page loaded into Safari. (More about the opacity settings in Chapter 9.)

What's interesting about the effect is that it's fixed in the page, whereas the content moves about as the page width is modified, as shown in Figure 8-9. This isn't a bad way to display images in the page, especially when you use scripting for a dynamic effect. We'll discuss this in Chapter 10, which covers dynamic effects with HTML and CSS.

Figure 8-8. Shadow effect using a div element and transparency

Figure 8-9. Impact of a fixed object in a fluid design

The shadow isn't as good as one we might create using SVG or a paint program, because it doesn't have the nice, soft Gaussian Blur, but it is a nice effect, it does look like a shadow, and it is easily created with CSS.

divs can also be used to create a frame-like effect, especially for photos or other images. The key to this effect is to make use of CSS outset and inset border styles, switching between the styles with each frame/panel surrounding the image. Example 8-5 demonstrates this effect, using two "frames" and two "panel inserts" around the image.

Example 8-5. Demonstrating "frames" with div elements and CSS

```
<!DOCTYPE html PUBLIC "-//W3C//DTD XHTML 1.0 Strict//EN"
        "http://www.w3.org/TR/xhtml1/DTD/xhtml1-strict.dtd">
<html xmlns="http://www.w3.org/1999/xhtml" lang="en" xml:lang="en">
<head>
<meta http-equiv="Content-Type" content="text/html; charset=utf-8" />
<title>Frames</title>
<style type="text/css">
body
{
    background-color: #ccf;
}

#outerframe { margin: 0 auto; width: 800px; background-color: #003; border: 2px outset
#ccc; }
#innerframe {
        color: #333;
        background:#ccc;
        margin: 5px;
        border: 2px outset #999
        }
#innerpanel, #innerpanel2 {
        background-color: #fff;
        margin: 20px;
        padding: 10px;
        text-align: center;
        border: 2px inset #ccc;
        }
img { border: 2px outset #ccc; }
</style>

</head>
<body>
<div id="outerframe">
<div id="innerpanel">
<div id="innerframe">
<div id="innerpanel2">

<img src="robin1wunder.jpg" alt="robin" />
</div>
</div>
```

Example 8-5. Demonstrating "frames" with div elements and CSS (continued)

```
</div>
</div>
</body>
</html>
```

Figure 8-10 shows the effect. The key, as pointed out in the figure, is to attempt to alternate the light/dark highlight/shadow areas to create a three-dimensional effect.

Figure 8-10. Creating an image frame with div elements and CSS

The effect can be varied. For instance, normally when a picture is framed, the frame itself is wood, metal, or plastic, and the insets are cloth of some kind. Textured background images can be used to emulate this, as shown in Figure 8-11.

In this version, the second inner panel is removed, the outside frame component is made quite small (more to add dimensional effect than a frame), and the inner panel is made wider. A wood background is used for the "frame," and cloth for the panel.

Figure 8-11. Using textured background images to add to the frames effect

(For more details, the example file, *materials.html*, is included in the downloadable examples for this book.)

The advantage of this approach is that you can add some framing effects to galleries or other online photo displays, which can resize to fit the images and be used again and again. Additionally, the background images used for the frames actually get cached locally, so using this effect is more bandwidth-friendly than attaching the effect directly to a photo using a photo editor.

 Where to get background images? Search for "textured background images" in your favorite search engine. There are several sites that provide background images for free as long as you provide credit.

Horizontal Lists

From a semantic perspective, when creating a web page menu, we should use the list type HTML elements, such as the unordered list and list item (ul/li). However, these have their own default presentation, including that the list items are laid out vertically. We'd rather have a horizontally presented menu.

Example 8-6 shows a web page with a high-level menu as a thin strip at the very top of the page. The idea is that high-level menu items are presented as part of the header, either right above or right below any header graphic and title. In the next chapter, we'll look at this design concept more closely, but for now, we'll look at using ul/li elements to implement this horizontal menu.

Example 8-6. Using lists as horizontal menu items

```
<!DOCTYPE html PUBLIC "-//W3C//DTD XHTML 1.0 Strict//EN"
        "http://www.w3.org/TR/xhtml1/DTD/xhtml1-strict.dtd">
<html xmlns="http://www.w3.org/1999/xhtml" lang="en" xml:lang="en">
<head>
<meta http-equiv="Content-Type" content="text/html; charset=utf-8" />
<title>List Items as Horizontal Menu</title>
<style type="text/css">
* { padding: 0; margin: 0; }
body
{
    background-color: #ccf;
    font-size: 14px;
    line-height: 140%;
}

p   {margin: 10px 5px;}

h1 { margin: 15px 0; }

#content
{
    width: 500px;
    margin: 0 auto;
    background-color: #fff;
    padding: 10px;
}

ul {      background-color: #003;      width: 100%; height: 20px;
             padding: 3px 20px;      list-style: none;       }

ul li{    display: inline;
    color: #fff;
    font-weight: bold;
    font-size: 14px;
    margin: 3px; padding: 5px 15px 5px;
    border-right: 1px solid #fff;
    font-family: Arial,Helvetica,sans-serif;
```

Example 8-6. Using lists as horizontal menu items (continued)

```
}
</style>

</head>
<body>
<ul id="menu">
<li>Home</li>
<li>Archives</li>
<li>About</li>
<li>FAQ</li>
<li>Photos</li>
</ul>
<div id="content">
<h1>Web Page Contents</h1>
<!-- add material -->
</div>
</body>
</html>
```

Figure 8-12 shows the page, with content added to pad out the page. Stripping the list-like default styles for the ul/li elements is accomplished by setting the list-style attribute to none on the ul element, and setting the display to inline for the list items. The page also uses the global reset trick, to remove any other default padding.

Figure 8-12. Using lists as horizontal menus

Earlier I mentioned specificity with CSS. In the previous example, the style change would apply to all list items. To make the style change more specific, you'll want to add a class name, such as:

```
#menu ul li { ...}
```

The Unit Font Trick

I can't remember where I picked this one up online, but it's a terrific CSS trick. From an accessibility perspective, we should be using "em" rather than pixels or points to set font sizes. By using "em" units, when people resize the page contents in order to see the text better, the text actually resizes rather than stays one fixed height. The only problem I've had with "em" units is understanding their sizes from a page perspective. I'm used to thinking in pixels when I lay out a page.

Since the default size of text in most browsers is 16 pixels, which is equivalent to 1em, and all other sizing is relative to this value, setting the overall font size of a document body to 62.5% changes the em unit size to 10 pixels. Then, a font size of 1.5em is equivalent to 15 pixels, 2em to 20 pixels, and so on.

```
body { font-size: 62.5% }
```

Of course, there are a couple of caveats with this CSS trick. First, anything that doesn't have a CSS font size set is going to appear much smaller with this overall body font setting. In addition, smaller and larger font attribute values have a different impact, and headers and general line-heights for text are smaller.

This goes back to the global reset discussed earlier and the importance of eliminating default settings in the page, so that you can tell which items still need to be styled. Don't depend on default settings—you'll end up regretting doing so at some point.

Multiple Stylesheets and Stylesheet Switchers

Sites can include references to multiple stylesheets: one stylesheet for printing, one for mobile, and a combination of other stylesheets controlling HTML elements for displaying images or controlling the web site. How the stylesheets are linked into the page determines their purpose. If the media attribute type is screen, the stylesheet is for viewing on the Web; handheld is for mobile; print for print; and so on.

You can also control what stylesheet is used with a conditional statement, though this approach is focused on managing IE differences. One of my web sites has the following stylesheet links:

```
<link rel="stylesheet" href="http://burningbird.net/wp/wp-content/themes/hubble/
style.css" type="text/css" media="screen" />
<!--[if gt IE 6]>
<link rel="stylesheet" type="text/css" href="http://burningbird.net/wp/wp-content/
themes/hubble/iestyle.css" />
```

```
<![endif]-->
<!--[if IE 6]>
<link rel="stylesheet" type="text/css" href="http://burningbird.net/wp/wp-content/
themes/hubble/ie6style.css" />
<![endif]-->
<link rel="stylesheet" href="http://burningbird.net/wp/mobile.css" type="text/css"
media="handheld" />
<link rel="stylesheet"
   type="text/css"
   media="print" href="http://burningbird.net/wp/print.css" />

<link rel="stylesheet" href="http://burningbird.net/wp/mtwimg.css" type="text/css"
media="screen" />

<link rel="stylesheet" href="http://burningbird.net/fullcomments/comments.css"
type="text/css" media="screen" />
```

The first stylesheet, *style.css*, is the main one, followed by a conditional stylesheet to manage IE differences. Next come the mobile and print stylesheets—pretty plain, stripping most images and gewgaws from the page display. The code also includes a link to stylesheets for my comments system and my image display for expanding thumbnails.

All of these sheets are meant to be accessed at the same time, with only the media type determining whether a sheet is loaded, or the HTML conditional statement for IE 6. Another option for loading multiple stylesheets is placing the control for which sheet is loaded into the hands of the web page readers. This option is called the *stylesheet switcher*.

A stylesheet switcher is a piece of code that works with browser cookies to record a person's preference on what stylesheet to use to view a site and loads the appropriate sheet. The code can be managed with JavaScript, or on the server side with a language such as PHP (if the site normally uses PHP, of course).

Most of the time the stylesheet switcher can be used to manage accessibility issues, such as providing zoomed-in text or eliminating images. However, you can also use it to provide stylesheets with different color schemes, or even completely different themes entirely. The world is open, and the choice is yours.

The key to a stylesheet switcher is providing alternate as well as primary stylesheets, and then using code and web cookies to select and record preferred stylesheets. At one point in time, I provided the same stylesheet theme but with the choice of two different types of fonts: serif or sans serif. The stylesheet was the same except for the fonts used, and I included both stylesheets in my page headers with the following:

```
<link rel="stylesheet" title="default"  media="screen" href="/themes/burningbird/
style-serif.css" type="text/css" />
<link rel="stylesheet" title="sans" media="screen" href="http://weblog.burningbird.net/
themes/burningbird/style-sans.css" type="text/css" />
```

It's important to provide a `title`, as this is how JavaScript can access the stylesheets. You'll also need to provide a way for people to select their preferred stylesheet. The following example uses a form and inline event handlers:

```
<form action="http://your site.com">
<input id="serif" name="serif" type="button" class="search-button" value="Serif"
onclick="setActiveStyleSheet('default'); return false;" />
<input id="sans" name="sans" type="button" class="search-button" value="Sans"
onclick="setActiveStyleSheet('sans'); return false;" />
</form>
```

Links could be used instead of the form buttons. As for the code, the popular web site A List Apart provided a downloadable JavaScript file that can be embedded into a web page and used to manage the mechanical pieces of the stylesheet switcher. I adapted this for my own use, and it's included in the examples for the book. The code is clean and simple to read, and I'll leave explorations of how it works as a personal exercise. For now, all that's left to do is add the script to the site. Example 8-7 shows a web page with two stylesheets, one in blues, one in yellows, and two links to select the stylesheets, as well as a `script` tag to include the stylesheet switching code.

Example 8-7. Using the style switcher code

```
<!DOCTYPE html PUBLIC "-//W3C//DTD XHTML 1.0 Strict//EN"
        "http://www.w3.org/IR/xhtml1/DID/xhtml1-strict.dtd">
<html xmlns="http://www.w3.org/1999/xhtml" lang="en" xml:lang="en">
<head>
<meta http-equiv="Content-Type" content="text/html; charset=utf-8" />
<title>List Items as Horizontal Menu</title>

<link rel="stylesheet" title="default" href="blue.css" type="text/css" media="screen" />
<link rel="alternate stylesheet" title="yellow" href="yellow.css" type="text/css"
media="screen" />

<script type="text/javascript" src="styleswitcher.js">
</script>
</head>
<body>
<ul id="menu">
<li><a href="#"
onclick="setActiveStyleSheet('default');
return false;">Blue</a></li>
<li><a href="#"
onclick="setActiveStyleSheet('yellow');
return false;">Yellow</a></li>
</ul>
<div id="content">
<h1>Web Page Contents</h1>
<!-- add content -->
</div>
</body>
</html>
```

A List Apart's style switcher web page is at *http://www.alistapart.com/stories/alternate/*.

Figure 8-13 shows the page with the non-default yellow stylesheet selected. Try the page yourself, switching back and forth between the sheets.

Figure 8-13. Style switcher code with yellow selected

Programming CSS

One of the more interesting tricks associated with CSS is the ability to generate CSS using server-side functionality. I've used it to change the background image for headers in my pages, to manipulate the SVG I use for decoration (covered in Chapter 12), and a variety of other odds and ends.

There are two components to generating CSS using a programming language like PHP. The first is how to incorporate the CSS into a stylesheet. For that, we need the CSS import:

```
@import "photographs.php";
```

It doesn't matter if the file imported is a static CSS file as long as the MIME type returned by the document is text/css. In PHP, this is managed through the header function:

```
header('Content-type: text/css');
```

The rest of the file can be any combination of programming blocks generating CSS and static CSS—it doesn't matter.

I mentioned that one use of this type of functionality is changing the background image of a header. The image files are given a *jpeg* extension and are loaded into the same directory as the CSS file. The application than randomly selects which image to use and creates the applicable CSS. Example 8-8 shows the PHP program that accomplishes all this. Notice the mix of code and static CSS. I've highlighted the static CSS to make it easier to see.

Example 8-8. PHP application generating CSS for randomly altering the header image

```php
<?php
// declare the output of the file as CSS
header('Content-type: text/css');
?>
#header {
<?php

$exts = array('jpeg');

//collect list of images in current (look) directory
//modification suggested by Kaf Oseo
$url = array();
if($handle = opendir(dirname(__FILE__))) {
        while(false !== ($image = readdir($handle)))
                foreach($exts as $ext)
                        if(strstr($image, '.' . $ext))
                                $url[] = $image;
        closedir($handle);
}

//generate a random number
srand((double)microtime( ) * 1000000);

//change the number after the % to the number of images
//you have
$ct = count($url);

$rn = (rand( )%$ct);

$imgname = trim($url[$rn]);

printf("background-image: URL('%s');\n", $imgname);

?>
```

```
            background-repeat: repeat-x;
            background-position: top left;
}
#footer {
<?php

printf("background-image: URL('%s');\n", $imgname);
?>
            background-repeat: no-repeat;
}
```

The application uses PHP's random-number generation functionality to randomly select a number between 0 and the count of images. The image filenames are stored in an array, accessed with the randomly generated number.

Example 8-9 is a web page with three div elements, each of which is assigned an image from the Hubble telescope (the images and this application are included in the examples, in the subdirectory named *hubble*), to demonstrate how each time the page is loaded, different images are loaded into the background of the div elements, based on the PHP-generated CSS.

Example 8-9. PHP-generated CSS pooled from available images

HTML Page:

```
<!DOCTYPE html PUBLIC "-//W3C//DTD XHTML 1.0 Strict//EN"
        "http://www.w3.org/TR/xhtml1/DTD/xhtml1-strict.dtd">
<html xmlns="http://www.w3.org/1999/xhtml" lang="en" xml:lang="en">
<head>
<meta http-equiv="Content-Type" content="text/html; charset=utf-8" />
<title>Images</title>
<link rel="stylesheet" href="photographs.css" type="text/css" media="screen" />
</head>
<body>
<div id="header1">
</div>
<div id="header2">
</div>
<div id="header3">
</div>
</body>
</html>
```

CSS:

```
@import "photographs.php";

body { background-color: #000; }
```

Example 8-9. PHP-generated CSS pooled from available images (continued)

```
div {
    margin: 50px auto;
    border: 1px solid #fff;
}
```

photographs.php

```php
<?php
// declare the output of the file as CSS
header('Content-type: text/css');
?>
#header1 {
<?php

$exts = array('jpeg');

//collect list of images in current (look) directory
$url = array();
if($handle = opendir(dirname(__FILE__))) {
        while(false !== ($image = readdir($handle)))
                foreach($exts as $ext)
                        if(strstr($image, '.' . $ext))
                                $url[] = $image;
        closedir($handle);
}

//generate a random number
srand((double)microtime() * 1000000);

//change the number after the % to the number of images
//you have
$ct = count($url);

$rn = (rand()%$ct);

$imgname = trim($url[$rn]);

printf("background-image: URL('%s');\n", $imgname);

?>
            background-repeat: repeat-x;
            background-position: top left;
            width: 600px; height: 100px;
}
#header2 {
<?php
$rn = (rand()%$ct);
$imgname = trim($url[$rn]);
```

Example 8-9. PHP-generated CSS pooled from available images (continued)

```
printf("background-image: URL('%s');\n", $imgname);
?>
        background-repeat: no-repeat;
        background-position: top left;
        width: 600px; height: 100px;
}

#header3 {
<?php
$rn = (rand( )%$ct);
$imgname = trim($url[$rn]);

printf("background-image: URL('%s');\n", $imgname);
?>
        background-repeat: no-repeat;
        background-position: top left;
        width: 600px; height: 100px;
}
```

Figure 8-14 shows the web page with three images loaded into the div element backgrounds.

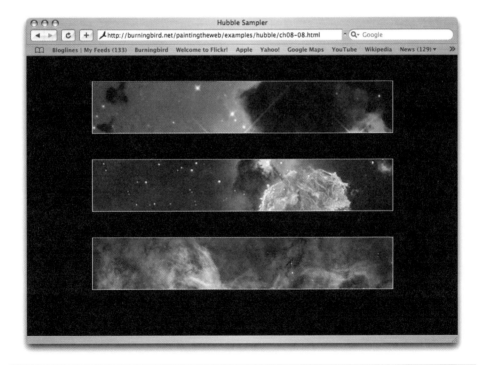

Figure 8-14. Hubble sampler using PHP-generated CSS

The benefit of an application like this is that you can drop images into the subdirectory without having to worry about changing the application. Figure 8-14 shows a sampler of header screen shots.

You can generate stylesheet settings for any effect, including changing colors, increasing font size, or, as mentioned earlier, modifying the CSS used for SVG elements. The only limitation is keeping the application small and fast—you don't want to slow down CSS while the page is loaded.

CSS Tools and Utilities

CSS isn't as complicated as a markup like XHTML, and a lot of CSS files are manually created. However, there are tools to help with CSS, including tools to create, to validate, to format, or to snoop.

Yes, snooping. Snooping is not only respectable when it comes to CSS, but it's also how most of us learn how to apply CSS to create effects. Once you're done snooping, you're ready to edit; once you've edited, it's time to format; and, finally, you need to validate.

Snooping CSS Through Firefox and the Web Developer Toolkit

There are toolkits and extensions to snoop through CSS in most of the primary browsers, but none more than with Firefox. My favorite of the browser-based CSS tools is Web Developer.

 The Web Developer Firefox extension can be accessed at *http://chrispederick.com/work/web-developer/*.

Once installed, this tool provides options for everything: validation, editing the HTML, magnifying it, cookies, disabling active page components, even seeing the page source after any client-side manipulation. It probably is the richest web toolkit I've seen and a must for page design and development.

Among the options is a set specific to CSS. Clicking on the top-level menu item labeled CSS provides the following options:

- Disable Styles
    - All Styles
    - Browser Default Styles
    - Embedded Styles
    - Inline Styles
    - Linked Style Sheets
    - Print Styles
    - Individual Style Sheets (leading to a list accessible in the page)

- Display CSS by Media Type
  - Handheld
  - Print
- View CSS
- View Style Information
- Add User Style Sheet
- Edit Css
- User Border Box Model

You can view every aspect of the CSS in the page in multiple ways, as well as disable stylesheets by name or category.

The ability to disable the browser's default styles is equivalent to the whitespace reset and then some. Not only is the whitespace impacted, but so are the font settings, including font size, family, and line height. This is an effective way of determining whether there's a component in the page that's relying on the default setting, and if there is, to add CSS entries.

 Even if the default browser setting looks good, it probably won't look good in all browsers or another user agent, in all operating systems, or even in all devices. That's why you'll always want to add style settings for all visible elements.

A great way to snoop around at a page's CSS is to set the View Style Information option on and then move your cursor around the page. As the cursor moves over every page element, a red box surrounds the element, and the element's position in the page hierarchy is displayed in the address bar. Once you find the element whose style you want information about, click on the element, and a panel opens below with the style information, as shown in Figure 8-15.

You can also edit the CSS and have it impact the loaded page. It won't permanently change the CSS, but it's a great way of trying out quick changes.

CSS Editors

Once you've scoped out new and nifty uses of CSS, you're ready to create or edit your own stylesheet. You can warm up your friendly text editor and dig in, but it's helpful to have an editor that understands the syntax behind CSS.

If you're a Mac user, one of the better CSS editors is CSSEdit. You can download a trial version at *http://macrabbit.com/cssedit/*. It's fully featured, but with a limitation that you can't save files with more than 2,500 characters. At a minimum, you can give the tool a good tryout.

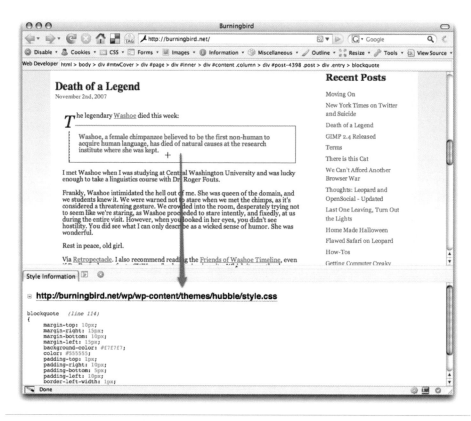

Figure 8-15. Snooping around CSS with Web Developer

This is very intuitive tool. You can almost learn at a glance how to use it by opening the *welcome.css* sample file. For instance, there are keywords you can embed in CSS comments that provide one-click access to sections in the CSS file, as shown in Figure 8-16.

Starting out is very simple: just open a file, create a new stylesheet, or open a file from the local computer. You can also specify a URL, and the page is loaded, including a reference to all of the page stylesheets. These can be loaded into the editor for live editing, as shown in Figure 8-17. In addition, clicking on any one item opens up relevant dialogs in the right side of the tool to fill in appropriate values, and once you're done playing around with your style settings, you can review the results in the page. Turning on X-Ray in the preview page (again, see Figure 8-17) highlights the item in the page, as well as changes the cursor and editor focus to the target item.

CSSEdit is the Jaguar of CSS editors.

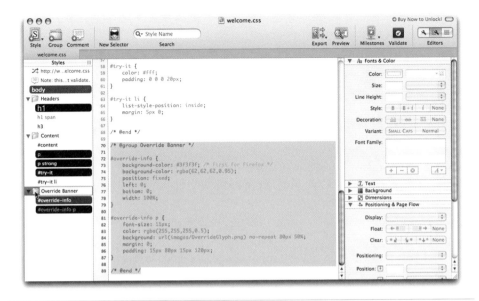

Figure 8-16. Opening the CSSEdit sample CSS file

Figure 8-17. Loading a stylesheet from a remote location, and live editing the sheet

CSS Validation

After editing the CSS, it's time to validate.

The primary validation page is provided by the W3C at *http://jigsaw.w3.org/css-validator/*. However, be prepared to get a lot of warnings and errors, especially if you're using SVG or versions of CSS newer than 2.1. For instance, in one of my stylesheets, I'm using the *rgba* method for defining color for my SVG elements. The CSS validator doesn't like this, because the *rgba* approach is a CSS 3.0 thing:

```
.color1 { rgb(64,50,22);
```

The validator also won't like any use of transparency because of the hacks necessary to make transparency work for most browsers, such as `moz-opacity` for older Mozilla browsers and `filter` for IE:

```
#mtwCover { margin: 0; width: 100%;  filter:alpha(opacity=100); -moz-opacity:1.0;
opacity:1.0;  }
```

The validator can help with debugging or finding obvious errors, such as typos when specifying a CSS property (for example, `wdth` instead of `width`). However, don't break down in tears if you can't eliminate all errors or warnings related to your CSS file.

The true validation of your CSS is how it appears in different browsers on different operating systems. If you don't have access to Linux, Mac, and Windows, or don't have access to all browsers, you can use one of the screenshot sites, such as Browsershots, or validators, such as TotalValidator, that provide such screenshots. Some charge a fee, others provide the screenshots as a service (though donations are usually welcome).

BrowserShots can be found at *http://browsershots.org* and TotalValidator at *http://totalvalidator.com*.

CSS Toys and Tools

You'll notice that in some of this book's examples the CSS is all bunched up together, and other times it's nicely spread out, with lots of whitespace surrounding the selectors.

There are no "rules" in how CSS is formatted. Some folks think you should scrunch it down, removing all the whitespace; after all, this will eliminate some of the bandwidth requirements. However, in the days of loading our pages with videos and images, it seems a little silly to strip all the whitespace from your CSS file.

A good place to start looking for CSS editors, validators, and other toys and tools is the WebsiteTips.com site at *http://websitetips.com/css/tools/*.

Going the opposite direction and putting in lots of whitespace to make the file easier to read can be a nice welcoming gesture to let other people learn from our CSS. At a minimum, it makes us look good—like hanging fresh towels in the guest bathroom.

The tool I often use for formatting is an online site called, appropriately enough, "Format CSS Online," at *http://www.lonniebest.com/FormatCSS/*. One side of the page has a space for CSS; the other side has instructions on how to format it, such as using tabs before property names, inserting a new line after a semicolon, etc. The result is elegantly formatted CSS, ready to paste into your CSS file, going from this:

```css
body {
    background-color: #ccf;
}
#outerframe { margin: 0 auto; width: 800px; background-color: #003; border: 2px
outset #ccc; }
#innerframe {
        color: #333;
        background:#ccc;
  margin: 5px;
        border: 2px outset #999
        }
#innerpanel {        background-color: #fff;
  margin: 20px;
        padding: 10px;
        text-align: center; border: 2px inset #ccc;
        }
img { border: 2px outset #ccc; }
```

to this:

```css
body
{
    background-color: #ccf;
}
#outerframe
{
    background-color: #003;
    border: 2px outset #ccc;
    margin: 0 auto;
    width: 800px;
}
#innerframe
{
    background: #ccc;
    border: 2px outset #999;
    color: #333;
    margin: 5px;
}
#innerpanel
{
    background-color: #fff;
    border: 2px inset #ccc;
    margin: 20px;
    padding: 10px;
    text-align: center;
}
img
{
    border: 2px outset #ccc;
```

Another interesting little tool is Imagelys Picture Styles, which can take any image and convert it into a background image. That's not as trivial as it sounds—most images don't make great background material.

 The Imagelys site is at *http://www.imagelys.com/*. The tool is freely available (though donations are welcome), but it only works in Windows.

Imagelys has several image editing tools, including Curves, so it's worth exploring as a general editor. However, the focus of the tool is to create backgrounds. As we remember from Chapter 1, backgrounds can be more enemy than friend, but backgrounds can add color, texture, and even interest to a visually dull page. As long as you go easy on the unicorns and animated sparkles, explore the option of background images.

You can create a background image using any number of built-in textures, including adding new texture packs, downloadable from the Imagelys site. Figure 8-18 shows me creating a blue marble effect with a couple of water drops, using materials provided for the tool. Figure 8-19 shows the background image, which was used as the background for one of the earlier web page examples.

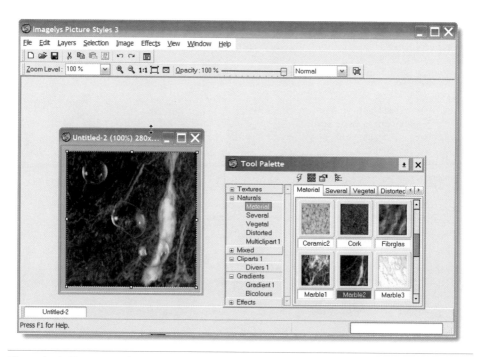

Figure 8-18. Using Imagelys to create an abstract background

Figure 8-19. Generated background image used in a web page

You can also create a seamless background from an existing image, or photograph. It's not as easy to do manually; you don't want to cut the image at the seams and then tile it, because it won't have that nice, clean join.

 Another option for a background image, especially if you like stripes, is the Stripe Generator, an online tool that can generate a wide variety of striped backgrounds. Access the Stripe Generator at *http:// stripegenerator.com/*.

Speaking of backgrounds, time to see how and when to use backgrounds, as well as incorporate the other tricks and tips covered in this chapter and earlier in this book, to create an overall web site look. Time to look at web page design.

CHAPTER 9

Design for the Non-Designer

I am not a designer, though I play one on the Web from time to time. I know what I like but can't always get it to work in my own space. My web sites don't inspire awards, but they typically don't send people running and screaming from the room either. In other words, I'm probably a lot like you and a whole lot of other folks who enjoy designing for the Web but aren't web designers.

In this chapter I'm going to look at web design, but rather than trot out my own admittedly plain efforts, I'll point out site designs others have created that I think are wonderful and give reasons why I, and others, like the sites. In addition, we'll take a look at the components of design, such as layout, color, mood, fonts and typography, purpose, as well as some of the design tools and techniques.

In addition to looking good, our sites have a responsibility to be readable and accessible, which also means utilizing valid technologies. These seem like old-fashioned ideas, but no site, no matter how pretty, is going to be successful if the font is too hard to read or if those with visual impairments can't access the site because of a graphic menu. I once visited a small-town online newspaper that took the front page copy and converted it into a huge JPEG, which was then inserted into a frame. If I could have reached through the Web and slapped them, I would have.

Aside from ensuring that our web sites are accessible, the most important aspect of site design is that we're happy with what we have. I may have listed top 10 no-nos in the first chapter of this book, but the Web really is the last frontier of freedom, and you shouldn't feel that your site must look a certain way. We all have different tastes, likes, and dislikes, and you're not constrained to make your site look like everyone else's. At the same time, you don't have to feel like you must maintain one consistent site design forever, or that you have to eschew what is currently popular; trends in web design change every couple of years, and it can be fun adapting your own site's look to current trends. In your own unique way, of course.

Have fun with site design. If you do, everything falls into place.

I'm indebted to many web page designers, too many to list in this chapter. Included with the book examples is a set of web pages with additional links to sites containing tutorials, articles, and so on that have inspired me in the past, and will hopefully inspire you in the future.

The Elements of Page Design

While I was writing this book, a friend sent me a page from the site Smashing Magazine that listed several screenshots of weblogs the editors felt had excellent site designs. Unlike other "favorites lists" of this nature, the page actually provided some annotation with the designs explaining why that particular site was picked. In addition, all of the sites used the same type of software—weblogging software—so that the purpose was held consistent and just the site design differed. This was an exceptionally good way to learn some of the key elements to good page design, and it offered a chance to check out some new and interesting design ideas.

Smashing Magazine's "45 Excellent Blog Designs" page can be found at *http://www.smashingmagazine.com/2007/08/28/45-excellent-blog-designs*.

In the designs at *Smashing Magazine*, and at others I've seen, there are certain elements present in most of the designs that transcend whatever is the current, popular trend, forming a set of timeless classics and essentials that every site should have and that we should abandon only with great reluctance. These are:

- Clear, immediately apparent site navigation
- Easy to find and read site content
- An uncluttered look, regardless of how heavily loaded down with items
- A design that fits the purpose of the site
- Minimal confusion: usability, accessibility, validity, and meaning

Clear Navigation: Missouri's Department of Conservation

One common element to most popular web site designs is immediate access to high-level navigation. In the last chapter, one example modified a list into a horizontal menu and placed the menu directly across the very top of the page. Depending on the colors used, as well as the rest of the site design, such a menu can be immediately apparent without being distracting. In fact, it can add a nice, clean edge to the site design.

One of my favorite page designs is the page created by the Missouri Department of Conservation (DC) that tracks the autumn colors in the state's region (see *http://mdc.mo.gov/nathis/seasons/fall/*). Not only does it provide all of the essential elements of page design, such as clear text, an uncluttered look, and easily determined purpose; it also provides excellent navigation—both at the top and bottom of the page.

In Figure 9-1, the menu shown along the top of the page is repeated in all pages at the DC site. Rather than mapping to some hierarchy within the department, the high-level menu splits the site's contents into general, broad areas of user, not organizational, interest. This is key to good site design: matching the needs of the people accessing the site, rather than matching an existing organizational hierarchy.

Figure 9-1. Screenshot of the Missouri Department of Conservation's Fall Colors page

Additionally, the menu is very accessible and immediately visible, but doesn't obstruct the site design. In fact, having the dark band of color at the top can actually add a clean edge to the site—better than having the DC site's normally earth-toned pages brush up against the typical chrome look of most web browsers.

Along the bottom, other links are given, but these are more in line with an "if you liked the above, you might like the following" category than being essential departmental links. Links to an event calendar, TV show, weblog, and so on invite the page visitor to keep exploring the site even though you found out where the pretty fall color drive is—look, there's a whole lot more to this site than colorful leaves in the fall.

Figure 9-2 also shows that the essential web site links are also included at the bottom of the page and easily spotted. The bottom of the page is almost always where you'll want such links, because most people have been "trained" over the years of viewing web sites to look for contact information, "about this site" links, and so on at the bottom of the page.

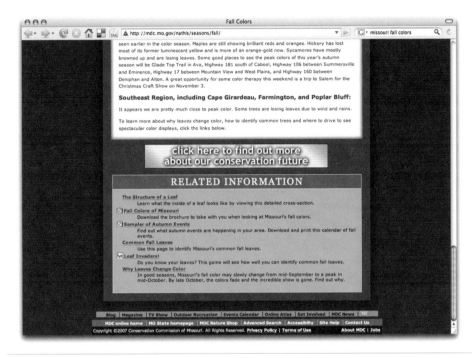

Figure 9-2. Bottom of the page for the DC Fall Colors page

It's tempting to get creative with page layout, and perhaps plunk such bottom links elsewhere in the page (in a floating SVG bubble, perhaps?). However, you never want to break with web page traditions to the point that you confuse people about where to find essential web site information, such as who to contact if there's a problem with the page (like when the person is using IE and can't see that lovely SVG bubble).

Notice something else from the Missouri Fall Colors page? No sidebar links. No sidebar, period, but no sidebar links.

We've gotten into the habit of plunking one, two, or even more sidebars into our pages. For many pages, though, they aren't essential, and can even distract from the page content. At the DC site, sidebars aren't used for secondary pages, only for the top-level pages, such as the one shown in Figure 9-3.

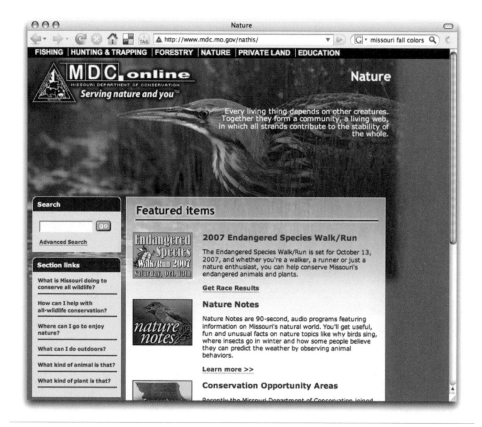

Figure 9-3. Top-level page for the DC Nature section

The sidebar links are phrased as questions, too, rather than formal titles or subject nouns. This is an effective approach, particularly when you're dealing with people who probably have differing levels of experience with the Internet.

All the main pages at the DC site have the same type of page look, too, again with the top high-level menu, bottom "about this site" menu items, and the new focused sidebar questions.

If I have one criticism of the DC site, it's that it doesn't provide a link back to the main section page from the individual pages, making it difficult to figure out whether the Fall Colors page is located under the Nature section or the Education section. However, the point also could be that not having this link shouldn't matter: each page can stand on its own, and the top menu can get you to where you want to go.

The text at the DC web site is also easily found and very readable, leading to the next essential web design element: being able to actually find, and read, the site contents.

The Readability of a Site: The CSS Zen Garden

Another excellent place to learn about web design is the CSS Zen Garden (*http://www.csszengarden.com/*). The brainchild of designer Dave Shea, Zen Garden was created to encourage people to use CSS to style their web sites.

The premise behind the CSS Zen Garden was to create one standard web page where the only thing that can be changed is the actual CSS to style the markup. People were then invited to submit different stylesheets, and the variety of designs at the site demonstrates how effective CSS is for design.

The designs are incredible, all the work of talented people. I noticed, however, that there was one primary factor that determined whether I liked the design or not: how easy was it to find the site content, and how easy was it to read?

For instance, one of the designs, Vertigo, by Antonio Cella, is an interesting mix of transparent images and has a nice use of space, but the background images show through the text, making it extremely difficult to read what was written, as shown in Figure 9-4.

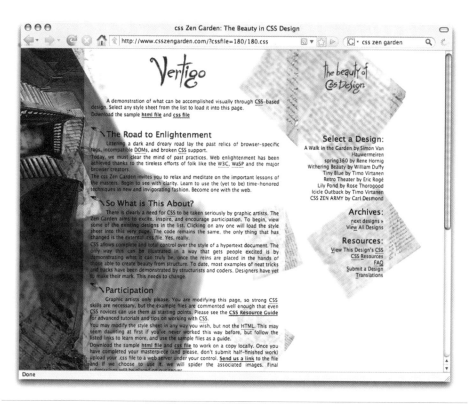

Figure 9-4. CSS Zen Garden design by Antonio Cella

Another design, Retro Theater by Eric Rogé, made really excellent use of fixed positioning and theme design, not to mention graphics, but the text was virtually illegible, as shown in Figure 9-5.

Figure 9-5. CSS Zen Garden design by Eric Rogé

Compare this with the clean reading area defined in the design Contemporary Nouveau, by David Hellsing, as shown in Figure 9-6. I picked this not only because I like the design and the text areas are kept clean and easy to find and read, but also to demonstrate that the background behind the text doesn't have to be white and text area black in order to be legible. What matters is the amount of contrast between the two. I'll get into readability in terms of background colors and text in more detail a little later in this chapter, in the section on typography.

No matter how attractive the design, it shouldn't come at the expense of making it difficult for your web page readers to find or read the all-important site text.

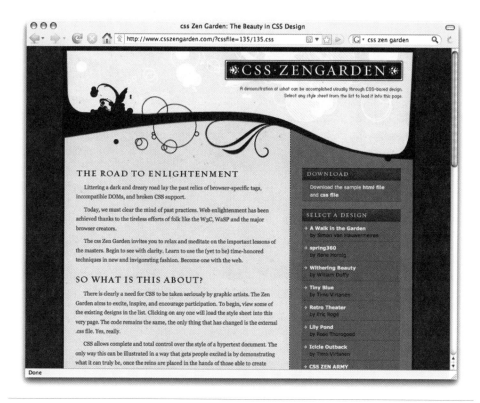

Figure 9-6. CSS Zen Garden design by David Hellsing

An Uncluttered Site: The Guardian Unlimited

Oh, give me the days before widgets. Return me to the days when I could load a web page and it would actually load into my browser in less than a minute. When I wouldn't be hit with lists of people's pictures, and weather gadgets, and dancing real estate agents; where my eyes wouldn't be assailed by a barrage of whirling, massive colors and quintuple rows of material featuring videos, scrolling text, and other assorted demands for my attention.

Give me the days when web pages were clean and uncluttered, no matter how wild the design or crazy the colors.

There are two issues with today's cluttered web sites. The first is the overuse of widgets, which slows down page loading, not to mention freezing up my browser so that I have to kill it and try again. However, this is an issue for a web performance book, not one on web graphics. This leads to the next issue: we only have one set of eyes and one brain, and both can be in only one place at one time.

Like most people, I like to think I'm a capable multitasker, but when I visit a site that has five columns of material, two or more of which feature something moving, scrolling, blinking, or doing their best to capture our mouse cursors for some playful action, my first reaction is to see whether the site has a syndication feed I can subscribe to, so I never have to actually visit the site again.

There's no harm in a multiple column layout or the use of visual ads. I had a friend tell me once that he included ads less because he wanted to make money and more to make the site look "more professional." However, someone somewhere decided that today's generation of young people has grown up with a barrage of noise, movement, and sound, and therefore aren't comfortable, or supposedly willing, to spend money unless hit with sight, sound, and movement from a dozen or so different spots at once. This belief has seeped into web design, and it leads to the most awful web sites I've seen. Too awful to list in the book. Yes, even more awful than the unicorns with purple and pink.

You can have multiple columns, especially containing excerpts that lead to pages with fewer columns and wider text areas. You can also use ads, even some animated ads. However, there is such a thing as too much content in too small an area.

No other type of web site represents the challenge of cramming in a lot of material while still being legible and not painful to access than online news sites. Among the sites that rate highly in this regard is the *New York Times*, with its clean white background, crisp text, and careful use of images and video. Most importantly, only one animated image is displayed on any one page at a time—you aren't hit with a barrage of animation that would make it difficult to focus on reading the actual text.

My favorite site from a design perspective, though, would be the *Guardian Unlimited*, shown in Figure 9-7. It has easy-to-spot navigation, clear text, little animation to distract, nice use of images in one column, ads that aren't overwhelming—not to mention it's quick to load, without any annoying pop ups.

What applies to the newspaper sites also applies to personal sites. We don't have to use the standard centered-content, two-column look with one sidebar. We can use multiple columns, as well as some widgets and images.

The key to making this work is providing secondary pages with fewer columns and ensuring that the text area is wide enough to be readable. In addition, use of whitespace between columns is essential, as is minimizing the use of wild color schemes and heavy use of background images.

A Purposeful Site: I Love Typography

If there is any rule to the Internet, it's that there are no rules. This "no rules" also includes your site design. At the same time, if you confuse the heck out of the poor people who stop by, your freedom from rules will also come with freedom from visitors.

Figure 9-7. Guardian Unlimited web site: uncluttered and clean

You can have individuality, as well as flexibility in what your site is all about, but still manage to give visitors a clear clue as to what to expect if they stay a while and explore. In fact, you can have a lot of fun with the purpose, integrating it heavily into the design. One of the best sites I've seen that manages this is I Love Typography (*http://ilovetypography.com/*), shown in Figure 9-8.

One can see at a glance the purpose of the site: an interest in all things typographic. However, one also gets a sense of playfulness, not the least of which is high-level topics such as "Who Shot the Serif?"

There are two reasons for providing such clearly defined signals about the purpose of a site. The first is that if a person accidentally stumbles onto the site from some odd or random search-engine result, she'll be able to quickly determine what the site is about and either stay, or leave, accordingly. One might think that how we receive visitors isn't important, as long as we have visitors. However, visitors who aren't going to be interested in what interests us take bandwidth and usually don't provide anything all that useful in return.

A second reason to provide a strong indication of purpose is a signal to others to link to your site when it comes to a specific topic. A site that writes on typography every three or four or so essays or posts is less likely to be linked than one that focuses on

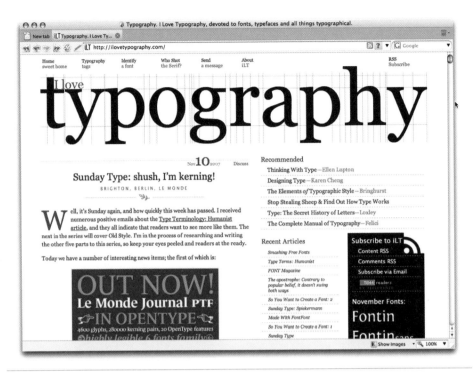

Figure 9-8. I Love Typography web site

typography—especially one that provides a clear indication that this focus is going to continue into the future. Being linked or listed with the topic ensures you will get visitors interested in what you're providing.

Of course, not every site has a clearly defined purpose. Surprisingly, though, most do and the people may not realize it. Even weblogs, which are notorious for not sticking to a single purpose, provide clues as to points of interest: pictures of family or food, lists of poets, knitting projects, and use of color all hint at what might lurk beyond the front page. Even listing categories and topics provides an indication of the site owner's interests.

Minimizing Confusion: Usability, Accessibility, Validity, and Meaning

Ensuring that a site has readable text, clear navigation, uncluttered content area, and generally a presentation that hints at topic areas and interest goes far in minimizing confusion. However, there are additional steps one can take to help our web site visitors, and not just the human visitors.

First, use underlines for links unless the context of the link is a clear signal that the listed items are links. It's a good rule of thumb to use underlines for links within text, but not to use underlines for links in sidebars. The reason for links in text is fairly obvious: no amount of bolding or color change of font is going to make a link look like a link without the underlining. As for not having underlines with sidebar links, generally sidebar links are listed, one right after the other. Using an underline is not only unnecessary to indicate the items are links, but it can make the text area messy looking. Figure 9-9 shows a tag cloud with and without underlines on links.

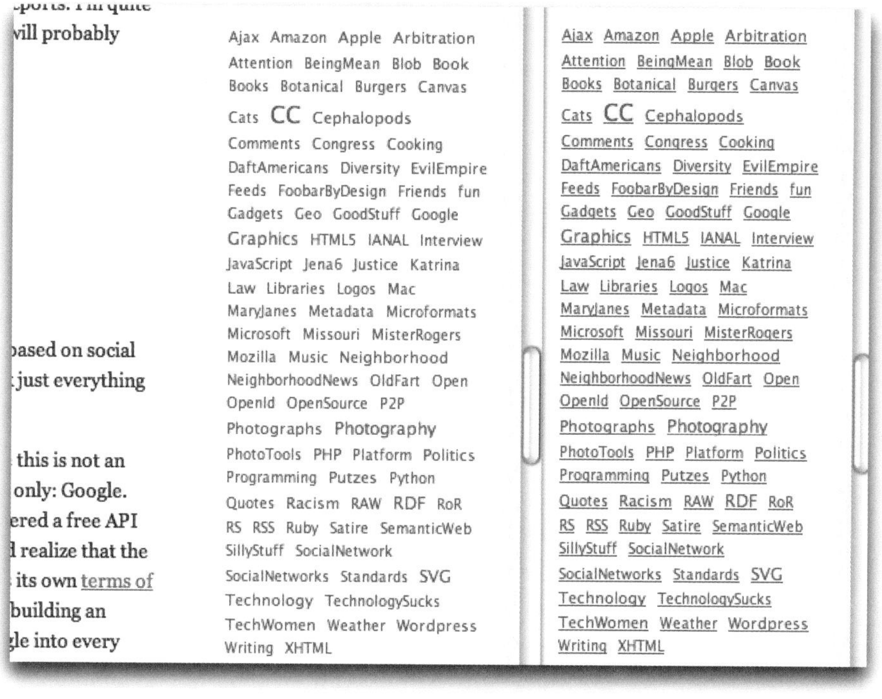

Figure 9-9. Tag cloud with and without underlines on links

Second, use meaningful link text. Yes, I've also been guilty of "Click here," but it really doesn't tell your web site visitor anything. At a minimum, use the web page or site title if you can't find any descriptive text to use, such as:

- "Burningbird wrote"
- "You can find more about it at the *New York Times*"
- "Interested in typography? You'll love I Love Typography"

With appropriate links, of course.

A third area of confusion has to do with accessibility and involves providing clearly labeled links for navigation.

Too often sites use images without links, which requires the mouse to navigate the site. Neither the use of images nor the mouse requirement is accessible via screen readers. Even if images and the mouse are used to provide dynamic link characteristics, still provide links (for keyboard access) and clear text labeling (for screen readers).

Continuing on with accessibility, use the alternative text attribute for visual elements. For instance, provide a meaningful description of the image in the img element's alt attribute.

These items have to do with people, but minimizing confusion relates to machines, too. Providing meaningful labels for links goes a long way toward ensuring that your pages show up properly in search engines. The same applies to titles and subtitles on stories and other writings. It's easy to get into being clever on titles—this is another bad habit I have—but h1 and h2 headers really can determine where your page shows up in search results. You'll want to feature the topic of the writing prominently in the text of the title.

Of course, you'll also want to use the correct markup for your page contents. Menus and lists should be ul/ol elements, blockquotes for long quotes, p for paragraphs, and so on. Remember, you can always redefine the appearance of the element, as I demonstrated in Chapter 8.

Finally, as much as possible, your page needs to validate. A page that doesn't validate is always going to be at more risk of not showing up at all in one browser or another. Plus, eventually you'll probably want to move your site to more rigorous specifications, such as XHTML. Making sure that the pages validate in HTML 4 now will make your job porting to XHTML much easier in the future. Also, using invalid markup could prevent your pages from showing up in search engines.

I could go on with classic page elements and minimizing confusion, but it's time to break from the wordy stuff and look at what we can do with different components of the page design.

Web Pages Are Like Ogres, and Ogres Have Layers

A typical web page five years ago was created with one big HTML table to manage the layout. Now, a typical web page could consist of one div element containing the main content (centered or not), and then multiple div elements split into columns, set side by side. It's an effective design strategy but neglects one important aspect of page design: that a web page has depth in addition to height and width.

HTML elements can be nested, of course, but the nesting can also be a part of site design, as well as the site's functionality. In particular, div elements lend themselves to creative nesting.

Only the Shadow Knows

OK, corny title. However, one of the more common effects created with nested `div` elements is to provide shadows, frames, or other overlapping effects. Only one background image can be used with each HTML element, but by being able to layer elements and making use of image transparency, we can add rounded corners, as well as add shadows to content areas.

Though web design trends constantly change, a popular page layout is to center content in the page, with a shadow around the content. An additional design element can also consist of rounded corners, but we'll focus just on adding shadows around a centered, sized content area.

There are a dozen ways to create the shadowed content, but in this how-to we'll use Photoshop and Photoshop's own drop-shadow capability. The same how-to can be adapted to other tools.

First, create a background image as wide as the content area will be and fill it with whatever shade is going to be the background color of the page. To match the example shown in Figure 9-10, fill the content area with a dark-red color (#a5212c). Next, to provide enough room for adding the drop shadow, extend the canvas area out 10 pixels on both sides.

Use the Layers menu to add a drop shadow. Since we want the shadow to be even on both sides, set the offset value to 0, leaving an even 10-pixel shadow area. If you're going to use the image as a PNG, you're finished. However, since not all popular browsers support PNG transparency, create a new layer and position it below the existing layer. Fill it with the same background color and then flatten the image, as shown in Figure 9-10. Since the image is repeated vertically, the background image can be trimmed to only about 10 pixels tall.

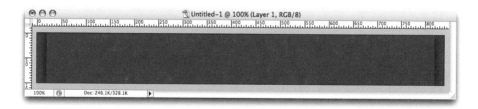

Figure 9-10. Background image, complete with "shadow"

To use the new background image, the web page has two containers. The first is the same width as the new background image, and the inner container is narrower, by the same amount as the shadow. For this example, 840 pixels for the outer container, 800 pixels for the inner, as shown in Example 9-1. Both containers are centered, with the outer main container in the page and the inner container within the outer main.

Example 9-1. Creating a web page with a centered, shadowed container

```
<!DOCTYPE html PUBLIC "-//W3C//DTD XHTML 1.0 Strict//EN"
        "http://www.w3.org/TR/xhtml1/DTD/xhtml1-strict.dtd">
<html xmlns="http://www.w3.org/1999/xhtml" lang="en" xml:lang="en">
<head>
<meta http-equiv="Content-Type" content="text/html; charset=utf-8" />
<title>Background Shadows</title>
<style type="text/css">
*
{
        margin: 0;
        padding: 0;
}
body
{
        background-color: #A31F2A;
        padding-top: 30px;
}
h1
{
        font-size: 48pt;
        margin: 30px;
}
#main
{
        background-image: url(shadow.jpg);
        margin: 0 auto;
        max-width: 840px;
}
#content
{
        background-color: #fcfcfc;
        margin: 0 20px;
        padding: 20px 0;
        width: 800px;
}
#content p
{
        margin: 10px 30px;
}
.cap
{
        background-color: #000;
        height: 10px;
}
</style>
</head>
<body>
<div class="cap">
</div>
<div id="main">
<div id="content">
<h1>Web Page Contents</h1>
<!-- add content here -->
```

Example 9-1. Creating a web page with a centered, shadowed container (continued)

```
</div>
</div>
<div class="cap"></div></body>
</html>
```

To even out the tops, one option is to create shadowed "caps" for the bottom and top of the content area. In this example, though, as shown in Figure 9-11, a solid black line is used, offset from the top and bottom to "frame" the interior content area. It's a clean end point, especially with colors that go well with the crispness of the black. The strong color also helps to blend in the shadows.

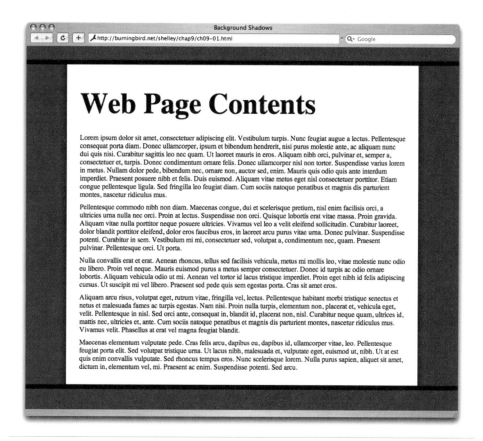

Figure 9-11. Using shadows with web page content

Shadows work better on lighter colors, such as light grays, pale pastel colors, or even white. To make the effect work with a patterned background, it helps if the pattern is small. In the last step listed with the original example, instead of filling the bottom layer with a solid color, copy pieces of the background pattern to the ends, as shown in Figure 9-12.

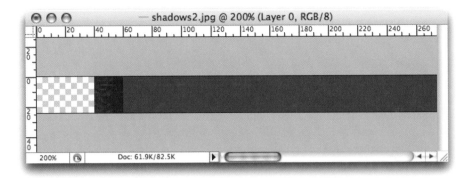

Figure 9-12. Adding a pattern to the shadow

When used in the page, the shadow/pattern combo should flatten into the background, as shown in Figure 9-13. Again, this works best if the pattern is small or very regular. This approach was used with the Missouri Department of Conservation web site, shown previously in Figures 9-1 and 9-2.

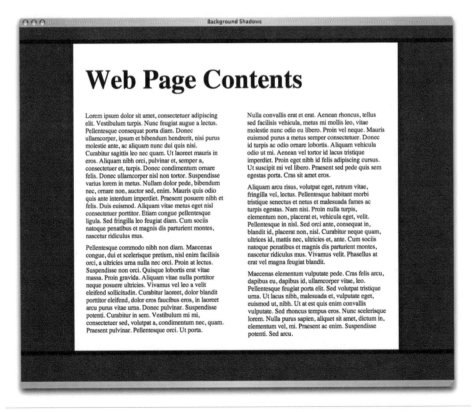

Figure 9-13. Adding a shadowed content area with a patterned background

Of course, if all browsers respected PNG transparency, you could forgo flattening the image or providing the extra "background" layer, and the shadow transparency would then blend into the background.

Multiple Backgrounds, Multiple Layers

There is one area where there still might be some overlap between presentation and content in web page design, and that's when using multiple elements in order to stage a page effect. However, if you consider the div element (and its blockless cousin, span) as nothing more than page play dough, using multiple div elements in order to create the effect should meet the spirit, as well as the letter, of the law when it comes to semantic web page design.

Case in point is the ability to create a shadowed bordered effect that surrounds page content and that also has an end cap—specifically, using this type of visual setup with a flexible web page layout.

I'll get into flexible versus fixed web page layouts in the next section. For now, we'll focus purely on using multiple div elements with differing backgrounds to create an effect like the one shown in Figure 9-14.

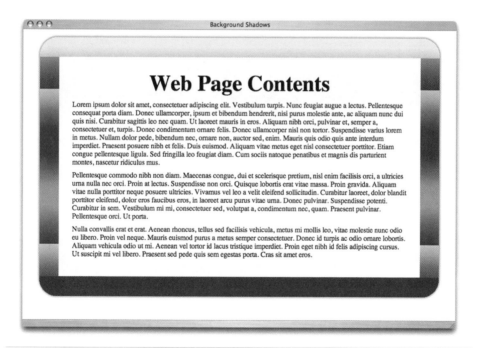

Figure 9-14. Using div elements and background images to create a flexible and bordered content area

To start, you need the image. To re-create the effect shown in Figure 9-14, use Photoshop to create a rounded rectangle, and then fill it with the Yellow, Violet, Orange, and Blue Gradient. It doesn't matter what you use, as long as the top and bottom center part of the image can repeat horizontally, and the right and left center portions of the image can repeat vertically. This is illustrated in Figure 9-15.

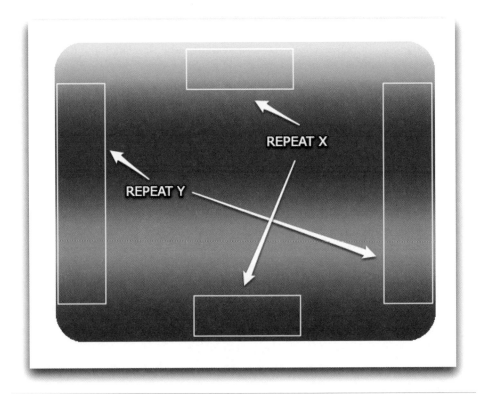

Figure 9-15. Image to use for borders, with repeating blocks highlighted

Once the image is created, add a generalized shadow effect by setting the offset to 0 and expanding the shadow width to 8 pixels. Since transparency is problematic with IE6, set the background color to what your web site page will be (in this case, white), and then flatten the image. Trim any excess white or other layout color from the image; you only want a uniform amount of space around the image, big enough to contain the shadow.

To create the page effect, cut the image into pieces. Start by cutting the rounded corners into four separate pieces. They don't have to be the same width, unless the pattern for the background demands this. The most effective way to chop up the image is to select and cut the entire upper block area, and then the bottom block area for further breakdown.

What's important is to work with whatever pattern you've chosen for your page border, and to ensure that the outside shadow area is the same for all of the pieces.

Once you're finished, you'll have eight pieces: left and right upper corner, left and right bottom corner, top and bottom center pieces, and the left and right side pieces. Now comes the part of putting them together.

You could try nesting all of the background images in their own containers all within one another, but trying to get all of the pieces to fit together is complicated, even if you do use the global whitespace reset to ensure that no unexpected margin or padding complicates the design.

Instead, as shown in the HTML markup document in Example 9-2, the header and footer caps are two separate page elements, as is the center piece of the document. The whole is then placed into an enclosing container. To ensure that the sections that repeat won't overlay those that don't, such as the cap center pieces overlapping the corners, use the center elements as the containers for the corners, as highlighted in the markup and illustrated in Figure 9-16.

Example 9-2. Defining the header and footer caps and main content area in the markup

```
<!DOCTYPE html PUBLIC "-//W3C//DTD XHTML 1.0 Strict//EN"
        "http://www.w3.org/TR/xhtml1/DTD/xhtml1-strict.dtd">
<html xmlns="http://www.w3.org/1999/xhtml" lang="en" xml:lang="en">
<head>
<meta http-equiv="Content-Type" content="text/html; charset=utf-8" />
<title>Background Shadows</title>
<link rel="stylesheet" href="borders.css" type="text/css" media="screen" />
</head>
<body>
<div id="whole">


<div id="mainupper">
   <div id="lefttop">
      <div id="righttop">
      </div>
   </div>
</div>


<div id="mainright">
   <div id="mainleft">
      <div id="content">
         <!-- add content -->
      </div>
   </div>
</div>


<div id="mainlower">
   <div id="leftbottom">
      <div id="rightbottom">
```

Example 9-2. Defining the header and footer caps and main content area in the markup (continued)

```
        </div>
    </div>
</div>

</div>
</body></html>
```

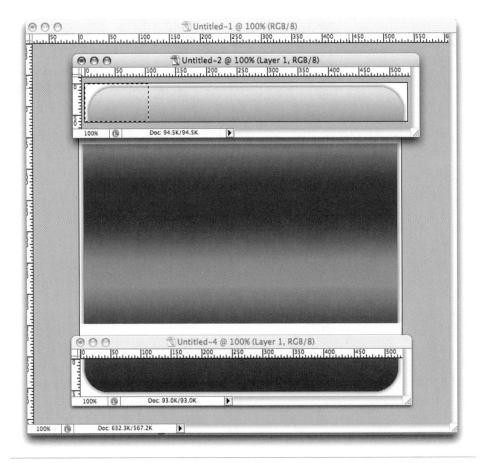

Figure 9-16. Cutting "caps" with rounded corners off the original image for further breakdown

For the center column, the actual content area is the innermost element, as it needs to overlap the sides. It doesn't matter the order, left or right, with either of the corner pieces of the center column.

The stylesheet in *borders.css* is shown in Example 9-3, split into general markup, the upper cap CSS, lower cap CSS, and the content area.

Example 9-3. CSS for the bordered example

```
* general markup */
html,body
{
        margin: 0;
        padding: 0;
}
body
{
        background-color: #fff;
        padding: 10px 30px;
}
h1
{
        font-size: 36pt;
        text-align: center;
}

#whole
{
        max-width: 1000px;
        margin: 0 auto;
}
/* upper cap */
#mainupper
{
        background-image: url(uppercenter.jpg);
        background-position: center top;
        background-repeat: repeat-x;
}

#lefttop
{
        background-image: url(upperleft.jpg);
        background-position: left top;
        background-repeat: no-repeat;
}
#righttop
{
        background-image: url(upperright.jpg);
        background-position: right top;
        background-repeat: no-repeat;
        height: 50px;
}
/* footer cap */
#mainlower
{
        background-image: url(bottom.jpg);
        background-position: center bottom;
        background-repeat: repeat-x;
}
#leftbottom
```

Example 9-3. CSS for the bordered example (continued)

```
{
        background-image: url(leftbottomcorner.jpg);
        background-position: left bottom;
        background-repeat: no-repeat;
}
#rightbottom
{
        background-image: url(rightbottomcorner.jpg);
        background-position: right bottom;
        background-repeat: no-repeat;
        height: 50px;
}
/* main content area */
#mainright
{
        background-image: url(rightside.jpg);
        background-position: center right;
        background-repeat: repeat-y;

}
#mainleft
{
        background-image: url(leftside.jpg);
        background-position: center left;
        background-repeat: repeat-y;

}

#content
{
    background-color: #fcfccc;
    margin: 0 50px;
    padding: 30px 0;
}
#content p
{
        margin: 10px 30px;
}
```

The stylesheet rules are quite simple: most are just adding the background image properties, split out for readability rather than using any shorthand technique. The "caps" also get a 50-pixel height; otherwise they wouldn't show, since they don't have content. You could also change this to include header and footer text, increasing the length of the "legs" for the corners.

This design is for a "flexible" content area, which will shrink as the page shrinks. That's why so many layers are used: the content can resize horizontally and vertically, as shown in Figure 9-17, after the page has been shrunk, resizing the content area. The use of the gradient enhances the effect, as the image seems to "flow" out of the top cap.

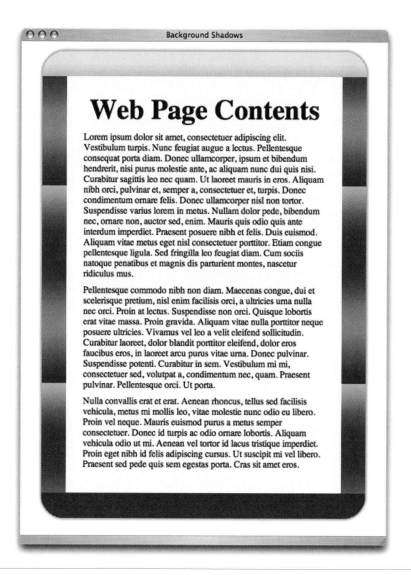

Figure 9-17. Page resized to show the flexible border

You can use this approach with any type of bordering image or images. If you want to use transparency, you can even use some overlap with corners, or even the sides and top or bottom, by using negative margins between elements to create the overlap effect. You'll still maintain the flexibility of the layout.

Speaking of flexibility, time to look at this concept more closely.

Flexible Designs

For the last several years, I have primarily used a fixed-width design at my web sites. It looks the same for everyone, and I can use a single piece image for the header and ensure that the text width area doesn't get too big or too small to read. The disadvantage to the approach, of course, is that the fixed width can be too small for some computer monitors or too large for others. There's also something constrained about a fixed width.

There are two main layout types: fixed and flexible. Within the flexible page layout category there are two subcategories: liquid and elastic.

The liquid design is one where no width is specified, or widths are specified as a percentage of the browser page size for all columns, or at least the main content column. The problem with this type of design is if the text area becomes too large, the text is too spread out, making it difficult to read. The advantage, though, is that it works quite well with float for flexible side-by-side columns.

The other flexible design type is the elastic design. The advantage of an elastic design is that text columns never get too large, and the overall page size can flex to meet whatever the browser window width is. The disadvantage is that horizontal scrollbars may appear where you least expect them when pages are shrunk down, not to mention columns shrinking to virtually nothing. The biggest problem, though, is mixing elastic widths with float for side-by-side columns.

One important component to the elastic layout design type is the unit of measurement used to specify the width, which I'll get into a little later. The other important component to the elastic design has to do with allowing a more flexible column and page width.

In the last section, in Example 9-3, `max-width` was used to size the main container element. As the page shrinks, so does the content area, and the text automatically wraps to compensate for a narrower space. As currently styled, the page will shrink until all that's left is the borders. To prevent the container from becoming *too* small, `min-width` can also be used. With both set, the content area will not expand or shrink past a certain point.

Another challenge with the use of max-min width/height is that IE 6.x and lower don't support the properties, though IE 7.x and up do. The simplest way to work around the problem is to use an IE-specific expression on the width, testing the width of the column and adjusting it to 900 pixels if it's wider:

```
#whole {
 width:expression(document.body.clientWidth > 900? "900px" : "auto");
}
```

Since this is a non-valid use of CSS, it can be packaged into a separate file and then, again, a conditional check in comments (supported only by IE) can be used to check the browser and load the IE-specific CSS. To make Example 9-2 IE-compatible, the markup is adjusted to:

```
<head>
<meta http-equiv="Content-Type" content="text/html; charset=utf-8" />
<title>Background Shadows</title>
<link rel="stylesheet" href="borders.css" type="text/css" media="screen" />
<!--[if IE 6]>
<link rel="stylesheet" type="text/css" href="ie6borders.css" />
<![endif]-->
</head>
```

It's not a pretty fix, but at least it works cross-browser, minimizing corruption of the more valid page elements.

Earlier I mentioned how the elastic layout is also dependent on units. One of the primary reasons for the elastic layout was to allow the content area widths to expand as the font size is increased. With fixed-width columns specified in pixels or percentages, when the font size is increased, the text wraps to compensate and may become uncomfortable to read. If the widths of the columns are specified in em units, though, when the font size increases, so do the widths of the columns.

Converting the CSS in Example 9-3 to a true elastic design leads to the CSS in Example 9-4, renamed as *bordersem.css*. The changes between the two pages are in bold to make them easier to see.

Example 9-4. Converting the CSS in Example 9-3 to a true elastic layout, with em sizing

```
/* general markup */
html,body
{
        margin: 0;
        padding: 0;
}
body
{
        background-color: #fff;
        padding: 1em 3em;
        font-size: 62.5%;
}
h1
{
        font-size: 4em;
        text-align: center;
}

#whole
{
        max-width: 80em;
        margin: 0 auto;
}
```

```css
/* upper cap */
#mainupper
{
        background-image: url(uppercenter.jpg);
        background-position: center top;
        background-repeat: repeat-x;
}

#lefttop
{
        background-image: url(upperleft.jpg);
        background-position: left top;
        background-repeat: no-repeat;
}
#righttop
{
        background-image: url(upperright.jpg);
        background-position: right top;
        background-repeat: no-repeat;
        height: 50px;
}

/* footer cap */
#mainlower
{
        background-image: url(bottom.jpg);
        background-position: center bottom;
        background-repeat: repeat-x;
}
#leftbottom
{
        background-image: url(leftbottomcorner.jpg);
        background-position: left bottom;
        background-repeat: no-repeat;
}
#rightbottom
{
        background-image: url(rightbottomcorner.jpg);
        background-position: right bottom;
        background-repeat: no-repeat;
        height: 50px;
}

/* main content area */
#mainright
{
        background-image: url(rightside.jpg);
        background-position: center right;
        background-repeat: repeat-y;
```

Example 9-4. Converting the CSS in Example 9-3 to a true elastic layout, with em sizing (continued)

```
}
#mainleft
{
        background-image: url(leftside.jpg);
        background-position: center left;
        background-repeat: repeat-y;

}

#content
{
   background-color: #fcfccc;
   margin: 0 5em;
   padding: 3em 0;
}
#content p
{
        margin: 1em 3em;
        font-size: 1.4em;
}
```

One of the first changes made is converting the font size to a pixel equivalency using the font-size: 62.5% trick from Chapter 8. This change makes it easier to convert the existing pixel sizes into the equivalent em size without resorting to a calculator. Of course, the font for the paragraphs also had to be resized because of the font size change.

Also note that the pixel height for the header and footer caps is kept at 50 pixels. This part of the page shouldn't change as the page is resized, because the background image isn't taller than 50 pixels. Figure 9-18 shows the page opened in a couple of browsers, with the text at different sizes using the browsers' built-in capability to resize text.

The elastic design is terrific but comes with one strong limitation: it doesn't work well with floats for multiple columns. If the columns are in an overall container, or one or more columns is flexibly sized using max-width, the columns will actually push down below each other rather than resize. With CSS3, implementation of columns will be simpler, but full implementation of that specification is years off. In the meantime, what's the best approach to mixed flexible and fixed column widths?

There have been ingenious design ideas dealing with fixed and fluid columns that are positioned using float (such as "Holy Grail," by Matthew Levine, at *http://www. alistapart.com/articles/holygrail*), but the simplest approach to floats and flexibility is using percentages. True, the design isn't nearly as elastic as using em units, but it doesn't require any overt tweaks to work. Not having to tweak overmuch is usually a good thing in my book.

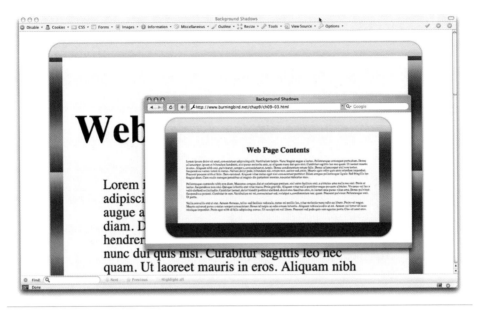

Figure 9-18. Elastic design in two different browsers with two different text sizes

Percentage widths can be mixed with `max-width` and `min-width`, to add some control onto the layout. This is especially important with text fields, where the length of the text lines can adversely impact readability. Example 9-5 is a web page that creates three different columns in three different colors, to make them easier to differentiate. Two of the columns—the main content and the third sidebar—are flexible, whereas the second is fixed. The overall container, bordered in gray, is also flexible.

Example 9-5. Fixed and flexible CSS widths

```
<!DOCTYPE html PUBLIC "-//W3C//DTD XHTML 1.0 Strict//EN"
        "http://www.w3.org/TR/xhtml1/DTD/xhtml1-strict.dtd">
<html xmlns="http://www.w3.org/1999/xhtml" lang="en" xml:lang="en">
<head>
<meta http-equiv="Content-Type" content="text/html; charset=utf-8" />
<title>Fixed and Flexible</title>
<style type="text/css">
*
{
        margin: 0;
        padding: 0;
}
body
{
        padding-top: 30px;
}
p {
        margin: 10px 30px;
}
```

Example 9-5. Fixed and flexible CSS widths (continued)

```
#main
{
    width: 90%;
    min-width: 800px;
    margin: 0 auto;
    border: 1px solid #ccc;
}
#one {
    width: 50%;
    max-width: 600px;
    min-width: 300px;
    float: left;
    background-color: #fcc;
    margin-right: 2%;
}
#two {
    width: 200px;
    float: left;
    background-color: #cfc;
    margin-right: 2%;
}
#three {
    width: 20%;
    max-width: 200px;
    min-width: 100px;
    float: left;
    background-color: #ccf;
}

#footer
{
    clear: both;
    height: 10px; background-color: #000;
}
</style>
</head>
<body>
<div id="main">
<div id="one">
<!-- content here --></div>
<div id="two">
<!-- content here -->
</div>
<div id="three">
<!-- content here -->
</div>
<div id="footer">
</div>
</div>
</body>
</html>
```

Figures 9-19 and 9-20 show the page in an expanded and collapsed width, respectively. Note the use of `mix-width` in the overall container element, `main`. This is set to a minimum width (800 pixels) to prevent the container from getting too small to hold all of the elements, and to keep the sidebars from being pushed under the content column. No matter how much the page is shrunk, the overall container will not shrink too far. Instead, a scrollbar will appear, allowing the person to scroll horizontally.

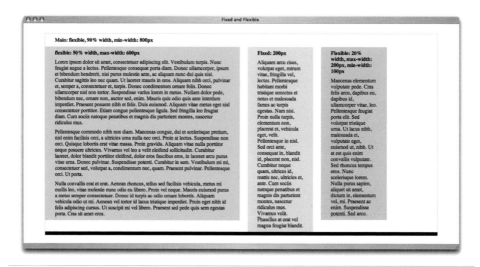

Figure 9-19. Fixed/flexible page layout design stretched out to maximum column widths

This isn't a comprehensive look at overall layout design issues by any means. Hopefully, though, this section gives you enough information on sizing issues so that you can minimize the confusing, and irritating, "pushed-down" sidebar column. To repeat one of the more important components to all of this: you do need to eliminate padding and margin differences, right at the start, to prevent frustration later. Either use the global whitespace reset, or you can be more selective with whitespace stripping, as covered in Chapter 8.

Once you have your layout, the next issue is: what color is your space?

Colors: Make Your Page Happy, Make Your Page Sad

You can mess around with layouts all you want, but what people will remember about your page is the color. The color could come from the backgrounds of elements or the color of fonts. Or the colors could come from the use of photos, images, graphics, and backgrounds. With the use of all white pages, color can even be ruthlessly suppressed, so as not to make a page overly busy or distract from photos.

Figure 9-20. Fixed/flexible page layout design, compressed until the minimum width is reached for the main element

There's more to the issue of color than what you like and don't like. I mentioned in Chapter 1 the hamster wheel and the overuse of color, which can make it more trash than treasure. Color can also make text hard to read, or even induce a headache in your web page visitors—not something I recommend if you want your site to be popular.

Color can also cheer people up, create a somber, serious mood, or send site visitors on a soothing quest through blue-green waves of contemplation. Thinking funky and fun? Bright, primary colors can stage the feel of a site before a person clicks even one link or reads one word. Into goth? Black and red. Into babies? Pastels rule. How about seasonal page looks? Coppery reds and yellow work for fall, and red and green or white and blue seem to be universal for winter, at least in my culture.

Horizontal Pages?

We're so used to vertical pages that when we come up against a horizontal layout, our minds go into a "does not compute" loop as we vainly look for the scrollbar on the side of the browser. Yet there's no reason not to have a horizontal page layout. With some forms of content, such as photos, a horizontal layout can actually be a very attractive alternative. What's important, regardless of layout direction, is minimizing the use of scrollbars that are active both horizontally and vertically.

Either develop a horizontal layout and work to ensure that the page height meets most of your readers' browsers, or go vertical and work for a consistent width.

The real challenge for horizontal layouts is the "paging" required for longer articles. With a vertical layout, the article just scrolls, as long as needed. With a horizontal layout, pages will need to be created specifically for certain amounts of text. That's why horizontal works best with photos and other discrete content.

Color is just as much a tool of site design as the markup you use to create the layout and the CSS you use to create the presentation. Use color wisely. Use color well. But above all, use color. The world was not meant for white web pages alone. No, not even when we were all peering into cramped 14-inch 8-bit computer monitors.

Web Colors: Worry? Not?

For the first 10 years of the Web, web designers labored under a form of tyranny. The monster that terrified page creators, pro or otherwise, was named Web Safe Colors. Gone were the days of subtle greens and the faint hint of cream. No, if it wasn't on the Web Safe Colors chart, with its severely limited 216-color palette, it wasn't used.

Web-safe colors were called this because these were colors supported across all 8-bit computer monitors and devices without the use of dithering. Lynda Weinman is credited with being the person to first chart all the colors, and there's many a day I spent poring over her charts, trying to find some color that I could use in a page design that didn't look awful, dithered or not.

 You can view Lynda's browser-safe color charts at *http://www.lynda.com/hex.asp*, or in Figure 9-21.

Of course, 8-bit computer monitors have gone the way of 64k memory, and we can finally contemplate putting the Web Safe Color monster to rest. Even the smaller handheld devices support 16-bit colors, or more. As long as subtle color differences aren't used to differentiate choices or highlight information, the page is your canvas and the world your color palette.

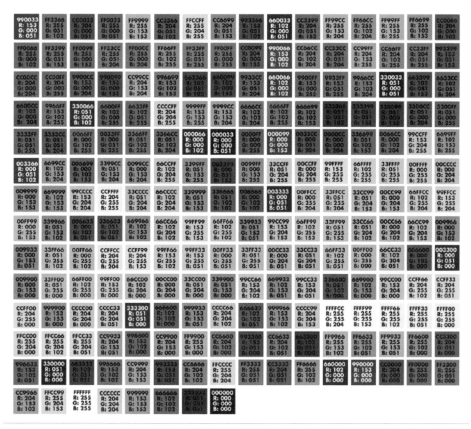

Figure 9-21. Lynda Weinman's chart of browser-safe colors; the monster is dead, long live the monster

Color and Accessibility

Being free of the Web Safe Color monster doesn't mean we can use colors willy-nilly all over our sites. One of the biggest mistakes web page creators make is to use green and red to mark "go" and "no go" conditions, completely disregarding that 7% of men can't differentiate between green and red.

Ralph Brandi, a friend of mine, once wrote an essay about how inaccessible the online Apple store is when it comes to signaling whether a product is available at a store location. Originally the site used red and green circles to signal whether an item (in this case, the early releases of the iPhone) was available or not. This use of color meant that color-blind people had no way of determining the availability of an item at their local stores. Ralph suggested that Apple use a square red icon to denote that an item wasn't available and a green circle to note that it was. While writing this chapter, I checked at the Apple store, and it is now using a red square for unavailable, green circle for available. Apple does learn from its mistakes.

Ralph's original writing is at *http://www.thereisnocat.com/showme874. html.*

Check iPhone availability at your local Apple Store

| New Jersey ▼ | ● iPhones available ▪ iPhones unavailable |

New Jersey Stores	Friday, June 29
Atlantic City, The Pier	▪
Bridgewater, Bridgewater	▪
Edison, Menlo Park	▪
Freehold, Freehold Raceway Mall	●
Marlton, Sagemore	●
Paramus, Garden State Plaza	●
Rockaway, Rockaway	●
Short Hills, Short Hills	▪
Woodcliff Lake, Tice's Corner	▪

Figure 9-22. Ralph Brandi's recommended status change, which eventually ended up being used at Apple

The point is, color can never be used by itself to indicate any state. Even for people who don't suffer from some visual impairment, trying to see the differences of color on small monitors, under bad lighting, or when they're tired can be a struggle. Color can be used to enhance—such as providing a yellow or red flash to signal the state of an operation, as is popular with Ajax-based applications—but it should never be the only indicator of important information.

Color should also be used carefully when marking something such as links in text. I've seen people use a dark maroon to signal a link not visited and a navy-blue link for a visited link. When mixed with black and white text, both colors can be hard to differentiate depending on lighting conditions and monitor resolution.

Aside from these caveats, though, color can be splashed happily about the page, limited only by your own tastes and preferences for a particular scheme, not to mention the theme and mood of your site.

Color, Schemes, Themes, and Mood

One of the more interesting web sites from a design perspective is COLOURlovers (at *http://www.colourlovers.com/*), where people can submit color palettes that others can then vote on. The site also has a weblog where different color themes are explored, themes such as "The Scariest Colors Imaginable" or how T-Mobile has trademarked the use of the color magenta. It's a wonderful site for exploring different color options, as well as learning to pick colors out of everyday things, such as a bowl of fruit.

Did you know there are actually phobias based on color? According to COLOURlovers, Cyanophobia is fear of the color blue, while Leukophobia is fear of the color white. These phobias are a result of an association between a specific color and a very tragic and profound event. The result is that the person can't see the color without experiencing a negative sensation, ranging from discomfort to more extreme reactions.

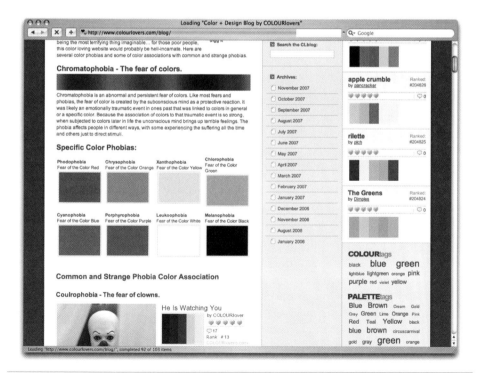

Figure 9-23. Fear of colors, at COLOURlovers

Colors have also been used to create psychological effects. Pink is used in jails to suppress negative emotions; black to convey elegance or mourning; red is sensual; green is fresh, ergonomic; blue is vast, intelligent; yellow is peppy. How much we each perceive these colors as a mood, though, differs based on culture as well as experience, so relying solely on color psychology when determining color use isn't a viable option when it comes to web design.

Frankly, though, there is no right or wrong color scheme. Have a baby site and want to use black and red? Go for it! How about a goth site in soft blues and pinks? If you can pull it off, more power to you. It's less the colors than how they're used that sets the mood and conveys the message.

There may be colors that don't work for your site or your site's theme; there may be colors that can be used together only with great care and deliberation. Color, though, is truly in the eye of the beholder.

Typography for the Page

I am not an expert in typography, other than knowing that no other web design topic drives out likes and dislikes—and passions—as much as the fonts you use and how you use them.

Some people prefer sans-serif fonts such as Arial or Verdana, whereas others can't stand them and prefer serif-based fonts, such as Georgia. I use a mix, which probably drives both groups mad.

Choosing a Font

The characteristics of fonts include such terms as ascenders and descenders, which describe the parts of the font that extend above the x-height of the font and below the font's baseline, respectively. Figure 9-24 shows a graphical depiction of these type terms, placed against an Arial font.

Most of us don't really care about the fundamentals of typography, other than wanting to ensure we're using the best fonts for our needs. Just like with color, what is the best depends on our own personal preferences as much as the mechanics of fonts.

Fonts generally fall into two main groupings, depending on whether the font has or doesn't have a *serif* at the end of the font strokes. A serif is a little stroke, a flourish if you will. Popular sans-serif fonts are Arial, Verdana, and Helvetica, while the more common serif fonts are Georgia and Times New Roman. Some fonts have a bolder variation, and others are *monospaced*, meaning that each letter takes up the same space regardless of letter. One variation of a bolder font is Arial Black, and Courier is the most common monospaced font.

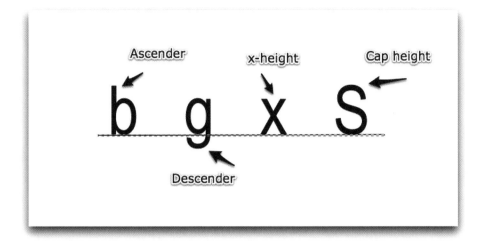

Figure 9-24. Depiction of some type characteristics

Another variety includes the cursives or fantasy fonts, such as Comic Sans MS. The symbol or wingdings fonts usually aren't used on the Web.

It might be tempting to open up Photoshop and explore its varied and many fonts to use for our web pages. Unfortunately, most of the fonts in tools such as Photoshop aren't part of the default font installation in most machines. Installed fonts can vary based on individual machine, but primarily vary by operating system.

The following are fonts commonly installed on Mac systems:

Sans serif
> Arial, Arial Black, Helvetica, Lucida Grande, Impact, Geneva, and Gadget

Serif
> Georgia, Times, New York, Palatino

Monospaced
> Courier, Courier New, Monaco

The following are fonts typically installed on Windows systems:

Sans serif
> Arial, Arial Black, Helvetica, Impact, Lucida Sans Unicode, Tahoma, Trebuchet MS, Verdana, MS Sans Serif

Serif
> Georgia, Palatino Linotype, Book Antiqua, Times New Roman, MS Serif

Monospaced
> Courier New, Lucida Console

Linux systems provide many of the fonts listed for the Mac and Windows operating systems, or their equivalents.

 Monday By Noon has a good page on Linux fonts at *http://mondaybynoon.com/2007/04/02/linux-font-equivalents-to-popular-web-typefaces/*, which also leads to a nicely definitive list of Windows/Mac fonts at *http://www.ampsoft.net/webdesign-l/WindowsMacFonts.html*, provided by Alberto Martinez Perez at AMPSoft (see Figure 9-25).

There is overlap in the fonts, though the same font name may not be used. An example of this is Windows' "Times New Roman," which is shortened to "Times" in the Mac. The safest way to ensure that at least some font of the general family is used is to do a compound property setting, such as the following in CSS:

```
font-family: Times New Roman, Times, serif
```

With this CSS setting, if Times New Roman is supported, it's used to define the font displayed. Otherwise, Times is used, followed by the generic serif, which instructs the browser to use the default serif font.

Windows fonts / Mac fonts / Font family

Normal style	Bold style
Arial, Arial, Helvetica, *sans-serif*	**Arial**, Arial, Helvetica, *sans-serif*
Arial Black, Arial Black, Gadget, sans-serif	**Arial Black, Arial Black, Gadget, sans-serif**
Comic Sans MS, Comic Sans MS[5], cursive	**Comic Sans MS**, *Comic Sans MS*[5], cursive
Courier New, Courier New, Courier[6], monospace	**Courier New**, Courier New, Courier[6], monospace
Georgia[1], Georgia, *serif*	**Georgia**[1], Georgia, *serif*
Impact, Impact[5]**, Charcoal**[6]**, sans-serif**	**Impact, Impact**[5]**, Charcoal**[6]**, sans-serif**
Lucida Console, Monaco[5], monospace	**Lucida Console**, Monaco[5], monospace
Lucida Sans Unicode, Lucida Grande, sans-serif	**Lucida Sans Unicode**, Lucida Grande, sans-serif
Palatino Linotype, Book Antiqua[3], Palatino[6], *serif*	**Palatino Linotype, Book Antiqua**[3], Palatino[6], *serif*
Tahoma, Geneva, sans-serif	**Tahoma**, Geneva, sans-serif
Times New Roman, Times, *serif*	**Times New Roman**, Times, *serif*
Trebuchet MS[1], Helvetica, *sans-serif*	**Trebuchet MS**[1], Helvetica, *sans-serif*
Verdana, Verdana, Geneva, *sans-serif*	**Verdana**, Verdana, Geneva, *sans-serif*
Symbol, Symbol **(Symbol**[2]**, Symbol**[2]**)**	Symbol, Symbol **(Symbol**[2]**, Symbol**[2]**)**
▶■✷♥①◐■? ✒ ▶■✷♥①◐■? **(Webdings**[2]**, Webdings**[2]**)**	▶■✷♥①◐■? ✒ ▶■✷♥①◐■? **(Webdings**[2]**, Webdings**[2]**)**
Wingdings, Zapf Dingbats **(Wingdings**[2]**, Zapf Dingbats**[2]**)**	Wingdings, Zapf Dingbats **(Wingdings**[2]**, Zapf Dingbats**[2]**)**
MS Sans Serif[4], Geneva, sans-serif	**MS Sans Serif**[4], Geneva, sans-serif
MS Serif[4], New York[6], *serif*	**MS Serif**[4], New York[6], *serif*

Figure 9-25. Font compatibility table from AMPSoft

Which font to use when? Like with color, there is no "rule" about what makes a good web page font. For my own use, I prefer a serif font (Georgia) for my general text, Lucida Grande/Verdana for my sidebar items, and a serif for larger titles. I've found that serif fonts seem to look better in larger text size, and that people generally prefer serif fonts for general text. However, sans-serif fonts seem to be crisper for sidebar items and lists of items, and I use a monospaced font, Courier New, for displaying code and markup. However, these are just my preferences; yours may, and probably will, differ.

Increasing Readability: Color Contrast, Line Length, Line Heights

Regardless of the font chosen, or in addition to font chosen, there are other characteristics associated with the font and page text that can impact readability.

The first is color and the amount of contrast between the background color and the font color. Contrary to expectation, a pure black font on a pure white background is not the optimal choice. The contrast between the two is so harsh that the combo can lead to eyestrain rather than enhanced viewing. At the same time, web accessibility guidelines recommend a minimum contrast of 5:1 between font and background for smaller text, 3:1 for larger fonts. Of course, the guidelines also say not to set either a font or background color, but that's something most of us aren't amenable to. Not to mention that most browsers have a way to override these settings if this becomes an issue.

The Web Content Accessibility Guidelines 2.0 can be accessed at *http://www.w3.org/TR/2007/WD-WCAG20-20070517/#visual-audio-contrast-contrast*. The Contrast Analyser can be found at *http://www.paciellogroup.com/resources/contrast-analyser.html*.

How can you determine the contrast ratio? With an algorithm, of course. Or you can use a tool, such as the Contrast Analyser 2.0. According to the site that provides the tool, a color brightness formula to consider is the following:

```
((Red value x 229) + (Green value x 587) + (Blue value x 114)) / 1000
```

In the formula, the color is broken down into its red, green, and blue values. Then, the red value is multiplied by 229, the green value multiplied by 587, and the blue by 114. The entire result is divided by 1,000. Apply this to both the font and background colors, and subtract the smaller from the larger. To meet the minimum contrast ratio, the difference should be greater than 125.

I tried this with one of my own sites, which currently uses a white background and a dark gray font (#ffffff and #333333, respectively):

```
Background color of #ffffff: ((255 x 229) + (255 x 587) + (255 x 114)) / 1000 = 237.15
Font color of #333333: (51 x 229) + (51 x 586) + (51 x 114)) / 1000 = 47.38
```

Subtracting 47.38 from 237.15 results in a value of 189.77, which safely exceeds the minimum contrast ratio requirement of 125.

Once the font and background colors are determined, the second most important component of web page readability is line length. Magazines and newspapers typically use a column with of 3 to 3 ½ inches (8.89 cm). Past studies have shown that this is the area that the eye can encompass for a page held about arm's length. The optimal line length for the Web isn't as clearly defined, because what people prefer and what works best aren't the same.

In a paper published by Dr. Bob Bailey, studies in 1998, 1999, and 2002 determined that shorter column widths, such as a 12-point font and a line length of 4 inches (10.16 cm), produced slower reading times than a longer line (7.3 inches, or 18.54 cm), but that people actually preferred the shorter line. According to Dr. Bailey's conclusion, based on the study results:

> Users tend to read faster if the line lengths are longer (up to 10 inches). If the line lengths are too short (2.5 inches or less) it may impede rapid reading. Finally, users tend to prefer lines that are moderately long (4 to 5 inches).

 Dr. Bailey's paper can be found at *http://www.webusability.com/article_line_length_12_2002.htm.*

Should we then design for preference or for efficiency? Personally, I design for preference. I figure if a person is irritated reading longer line lengths, even if it's more efficient, he won't return. My web sites tend to feature text fields between 500 and 650 pixels wide, with sidebar items generally in the range of 200 to 250 pixels. I also make sure that there's a decent amount of whitespace surrounding the text, through the use of both margins and padding.

Finally, a last issue is line height. The CSS line height attribute, `line-height`, determines the distance between the text baselines. Too little, and the words are crammed on top of one another; too much, and you feel like you're swimming through whitespace. A good rule of thumb is to set the `line-height` at 1.5 times the size of the font; others recommend a `line-height` of 140% of the font size. For a 14-point font, a good line height could then be 16 points, which translates to a font size of 12 pixels and a line height of 14 pixels.

However, like with everything else, your mileage can vary. Color of font, type of font, size of font, padding, general use of whitespace, all of these can change the best value to use for line heights. Figure 9-26 shows several paragraphs with different font settings, some meeting the golden rules and some not. The trick is: can you tell which is which?

Lorem ipsum dolor sit amet, consectetuer adipiscing elit. Vestibulum turpis. Nunc feugiat augue a lectus. Pellentesque consequat porta diam. Donec ullamcorper, ipsum et bibendum hendrerit, nisi purus molestie ante, ac aliquam nunc dui quis nisi. Curabitur sagittis leo nec quam. Ut laoreet mauris in eros. Aliquam nibh orci, pulvinar et, semper a, consectetuer et, turpis. Donec condimentum ornare felis. Donec ullamcorper nisl non tortor. Suspendisse varius lorem in metus. Nullam dolor pede, bibendum nec, ornare non, auctor sed, enim. Mauris quis odio quis ante interdum imperdiet. Praesent posuere nibh et felis. Duis euismod. Aliquam vitae metus eget nisl consectetuer porttitor. Etiam congue pellentesque ligula. Sed fringilla leo feugiat diam. Cum sociis natoque penatibus et magnis dis parturient montes, nascetur ridiculus mus.

> Pellentesque commodo nibh non diam. Maecenas congue, dui et scelerisque pretium, nisl enim facilisis orci, a ultricies urna nulla nec orci. Proin at lectus. Suspendisse non orci. Quisque lobortis erat vitae massa. Proin gravida. Aliquam vitae nulla porttitor neque posuere ultricies. Vivamus vel leo a velit eleifend sollicitudin. Curabitur laoreet, dolor blandit porttitor eleifend, dolor eros faucibus eros, in laoreet arcu purus vitae urna. Donec pulvinar. Suspendisse potenti. Curabitur in sem. Vestibulum mi mi, consectetuer sed, volutpat a, condimentum nec, quam. Praesent pulvinar. Pellentesque orci. Ut porta.

Nulla convallis erat et erat. Aenean rhoncus, tellus sed facilisis vehicula, metus mi mollis leo, vitae molestie nunc odio eu libero. Proin vel neque. Mauris euismod purus a metus semper consectetuer. Donec id turpis ac odio ornare lobortis. Aliquam vehicula odio ut mi. Aenean vel tortor id lacus tristique imperdiet. Proin eget nibh id felis adipiscing cursus. Ut suscipit mi vel libero. Praesent sed pede quis sem egestas porta. Cras sit amet eros.

Aliquam arcu risus, volutpat eget, rutrum vitae, fringilla vel, lectus. Pellentesque habitant morbi tristique senectus et netus et malesuada fames ac turpis egestas. Nam nisi. Proin nulla turpis, elementum non, placerat et, vehicula eget, velit. Pellentesque in nisl. Sed orci ante, consequat in, blandit id, placerat non, nisl. Curabitur neque quam, ultrices id, mattis nec, ultricies et, ante. Cum sociis natoque penatibus et magnis dis parturient montes, nascetur ridiculus mus. Vivamus velit. Phasellus at erat vel magna feugiat blandit.

Figure 9-26. Example fonts from file ch09-06.html

Web Design Tools

This last section is a brief review of some tools and utilities that can help you create your web designs. In addition, the very end of this chapter includes a list of additional reading that will help you continue your explorations in the mysteries and magic of web design.

Editors

Any text editor can be used for building web pages. My first web page editor was vi, a Unix command-line tool, a variation of which (vim) I still use for most of my web page editing. Others use Notepad or some variation in Windows, Textpad in the Mac, or emacs, a competitor of the earlier vi.

Some editors provide a What You See Is What You Get (WYSIWYG) interface that can be used to display the changes as they're made. Others go beyond this and provide forms and fields to fill in, which then generate the HTML and CSS.

For the simplest type of text editing, you can use Notepad and its more modern variations on Windows, and Textpad, as well as vi and emacs for the Mac and Linux, respectively.

For a step above a plain-text tool, you have the WYSIWYG tools, such as BBEdit for the Mac and HotDog Pro for Windows. One of the first HTML editing tools I used was the earliest version of HotDog. Most tools are either freely available or provide a 30-day trial, which allows you to check out several before settling on one.

A new tool I tried while writing this book was the open source Bluefish, available for Linux/FreeBSD and other Unix environments, as well as the Mac. I was able to install it on my Mac using the Macports command:

```
sudo port install bluefish
```

Bluefish does require X11 Windows support, of course, but if you're running a Mac and working with web graphics, you most likely have X11 installed by now. Bluefish is actually quite sophisticated, and I was tempted to put it into the web authoring tools because of its support for PHP, SQL, Apache, and so on. However, it lacks some of the visual helpfulness of the other more fully featured web authoring tools. If you're an experienced web page designer/developer, though, Bluefish does have what you need.

 BBEdit can be found at *http://www.barebones.com/products/bbedit/index.shtml*. HotDog can be accessed at *http://www.sausage.com/hotdog-professional.html*. Bluefish can be downloaded from *http://bluefish.openoffice.nl/*.

Web Authoring Tools

I differentiate web editors and web authoring tools primarily based on the level of site management support, as well as page editing. I would expect more features with a web authoring tool, as well as more support for ancillary specifications, such as the canvas element, XSLT, and SVG. Built-in or integrated preview capability is essential, as well as some non-markup way of creating the page content, such as dragging and dropping objects.

Probably the king daddy of web authoring tools is Dreamweaver, from Adobe. This complex, full-service authoring tool isn't cheap, but it's the tool of choice for many professional web page designers. It includes integration with other Adobe products, such as Photoshop, another reason for its popularity. Among its functions is a visual CSS editor, a layout editor, and Ajax support, though this is primarily focused on Adobe's Ajax products.

For the longest time, Microsoft's Frontpage was the de facto tool for building web pages within a Microsoft environment. Microsoft eventually replaced the functionality of Frontpage with Expression Web.

Microsoft does offer a 90-day trial of the tool, but you need to download and install .NET Framework 2.0, which isn't installed on most systems by default. In addition, I had some problems with the tool when I tried it out. Therefore, I decided to skip coverage of Expression Web. However, if you mainly work with Microsoft tools in the .NET and the ASP.NET environment, and don't mind downloading and installing the .NET Framework, give Expression Web a try.

The equivalent of Expression Web for the Mac would probably be iWeb. However, since Apple doesn't provide trial versions of its software, I'll forgo any further mention of this product.

Web Content Management Tools

Though not necessarily associated with web design, a variation on producing content for the Web is based on using some form of content management tool—for example, a weblogging tool such as WordPress or something more fully featured, such as the popular Drupal. Many are freely available, take care of most of the page generation, and can sometimes be installed with one click of a cPanel button. Another option is using a site that hosts generated web pages, such as Blogger or Typepad.

These web content management tools are a good alternative to hand-editing your pages. Even if you're an experienced web page editor or designer, you won't want to hand-edit every page at your site. With the hosted tools, all you have to do is design the template; the tool takes care of the rest. Plus, many of the tools provide "theme" sites, where you can download a theme that you can then either use as is or personalize. It's a fast way to get up and running.

Other Tools and Utilities

There's a wealth of other tools and utilities you can download or use online that can help with your page designs. Among those I can recommend are:

- The online Color Schemer, at *http://www.colorschemer.com/online.html*, provides a way of looking at lighter and darker variations of a given color.
- A-Prompt, at *http://aprompt.snow.utoronto.ca/*, tests your page for accessibility.
- The University of Minnesota Duluth has a page with a ton of tools and utilities at *http://www.d.umn.edu/is/support/Training/Online/webdesign/tools.html*.
- Eric Meyer has a color-blending tool that can be used online or saved for offline use; see *http://meyerweb.com/eric/tools/color-blend/*.

- A quick and easy color contrast tool can be found at *http://www.colorsontheweb.com/colorcontrast.asp*.

- GRSites has a lot of background images at *http://www.grsites.com/textures/*, though watch out for the pop ups.

- Adobe provides a free font browser with the Adobe Type Manager Light, at *http://www.adobe.com/products/atmlight/download.html*.

Additional Readings

I barely scratched the surface of web design in this chapter. To assist in your efforts in creating the world's best web design, I'd recommend the following for additional reading:

- "The Elements of Typographic Style Applied to the Web," at *http://webtypography.net/*. This site is a work in progress, containing a nicely organized collection of typographical "rules."

- "The Evolution of Type," presented by mediumbold, at *http://www.mediumbold.com/04_thinking/type/index.html*. This interesting history and overview of type also includes a dictionary of type terms.

- Websitetips.com has loads of useful articles and tips.

- Juicy Studio has much on accessibility issues, at *http://juicystudio.com/index.php*.

CHAPTER 10

Dynamic Web Page Graphics

I stumbled onto the Bubblemark animation test site while writing this book. It's a site set up for one purpose: to compare the performance on the same task between different Rich Internet Application (RIA) frameworks. What's the task? Animating from 1 to 128 balls within a given box.

The systems compared were: dynamic HTML (DHTML, shown in Figure 10-1), Microsoft's Silverlight (both the Common Language Runtime [CLR] and JavaScript), Adobe's Flash (Flex) and Apollo, several variations of Java (including JavaFX and Swing), the older IE-WPF, and the very new Python-based Cairo. That's a lot of user interface frameworks, including a couple I hadn't yet heard about.

With all of these different styles to choose from, why am I only focusing on the first option, DHTML (with and without SVG/canvas) for this book?

Trying out the various test pages provides some explanation. Some of the options, such as Silverlight and Flash, require installation of plug-ins or other external libraries. Other options lack maturity, or the performance suffers when compared with DHTML.

My main reason, though, is because DHTML (or Ajax, or client-side JavaScript, or ECMAScript, or whatever you want to call it) is a framework for interactive and animated web page graphics that has been under development and refinement for over 10 years, with support in all of the browsers. Yes, even IE. Add in the non-proprietary nature of the technology, the addition of graphical cousins such as the canvas element and SVG, and the fact that whatever you learn with DHTML typically can be applied to the other frameworks (at least those supporting some form of JavaScript, and which can't be said of the converse), and DHTML is a win-win.

 I use JavaScript in this book, but the proper name is ECMAScript, since this scripting language is now an ECMA specification.

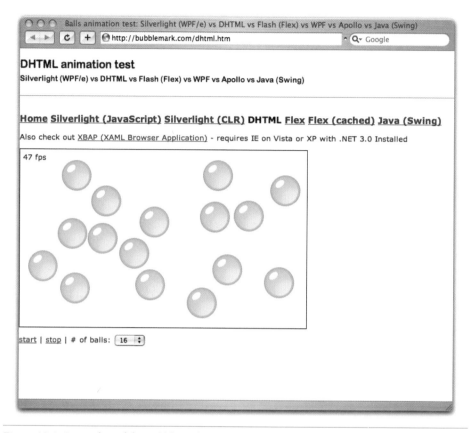

Figure 10-1. Screenshot of the Bubblemark DHTML page

The Quick Intro to the DOM

Web pages are based on a structure in which elements are nested within elements:

```
<div>
<h1>Title</h1>
<p>This is a paragraph.</p>
</div>
```

Figure 10-2 contains a screenshot of an SVG document (*webstructure.svg*, included in the book examples) that maps the HTML elements from Example 10-1 into a tree-like structure. Notice how the text contained within elements such as title and p are also nodes within the tree? The reason is because the content between an element's opening and closing tags is also a unique piece of the page, separate from and in addition to the elements themselves.

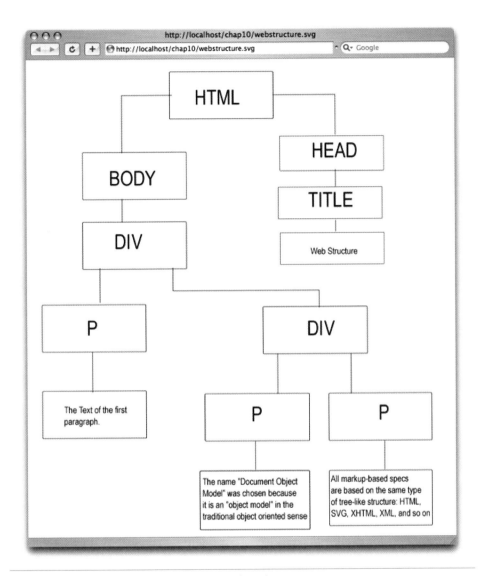

Figure 10-2. An SVG mapping of the structure of a web page

Example 10-1. Simple HTML 4.01 web page to demonstrate the hierarchical nature of web pages

```
<!DOCTYPE html PUBLIC "-//W3C//DTD XHTML 1.0 Strict//EN"
  "http://www.w3.org/TR/xhtml1/DTD/xhtml1-strict.dtd">
<html xmlns="http://www.w3.org/1999/xhtml" xml:lang="en" lang="en">
<head>
<title>Web Structure</title>
```

Example 10-1. Simple HTML 4.01 web page to demonstrate the hierarchical nature of web pages (continued)

```
</head>
<body>
<div>
<p>The text of the first paragraph</p>
<div>
<p>The name "Document Object Model" was chosen because it is an "object model" in the
traditional object oriented sense</p>
<p>All markup-based specs are based on the same tree-like structure: HTML, SVG, XHTML,
XML, and so on</p>
</div>
</div>
</body>
</html>
```

Though not demonstrated in Example 10-1, elements also have one or more attributes, which are properties defining the appearance and behavior of the element. For instance, the following code snippet contains an image element, `img`, with three attributes set, `id`, `alt`, and `src`:

```
<img id="someimage" src="some.jpg" alt="some text" />
```

Some attributes can be used only with specific elements, whereas other attributes can be used with most, if not all, elements. The `src` attribute can be used only with some elements, such as `img`, but the `id` attribute is universal.

The whole document structure is governed by some basic rules, such as ending what is known as an *empty element* with a forward slash:

```
<img src="some.jpg" alt="some text" />
```

An empty element is one that doesn't have both opening and closing tags, unlike the following:

```
<h1>Title</h1>
```

Another rule is that all elements that aren't empty must have closing tags, regardless of whether they contain anything, though not all variations of web page specifications rigidly enforce the rules.

You probably know all of this from earlier chapters or your own experiences before picking up this book. The point is, any web page can be broken down into basic components consisting of elements, content, and attributes, regardless of the specification governing the page: XHTML, HTML, or even HTML5, currently under development. For our purposes, whatever can be modeled as a separate and unique element in the page can be accessed using JavaScript.

Every element in a web page is accessible via JavaScript, and not just the visual elements you see, such as the `div`s and `ul`s and stylesheets. Even the `meta` elements in the `head` section of the document can be accessed as a node of the tree formed by all of the elements, contained in what is known as the DOM.

Enter: The DOM

The Document Object Model (DOM) is a programming interface specification created by the W3C that allows us to access the elements of a web page programmatically. There are three different DOM specifications: DOM Level 1, DOM Level 2, and DOM Level 3, with each new level building on the specification in the previous one. The aspect of the DOM we're concerned with in this chapter is the functionality implemented in browsers that allows us programmatic access to the page elements and their attributes.

Implicit within every document, be it SVG, XML, or HTML, are two elements key to working with a web page's contents: `window` and `document`. The `window` object is the overall parent, and includes things like the chrome and navigation, as well as events such as those that are fired when the web page is loaded. The `document` object encapsulates all of the elements *within* the document, such as the `body`, `divs`, and so on. It's through the `document` that we can access elements either by a given class or type, or uniquely, by identifier.

Focusing for the moment on accessing specific page elements, to ensure that an element is uniquely accessible, you'll need to give the element an identifier:

```
<div id="contents">
...
</div>
```

The `document` method to access the element is `getElementById`, as follows:

```
var contents = document.getElementById("contents");
```

Now you have an actual representation of that element within the script, ready to manipulate in all sorts of ways. One such manipulation is to access and/or alter attributes. Two DOM methods can be used to both set and retrieve an element's attributes: `setAttribute` and `getAttribute`.

```
var attr = div1.getAttribute("id");
div1.setAttribute("class","test");
```

The `getAttribute` method takes one parameter, the name of the attribute. The `setAttribute` method takes two, one for the attribute name and one for the attribute's new value.

With just these three methods, `getElementById`, `setAttribute`, and `getAttribute`, you can create a surprising number of graphical effects, simply by modifying one attribute: `style`.

Working with CSS Style Settings

One attribute shared by all the visual elements is the `style` attribute. Even if the attribute isn't explicitly set within the element directly:

```
<div style="color: #ffffff">
```

Every element has a CSS style.

The style attribute contains a reference to the CSS properties that can be modified by script, such as style.color for font color or style.backgroundColor for the element's background color. For multiple-word properties, such as background-color or font-family, the property is converted into a notation that removes all of the dashes, and replaces the lowercase letter in the word following the dash with a capital letter. For example:

- background-color becomes backgroundColor
- font-family becomes fontFamily
- list-style-type becomes listStyleType

This notation is commonly called *CamelCase*, because of the up/down nature of the names, similar to the humps of a camel.

Earlier I mentioned three important DOM methods: getElementById, setAttribute, and getAttribute. In the web page in Example 10-2, the outer div element is styled within the stylesheet embedded into the head section of the document. The page also has a small scripting block that doesn't do anything more than access the style attribute and change the background color.

Example 10-2. Simple web page with script to alter the background color of one of the elements

```
<!DOCTYPE html PUBLIC "-//W3C//DTD XHTML 1.0 Strict//EN"
  "http://www.w3.org/TR/xhtml1/DTD/xhtml1-strict.dtd">
<html xmlns="http://www.w3.org/1999/xhtml" xml:lang="en" lang="en">
<head>
<title>Web Structure</title>
<style type="text/css">
#first
{
   background-color: #ff0000;
}
</style>
<script type="text/javascript">
//<![CDATA[

window.onload=function() {
   var div1 = document.getElementById("first");
   var div1style = div1.getAttribute("style");
   div1style.backgroundColor="#ffff00";
}
//]]>
</script>
</head>
<body>
<div id="first">
<p>The text of the first paragraph</p>
```

Example 10-2. Simple web page with script to alter the background color of one of the elements (continued)

```
<div>
<p>The name "Document Object Model" was chosen because it is an "object model" in the
traditional object oriented sense</p>
<p>All markup-based specs are based on the same tree-like structure: HTML, SVG, XHTML,
XML, and so on</p>
</div>
</div>
</body>
</html>
```

I load the page in the browser, confident that the color of the background for the first div element will be changed, only to receive a JavaScript error displayed in the Firefox extension Firebug, as shown in Figure 10-3.

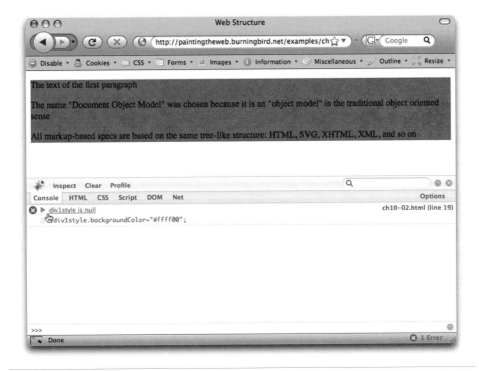

Figure 10-3. JavaScript error reflected in the Firebox debugging window

Example 10-2 generated the error because there is no background color style setting to the application. Though the background color is set using a stylesheet, this property is not available to script until either it's set directly in script, first, or set within a style attribute added directly to the element. Even with the latter, you can access the style attribute on the element, but all you'll get is a string containing all of the CSS properties—not individually accessible CSS attributes.

The reason the background color isn't accessible via script in this web page is because the style setting used to render the div element is a *computed* setting, consisting of a combination of stylesheet settings, element inheritance, and browser defaults. As such, they're not something you can just access directly from the style attribute.

 CSS style properties are blank or undefined except when set previously in the script, even if you set the value through a stylesheet or set the style attribute directly in the element.

To read individual CSS style properties, you'll need to use other properties, each specific to different types of browsers. Internet Explorer (IE) and Opera support a currentStyle property on the element, though how the value is accessed differs between the two. The current style is an array value with IE, whereas Opera supports the DOM-compatible getPropertyValue method. Firefox and Safari support window.getComputedStyle, which then returns an object from which we can derive the CSS style using getPropertyValue.

We could account for differences in style access among browsers if this were the only difference. Unfortunately, it's not.

For the getPropertyValue methods, regardless of how you get the object that supports this method, you must pass in the CSS attribute using the same syntax you use when setting the style in the stylesheet. In other words, say you use background-color to access the background color. However, for the IE-specific currentStyle array method, you'll use the CamelCase notation, described earlier: backgroundColor rather than background-color.

 As this book was being prepared for publication, Microsoft released the first beta of IE8, which addresses some of the browser differences between IE8 and the other browsers. As long as JavaScript libraries use object detection (looking for a specific method or property), the library should work equally well with IE7 and IE8 and the other browsers.

In order to work around the browser differences, developers typically create functions that check for the existence of specific functionality with which to access the style property. If one method isn't supported, a second is tested, and so on until all browser differences have been accounted for. That's the approch we'll use. In Example 10-3, a new function is created, getStyle, taking three parameters: the element whose CSS style we're trying to find, the style property name in CSS format, and, finally, the property name in CamelCase notation. The function tests to see whether currentStyle is supported, and then whether getPropertyValue is supported, and pulls the value based on the response. For computedStyle, the function uses the same test for an appropriate response. Finally, one last test is made: to see whether the property is actually set *in* the style attribute.

Example 10-3. Using a cross-browser CSS style technique

```
<!DOCTYPE html PUBLIC "-//W3C//DTD XHTML 1.0 Strict//EN" "http://www.w3.org/TR/xhtml1-
strict.dtd">
<html xmlns="http://www.w3.org/1999/xhtml" xml:lang="en" lang="en">
<head>
<title>Web Structure</title>
<style type="text/css">
#first
{
    background-color: #ff0000;
    color: #fff;
}
</style>
<script type="text/javascript">
//<![CDATA[

function getStyle(node,styleName,camelStyleName) {

    if (node.currentStyle) {
        if (node.currentStyle.getPropertyValue) {
            return node.currentStyle.getPropertyValue(styleName);
        } else {
            return node.currentStyle[camelStyleName];
        }
    } else if (document.defaultView) {
        return document.defaultView.getComputedStyle(node,null).getPropertyValue(styleName);
    } else if (node.style.getPropertyValue) {
        return node.style.getPropertyValue(styleName);
    } else {
        return undefined;
    }
}

window.onload=function( ) {
    var div1 = document.getElementById("first");
    alert(getStyle(div1,"background-color", "backgroundColor"));
    div1.style.backgroundColor = "#000000";
}
//]]>
</script>
</head>
<body>
<div id="first">
<p>The text of the first paragraph</p>
<div>
<p>The name "Document Object Model" was chosen because it is an "object model" in the
traditional object oriented sense</p>
<p>All markup-based specs are based on the same tree-like structure: HTML, SVG, XHTML,
XML, and so on</p>
</div>
</div>
</body>
</html>
```

The page should now work properly, popping up a message box containing the original background color setting and then changing this color. Notice how easy it is to set the background color—no cross-browser challenges with changing the style properties, only with accessing them.

Once you have resolved the challenges with accessing the style properties, exactly what is returned also varies from browser to browser. For instance, Opera and IE8 return the hexadecimal format for the color:

```
#ff0000
```

whereas Firefox and Safari return the RGB setting:

```
RGB(255,0,0)
```

You'll then need to convert between the two formats if you want a consistent result. In addition, other formatting issues can arise, such as float values and opacity.

Retrieving style settings from the page is a minefield. It's problems such as this that led to the creation of JavaScript/Ajax libraries, such as Prototype, Dojo, and JQuery. If you don't want to use an external library, you can bypass the whole style access problem by using program variables to hold initial values and only using the style attribute to set CSS properties.

Example 10-4 demonstrates this approach. The application has been changed, the convoluted method to resolve the `style` attribute is gone, and any settings essential to the application are stored in global variables. Additionally, the `div` element's background color is changed only when the element is clicked, and then it's cycled back and forth between red and black.

Example 10-4. Resolving the problem of accessing the style property by storing it ourselves

```
<!DOCTYPE html PUBLIC "-//W3C//DTD XHTML 1.0 Strict//EN"
"http://www.w3.org/TR/xhtml1/DTD/xhtml1-strict.dtd">
<html xmlns="http://www.w3.org/1999/xhtml" xml:lang="en" lang="en">
<head>
<title>Web Structure</title>
<style type="text/css">
#first
{
    background-color: #ff0000;
    color: #fff;
}
</style>
<script type="text/javascript">
//<![CDATA[
var funBackgroundColor = "#ff0000";

window.onload=function() {
    var div1 = document.getElementById("first");
    div1.onclick = function() {
```

```
        div1.style.backgroundColor = funBackgroundColor = (funBackgroundColor == "#ff0000")
? "#000000" : "#ff0000";
    }
}
//]]>
</script>
</head>
<body>
<div id="first">
<p>The text of the first paragraph</p>
<div>
<p>The name "Document Object Model" was chosen because it is an "object model" in the
traditional object oriented sense</p>
<p>All markup-based specs are based on the same tree-like structure: HTML, SVG, XHTML,
XML, and so on</p>
</div>
</div>
</body>
</html>
```

Now all the browsers are happy, we don't have to resolve differences between "rgb(0,0,0)" and "#000000", and, most importantly, the CSS effect works. Even with IE, as shown in Figure 10-4.

The Ajax purists will howl about the global variable because these can conflict with other variables of the same name if you use multiple libraries in your web pages. However, I've prefaced the value with fun to act as a pseudonamespace, which hopefully will differentiate it from any other attribute like backgroundcolor.

This has been a quick introduction to the technology used for accessing and modifying page elements in the rest of this chapter and book, but I hope it provides enough to help you play with the examples on your own.

> Some of the examples that follow use larger JavaScript libraries, of which I'll repeat only the parts related to the modification of CSS. All of the libraries are included in the examples for this book, so you can review the pieces of the script not covered.

Coloring Highlights

Using color as a means to communicate is incredibly risky because not all people can differentiate among colors. Color blindness impacts up to 8% of the Caucasian male population (more or less), and even those not so challenged may have some problems with more subtle variations. Poor eyesight, eyestrain, bad computer monitors, room or outdoor lighting—all can impact the perception of color.

Figure 10-4. Even IE likes the use of a global variable to capture current style information

If color is not the only means by which information is communicated, though, it can be a terrific way to add a little extra oomph to a process. One such use of color is the use of the color flash, or fade, as it's come to be known in Ajax circles.

A color fade, usually red to white or yellow to white, is a quickly displayed flash of graduated color that highlights information or marks an action. Examples include a red flash just before a row of data is deleted from a database, or a yellow flash to signal an update or modification. A fade should be accompanied by some other indicator that an action has taken place, such as an update to a counter for the number of comments or a statement about successful database deletion.

The color fades flash between no color and fully saturated color, which means that even if you can't differentiate the shade, usually you can differentiate between the differing saturations.

Dynamically creating a color fade starts with selecting a color at peak saturation and then adjusting the remaining channels until the color approaches white. Figure 10-5 shows several bars of green, starting with an RGB value of (0,255,0) at the top, and ending with an RGB value of (238,255,238) at the bottom, expressed in hexadecimal notation. The saturated color—in this instance, green—remains constant; it is the other channels that change.

#00ff00

#33ff33

#66ff66

#99ff99

#aaffaa

#ccffcc

#eeffee

Figure 10-5. Different saturations of green

The same effect applies to red and blue, and also for colors such as yellow, which is an RGB of (255,255,0) at its most saturated and (255,255,238) at its least; magenta, with an RGB of (255,0,255) at its most saturated and (255,238,255) at its least; and so on. The key to create the effect is to hold the target color channel (or channels) the same, and just adjust the other non-saturated color channels in increments.

Example 10-5 shows a web page that has a form with a text area and text input box, as well as two div elements: one to act as a comment preview "button" and the other as a comment preview area. I use a div rather than a button because I don't want to mess around with canceling form submission events, since I'm demonstrating the graphical elements in the example.

Clicking the preview "button" copies the text to the preview element, flashing the color specified in the text input box at the same time. Both the CSS styles and Java-Script are located in separate files.

Example 10-5. Web page application to demonstrate color fades/flashes

```
<!DOCTYPE html PUBLIC "-//W3C//DTD XHTML 1.0 Strict//EN"
  "http://www.w3.org/TR/xhtml1/DTD/xhtml1-strict.dtd">
<html xmlns="http://www.w3.org/1999/xhtml" xml:lang="en" lang="en">
<head>
<title>Color Flash</title>
<link rel="stylesheet" href="color.css" type="text/css" media="screen" />
<script type="text/javascript" src="color.js">
</script>
</head>
<body>
<form action="">

<p><textarea id="comment" cols="70" rows="10"></textarea></p>
<p><input type="text" id="color" /></p>
</form>

<div id="save">Preview Text</div>

<h3>Preview</h3>
<div id="preview"></div>
</body>
</html>
```

The CSS to style the page isn't anything special, and is included with the examples for review. The JavaScript, though, demonstrates how a color flash/fade is created and is replicated in Example 10-6. Note that the color functions are grouped apart from the functions that manage the non-color-specific components, such as copying the text and capturing the "button" click event.

Example 10-6. The color flash/fade JavaScript

```
// color functions

// fade color
function colorFlash(color,val) {

    var satval = val.toString(16);
    if (satval.length <=1) satval="0"+ satval;

    var r = "ff"; var g = "ff"; var b = "ff";

    switch(color) {
        case "green" :
          r = satval;
          b = satval;
          break;
        case "orange" :
          g = "a7";
          b = satval;
          break;
        case "magenta" :
          g = satval;
          break;
        case "blue" :
          r = g = satval;
          break;
        case "yellow" :
          b = satval;
          break;
        case "red" :
          b = g = satval;
          break;
     }

    var newval = "#"+r+g+b;
    return newval;
}

// bind event to object without overriding 'this'
function bindEventListener(obj, method) {
   return function(event) { method.call(obj, event || window.event)};
}

// color fade timer
function Counter(id,color,start,finish) {
    var timerval = 30;
    this.count = this.start = start;
    this.finish = finish;
    this.id = id;
    this.countDown = function() {
       this.count+=25;
```

Example 10-6. The color flash/fade JavaScript (continued)

```
        if (this.count >= this.finish) {
            document.getElementById(this.id).style.background="transparent";
            this.countDown=null;
            return;
        }
        document.getElementById(id).style.backgroundColor=colorFlash(color,this.count);
        setTimeout(bindEventListener(this,this.countDown),timerval);
    }
}


// general application functions
window.onload = function ( ) {
    document.getElementById("save").onclick=echoPreview;
}

// preview and set color
function echoPreview( ) {
    var color = document.getElementById("color").value;
    var commentText = document.getElementById("comment").value;
    modText = commentText.split(/\n/).join("<br />");
    var previewElem = document.getElementById("preview");
    previewElem.innerHTML = modText;
    var ctrObj = new Counter("preview", color, 0, 255);
    ctrObj.countDown( );
}
```

The color routine is made up of a JavaScript `switch` statement that checks to see what color it should be fading and then adjusts the other channels appropriately. The current "saturation" value is passed to the function and converted into a hexadecimal value using the `toString` function with a parameter of 16 (decimal is 10, octal is 8):

```
        var satval = val.toString(16);
```

By default, all channels are set to their highest saturation levels, a hexadecimal value of `"ff"`:

```
        var r = "ff"; var g = "ff"; var b = "ff";
```

For each of the colors, the `satval` is used for whatever channel is being adjusted, such as the red and blue channels when a green flash is implemented:

```
        case "green" :
          r = satval;
          b = satval;
          break;
```

The only color that differs is the orange color, which doesn't have an equal amount of saturation in the red and green channels. Because of this, and the process used to create the flash, the orange color doesn't fade as pure orange—it cycles through an orange, a magenta-like color, and an aqua before fading to white. It's an interesting effect, and one that can be used to experiment with other colors and the resulting flash.

The other functions in the JavaScript file manage the timer and the event handling. The function bindEventListener is used to make sure that when an event is bound to an object, the event listener doesn't override the this, which holds the timer object itself:

```
// bind event to object without overriding 'this'
function bindEventListener(obj, method) {
  return function(event) { method.call(obj, event || window.event)};
}
```

If the event overrode the object, we'd never have access to the current color and the color used with each timer iteration:

```
// color fade timer
function Counter(id,color,start,finish) {
   var timeval = 30;
   this.count = this.start = start;
   this.finish = finish;
   this.id = id;
   this.countDown = function( ) {
       this.count+=25;
       if (this.count >= this.finish) {
          document.getElementById(this.id).style.background="transparent";
          this.countDown=null;
          return;
       }
       document.getElementById(id).style.backgroundColor=colorFlash(color,this.count);
       setTimeout(bindEventListener(this,this.countDown),timeval);
   }
}
```

The highlighted code is the timer amount. The current implementation triggers the timer code every 30 microseconds. Also notice from the timer code that the flash sets the saturated color immediately and then fades to white. A variation could be to start with white, flash to the color in degrees, and then fade to white. You could do this by reversing the color timer amount, starting with 255 and then counting down to 0, before switching to starting with 0 and counting up to 255. Included in the examples is a file, *ch10-05a.html*, with a matching JavaScript file, *colors2.js*, that does just this.

Even if you're not experienced with JavaScript, there are two modifications to this application you can make in order to experiment with the color effect. The first is to add another color to the switch statement at the beginning of the *color.js* file in order to try out different effects with different colors. Just remember to add the break at the end of the new case, to stop the processing of the switch statement at that point.

The second modification applies to the timer value, the highlighted code in the previous snippet. Setting a higher value will slow down the flash; a lower value will speed it up. I used a timer value of 2000 in order to slow the flash enough to get the screenshot shown in Figure 10-6.

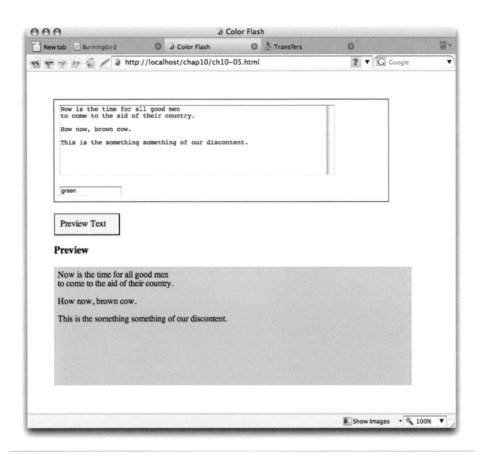

Figure 10-6. Partial fade from bright green to white

Another use of color and color saturation is signaling completion of an act, especially if there are other indicators that show this type of information. In the last chapter of this book, I demonstrate this with my "Rosy Glow of Completion" form effect.

Changing Class and Transparency

Opacity is sometimes overlooked when it comes to visual effects. Opacity can be a great way of indicating whether something is applicable, for example, to indicate whether a button is active or a link can be clicked. Opacity can be a great way to indicate whether something is applicable—whether a button is active or a link can be clicked, for example.

To demonstrate working with opacity, Example 10-7 shows a web page with several different chocolates, each with different ingredients. Along the top of the page are seven checkboxes associated with ingredients found in the candies: chocolate, berry, lemon, hazelnut, caramel, coffee, and sea salt. These same ingredients are also given as HTML classes to the div element containing each chocolate.

Checking one or more checkboxes highlights which chocolate has the ingredient. The application does this by de-emphasizing the chocolates that don't have the ingredient. The result is cumulative: a chocolate only has to match one of the checked options to be displayed with 100% opacity.

Example 10-7. Page with several chocolates, with ingredients listed as class names

```
<!DOCTYPE html PUBLIC "-//W3C//DTD XHTML 1.0 Strict//EN"
"http://www.w3.org/TR/xhtml1/DTD/xhtml1-strict.dtd">
<html>
<head>
<title>A Taste Of</title>
<meta http-equiv="X-UA-Compatible" content="IE=7"/>
<link rel="stylesheet" href="taste.css" type="text/css" media="screen" />
<script type="text/javascript" src="taste.js">
</script>
</head>
<body>
<form action="">
<div><label for="chocolate">Chocolate:</label><input type="checkbox" name="chocolate"
value="chocolate"></div>
<div><label for="berry">Berry</label><input type="checkbox" name="berry" value="berry">
<div><label for="lemon">Lemon:</label><input type="checkbox" name="lemon" value="lemon">
</div>
<div><label for="hazelnut">Hazelnut:</label><input type="checkbox" name="hazelnut"
value="hazelnut"></div>
<div><label for="caramel">Caramel:</label><input type="checkbox" name="caramel"
value="caramel" /></div>
<div><label for="coffee">Coffee:</label><input type="checkbox" name="coffee"
value="coffee" /></div>
<div><label for="salt">Sea Salt:</label><input type="checkbox" name="salt" value="salt" />
</div>
</form>

<ul>
<li class="chocolate coffee salt">Chocolate Delight: A tasty blend of chocolate with
creamy ganache flavored with coffee. The top is sprinkled with smoky gray salt from the
waters near the French Riviera. </li>
<li class="chocolate berry">Ma Dear A: Sweet 16 and never been kissed comes to mind with
this sweet wine/berry infused chocolate drop, shaped like a kiss, but twice as smooth.</li>
<li class="hazelnut chocolate">Pralines and Creme: Wonderful mix of hazelnut cream,
chopped hazelnuts, crisped rice, all enveloped in a smooth robe of the richest, thickest,
creamiest milk chocolate. </li>
<li class="lemon chocolate">Lemon Pi: Figure this one out: how many Lemon Pis can you eat
in one sitting? Creamy lemon fondant filling with darkest chocolate coating, sprinkled
with fractured wafer thin lemon candy.</li>
<li class="lemon">Lemon Cream: Candied lemon peel chopped fine and folded into a creamy
nougat, which is then dipped in white chocolate.</li>
```

Example 10-7. Page with several chocolates, with ingredients listed as class names (continued)

```
<li class="chocolate salt caramel">Dirty Caramels: The richest, buttery caramels are
coated with milk chocoate and the finest flor de sal mixed with grated peppercorn
sprinkled on top to bring out the sweetness.</li>
<li class="hazelnut caramel coffee">Coffee Drops: Who says you need chocolate when you
have a coffee and hazelnut infused caramel? Tastes reminds you of the Walnettos you ate as
a kid, only better.</li>
<li class="berry lemon">Berry Lemonade: Similar to the Turkish delights of yesterday,
these lemon and berry jellies are filled with pecans (berry) or walnuts (lemon), cut into
squares, dusted with powdered sugar, and pretty as a picture.</li>
<li class="coffee chocolate hazelnut">Wake me up: Coffee ganache lovingly wraps a whole
hazelnut, before being tenderly covered in the finest dark chocolate.</li>
<li class="chocolate salt">Black Widow: Death by chocolate, what a way to go. Creamy
chocolate ganache infused with black pepper, enrobed in darker chocolate, sprinkled with a
few grains of pink Hawaiian salt.</li>
<li class="berry caramel">Berry Widow: Raspberry caramel with bits of pecan and white
chocolate rose dabbed on top.</li>
</ul>
</body>
</html>
```

Note in the example how each chocolate can have more than one class, depending on which ingredients it has.

Figure 10-7 shows the page when first loaded. The CSS file for the application doesn't do anything with the class names; they're only used for processing. As such, we'll move on to the JavaScript implementing the application.

This new example demonstrates another DOM method for accessing page elements: getElementsByTagName. This method finds all of the elements of a given tag (element) in the page and returns them as an array in the same order in which they appear in the DOM—typically the order in which they appear in the page, unless the document has been modified previously. The tag name used for this application is li for all of the list items in the page, and input for the input elements (in this case, the checkboxes). In addition, the property className is accessed directly on elements to get the class names assigned to the element. Another approach (demonstrated in a later application) would be to use the getAttribute method, passing in the class attribute name.

Example 10-8 shows the JavaScript for the page, located in the file *taste.js*. To start, the onclick event handler is attached to each checkbox and assigned to the function, checkValues. In this function, the checkboxes are reviewed to see which are checked, and a list of options is captured. Then, each chocolate's class attribute is accessed and checked to see whether any of the classes match any of the options. If there is a match, the chocolate is set to full opacity; otherwise, it's set to a third opacity.

Figure 10-7. Taste Of application, demonstrating the power of opacity

Example 10-8. Processing the Taste Of application, highlighting chocolates based on class match

```
/ attach click event to each checkbox
window.onload =function( ) {
  var boxes = document.getElementsByTagName("input");
  for (var i = 0; i < boxes.length; i++) {
      boxes[i].onclick=checkValues;
  }
}

// cross-browser adjust opacity function
function setOpacity(obj,val) {
  obj.style.opacity = val;
  obj.style.MozOpacity=val;
  obj.style.KhtmlOpacity=val;
  val*=100;
  obj.style.filter = "alpha(opacity="+val+")";
}
```

Example 10-8. Processing the Taste Of application, highlighting chocolates based on class match (continued)

```
// reset all list items back to fully opaque
function resetAll( ) {
   var chocolates = document.getElementsByTagName("li");
   for (var i = 0; i < chocolates.length; i++)
      setOpacity(chocolates[i],1.0);
}

// checkbox is checked
function checkValues ( ) {
  var boxes = document.getElementsByTagName("input");
  var options = new Array( );

  // create array of checked options
  for (var i = 0; i < boxes.length; i++) {
      if (boxes[i].checked)
         options[options.length] = boxes[i].value;
  }

  // if no flavors checked, reset all chocolates to display
  if (options.length == 0) {
     resetAll( );
     return;
  }
  // for each chocolate, compare against flavor options
  // if found, mark chocolate for full opacity
  var chocolates = document.getElementsByTagName("li");
  var opaques = new Array(chocolates.length);
  for (j = 0; j < chocolates.length; j++)
     for(var k = 0; k < options.length; k++) {
        if (chocolates[j].className.indexOf(options[k]) >= 0) {
           opaques[j] = 1;
        }
     }

  // for all opaque chocolates, set opacity for full
  // otherwise, cut opacity down to a third
  for (var l = 0; l < opaques.length; l++)
     if (opaques[l])
        setOpacity(chocolates[l],1.0);
     else {
        setOpacity(chocolates[l],0.3);
     }
}
```

Figure 10-8 shows the page with a couple of ingredients checked.

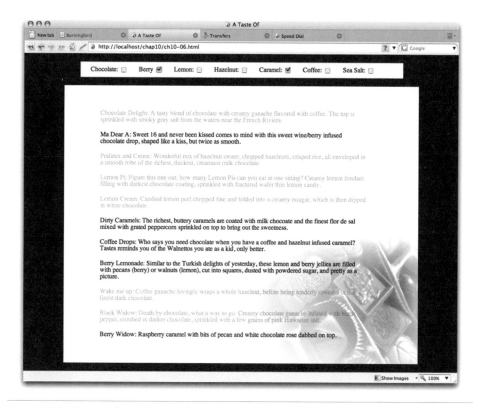

Figure 10-8. Give me chocolates with berries and/or caramel

Opacity differs rather drastically between the different browsers. Some browsers support the CSS `opacity` attribute, older Mozilla browsers support `MozOpacity`, and other older browsers support `KhtmlOpacity`, while Internet Explorer 7 and lower manage opacity through a specialized filter. Rather than test for each attribute, I just set the properties regardless:

```
// cross-browser adjust opacity function
function setOpacity(obj,val) {
  obj.style.opacity = val;
  obj.style.MozOpacity=val;
  obj.style.KhtmlOpacity=val;
  val*=100;
  obj.style.filter = "alpha(opacity="+val+")";
}
```

This highlights an interesting aspect of JavaScript: new properties can be assigned dynamically to any JavaScript object at any time. Of course, you have to be careful in case some other application might be using the properties. In this case, though, we'll take the shortcut, which leads us to a modification to the Taste Of application.

One major change in IE8 was the removal of a proprietary functionality called hasLayout. Unfortunately, the opacity filters in IE were dependent on this, and because of this change, the first beta of IE8 does not support opacity in any form. To test the examples that use opacity, like those included in this section, you'll need to turn on IE7 emulation mode. You can do so in the IE8 toolbar, or by opening the Developer Tools, selecting the View menu option in the debug window that opens, and then selecting the IE7 compatibility mode. If you want to ensure that your examples work with IE, at least until Microsoft supports CSS3 opacity, you can also add the following meta tag, which tells IE to process the page in IE7 mode:

```
meta http-equiv="X-UA-Compatible" content="IE=7"/>
```

Hopefully the CSS3 version of opacity will be added to future versions of IE8.

Many of the examples involving dynamic modification of CSS properties show one property changing at a time. In most cases, that's all that's needed. Other times, though, several CSS properties might need to be changed at once, rather than individually. In cases like this, it's better to change one attribute: the element's class.

Using opacity to de-emphasize the chocolates that don't match an option is OK, but it would be better to emphasize the picked chocolates as well as de-emphasize the ones not picked, as shown in Figure 10-9. We could do this by changing more properties individually, but this approach gets processing-intensive after a time. A better technique would be to have one class for the matched chocolates and one class for those not matched, and then just change the class.

The following two CSS entries are added to the *taste.css* file:

```
.matched
{
        font-size: larger; font-weight: bold;
        filter:alpha(opacity=100);
        -moz-opacity:1.0;
        -khtml-opacity: 1.0;
        opacity: 1.0;
        border: 1px dashed #300;
        padding: 5px;
}
.notmatched
{
        filter:alpha(opacity=30);
        -moz-opacity:0.3;
        -khtml-opacity: 0.3;
        opacity: 0.3;
}
```

Figure 10-9. De-emphasizing not-picked and emphasizing picked

Both entries are needed because an entry is modified both when it isn't found, and when it is, once the filtering begins. The HTML file is unchanged, but the JavaScript is modified—first to remove the opacity change, since it's no longer needed, and then to add the processing to add and remove the class names, without removing the other classes describing the chocolates. Example 10-9 shows the modified application, with modified lines in bold text.

Example 10-9. Modification of Taste Of application to use classes rather than setting CSS properties

```
// attach click event to each checkbox
window.onload =function( ) {
  var boxes = document.getElementsByTagName("input");
  for (var i = 0; i < boxes.length; i++) {
      boxes[i].onclick=checkValues;
  }
}
```

Example 10-9. Modification of Taste Of application to use classes rather than setting CSS properties (continued)

```
// alter class string
function removeMatched(chocolate) {
   var class = chocolate.className.replace(/matched/,"");
   chocolate.className = class;
}

function removeNotMatched(chocolate) {
   class = chocolate.className.replace(/notmatched/,"");
   chocolate.className = class;
}

// reset all list items back to fully opaque
function resetAll( ) {
   var chocolates = document.getElementsByTagName("li");
   for (var i = 0; i < chocolates.length; i++) {
      removeNotMatched(chocolates[i]);
      removeMatched(chocolates[i]);
   }
}
// checkbox is checked
function checkValues ( ) {
  var boxes = document.getElementsByTagName("input");
  var options = new Array( );

  // create array of checked options
  for (var i = 0; i < boxes.length; i++) {
      if (boxes[i].checked)
         options[options.length] = boxes[i].value;
  }

  // if no flavors checked, reset all chocolates to display
  if (options.length == 0) {
     resetAll( );
     return;
  }

  // for each chocolate, compare against flavor options
  // if found, mark chocolate for full opacity
  var chocolates = document.getElementsByTagName("li");
  var opaques = new Array(chocolates.length);
  for (j = 0; j < chocolates.length; j++)
     for(var k = 0; k < options.length; k++) {
        if (chocolates[j].className.indexOf(options[k]) >= 0) {
           opaques[j] = 1;
        }
     }

  // for all opaque chocolates, set opacity for full
  // otherwise, cut opacity down to a third
  for (var l = 0; l < opaques.length; l++)
```

```
    if (opaques[1]) {
        removeNotMatched(chocolates[1]);
        chocolates[1].className+= " matched";
    } else {
        removeMatched(chocolates[1]);
        chocolates[1].className+=" notmatched";
    }
}
```

The JavaScript `replace` method looks for the `matched` or `notmatched` substring and replaces it with an empty string, effectively erasing it. Notice in the `resetAll` function that the `removeNotMatched` is called before the `removeMatched`—otherwise, the "matched" part of "notmatched" will get replaced, leaving "not." The visual effect is the same, but switching the order leaves a "not" class hanging around. Untidy.

Modifications to the application could make actual design use of the chocolate ingredient class names, both with the highlighting and in the regular entries.

Opacity is also a component of most image thumbnail expansion applications, covered in the next section.

Programming with Images

Earlier in this book, I demonstrated the use of the Lightbox2 application that expands thumbnails while overlaying the existing page with a partially transparent background. Two elements make up this type of application.

The first is the semi-transparent overlay. In the last section, I covered issues of opacity, including managing the cross-browser differences. In that example, though, only pieces of the page were made semi-transparent, to de-emphasize the elements. With an overlay, an HTML element, usually a `div`, is set as semi-transparent in CSS and either hidden or made completely transparent when an image isn't being shown.

To use the thumbnail expansion program, a special class called `thumb` is added to the image thumbnails. Each thumbnail is surrounded by a link, so that if scripting is disabled, the larger images are still available:

```
<a href="largerimage.jpg"><img src="smallerimage.jpg" class="thumb" alt="some text" />
</a>
```

Two other `div` elements are added to the page. One, with an identifier of `mtwCover`, is used to surround the entire page contents. The easiest way to do this is to add the opening `div` element right after the opening `body` tag:

```
<body>
<div id="mtwCover">
```

The ending tag for `mtwCover` and the other required element for the application are added in just before the closing `body` tag:

```
</div> <!-- end mtwCover -->
<div id='mtwPicture'><img id='mtwPictureimage' class='mtwPictureimage1' src='http://
burningbird.net/wp/ajax-loader.gif' alt='' /></div>
</body>
```

The `mtwPicture` element contains an `img` element with a temporary image, in this case an animated GIF signaling that a file is loading. Eventually, the source will be replaced by the expanded image.

Once the new page elements and classes are added, the page is ready. The mtwimg application determines which images are thumbnails by looking for a `thumb` class. In the setup routine, the `click` event associated with the link is assigned a function to be invoked when the link is clicked. This function opens an image directly into the page rather than in a separate page.

I don't want to repeat all of the software here—it is available with the book examples in the file named *mtwimg.js*—but the function setup routine that looks for the target images is replicated in Example 10-10. The DOM method `getElementsByTagName` is used to access all image elements, looking for those with a `className` of thumb. When found, the application assigns the `onclick` event handler to the element.

Example 10-10. Setup routine that discovers thumbnails and assigns event handlers for each

```
// Finds all images on the page with "thumb" class
// adds click event handlers for each
// adds click event handler for the expanded picture element
//  added as part of the setup process
function setUp( ) {

   var elem = elementClass = null;
   var elems = document.getElementsByTagName('img');
   for (i = 0; i < elems.length; i++) {
      elem = elems[i];
      elementClass = elem.getAttribute("class");
      elementClass = elementClass ? elementClass : elem.getAttribute("className");
      if (elementClass == 'thumb') {
         elem.onclick=expandPic;
      }
   }

}
```

When one of the images with the `thumb` class is clicked, the expansion function is called, which "hides" the web page by overlaying it with a `div` element that is expanded to page size and which is set to be partially opaque. The larger image is then uploaded into the page by setting the `src` attribute of the `img` in the `mtwPicture` div to that of the image filename, as shown in Example 10-11. Since the image has an animated "loading" throbber already, this will show while the larger image is being loaded.

Example 10-11. Function to expand and load a larger image when a thumbnail is clicked

```
function expandPic(evnt) {

   listenkey();
   evnt = (evnt) ? evnt : ((window.event) ? window.event : "");

// find photo position
   var pos = 0;
   if (window.pageYOffset) {
      pos = window.pageYOffset;
   } else if (document.documentElement && document.documentElement.scrollTop) {
      pos = document.documentElement.scrollTop;
   } else if (document.body) {
      pos = document.body.scrollTop;
   }

   var evntTarget = (evnt.target) ? evnt.target : evnt.srcElement;

   // discover image src name
   var oParent = evntTarget.parentNode;

   var imgs = document.getElementsByTagName('img');
   imgs['mtwPictureimage'].src=oParent;

   // fade background, display expanded image
   var obj = document.getElementById('mtwPicture');
   obj.style.top = pos + "px";
   var cover = document.getElementById('mtwCover');
   setOpacity(cover,.1);
   obj.style.visibility='visible';

   // add event handler for image
   obj.onclick=restore;

   imgs['mtwPictureimage'].className = "mtwPictureimage2";

   // end event bubbling
   return false;
}
```

The key line in the code is:

```
   imgs['mtwPictureimage'].src=oParent;
```

For the thumbnail that had been clicked, the larger image name is found by accessing the parent node (the hypertext link) of the element that contains the image. In a hierarchical structure such as a web page, the parent node is the element that is wrapped around the current node, such as the link that wraps the image elements:

```
   <a href="bigger.jpg"><img src="smaller.jpg" class="thumb" alt="" /></a>
```

Finding the image to open is the first part of the functionality. The second is to determine where to place the overlay.

The page's current vertically scrolled position is accessed via the window object's YOffset attribute, if this attribute is supported by the browser. If the attribute is not supported, the application then looks for the scrollTop attribute, provided either by the body element or the documentElement—both of which represent the very first element in the document, again depending on which browser you're using.

The conditional test just described is a cross-browser technique for finding where in the page a certain element is placed, in order to correctly position the expanded photo. Once the correct vertical position is determined, the expanded image's CSS top property is set to this calculated value, after first appending a px pixel unit measurement. The application also makes use of the setOpacity function, described in the previous section.

The rest of the JavaScript application is included with the examples, and mainly has to do with event handling, so I'll leave that to your own explorations. To use the software, all that's needed is to include the JavaScript file in the header, add the two new div elements (described earlier), and add the thumb class to the img element:

```
<a href="http://burningbird.net/photos/botanical/rose2.jpg"><img src="http://
burningbird.net/photos/botanical/rose.png" class="thumb" alt='Rose' /></a>
```

The class isn't used just to mark the image for processing; it also adds a visual indicator that the expansion functionality is present, as shown in Figure 10-10. It's important to provide a visual cue that clicking on an object will result in some action.

The best thing about this application is that if scripting is disabled, the hypertext link operates normally, and clicking the smaller image opens the larger image in a separate page. Example 10-12 shows a web page with one embedded thumbnail image.

Example 10-12. Sample page with one image and set up to use the mtwimg JavaScript library

```
<!DOCTYPE html PUBLIC "-//W3C//DTD XHTML 1.0 Strict//EN"
"http://www.w3.org/TR/xhtml1/DTD/xhtml1-strict.dtd">
<html>
<head>
<title>MTW Image Expander</title>
<link rel="stylesheet" href="mtwimg.css" type="text/css" media="screen" />
<script type="text/javascript" src="mtwimg.js">
</script>
</head>
<body>
<div id="mtwCover">
<p>
<a href="purpledragon.png"><img src="purpledragonthumb.jpg" class="thumb" alt="dragonfly" />
</a>
<!-- enter other text -->
</p>
</div>
<div id='mtwPicture'><img id='mtwPictureimage' class='mtwPictureimage1'
src='ajax-loader.gif' alt='' /></div>
```

Example 10-12. Sample page with one image and set up to use the mtwimg JavaScript library (continued)

```
</body>
</html>
```

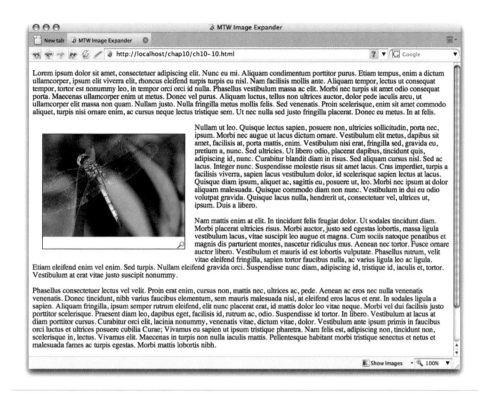

Figure 10-10. Page with image added with thumb class, before expansion

A CSS file providing formatting for the mtwimg elements is added to the page, in addition to the image and the expanding program JavaScript. Figure 10-11 shows the page with the image expanded and the underlying page covered with semi-transparent overlay.

The overlay, coupled with the ability to determine vertical position that was just demonstrated for the thumbnail expansion program, can also be used as a way of capturing your web page reader's attention. Instead of opening an image into the overlay, a `div` element can be opened with an important message, ensuring that your web page readers see whatever it is.

There's one last example using a packaged library, this time to create one of my favorite page customizations: the accordion.

Figure 10-11. Expanded image using mtwim

Accordions: Smooshable Spaces

Another neglected graphical element in web pages is space. Nowadays, people cram as much as they can on a page, especially if any of the objects so crammed are ads or other moneymakers. We debate the benefits of color, argue about fonts, discuss endlessly the merits of photos and other visual devices, but rarely do we sit down and talk about space.

Space is just as much a component of a site's visual design and display as the color and the images. One of the central questions with space is, how do we continue to cram in all we want in the page while still providing enough empty space to be visually pleasing?

There are two ways to manage the space problem in a web page. One is to provide tabbed pages and add functionality to "open" pages when a tab is clicked, as in Figure 10-12.

The problem I have with tabbed pages is that they can be confusing, especially if you have a horizontal menu bar in addition to the tabs. My preferred alternative, and also the more accessible, is to provide a horizontal accordion: content separated into individual blocks that can be opened when clicking on the title bar.

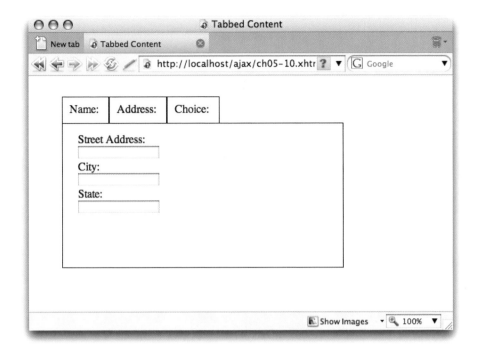

Figure 10-12. A very simple tabbed interface

The accordion does require scripting, but if scripting is not enabled, the content displays vertically, as it would anyway—no harm, no loss of access.

Along with the reusable image expander, I also have a packaged accordion application that's relatively simple to use. Just like with the image application, specialized class names are used to mark the separate components of the accordion: panel (class name of panel), title (either nameCollapsed or nameExpanded), and content (class name of elements). Example 10-13 shows an example web page with three panels.

Example 10-13. Page set up with three accordion panels

```
<!DOCTYPE html PUBLIC "-//W3C//DTD XHTML 1.0 Strict//EN"
      "http://www.w3.org/TR/xhtml1/DTD/xhtml1-strict.dtd">
<html xmlns="http://www.w3.org/1999/xhtml" lang="en" xml:lang="en">
<head>
<meta http-equiv="Content-Type" content="text/html; charset=utf-8" />
<title>Accordion</title>
<link rel="stylesheet" href="accordion.css" type="text/css" media="screen" />
<script type="text/javascript" src="accordion.js">
</script>
</head>
<body>

<form action="GET">
```

Example 10-13. Page set up with three accordion panels (continued)

```
<div id="accordionDiv">

<div class="panel">
<div class="nameCollapsed">
Name:
</div>
<div class="elements">
<fieldset>
<legend>Names</legend>
<label for="firstname">First Name:</label><br /><input type="text" name="firstname"
id="firstname"/>
<label for="lastname">Last Name:</label><br /><input type="text" name="lastname"
id="lastname" />
</fieldset>
</div>
</div>
div class="panel">
<div class="nameCollapsed">
Address
</div>
<div class="elements">
<fieldset>
<legend>Address</legend>
<label for="street">Street Address:</label><br /><input type="text" name-"street"
id="street" />
<label for="city">City:</label><br /><input type="text" name="city" id="city" />
<label for="state">State:</label><br /><input type="text" name="state" id="state" />
</fieldset>
</div>
</div>

<div class="panel">
<div class="nameCollapsed">
Options
</div>
<div class="elements">
<fieldset>
<legend>Options</legend>
<label for="opt1">Option 1</label><input type="checkbox" name="opt1" id="opt1"
checked="checked" />
<label for="opt2">Option 2</label><input type="checkbox" name="opt2" id="opt2"  />
<label for="opt3">Option 3</label><input type="checkbox" name="opt3" id="opt3"  />
<label for="opt4">Option 4</label><input type="checkbox" name="opt4" id="opt4"
checked="checked" />
</fieldset>
</div>
</div>

</div>
</form>
<p>Other data or information.</p>
</body>
</html>
```

When the page is loaded, the div elements are accessed, and those with the class name nameCollapsed are assigned onclick event handlers, and those assigned the class name elements are collapsed (height reduced to 0). I don't want to repeat all of the code here, because the application is included in the examples. I do want to point out the setup routine and a unique bit of code to find the height of the elements. The function is shown in Example 10-14.

Example 10-14. Function setting up the accordion

```
// setup accordion elements
window.onload= function( ) {
    var divs = document.getElementsByTagName('div');

    for (var i = 0; i < divs.length; i++) {

        // setup click for name bar
        if (divs[i].className == 'nameCollapsed') {
            aaManageEvent(divs[i],'click',Accordion.expandOrCollapse);

        // assign height as custom property to element and then collapse
        } else if (divs[i].className == 'elements') {

            // IE6.x handles elements returned from getElementsByTagName differently
            // and clientHeight doesn't work; using offsetHeight, instead
            var height = divs[i].offsetHeight;
            divs[i].height = height;
            if (divs[i].id == "") divs[i].id = "div" + i;
            divs[i].style.height = "0";
        }
    }
}
```

Before collapsing the elements, each element's loaded content height needs to be measured and then stored in some way with the element. If we didn't have the height, we wouldn't be able to determine how big to make the panel when it's opened. Using a default height doesn't work for a library, and it's not very flexible.

The height of the element is accessed through the attribute offsetHeight, which is the better cross-browser choice, though clientHeight is more standard. Where to put this value once we have it, though?

I could have created a global array, but instead I used the approach demonstrated earlier with the opacity function: dynamically adding it to the element in a custom runtime attribute called height. Not style.height, but height, directly. Because of the underlying nature of JavaScript, custom properties such as height can be added at runtime to page elements. You just have to be careful because your code might not be the only application code adding such properties.

Once the height is captured, the content can be collapsed by setting the height to 0, as shown in Figure 10-13.

Figure 10-13. Accordion panels with all panels currently closed

Clicking on the panel titles opens the panel. This particular application uses a timer to slide the panel open, rather than just snapping it open. No particular reason, just personal preference.

Figure 10-14 shows the same application page with two panels expanded. Note how both are different sizes, and there's no extraneous material around the panel contents.

The importance of capturing the proper height is more apparent when seeing the accordion application used in another context, such as that shown in Figure 10-15, with panels closed, and Figure 10-16, with one panel expanded. In this case, different values are used to style the panels, but as long as the proper names are used, the application works without a hitch. This application is used with a content management system, WordPress, so the accordion application is added to the WordPress template.

Another piece of the code I want to highlight is the accordion object itself, as shown in Example 10-15. This functionality again demonstrates switching the classes for an element. In this case, though, more than appearance is at stake: when the title is clicked, the application checks to see whether the class name is nameCollapsed. If the class matches, the expand method is invoked; otherwise, the collapse method is invoked. Of course, the first thing these methods do is switch the class names to reflect the current state.

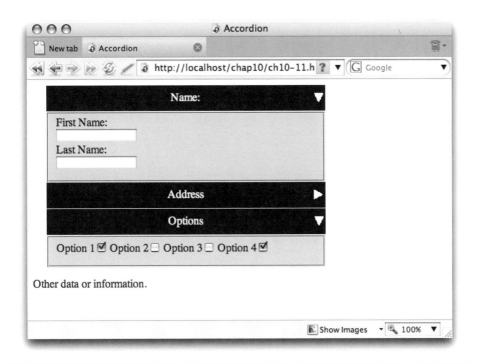

Figure 10-14. Accordion panel application with two panels expanded

Figure 10-15. Accordion application used in WordPress weblog

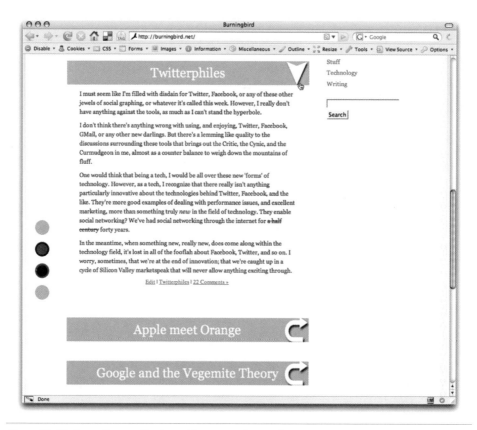

Figure 10-16. Accordion application with one panel opened

Example 10-15. The accordion object in JavaScript

```
// manage the accordion
var Accordion = {

    // adjust height
    adjustItem  : function(val, newItem) {
          document.getElementById(newItem).style.height=val + "px";
    },

    // check if expand or collapse
    expandOrCollapse : function (evnt) {
          evnt = evnt ? evnt : window.event;
          var target = evnt.target ? evnt.target : evnt.srcElement;
          if (target.className == 'nameCollapsed')
              Accordion.expand(target);
          else
              Accordion.collapse(target);
    },
```

Example 10-15. The accordion object in JavaScript (continued)

```
    // expand panel
    expand : function(target) {
            target.className = 'nameExpanded';
            // switch signal
            var children = target.parentNode.childNodes;
            var panel;
            for (var i = 0; i < children.length; i++) {
              if (children[i].className == 'elements') {
                 panel = children[i];
                 break;
              }
            }
            var height = panel.height;
            // find increment based on computed height divided by loop count of 20
            var incr = height / 20;
            for (var i=0; i < 20; i++) {
              var val = (i+1) * incr;
              var func = "Accordion.adjustItem("+val+",'"+ panel.id +"')";
              setTimeout(func,(i+1)*30);
            }

    },

    // collapse panel
    collapse : function (target) {
            target.className = 'nameCollapsed';
            // switch signal
            var children = target.parentNode.childNodes;
            var panel;
            for (var i = 0; i < children.length; i++) {
              if (children[i].className == 'elements') {
                 panel = children[i];
                 break;
              }
            }
            var height = panel.height;

            // find increment based on computed height divided by loop count of 20
            var decr = height / 20;
            for (var i=0; i < 20; i++) {
              var val = height-(decr*(i+1));;
              var func = "Accordion.adjustItem("+val+",'"+ panel.id +"')";
              setTimeout(func,(i+1)*30);
            }
    }

};
```

The object also accessed the runtime height attribute, discussed earlier.

The image and accordion examples demonstrate one nice aspect of creating web pages: there's no end to free libraries that implement the functionality we need.

The two mentioned in this chapter are included in the example files for this book, but you also might want to check out the following visual effects libraries:

- The Rico library, at *http://openrico.org/*, has several very nice effects, including its own accordion, as well as a way to programmatically create rounded corners.

- The *script.aculo.us* library, at *http://script.aculo.us/*, is the visual frontend to the popular *prototype.js* library, and is used by Apple, Gucci, and several other companies.

- The big daddy of open source Ajax libraries is Dojo, at *http://dojotoolkit.org/*. Because of the community nature of the framework, effects are added all the time, including some interesting fisheye menu effects.

- The jQuery library, at *http://jquery.com/*, makes an excellent infrastructure, but it doesn't quite have the same number of visual effects as the others.

CHAPTER 11

Canvassing

While work was underway on SVG, Apple was doing its own thing, and the result was the canvas object.

Rather than an XML-based specification, the canvas object is just that—an object that provides a graphical "canvas" on which to create. Instead of adding separate elements, as was demonstrated with SVG earlier in this book, you create an instance of the canvas object and then manipulate it with script to create the desired effect.

The benefit to the canvas object is you don't have to work with XML, nor the potentially large amounts of markup this might create in your web page. The disadvantage is that if a person accessing the page has scripting turned off—which many people do for security reasons—the canvas effect won't show.

The canvas object lacks the sophistication of SVG, especially as we'll see later in this book. However, it's also a simple object to learn how to use, as this chapter will demonstrate. In addition, the canvas object is supported for the next generation of HTML, HTML5.

This chapter uses JavaScript extensively. See *http://www.oreilly.com/catalog/9780596515096* for links to good tutorials to get you up to speed on working with this client-side scripting language.

Cross-Browser canvas Support and Microsoft's Silverlight

There is extensive cross-browser support for the canvas object. Safari, Opera, and Mozilla support canvas out of the box, and Google supplies a JavaScript library, ExplorerCanvas, that can be added to a page and which converts canvas commands into Microsoft's VML. Google uses this plug-in when it annotates maps with routes at *http://maps.google.com* (covered in detail in Chapter 14). Google provides two versions: one uncompressed and readable, one compressed to save bandwidth.

You can download ExplorerCanvas from *http://excanvas.sourceforge.net/*.

To use ExplorerCanvas, just download the script to your server and add the following into your web pages wherever you use canvas commands:

```
<!--[if IE]><script type="text/javascript" src="../excanvas.js"></script><![endif]-->
```

This line adds a conditional comment to include the script element if the browser accessing the page is IE; otherwise the library isn't opened and its contents are not included in the page. You need the conditional statement to ensure the script isn't opened by other browsers, as the file provides VML-specific scripting, which only IE supports. Using ExplorerCanvas, canvas effects should be viewable by IE.

---

canvas, ExplorerCanvas, and IE8

After this chapter was originally written, but before going through the publication process, Microsoft released the first beta for IE8. This new browser version has significantly impacted some applications, among them *excanvas.js*, from Google.

Microsoft has made a commitment to support HTML5, but hasn't made a commitment, yet, to support the canvas element. The element is not implemented in IE8 beta 1, and underlying code changes in the new browser adversely impacted ExplorerCanvas.

Currently, a Silverlight version of *excanvas.js* is being developed, but hasn't been released. In the meantime, some, not all, of the canvas applications created in this chapter will work with IE8, but only if you modify the application to run in "quirks" mode (without a DOCTYPE); or you run in IE7 emulation mode. Even in the emulation mode, though, most of the applications won't work unless you modify the application to run in quirks mode.

Included in the examples for this book are the canvas examples as detailed in this chapter. However, there are also at least two additional variations of each, with the same filename but the addition of the letters *b*, *c*, or *d*. One of the variations is the same application as detailed in this chapter, but without the DOCTYPE as the type of the file. Another variation leaves the DOCTYPE, but uses the Microsoft compatibility meta tag, as described in Chapter 10.

Not all of the examples work in IE8, but these small modifications did make it so that most of them work, or at a minimum, partially work. Hopefully with the newer Silverlight-based ExplorerCanvas library from Google, all of the applications will work.

Before I get into the basics of canvas, one last cross-browser issue. Microsoft released a proprietary technology called "Silverlight" in 2007, which provides graphical effects focused more on Rich Internet Application (RIA) functionality. Included in the Silverlight libraries is support for a Canvas object. It might be confusing and it might seem like Microsoft is supporting the more universal canvas object, but the company is not.

Microsoft's Canvas object acts more like SVG, since it's also markup-based. Unfortunately, the markup is not SVG; instead, it's Microsoft's own proprietary XAML markup. To use Microsoft's Silverlight Canvas object, following the quick start provided by Microsoft, add the Silverlight script file to your web page:

```
<script type="text/javascript" src="Silverlight.js"></script>
```

Create a dummy div block, which will end up "holding" the canvas content:

```
<div id="mySilverlightPluginHost">
</div>
```

Create a Silverlight object in script:

```
<script type="text/javascript">


        // Retrieve the div element you created in the previous step.
        var parentElement =
            document.getElementById("mySilverlightPluginHost");

        // This function creates the Silverlight plug-in.
        createMySilverlightPlugin();

</script>
```

Create the Silverlight object, passing in the Canvas definition:

```
function createMySilverlightPlugin()
{
    Silverlight.createObject(
        "myxaml.xaml",                  // Source property value.
        parentElement,                  // DOM reference to hosting DIV tag.
        "mySilverlightPlugin",          // Unique plug-in ID value.
        {                               // Per-instance properties.
            width:'300',                // Width of rectangular region of
                                        // plug-in area in pixels.
            height:'300',               // Height of rectangular region of
                                        // plug-in area in pixels.
            inplaceInstallPrompt:false, // Determines whether to display
                                        // in-place install prompt if
                                        // invalid version detected.
            background:'#D6D6D6',       // Background color of plug-in.
            isWindowless:'false',       // Determines whether to display plug-in
                                        // in Windowless mode.
```

```
            framerate:'24',            // MaxFrameRate property value.
            version:'1.0'              // Silverlight version to use.
        },
        {
            onError:null,              // OnError property value --
                                       // event handler function name.
            onLoad:null                // OnLoad property value --
                                       // event handler function name.
        },
        null);                         // Context value -- event handler function
                                       // name.
    }
```

The XAML file contains the Canvas definition:

```
<Canvas
    xmlns="http://schemas.microsoft.com/client/2007"
    xmlns:x="http://schemas.microsoft.com/winfx/2006/xaml">

  <Ellipse
      Height="200" Width="200"
      Stroke="Black" StrokeThickness="10" Fill="SlateBlue" />
</Canvas>
```

All of this will draw a circle that's colored slate blue with a black border, similar to what can be drawn with SVG or the canvas element.

Microsoft does provide a browser plug-in, both Mac- and Windows-based, that enables Silverlight support in browsers other than just IE. Silverlight works with IE, Firefox, and Safari at this time, and work is underway to enable it to work with Opera. Unfortunately, there is no Linux support for Silverlight.

When Microsoft announced Silverlight, the company released two versions, one JavaScript-based and one based on Microsoft's .NET Framework. I think this move confused non-developers, and because of this and the strong support for open specifications in other browsers, adoption of Silverlight has been slow.

 If you want to learn more about Microsoft's Silverlight, I strongly recommend WynApse.com, at *http://www.wynapse.com/*, for a discussion on how Silverlight works and some of the clearest tutorials I've seen on the implementation.

canvas Basics

The canvas specification is currently being developed by a merging of the WHATWG group and the W3C. The specification can be found at *http://www.whatwg.org/specs/web-apps/current-work/multipage/section-the-canvas.html*. The documentation for the object is fuzzy, to put it delicately. There is documentation, but not necessarily anything as explicit, or precise, as that given for SVG.

The canvas object is an HTML element, added to a page just like you'd add a div or an img. When adding a canvas element, make sure to give it an identifier, a width, and a height, though this could cause XHTML or HTML validation warnings and errors:

```
<canvas id="workObj" width="400" height="400">
</canvas>
```

You're not going to want to use CSS style settings, as the two aren't compatible, at least from my own explorations.

For those environments that don't support the canvas element, or more importantly, have scripting turned off, add content within the element that will then be displayed that either reflects the canvas content or perhaps replaces it with an image:

```
<canvas id="workObj" width="400" height="400">
<img src="some.jpg" alt="Replacement image for canvas" />
</canvas>
```

Once you've added a canvas element, you can access it in script and begin to draw.

Beginning to Draw

The only non-script portion of the canvas element is adding the element to the page. The rest of the work with the object happens in script.

To start, you have to access the canvas element through the Document Object Model (DOM) functions, and then you have to access the 2D *rendering context* for that object:

```
var canvas = document.getElementById('workObj');
if (canvas.getContext) {

  var ctx = canvas.getContext('2d');
}
```

The only supported context at this time is the 2D context, but there are plans for a 3D one that's based on OpenGL, which will be fun to play with.

 What about the seeming 3D applications you might have seen made with the canvas element? Though 3D actions and element behavior are demonstrated, these aren't really 3D applications. You can always tell the difference by looking at the light on the object—if it changes as an object turns, the application is a true 3D; otherwise, it's just an emulated effect.

Once you have the rendering context, you can use it to draw any number of objects. The following sets the fill color to red and then draws a simple rectangle using the canvas fillStyle property and fillRect function:

```
ctx.fillStyle="#ff0000";
ctx.fillRect(25,25,100,100);
```

The rectangle is drawn at a coordinate point (x,y) of 25,25 and is 100 pixels square. Like SVG, the canvas coordinate system starts at a point of 0,0 in the left-top corner.

To add a border to the rectangle, set the border color using strokeStyle, and then use strokeRect to draw the border rectangle over the existing filled rectangle:

```
ctx.strokeStyle="#006600";;
ctx.strokeRect(25,25,100,100);
```

Example 11-1 has a web page with one canvas element. In the element, three squares are drawn, two with borders and one overlapping another. The overlapping square is created with the rgba color function, setting the alpha, or a, value to 50%. The canvas elements are drawn after the window is loaded, to ensure that the canvas element has been created in the page before it's accessed.

Example 11-1. canvas application that draws three rectangles

```
<!DOCTYPE html PUBLIC "-//W3C//DTD XHTML 1.0 Strict//EN"
        "http://www.w3.org/TR/xhtml1/DTD/xhtml1-strict.dtd">
<html xmlns="http://www.w3.org/1999/xhtml" lang="en" xml:lang="en">
<head>
<meta http-equiv="Content-Type" content="text/html; charset=utf-8" />
<title>Canvas Drawing</title>
<style type="text/css">
#workObj
{
    border: 1px solid #000;
}
</style>

<script type="text/javascript">
//<![CDATA[


window.onload= setup( ) {
    var canvas = document.getElementById('workObj');
    if (canvas.getContext) {

    canvas.setAttribute("width",400);
    canvas.setAttribute("height",400);

    var ctx = canvas.getContext('2d');

    // yellow rectangle with green border
    ctx.fillStyle="#ffff00";
    ctx.fillRect(25,25,100,100);

    ctx.strokeStyle="#006600";;
    ctx.strokeRect(25,25,100,100);

    // red rectangle with black border
    ctx.fillStyle="rgb(255,0,0)";
    ctx.fillRect(150,150,100,100);
```

Example 11-1. canvas application that draws three rectangles (continued)

```
    ctx.strokeStyle="#000";
    ctx.strokeRect(150,150,100,100);
    // overlapping semi-transparent rectangle
    ctx.fillStyle="rgba(255,255,0,0.5)";
    ctx.fillRect(200,200,100,100);

    }
}

//]]>
</script>

</head>
<body>
<canvas id="workObj" width="500" height="500">
Working with Canvas here
</canvas>
</body>
</html>
```

The example also shows how to reset the width and height of the canvas object itself, before the context is accessed and the figures drawn. In addition, the canvas area is given a border, to make it visible. By default, the canvas is given a black background. However, the black doesn't show, because the background is also transparent.

Figure 11-1 shows the canvas area created with the page in Example 11-1.

Example 11-1 used the fillRect and strokeRect functions to create a rectangle. Since the canvas element is a scripted functionality, it makes sense then that there's a way to clear a rectangle. In addition to creating a rectangle with fillRect and strokeRect, you can also clear an existing rectangle with clearRect:

```
    ctx.clearRect(x,y,width,height);
```

What's interesting about clearRect is that it clears a rectangle at the given position, width, and height, regardless of what might be in the spot—bigger rectangles, circles, or other items will end up with a rectangular "hole" in them. Not a bad result, but one to be aware of before you get the unexpected.

Though canvas supports rectangles, it doesn't have all the shape options that SVG does. Or, I should say, most shapes we need can be emulated, but we're not going to find "circle" or "ellipse" just waiting for us to plunk down.

Basic Shapes

Among the shapes not natively supported with the canvas element are circles or ellipses. What the canvas element does have is an arc function, which can be used to create circles or elliptical curves.

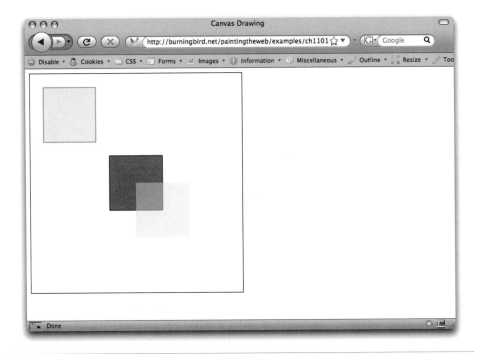

Figure 11-1. Drawing with the canvas element

The arc function takes as parameters the coordinates x,y for the center of the circle, the radius, the start and end angle, and lastly the direction the curve is drawn. The start and end angles are in *radians*, not degrees, and the direction is true for drawing counterclockwise, false for clockwise:

```
ctx.arc(250,250, 100, 1.57079633, 4.71238898,false);
```

This line creates a half-circle arc, starting at circle center position of 250,250 pixels, with a 100 pixel radius; starting at 90 degrees and ending at 270 degrees; and drawing the arc in a positive direction. However, the half-circle won't be drawn when you call the function, because you have to call stroke to create an angle outline or fill to create a solid arc. The following creates a solid half-circle:

```
ctx.arc(250,250, 100, 1.57079633, 4.71238898,false);
ctx.fill();
```

The lack of built-in rounding also applies to the rectangle: there is no rounded rectangle in canvas as there is with SVG. However, a rounded rectangle can be derived using other functionality.

In the tutorials Mozilla provides, one of the examples provides a custom function, roundedRect, that can be used to create a rounded rectangle:

```
function roundedRect(ctx,x,y,width,height,radius,fill){
  ctx.beginPath( );
  ctx.moveTo(x,y+radius);
  ctx.lineTo(x,y+height-radius);
  ctx.quadraticCurveTo(x,y+height,x+radius,y+height);
  ctx.lineTo(x+width-radius,y+height);
  ctx.quadraticCurveTo(x+width,y+height,x+width,y+height-radius);
  ctx.lineTo(x+width,y+radius);
  ctx.quadraticCurveTo(x+width,y,x+width-radius,y);
  ctx.lineTo(x+radius,y);
  ctx.quadraticCurveTo(x,y,x,y+radius);
  if (fill)
     ctx.fill( );
  else
     ctx.stroke( );
}
```

A rather significant amount of functionality is needed just to create the rounded rectangle. In addition, I modified the function to allow for both a stroke and a fill. However, this custom function does demonstrate another key difference between a
programmatic element, such as canvas, and a markup, like SVG.

In SVG, we can derive most shapes from the use of a line and an arc, but having to
do so every time we need a rounded rectangle would not lead to quick acceptance of
the functionality. With canvas, the new figure type can be created as a user custom
function that is coded once and used many times. In addition, the application figures out all of the pieces, so we don't have to get out our calculators and rusty math
skills.

Example 11-2 combines the shapes just covered into a rainbow-hued sampler that
explores variations of each of the functions and their parameters. The first consists of
a mix of rectangles and elliptical curves, the second of circles and square cutouts,
and the third of rounded rectangles using the roundedRect function. To make it more
interesting, a function is used to derive a random color for the fill or stroke, and a
second function is used to convert degrees to radians, because it's a lot easier to visualize what's happening with degrees. Notice the use of clearRect to "cut" squares
into the circles.

Example 11-2. Shape and color sampler for the canvas element

```
<!DOCTYPE html PUBLIC "-//W3C//DTD XHTML 1.0 Strict//EN"
      "http://www.w3.org/TR/xhtml1/DTD/xhtml1-strict.dtd">
<html xmlns="http://www.w3.org/1999/xhtml" lang="en" xml:lang="en">
<head>
<meta http-equiv="Content-Type" content="text/html; charset=utf-8" />
<title>Canvas Drawing</title>
<style type="text/css">
#workObj
{
    border: 1px solid #000;
}
```

Example 11-2. Shape and color sampler for the canvas element (continued)

```
</style>

<script type="text/javascript" src="addingajax.js">
</script>
<script type="text/javascript">
//<![CDATA[

// start drawing event
aaManageEvent(window,"load",setup);

// custom rounded rect function
function roundedRect(ctx,x,y,width,height,radius,fill){
  ctx.beginPath();
  ctx.moveTo(x,y+radius);
  ctx.lineTo(x,y+height-radius);
  ctx.quadraticCurveTo(x,y+height,x+radius,y+height);
  ctx.lineTo(x+width-radius,y+height);
  ctx.quadraticCurveTo(x+width,y+height,x+width,y+height-radius);
  ctx.lineTo(x+width,y+radius);
  ctx.quadraticCurveTo(x+width,y,x+width-radius,y);
  ctx.lineTo(x+radius,y);
  ctx.quadraticCurveTo(x,y,x,y+radius);
  if (fill)
    ctx.fill();
  else
    ctx.stroke();
}
// generate random
function random(max) {
    return Math.round(max*Math.random());
}

// generate random color
function randomColor() {
    var color= "rgb(" + random(255) + "," + random(255) + "," + random(255) + ")";
    return color;
}

// generate radians
function genRadians(degrees) {
    return (Math.PI/180)*degrees;
}
//draw
function setup() {
    var canvas = document.getElementById('workObj');
    if (canvas.getContext) {

        // get context
        var ctx = canvas.getContext('2d');

        // draw half circle topped boxes
        var x;
```

Example 11-2. Shape and color sampler for the canvas element (continued)

```
        for (i=1;i<=5;i++) {
            ctx.beginPath();
            ctx.fillStyle=randomColor();
            ctx.strokeStyle=ctx.fillStyle;
            x = i*100;
            ctx.fillRect(x,50,50,50);
            ctx.arc(x+25,50,25,0,genRadians(180),true);
            ctx.stroke();
        }

        // Full circle with square cut out
        for (i=1; i<= 5; i++) {
            ctx.beginPath();
            ctx.fillStyle=randomColor();
            x = i*100;
            ctx.arc(x + 25, 220,50,0,genRadians(360),false);
            ctx.fill();
            ctx.clearRect(x + 12, 210,20,20);
        }

        // rounded rectangle
        for (i = 0; i < 5; i++) {
            x=i*125;
            ctx.strokeStyle=randomColor();
            roundedRect(ctx,x + 25, 330, 100,50,20,false);
        }
    }
}

//]]>
</script>
</head>
<body>
<canvas id="workObj" width="650" height="450">
Working with Canvas here
</canvas>
</body>
</html>
```

Figure 11-2 shows the results of opening the page. Of course, with the random-color generator, the image won't look the same twice. In fact, considering that we're using a random-color generator, it's rather interesting how the colors complement one another.

In the example, other variations on the concept of curves are used, as is the function beginPath. The arc, like the other curves, is a path-based function. If the beginPath function weren't used with each use of the arc, moving the "drawing pen" between circles would create a line between them. Try removing it in the example, and you'll get an unexpected result.

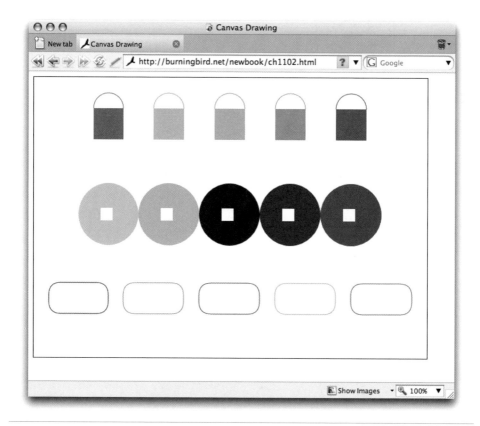

Figure 11-2. canvas shape and color sampler

Paths

In the example in the last section, beginPath was used to begin a new path. Paths in the canvas object are similar paths in SVG: they're ways of drawing freeform shapes. Once started, a path continues until either another beginPath is called or the closePath is called. Similar to SVG, the path is drawn as a line with stroke, or as a shape with fill.

The arc function is one of the path functions. Others are:

moveTo
  Moves the pen to a new location in the canvas without drawing

lineTo
  Draws a line from the current position to a given position

arc
  Draws an arc with a given radius, from angle to angle, and a given direction

quadraticCurveTo

Our friend, the quadratic Bézier curve

bezierCurveTo

The quadratic's friend, the cubic Bézier curve

The `moveTo` and `lineTo` functions are very similar to what we had with paths in SVG: move the pen, draw a line. The line can be further modified and given different end caps, joins, and thicknesses:

```
ctx.lineWidth = "5";
ctx.lineCap = "round";
ctx.lineJoin = "bevel";
```

The default width is 1 pixel, the default `lineCap` is `butt`, and the default `lineJoin` is `miter`. The `lineCap` options are:

- round
- butt
- square

The `lineJoin` options are:

- miter
- bevel
- round

Example 11-3 contains a web page sampler exploring variations of the `line` and `move` functions and the line options just given. Note how `beginPath` is used each time an attribute is changed, such as line width or stroke color.

Example 11-3. Line drawings

```
<!DOCTYPE html PUBLIC "-//W3C//DTD XHTML 1.0 Strict//EN"
        "http://www.w3.org/TR/xhtml1/DTD/xhtml1-strict.dtd">
<html xmlns="http://www.w3.org/1999/xhtml" lang="en" xml:lang="en">
<head>
<meta http-equiv="Content-Type" content="text/html; charset=utf-8" />
<title>Canvas Lines Drawing</title>
<style type="text/css">
#workObj
{
    border: 1px solid #000;
}
</style>

<script type="text/javascript" src="addingajax.js">
</script>
<script type="text/javascript">
//<![CDATA[
```

Example 11-3. Line drawings (continued)

```
// start drawing event
aaManageEvent(window,"load",setup);

//draw
function setup( ) {
    var canvas = document.getElementById('workObj');
    if (canvas.getContext) {

        // get context
        var ctx = canvas.getContext('2d');

        // draw different thickness of lines
        ctx.strokeStyle = "#000";
        ctx.beginPath( );
        for (var i = 1; i <=10; i++) {
            ctx.beginPath( );

            y = i*20;
            ctx.moveTo(20,y);
            ctx.lineWidth=i;
            ctx.lineTo(600,y);
            ctx.stroke( );
        }
        // vertical line
        ctx.beginPath( );
        ctx.strokeStyle = "#f00";
        ctx.lineWidth = "3";
        ctx.moveTo(600,250);
        ctx.lineTo(600,360);
        ctx.stroke( );

        // reset line style
        ctx.beginPath( );
        ctx.strokeStyle="#000";
        ctx.lineWidth="10";

        // linecaps
        var linecaps = ['butt','round','square'];
        for (i = 0; i<3;i++) {
            ctx.beginPath( );
            ctx.lineCap = linecaps[i];
            y = 270 + i*30;
            ctx.moveTo(20,y);
            ctx.lineTo(610,y);
            ctx.stroke( );
        }

        //linejoin
        var linejoin = ['miter','bevel','round'];
        for (i = 0; i < 3; i++) {
            ctx.beginPath( );
            ctx.lineJoin = linejoin[i];
```

Example 11-3. Line drawings (continued)

```
        y = 400 + i * 30;
        ctx.moveTo(20,y);

        x = 600 - i * 30;
        ctx.lineTo(x,y);
        ctx.lineTo(x,y + 50);
        ctx.stroke( );
      }
    }
}

//]]>
</script>
</head>
<body>
<canvas id="workObj" width="650" height="550">
Working with Canvas here
</canvas>
</body>
</html>
```

The results of the canvas application are shown in Figure 11-3.

A last property associated with the lines is miterLimit, which sets how thick the extended line join is before it's converted into a bevel. Figure 11-4 shows an example at Mozilla where you can change the miterLimit and get a different effect. The example is part of the canvas tutorial at *http://developer.mozilla.org/en/docs/Canvas_tutorial*.

One property not supported for the canvas line that is supported in SVG is the ability to create dashed lines. I researched this when writing this book and discovered that the creators of HTML5, the organization defining the specification for the canvas element, felt that this wasn't a needed item. Like the rounded rectangle, dashed lines can be emulated with code, but the code isn't necessarily trivial and also requires access to both curves and transforms I haven't covered yet. Later in the section on transformations, I'll demonstrate how to use code to create a circle with a dashed stroke.

The Curves

The canvas Bézier curves are no different from those described in Chapter 7, "SVG Bootcamp." The quadratic curve takes four parameters, the x and y of the control point and the x and y point of the end of the curve. The cubic curve has two control points, and therefore four settings: two for x and two for y for each control point. The math involved in the curves is no different in canvas than in SVG. What better way to demonstrate than to adapt the examples for these curves from Chapter 7.

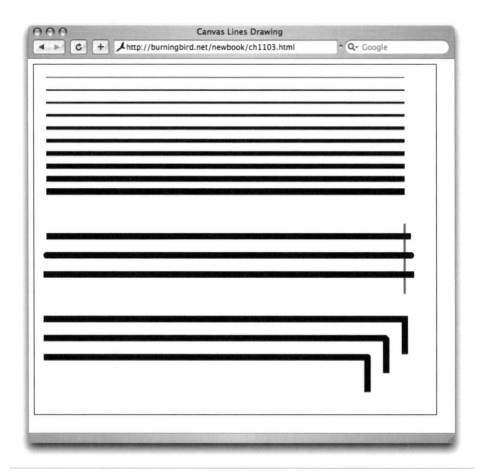

Figure 11-3. Line caps, width, and joins

 If you haven't explored Chapter 7 yet, take a few minutes to look at the section on the Bézier curves and the examples before proceeding with the examples in this section.

Example 11-4 duplicates the curves from Example 7-12 in Chapter 7, but without the annotation. The SVG markup consists of one path for each curve, which also includes the movement to stage the curve. The canvas function is identical except the movement is handled with moveTo and then the curve is drawn.

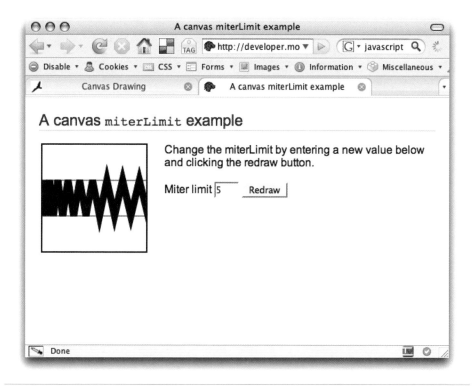

Figure 11-4. Example of miterLimit at Mozilla

Example 11-4. Drawing four quadratic Bézier curves

```
<!DOCTYPE html PUBLIC "-//W3C//DTD XHTML 1.0 Strict//EN"
        "http://www.w3.org/TR/xhtml1/DTD/xhtml1-strict.dtd">
<html xmlns="http://www.w3.org/1999/xhtml" lang="en" xml:lang="en">
<head>
<meta http-equiv="Content-Type" content="text/html; charset=utf-8" />
<title>Canvas Lines Drawing</title>

<script type="text/javascript" src="addingajax.js">
</script>
<script type="text/javascript">
//<![CDATA[

// start drawing event
aaManageEvent(window,"load",setup);

//draw
function setup() {
    var canvas = document.getElementById('workObj');
    if (canvas.getContext) {
```

Example 11-4. Drawing four quadratic Bézier curves (continued)

```
    // get context
    var ctx = canvas.getContext('2d');

    // transform origin
    ctx.translate(-50,-50);

    ctx.strokeStyle="#000";
    ctx.beginPath( );

    // first curve
    ctx.moveTo(100,200);
    ctx.quadraticCurveTo(300,100,500,200);
    ctx.stroke( );

    // second curve
    ctx.moveTo(600,200);
    ctx.quadraticCurveTo(800,0,1000,200);
    ctx.stroke( );

    // third curve
    ctx.moveTo(100,400);
    ctx.quadraticCurveTo(200,300,500,400);
    ctx.stroke( );
    // fourth curve
    ctx.moveTo(600,400);
    ctx.quadraticCurveTo(960,200,1000,400);
    ctx.stroke( );
  }
}

//]]>
</script>

</head>
<body>
<canvas id="workObj" width="1050" height="550">
Working with Canvas here
</canvas>
</body>
</html>
```

Compare the results of the application shown in Figure 11-5 with that shown in Figure 7-17. The functionality between the two is virtually identical, including the use of the *transform translate*, which moves the origin of the coordinate system for the rendering context up 50 pixels and to the left 50 pixels. I'll be getting into transforms in the next section, but like the curves, they're remarkably similar to the SVG transforms.

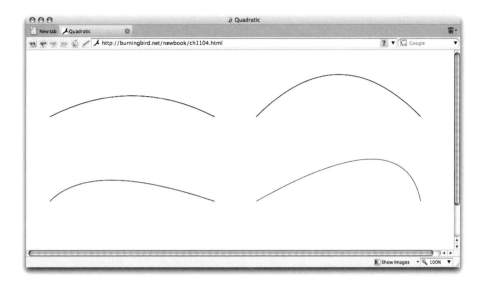

Figure 11-5. Using quadratic curves in canvas

The cubic Bézier curve is the same, except two control points are used, followed by the end point:

```
ctx.bezierCurveTo(70,27,20,30,300,400);
```

Again converting an SVG example, Example 7-13, into a canvas implementation, Example 11-5 duplicates the two cubic Bézier curves, but without the added annotation.

Example 11-5. Cubic Bézier curves

```
<!DOCTYPE html PUBLIC "-//W3C//DTD XHTML 1.0 Strict//EN"
        "http://www.w3.org/TR/xhtml1/DTD/xhtml1-strict.dtd">
<html xmlns="http://www.w3.org/1999/xhtml" lang="en" xml:lang="en">
<head>
<meta http-equiv="Content-Type" content="text/html; charset=utf-8" />
<title>Cubic</title>

<script type="text/javascript" src="addingajax.js">
</script>
<script type="text/javascript">
//<![CDATA[

// start drawing event
aaManageEvent(window,"load",setup);

//draw
function setup() {
   var canvas = document.getElementById('workObj');
   if (canvas.getContext) {
```

Example 11-5. Cubic Bézier curves (continued)

```
    // get context
    var ctx = canvas.getContext('2d');

    ctx.translate(-50,0);
    ctx.strokeStyle="#000";
    ctx.beginPath();

    // first curve
    ctx.moveTo(100,300);
    ctx.bezierCurveTo(300,50,500,50,700,300);
    ctx.stroke();

    // second curve
    ctx.moveTo(700,200);
    ctx.bezierCurveTo(600,10,1000,400,900,200);
    ctx.stroke();

  }
}

//]]>
</script>
</head>
<body>
<canvas id="workObj" width="1050" height="550">
Working with Canvas here
</canvas>
</body>
</html>
```

The canvas Bézier method is identical in behavior to that supported for SVG, outside of that fact that one is managed by markup, the other by script. Compare Figure 11-6 showing the canvas results with Figure 7-18, created using SVG. In addition, Example 11-5 made use of a new canvas function, the translate transform, covered in a later chapter.

Saving State

canvas isn't necessarily loaded down with properties, but once we add in fill and stroke color, line widths, transformations, and so on, the state of the canvas context can be relatively complex at any point in time. It'd be nice to save the state of the canvas, so we can restore it once we've made a set of adjustments.

Luckily, saving canvas state is supported through the save and restore methods. Each time save is called on the context, the state and all the property settings are pushed onto a stack; each time restore is called, states are popped off the stack in the reverse order.

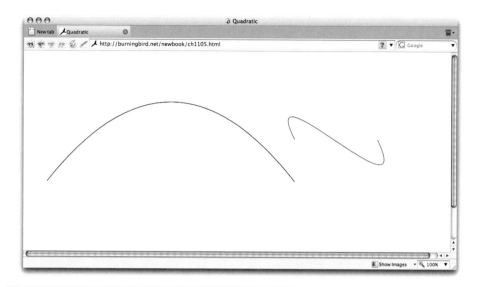

Figure 11-6. Cubic Bézier curves

To demonstrate, Example 11-6 creates several different lines, each with different style settings. As the first two lines are created, their state is saved before a new path is created using new settings. The last two lines are drawn with these restored states.

Example 11-6. Saving and restoring canvas context state

```
<!DOCTYPE html PUBLIC "-//W3C//DTD XHTML 1.0 Strict//EN"
      "http://www.w3.org/TR/xhtml1/DTD/xhtml1-strict.dtd">
<html xmlns="http://www.w3.org/1999/xhtml" lang="en" xml:lang="en">
<head>
<meta http-equiv="Content-Type" content="text/html; charset=utf-8" />
<title>Saving State</title>
<style type="text/css">
#workObj
{
    border: 1px solid #000;
}
</style>

<script type="text/javascript" src="addingajax.js">
</script>
<script type="text/javascript">
//<![CDATA[

aaManageEvent(window,"load",setup);
function setup( ) {
   var canvas = document.getElementById('workObj');
   if (canvas.getContext) {

    var ctx = canvas.getContext('2d');
```

Example 11-6. Saving and restoring canvas context state (continued)

```
    // first line
    ctx.beginPath( );
    ctx.lineWidth="6";
    ctx.strokeStyle = "rgb(255,0,0)";
    ctx.fillStyle = "#003";
    ctx.lineCap = "round";
    ctx.moveTo(100,50);
    ctx.lineTo(600,50);
    ctx.stroke( );
    ctx.save( );

    // second line
    ctx.beginPath( );
    ctx.lineWidth = "3";
    ctx.strokeStyle = "#ff0";
    ctx.lineCap = "square";
    ctx.moveTo(100, 100);
    ctx.lineTo(600,100);
    ctx.stroke( );
    ctx.save( );

    // third line
    ctx.beginPath( );
    ctx.lineWidth = "10";
    ctx.strokeStyle = "#060";
    ctx.lineCap = "butt";
    ctx.moveTo(100, 150);
    ctx.lineTo(600,150);
    ctx.stroke( );

    // square
    ctx.globalAlpha = 0.2;
    ctx.fillStyle = "#0ff";
    ctx.fillRect(150,80,80,80);
    ctx.save( );

    // restore last  two and draw
    ctx.beginPath( );
    ctx.restore( );
    ctx.moveTo(100,200);
    ctx.lineTo(600,200);
    ctx.stroke( );

    // restore again and draw
    ctx.beginPath( );
    ctx.restore( );
    ctx.moveTo(100,250);
    ctx.lineTo(600,250);
    ctx.stroke( );
  }
}
```

Example 11-6. Saving and restoring canvas context state (continued)

```
//]]>
</script>

</head>
<body>
<canvas id="workObj" width="700" height="400">
Working with Canvas here
</canvas>
</body>
</html>
```

The page is shown in Figure 11-7. Unfortunately, the state is saved and restored as a stack, so you can't access any individual state, regardless of its position in the stack. Still, when creating objects with alternating styles, or even duplicating complex objects, the ability to save and access state can save time and code.

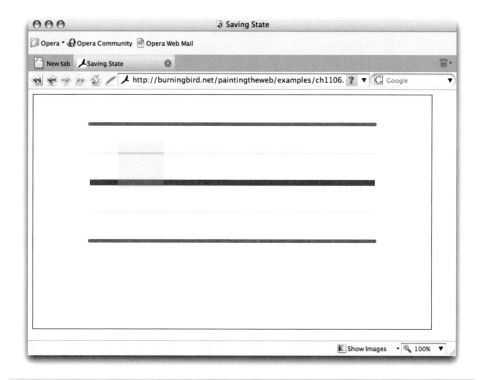

Figure 11-7. Use of save and restore to maintain context state

The example also introduced another property, globalAlpha. This property sets the alpha state (state of transparency), which is used for all objects until it's changed again. But, since we're restoring state, we're restoring the context to a point where the global alpha has not been set, which is why the last two lines were drawn completely opaque.

Layering and Clipping

Two other object modifications that can control the appearance of the canvas are clipping—controlling what is or is not drawn—and the `globalCompositeOperation` property, which determines how new objects are layered in relation to existing objects.

Clipping

Clipping isn't quite descriptive: you define an area where drawing is allowed, creating a "mask" over the rest of the canvas area and preventing any drawing in the masked area. It's somewhat like cutting a hole in cardboard, putting it over paper, and then drawing over the hole—the coloring only shows in the uncovered area. Clipping works on a path, which can be built with any path function: arc, line, or the curves.

Example 11-7 creates a large circular clipping path, then creates 20 random circles, many within the clipping path, some on the edge, and others outside the clipping path.

Example 11-7. Clipping circles

```
<!DOCTYPE html PUBLIC "-//W3C//DTD XHTML 1.0 Strict//EN"
        "http://www.w3.org/TR/xhtml1/DTD/xhtml1-strict.dtd">
<html xmlns="http://www.w3.org/1999/xhtml" lang="en" xml:lang-"en">
<head>
<meta http-equiv="Content-Type" content="text/html; charset=utf-8" />
<title>Clipping Circles</title>

<script type="text/javascript" src="addingajax.js">
</script>
<script type="text/javascript">
//<![CDATA[

aaManageEvent(window,"load",setup);

// generate random
function random(max) {
   return Math.round(max*Math.random());
}

// generate random color
function randomColor() {
    var color= "rgb(" + random(255) + "," + random(255) + "," + random(255) + ")";
    return color;
}
```

Example 11-7. Clipping circles (continued)

```
// draw random circle
function drawRandomCircle(ctx, maxX, maxY) {
   ctx.beginPath();
   ctx.fillStyle=randomColor();
   ctx.arc(random(maxX),random(maxY),30,0,Math.PI*2,true);
   ctx.fill();
}
function setup() {
   var canvas = document.getElementById('workObj');
   if (canvas.getContext) {

    // create clipping path
    var ctx = canvas.getContext('2d');
    ctx.beginPath();
    ctx.arc(250,250,200,0,Math.PI*2,true);
    ctx.strokeStyle="#000";
    ctx.stroke();
    ctx.clip();

    // creates 20 random circles
    for (var i = 0; i < 20; i++) {
       drawRandomCircle(ctx,550,550);
    }

   }
}

//]]>
</script>

</head>
<body>
<canvas id="workObj" width="600" height="600">
Working with Canvas here
</canvas>
</body>
</html>
```

Figure 11-8 shows one iteration of the application. Reloading the page creates a different grouping of circles, in different colors, clipped and not. Try it out several times. It's rather like playing with meditation beads, but without the chants.

 Though not demonstrated in Chapter 6, SVG also supports masking and clipping.

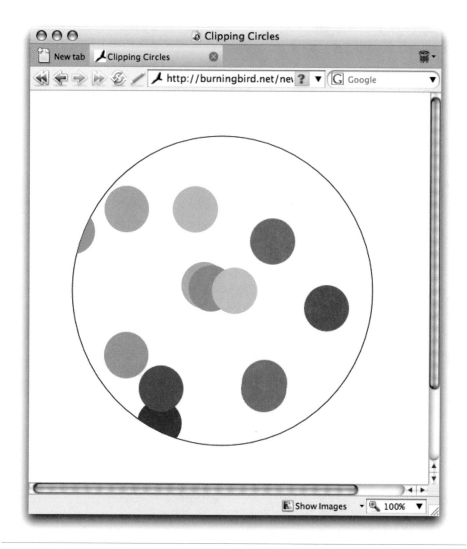

Figure 11-8. Demonstration of the clipping circle example

globalCompositeOperation and a Quick Word on Text and HTML Integration

When you create a new object that shares the same space with another, existing object, the new object is layered on top of the older, and the only way the older object shows through the newer is if the latter is semi-transparent. The behavior between the two can be altered by setting the globalCompositeOperation property with one of the following values:

source-over *(default)*
> The new shape overlaps the old shape.

destination-over
> New shapes are drawn behind the old shape.

source-in
> The overlapping area of the new shape is drawn.

destination-in
> The overlapping area of the old shape is drawn.

source-out
> The part of the new shape that does not overlap is drawn.

destination-out
> The part of the old shape that does not overlap is drawn.

source-atop
> That part of the new shape that overlaps the existing canvas content is drawn.

destination-atop
> Only that part of the old shape that overlaps the new shape is drawn.

lighter
> The overlapping area is drawn with a color derived from adding the color values from both shapes.

darker
> The overlapping area is drawn with a color derived from subtracting the color values.

xor
> The area where the shapes overlap is made transparent.

copy
> Draws the new shape and deletes everything else.

The Mozilla canvas tutorial on globalCompositeOperation (at *http://developer.mozilla. org/samples/canvas-tutorial/6_1_canvas_composite.html)* has a nice application demonstrating the different composite effects, as shown in Figure 11-9. Another interesting thing about the page created is that it also demonstrates integration between the canvas elements and other HTML elements.

The application is created as an HTML table (which is frowned upon for page layout purposes), containing rows of canvas elements that are followed by label elements. In the application, a snippet of which is shown below, an array of globalCompositeOperation is used to set each canvas element in turn, and the same blue square and red circle are drawn for each canvas. In addition, text nodes are created to hold the property type value for each iteration, and are appended to the label.

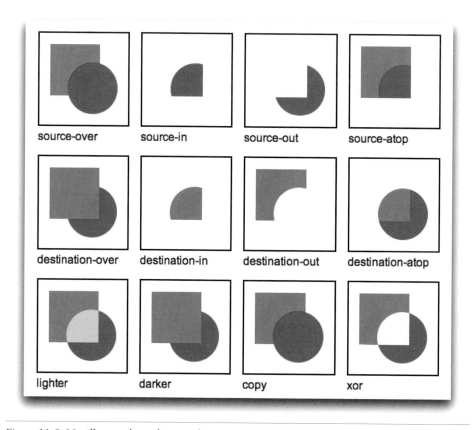

Figure 11-9. Mozilla sample application demonstrating different globalCompositeOperation settings

```
var compositeTypes = [
  'source-over','source-in','source-out','source-atop',
  'destination-over','destination-in','destination-out','destination-atop',
  'lighter','darker','copy','xor'
];
function draw( ){
  for (i=0;i<compositeTypes.length;i++){
    var label = document.createTextNode(compositeTypes[i]);
    document.getElementById('lab'+i).appendChild(label);
    var ctx = document.getElementById('tut'+i).getContext('2d');

    // draw rectangle
    ctx.fillStyle = "#09f";
    ctx.fillRect(15,15,70,70);

    // set composite property
    ctx.globalCompositeOperation = compositeTypes[i];
```

```
    // draw circle
    ctx.fillStyle = "#f30";
    ctx.beginPath();
    ctx.arc(75,75,35,0,Math.PI*2,true);
    ctx.fill();
  }
}
```

This application demonstrates not only how the `globalCompositeOperation` property is used, but also how text is integrated into a `canvas` effect. Unlike SVG, which can be used to create standalone applications and must therefore support some form of text object, the `canvas` element is integrated into HTML pages, and text is provided like it's provided for every other HTML element.

Integrated for the specification and most browsers, I should say. The reason I specifically grabbed the Mozilla application for this example is that Mozilla is working with its own proprietary `canvas` APIs and properties and functions to control text associated with a `canvas` element. For instance, the following code changes the font type and "draws" text:

```
ctx.mozTextStyle = "16pt Georgia";
ctx.mozDrawText("This is the text");
```

There are even functions, `mozPathText` and `mozTextAlongPath`, that can be used to create text as a path and then move text along that path.

Most of the functionality has been implemented in Firefox 3, but only in Firefox 3. As such, I mention it here for comprehensiveness, but won't be using any of the Mozilla-specific functionality in this chapter or later in this book.

canvas Effects

The `canvas` object is relatively simple to work with, but it isn't as sophisticated as SVG. For instance, it lacks many of the SVG filter effects, as well as several of the primitive shapes. It also doesn't have the ability to add dashes or markers to objects. Most of these problems can be somewhat countered by using functions, but doing so adds to the complexity of creating images.

On the other hand, the `canvas` object does provide support for two important effects: gradients and transforms. It also has some fun image functions that allow us to do some interesting tweaks.

Gradients

Gradients in `canvas` are quite similar to those in SVG. They're created as linear or radial gradients, and color stops can be defined to make more complex effects. Once a gradient is created, it can be used with either stroke or fill, directly assigned to either `strokeStyle` or `fillStyle`.

The function to create a linear gradient is createLinearGradient, and it takes the coordinates for the stop and end points of the gradient, given as relative pixel locations:

```
var lgFirst = ctx.createLinearGradient(0,0, 0.95, 0.95);
```

The function to create a radial gradient is createRadialGradient. It takes six arguments: three to define one circle and three to define a second. Of the circle measurements, the first two are for the relative coordinate (x,y), and the third is the circle radius:

```
var rgFirst = ctx.createRadialGradient(0,0,20,150,210,10);
```

To modify the gradient stops, use the addColorStop, passing in a position (as a value between 0.0 and 1.0) and a color:

```
rgFirst.addColorStop(0.5,"#ff0000");
```

The complicated problem with gradients and the canvas element is that the positioning of the gradient is independent of the coordinate system for the individual shapes. This means that you have to position gradients relative to the shapes, rather than assume that "0,0" marks the top-left of the shape.

Example 11-8 combines pieces of Examples 11-2 and 11-3, but this time using gradients to fill the various circle, rectangle, and line shapes—including the use of gradients to create strokes, as well as fills.

Example 11-8. Linear and gradient fills, with various shapes

```
<!DOCTYPE html PUBLIC "-//W3C//DTD XHTML 1.0 Strict//EN"
        "http://www.w3.org/TR/xhtml1/DTD/xhtml1-strict.dtd">
<html xmlns="http://www.w3.org/1999/xhtml" lang="en" xml:lang="en">
<head>
<meta http-equiv="Content-Type" content="text/html; charset=utf-8" />
<title>gradients</title>
<style type="text/css">
#workObj
{
    border: 1px solid #000;
}
</style>

<script type="text/javascript" src="addingajax.js">
</script>
<script type="text/javascript">
//<![CDATA[

// start drawing event
aaManageEvent(window,"load",setup);

// generate random
function random(max) {
    return Math.round(max*Math.random());
}
```

Example 11-8. Linear and gradient fills, with various shapes (continued)

```
// generate random color
function randomColor() {
    var color= "rgb(" + random(255) + "," + random(255) + "," + random(255) + ")";
    return color;
}
//draw
function setup() {
   var canvas = document.getElementById('workObj');
   if (canvas.getContext) {

       // get context
       var ctx = canvas.getContext('2d');

       // draw half circle topped boxes (circle drawn from 0 to 180 degrees, counter-
clockwise)s
       var x = 50;
       var lgFirst = new Array();
       for (i=1;i<=5;i++) {
          ctx.beginPath();

          // create linear gradient
          lgFirst[i] = ctx.createLinearGradient(x,x+100,100,200);
          lgFirst[i].addColorStop(0,randomColor());
          lgFirst[i].addColorStop(0.5,randomColor());

          ctx.fillStyle=lgFirst[i];
          ctx.strokeStyle=lgFirst[i];
          ctx.fillRect(x,100,100,100);
          ctx.arc(x+50,100,50,0,Math.PI,true);
          ctx.stroke();
          x+=100;
          }

       // Full circle
       var rgFirst = new Array();
       x = 60;
       for (i=1; i<= 6; i++) {
          ctx.beginPath();
          rgFirst[i] = ctx.createRadialGradient(x-55,275,10,x,370,100);
          rgFirst[i].addColorStop(0,randomColor());
          rgFirst[i].addColorStop(0.3,randomColor());
          rgFirst[i].addColorStop(0.5,randomColor());
          rgFirst[i].addColorStop(1,randomColor());

          ctx.fillStyle=rgFirst[i];
          ctx.arc(x, 320,50,0,Math.PI*2,false);
          ctx.fill();
          x+=100;
       }

    // draw different thickness of lines
```

Example 11-8. Linear and gradient fills, with various shapes (continued)

```
        ctx.beginPath();
        ctx.lineWidth = 10;
        for (var i = 1; i <=5; i++) {
            ctx.beginPath();
            ctx.strokeStyle = lgFirst[i];
            y = i*20 + 405;
            ctx.moveTo(20,y);
            ctx.lineTo(620,y);
            ctx.stroke();
        }

    }
}

//]]>
</script>

</head>
<body>
<canvas id="workObj" width="650" height="600">
Working with Canvas here
</canvas>
</body>
</html>
```

Three different types of shapes are created: a square with an open half-circle, a circle, and thick lines. Two different gradients are created. The linear gradients are used for the square and the lines, the radial for the full circles. Figure 11-10 shows the page opened in Safari 3. Note that the results can differ if you look at the application with Firefox, IE, and Opera, though Firefox 3 and Safari 3 are almost identical. Notice how the gradient is used, even with the stroke on the half circle "handle" in the first set of shapes.

Try out different variations of gradients yourself to see what happens when you change the parameters even a small amount.

Transformations

There are three different transformations supported with the canvas element:

translate
> Moves the origin of the canvas to a new location

scale
> Changes the size of the units within the coordinate system

rotate
> Rotates the coordinate system

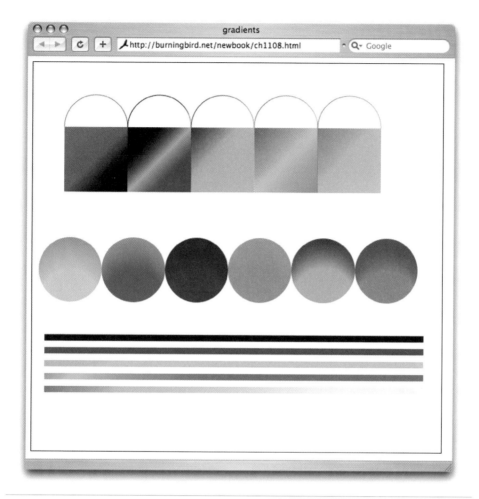

Figure 11-10. Using radial and linear gradients to fill various shapes

The `translate` transformation was used earlier with the Bézier curve examples, to move the drawings closer to the top and left. It takes two parameters, the x and y coordinates to the new location of the origin:

```
ctx.translate(-50,0);
```

The `scale` also takes two parameters, a scaling factor for both the x- and y-axis. A value of 1.0 is no change; less than 1.0 decreases size; and greater than 1.0 increases size:

```
ctx.scale(0.5,0.5);
```

The `rotate` function rotates the entire coordinate system around the angle, given as its one and only parameter:

```
ctx.rotate(Math.PI);
```

The canvas transforms are identical in operation to those of SVG, except that SVG allows transforms to be attached to specific elements, and the canvas transforms are applied to the entire canvas. However, you can use the save and restore methods in order to return the coordinate system to its original state after using each transform.

Earlier I mentioned using functions to create dashed lines with the canvas element. One way to create dashed lines for a circle is to use the rotate function and "turn" the coordinate system as each dash outlining the circle's circumference is drawn. In Example 11-9, I use this approach to create several circles, changing the scale and coordinate system in order to move the circles, as well as resize them. The canvas state is saved before each modification, so that the canvas is returned to its initial state, ready for the next circle. In the end, I rotate four rectangles, just so you can see how rotation works with a more solid-looking object.

Example 11-9. Exploring the canvas element's transforms

```
<!DOCTYPE html PUBLIC "-//W3C//DTD XHTML 1.0 Strict//EN"
        "http://www.w3.org/TR/xhtml1/DTD/xhtml1-strict.dtd">
<html xmlns="http://www.w3.org/1999/xhtml" lang="en" xml:lang="en">
<head>
<title>Transform</title>
<meta http-equiv="Content-Type" content="text/html; charset=utf-8" />
<style type="text/css">
#workObj
{
    border: 1px solid #000;
}
</style>

<script type="text/javascript" src="addingajax.js">
</script>
<script type="text/javascript">
//<![CDATA[

aaManageEvent(window,"load",setup);

function drawCircle(ctx) {
    for (i=0;i<60;i++){
        ctx.beginPath();
        ctx.moveTo(117,0);
        ctx.lineTo(121,0);
        ctx.stroke();
        ctx.rotate(Math.PI/30);
    }
}

// draw dashed circles
function setup() {
    var canvas = document.getElementById('workObj');
    if (canvas.getContext) {
```

Example 11-9. Exploring the canvas element's transforms (continued)

```
    var ctx = canvas.getContext('2d');
    ctx.lineWidth = 5;
    ctx.strokeStyle = "#f00";
  // first circle
    ctx.save( );
    drawCircle(ctx);
    ctx.restore( );

    // second translate
    ctx.save( );
    ctx.strokeStyle="#030";
    ctx.translate(150,150);
    drawCircle(ctx);
    ctx.restore( );

    // translate and scale
    ctx.save( );
    ctx.strokeStyle="#f0f";
    ctx.translate(370,250);
    ctx.scale(2.0,0.5);
    drawCircle(ctx);
    ctx.restore( );

    // one last circle
    ctx.save( );
    ctx.strokeStyle="#00f";
    ctx.translate(600,300);
    ctx.scale(1.0,5.0);
    drawCircle(ctx);
    ctx.restore( );

    // rotated squares
    ctx.strokeStyle="#ff0";
    ctx.translate(250, 450);
    for (var i = 1; i <= 4; i++) {
       ctx.save( );
       ctx.rotate(Math.PI/i);
       ctx.strokeRect(0,0,50,100);
       ctx.restore( );
    }
   }
}

//]]>
</script>
</head>
<body>
<canvas id="workObj" width="800" height="600">
Working with Canvas here
</canvas>
</body>
</html>
```

Figure 11-11 shows the results of all the transformations. Note that, just as with SVG, the order that you apply a transform can make a difference in the end result.

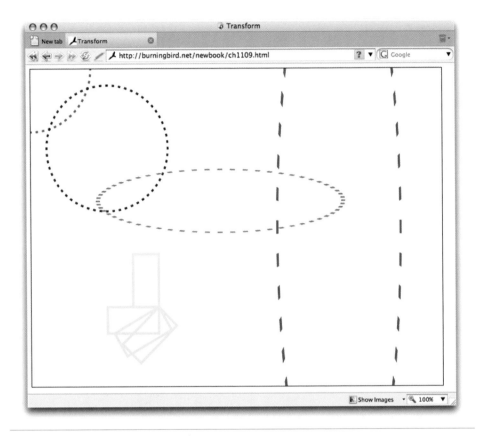

Figure 11-11. Results of various transforms

Images

The canvas element has a nice integration with other objects, especially images because you can capture loading events for images, slice and dice them, add frames, and even scale the images in the page. For those who are worried about copyright, you can also display photos without worrying too much about them being copied because right-click+Save doesn't work if the image is displayed using the canvas element.

There is only one canvas image function, drawImage, which has different behaviors depending on the number of arguments:

```
drawImage(img, x, y)
```
   Draws an image to page

```
drawImage(img, x, y, width, height)
```
   Draws an image to page, scaled to its width and height

```
drawImage(img, sx, sy, width, height, dx, dy, width, height)
```
   Draws a portion of an image bounded by *sx* and *sy*, at the given width and
   height to the canvas at the location given, and with the width and height, scaling the image accordingly

The abilities to scale the image, as well as to crop it via the second and third variations of the `drawImage` methods, are the functionalities of most interest, at least to
me. This is something we've not easily had in the client side of the application.

The last example for this chapter, Example 11-10, creates a gradient backdrop for
the canvas, and then creates a new image. When the image is loaded, the application
scales it half size and draws to the page. It also outlines the image in yellow, as well
as extracts a segment of the parent photo, displayed at full size just below the original photo. A yellow line is drawn between the two.

Example 11-10. Working with the canvas element image functions

```
<!DOCTYPE html PUBLIC "-//W3C//DTD XHTML 1.0 Strict//EN"
        "http://www.w3.org/TR/xhtml1/DTD/xhtml1-strict.dtd">
<html xmlns="http://www.w3.org/1999/xhtml" lang="en" xml:lang="en">
<head>
<meta http-equiv="Content-Type" content="text/html; charset=utf-8" />
<title>Images</title>
<style type="text/css">
#workObj
{
    border: 1px solid #000;
}
</style>

<script type="text/javascript" src="addingajax.js">
</script>
<script type="text/javascript">
//<![CDATA[

aaManageEvent(window,"load",setup);

function setup() {
   var canvas = document.getElementById('workObj');
   if (canvas.getContext) {
    var ctx = canvas.getContext('2d');
```

Example 11-10. Working with the canvas element image functions (continued)

```
    // add gradient backdrop
    var grd = ctx.createLinearGradient(0,0,700,600);
    grd.addColorStop(0,"#030");
    grd.addColorStop(0.5,"#0ff");
    grd.addColorStop(0.8,"#0f0");
    grd.addColorStop(1,"#ff0");
    ctx.fillStyle=grd;
    ctx.fillRect(0,0,700,600);

    // add image and expansion
    ctx.strokeStyle = "#ff0";
    var img = new Image();
    img.onload = function(){
      ctx.beginPath();

      // add image to page, reduced 50%
      ctx.drawImage(img,20,20,400,259);

      // frame inset picture
      ctx.lineWidth="5";
      ctx.moveTo(120,70);
      ctx.lineTo(345,70);
      ctx.lineTo(345,195);
      ctx.lineTo(120,195);
      ctx.lineTo(120,68);

      //draw connecting line
    ctx.moveTo(325,195);
    ctx.lineTo(325,300);

      ctx.stroke();

      // draw expanded image
      ctx.drawImage(img, 200,100,450,250,220,300,450,250);
    }

    // load image source
    img.src = '/images/misc/shawdragon1b.jpg';

}

//]]>
</script>

</head>
<body>
<canvas id="workObj" width="700" height="600">
Working with Canvas here
</canvas>
</body>
</html>
```

Figure 11-12 shows the color result of running this application.

Figure 11-12. Drawing images with canvas

 It's important to perform the canvas modifications on the image after it's loaded. If the image is part of the page, it can be accessed through the DOM, and the image is already loaded by the time the window load event is fired.

Example 11-10 is a fun demonstration of what you can do with the canvas element. Consider how useful something like this static application would be if a person could drag and drop a rectangle, click a button, and have an expansion of the marked area of the image displayed directly in the page.

Christian Effenberger created several libraries to manipulate images using the canvas object, at *http://www.netzgesta.de/cvi/*. This includes a magnifier example that uses the same type of functionality demonstrated with Example 11-10. Do take some time to explore these excellent libraries.

We'll look at this and plenty of other dynamic uses of both the canvas element and SVG in the last few chapters of this book.

CHAPTER 12

Dynamic SVG and canvas

If all we needed was a way to create an image to add to a web page, we have paint programs and photo editors, and wouldn't need either an XML schema or scripted object: we'd just create the image, link it into our pages, and go happily on our way.

In earlier chapters, I introduced both SVG and the canvas element, but only static variations. The real power to both graphics systems is the fact that graphics can be created and modified dynamically, responding to a reader's interactions, a changing environment, or even new data.

The canvas object is already dependent on scripting, but adding interactivity to the element adds a new dimension of usefulness and interest. SVG, though, is as static as any web page in HTML or JPEG photo. Or is it?

SVG can be animated in two ways. The first is through the use of specialized animating elements that don't require scripting in any form in order to scale, fade, color, or move. The second form of SVG interactivity and animation occurs through the use of JavaScript and scripting.

Scripting can be added directly into the svg element, or the element can be accessed by a code block external to the element. Which is the better approach—embedded in the script or accessing the SVG externally—depends on whether the SVG is added to a web page from a file or added directly into the page.

 This chapter uses the Document Object Model (DOM) methods, introduced in Chapter 10. If you've not worked with the DOM previously, you'll most likely want to read that chapter first.

Embedded Animation

Animation with SVG is usually a product of scripting, but can also be built into the document using the animation-specific objects. In this section, I'm going to introduce the five animating SVG elements:

- set
- animateTransform
- animateColor
- animateMotion
- animate

The animation elements aren't in widespread use. At the time this was written, only Opera and Safari had made any efforts in their implementation. Still, the more we discuss these elements, the more interest is generated, and the more quickly they'll be implemented in more of our browsers.

 I was disappointed to see Firefox 3.0 come out without support for the animation objects in SVG. However, Mozilla has made strides in its support for SVG Filters (demonstrated in Chapter 15), and I guess that's a start.

animateColor

The `animateColor` element will transform the attribute given in `attributeName` of whatever parent element contains it from one specified color to another. It supports a variety of attributes, including the beginning and ending color of the animation with the `from` and `to` attributes. The animation itself is controlled through other attributes, primarily the `begin` and `dur` attributes, which specify the beginning time and how long it takes, respectively. Another is `fill`, except rather than specifying a fill color, the `fill` attribute defines what happens to the object's coloring after the color animation finishes. A value of `"freeze"` persists the last animated color; the default is no fill value at all, which returns the element to its original color:

```
<animateColor attributeName="fill" attributeType="CSS" from="rgb(255,0,0)"
to="rgb(0,255,0)"
    begin="1s" dur="10s" fill="freeze" />
```

To better demonstrate `animateColor`, Example 12-1 contains three rectangles, each with an `animateColor` transformation element. The three rectangles all transform from red to green, but the duration of the transforms overlap, with each square starting as the other is finishing.

Example 12-1. Three rectangles using animateColor to transform from red to green

```
<?xml version="1.0" standalone="no"?>
<!DOCTYPE svg PUBLIC "-//W3C//DTD SVG 1.1//EN"
  "http://www.w3.org/Graphics/SVG/1.1/DTD/svg11.dtd">
<svg width="800" height="500" version="1.1"
    xmlns="http://www.w3.org/2000/svg" xmlns:xlink="http://www.w3.org/1999/xlink">
 <title>animating color</title>
<!-- three boxes, each with similar animations but different and overlapping durations -->
```

Example 12-1. Three rectangles using animateColor to transform from red to green (continued)

```
<rect width="200" height="200" x="50" y="20" fill="red">
<animateColor attributeName="fill" attributeType="CSS" from="rgb(255,0,0)"
to="rgb(0,255,0)"
    begin="1s" dur="10s" fill="freeze" />
</rect>
<rect width="200" height="200" x="250" y="20" fill="red">
<animateColor attributeName="fill" attributeType="CSS" from="rgb(255,0,0)"
to="rgb(0,255,0)"
    begin="8s" dur="10s" fill="freeze" />
</rect>
<rect width="200" height="200" x="450" y="20" fill="red">
<animateColor attributeName="fill" attributeType="CSS" from="rgb(255,0,0)"
to="rgb(0,255,0)"
    begin="16s" dur="10s" fill="freeze" />
</rect>
</svg>
```

Try the example out with Safari or Opera—animation without scripting.

The `attributeType` attribute is set to `"CSS"` because the type of the attribute being changed is a CSS value. In later examples, the `attributeType` is set to `"XML"` when SVG attributes are altered.

The animation elements are included within the elements they're transforming. They're also cumulative, which I'll discuss in more detail later. Figure 12-1 shows the three boxes in mid-color transformation.

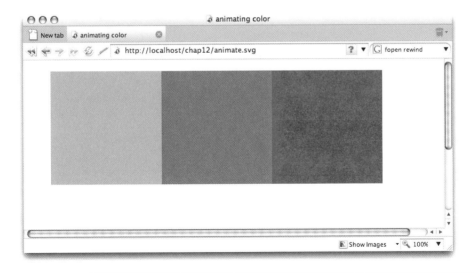

Figure 12-1. Three rectangles in mid-color transformation

animateMotion

Not hard to guess what animateMotion does, but it's still cool to see it in action. The animateMotion element has one child element, mpath, that links to the document fragment (such as #motion) for the path the animation is supposed to take when moving whatever it animates.

I made a mistake when I started fooling around with the W3C's animation example. The W3C example is a triangle that follows along a given path, and I was trying to get the triangle to follow a circle. I was attempting to wrap my mind around the cubic Bézier curve to complete a circle and made a mistake, ending up with this path:

```
<path id="path1" d="M100,250 C 100,50 400,50 400,250 C400,50 100,50 400,250"
      fill="none" stroke="blue" stroke-width="7.06"  />
```

When I used the path for the example, the little triangle twisted around the loop, like a car on a roller coaster (see for yourself in the examples, in a file called *mistake.svg*, and in Figure 12-2). It was a gas, but it was also an excellent way to see how well the animateMotion element works.

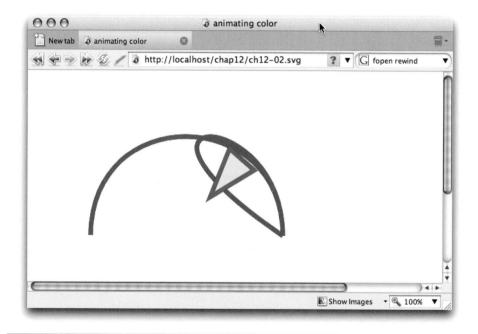

Figure 12-2. A mistake, yes, but a fun one

Example 12-2 has the SVG to create the animated document I had intended. It uses a circular shaped path to animate a group consisting of a line and three circles. The circles and line are aligned on the x-axis, extending into the circle. The animation is set to run for 20 seconds.

Example 12-2. Using animateMotion to animate a group of elements

```
<?xml version="1.0" standalone="no"?>
<!DOCTYPE svg PUBLIC "-//W3C//DTD SVG 1.1//EN"
  "http://www.w3.org/Graphics/SVG/1.1/DTD/svg11.dtd">
<svg width="800" height="500" version="1.1"
    xmlns="http://www.w3.org/2000/svg" xmlns:xlink="http://www.w3.org/1999/xlink">
 <title>animating objects</title>

<path id="path1" d="M100,250 C100,50 400,50 400,250 S100,450 100,250"
 fill="none" stroke="blue" stroke-width="7.06"  />

<g>
<line x1="0" y1="0" x2="0" y2="90" stroke="black" />
<circle cx="0" cy="0" r="15"  fill="navy" />
<circle cx="0" cy="45" r="13" fill="red" />
<circle cx="0" cy="90" r="10" fill="lightgreen" />
    <!-- Define the motion path animation -->
    <animateMotion dur="20s" repeatCount="indefinite" rotate="auto" >
       <mpath xlink:href="#path1"/>
    </animateMotion>
</g>
</svg>
```

The repeatCount attribute is set to indefinite, which means the animation will continue forever, until unloading the SVG document. In addition, the rotate attribute is set to auto, which means the element is automatically rotated according to variations in the path—the roller coaster effect I wrote about earlier (and located in *mistake.svg*). Other options are auto-reverse, which is similar to auto but incremented by 180 degrees, or, if the attribute value is a number, at a specific angle, which keeps the element related to the path at a rigid angle. Try out the different settings with the example or *mistake.svg* to see how each impacts the motion.

The image created in Example 12-2 is shown in Figure 12-3, but the picture doesn't really do justice to the motion. When you run the example, you'll most likely notice, as I did, how smooth the object is closer to the path, and the jerky motion of the circles and line further from the path.

animateTransform

animateTransform is a fun element. Any of the transform operations—scale, rotate, translate, or the skews—can be animated. If more than one animateTransform is attached to an element, the combined effect can be controlled through the additive attribute: the effect is cumulative when set to sum, and succeeding transforms override earlier transforms when set to replace.

Example 12-3 shows two elements, each with more than one animateTransform applied. The green square seemingly spirals down from the top, and as soon as it settles horizontally, a "Hello World!" text string moves in quickly from the side, ending up skewed horizontally, as if the text string had hit its breaks at the end of the animation.

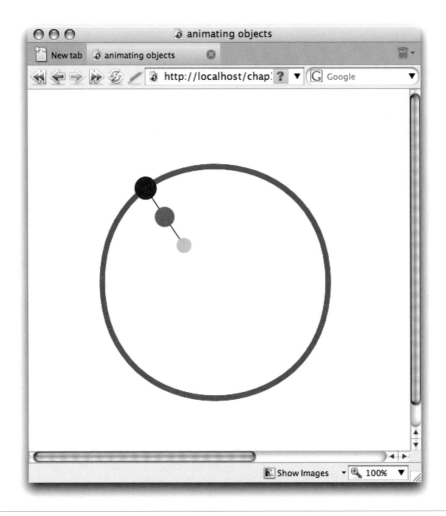

Figure 12-3. Animated circles and line, as a group, moving along a circular path

Example 12-3. Using animateTransform on two elements, rotating, scaling, and moving

```
<?xml version="1.0" standalone="no"?>
<!DOCTYPE svg PUBLIC "-//W3C//DTD SVG 1.1//EN"
  "http://www.w3.org/Graphics/SVG/1.1/DTD/svg11.dtd">
<svg width="800" height="500" version="1.1"
    xmlns="http://www.w3.org/2000/svg" xmlns:xlink="http://www.w3.org/1999/xlink">
 <title>animating objects</title>
<rect x="100" y="0" width="50" height="180" fill="seagreen">
<animateTransform attributeName="transform" attributeType="XML"
    type="rotate" from="0" to="90" dur="5s"
    additive="sum" fill="freeze" />
```

Example 12-3. Using animateTransform on two elements, rotating, scaling, and moving (continued)

```
<animateTransform attributeName="transform" attributeType="XML"
                  type="scale" from="1" to="2" dur="5s"
                  additive="sum" fill="freeze"/>
<animateTransform attributeName="transform" attributeType="XML"
                  type="translate" from="0,0" to="10,-180" dur="5s"
                  additive="sum" fill="freeze" />
</rect>
<text x="-350" y="100" font-family="Georgia" font-size="56" fill="orange">
Hello World!
<animateTransform attributeName="transform" attributeType="XML"
                  type="translate" from="-250,0" to="320,180" begin="3s" dur="2s"
                  additive="sum" fill="freeze"  />
<animateTransform attributeName="transform" attributeType="XML"
                  type="skewX" from="0" to="30" begin="5s" dur="1s"
                  additive="sum" fill="freeze" />
</text>
</svg>
```

It's hard to capture this effect in a screenshot, but Figure 12-4 shows the SVG document during transition, and Figure 12-5 shows the effect when its finished.

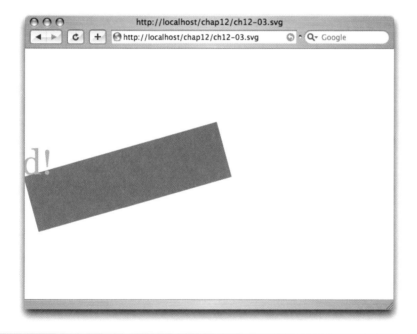

Figure 12-4. The animateTransform transition in process

Figure 12-5. After the animateTransform process is finished

set and animate

The last two animation elements are the set and animate elements. The set element does nothing more than set an animate-allowed attribute on an SVG element for a given duration. It's not a permanent change, and will revert to the original settings unless you set fill to freeze. Setting fill to remove removes the result of the set element at the end of the animation:

```
<set attributeName="fill" to="red" dur="5s" fill="remove" />
```

The animate element is a general all-purpose animator that can be applied to any animate-allowed attribute, CSS or SVG/XML, specified by attributeType. In the following code, opacity of an element is altered over time, creating a nice fade in/fade out effect:

```
<animate attributeType="CSS" attributeName="opacity"
    from="1" to="0" dur="5s" fill="freeze"  />
```

Example 12-4 combines the use of animateTransform, animate, and set into an application that fades the rectangle to nothing as it spirals down, and then sets the text to red after it's moved into position.

Example 12-4. Combining animateTransform, animate, and set

```
<?xml version="1.0" standalone="no"?>
<!DOCTYPE svg PUBLIC "-//W3C//DTD SVG 1.1//EN"
  "http://www.w3.org/Graphics/SVG/1.1/DTD/svg11.dtd">
<svg width="800" height="500" version="1.1"
    xmlns="http://www.w3.org/2000/svg" xmlns:xlink="http://www.w3.org/1999/xlink">
 <title>animating objects</title>
<rect x="100" y="0" width="50" height="180" fill="seagreen">
<animateTransform attributeName="transform" attributeType="XML"
    type="rotate" from="0" to="90" dur="5s"
    additive="sum" fill="freeze" />
<animateTransform attributeName="transform" attributeType="XML"
                  type="scale" from="1" to="2" dur="5s"
                  additive="sum" fill="freeze"/>
<animateTransform attributeName="transform" attributeType="XML"
                  type="translate" from="0,0" to="10,-180" dur="5s"
                  additive="sum" fill="freeze" />
  <animate attributeType="CSS" attributeName="opacity"
        from="1" to="0" dur="5s" fill="freeze"  />
</rect>
<text x="-350" y="100" font-family="Georgia" font-size="56" fill="orange">
Hello World!
<animateTransform attributeName="transform" attributeType="XML"
                  type="translate" from="-250,0" to="320,180" begin="3s" dur="2s"
                  additive="sum" fill="freeze"  />
<animateTransform attributeName="transform" attributeType="XML"
                  type="skewX" from="0" to="30" begin="5s" dur="1s"
                  additive="sum" fill="freeze" />
<set attributeType="XML" attributeName="fill" to="red" begin="6s" dur="1s"
fill="freeze" />
</text>
</svg>
```

Now, when the animation is finished, all that shows is the text, "Hello, World!", in red.

This has been a quick introduction to a wonderful functionality. As nice as these animation objects are, until they've reached wider implementation in more browsers (Firefox, at least), we're better off doing our animations with script, as covered in the next few sections.

The animation elements in SVG are based on an older specification, SMIL, or Synchronized Multimedia Integration Language, a recommended W3C specification described at *http://www.w3.org/TR/SMIL/*.

Scripting SVG

Until there's more widespread implementation of the animation objects, we're dependent on script to move our SVG about.

There are two ways to integrate JavaScript with SVG. The first is by adding a scripting block into the svg element. The scripting element so popular with HTML pages is also a component of the SVG specification. The second approach is to access the svg elements using JavaScript external to the SVG, such as in a scripting block within the higher-level XHTML document. The main difference between the two approaches is that the highest-level document object is the svg element when the script is embedded in SVG; otherwise, it's the containing web page.

Embedded Scripting

Adding a script block directly into an SVG document does not differ from how we add one to an XHTML document. Both are XML-based, and both require that the actual script be contained in cdata opening and closing tags or the XML won't validate. Browsers provide access to the DOM though the top-level document differs. Both can be used to create, modify, remove, or animate existing document elements.

Example 12-5 shows a standalone SVG document with embedded script. The high-level document is the svg element. Just as with an XHTML or HTML document, the high-level window object is accessed for its onload event and used to set the onclick event on the SVG circle. Clicking on the circle shrinks the radius by 10 pixels between each click, until the circle effectively disappears.

Example 12-5. Scripting block embedded in SVG

```
<?xml version="1.0" encoding="UTF-8" standalone="no"?>
<svg xmlns="http://www.w3.org/2000/svg" xmlns:xlink="http://www.w3.org/1999/xlink"
width="600" height="600">
  <script type="text/ecmascript">
    <![CDATA[

     // set element onclick event handler
     window.onload=function () {
        var circle = document.getElementById('redcircle');

        // onclick event handler, change circle radius
        circle.onclick = function() {
           var r = parseInt(this.getAttribute("r"));
           r-=10;
           circle.setAttribute("r",r);
        }
     }
    ]]>
  </script>
  <circle id="redcircle" cx="300" cy="300" r="300" fill="red" />
</svg>
```

The page works with Opera and Firefox, but not with IE, not even when accessed as the proper embedded object. It also doesn't work with Safari.

The reason it doesn't work with IE is that IE doesn't use its scripting engine to process scripting blocks within SVG. In order to process script within the svg element, Adobe's scripting engine needs to be enabled. Unfortunately, Adobe's scripting engine doesn't support the event handler assignment in code. Instead, the event handler assignments have to be made directly in the objects, as shown in Example 12-6, even though such direct assignment tends to be frowned upon in development circles.

Example 12-6. Animated SVG element altered to work with IE and the Adobe SVG Viewer ASV

```
<?xml version="1.0" encoding="UTF-8" standalone="no"?>
<svg xmlns="http://www.w3.org/2000/svg" xmlns:xlink="http://www.w3.org/1999/xlink"
     xmlns:a3="http://ns.adobe.com/AdobeSVGViewerExtensions/3.0/"
     a3:scriptImplementation="Adobe" width="600" height="600">
<script a3:scriptImplementation="Adobe" type="text/ecmascript">
<![CDATA[
   function shrink() {
       var circle = document.getElementById("redcircle");
       var r = parseInt(circle.getAttributeNS(null,"r"));
        r-=10;
        circle.setAttributeNS(null,"r",r);
   }
]]>
</script>
<circle id="redcircle" cx="300" cy="300" r="300" fill="red" onclick="shrink()"/>
</svg>
```

The additional namespaces and other extensions necessary to turn on the Adobe scripting engine are in bold text. Notice now that the onclick event handler is added directly to the circle. The window onload event handler is no longer needed, but if it were, the onload event handler assignment would have to be on the outer svg element opening tag:

```
<svg onload="init()" ...
```

Both examples work in Firefox and Opera, and the last works with Safari. With the modifications in Example 12-6, the application now works with IE, as long as the Adobe SVG plug-in is installed. The interactive element in the svg element works whether the element is accessed directly or embedded into a web page, as demonstrated in Example 12-7.

Example 12-7. SVG element embedded into an HTML page

```
<!DOCTYPE html PUBLIC "-//W3C//DTD XHTML 1.0 Strict//EN"
      "http://www.w3.org/TR/xhtml1/DTD/xhtml1-strict.dtd">
<html xmlns="http://www.w3.org/1999/xhtml" lang="en" xml:lang="en">
<head>
<meta http-equiv="Content-Type" content="text/html; charset=utf-8" />
```

Example 12-7. SVG element embedded into an HTML page (continued)

```
<title>Embedded SVG</title>
</head>
<body>
<p>
<object data="anim2.svg"
style="width: 600px; height: 600px; border: 1px solid #ff0000; padding: 20px; ">
<p>No SVG support</p>
</object>
</p>
</body>
</html>
```

Figure 12-6 shows the svg element in IE, after the circle has been clicked a couple of times.

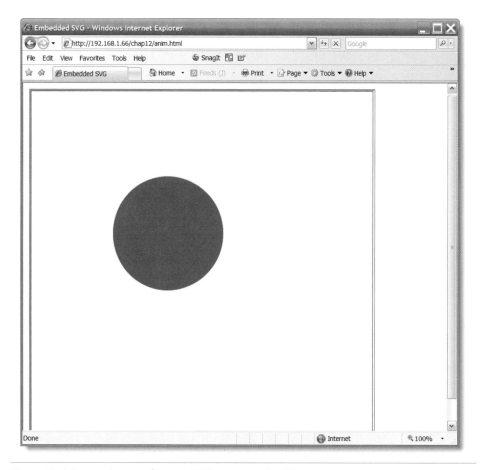

Figure 12-6. Interactive cross-browser SVG as accessed in IE

Cross-Document Scripting

The second way to mix scripting and SVG is via a script external to the SVG. For pages served up as XHTML, accessing the SVG in an embedded svg block is the same as accessing any other page element: use the DOM methods to get, create, and modify the contained svg elements.

Example 12-8 shows our red circle, this time inserted inline into an XHTML document. The script to change the circle size is now a part of the XHTML document, but the functionality is still similar to that in Example 12-6, including the use of the namespace-specific DOM methods, such as getAttributeNS.

The namespace-specific methods are recommended when working with SVG, because it is an XML document, unlike the earlier HTML documents. One major difference between the two applications is the event handling: the browsers that can process XHTML and inline SVG provide for event handling within script, without having to attach event handlers directly to the elements.

Example 12-8. Inline SVG circle altered by an external script

```
<!DOCTYPE html PUBLIC
    "-//W3C//DTD XHTML 1.1 plus MathML 2.0 plus SVG 1.1//EN"
    "http://www.w3.org/2002/04/xhtml-math-svg/xhtml-math-svg.dtd">
<html xmlns="http://www.w3.org/1999/xhtml"
     xmlns:xlink="http://www.w3.org/1999/xlink" xml:lang="en">
<head>
<title>Accessing Inline SVG</title>
<meta http-equiv="Content-Type" content="application/xhtml+xml; charset=utf-8" />
<script type="text/javascript">
    <![CDATA[

    // set element onclick event handler
    window.onload=function () {
        var circle = document.getElementById('redcircle');

        // onclick event handler, change circle radius
        circle.onclick = function() {
            var r = parseInt(this.getAttributeNS(null,"r"));
            r-=10;
            circle.setAttributeNS(null,"r",r);
        }
    }
    ]]>

</script>
</head>
<body>
<svg xmlns="http://www.w3.org/2000/svg" xmlns:xlink="http://www.w3.org/1999/xlink"
width="600" height="600">
  <circle id="redcircle" cx="300" cy="300" r="300" fill="red" />
</svg>
</body>
</html>
```

This example works in browsers that support both XHTML and inline SVG, but not all browsers (IE) can process inline SVG, and not all uses of SVG in a page are inline. There are some differences in functionality when the SVG is added to the page via an object element.

The SVG wiki has a page that covers interdocument interactivity (at *http://wiki.svg. org/Inter-Document_Communication*) with examples that work in all of the target browsers, including IE if the Adobe SVG plug-in is enabled. Example 12-9 uses the functionality to access the SVG document, using contentDocument, if supported; otherwise, it uses getSVGDocument. Once the SVG document is accessed, the same DOM methods available for the HTML document are available for the SVG document.

Example 12-9. Accessing SVG elements in an embedded SVG document from an external page

```
<!DOCTYPE html PUBLIC "-//W3C//DTD XHTML 1.0 Strict//EN"
        "http://www.w3.org/TR/xhtml1/DTD/xhtml1-strict.dtd">
<html xmlns="http://www.w3.org/1999/xhtml" lang="en" xml:lang="en">
<head>
<meta http-equiv="Content-Type" content="text/html; charset=utf-8" />
<title>Embedded SVG</title>
<script type="text/javascript">
//<![CDATA[

var svgdoc = null;

// set element onclick event handler
window.onload=function() {
   var object = document.getElementById('object');
   if (object && object.contentDocument)
     svgdoc = object.contentDocument;
   else try {
     svgdoc = object.getSVGDocument();
   }
   catch(exception) {
     alert('Neither the HTMLObjectElement nor the GetSVGDocument interface are
implemented');
   }

   var circle = svgdoc.getElementById('redcircle');

  // onclick event handler, change circle radius
   circle.onclick = function() {
      var r = parseInt(this.getAttributeNS(null,"r"));
      r-=10;
      circle.setAttributeNS(null,"r",r);
   }
}
//]]>
</script>
</head>
<body>
```

Example 12-9. Accessing SVG elements in an embedded SVG document from an external page (continued)

```
<p>
<object id="object" data="anim3.svg"
style="width: 600px; height: 600px; border: 1px solid #ff0000; padding: 20px; ">
<p>No SVG support</p>
</object>
</p>
</body>
</html>
```

Just like with the other examples, clicking on the red circle in Example 12-9 shrinks the circle. It has the added advantage of working with most browsers, too.

 Again, the example doesn't work with Safari 3.

Now that we can animate SVG, what can we do with it?

Animated Clock: The Hello World of Animated and Interactive SVG

Whatever you can do with a web page, you can do with an SVG document. Move elements about, change opacity, shrink, grow, or rotate. You can also create new elements to either replace existing elements or add new ones. If you don't want an element, remove it from the document.

Too many modifications to cover in-depth, but we can look at a few examples and see what kind of trouble we can generate.

The Dots, the Dots

I created a small application that does nothing more than add or remove dots from within an SVG canvas. I implemented it first as an HTML application using an `object` to hold an external SVG file, and then using inline SVG. How it works is that if you click on the SVG canvas area, a new randomly colored dot is added at that position. However, if you click on any existing circle, it's removed from the page. Simple, but it does demonstrate event handling, capturing mouse events in the SVG document, and adding and removing elements.

The SVG, whether inline or included through an object, is very simple:

```
<svg xmlns="http://www.w3.org/2000/svg" xmlns:xlink="http://www.w3.org/1999/xlink"
     width="600" height="600">
<circle id="redcircle" cx="30" cy="30" r="30" fill="red" />
</svg>
```

Example 12-10 has the contents of the application that uses the object element to embed an external SVG document.

Example 12-10. Dots application with SVG document as an external object

```
<!DOCTYPE html PUBLIC "-//W3C//DTD XHTML 1.0 Strict//EN"
        "http://www.w3.org/TR/xhtml1/DTD/xhtml1-strict.dtd">
<html xmlns="http://www.w3.org/1999/xhtml" lang="en" xml:lang="en">
<head>
<meta http-equiv="Content-Type" content="text/html; charset=utf-8" />
<title>Dots!</title>
<script type="text/javascript">
//<![CDATA[

var svgdoc = null;

// generate random
function random(max) {
   return Math.round(max*Math.random( ));
}

// generate random color
function randomColor( ) {
    var color= "rgb(" + random(255) + "," + random(255) + "," + random(255) + ")";
    return color;
}

// set element onclick event handler
window.onload=function( ) {
  var object = document.getElementById('object');
  if (object && object.contentDocument)
    svgdoc = object.contentDocument;
  else try {
    svgdoc = object.getSVGDocument( );
  }
  catch(exception) {
    alert('Neither the HTMLObjectElement nor the GetSVGDocument interface are
implemented');
    return;
  }

   svgdoc.onclick=addDeleteDots;
}

// add or delete dot
function addDeleteDots(evnt) {
    evnt = (evnt) ? evnt : ((window.event) ? window.event : "");
    var obj = (evnt.target) ? evnt.target : evnt.srcElement;
    if (obj.nodeName == 'circle')
        deleteCircle(obj);
```

Example 12-10. Dots application with SVG document as an external object (continued)

```
    else
        addCircle(evnt,obj);
}

function deleteCircle(obj) {
   obj.parentNode.removeChild(obj);
}

function addCircle(evnt,parent) {
   var posx = 0;
   var posy = 0;

   // all this processing is brought to you
   // courtesy of cross-browser differences
   if (evnt.pageX || evnt.pageY)        {
       posx = evnt.pageX;
       posy = evnt.pageY;
   }
   else if (evnt.clientX || evnt.clientY)       {
       posx = evnt.clientX + document.body.scrollLeft
               + document.documentElement.scrollLeft;
       posy = evnt.clientY + document.body.scrollTop
               + document.documentElement.scrollTop;
   }

   // specify a namespace when creating svg element
   var obj = svgdoc.createElementNS('http://www.w3.org/2000/svg','circle');

   // set attributes
   var color = randomColor();
   obj.setAttributeNS(null,'fill',color);
   obj.setAttributeNS(null,'cx',posx);
   obj.setAttributeNS(null,'cy',posy);
   obj.setAttributeNS(null,'r',30);

   // append to parent document
   parent.appendChild(obj);
}
//]]>
</script>

</head>
<body>
<p>
<object id="object" data="anim4.svg"
style="width: 600px; height: 600px; border: 2px solid #000;  ">
<p>No SVG support</p>
</object>
</p>
</body>
</html>
```

Clicking on an existing element removes it from the document; clicking on the SVG canvas, though, creates a new dot using `createElementNS`, passing in the SVG namespace as the first parameter and `'circle'`, as the second. It's positioned where the click event occurs in the SVG document. Figure 12-7 shows the page in Opera, with lots and lots of dots.

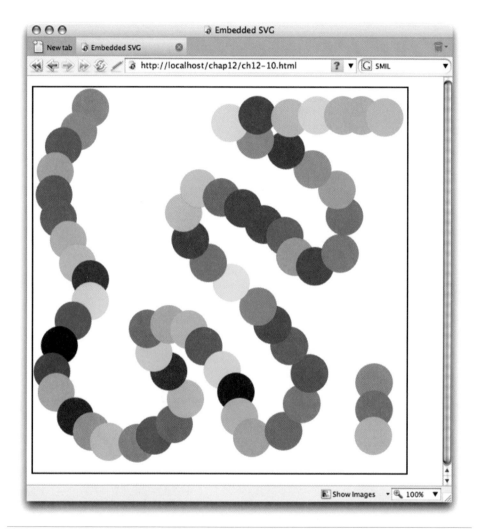

Figure 12-7. SVG creating lots of colored dots, shown in Opera

Compare the application that embeds an external SVG document with the one that uses an inline SVG document in Example 12-11. The functionality is quite similar, except that accessing the svg element is no different than accessing any other page element.

Additionally, the document object is used for creating the SVG circles, rather than a separate SVG document.

Example 12-11. Inline SVG and the same dots application

```
<!DOCTYPE html PUBLIC
    "-//W3C//DTD XHTML 1.1 plus MathML 2.0 plus SVG 1.1//EN"
    "http://www.w3.org/2002/04/xhtml-math-svg/xhtml-math-svg.dtd">
<html xmlns="http://www.w3.org/1999/xhtml"
      xmlns:xlink="http://www.w3.org/1999/xlink" xml:lang="en">
<head>
<title>Accessing Inline SVG</title>
<meta http-equiv="Content-Type" content="application/xhtml+xml; charset=utf-8" />
<style type="text/css">

svg { border: 1px solid #000; }
</style>

<script type="text/javascript">
//<![CDATA[

// generate random
function random(max) {
   return Math.round(max*Math.random());
}

// generate random color
function randomColor() {
    var color= "rgb(" + random(255) + "," + random(255) + "," + random(255) + ")";
    return color;
}

// set element onclick event handler
window.onload=function() {
  var svg = document.getElementById('object');
  svg.onclick=addDeleteDots;
}
// add or delete dot
function addDeleteDots(evnt) {
    evnt = (evnt) ? evnt : ((window.event) ? window.event : "");
    var obj = (evnt.target) ? evnt.target : evnt.srcElement;
    if (obj.nodeName == 'circle')
       deleteCircle(obj);
    else
       addCircle(evnt,obj);
}

function deleteCircle(obj) {
   obj.parentNode.removeChild(obj);
}

function addCircle(evnt,parent) {
   var posx = 0;
   var posy = 0;
```

Example 12-11. Inline SVG and the same dots application (continued)

```
    // all this processing is brought to you
    // courtesy of cross-browser differences
    if (evnt.pageX || evnt.pageY)          {
        posx = evnt.pageX;
        posy = evnt.pageY;
    }
    else if (evnt.clientX || evnt.clientY)          {
        posx = evnt.clientX + document.body.scrollLeft
                + document.documentElement.scrollLeft;
        posy = evnt.clientY + document.body.scrollTop
                + document.documentElement.scrollTop;
    }

    // specify a namespace when creating svg element
    var obj = document.createElementNS('http://www.w3.org/2000/svg','circle');

    // set attributes
    var color = randomColor();
    obj.setAttributeNS(null,'fill',color);
    obj.setAttributeNS(null,'cx',posx);
    obj.setAttributeNS(null,'cy',posy);
    obj.setAttributeNS(null,'r',30);
    // append to parent document
    parent.appendChild(obj);
}
//]]>
</script>

</head>
<body>
<svg id="object" xmlns="http://www.w3.org/2000/svg" style="border: 1px solid #000"
width="600" height="600">
  <circle id="redcircle" cx="30" cy="30" r="30" fill="red" />
</svg>
</body>
</html>
```

Other than a few document-based changes, the two applications are the same. Both pages work in both Opera and Firefox, but the latter does not work with IE, and neither application works with Safari. In the first application, Safari doesn't provide a way to get the SVG document, and in the second application, clicking on the SVG panel, but not a circle, doesn't trigger an event. The circle can be deleted, but no new ones added. With the increasing support for SVG in WebKit (the underlying engine behind Safari), these issues should be resolved in the future.

SVG Animation

For some reason, an animated clock seems to be the "Hello World" of SVG animation. I imagine it's because SVG provides circular objects, something missing in the HTML world (there are no curves in HTML; it's right angles all the way). Additionally, there's so much one can do to decorate the clock. From the simple, as shown by the clock created by Jason Davis (at *http://www.browserland.org/scripts/svgclock/*) in Figure 12-8, to a rather fascinating multiple gear contrivance, shown in Figure 12-9 and found at *http:// tavmjong.free.fr/INKSCAPE/DRAWINGS/clock_plain.svg*. Be careful accessing the latter with Firefox, as the application is a little memory intensive for that browser.

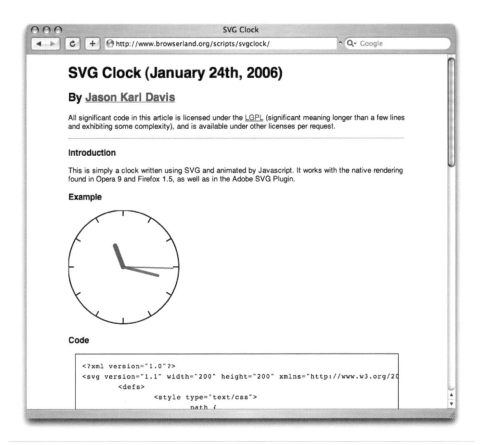

Figure 12-8. Simple, clean animated analog clock in SVG

Jason was kind enough to release his clock under a generous license, so I thought I'd take his effort and modify it. His original source is shown in Example 12-12.

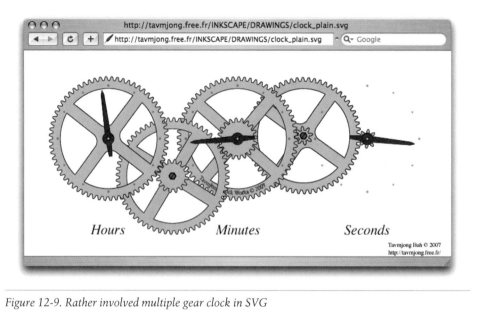

Figure 12-9. Rather involved multiple gear clock in SVG

Example 12-12. Animated analog clock via Jason Davis

```
<?xml version="1.0"?>
<svg version="1.1" width="200" height="200" xmlns="http://www.w3.org/2000/svg"
viewBox="0 0 2.02 2.02">
    <defs>
        <style type="text/css">
            path {
                stroke: black;
                stroke-width: 0.02;
                fill: none;
            }
            line {
                stroke-linecap: round;
            }

            #seconds {
                stroke: red;
                stroke-width: 0.02;
            }
            #minutes {
                stroke: green;
                stroke-width: 0.05;
            }
            #hours {
                stroke: blue;
                stroke-width: 0.08;
            }
        </style>
    </defs>
```

Example 12-12. Animated analog clock via Jason Davis (continued)

```
    <g transform="rotate(-90) translate(-1,1)">

        <path d="
            M  1 0 A 1 1 0 1 1 -1 0 A 1 1 0 1 1 1 0
            M  1.000  0.000 L  0.900  0.000
            M  0.866  0.500 L  0.779  0.450
            M  0.500  0.866 L  0.450  0.779
            M  0.000  1.000 L  0.000  0.900
            M -0.500  0.866 L -0.450  0.779
            M -0.866  0.500 L -0.779  0.450
            M -1.000  0.000 L -0.900  0.000
            M -0.866 -0.500 L -0.779 -0.450
            M -0.500 -0.866 L -0.450 -0.779
            M  0.000 -1.000 L  0.000 -0.900
            M  0.500 -0.866 L  0.450 -0.779
            M  0.866 -0.500 L  0.779 -0.450
        "/>
        <line id="hours"   x1="0" y1="0" x2="0.40" y2="0"/>
        <line id="minutes" x1="0" y1="0" x2="0.65" y2="0"/>
        <line id="seconds" x1="0" y1="0" x2="0.90" y2="0"/>

    </g>
    <script>
        var seconds = document.getElementById("seconds");
        var minutes = document.getElementById("minutes");
        var hours   = document.getElementById("hours");

        function setClock(date) {
            var s = (date.getSeconds() + date.getMilliseconds() / 1000) * Math.PI / 30;
            var m = date.getMinutes() * Math.PI / 30 + s / 60;
            var h = date.getHours() * Math.PI / 6 + m / 12;

            seconds.setAttribute("x2", 0.90 * Math.cos(s));
            seconds.setAttribute("y2", 0.90 * Math.sin(s));
            minutes.setAttribute("x2", 0.65 * Math.cos(m));
            minutes.setAttribute("y2", 0.65 * Math.sin(m));
            hours  .setAttribute("x2", 0.40 * Math.cos(h));
            hours  .setAttribute("y2", 0.40 * Math.sin(h));
        }

        setInterval("setClock(new Date())", 10);
    </script>
</svg>
```

The first thing I did was remove the outer circle and tick marks, in preparation for trying a different clock background. The next thing I did was to change the setInterval from 10 microseconds to a full second. With this modification, the sweep or second hand makes more of the click move than I'm used to with a clock:

```
        setInterval("setClock(new Date())", 1000);
```

The change also has an added bonus of being less of a burden on the CPU. Now I have a clock that has the movement I expected from a sweep hand, as shown in Figure 12-10.

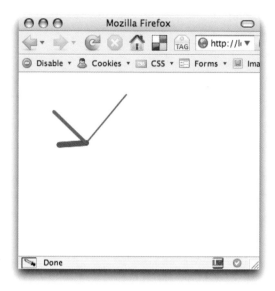

Figure 12-10. Stripped-down clock

I adjusted both the viewport and the group's translate transform to give me a little working area, as well as changing the color and width of the hands. I also used circles to create an inner clock area and a frame, shown in Figure 12-11.

Since the clock seemed flat without some form of reflection, I added other circles, using gradients, to create a shadow effect at the bottom and light reflection at the top, as shown in Figure 12-12.

Much better. Still, while looking at it, I decided that the tick marks really do add to the usability of the clock and added these back in, but without the circle portion of the path. Instead, I created another circle and used `stroke-dasharray` to add a decorative border. One last touch to support the 3D feel was to add a shadow, using an SVG Gaussian Blur and Filter on a new underlying circle. I haven't covered these previously, but a filter is similar to a gradient in that you create the effect and then attach it to an element. In this case, the effect is `feGaussianBlur`, which takes as attributes `stdDeviation` for the offset, and `blur` for the `result`. There are several other filters, each also capable of fascinating effects, but further explorations of their use are outside the scope of this book.

The filter shadow doesn't show up on all browsers, but for those where it does, it adds a nice effect. Example 12-13 contains the now visually and behaviorally modified clock, ready for someone to copy and try his or her own innovative modifications.

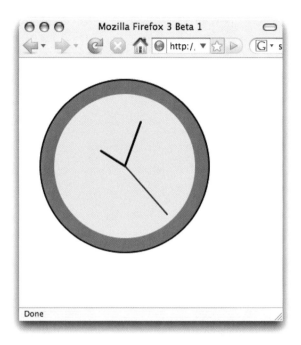

Figure 12-11. Interim modified SVG analog clock

Example 12-13. Finished, modified working analog clock

```
<?xml version="1.0"?>
<svg version="1.1" width="300" height="300" xmlns="http://www.w3.org/2000/svg" viewBox="0
0 3 3">
        <defs>
                <style type="text/css">
                        path {
                                stroke: black;
                                stroke-width: 0.02;
                                fill: none;
                        }
                        line {
                                stroke-linecap: round;
                        }

                        #seconds {
                                stroke: maroon;
                                stroke-width: 0.02;
                        }
                        #minutes {
                                stroke: black;
                                stroke-width: 0.03;
                        }
```

Example 12-13. Finished, modified working analog clock (continued)

```
                    #hours {
                            stroke: black;
                            stroke-width: 0.03;
                    }
            </style>

            <!-- outer silver band -->
            <linearGradient id="gg1">
             <stop stop-color="#333" offset="0" />
             <stop stop-color="#eee" offset="100%" />
            </linearGradient>

            <!-- highlight -->
            <linearGradient id="gg2" x1="0" y1="1" x2="1" y2="0">
             <stop stop-color="white" stop-opacity="0" offset="50%" />
             <stop stop-color="white" offset="100%"  />
            </linearGradient>
            <!-- shadow effect -->
            <linearGradient id="gg3">
             <stop stop-color="lightpink" offset="0" />
             <stop stop-color="mistyrose" offset="50%" />
            </linearGradient>

            <!-- drop shadow -->
            <filter id="shadow">
                <feGaussianBlur stdDeviation="0.08" result="blur" />
            </filter>
        </defs>

        <g transform="rotate(-90) translate(-1.5,1.5) ">
                <!-- shadow -->
                <circle cx="-0.04" cy="0.01" fill="#333333"  r="1.14"
filter="url(#shadow)" />

                <!-- outer silvered band -->
                <circle cx="0" cy="0" r="1.2" fill="url(#gg1)" stroke-width="0.02"
stroke="black" />

                <!-- clock interior -->
                <circle cx="0" cy="0" r="1.0" fill="mistyrose" />

                <!-- interior shadow -->
                <circle cx="-0.1" cy="0" r="0.91" fill="url(#gg3)" />

                <!-- decorative border -->
                <circle cx="0" cy="0" r="1.0" fill-opacity="0"  stroke-width="0.04"
                    stroke-dasharray="0.01,0.02,0.01" stroke="black" />
```

Example 12-13. Finished, modified working analog clock (continued)

```
                <!-- tick marks -->
                <path d="
                        M  1.000  0.000 L  0.900  0.000
                        M  0.866  0.500 L  0.779  0.450
                        M  0.500  0.866 L  0.450  0.779
                        M  0.000  1.000 L  0.000  0.900
                        M -0.500  0.866 L -0.450  0.779
                        M -0.866  0.500 L -0.779  0.450
                        M -1.000  0.000 L -0.900  0.000
                        M -0.866 -0.500 L -0.779 -0.450
                        M -0.500 -0.866 L -0.450 -0.779
                        M  0.000 -1.000 L  0.000 -0.900
                        M  0.500 -0.866 L  0.450 -0.779
                        M  0.866 -0.500 L  0.779 -0.450
        "  />

        <!-- clock hands -->
        <line id="hours"   x1="0" y1="0" x2="0.70" y2="0"/>
        <line id="minutes" x1="0" y1="0" x2="0.85" y2="0"/>
        <line id="seconds" x1="0" y1="0" x2="0.90" y2="0"/>

        <!-- reflection -->
        <circle cx="0.5" cy="-0.25" r="0.8" fill="url(#gg2)" />
        </g>
        <script>
                var seconds = document.getElementById("seconds");
                var minutes = document.getElementById("minutes");
                var hours   = document.getElementById("hours");

                function setClock(date) {
                        var s = (date.getSeconds() + date.getMilliseconds() / 1000) *
Math.PI / 30;
                        var m = date.getMinutes() * Math.PI / 30 + s / 60;
                        var h = date.getHours() * Math.PI / 6 + m / 12;

                        seconds.setAttribute("x2", 0.90 * Math.cos(s));
                        seconds.setAttribute("y2", 0.90 * Math.sin(s));
                        minutes.setAttribute("x2", 0.65 * Math.cos(m));
                        minutes.setAttribute("y2", 0.65 * Math.sin(m));
                        hours  .setAttribute("x2", 0.40 * Math.cos(h));
                        hours  .setAttribute("y2", 0.40 * Math.sin(h));
                }

                setInterval("setClock(new Date())", 1000);
        </script>
</svg>
```

Figure 12-12. An SVG clock with more depth

Figure 12-13 shows the now-finished modified clock, ready for you to alter to create your own unique look and behavior.

Modifications to the application can include a way of setting the clock to a specific time zone, using a function like the following in place of the `new Date( )` syntax in the timer call function:

```
function calcTime(offset) {

    d = new Date( );
    utc = d.getTime( ) + (d.getTimezoneOffset( ) * 60000);
    nd = new Date(utc + (3600000*offset));
    return nd;
}
...
setInterval("setClock(calcTime(-6))", 1000);
```

Now the clock is set to my own St. Louis (Central) time zone. You can also modify the background coloring to reflect A.M. and P.M., such as using grays for the latter and leaving the lighter colors for the daylight hours.

An interesting discovery I made while making these screenshots is that now each browser does the drawing within SVG. Both Opera and Firefox remove and add back the SVG drawing as they perform animation. Because of this, depending on the exact

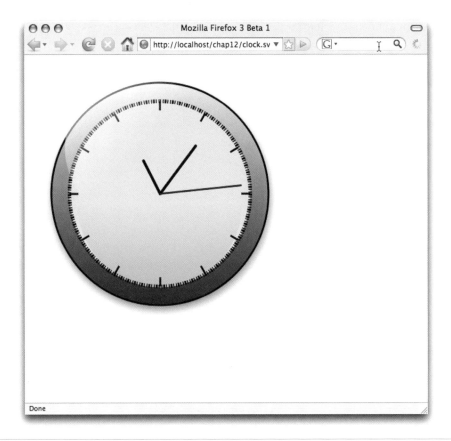

Figure 12-13. Finished modified clock

moment when the screenshot is made, the SVG won't show. Only Safari, which either has a faster refresh rate or does some other magic, consistently showed up in the screen captures.

Scripting canvas: Zoom!

Unlike SVG, which generates objects even if scripting is disabled, the canvas element is dependent on JavaScript. JavaScript is used to create the canvas element, the contained objects, annotate the objects, position them, and add the pretties. I covered all of this in Chapter 12. What I didn't cover in the last chapter is that, just like SVG, canvas is also interactive and dynamic.

I must seem as if I prefer SVG over canvas, and I do. The SVG specification is much broader in scope and capability, not to mention it works without scripting. Still, there are characteristics of the canvas element I really like, such as being able to dynamically generate the tick marks on a clock via an algorithm rather than have to place them manually. What I especially like about the canvas element, though, is the ability to zoom into a picture.

Capturing Events on the canvas Element

The biggest difference when working with the canvas element and other web page elements is that it's one single piece, no matter what's added to the canvas. As such, when you're capturing events, you're capturing them for the canvas element, not the individual canvas items. As you can imagine, capturing the position of an event is pretty important.

Example 12-14 is web page with a canvas element consisting of an external photo pulled into the canvas. Clicking on the image adds a small rectangle to the canvas. It's important to be aware of one challenge associated with the application: the mouse event position will be off by a factor based on where in the web page the canvas element is. As such, the click event has to adjust the mouse event by the left and top values for the canvas element in order to properly position the square. Note that the external JavaScript file, *excanvas.js*, allows the application to work with IE. However, as was mentioned in Chapter 11, the application usually needs to be run in quirks mode (remove DOCTYPE), or emulating IE7 to work; even then, the positioning is way off with IE8. In the examples are variations of the applications in this chapter, modified to work with IE8, but you may need to modify further when new versions of IE8 are released.

Example 12-14. Capturing a mouse click and drawing a small square

```
<!DOCTYPE html PUBLIC "-//W3C//DTD XHTML 1.0 Strict//EN"
        "http://www.w3.org/TR/xhtml1/DTD/xhtml1-strict.dtd">
<html xmlns="http://www.w3.org/1999/xhtml" lang="en" xml:lang="en">
<head>
<meta http-equiv="Content-Type" content="text/html; charset=utf-8" />
<title>Canvas Events</title>
<style type="text/css">
#workObj
{
    border: 1px #660066;
    padding: 0;
}
</style>

<script type="text/javascript" src="excanvas.js">
</script>

<script type="text/javascript">
//<![CDATA[


// for adjusting based on canvas position
```

Example 12-14. Capturing a mouse click and drawing a small square (continued)

```
function findPos(obj) {
   var curleft = curtop = 0;
   if (obj.offsetParent) {
        curleft = obj.offsetLeft
        curtop = obj.offsetTop
        while (obj = obj.offsetParent) {
           curleft += obj.offsetLeft
           curtop += obj.offsetTop
        }
   }
   return [curleft,curtop];
}
window.onload = function ( ) {
   var canvas = document.getElementById('workObj');
   if (canvas.getContext) {
    var ctx = canvas.getContext('2d');

     canvas.onclick = drawRectangle;

     // add image and expansion
     var img = new Image( );
     img.onload = function( ){

       // add image to page, reduced 50%
       ctx.drawImage(img,0,0);

     }

     // load image source
     img.src = 'purpledragon.png';

   }

   function drawRectangle(evnt) {
      evnt = (evnt) ? evnt : ((window.event) ? window.event : "");
      var posx = 0;
      var posy = 0;

      // all this processing is brought to you
      // courtesy of cross-browser differences
      if (evnt.pageX || evnt.pageY)          {
        posx = evnt.pageX;
        posy = evnt.pageY;
      }
      else if (evnt.clientX || evnt.clientY)          {
        posx = evnt.clientX + document.body.scrollLeft
               + document.documentElement.scrollLeft;
        posy = evnt.clientY + document.body.scrollTop
               + document.documentElement.scrollTop;
      }
   var canvas = document.getElementById('workObj');
   var pos = findPos(canvas);
```

Example 12-14. Capturing a mouse click and drawing a small square (continued)

```
    posx-=pos[0];
    posy-=pos[1];

    var ctx = canvas.getContext('2d');
    ctx.fillStyle="#ffccff";
    ctx.fillRect(posx,posy,5,5);

    }

}

//]]>
</script>

</head>
<body>
<canvas id="workObj" width="800" height="600">
Working with Canvas here
</canvas>
</body>
</html>
```

When the window is loaded, the canvas element is created and the onclick event is assigned a function, drawRectangle. In this function the position of the mouse event is captured, and then the position is adjusted based on the position of the canvas element in the page. This derived position is used to determine where to draw the small rectangle.

Figure 12-14 shows the page loaded in Opera, with several clicks leaving small purple rectangles behind.

Once we have a good idea of how mouse events work with the canvas element, the next step is to track a mouse in order to draw a rectangle around a dragged area.

Dragging a Selection Rectangle and Frame Animation

When finished, the application will allow a person to draw a rectangle around a portion of a picture and then zoom in for a better look. The next step in this implementation, then, is to create the functionality to draw the rectangle.

Example 12-14 is modified to capture mousedown and mouseup events: the classic drag and drop, but without actually dragging anything. In addition, as the mouse moves, a new rectangle is continuously being drawn to match the mouse movement. This runs us into one of the major challenges with animation and the canvas element: frame refreshing.

The canvas element was not originally intended for animation, so it doesn't have a way to automatically clear old images based on new actions. The only way to redraw the rectangle to match the mouse movements is to "refresh the frame." In other

Figure 12-14. Capturing mouse events and leaving a trace

words, to clear the existing canvas element ("frame"), restore the original visual image, and then make the new drawing. This is basically how frame animation works, and actually sounds worse than it is if you keep your "frame" simple to redraw.

Example 12-15 implements the frame animation to draw a rectangle around a piece of the background image. The mouse down, mouse move, and mouse up events are all captured, and functionality added for each. In the case of mouse down, global variables are set to the current position. For mouse up, these values are nulled out. It's during the mouse movement that the real fun happens.

Example 12-15. Frame animation with the canvas element

```
<!DOCTYPE html PUBLIC "-//W3C//DTD XHTML 1.0 Strict//EN"
        "http://www.w3.org/TR/xhtml1/DTD/xhtml1-strict.dtd">
<html xmlns="http://www.w3.org/1999/xhtml" lang="en" xml:lang="en">
<head>
<meta http-equiv="Content-Type" content="text/html; charset=utf-8" />
```

Example 12-15. Frame animation with the canvas element (continued)

```
<title>Canvas Events</title>
<style type="text/css">
#workObj
{
    border: 1px #660066;
    padding: 0;
}
#image { display: none }
</style>

<script type="text/javascript" src="excanvas.js">
</script>

<script type="text/javascript">
//<![CDATA[

var startx = starty = null;

// for adjusting based on canvas position
function findPos(obj) {
    var curleft = curtop = 0;
    if (obj.offsetParent) {
        curleft = obj.offsetLeft
        curtop = obj.offsetTop
        while (obj = obj.offsetParent) {
            curleft += obj.offsetLeft
            curtop += obj.offsetTop
        }
    }
    return [curleft,curtop];
}
function addImage(ctx) {
    // add image and expansion
    var img = new Image();
    img = document.images['image']
    ctx.drawImage(img,0,0);

}

function mousePosition(evnt) {
    evnt = (evnt) ? evnt : ((window.event) ? window.event : "");
    var canvas = document.getElementById('workObj');

    var posx; var posy;

    // all this processing is brought to you
    // courtesy of cross-browser differences
    if (evnt.pageX || evnt.pageY)          {
      posx = evnt.pageX;
      posy = evnt.pageY;
    }
```

Example 12-15. Frame animation with the canvas element (continued)

```
        else if (evnt.clientX || evnt.clientY)        {
          posx = evnt.clientX + document.body.scrollLeft
                + document.documentElement.scrollLeft;
          posy = evnt.clientY + document.body.scrollTop
                + document.documentElement.scrollTop;
        }
        var  pos = findPos(canvas);

        posx-=pos[0];
        posy-=pos[1];

        return [posx,posy];
}
window.onload = function () {
    var canvas = document.getElementById('workObj');
    if (canvas.getContext) {
      var ctx = canvas.getContext('2d');
      canvas.onmousedown = startRectangle;
      canvas.onmousemove = drawRectangle;
      canvas.onmouseup = finishRectangle;
      addImage(ctx);

    }
}

function startRectangle(evnt) {
    var canvas = document.getElementById('workObj');
    var pos = mousePosition(evnt);
    startx = pos[0];
    starty = pos[1];
}

function finishRectangle(evnt) {

    startx = starty = null;
}
function drawRectangle(evnt) {
        if (!startx) return;

        var canvas = document.getElementById('workObj');
        var ctx = canvas.getContext('2d');
        ctx.clearRect(0,0,800,600);
        addImage(ctx);

        var pos = mousePosition(evnt);

        var posx=pos[0];
        var posy=pos[1];

        ctx.strokeStyle="#ffccff";
        ctx.strokeWidth="#ffccff";
        ctx.lineWidth="2";
```

Example 12-15. Frame animation with the canvas element (continued)

```
      posx = -1 * (startx - posx);
      posy = -1 * (starty - posy);

      ctx.strokeRect(startx,starty,posx,posy);
}


//]]>
</script>

</head>
<body>
<canvas id="workObj" width="800" height="600">
Working with Canvas here
</canvas>
<img src="purpledragon.png" id="image" />
</body>
</html>
```

During the mouse movement, the canvas is cleared with the `clearRect` method, and then the image is added back before the new drawing occurs. To make the application more efficient, the image is added into an element in the web page, which is then set to `"display:none"` so that it doesn't show. This effectively "caches" the image in the page.

Once the `canvas` element is refreshed and all previous rectangle drawing erased, the application then draws the new rectangle using the pre-existing starting position for the left/top of the rectangle and adjusted values to determine the height and width of the rectangle. These values are based on subtracting the current position from the starting position and then multiplying by minus one (–1).

It doesn't sound like the animation would be very fast, but it is. Figure 12-15 is a screenshot of the page with a rectangle that's drawn by clicking down on the mouse and dragging until the rectangle is as big as you want.

The correct rectangle is drawn regardless of which direction the mouse is dragged—from left to right or right to left.

Now that we have a way to "grab" a section of a photo, all that's left is to create the magnification.

Zooming In for the Finish

The canvas `drawImage` function has a way of accessing just an area of a photo and then magnifying this area. In the last section, we created the code to pull out a piece of the photo. Now we need to magnify this section.

Figure 12-15. Drag and draw a rectangle, thanks to frame animation

To create a magnification, the application adds a new canvas element to the page within a div element that's had its display set to "none", to remove it from both the page display and layout. When the rectangle for the first canvas element is finished, the new canvas element is accessed, the image loaded, and the globally stored section information from the previous canvas element is used to determine which slice of the photo to display. The image is set to the same width and height as the canvas element, which in this case is 800×600 pixels. Example 12-16 contains the finished application.

Example 12-16. Image magnification application, with magnifier

```
<!DOCTYPE html PUBLIC "-//W3C//DTD XHTML 1.0 Strict//EN"
        "http://www.w3.org/TR/xhtml1/DTD/xhtml1-strict.dtd">
<html xmlns="http://www.w3.org/1999/xhtml" lang="en" xml:lang="en">
<head>
<meta http-equiv="Content-Type" content="text/html; charset=utf-8" />
<title>Canvas Events</title>
<style type="text/css">
#workObj
```

Example 12-16. Image magnification application, with magnifier (continued)

```
{
    border: 1px #660066;
    padding: 0;
}
#image { display: none }
#glasscontainer { position: absolute; left: 50px; top: 50px;  padding: 10px;
border: 2px #ffccff solid; display: none}
</style>

<script type="text/javascript" src="excanvas.js">
</script>

<script type="text/javascript">
//<![CDATA[

// globals to maintain dimensions across events and objects
var startx = starty = null;
var endx = endy = null;

// start this puppy
window.onload = function () {
   var canvas = document.getElementById('workObj');
   if (canvas.getContext) {
     var ctx = canvas.getContext('2d');
     canvas.onmousedown = startRectangle;
     canvas.onmousemove = drawRectangle;
     canvas.onmouseup = finishRectangle;
     addImage(ctx);

   }
}

// general functions
// for adjusting based on canvas position
function findPos(obj) {
   var curleft = curtop = 0;
   if (obj.offsetParent) {
       curleft = obj.offsetLeft;
       curtop = obj.offsetTop;
       while (obj = obj.offsetParent) {
          curleft += obj.offsetLeft;
          curtop += obj.offsetTop;
       }
   }
   return [curleft,curtop];
}

// draw image
function addImage(ctx) {
    // add image and expansion
    var img = new Image();
    img = document.images['image'];
    ctx.drawImage(img,0,0);
```

Example 12-16. Image magnification application, with magnifier (continued)

```
}

// find mouse position
function mousePosition(evnt) {
    evnt = (evnt) ? evnt : ((window.event) ? window.event : "");
    var canvas = document.getElementById('workObj');

    var posx; var posy;

    // all this processing is brought to you
    // courtesy of cross-browser differences
    if (evnt.pageX || evnt.pageY)        {
      posx = evnt.pageX;
      posy = evnt.pageY;
    }
    else if (evnt.clientX || evnt.clientY)       {
      posx = evnt.clientX + document.body.scrollLeft
             + document.documentElement.scrollLeft;
      posy = evnt.clientY + document.body.scrollTop
             + document.documentElement.scrollTop;
    }
    var  pos = findPos(canvas);

    // adjusted position
    posx-=pos[0];
    posy-=pos[1];

    return [posx,posy];
}

// begin drawing, record start position
function startRectangle(evnt) {
    var canvas = document.getElementById('workObj');
    var pos = mousePosition(evnt);
    startx = pos[0];
    starty = pos[1];
}

// refresh frame, and redraw rectangle
function drawRectangle(evnt) {
    if (!startx) return;

    var canvas = document.getElementById('workObj');
    var ctx = canvas.getContext('2d');
    ctx.clearRect(0,0,800,600);
    addImage(ctx);

    var pos = mousePosition(evnt);

    var posx=pos[0];
    var posy=pos[1];
```

Example 12-16. Image magnification application, with magnifier (continued)

```
        ctx.strokeStyle="#ffccff";
        ctx.strokeWidth="#ffccff";
        ctx.lineWidth="2";

        posx = -1 * (startx - posx);
        posy = -1 * (starty - posy);

        ctx.strokeRect(startx,starty,posx,posy);
        endx = posx; endy = posy;
}
// rectangle finished, display magnifier glass, display image section
// reset globals
function finishRectangle(evnt) {
   var canvas = document.getElementById('glass');
   var ctx = canvas.getContext('2d');
  canvas.onclick = closeGlass;

   ctx.clearRect(0,0,800,600);
   var img = new Image( );
   img = document.images['image'];

   ctx.drawImage(img, startx, starty, endx, endy, 0,0,800,600);
   var container = document.getElementById("glasscontainer");
   container.style.display="block";
   startx = starty = null;
   endx = endy = null;
}

// close magnifier
function closeGlass( ) {
    document.getElementById('glasscontainer').style.display="none";
}

//]]>
</script>

</head>
<body>
<canvas id="workObj" width="800" height="600">
Working with Canvas here
</canvas>
<img src="purpledragon.png" id="image" />
<div id="glasscontainer">
<canvas id="glass" width="800" height="600">
</canvas>
<p>Click on image to close magnification.</p>
</div>
</body>
</html>
```

Clicking on the enlarged image closes the magnification element. Figure 12-16 shows the page with part of the original picture magnified.

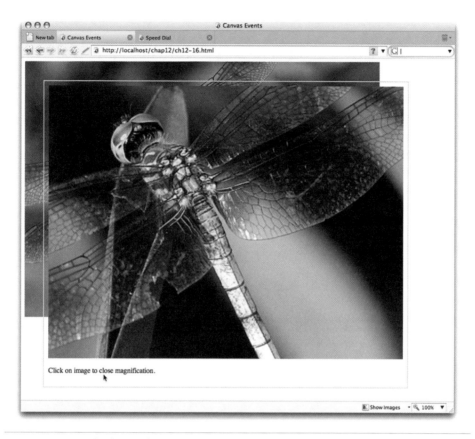

Figure 12-16. Result of magnification using canvas

Of course, when you scale a picture, the result is going to pixelate. If the original has a high enough resolution and quality, the magnification should be good enough to at least see the general detail.

You can also quickly click the picture, and open the pixel—just the pixel—wherever the mouse event occurs, as shown in Figure 12-17.

A better approach to the application (the implementation of which I leave to your discretion) would be to use a thumbnail image for the smaller image and a much larger image for the "magnification." The section information will have to be adjusted to match the larger image, but the result will be a much clearer picture.

Regardless, it's a fun little application that also gives us a chance to learn how to animate and interact with the canvas element.

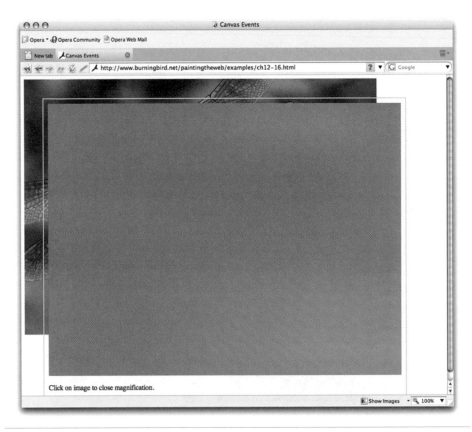

Figure 12-17. Accessing a single pixel

CHAPTER 13

Image Magic: Programming and Power Tools

There are an extraordinary number of tools that can create and manipulate images on the typical Linux-based web server. From native image support built into programming languages to tools that can be accessed via the command line, you can turn a photo into a postcard, resize and annotate images, create an instant slideshow, or toss in complex image manipulations at the call of a function.

For instance, popular web scripting languages such as PHP have built-in interfaces to external graphics libraries. With this support, we can create simple applications that can open a photo, access individual pixels to find colors at these points, and generate an entire web color scheme.

Going beyond this built-in language-based functionality, there's the incredibly powerful ImageMagick software suit, with functionality that can be accessed via the command line, built into reusable scripts, or created as applications via libraries in PHP, Perl, Ruby, and Python, among others.

Most of the functionality covered in this chapter is available with the typical web-hosting package that provides Secure Shell (SSH) access, and is built into the Linux operating system. Most is also available easily on the Mac with the Macports package management system or comparable Fink system. In addition, the version of PHP for Windows includes access to the graphics functionality, and ImageMagick provides a one-click installation of the graphics suite for Windows.

The only restriction to these graphics capabilities is that they do require some programming experience and a level of comfort with the Linux or MS-DOS command line. However, none of the capabilities requires that a person be a pro at software development or a wiz at Unix. A strong interest and curiosity are the primary requirements.

 This chapter, as with the rest of this book, focuses on PHP as the programming language, primarily because PHP is the easiest web scripting language to read for those not as familiar with software development.

Serving Up Photos: Insta-Slideshows

It might surprise you how much you can manipulate images using server-side technology. Not just how images are displayed on a page, but the fact that you can easily open an image file, manipulate its contents, and generate an entirely new image as a result.

The only limitation to this type of image functionality is the fact that photo and graphics manipulation is heavily mathematical in nature, and as such, can put a burden on the hosting machine's CPU and memory. However, for most of us, and most of our needs, servers can easily handle the extra load. You might want to restrict access to editing or conversion applications, though.

One of the simplest uses of server-side functionality is to create a drop-in insta-slideshow. This type of application can examine all the photos in a directory and instantly generate the necessary navigation controls. I provided just such an application for my tech reviewers, to make it easier to review the figures for this book.

The first component to the application is code to open the current directory, look for all filenames with file extensions provided in $exts, and then create a sorted array of these filenames. Example 13-1 shows this functionality, created as a separate PHP file, *photos.php*. It's created separately so that the functionality can be used in multiple applications. The current version just creates the array, but other versions could encapsulate the functionality into an object method or make it accessible via an external library function.

Example 13-1. Functionality to create an array from files in a directory

```php
<?php

$exts = array('jpg','png','gif');

//collect list of images in current (look) directory
$url = array();
if($handle = opendir(dirname(__FILE__))) {
        while(false !== ($image = readdir($handle)))
                foreach($exts as $ext)
                        if(strstr($image, '.' . $ext))
                                $photos[] = $image;
        closedir($handle);
}

sort($photos);


?>
```

There's nothing specifically image-related to the functionality in *photos.php*; it could be used for files with any extension just by changing the entries in the $exts array:

```
$exts = array('jpeg','pdf');
```

The next piece of the application is the slideshow page itself, *slideshow.php*, as shown in Example 13-2. It includes a reference to the *photos.php* file at the top, and then reads the current photo (if any) from the URL (via the photo parameter). From this information, the application rebuilds the appropriate navigation, checking first to see whether it makes sense to show the Previous or Next buttons. If the viewer is at the last of the photos in the directory, the Next button isn't shown; at the first, the Previous button is not displayed.

Example 13-2. Slideshow application page, including code to create the navigation

```php
<?php

require_once "photos.php";

    $index = $_GET['photo'];
    $uri = $_SERVER['SCRIPT_NAME'];

    if (empty($index))
        $index = 0;

    $prev = $index - 1;

    if ($index < (count($photos) - 1)) {
      $next = $index + 1;
    }

?>
<!DOCTYPE html PUBLIC "-//W3C//DTD XHTML 1.0 Strict//EN"
  "http://www.w3.org/TR/xhtml1/DTD/xhtml1-strict.dtd">
<html xmlns="http://www.w3.org/1999/xhtml" lang="en">
<head>
<title>Slideshow</title>
<meta http-equiv="Content-Type" content="text/html; charset=utf-8" />
<link rel="stylesheet" type="text/css" href="photoslideshow.css" />
</head>
<body>
<div id="slideshow">
   <div id="content">
      <div id="navigation">
         <?php if ($prev >= 0) : ?>
            <div id="previous" class="navlink">
               <a href="<?php echo "$uri?photo=$prev"; ?>">Previous</a>
            </div>
         <?php endif; ?>
```

```
        <div id="home" class="navlink"><a href="<?php echo $uri ?>?photo=0">Home</a>
</div>

        <?php if (!empty($next)) : ?>
            <div id="next" class="navlink">
                <a href="<?php echo "$uri?photo=$next"; ?>">Next</a>
            </div>
        <?php endif; ?>
    </div>

    <div id="main">
      <p><?php echo $photos[$index]; ?></p>
      <img src="<?php echo $photos[$index]; ?>" id="photo" alt="<?php echo
$photos[$index]; ?>" />
    </div>
  </div>
</div>

</body>
</html>
```

The application creates the navigation bar, which basically just prints out the array entry photo number for the next and previous photo, and displays whatever photo is current: either the first when the page is opened, or whichever photo is next in the navigation stream.

Figure 13-1 shows the application in process. The page is styled through the use of CSS, included as a separate file and not repeated here. The example files for the book include all of the necessary files for this application.

To run the application, all you have to do is drop the *photos.php*, *slideshow.php*, and *photoslideshow.css* files into the directory where the images are stored, and, instantly, you have a slideshow.

> Rename the *slideshow.php* file to *index.php*, and you also prevent a "directory contents" view of the image directory. Security and slideshow in one.

Manipulate Images with PHP/GD

The insta-slideshow is a helpful little beast, but it doesn't demonstrate actual manipulation of the photos.

Before attempting to create or manipulate images using PHP, see what your hosting company has installed for your use, or if you are running the applications locally, install the necessary graphics libraries.

Figure 13-1. The drop-in insta-slideshow application

To explore what's installed, the following small PHP application page pulls up information about your PHP installation, including supported libraries:

```
<?

php phpinfo();

?>
```

Saving the file as *info.php* and accessing this page on my local Mac-based development machine, as well as my Linux-based hosted web account, I can see support for EXIF, GD, and IMagick PHP libraries, as shown in Figure 13-2. I'll cover metadata manipulation with EXIF in Chapter 15, and IMagick later in this chapter, but for now all I need is the GD Graphics Library support.

 The GD library is an open source graphics library, with interfaces built into several programming languages, such as PHP. Beginning with version 4.3 of PHP, a GD library is implemented as part of the basic language package. This includes PHP for Windows, as well as the Unix and Mac-based installations. Most ISPs offering basic web hosting provide support for the GD functions, ready for you to use, right out of the box. For more on this package, see the main library page at *http://www.boutell.com/gd/*.

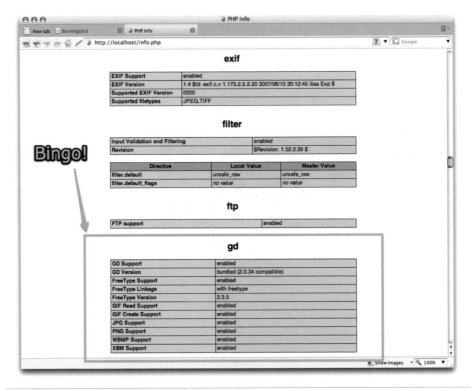

Figure 13-2. Looking for GD graphics as part of the PHP installation

Adding Borders

The slideshow application displayed earlier just output the images as found in the files, without any regard to touches such as drop shadows, borders, and the like. Depending on your images, this might work for some of the images but not so well for others.

To demonstrate the modifications we can make to images with PHP/GD, we'll walk through code to first create a border, then add a drop shadow, and finally tilt the image, like the "polaroid" look that has become quite popular with photos.

The first variation of the application uses several GD functions to create a white border with a black edge around any image, whose name and location is passed into the application.

To create a bordered image, the application creates a new background image, fills it, and then copies the original photo into it, topping off the application with the black border. The GD functions used are:

`imagecreatefromjpeg($filename)`

> Creates a working JPEG image given a JPEG filename. If supported on your system, the name can be passed in as a URL if the version of PHP you're using supports fopen wrappers (see php.net for more on fopen wrappers). The image must be a JPEG.

`imagesx($filename)` *and* `imagesy($filename)`

> Returns the width and height of a given image.

`imagecreatetruecolor($width,$height)`

> Creates a new image with the given width and height.

`imagecolorallocate($img,$red,$green,$blue)`

> Creates a color object that can be used with the given image.

`imagefillrectangle($img,$x,$y,$width,$height,$color)`

> Creates a filled rectangle, starting at x, y, and to the width and height specified.

`imagecopy($newimg, $img, $destx, $desty, $srcx, $srcy, $width, $height)`

> Copies a portion (or all) of one image into another, in the position specified.

`imagerectangle($img, $x, $y, $width, $height)`

> Creates a non-filled rectangle.

`imagejpeg($img,$filename,$quality)`

> Writes the image out to the given filename (if provided) and at the quality specified.

`imagedestroy($img)`

> Frees up memory used for image. Note that when the application finishes, the memory will also be freed, so this isn't necessary. It's just a good idea to get in the habit of cleaning up at the end of an application.

The easiest way to understand how all of these functions work together is to see the complete application. Example 13-3 shows the entire application, which borders the image passed in as part of the URL and returns the image formatted as a JPEG.

Example 13-3. PHP GD application to border a given image

```
// get image
$filename = $_GET['photo'];

$border=20;

// load image
$im=imagecreatefromjpeg($filename);

// check for image
if (!$im) exit ("Not a JPEG image");

// calculate and create new image
$width=imagesx($im);
$height=imagesy($im);
```

Example 13-3. PHP GD application to border a given image (continued)

```
$newwidth=$width+(2*$border);
$newheight=$height+(2*$border);
$newimage=imagecreatetruecolor($newwidth,$newheight);

// create filled rectangle
$white = imagecolorallocate($newimage, 255, 255, 255);
imagefilledrectangle($newimage,0,0,$newwidth,$newheight,$white);

// copy old image to new
imagecopy($newimage,$im,$border,$border,0,0,$width,$height);

// add black border
$black = imagecolorallocate($newimage, 0, 0, 0);
imagerectangle($newimage, 0,0,$newwidth-1, $newheight-1,$black);

// output image
header('Content-type: image/jpeg');
imagejpeg($newimage,null,100); // change here to $add2 if a new image is to be created

// though not required
// cleanup
imagedestroy($newimage);
imagedestroy($im);

?>
```

The application is run like so:

```
http://somehost.com/ch13-03.php?photo=photo1.jpg
```

or:

```
http://somehost.com/ch13-03.php?photo=http://somehost.com/images/photo1.jpg
```

Figure 13-3 shows a photo run through the application, which can be saved to our computers using the same right-click operation used for a static image.

To save a static copy of the image, a variation of the function, imagejpeg, can be used. Pass in the name of the file and the quality (up to 100 for 100%):

```
imagejpeg($newimage,"filename.jpg",100);
```

To write the file, the subdirectory needs to have global write permission. A variation on this application could test to see whether the modified image already exists and if so, serve it up with the page. This *caching* would be a preferred performance enhancement if the application were accessible by the general public. Example 13-4 shows the application from Example 13-3 with this caching modification.

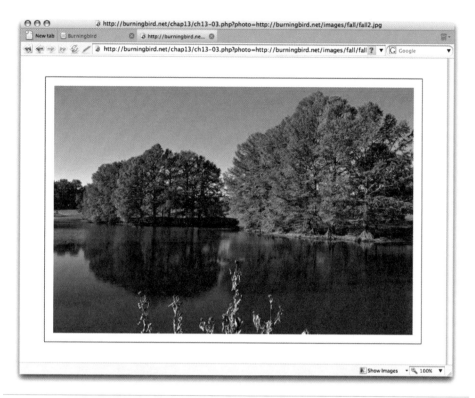

Figure 13-3. Dynamically bordered image

Example 13-4. Example 13-3 modified to cache bordered images

```
<?php

header('Content-type: image/jpeg');

// get image
$filename = $_GET['photo'];

// tokenize and create mod filename
$str = strtok($filename,".");
$newfile = $str . "mod.jpg";

$border=20;

// if mod file exists, read
if (file_exists($newfile)) {
    readfile($newfile);

} else { // generate file
```

Example 13-4. Example 13-3 modified to cache bordered images (continued)

```
    $im=imagecreatefromjpeg($filename);

    if (!$im) exit("not a JPEG image");

    // calculate and create new image
    $width=imagesx($im);
    $height=imagesy($im);

    $newwidth=$width+(2*$border);
    $newheight=$height+(2*$border);
    $newimage=imagecreatetruecolor($newwidth,$newheight);

    // create filled rectangle
    $white = imagecolorallocate($newimage, 255, 255, 255);
    imagefilledrectangle($newimage,0,0,$newwidth,$newheight,$white);

    // copy old image to new
    imagecopy($newimage,$im,$border,$border,0,0,$width,$height);

    // add black border
    $black = imagecolorallocate($newimage, 0, 0, 0);
    imagerectangle($newimage, 0,0,$newwidth-1, $newheight-1,$black);
    // output image
    imagejpeg($newimage);

    // save image

    imagejpeg($newimage,$newfile,100);

    // though not required
    // cleanup
    imagedestroy($newimage);
    imagedestroy($im);
}
?>
```

The application expects that the images will be local to the directory. Now when an image is passed to the program, the modified image is stored locally, in order to reduce processing time.

The next step is to incorporate the application into web pages. Since the application returns an image MIME type, it can be used in place of a static image file:

```
<img src="ch13-04.php?photo=image.jpg" alt="some image" />
```

With caching and direct web page access, this functionality could be added to the insta-slideshow described earlier. However, I'll leave that for an "off-book exercise."

One thing about this example is that it's focused on JPEGs. There are functions for working with GIFs and PNGs, such as imagepng and imagegif. In addition, because PNG images support alpha transparency, there are specialized functions that preserve transparency when working with the image.

There's also a way of finding the type of image and then adjusting the code for each type. The function, `getimagesize`, returns an array with five elements: width, height, image type as an `IMAGETYPE_XXX` constant, a string with width and height that can be used with an IMG element, and the MIME type. The third array element is the key one, returning values of `IMAGETYPE_GIF`, `IMAGETYPE_JPEG`, and `IMAGETYPE_PNG`, in addition to several others. For now, though, since most photos are JPEGs, we'll focus on JPEGs.

Adding a Drop Shadow, Cheatin' Style

There is no built-in blur with the PHP/GD functions. The effect is usually implemented by creating several, or sometimes dozens, of rectangles, each offset by a minute amount from the others and varying in color by a small amount. We still have a lot to cover, so I'm taking a simpler approach. In other words: I'm cheating.

To emulate this graphics cheat, take advantage of another GD function, `imagecopyresized`, which resizes the copied image if necessary. Create a rectangle that's about the size of the images you'll most likely work with, using whatever is your favorite paint program. Apply a Gaussian Blur to the image, with a radius of about 6 pixels.

This "shadow" template image (see Figure 13-4) is then used to create a shadow for each modified image.

Figure 13-4. Working shadow image

The application shown in Example 13-4 is modified to add in shadow capability. Since multiple constant values are now being used, border and shadow widths are stored in PHP constants, to keep them from being mixed up and to make it easier to modify. The added shadow component is emphasized in the code, shown in Example 13-5.

Example 13-5. Bordered image with drop shadow

```php
<?php

define("BORDER",20);
define("SHADOW",15);
define("OFFSET",10);

header('Content-type: image/jpeg');

// get image
$filename = $_GET['photo'];

// tokenize and create mod filename
$str = strtok($filename,".");
$newfile = $str . "mod.jpg";

// if mod file exists, read
if (file_exists($newfile)) {
    readfile($newfile);

} else { // generate file

    $im=imagecreatefromjpeg($filename);

    if (!$im) exit("not a JPEG image");

    // calculate and create new image
    $width=imagesx($im);
    $height=imagesy($im);

    $newwidth=$width+(2*BORDER);
    $newheight=$height+(2*BORDER);
    $newimage=imagecreatetruecolor($newwidth,$newheight);

    // create filled rectangle
    $white = imagecolorallocate($newimage, 255, 255, 255);
    imagefilledrectangle($newimage,0,0,$newwidth,$newheight,$white);

    // copy old image to new
    imagecopy($newimage,$im,BORDER,BORDER,0,0,$width,$height);
    // add black border
    $black = imagecolorallocate($newimage, 0, 0, 0);
    imagerectangle($newimage, 0,0,$newwidth-1, $newheight-1,$black);
```

Example 13-5. Bordered image with drop shadow (continued)

```
    // add shadow
    // create new canvas and fill with white
    $shadowimage = imagecreatetruecolor($newwidth+SHADOW, $newheight+SHADOW);

    imagefilledrectangle($shadowimage, 0, 0, $newwidth+SHADOW, $newheight+SHADOW,
    $white);

    // open the working shadow image and copy to new canvas
    $shadowimg = imagecreatefromjpeg("workingshadow.jpg");

    imagecopyresized($shadowimage,$shadowimg,OFFSET,OFFSET,0,0,$newwidth+OFFSET,
    $newheight+OFFSET,  imagesx($shadowimg),imagesy($shadowimg));

    // copy in newly bordered photo
    imagecopy($shadowimage,$newimage,0,0,0,0,$newwidth,$newheight);

    // output image
    imagejpeg($shadowimage);

    // save image
    imagejpeg($shadowimage,$newfile,100);

    // though not required
    // cleanup
    imagedestroy($newimage);
    imagedestroy($im);
    imagedestroy($shadowimage);
}
?>
```

Unless the working shadow image differs drastically in size from the shadow needed for the image, the drop shadow effect with this approach works quite nicely. It is important to ensure that the new "background" image that will contain the shadow is larger than the original image and shadow combined. If the background color matches the background color where the image will be used, it shouldn't matter if the overall image is a few pixels larger than the actual visual elements.

The drop shadow approach described is a "cheat," but it has an added benefit of less processing, as well as simplification of the program. Figure 13-5 shows the image using the drop shadow.

All that's left to finish the effect is to tilt the picture.

Tilt!

This is easy. The PHP GD functions have a rotate function, imagerotate, which takes the image as a first parameter, the degrees to tilt as the second, the background color third, and finally, a flag indicating whether to preserve transparency.

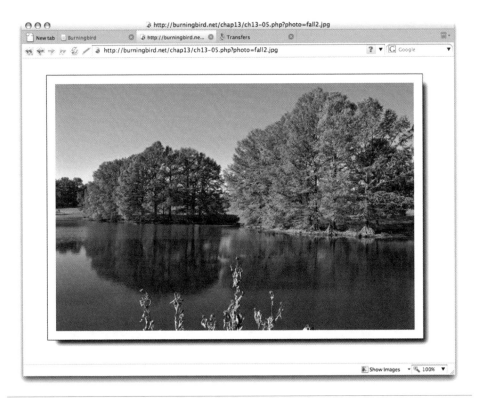

Figure 13-5. Modified bordered photo with drop shadow

Much of the code in the newest version of the application is a duplicate of the old, but Example 13-6 is the finished application, with the new rotate functionality emphasized.

Example 13-6. Adding the ability to rotate the image, after adding drop shadow and border

```php
<?php

define("BORDER",20);
define("SHADOW",15);
define("OFFSET",10);

header('Content-type: image/jpeg');

// get image
$filename = $_GET['photo'];

// tokenize and create mod filename
$str = strtok($filename,".");
$newfile = $str . "mod.jpg";

// if mod file exists, read
```

Example 13-6. Adding the ability to rotate the image, after adding drop shadow and border (continued)

```php
if (file_exists($newfile)) {
    readfile($newfile);

} else { // generate file

    $im=imagecreatefromjpeg($filename);

    if (!$im) exit("not a JPEG image");

    // calculate and create new image
    $width=imagesx($im);
    $height=imagesy($im);

    $newwidth=$width+(2*BORDER);
    $newheight=$height+(2*BORDER);
    $newimage=imagecreatetruecolor($newwidth,$newheight);

    // create filled rectangle
    $white = imagecolorallocate($newimage, 255, 255, 255);
    imagefilledrectangle($newimage,0,0,$newwidth,$newheight,$white);

    // copy old image to new
    imagecopy($newimage,$im,BORDER,BORDER,0,0,$width,$height);

    // add shadow
    // create new canvas and fill with white
    $shadowimage = imagecreatetruecolor($newwidth+SHADOW, $newheight+SHADOW);
    imagefilledrectangle($shadowimage, 0, 0, $newwidth+SHADOW, $newheight+SHADOW, $white);

    // open the working shadow image and copy to new canvas
    $shadowimg = imagecreatefromjpeg("workingshadow.jpg");

imagecopyresized($shadowimage,$shadowimg,OFFSET,OFFSET,0,0,$newwidth+OFFSET,$newheight+OF
FSET, imagesx($shadowimg),imagesy($shadowimg));

    // copy in newly bordered photo
    imagecopy($shadowimage,$newimage,0,0,0,0,$newwidth,$newheight);

    // now rotate the image
    $rotated = imagerotate($shadowimage, 15, 0xFFFFFF,0);

    // output image
    imagejpeg($rotated);

    // save image
    imagejpeg($rotated,$newfile,100);

    // though not required
    // cleanup
    imagedestroy($newimage);
    imagedestroy($im);
    imagedestroy($shadowimage);
}
?>
```

The background color used is white. The imagerotate function returns the modified image, which is then used to both save the modified image and return to the browser. Figure 13-6 shows the new effect applied to the photo.

Figure 13-6. Photo modified with a border, drop shadow, and tilt

Further additions to the application could convert some of the other static properties into parameters passed to the application, such as the offset use, color of border, width of border, and even the amount of tilt.

One more example using the GD, and then we'll move on to ImageMagick.

 The GD manual entries for the functions described in this section can be found at *http://us2.php.net/manual/en/ref.image.php*.

Mashup: Photos, PHP, and SVG

In Chapter 8, I demonstrated how to dynamically modify the CSS stylesheet using PHP, and in Chapter 12, how to use SVG to create web page elements. In this chapter, I've introduced you to the graphics server-side power tools, including PHP/GD. In this section, I'm going to create a "mashup"—a combination of separate technologies—that pulls together all of these pieces.

One of the GD functions is `imagecolorat`. Given a point in the image, the function returns the index of the color at that point. After conversion, this color can be used for any reason, including modifying the CSS for HTML, as well as SVG elements.

At one of my web sites, I use a rotating image application that changes the background image of the header based on a random array access, as discussed in Chapter 8. Combined with `imagecolorat`, the capability is used to generate decorative elements with SVG, as well as modify the color of my article. Figures 13-7 and 13-8 demonstrate my use of sampled coloring.

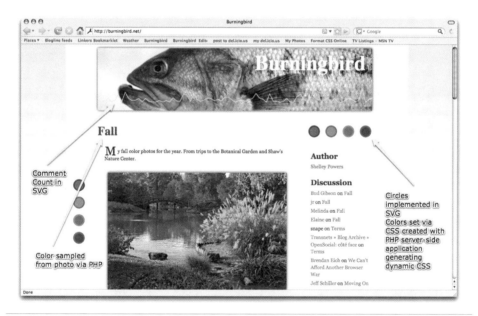

Figure 13-7. The use of sampled coloring at a web site

In photography, there's a "rule of thirds," based on the premise that the most important image elements lie along imaginary lines dividing an image into thirds, both horizontally and vertically. That's why you'll see many an image with the subject placed to the side rather than dead center.

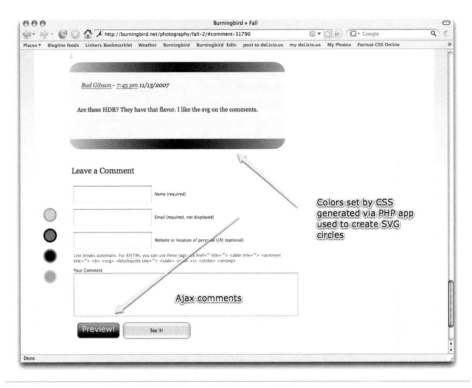

Figure 13-8. The use of sampled coloring and SVG at a web site

Based on this principle, I selected the intersection of these imaginary lines as the place to sample for colors, in addition to a fifth point, which is dead center (see Figure 13-9). I figured that by doing this, I would most likely capture the colors that define the essence of the image.

Modifying the application used at my site into a standalone application that can be dropped into a directory with JPEGs, Example 13-7 shows the CSS generation application, *photographs.php*, that gets incorporated into the CSS file. It first makes an array of the photos in the directory, and then randomly selects one. After the image is used to create a GD work image, the color samplings are made and used to generate several CSS settings. PHP bitshifting and masking, denoted by the >> operator, in conjunction with &, are used to convert the value to an RGB color.

The settings are used to alter an h2 header, as well as to create various SVG objects.

Figure 13-9. A photo marked out with the "rule of thirds" points, as well as the mid-point

Example 13-7. PHP application that uses the GD functions to generate CSS

```php
<?php
// declare the output of the file as CSS
header('Content-type: text/css');
?>
#header {
<?php

$exts = array('jpg');

//collect list of images in current (look) directory
//modification suggested by Kaf Oseo
$url = array();
if($handle = opendir(dirname(__FILE__))) {
        while(false !== ($image = readdir($handle)))
                foreach($exts as $ext)
                        if(strstr($image, '.' . $ext))
                                $url[] = $image;
        closedir($handle);
}
```

Example 13-7. PHP application that uses the GD functions to generate CSS (continued)

```
//generate a random number
srand((double)microtime( ) * 1000000);

// number of images
$ct = count($url);

// random image number
$rn = (rand( )%$ct);

// get the image name
$imgname = trim($url[$rn]);

// create a working image
$im = imagecreatefromjpeg($imgname);

$width = imagesx($im);
$height = imagesy($im);

$upperx = floor($width / 3);
$lowerx = floor(2 * ($width / 3));
$midx = floor($width / 2);
$lefty = floor($height / 3);
$righty = floor(2 * ($height / 3));
$midy = floor($height / 2);

// sample five points in the image, based on rule of thirds and center
$rgb = array( );

$rgb[1] = imagecolorat($im, $upperx, $lefty);
$rgb[2] = imagecolorat($im, $lowerx, $lefty);
$rgb[3] = imagecolorat($im, $upperx, $righty);
$rgb[4] = imagecolorat($im, $lowerx, $righty);
$rgb[5] = imagecolorat($im, $midx, $midy);

// extract each value for r, g, b
$r = array( );
$g = array( );
$b = array( );

for ($i = 1; $i <= 5; $i++) {
   $r[$i] = ($rgb[$i] >> 16) & 0xFF;
   $g[$i] = ($rgb[$i] >> 8) & 0xFF;
   $b[$i] = $rgb[$i] & 0xFF;
   }

printf("background-image: URL('%s');\n", $imgname);
echo "width: " . $width . "px; height: " . $height . "px;";

?>
            background-repeat: no-repeat;
            background-position: top left;
}
```

Example 13-7. PHP application that uses the GD functions to generate CSS (continued)

```php
<?php
    printf(".color1 { fill: rgb($r[1],$g[1],$b[1]); stroke: rgb($r[4],$g[4],$b[4]); }\n");
    printf(".color2 { fill: rgb($r[2],$g[2],$b[2]); stroke: rgb($r[3],$g[3],$b[3]); }\n");
    printf(".color3 { fill: rgb($r[3],$g[3],$b[3]); stroke: rgb($r[2],$g[2],$b[2]); }\n");
    printf(".color4 { fill: rgb($r[4],$g[4],$b[4]); stroke: rgb($r[1],$g[1],$b[1]); }\n");
    printf(".color5 { fill: rgb($r[5],$g[5],$b[5]); }\n");

    printf("stop.begin { stop-color: rgb($r[1],$g[1],$b[1]); }\n");
    printf("stop.middle { stop-color: rgb($r[5],$g[5],$b[5]); }\n");
    printf("stop.end { stop-color: rgb($r[4],$g[4],$b[4]); }\n");
    printf(" h2 { color: rgb($r[4],$g[4],$b[4]); } \n");

?>
```

Notice that the sampled colors are used to define stop points for an SVG gradient. The stylesheet is incorporated into the overall page stylesheet, *mashup.css*:

```css
@import "photographs.php";

svg
{
        display: block;
}

div
{
        margin: 20px;
}
#header h1 {
        font-size: 6em;
        text-align: right;
        margin: 0 40px 15px 0;
        padding-top: 25px;
        color: #ff0;
        }
```

The stylesheet is then incorporated into an XHTML file, shown in Example 13-8. XHTML is used because the SVG elements are embedded directly into the page. The page consists of a header showing the image; a title overlaying the image; an h2 header following, whose color is dynamically changed based on the picture; four SVG circles and a gradient, all using the sampled color points.

Example 13-8. XHTML page using the dynamically generated CSS entries

```
<!DOCTYPE html PUBLIC
    "-//W3C//DTD XHTML 1.1 plus MathML 2.0 plus SVG 1.1//EN"
    "http://www.w3.org/2002/04/xhtml-math-svg/xhtml-math-svg.dtd">
<html xmlns="http://www.w3.org/1999/xlink" lang="en">
<head>
<title>Mashup</title>
<meta http-equiv="Content-Type" content="application/xhtml+xml; charset=utf-8" />
<link rel="stylesheet" type="text/css" href="mashup.css" />
```

Example 13-8. XHTML page using the dynamically generated CSS entries (continued)

```
</head>
<body>
<div id="header">
<h1>Mashup</h1>
</div>
<h2>Mixing SVG, PHP/GD, and dynamic CSS</h2>
<div >
<svg:svg version="1.1" baseProfile="full" width="190" height="60" >

<svg:circle cx="20" cy="20" r="15" class="color1" stroke-width="4" />
<svg:circle cx="70" cy="20" r="15" class="color2" stroke-width="4" />
<svg:circle cx="120" cy="20" r="15" class="color3" stroke-width="4" />
<svg:circle cx="170" cy="20" r="15" class="color4" stroke-width="4" />

</svg:svg></div>

<div>
<svg:svg version="1.1" baseProfile="full" width="540" height="50" >
    <svg:defs>
    <svg:linearGradient id="gradient">
      <svg:stop class="begin" offset="0%"/>
        <svg:stop class="middle" offset="50%" />
        <svg:stop class="end" offset="100%"/>
    </svg:linearGradient>
    </svg:defs>

    <svg:rect width="540" style="fill:url(#gradient);"  height="50" rx="30" ry="30"  />

</svg:svg>
</div>
</body>
</html>
```

The page uses the sampled colors to create SVG, but it can be used to dynamically alter an entire web site based on color samplings from one image. Figure 13-10 shows the results of the page with one image, and Figure 13-11 with another.

The applications in this section demonstrate what you can do with the GD functions in PHP, but they don't touch on all of the capabilities. I recommend spending time with the PHP manual pages for the functions, as well as exploring other examples online.

Now, time for a little magic. A little ImageMagick.

Forget the Interface: The Magic of ImageMagick

All the tools we've explored earlier in this book have user interfaces. However, graphics work, including photo editing, doesn't always require a user interface—especially if you're doing a bulk edit on images. For some purposes, you'll want a set of tools that can be run directly from the command line in whatever operating system

Figure 13-10. Color sampling application with graphical image

you're using. The king of image manipulation from the command line is, in my opinion, ImageMagick.

ImageMagick is a software suite that allows us to create and edit images of all types, including SVG, TIFF, PDF, the webby JPEG (including JPEG-2000), GIF, and PNG. The suite can be downloaded and is documented at *http://www.imagemagick.org*. It can be installed from source on Unix and Windows, and from binary releases for Unix, Windows, and Mac OS X.

The suite's application interface is accessible via several language-specific libraries, including libraries for Ruby, PHP, Python, Perl, Java, C++, and even Ada and Pascal. If you program in it, chances are there's a library for working with ImageMagick. However, once the suite is installed, you can access its functionality directly from the command line, which is the approach I'll use first to demonstrate the capabilities of ImageMagick before diving into the programming aspects.

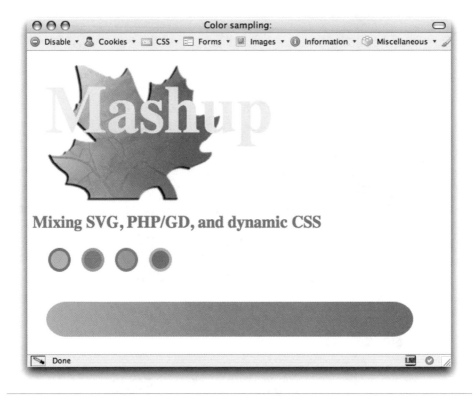

Figure 13-11. Color sampling application with different image

What are some of the capabilities of this rich suite of applications?

- Converting images between formats
- Transforming the image by rotating, cropping, flipping
- Making portions of the image transparent
- Resizing images
- Adding borders, text, comments
- Animating and adding special effects
- Creating a montage or composite of different images

Some of the commands require the presence of an X11 server, discussion of which is beyond the scope of this book. Many of the functions, though, are used to manipulate existing images and then either create new versions of the image with the modification or make the modifications directly to the image. These don't have any special requirements for display; you just need an ImageMagick installation and access to the command line.

Many shared hosting sites have ImageMagick installed, if you don't want to install on your own computer. All you'll need is Secure Shell (SSH) access to your site if you want to run the commands via the command line. If you're not familiar with the Unix/Linux command line, a page at *http://www.comptechdoc.org/os/linux/usersguide/linux_ ugbasics.html* has a listing of basic Linux commands.

Understanding the Command-Line ImageMagick

The command-line tools provided by ImageMagick and the uses of each could probably fill a book, but we'll try out some fun ones that should be reasonably simple to use. First, though, a quick look at how ImageMagick commands are formed.

An ImageMagick command combines options with both input image files and an (optional) output image file, depending on what you're attempting to do. A typical line would be like the following, using the most important ImageMagick utility, convert. This particular command uses the -thumbnail option, which creates a thumbnail image, maintaining an image perspective that is no wider than 90 pixels, stripping away any image profile data. The command then saves the modified image as *testthumb.jpg*:

```
convert test.jpg -thumbnail 90x90 testthumb.jpg
```

The options in ImageMagick are preceded by a dash, such as -thumbnail, and followed by any necessary parameters, in this case 90x90. This is about what you would expect from a command-line tool, except that using ImageMagick can involve some pretty complex operations on multiple images. Because of this, options can be used before input images, as well as after, to denote that the operation is specific to that image.

In the following, the -size option is used to tell ImageMagick to use a smaller version of the original JPEG image when creating the thumbnail, so that the memory buffer isn't overwhelmed with having to work with very large images:

```
convert -size 360x360 botfall1.jpg -thumbnail 120x120 botfall1thumb.png
```

Since we're creating smaller thumbnails anyway, the result of working with smaller versions of the original is virtually undetectable by the people looking at the thumbnail, and it's much friendlier to the machine creating the thumbnail.

This mix of input images and options is also useful when performing operations on multiple images, to control which images have what action performed.

The ImageMagick Commands

I'm not demonstrating all of the ImageMagick commands, only those used to modify images:

```
convert
```
Convert or modify images

```
mogrify
```
In-place batch processing

```
composite
```
Overlay images

```
montage
```
Create an array of images

One other command is `conjure`, which has its own ImageMagick-specific scripting language. This command is currently under development, and is also complex enough to deserve its own chapter. Due to limitation, I've decided to forgo coverage of it, but you should spend some time with the ImageMagick document on this interesting utility.

The primary ImageMagick application is `convert`. With it you can do most of the common operations on an image. The following converts a JPEG image to a PNG, for archival purposes:

```
convert image.jpg image.png
```

The next creates a thumbnail of the original image:

```
convert image.jpg -thumbnail 500x300 imagethumb.jpg
```

The parameter passed with the -thumbnail option, 500x300, tells the tool that the image must be a maximum width of 500 pixels and a maximum height of 300 pixels. The ratio of the width to height for the image is maintained once these outside limits are met, unless an exclamation point (!) follows, which tells the tool that the image must be resized to 500 pixels wide and 300 pixels high, regardless of aspect:

```
convert image.jpg -thumbnail 500x300! imagethumb.jpg
```

The -thumbnail option is similar to -resize, except that photo metadata is stripped from the image—useful for a thumbnail image.

Rather than creating separate files, you can overwrite the existing file using the `mogrify` utility:

```
mogrify -border 10 -bordercolor "#ff0000" image.jpg
```

Be very careful with this command, of course. If you run the same command multiple times, you may end up with multiple borders, which may or may not be pleasing. Figure 13-11 shows an image with two borders created using `mogrify`: one maroon, which was intended, and one magenta, which was not.

The `composite` utility lays one image over another. It helps first to have a couple of images that work well in a composite, which leads us back to `convert`.

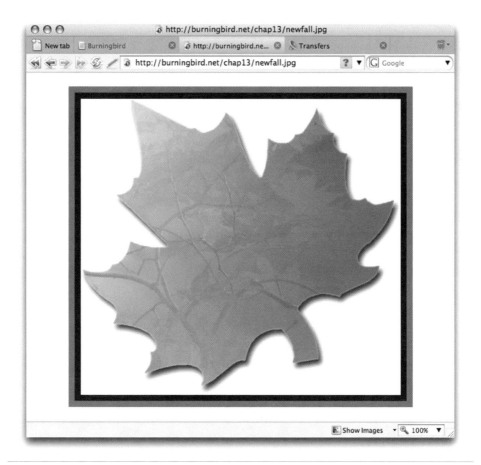

Figure 13-12. Double-bordered image, with one mogrify too many

convert doesn't just modify existing images, it can also be used to create images. The following will create a blue circle with a yellow background:

```
convert -size 300x300 xc:none -fill blue -draw 'circle 150,150,50,50' bluecircle.png
```

The size of the image, defined through -size, is 300 by 300 pixels, and the transparent background is specified with the xc:none option, with a blue circle centered at 150,150. convert also has a set of patterns that can be used to provide a background, ranging from checkerboards to vertical stripes, shingles to hatch patterns, and so on. The pattern option can be used to create a nice vertical brick pattern:

```
convert -size 500x500 pattern:verticalbricks bricks.png
```

If you've always wanted to know how to create a hatch-like or other patterned background, there you go.

We can now use `composite` to pull together these two images. Another option, `-gravity`, is an interestingly named option that determines where one image is positioned relative to the other. The available parameters for use with `-gravity` are:

- `NorthWest`
- `North`
- `NorthEast`
- `West`
- `Center`
- `East`
- `SouthWest`
- `South`
- `SouthEast`

`North` would be top, `South` bottom, `West` left, and `East` to the right. `Center` is self-explanatory and is the parameter used to center the blue circle on the new vertical brick background:

```
composite -gravity center bluecircle.png bricks.png circlebricks.png
```

Figure 13-13 shows the newly created composite image.

The `montage` utility is a fun little tool. Unlike `composite`, `montage` is meant to create a sequence of images, as well as decorate and annotate the result. The following uses three new options: `-frame`, which creates a frame around the image, 5 pixels wide in this case; `-background`, to set the background color, using hexadecimal notation, #cccccc; and `-geometry`, which specifies the width, height, and x,y of the offset between the images:

```
montage -frame -background "#cccccc" -geometry 300x300+5+5 botfall1thumb.jpg
botfall2thumb.jpg botfall3thumb.jpg montage.png
```

Figure 13-14 shows the results of this latest command, resulting in a little instant photo gallery.

All of the ImageMagick tools are interesting and useful, but `convert` is the workhorse, and as such, I'll focus primarily on it in the rest of this section as we explore other options.

Simple Liners

I like ImageMagick for the complex graphical tasks it can accomplish, but I also like it for the fun, simple, one-line actions that seem to do so much. Want to make a quick and dirty animated GIF? Use the following:

```
convert *.jpg images.gif
```

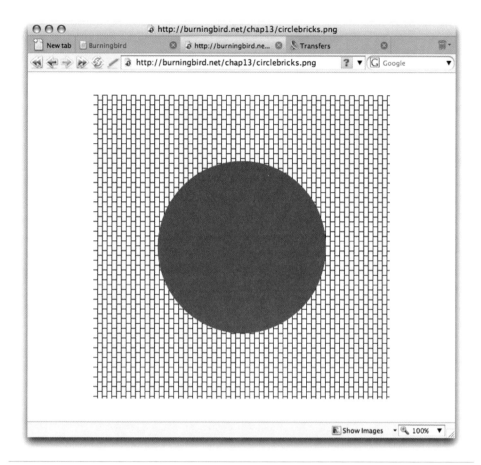

Inside the browser window:

http://burningbird.net/chap13/circlebricks.png

New tab | Burningbird | http://burningbird.ne... | Transfers

http://burningbird.net/chap13/circlebricks.png | Google

Show Images | 100%

Figure 13-13. Blue circle on vertical brick background

This creates an animated GIF of all JPEG images within a subdirectory. It creates an interesting, if rather dizzying (and potentially quite large), animation. I recommend you try it. Once.

Being able to crop a picture is an a nice capability, and simple to use, too:

```
convert botfall3.jpg -crop 200x200+50+50 botfall3crop.jpg
```

The parameters passed are width, height, and x and y of the offset position, just like with -geometry earlier. You do need to be a little careful, though, because if you do what I did once, and use the x instead of the + for the last two x,y values, you'll end up with many little slices of the image, because crop can also be used to slice up the whole image.

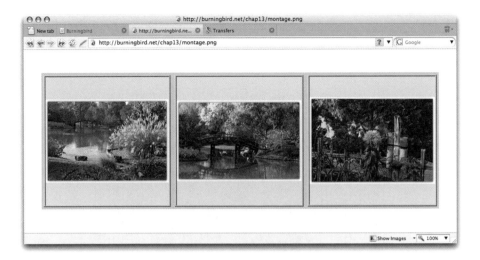

Figure 13-14. Mini-photo gallery, created with montage

Unlike the GD functions covered earlier, there are a couple of blur options with ImageMagick: `-blur` and `-gaussian-blur`. These are very computationally involved processes, which means you probably want to restrict their use as much as possible. Figure 13-15 is a result of running the following:

```
convert leaf.jpg -blur 0x8 blurleaf.jpg
```

The parameters to pass with the option are the radius and the standard deviation for the Gaussian distribution. If you pass in a 0 for the radius, as I do, this value triggers ImageMagick to select the best radius.

Earlier in the GD section, we had some fun creating borders. It's dirt simple to create borders with ImageMagick. The following first resizes the image, this time using `-resize` instead of `-thumbnail`, and then creates a gold border 30 pixels wide:

```
convert tree.jpg -resize 500x500 -bordercolor gold -border 30 borderedtree.jpg
```

I've found that order matters when creating borders. If the `-border` option is specified before `-bordercolor`, the color ends up gray. With the color first, the border ends up the gold we're expecting (see Figure 13-16).

The border example uses a named color, gold. You can find a list of named colors using the convert option `-list`:

```
convert -list color
```

Figure 13-15. Applying the -blur option to an image

Depending on which version of ImageMagick you have installed, you can list values for color, formats, layers, and other options with named values. However, which items -list supports does vary considerably among ImageMagick versions. Later versions even allow the following, to get a list of applicable options that can be listed, while earlier versions do not:

```
convert -list list
```

This command worked on my local Mac development machine, which was running ImageMagick 6.3.6, but not on my hosted machine, running 6.2.6.

Figure 13-16. Applying a gold border to an image

To return to our one-liner code samples, borders are easy with ImageMagick, true. However, we are graphic geniuses. We laugh—laugh, do you hear?—at such simple borders…especially when we can frame an image:

```
convert doggies.png -frame 15+5+5 frameddoggies.jpg
```

Or create a beveled-edge picture with the -raise option:

```
convert doggies.png -raise 20x20 doggiesraise.jpg
```

To create an inset look instead of a raised one, use +raise instead of -raise.

We can also create a vignette, using two new options: -alpha, set to a value of on, which means to use alpha channel data; and -vignette, to create a vignetted image:

```
convert doggies.png -alpha on -background none -vignette 0x4 doggievignette.png
```

Figure 13-17 shows the same image framed in a solid color, given a beveled edge, and with a raised-edge frame. In addition to framing, cropping, sizing, grouping images, we can also perform more photo-like alterations on images, similar to what we can create with any of the photo editors I covered in Chapter 3. To create a sketched outline, use the -charcoal option, passing in an integer parameter equal to the width of the pencil used:

```
convert doggies.png -charcoal 1 doggiescharcoal.jpg
```

Figure 13-17. Same photo framed, beveled, and vignetted

To convert a photo to sepia-toned, use the -sepia-tone option, with a percentage representing the degree of intensity:

```
convert doggies.png -sepia-tone 80% sepiadoggie.jpg
```

You can also convert an image into monochrome, though the result isn't what you might expect:

```
convert doggies.png -monochrome bwdoggie.jpg
```

I found the resulting image to be excessively grainy, which is interesting but not what I was expecting. Another option to convert the image to black and white would be to adjust the color channels through the -channel and the -separate option:

```
convert doggies.png -channel R -separate separate_R_doggie.jpg
```

This results in a much better monochrome, similar to what you might get with a photo-editor channel mixer.

If black and white or sepia isn't your thing, you can tint the picture by setting the -fill option to whatever color you wish and then using -tint with whatever percentage you wish to create the effect you want:

```
convert doggies.png -fill red -tint 50% reddoggie.jpg
```

Figure 13-18 shows the same dog image, this time tinted, charcoaled, converted to black and white, given a sepia tint, and converted to black and white using channels. Of course, all of these modifications can be made in a photo editor or paint program. Where ImageMagick's power really comes in is when you want to create more complex effects, especially ones that might be duplicated across several images or pictures. To create these effects, though, the command will extend beyond one line. To repeat the action, the command should be created as a shell script. Both of these options are discussed in the next section.

Figure 13-18. Montage of photos featuring original, and altered with tint, charcoal, monochrome, sepia, and channels

Multi-Line Commands

An ImageMagick command can be complex, and though you can just continue typing and letting the command wrap, this is a good way to spend a lot of time typing a command, creating an error right at the end, and having a heck of a time recovering your work.

Instead, continue the command over multiple lines using the backslash (\) escape character. The following adds a shadowed signature with my name to an image, with the shadow colored in blue and the forecolor in white (see Figure 13-19):

```
convert doggies.png -font "Palatino-BoldItalic"  -pointsize 48 \
-gravity SouthEast -fill blue  -draw "text 47,47 'Shelley'" \
-fill white -draw "text 45,45 'Shelley'" signedimage.jpg
```

Figure 13-19. Signed picture using multi-line ImageMagick command

The command just displayed uses the -fill option to define the fill used for the text, specifies a font (in this case, Palatino-BoldItalic) and a font size, and also sets the location of image. In this example, I used SouthEast gravity, which means that the vertical and horizontal placements originate from the lower-right side of the image. The two text elements are created with -draw, which has as parameters the vertical and horizontal placement of the beginning of the text, plus the actual text itself.

Because having to repeat the command multiple times can be cumbersome, ImageMagick commands can be incorporated into shell scripts, which can then be applied to all images in a subdirectory, as shown in Example 13-9. In this shell script, all JPEG images in a subdirectory are "signed" with a signature. A for loop is used to access all files with a *.jpg* extension, names of which are passed to the ImageMagick command.

Example 13-9. Shell script to add a signature to every JPEG in a subdirectory

```
#!/bin/sh
for name in *jpg
do
echo $name
convert -font "Palatino-BoldItalic" -pointsize 48 -gravity center -fill white \
        -background none label:'Shelley' -trim \
        \( +clone -background black -shadow 100x4+0+0 \
        -channel A -evaluate multiply 4 +channel \) +swap \
        +repage -gravity center -composite +geometry \
        -background none  \
        $name -gravity SouthEast +swap -composite $name
done
```

If you've not worked with shell scripts, this text is saved in a file with a *.sh* extension—in this case, *label.sh*—using whatever text editor you prefer. To run the script, you need to change the permissions on this so it's executable, either via the command line (typing in chmod 755 label.sh) or using whatever file-management tool your ISP provides. To run, type the following at the command line:

```
./label.sh
```

This only works in the Terminal for the Mac, or via the Linux command line. It won't work in the DOS command window.

In this rather involved ImageMagick example, the signature is bordered by an indirect shadow, created using the -shadow option, which takes an opacity, sigma, and an x, y offset—in this case, 100x4+0+0 for 100% opacity, a sigma of 4, and no offset (an indirect overall shadow). To apply this to just the signature, though, it has to be created as its own separate canvas; otherwise, the effect is applied to the overall image. The label option not only assigns a label to the image, it also creates a new canvas for the current effort, in this case creating the signature. Once the label canvas is created, it's trimmed to just the text, and the background is set to none because we don't want the default (which is black).

The shadow is actually created on a cloned image, and to restrict the shadow operations to just this clone, parentheses are used to group options and image. The parentheses have to be escaped, again with the escape backslash character:

```
\( +clone -background black -shadow 100x4+0+0 \
        -channel A -evaluate multiply 4 +channel \)
```

After the shadowed text is created, the color channel is limited to just the alpha, transparent channel, and the results are passed to the -evaluate option to multiply the effect by a factor of 4.

```
-channel A -evaluate multiply 4 +channel
```

Once the shadow is created, it's swapped with the filled text, using +swap, which operates on the preceding images, and then the fun part begins.

The repage option resizes the canvas to include the shadow effect, and then the signature is centered within the existing canvas, one overlayed over the other via the composite option. Remember, we're still only working with the canvas created with the original label.

```
+repage -gravity center -composite +geometry \
         -background none   \
```

Finally, we're able to open the actual image where the signature is placed, which is swapped with the signature canvas so the signature is on top. The two are merged, again using composite, and we have the final picture, as shown in Figure 13-20.

Figure 13-20. Merging to create a final image

If you think this was complicated, you should see the routine to create a Polaroid effect with ImageMagick, especially since the tool supports skewing and a more sophisticated Gaussian Blur. Luckily, the creators of ImageMagick liked the trick so much, they've added it as an option in the newest releases of the tool:

```
convert doggies.png -bordercolor white -background DarkGray -polaroid 5 polaroid.png
```

As you can see in Figure 13-21, ImageMagick makes a fine Polaroid.

Figure 13-21. Using the newer Polaroid option to create a nice Polaroid effect

 To see the steps originally required, a Ruby version of the process can be found at RMagick, at *http://rmagick.rubyforge.org/Polaroid/ polaroid.html*.

This just touches on the command-line capability of ImageMagick. I strongly recommend spending time in the ImageMagick usage section (at *http://www.imagemagick. org/Usage/*), to get even more exposure to this wonderful graphics suite.

Now, a brief look at ImageMagick as it's accessed via the API and a programming language—in this case, IMagick for PHP.

Programming with ImageMagick and IMagick

Most, if not all, of the ImageMagick functionality is available via a language-based API for languages such as Ruby, Python, Perl, C, List, C++, and even Pascal. There are two ImageMagick interface libraries for PHP, and I'm going to take a quick look at one, IMagick. The last chapter in this book has further examples of using both PHP/GD and IMagick for creating dynamic images.

Chances are good that, unlike GD, your hosting solution doesn't have support for IMagick, which does need to be compiled into your version of PHP. However, if you ask nice and promise your host not to abuse the privilege (by blurring thousands of 1,600-pixel-wide PNG files), they might install it for your use. At a minimum, do try to install it locally on your machine.

Unfortunately, IMagick is not simple to install and comes with little documentation. However, with the new, more stable release of version 2.0 in October of 2007, I'm hoping that increased interest in the product will drive out simpler installation and documentation.

 The source for IMagick can be found at *http://pecl.php.net/package/imagick*. There are installation instructions in the file named *INSTALL*, and at the PHP.net site, at *http://us.php.net/manual/en/imagick.install.php*. Windows-built libraries are also available. The documentation is very limited, but the class methods and parameters are at least described at *http://us2.php.net/imagick*. The creator of the extension, Mikko Koppanen, does have some nice examples at his site, at *http://valokuva.org/?cat=1*.

Once installed, applications using IMagick begin with creating a new IMagick object from whatever image is being modified, similar to specifying the image in an ImageMagick command:

```php
$im = new IMagick("someimage.png");
```

From there, you have access to most of the ImageMagick options, given as separate object methods. As an example, Example 13-10 shows how you would apply the charcoal option to the image and then print it out to the web page:

Example 13-10. Create a charcoal image using IMagick and PHP

```php
<?php
    /* Create an empty canvas with white background */
    $im = new Imagick('doggies.png');

    $im->charcoalImage(1,0);
```

Example 13-10. Create a charcoal image using IMagick and PHP (continued)

```
    header( "Content-Type: image/png" );
    echo $im;
?>
```

The options are created as separate methods, each with its required arguments. In this example, the -charcoal option is converted into the charcoalImage method, taking the radius of the charcoal strokes and the standard deviation of the Gaussian effect applied with the stroke. To match the earlier example, I used 1 for the radius and 0 (or none) for the Gaussian setting. The result between the two is identical, because IMagick is a programming interface to ImageMagick.

In a way, it can be easier to create effects with IMagick, because the separate options are created as separate methods, and it's easier, and cleaner, to follow some of the examples. Additionally, other commonly reapplied steps have been encapsulated into single function calls, further simplifying its use.

A good demonstration of this is one of the example applications that Mikko created that makes an attractive thumbnail image with a shadow and rounded corners. Normally, with ImageMagick, you'd have to create the rounded-corner effect using masks and channels, in a multistep process that's a little daunting. With IMagick, the effect is accomplished by one call to a function. In Example 13-11, I'm using Mikko's effect in an application to create thumbnails from all the images in a subdirectory.

Example 13-11. Application to generate attractive thumbnails from PNG files

```
<?php

try {
    // get image
    $filename = $_GET['photo'];

    // create IMagick object
    $im = new IMagick($filename);

    // create thumbnail
    $im->thumbnailImage(300,null);

    // round corners
    $im->roundCorners(5,5);

    // clone object
    $shadow = $im->clone( );

    // add shadow
    $shadow->setImageBackgroundColor(new ImagickPixel('black'));
    $shadow->shadowImage(80,3,5,5);

    // compose image
    $shadow->compositeImage($im, Imagick::COMPOSITE_OVER,0,0);
```

Example 13-11. Application to generate attractive thumbnails from PNG files (continued)

```
    // print image
    header( "Content-Type: image/png" );
    echo $shadow;

    // clean up
    $shadow->destroy( );
    $im->destroy( );
} catch(Exception $e) {
   echo "Problems with image file ", $e->getMessage, "\n";
}
?>
```

The PHP is saved in a file called *thumbs.php*. PNG files are used because PNG supports alpha transparency. The application page that uses the thumb is shown in Example 13-12. This application uses the PHP function glob, rather than opendir, to cycle through the PNG files in the directory.

Example 13-12. PHP page to cycle through all PNGs in a subdirectory and create thumbnail versions for display

```
<!DOCTYPE html PUBLIC "-//W3C//DTD XHTML 1.0 Strict//EN"
       "http://www.w3.org/TR/xhtml1/DTD/xhtml1-strict.dtd">
<html xmlns="http://www.w3.org/1999/xhtml" lang="en" xml:lang="en">
<head>
<meta http-equiv="Content-Type" content="text/html; charset=utf-8" />
<title>Thumb It</title>
<style type="text/css">
body { margin: 20px; }
img { margin: 20px; }
</style>
</head>
<body>

<?php
foreach (glob("*.png") as $filename) {
?>

<img src="thumbs.php?photo=<?php echo $filename; ?>" alt="" />
<?php
}
?>
</body>
</html>
```

Figure 13-22 shows the result of the application with four separate PNG files in the subdirectory. The application doesn't cache the results, but it could be modified using the example given earlier in the section on GD to do so, saving resources and enhancing performance.

Figure 13-22. Running the magic thumbnail application on four PNGs in a subdirectory

As currently coded, the application doesn't work with JPEGs because of the alpha transparency. It could be modified to work with JPEGs and return PNGs, or even work with any image file: PNG, JPEG, or GIF. To convert the image format to PNG, modify the *thumbs.php* application to add the following just after the image is created (in bold text):

```
// create IMagick object
$im = new IMagick($filename);

if ($im->getImageFormat( ) == 'JPEG')
    $im->setImageFormat("png");
```

You can also convert the result to GIFs because of Internet Explorer 6's limitation with alpha transparencies (covered earlier in the book) if you wish. The results won't be as good because of the limited palette with GIFs, resulting in dithering for photos.

This is just a taste of what ImageMagick can do. The ImageMagick site provides both documentation and examples to explore all aspects of this handy beast. The usage examples are the most helpful, and extensive.

ImageMagick is a powerful tool that is largely underutilized, primarily because people aren't necessarily aware of how useful it is. It forms the core functionality for many graphics and gallery applications. However, if you're willing to hit the command line or one of the language-specific APIs, you can also make use of all of its functionality directly yourself.

Just be aware that ImageMagick and GD, like most graphics software, are CPU- and memory-intensive. You'll want to keep any shell scripts as simple as possible, and be cautious with making any of this functionality available to others online if you're running from a shared hosting system. However, with the addition of caching, both GD and ImageMagick/IMagick could be very useful and fun additions to your web site.

CHAPTER 14

The Geo Zone

The big thing in web graphics the last few years has been mapping. Online maps don't specifically introduce anything new to the world of web graphics; it's the visualization of mapping that's the fun part, because maps form a canvas on which we can paint.

There is mapping software that works with your GPS device, hosted maps, and even Google Earth, which provides hidden goodies, such as piloting (and crashing) an F15 fighter over a "real" area. In this chapter, though, I walk through a couple of the mapping systems that allow us to create maps within our own spaces, supported by our own applications.

I'm covering Google Maps, of course, it being the daddy of the bunch. Yahoo! also provides a way of hosting maps, so we'll take a look at it, too. I'm also going to spend some time discussing how you can integrate mapping data, and thus mapping, into your photos, your events, your recent hike—virtually anything that has an associated location.

Both Yahoo! and Google Maps provide a way to embed a map directly in your web pages, and then alter it with markers, notes, and routes, as well as controlling the view and number of controls. Other than that, they really are quite different.

Google was the originator of freely accessible mapping services, but it has one major limitation: you have to get a Google API key for one directory, and it only works with that directory. It won't work for subdirectories (subfolders), which means that a key that works with *http://somecompany.com* won't work with *http://somecompany.com/maps/*.

Yahoo! doesn't have this limitation as long as you provide the overall location of where the map will be located. It also provides a Flash-based map system, as well as one based in Ajax. The former is nice, but for this book, I focused on the non-Flash alternative.

Yahoo! also has a web-services-based version of its Maps.

Find out about and sign up for a Google Maps API key at *http://www. google.com/apis/maps/*. Yahoo!'s own Mapping API can be accessed at*http://developer.yahoo.com/maps/*.

Mapping with Google

Google created the mold when it comes to self-hosted maps. First, it invented the concept of the never-ending map, by creating map tiles and a container that knows to fetch the next pieces as a person scrolls through the existing view. Second, it provided an easy way to embed a Google map in your web page and add annotation, route mapping, and even dynamic elements all through a fairly easy-to-use JavaScript-based API.

Google Maps: Up and Running

To start with Google Maps, you have to sign up for a free API key. It's important that you have a good idea where the maps will be placed, because the keys are specific to the web location.

Once you have your key in hand, to add a Google map to a page, add an empty div element where you'll want the map located, and add in the Google map's JavaScript source file. Next, you'll use Google Maps' API methods to customize the map, such as centering it on a location, or adding a marker, route, or a control panel. Google is even nice enough to generate your first "Hello World"-style maps application. It's pretty useless, though, so I'll see if I can do one better.

 The Google examples all use an XHTML DOCTYPE, but that's to ensure that the page is accessed in standards mode. Google Maps does not work if the document is served up with an XHTML MIME type.

Example 14-1 takes the initial Google-generated map, re-centers it to a new location, and adds both map type and map distance controls, as well as a marker for the center location. The location is the St. Louis Arch. I recommend the satellite view, myself.

Example 14-1. Creating a map centered on the St. Louis Arch, with controls and a marker

```
<!DOCTYPE html PUBLIC "-//W3C//DTD XHTML 1.0 Strict//EN"
  "http://www.w3.org/TR/xhtml1/DTD/xhtml1-strict.dtd">
<html xmlns="http://www.w3.org/1999/xhtml">
  <head>
    <title>Google Maps JavaScript API Example</title>
    <meta http-equiv="content-type" content="text/html; charsct=utf-8"/>
    <meta http-equiv="X-UA-Compatible" content="IE=7"/>
    <style type="text/css">
    #map {
```

Example 14-1. Creating a map centered on the St. Louis Arch, with controls and a marker (continued)

```
          border: 4px solid #000;
          margin: 40px auto;
          width: 600px; height: 400px;
     }
     </style>

 <script src="http://maps.google.com/maps?file=api&amp;v=2&amp;key="
     type="text/javascript"></script>
<script type="text/javascript">
//<![CDATA[

window.onload = function load() {
   if (GBrowserIsCompatible()) {

      // new map with type and distance controls
      var map = new GMap2(document.getElementById("map"));
      map.addControl(new GSmallMapControl());
      map.addControl(new GMapTypeControl());

      // location - St. Louis Arch
      var point = new GLatLng(38.6247732, -90.183444);

      // center location - St. Louis Arch
      map.setCenter(point, 14);

      // add marker
      map.addOverlay(new GMarker(point));
      }
}

window.onunload=GUnload;
//]]>
</script>
</head>
   <body onload="load()" onunload="GUnload()">
     <div id="map"></div>
   </body>
</html>
```

The Google Maps API is based on a set of objects. The GMap2 object is the main Google Maps 2.0 object. The examples also include two types of controls, a location determined by a specific point object, and then the GMarker object. Each object has a set of parameters, such as passing in the identifier of the div element to hold the map when creating the new map object, or passing in the latitude and longitude to create a new location object (GLatLng).

Google Maps makes use of the ExplorerCanvas JavaScript library detailed in Chapter 10. Therefore, to ensure that the maps work to the best of their ability, the IE-specific compatibility meta tag shown below had to be added to the example applications:

```
<meta http-equiv="X-UA-Compatible" content="IE=7"/>
```

However, when you test the applications in this chapter, you may want to try removing this element to see whether the application can function without it.

Figure 14-1 shows the result after zooming in, switched to the satellite view, of course, to better display the arch.

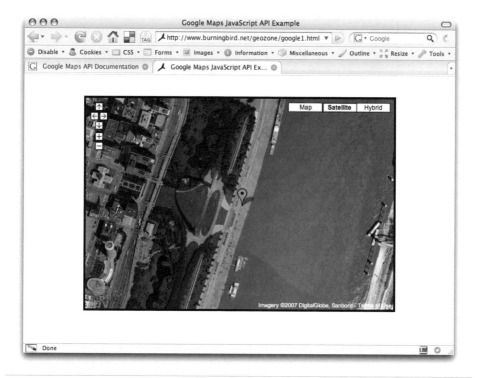

Figure 14-1. Google Maps located at the St. Louis Arch and switched to satellite view

Fun with Markers

The map marker doesn't have to just sit there. A second, optional argument makes it into a *draggable* object:

```
var marker = new GMarker(point, {draggable: true} );
```

Clicking and dragging the marker now converts the marker into a nice shadowed image, with "X" marking the spot where the marker is currently located, as shown in Figure 14-2.

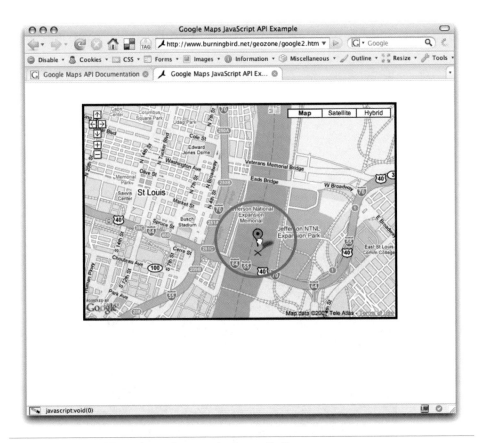

Figure 14-2. Draggable marker with "X marks the spot" effect

When you drag a marker around, it helps to be able to mark the physical location of the marker's new location once it's dropped. Accomplishing this introduces a couple of new concepts: event handling in Google Maps, as well as the marker information window.

If you can assign a point to a marker, you can get the point from the marker at any time, using either getLatLng or getPoint. Once you have the new point (the GLatLng object), you can get the latitude and longitude using its lat and lng methods.

To get this new point after dragging, the dragging start and end events are captured using the GEvent objects, one for each event. When dragging starts, whatever info window is open is closed; when dragging stops, a new info window is opened with the longitude/latitude values.

The marker's info windows method opens a text bubble above the marker, containing whatever text you give it. You can open either a text window (openInfoWindow), one using tabs (openInfoWindowTabs), an HTML-based window (openInfoWindowHtml), or one mixing HTML and tabs (openInfoWindowTabsHtml). Example 14-2 uses the openInfoWindowHtml option, passing in the formatted string with the longitude and latitude of the dragged marker's new location.

Example 14-2. Popping open an info window with the new location after a drag

```
<!DOCTYPE html PUBLIC "-//W3C//DTD XHTML 1.0 Strict//EN"
  "http://www.w3.org/TR/xhtml1/DTD/xhtml1-strict.dtd">
<html xmlns="http://www.w3.org/1999/xhtml">
  <head>
    <title>Google Maps JavaScript API Example</title>
    <meta http-equiv="content-type" content="text/html; charset=utf-8"/>
    <meta http-equiv="X-UA-Compatible" content="IE=7"/>
    <style type="text/css">
    #map {
        border: 4px solid #000;
        margin: 40px auto;
        width: 600px; height: 400px;
    }
    </style>

 <script src="http://maps.google.com/maps?file=api&amp;v=2&amp;key=yourkey"
      type="text/javascript"></script>

<script type="text/javascript">
//<![CDATA[

window.onload = function(){

if (GBrowserIsCompatible()) {

   // new map with type and distance controls
   var map = new GMap2(document.getElementById("map"));
   map.addControl(new GSmallMapControl());
   map.addControl(new GMapTypeControl());

   // location - St. Louis Arch
   var point = new GLatLng(38.6247732, -90.183444);

   // center location - St. Louis Arch
   map.setCenter(point, 14);

   // add marker
   var marker = new GMarker(point, {draggable: true});
   map.addOverlay(marker);
```

Example 14-2. Popping open an info window with the new location after a drag (continued)

```
  GEvent.addListener(marker, "dragstart", function() {
    map.closeInfoWindow();
    });

  GEvent.addListener(marker, "dragend", function() {
    var newPoint = marker.getPoint();
    var msg = "Lat: " + newPoint.lat() + "<br />Lng: " + newPoint.lng();
    marker.openInfoWindowHtml(msg);
    });

  }
}

window.onunload=GUnload;
//]]>
</script>
  </head>
  <body>
    <div id="map"></div>
  </body>
</html>
```

Now, when the dragging ends, information about the new location is shown in an info bubble. This is particularly helpful if you're trying to record new longitude/latitude points to use for additional mapping. Figure 14-3 shows the result of this application.

Routes on Google Maps

Google provides multiple methods for marking routes on maps. The first and simplest is to add a polyline that marks the route as an overlay on the map. All you have to do is provide a series of GLatLng points, and Google Maps draws a solid line, connecting all of the dots.

One additional effort involved with the use of polylines is that Google uses Microsoft's VML to draw the line for that browser. To ensure that the application works with IE, you'll need to add the VML namespace:

```
<html xmlns="http://www.w3.org/1999/xhtml" xmlns:v="urn:schemas-microsoft-com:vml">
```

Once VML is enabled, a polyline is implemented with the GPolyline object, passing in an array of points, line color, line width, opacity of line, and any other options. In Example 14-3, a polyline is used to map out a route from one side of the Mississippi River to the other in the map. In this example, opacity is set to fully opaque (a value of 1.0), which makes the route more noticeable, though it does cover street names. The default value is 50%, or semi-transparent.

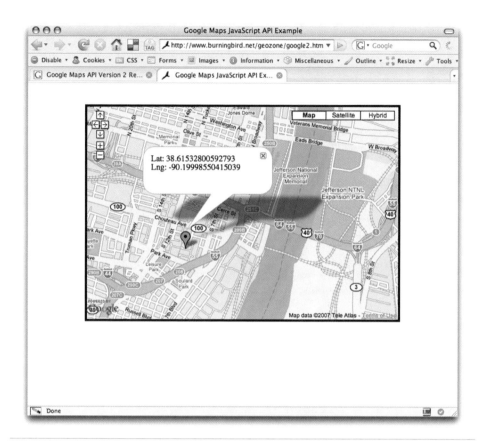

Figure 14-3. X marks the spot: location where the marker has been dragged

Example 14-3. Drawing a route out on the map with a GPolyline

```
<!DOCTYPE html PUBLIC "-//W3C//DTD XHTML 1.0 Strict//EN"
  "http://www.w3.org/TR/xhtml1/DTD/xhtml1-strict.dtd">
<html xmlns="http://www.w3.org/1999/xhtml" xmlns:v="urn:schemas-microsoft-com:vml">
  <head>
    <title>Google Maps JavaScript API Example</title>
    <meta http-equiv="content-type" content="text/html; charset=utf-8"/>
    <meta http-equiv="X-UA-Compatible" content="IE=7"/>
    <style type="text/css">
    #map {
        border: 4px solid #000;
        margin: 40px auto;
        width: 600px; height: 400px;
    }
    </style>
```

Example 14-3. Drawing a route out on the map with a GPolyline (continued)

```
<script src="http://maps.google.com/maps?file=api&amp;v=2&amp;key=yourkey"
    type="text/javascript"></script>
<script type="text/javascript">
//<![CDATA[

window.onload=function ( ) {
   if (GBrowserIsCompatible( )) {

       // new map with type and distance controls
       var map = new GMap2(document.getElementById("map"));
       map.addControl(new GSmallMapControl( ));
       map.addControl(new GMapTypeControl( ));

       // location - St. Louis Arch
       var point = new GLatLng(38.6247732, -90.183444);

       // center location - St. Louis Arch
       map.setCenter(point, 14);

       var polyline = new GPolyline([
          new GLatLng(38.6242, -90.1838),
          new GLatLng(38.6252, -90.1886),
          new GLatLng(38.6298, -90.1870),
          new GLatLng(38.6281, -90.1717),
          new GLatLng(38.6229, -90.1738)
          ], "#0000ff", 5, 1.0);
          map.addOverlay(polyline);
   }
}

window.onunload=GUnload;
//]]>
</script>
  </head>
  <body>
    <div id="map"></div>
  </body>
</html>
```

Really simple to use, and you can also add in markers to highlight turn points or references along the way. Figure 14-4 shows the route as coded in Example 14-3.

An interesting variation on the path-based APIs is the polygon, which also takes a set of points, and a fill color and opacity in addition to the argument controlling the stroke:

```
var polygon = new GPolygon([
            new GLatLng(38.6242, -90.1838),
            new GLatLng(38.6252, -90.1886),
            new GLatLng(38.6298, -90.1870),
            new GLatLng(38.6281, -90.1717),
            new GLatLng(38.6229, -90.1738)
          ], "#0000ff", 5, 1.0,"#ffff00",0.5);
```

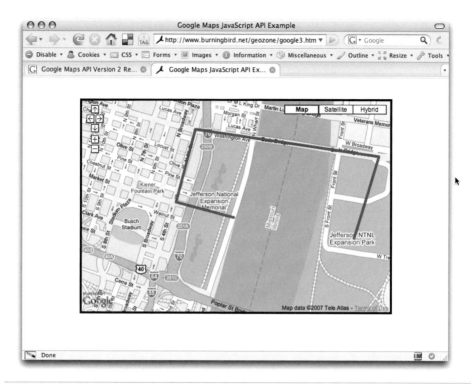

Figure 14-4. Route marked in blue in Google Maps

The shape automatically connects between the last and first point, though the end line won't be stroked until the connection is explicitly stated, as shown in Figure 14-5.

There's a lot of other functionality to Google Maps, but this gets us started, and it provides the mapping functionality necessary to implement the example uses of maps at the end of this chapter. Do take some time, though, and play around with the other examples at the Google Maps developer site.

Yahoo!'s Maps

Yahoo! may have come later to the open maps game, but when it came, it came with a vengeance, providing both a Flash and non-Flash alternative. In this section, I'm focusing on the JavaScript-only API, but if you have time, I recommend checking out the Flash-based functionality, too.

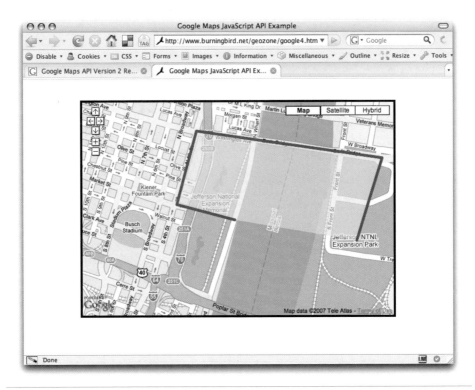

Figure 14-5. Using GPolygon instead of GPolyline to map out a route

Yahoo!'s Run

To begin with Yahoo! Maps, you have to get an application key. Unlike Google's API, Yahoo!'s map keys work in subdirectories under the URL specified when signing up for the key. Once you have the key, add the Yahoo! Maps script URL to the page, along with a `div` element serving as a container.

Superficially, it may seem as if Yahoo!'s API is similar to Google's. However, as the first example—Example 14-4, which duplicates the same functionality as Example 14-1—demonstrates, the two are quite different. The example creates a map, centers it, and adds controls for both type and zooming, as well as a marker at the center location—a good basic map, probably meeting 90% of most map needs.

Example 14-4. Map with controls, centered at the St. Louis Arch, and with a marker

```
<!DOCTYPE html PUBLIC "-//W3C//DTD XHTML 1.0 Strict//EN"
  "http://www.w3.org/TR/xhtml1/DTD/xhtml1-strict.dtd">
<html xmlns="http://www.w3.org/1999/xhtml">
<head>
<title>Google Maps JavaScript API Example</title>
```

Example 14-4. Map with controls, centered at the St. Louis Arch, and with a marker (continued)

```
<meta http-equiv="content-type" content="text/html; charset=utf-8"/>
<meta http-equiv="X-UA-Compatible" content="IE=7"/>
<style type="text/css">
    #map {
        border: 4px solid #000;
        margin: 40px auto;
        width: 600px; height: 400px;
        }
</style>
<script type="text/javascript"
src="http://api.maps.yahoo.com/ajaxymap?v=3.7&appid="></script>
<script type="text/javascript">
//<![CDATA[

window.onload=function() {

    // Create a Map that will be placed in the "map" div.
    var map = new YMap(document.getElementById('map'));

    // Add the ability to change between Sat, Hybrid, and Regular Maps
    map.addTypeControl();

    // Add the zoom control. Long specifies a Slider versus a "+" and "-" zoom control
    map.addZoomLong();

    // Add the Pan control to have North, South, East and West directional control
    map.addPanControl();

    // create geopoint
    var point = new YGeoPoint(38.6247732, -90.183444);

    // Specifying the Map starting location and zoom level
    map.drawZoomAndCenter(point, 3);

    // set marker
    map.addMarker(point);

}
//]]>

</script>

</head>
<body>
<div id="map"></div>
</body>
</html>
```

One difference immediately apparent between the two APIs is the code to create the controls. Google has two controls, while Yahoo! has three, splitting the pan navigation feature apart from the zooming. The other methods seem similar to Google's because of how I'm using them: create a geo location, center the map, place a marker. What the example doesn't show is that `drawZoomAndCenter` takes a string with an address in addition to the geo location object as its first parameter. This means that we don't have to muck around with longitudes and latitudes if we don't want to. However, using specific mapping values is more precise, and I'll continue to use them. Just be aware of the additional capability.

Figure 14-6 shows the map just created. As you can see, the look of the Yahoo! maps is very different than Google's maps. The satellite images used are different, too, with the Arch shadow in a different position in the Yahoo! maps.

 Even when using the IE compatibility meta tag in the maps application, IE8 does not process the transparency related to the shadow for the marker in the Yahoo! Maps application. Hopefully this will improve in future beta releases of IE8.

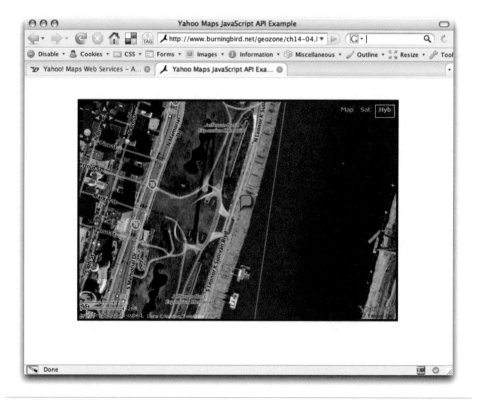

Figure 14-6. Yahoo! map, centered on the St. Louis Arch, showing the satellite view

I'm not crazy about the Yahoo! controls. For the satellite view, they don't show at all. Later screenshots will show they do look better with the mapping views. I like the fact that this example can be moved to a subdirectory and still work. To me, that's a significant difference.

Now let's see how Yahoo! does with the other examples, starting with event handling, dragging markers, and getting locations.

X Marks the...

Unlike Google's API, drag and drop for Yahoo! markers doesn't seem to be part of the API, or at least it isn't apparent. Instead, I modified the functionality to add a click event for the map itself, and then moved the marker to the position.

 One possibility for managing drag and drop of the marker is providing the third parameter, a DOM identifier, and then using custom drag and drop code. Seems overly complicated, though, when using an alternative event works.

To get this to work, a marker is created explicitly and then added to the map using the addOverlay method. When the map is clicked, the marker's position is reset, and what Yahoo! terms a "smart" window is opened, with the longitude and latitude of the new position. Example 14-5 has the code for this application.

Example 14-5. Moving the marker about based on a map click event

```
<!DOCTYPE html PUBLIC "-//W3C//DTD XHTML 1.0 Strict//EN"
   "http://www.w3.org/TR/xhtml1/DTD/xhtml1-strict.dtd">
<html xmlns="http://www.w3.org/1999/xhtml">
<head>
<title>Yahoo! Maps JavaScript API Example</title>
<meta http-equiv="content-type" content="text/html; charset=utf-8"/>
<meta http-equiv="X-UA-Compatible" content="IE=7"/>
<style type="text/css">
    #map {
        border: 4px solid #000;
        margin: 40px auto;
        width: 600px; height: 400px;
        }
</style>
<script type="text/javascript"
src="http://api.maps.yahoo.com/ajaxymap?v=3.7&appid="></script>
<script type="text/javascript">
//<![CDATA[

window.onload=function() {
```

Example 14-5. Moving the marker about based on a map click event (continued)

```
    // Create a Map that will be placed in the "map" div.
    var map = new YMap(document.getElementById('map'));

    // Add the ability to change between Sat, Hybrid, and Regular Maps
    map.addTypeControl();

    // Add the zoom control. Long specifies a Slider versus a "+" and "-" zoom control
    map.addZoomLong();

    // Add the Pan control to have North, South, East and West directional control
    map.addPanControl();

    // create geopoint
    var point = new YGeoPoint(38.6247732, -90.183444);

    // Specifying the Map starting location and zoom level
    map.drawZoomAndCenter(point, 3);

    // create smart marker
    var theMarker = new YMarker(point);

    // set marker
    map.addOverlay(theMarker);

    // add event listeners
    YEvent.Capture(map, EventsList.MouseClick,  function(evnt,pnt) {
        theMarker.closeSmartWindow();
        theMarker.openSmartWindow("Lat: " + pnt.Lat + " Lon: " + pnt.Lon);
        theMarker.setYGeoPoint(pnt);
    });

}
//]]>

</script>

</head>
<body>
<div id="map"></div>
</body>
</html>
```

The smart window has to be closed each time an event occurs, or the same window (and contents) is used each time. The application isn't quite as slick as Google's, but I've never been fond of dragging and dropping anyway. Did I also happen to mention that this application works in subdirectories, as well as the main directory?

Figure 14-7 shows the results of the click/location application, after the marker has been moved.

One last look at the Yahoo! API functions, and then we'll get into some examples.

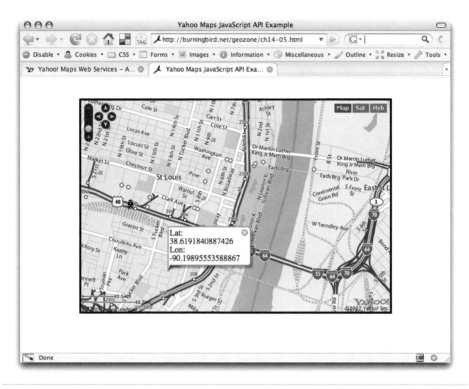

Figure 14-7. Application after clicking and relocating the marker

Routing with Yahoo!

A route in Yahoo! Maps is created from a sequence of geo location points, used to create a polyline, which is then overlayed on the map. This is probably familiar because the process is exactly the one we followed when creating the Google map. I actually copied the Google Maps code and then did a global change, replacing the Google object names with Yahoo! ones, as shown in Example 14-6. Piece of cake.

Example 14-6. Route marked out on Yahoo! Maps

```
<!DOCTYPE html PUBLIC "-//W3C//DTD XHTML 1.0 Strict//EN"
  "http://www.w3.org/TR/xhtml1/DTD/xhtml1-strict.dtd">
<html xmlns="http://www.w3.org/1999/xhtml">
<head>
<title>Yahoo! Maps JavaScript API Example</title>
<meta http-equiv="content-type" content="text/html; charset=utf-8"/>
<meta http-equiv="X-UA-Compatible" content="IE=7"/>
<style type="text/css">
    #map {
        border: 4px solid #000;
        margin: 40px auto;
        width: 600px; height: 400px;
        }
```

Example 14-6. Route marked out on Yahoo! Maps (continued)

```
</style>
<script type="text/javascript"
src="http://api.maps.yahoo.com/ajaxymap?v=3.7&appid="></script>
<script type="text/javascript">
//<![CDATA[

window.onload=function() {

    // Create a Map that will be placed in the "map" div.
    var map = new YMap(document.getElementById('map'));

    // Add the ability to change between Sat, Hybrid, and Regular Maps
    map.addTypeControl();

    // Add the zoom control. Long specifies a Slider versus a "+" and "-" zoom control
    map.addZoomLong();

    // Add the Pan control to have North, South, East and West directional control
    map.addPanControl();

    // create geopoint
    var point = new YGeoPoint(38.6247732, -90.183444);

    // Specifying the Map starting location and zoom level
    map.drawZoomAndCenter(point, 3);

    // add route
  var polyline = new YPolyline([
        new YGeoPoint(38.6242, -90.1838),
        new YGeoPoint(38.6252, -90.1886),
        new YGeoPoint(38.6298, -90.1870),
        new YGeoPoint(38.6281, -90.1717),
        new YGeoPoint(38.6229, -90.1738)
      ], "#ff0000", 5, 1.0);

    // attach to map
    map.addOverlay(polyline);

}
//]]>

</script>

</head>
<body>
<div id="map"></div>
</body>
</html>
```

The only difference, demonstrated in Figure 14-8, is that I used a red route with Yahoo! maps, as the coloring shows up better with the predominantly blue/gray background of the map.

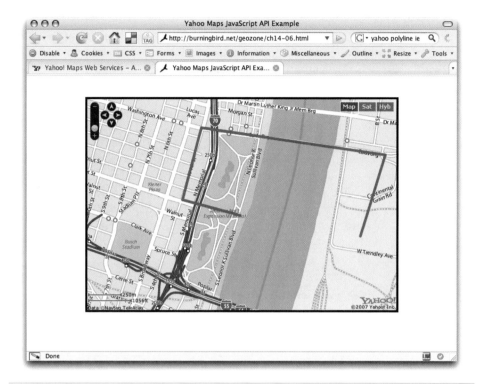

Figure 14-8. Route mapped out with Yahoo! Maps

There's more to Yahoo! maps, as well as Google maps, but we have enough to implement a couple of examples and see the maps in action.

Living Within the Geoweb

It's surprising how much of our everyday lives is associated with locations. Where we live, where our friends live, work, shopping, and entertainment—all have a location. Some of these locations are interesting to people outside our local sphere, and some are not. Among the locations of interest:

- The location of an event or party we're invited to
- Addresses for friends and family members
- Where a photo was taken
- Locations for great coffee shops, restaurants, parks, etc.
- Where something important is happening now

Finding Longitudes and Latitudes

Before you even begin to work with mapping tools, you need the ability to "map" between an address and its associated longitude and latitudes. Some of the map APIs work with addresses, but support is limited. Most of the mapping APIs work best with longitude and latitudes, but we don't always run around with GPS devices capturing these values as we travel about.

There are sites online that provide both values when given an address. Figure 14-9 shows the results from one of the more comprehensive of these sites, MelissaDATA (at *http://www.melissadata.com/Lookups/addressverify.asp*). The page not only provides the longitude and latitude, but also information about political representatives, school zones, police stations, postal data, and so on. Another site, maintained by Stephen Morse (at *http://stevemorse.org/jcal/latlon.php*), provides a results page from a lookup on addresses at various sites. It also provides a link to the resources the site uses.

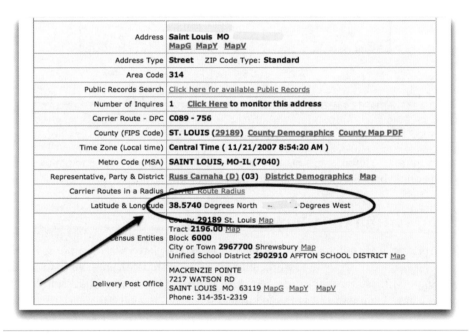

Figure 14-9. Result of a geo location lookup of an address at MelissaDATA

The GPS Visualizer, a terrific site if you're into geocaching, geocoding, hiking, and other activities related to maps, also provides an address-to-latitude/longitude converter at *http://www.gpsvisualizer.com/geocoding.html*. The site can also generate a map given a GPS file that has been generated by a GPS device. It makes use of Yahoo!'s geocoding API, introduced earlier in this chapter. You don't have to program an application, though, to use the service to look up a longitude/latitude from an address. A web browser query using the following format will return a small XML document with both values clearly listed.

This query, included at the Yahoo! site at *http://developer.yahoo.com/maps/rest/V1/geocode.html*:

```
http://local.yahooapis.com/MapsService/V1/
geocode?appid=YahooDemo&street=701+First+Street&city=Sunnyvale&state=CA
```

returns the following XML document, which can then be read for the location, or converted into a presentation using an application or something such as an XSL Transformation (XSLT):

```
<?xml version="1.0"?>
<ResultSet xmlns:xsi="http://www.w3.org/2001/XMLSchema-instance" xmlns="urn:yahoo:
maps" xsi:schemaLocation="urn:yahoo:maps http://api.local.yahoo.com/MapsService/V1/
GeocodeResponse.xsd"><ResultSet xsi:schemaLocation="urn:yahoo:maps http://api.local.
yahoo.com/MapsService/V1/GeocodeResponse.xsd">
<Result precision="address" warning="The exact location could not be found, here is
the closest match: 701 1st Ave, Sunnyvale, CA 94089">
<Latitude>37.416402</Latitude>
<Longitude>-122.025078</Longitude>
<Address>701 1st Ave</Address>
<City>Sunnyvale</City>
<State>CA</State>
<Zip>94089</Zip>
<Country>US</Country>
</Result>
</ResultSet>
```

Being able to get a mapping location via an address using a RESTful solution makes this a viable option for an application such as GPS Visualizer, or for one of your own applications—even if you don't make use of the Yahoo! mapping APIs. Speaking of using mapping APIs, it's time to look at a couple of examples for using online mapping.

Mapping a Photowalk with Yahoo!'s Maps

I purchased a GPS device because I like to take walks. I also use it to record GPS information when I'm out taking pictures. I especially like it because I can record a route I've taken, and then upload the data for the route. I can then use the data with Google Earth, or to plot a route using mapping software, such as Google or Yahoo! Maps.

Of course, mapping a route isn't as interesting if the route is just laid out, without any supporting information, such as accompanying text or, better yet, photos.

Example 14-7 creates a web page with a route marked between four of my favorite St. Louis places: the Arch, St. Louis Zoo, the Botanical Gardens, and the Art Museum. The application uses the YMarker object's addAutoExpand method to associate a small thumbnail image and location title with each marker. Moving the mouse over the marker pops open the photo, which remains until you move the mouse over another item.

Example 14-7. Annotating markers with photos

```
<!DOCTYPE html PUBLIC "-//W3C//DTD XHTML 1.0 Strict//EN"
  "http://www.w3.org/TR/xhtml1/DTD/xhtml1-strict.dtd">
<html xmlns="http://www.w3.org/1999/xhtml">
<head>
<title>Yahoo! Maps JavaScript API Example</title>
<meta http-equiv="content-type" content="text/html; charset=utf-8"/>
<meta http-equiv="X-UA-Compatible" content="IE=7"/>
<style type="text/css">
    #map {
        border: 4px solid #000;
        margin: 40px auto;
        width: 800px; height: 600px;
        }
</style>
<script type="text/javascript"
src="http://api.maps.yahoo.com/ajaxymap?v=3.7&appid="></script>
<script type="text/javascript">
//<![CDATA[

window.onload=function() {

    // Create a Map that will be placed in the "map" div.
    var map = new YMap(document.getElementById('map'));

    // Add the ability to change between Sat, Hybrid, and Regular Maps
    map.addTypeControl();

    // Add the zoom control. Long specifies a Slider versus a "+" and "-" zoom control
    map.addZoomLong();

    // Add the Pan control to have North, South, East and West directional control
    map.addPanControl();

    // create geopoint
    var point = new YGeoPoint(38.62069, -90.24685);

    // Specifying the Map starting location and zoom level
    map.drawZoomAndCenter(point, 5);
    // create points
    var botanical = new YGeoPoint(38.615646, -90.258865);
    var museum = new YGeoPoint(38.641629,-90.296244);
    var zoo = new YGeoPoint(38.634422,-90.2890778);
    var arch = new YGeoPoint(38.62507, -90.184621);

    var marker1 = new YMarker(botanical);
    var marker2 = new YMarker(museum);
    var marker3 = new YMarker(zoo);
    var marker4 = new YMarker(arch);
```

Example 14-7. Annotating markers with photos (continued)

```
    // add route
    var polyline = new YPolyline([botanical, zoo, museum, arch
        ], "#ff0000", 5, 1.0);

    // attach to map
    map.addOverlay(polyline);

    // add annotated markers
    marker1.addAutoExpand("<img src='botanical.jpg'><br />Botanical Gardens");
    map.addOverlay(marker1);

    marker2.addAutoExpand("<img src='museum.jpg'><br />Art Museum");
    map.addOverlay(marker2);

    marker3.addAutoExpand("<img src='zoo.jpg'><br />St. Louis Zoo");
    map.addOverlay(marker3);

    marker4.addAutoExpand("<img src='arch.jpg'><br />The Arch");
    map.addOverlay(marker4);

}
//]]>

</script>

</head>
<body>
<div id="map"></div>
</body>
</html>
```

Simple, 1-2-3. Figure 14-10 shows the map without a marker selected, and Figure 14-11 shows it with a marker selected.

The next section demonstrates how an event can be microformatted and a map generated to support the event.

> The drawn route doesn't quite match the markers when running Example 14-7 in IE8, beta 1. However, the markers and the images work fine. Your own experience may vary, depending on the version of IE8 you're using.

Mapping an Event

Microformats are ways of using document structure and class names to annotate an event. Microformat-enabled applications can then pick up the event more easily. We can add an application to mine the event location and pop up a related map.

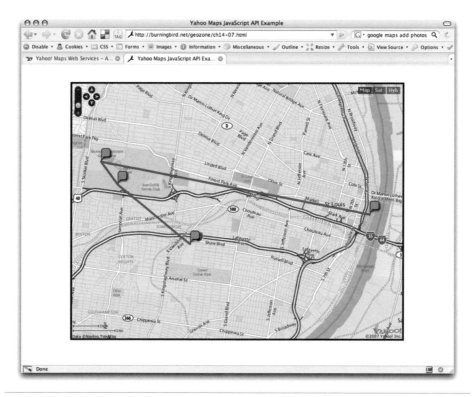

Figure 14-10. Route with markers without the photo annotation

The microformat structure for recording an event is known as *hCalendar*. An example of what you can find in a web page would be the following:

```
<div class="vevent">
 <a class="url" href="http://www.mobot.org/events/GardenlandExpress/glexpress.asp" >
www.mobot.org/events/GardenlandExpress/glexpress.asp</a>
  <span class="summary">Missouri Botanical Garden's Wilderness Escape miniature train
show</span>:
  <abbr class="dtstart" title="2007-11-21">November 21, 2007</abbr>-
  <abbr class="dtend" title="2008-01-01">January 1, 2008</abbr>,
 at the <span class="location">Missouri Botanical Gardens, St. Louis</span>
 <div class="geo"><span class="latitude"></span><span class="longitude"></span></div>
 </div>
```

Anything in the page tree can be accessed by this script, including the geo location included in the element with the geo class name. The geo data doesn't even have to be displayed: it can be hidden using CSS, which still leaves it available for application use.

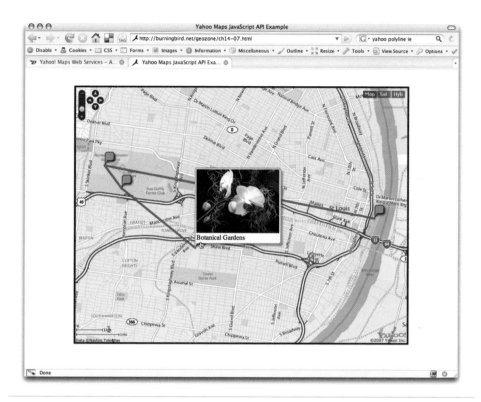

Figure 14-11. Route with the Botanical Garden marker active and the photo displayed

Example 14-8 is the last example we'll look at in this chapter. In the web page created, a div element is added as a button associated with a calendared event. Clicking on the button opens the Yahoo! map, and then triggers processing to pull in the latitude and longitude to add and center a new map. The map also has a photo attached from the previous year's event: a model train show.

Example 14-8. Mapping microformats and maps

```
<!DOCTYPE html PUBLIC "-//W3C//DTD XHTML 1.0 Strict//EN"
  "http://www.w3.org/TR/xhtml1/DTD/xhtml1-strict.dtd">
<html xmlns="http://www.w3.org/1999/xhtml">
<head>
<title>Yahoo Maps JavaScript API Example</title>
<meta http-equiv="content-type" content="text/html; charset=utf-8"/>
<meta http-equiv="X-UA-Compatible" content="IE=7"/>
<style type="text/css">
```

Example 14-8. Mapping microformats and maps (continued)

```
    #map {
        border: 3px solid #ffcc00;
        margin: 40px auto;
        width: 600px; height: 400px;
        display: none;
        }
    .mapit {
        padding: 5px;
        background-color: #ffcc00;
        margin-top: 20px;
        border: 2px outset #000;
        font-size: smaller;
        cursor: pointer;
        width: 40px;
    }
    .geo {
        display: none;
    }
    a { text-decoration: none }
</style>
<script type="text/javascript"
src="http://api.maps.yahoo.com/ajaxymap?v=3.7&appid="></script>
<script type="text/javascript">
//<![CDATA[

window.onload=function( ) {

    // attach event handler for mapits
    var mapits = document.getElementsByTagName("div");
    for (var k = 0; k < mapits.length; k++) {
        if (mapits[k].className == 'mapit')
            mapits[k].onclick=mapit;
    }
}

function mapit(evnt) {
    evnt = evnt ? evnt : window.event;
    var target = evnt.target ? evnt.target : evnt.srcElement;
    var children = target.parentNode.childNodes;

    var latitude = longitude = null;
    for (var i = 0; i < children.length; i++) {
        if (children[i].className == "geo") {
            var geokids = children[i].childNodes;
            for (var j = 0; j < geokids.length; j++) {
                if (geokids[j].className == 'latitude')
                    latitude = geokids[j].firstChild.data;
```

Example 14-8. Mapping microformats and maps (continued)

```
            else if (geokids[j].className == 'longitude')
                longitude = geokids[j].firstChild.data;
        }
      break;
      }
    }

    if (!latitude) return;

    document.getElementById("map").style.display = "block";

    // Create a Map that will be placed in the "map" div.
    var map = new YMap(document.getElementById('map'));

    // Add the ability to change between Sat, Hybrid, and Regular Maps
    map.addTypeControl( );

    // Add the zoom control. Long specifies a Slider versus a "+" and "-" zoom control
    map.addZoomLong( );

    // Add the Pan control to have North, South, East and West directional control
    map.addPanControl( );

    // create geopoint
    var point = new YGeoPoint(latitude,longitude);

    // Specifying the Map starting location and zoom level
    map.drawZoomAndCenter(point, 3);

    var marker1 = new YMarker(point);
    marker1.addAutoExpand("<a href='trains.jpg'><img src='trainsthumb.jpg' alt='train show'
/></a><br />2006/2007 Train Show");
    map.addOverlay(marker1);
}
//]]>

</script>

</head>
<body>
<div id="event1" class="vevent">
  <h2 class="summary">Missouri Botanical Garden's Wilderness Escape</h2>
  <p class="description"> The Botanical Society's world famous holiday miniature train
show.</p>
<p>
  <abbr class="dtstart" title="2007-11-21">November 21, 2007</abbr>-
  <abbr class="dtend" title="2008-01-01">January 1, 2008</abbr>,
 at the <span class="location">Missouri Botanical Gardens, St. Louis</span></p>
```

Example 14-8. Mapping microformats and maps (continued)

```
<div class="geo"><span class="latitude">38.615646</span><span class="longitude">
-90.258865</span></div>
<a class="url" href="http://www.mobot.org/events/GardenlandExpress/glexpress.asp">More at
the Botanical Web Site</a>
<div class="mapit">MapIt</div>
 </div>
<div id="map"></div>
</body>
</html>
```

The way the application is coded, multiple events can be added to the page, and as long as the geo latitude and longitude are provided, the event is mappable.

Figure 14-12 shows the page before the map is pulled up. Notice how the geo location elements aren't visible? Since these aren't human friendly, there's no reason they need to be displayed. Figure 14-13 shows the page after the MapIt button has been clicked, and the photo attached to the marker has been expanded.

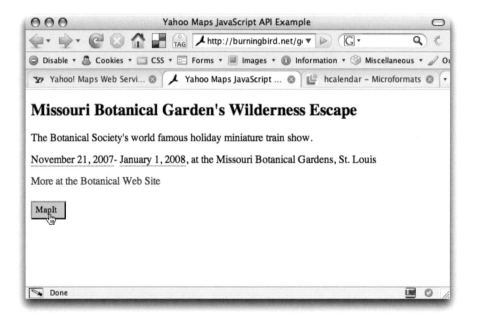

Figure 14-12. MapIt microformat example before the map is opened

This is just a start for what you can do with maps, but hopefully enough to get your creative juices flowing for your own web pages.

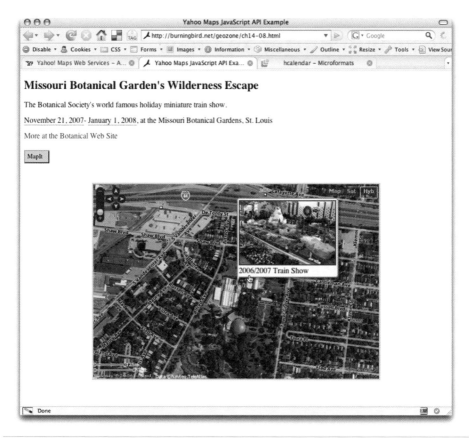

Figure 14-13. MapIt microformat/maps application with the map expanded

CHAPTER 15

Like Peanut Butter and Jelly: Data and Graphics

The Web is full of imagery. Images serve as buttons and bars; show the world around us; sell us homes and cars; make us laugh and cry, and, on occasion, irritate us. Most importantly, images inspire us. When we add web design, a good 50% of the content we see through the Web could be considered "web graphics."

Much of the imagery is static, mainly because we've not really pushed the boundaries of our use of dynamic imagery. We might put up a simple bar chart created through Flash, but most of our data representations are created using Photoshop, GIMP, Illustrator, or any number of tools, saved as our old friends JPEG, GIF, or PNG, and embedded into a page, to remain there until replaced when the data represented is outdated.

Text in web pages isn't statically rigid. Text is ever changing—words replaced, errors corrected, and thoughts reorganized. Why, then, must all our imagery be frozen, for all time?

It doesn't have to be frozen. Visual representation of data isn't a replacement but an enhancement. It's a way to provide a look at data that can be absorbed at a glance. It's not a replacement, because not everyone who accesses your pages is capable of appreciating the visualization. It is an alternative view—a rich expression of both a practical data application and creativity.

Years ago, while working with the data modeling group at Boeing, we experimented with visual data modeling tools, as well as text-based management products. We found that some people preferred the text format, but many were more comfortable with the visual. Providing both is a way of ensuring that all people get a chance to appreciate the data, and what it means, to the fullest. It gives people a choice.

Of course, one of the drawbacks to visualizing data has been the absence of an easy way to dynamically generate images to represent the data. You had to stop, get out the old paint routine, fiddle around with pie charts in Excel, and dump it into a static file, then get ready to do the whole thing again the next time the data changes.

Now, though, the Web is your oyster, and visualizing data has never been easier. Even old data structures, such as line graphs, take on a dynamic new life.

Graphs: Every Which Way but Static

A popular type of data chart is the line graph. A line graph compares two variables, each plotted along a different axis. Line graphs are used to depict things such as sales of an item over time or correct answers on a test taken by a class. They can also be used to graphically depict communications at a site, such as a weblog, by graphing out the number of comments per entry or post, as shown in Figure 15-1.

Figure 15-1. Line graph mapping the frequency of comments per entry or post

It's interesting what a visual representation of the data can provide at a glance. Looking at the line graph, one can quickly see that communication seems to be happening in cycles, with a couple of entries getting several comments, followed by several with a lower count, and then back again for a couple of popular posts, and so on. Providing data in two formats—as text or a downloadable file, and as a visual representation—gives people more than one way to receive the data, providing a richer experience.

Of course, after all these chapters you know that we can create line graphs for our web pages from dynamically changing data. However, you might be surprised at how many ways we can create the same image.

Line Graph As Inline SVG

An inline SVG-based line graph can be created in two different ways. One way is to use something like JavaScript to pull in the points with an Ajax web service call and then use the same script to plot the graph. The challenge with this approach is that the graph isn't available if scripting is disabled.

Another approach is to use a server-side language, such as PHP, to generate the line graph and include the code in the web page. When the page is accessed, the application code is processed and the line drawn.

The example shown earlier in Figure 15-1 was created using inline SVG generated using PHP in a server-side application, with the plotted points pulled from a database query. A better approach, though, is to cache the query values each time a new comment is made, and then just access this cached file each time the graph is re-created.

 A test file with comment counts is included in this book's examples.

To create a line graph with PHP and using a cached file of comment counts, each separated by a comma, a `div` element is added to the web page to hold the graph. On the server side, the PHP to generate the SVG is then embedded into this element. On the client side, the element is given a background color or image that makes the graph easier to see. For this example the background is set to a dark blue, and the line graph is a bright yellow.

In Example 15-1 an SVG polyline is created using the comment counts as points along the vertical axis, while each entry forms a point along the horizontal axis. Since vertical values in SVG grow "down," the comment count is actually subtracted from a baseline value before plotting, to make the graph grow "up" as the values increase. Whatever the baseline value will be is dependent on the size of the overall SVG element, as well as the comment counts.

For instance, if the comment count is 10 and the maximum comments are 50, subtracting 10 from 50 leaves 40, which is what's plotted. A comment count of 100 would plot out at 50, and a comment count of 50 would plot out at 0. Since the vertical axis increases "down" the SVG document, this ensures that the graph has a baseline of 50 for no comments and all other values plot "up" from that point.

The actual code to create the line graph is set in bold text.

Example 15-1. Comments line graph created with inline SVG

```
<?php    header( "Content-Type: application/xhtml+xml" ); ?>
<!DOCTYPE html PUBLIC
  "-//W3C//DTD XHTML 1.1 plus MathML 2.0 plus SVG 1.1//EN"
  "http://www.w3.org/2002/04/xhtml-math-svg/xhtml1-math-svg.dtd">
<html xmlns="http://www.w3.org/1999/xhtml" xmlns:svg="http://www.w3.org/2000/svg"
  xmlns:xlink="http://www.w3.org/1999/xlink" xml:lang="en">
<head>
<title>Line Graph: inline SVG</title>
<meta http-equiv="Content-Type" content="application/xhtml+xml; charset=utf-8" />
<style type="text/css">
```

Example 15-1. Comments line graph created with inline SVG (continued)

```
#graph
{
    background-color: #006;
    width: 800px;
    height: 100px;
    margin: 50px auto;
    padding-top: 100px;
}
</style>
</head>
<body>
<div id="graph">

<svg:svg baseProfile="full" version="1.1" width="800" height="100" >
<?php

$handle = fopen("comments.csv", "r");
$cts = fgetcsv($handle, 1000, ",");
fclose($handle);

if ($cts) {
    $points = "";
    $x = 0;
    foreach ($cts as $ct) {
        $count = 50 - $ct;
        $points .= "$x,$count ";
        $x += 10;

    }
    echo "<svg:polyline points='$points' fill='none' stroke='#ff0' stroke-width='2'
stroke-opacity='1.0' />";

}
?>
</svg:svg>
</div>
</body>
</html>
```

Notice how the svg beginning and end tags fall outside of the code? Since these are static, it makes no sense to generate them using server-side code.

The result, shown in Figure 15-2, looks the same when accessed from Opera, Firefox, and Safari. It doesn't, of course, show in IE since the example is using inline SVG.

The first line in the file is PHP code to change the header. Remember that inline SVG only works in XHTML documents. Since the extension for a PHP file is *.php*, we need another way to trigger MIME type, especially if we don't have the capability to set it with an *.htaccess* file.

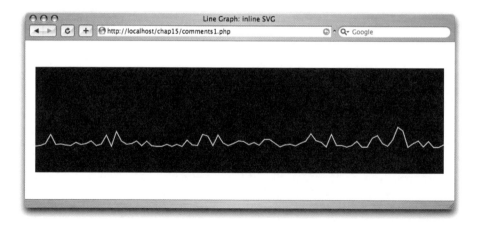

Figure 15-2. Comment counts built into a line graph using SVG and PHP

An interesting variation on this line graph is to create it as a polygon, using it to "tear" off the bottom of the div element by filling the polygon with the same color as the background color.

To create this variation, you just need to use a polygon instead of a polyline, and add two points: one to draw from the last data point to the end of the div element, and then over to the beginning horizontal position. The polygon is then automatically closed by filling in the last line, from the bottom of div to the top of div. Example 15-2 contains just the SVG and PHP for this variation (the rest of the document is exactly the same).

Example 15-2. Modification to the line graph, using a filled polygon

```
<svg:svg baseProfile="full" version="1.1" width="800" height="100" >

<?php

$row = 1;
$handle = fopen("comments.csv", "r");
$cts = fgetcsv($handle, 1000, ",");
fclose($handle);

if ($cts) {
    $points = "";
    $x = 0;
    foreach ($cts as $ct) {
        $count = 50 - $ct;
        $points .= "$x,$count ";
        $x += 10;

    }
    $points .= "$x,100 0,100";
    echo "<svg:polygon points='$points' fill='white' />";
```

Example 15-2. Modification to the line graph, using a filled polygon (continued)

```
}

?>
</svg:svg>
```

Figure 15-3 shows the results from this modification. It provides an intriguing and unusual visual effect, especially as it breaks the "boxy" mold.

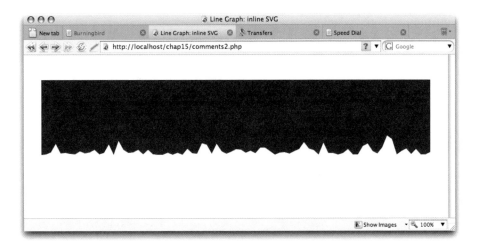

Figure 15-3. "Tearing off" the line graph along the bottom of a div element

One additional effect can be made by combining the polygon and polyline, and adding in a filter to create a highlighted, drop shadow below the line. This is an application of the shadowed edge demonstrated in earlier chapters, but used here with dynamically generated SVG. The modification to the application is shown in bold text in Example 15-3.

Example 15-3. Adding a color outline and drop shadow to the earlier torn examples

```
<svg:svg baseProfile="full" version="1.1" width="800" height="100" >
    <svg:filter id = "i1" width = "150%" height = "150%">
        <svg:feOffset result = "offOut" in = "SourceGraphic" dx = "0" dy = "5"/>
        <svg:feColorMatrix result = "matrixOut" in = "offOut" type = "matrix" values = "0.2
0 0 0 0 0 0.2 0 0 0 0 0 0.2 0 0 0 0 0 1 0"/>
        <svg:feGaussianBlur result = "blurOut" in = "matrixOut" stdDeviation = "3"/>
        <svg:feBlend in = "SourceGraphic" in2 = "blurOut" mode = "normal"/>
    </svg:filter>

<?php

$row = 1;
$handle = fopen("comments.csv", "r");
$cts = fgetcsv($handle, 1000, ",");
```

Example 15-3. Adding a color outline and drop shadow to the earlier torn examples (continued)

```
fclose($handle);

if ($cts) {
    $points = "";
    $x = 0;
    foreach ($cts as $ct) {
        $count = 50 - $ct;
        $points .= "$x,$count ";
        $x += 10;

    }
    $holdpoints = $points;
    $points .= "$x,100 0,100";
    echo "<svg:polygon points='$points' fill='white'  />";
    echo "<svg:polyline points='$holdpoints' fill='none' stroke='#ff0'
stroke-width='2' stroke-opacity='1.0' filter='url(#shadow)' />";
}

?>
</svg:svg>
```

The filter creates an offset clone of the original element, the polyline, and then desaturates the color before applying a Gaussian Blur and blending the results. It's a really stunning effect when you consider it's all dynamic and created using nothing more than a little markup, as shown in Figure 15-4. The effect shows up with Firefox version 3.0 and up, as well as Opera. Only the yellow edge shows up in Safari. In IE, all that shows is the blue background of the div element.

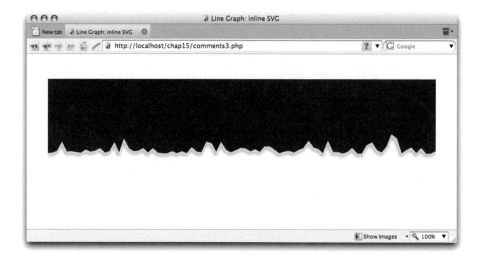

Figure 15-4. Outlining the line graph in yellow, and adding a drop shadow, overlaying the polygon

Of course, there is one way to make sure the line graph effect shows up with IE: use an embedded object, and have your readers install an SVG plug-in. Using an embedded object also works for all SVG-capable browsers if the page is served up as HTML rather than XHTML.

IE- and HTML-Friendly Embedded SVG Version

The PHP application to generate the SVG line graph demonstrated in the last section is no different when the SVG is included in a web page via an embedded object. The only difference is that the MIME type of the page creating the line graph is set to return SVG instead of XHTML.

The standard element to embed an external SVG file is object, which some older browsers don't support. To get around this problem, embed can be used as the fallback for when object isn't supported.

 Supporting embedded SVG files for all browsers is covered at the SVG Wiki, at *http://wiki.svg.org/SVG_and_HTML.*

Example 15-4 is an HTML page using the embedded object approach to include an SVG file.

Example 15-4. Embed as fallback for lack of support for the object element

```
<!DOCTYPE html PUBLIC "-//W3C//DTD XHTML 1.0 Strict//EN"
       "http://www.w3.org/TR/xhtml1/DTD/xhtml1-strict.dtd">
<html xmlns="http://www.w3.org/1999/xhtml" lang="en" xml:lang="en">
<head>
<title>Line Graph: using object</title>
<meta http-equiv="Content-Type" content="text/html; charset=utf-8" />
<style type="text/css">
#graph
{
   width: 800px;
   margin: 50px auto;
}
</style>
</head>
<body>
<div id="graph">
<object data="comments.php" type="image/svg+xml"
   width="800px" height="200px" >
  <embed src="comments.php" type="image/svg+xml" width="800px" height="200px"
     pluginspage="http://www.adobe.com/svg/viewer/install/" />
</object>
</div>

</body>
</html>
```

The pluginspage attribute for embed should trigger a download for the viewer from the appropriate place, in this case the Adobe SVG plug-in. Unlike the inline SVG, the background color of the div element isn't set. Safari doesn't handle the embedded SVG well, and adds a white background to the SVG element. In addition, IE's sense of width and height is different than the other browsers, which causes the line to come up short.

However, by adding a rectangle behind the line graph in the SVG file, as shown in Example 15-5, the application looks the same in all browsers.

Example 15-5. SVG generated by PHP to be embedded or opened directly

```
<?php header("Content-Type: image/svg+xml"); ?>
<svg xmlns="http://www.w3.org/2000/svg" baseProfile="full" version="1.1"
style="background-color: #006" height="200" width="800">
<?php

$row = 1;
$handle = fopen("comments.csv", "r");
$cts = fgetcsv($handle, 1000, ",");
fclose($handle);

if ($cts) {
    $points = "";
    $x = 0;
    foreach ($cts as $ct) {
        $count = 150 - $ct;
        $points .= "$x,$count ";
        $x += 10;

    }
    echo "<rect width='800' height='200' x='0' y='0' fill='#000066' />";
    echo "<polyline points='$points' fill='none' stroke='#ff0' stroke-width='2'
stroke-opacity='1.0'  />";
}
?>
</svg>
```

Figure 15-5 shows the page loaded into IE7 using the Adobe SVG plug-in.

 As has been noted elsewhere in this book, many of the examples don't work or only partially work with IE8. The application demonstrating adding a line graph using SVG in an object *does* work with IE8, beta 1, but it loads very slowly.

Another HTML-friendly, cross-browser alternative that doesn't require the web page reader to download and install a plug-in is to use the canvas element to generate the line graph.

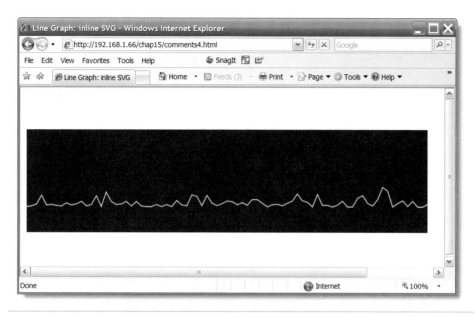

Figure 15-5. Cross-browser embedded SVG document loaded into IE7

The Googlefied canvas Alternative

The canvas element, unlike SVG, doesn't require a browser plug-in to work in IE. Google provides a JavaScript library that takes canvas element functions and converts them into VML without requiring any work on the part of the web page reader. Unlike SVG, though, the canvas element is a client-side technology. How, then, can the data points necessary for the line graph be included?

Again, this is where the aforementioned JavaScript approach could be used. JavaScript and Ajax web service requests could be used to invoke a web service, which then returns the points ready to process. However, you don't have to get so fancy or hip: the same PHP application that can generate points for the svg element can also embed the JavaScript necessary to create the canvas element.

Example 15-6 displays the code, markup, and script necessary to use the canvas element to create the line graph, using basically the same functionality we've been working with in previous examples. Just as with an embedded svg element, it's better to create the background in the canvas element, in this case using a filled rectangle. The PHP application is simple: read a line in from the file, and use it to create a JavaScript array. Since JavaScript arrays are comma-delimited, no loop is needed to process the data.

Example 15-6. Application using the canvas element to create the line graph

```
!DOCTYPE html PUBLIC "-//W3C//DTD XHTML 1.0 Strict//EN"
        "http://www.w3.org/TR/xhtml1/DTD/xhtml1-strict.dtd">
<html xmlns="http://www.w3.org/1999/xhtml" lang="en" xml:lang="en">
<head>
<title>Line Graph: Canvas</title>
<meta http-equiv="Content-Type" content="text/html; charset=utf-8" />
<style type="text/css">
#graph
{
    width: 800px;
    margin: 50px auto;
}
</style>
<script type="text/javascript" src="excanvas.js">
</script>

<script type="text/javascript">
//<![CDATA[

<?php

$row = 1;
$handle = fopen("comments.csv", "r");
$cts = fread($handle, 1000);
fclose($handle);

if ($cts) {
    print("var points = new Array($cts);");
}
?>
window.onload = function( ) {
    var canvas = document.getElementById("graphcanvas");
    if (canvas.getContext) {
        var ctx = canvas.getContext("2d");

        // blue background
        ctx.fillStyle="#000066";
        ctx.fillRect(0,0,800,200);

        // create line graph
        var startx = 0; starty = 150;
        ctx.strokeStyle = "#ff0";
        ctx.lineWidth="2";
        for (var i = 0; i < points.length; i++) {
          ctx.moveTo(startx, starty);
          startx+=8;
          starty=150 - (points[i] * 2);
          ctx.lineTo(startx,starty);
        }
```

Example 15-6. Application using the canvas element to create the line graph (continued)

```
      // write out the line
      ctx.stroke( );
   }
}
//]]>

</script>
</head>
<body>
<div id="graph">
<canvas id="graphcanvas" width="800" height="200"></canvas>
</div>
</body>
</html>
```

The element necessary to make this example cross-browser is the inclusion of the Google canvas element JavaScript library, *excanvas.js*. The example works with all the target browsers and looks exactly the same in each—a true cross-browser implementation. Of course, nothing is more browser friendly than using a JPEG, PNG, or GIF image.

 To make the canvas application work with IE8, you have a couple of options. One is to remove the DOCTYPE (demonstrated in the file *ch15-05b.html*), which runs the page in quirks mode, and the example works as both IE8 and emulated IE7. A second way is to add the compatibility meta tag, and use the Silverlight version of the ExplorerCanvas JavaScript library, as described in Chapter 11. The file *ch15-05c.html* demonstrates this option, and both approaches work with other browsers in addition to IE8, as long as the Silverlight plug-in is installed in the browser.

Heck, Just Create a Picture, It'll Last Longer

We haven't exhausted the by now over-familiar yellow-on-blue line graph. One last way to incorporate dynamic data with a visual presentation is to create a static image, but do so dynamically.

We have two options for creating the image from a PHP-based application: using either the built-in GD functions or the ImageMagick iMagick library. For this example I picked the iMagick library, but try the example out with both.

iMagick provides an object specifically created for drawing, ImagickDraw. Among its methods is polyline, which takes a multidimensional associate array of x,y pairs representing points. By default, both fill and stroke are black, so we'll also need to set the fill to dark blue and the stroke to yellow before drawing the line.

Example 15-7 contains the PHP application to create the image, including opening the points file and drawing the line graph with the ImageMagick functionality.

Example 15-7. Generating a static image using PHP, ImageMagick, and IMagick

```php
<?php

try {

    // create canvas
    $canvas = new Imagick( );

    // blue pixel
    $blue = new ImagickPixel("DarkBlue");

    // new image
    $canvas->newImage( 800, 200, $blue);

    // get data points from file
    $handle = fopen("comments.csv", "r");
    $cts = fgetcsv($handle, 1000, ",");
    fclose($handle);

    if ($cts) {
        $x = 0;
        $points = array( );
        $ctr = 0;

        // create array of points
        foreach ($cts as $ct) {
            $y = 150 - $ct;
            $point = array('x' => $x, 'y' => $y);
            $points[$ctr] = $point;
            $x += 10;
            $ctr++;
        }
    }

    // create drawing object, set stroke and fill
    $draw = new ImagickDraw( );
    $draw->setStrokeColor(new ImagickPixel("yellow"));
    $draw->setStrokeWidth(2);
    $draw->setFillColor($blue);

    // draw polyline
    $draw->polyline($points);
    // draw image on canvas
    $canvas->drawImage($draw);

    // Set the image format to png
    $canvas->setImageFormat( "png" );

    // print image
    header( "Content-Type: image/png" );

    // output image
    echo $canvas;
```

Example 15-7. Generating a static image using PHP, ImageMagick, and IMagick (continued)

```
} catch(ImagickException $e) {
    echo "Problems with image file ", $e->getMessage, "\n";
}
?>
```

To use the image, link the file like you would link any PNG image, through an `img` `src` attribute. Example 15-8 shows a web page that links to the application that generates the image. Figure 15-6 shows the generated image.

Example 15-8. Page opening an "image" generated by PHP and IMagick

```
<!DOCTYPE html PUBLIC "-//W3C//DTD XHTML 1.0 Strict//EN"
        "http://www.w3.org/TR/xhtml1/DTD/xhtml1-strict.dtd">
<html xmlns="http://www.w3.org/1999/xhtml" lang="en" xml:lang="en">
<head>
<title>Line Graph: Generating a static image</title>
<meta http-equiv="Content-Type" content="text/html; charset=utf-8" />
<style type="text/css">
#graph
{
    width: 800px;
    margin: 50px auto;
}
</style>
</head>
<body>
<div id="graph">
<img src="linegraph.php" alt="Line Graph" />
</div>

</body>
</html>
```

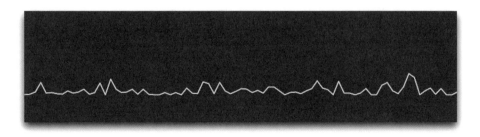

Figure 15-6. Actual generated PNG image

One benefit of this approach is that if the data doesn't change frequently, the PHP application could save the image to a directory the first time it's accessed, and then serve the saved image. When the data changes, the image can be updated.

Bars, Charts, and Pies

The examples so far demonstrate dynamic methods for showing data in a line graph, and the same approaches can be used when creating bar charts, pie graphs, scattergrams, and other statistical visualizations. Of course, the data may not suit the graph, but the technology has little to do with data/graph compatibility.

Example 15-9 describes a web page that uses the data from the earlier examples (100 comment counts per weblog post), but this time charts the data as a bar chart. Rather than "flip" the chart by manipulating the data, the chart is flipped by grouping the rectangles, and then flipping the entire thing using an SVG transform.

Example 15-9. Bar charting the comment counts

```
<?php     header( "Content-Type: application/xhtml+xml" ); ?>
<!DOCTYPE html PUBLIC
        "-//W3C//DTD XHTML 1.1 plus MathML 2.0 plus SVG 1.1//EN"
        "http://www.w3.org/2002/04/xhtml-math-svg/xhtml-math-svg.dtd">
<html xmlns="http://www.w3.org/1999/xhtml" xmlns:svg="http://www.w3.org/2000/svg"
        xmlns:xlink="http://www.w3.org/1999/xlink" xml:lang="en">
<head>
<title>Bar Chart: inline SVG</title>
<meta http-equiv="Content-Type" content="application/xhtml+xml; charset=utf-8" />
<style type="text/css">
#graph
{
   background-color: #006;
   width: 800px;
   height: 100px;
   margin: 50px auto;
   padding-top: 100px;
}
</style>
</head>
<body>

<svg:svg baseProfile="full" version="1.1" width="100%" height="200" >
<svg:g transform="rotate(180 510 90)">
<?php

$handle = fopen("comments.csv", "r");
$cts = fgetcsv($handle, 1000, ",");
fclose($handle);

if ($cts) {
   $points = "";
   $x = 0;
   foreach ($cts as $ct) {
       $y = ($ct * 2);
       printf ("<svg:rect width='10' height='$y' x='$x' y='10' fill='orange'
stroke='black' />");
       $x += 10;
       }
```

Example 15-9. Bar charting the comment counts (continued)

```
    printf("<svg:line x1='10' y1='10' x2='1010' y2='10' stroke='black' />");

}

?>
</svg:g>
</svg:svg>
</body>
</html>
```

Figure 15-7 shows the results of this inline SVG usage. As you can see, bar charts don't work out as well when there are a lot of data points, or when there are strong variations in the data controlling the height of the bar chart. To get this to show the frequency pattern, I've had to multiply the comment count by a factor of two.

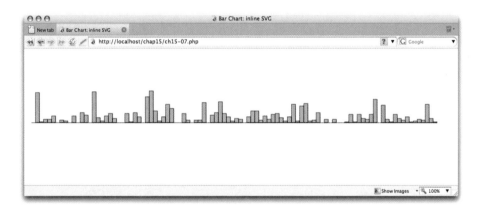

Figure 15-7. Sometimes bar charts just don't work

However, a different set of data could work nicely for bar charts. To demonstrate, I created a different data export, this one showing categories of posts and post count for each. There are only 11 categories, each one given a label in the exported file:

```
    Society,1322
    Environment,157
    Technology,905
    History,12
    Life,565
    Stuff,1025
    Photography,70
    Diversity,71
    Missouri,51
    Highlights,50
    Writing,153
    Graphics,375
```

We now have two pieces of data to incorporate—label and count—in addition to fewer data members. Let's also add a little visual appeal, rather than just placing a few plain bars on the page. While we're at it, let's make it more interactive.

In Example 15-10, the processing of the CSV file is altered because we now have rows, and each row has two values. However, the file contents are processed twice: once to determine the maximum width and height of the bar chart, and then a second time to get the individual bar values. The first run-through (getting the maximum height and width) allows us to dynamically alter the SVG group element, applying a translate transform to move the group to the right and down, since we'll be rotating it 180 degrees. If we didn't do this, the group would rotate right out of the picture.

Two linear gradients are used, one for the bars and one for a rectangle, which will act as the background for the graph. The calculated width and height are used to create the background image first, and then are used for the grouping. After that, the processing isn't all that different from what happens in Example 15-10, except the values are pulled from an array for each row. In addition, a JavaScript event handler for the mouseover event is added for each rectangle (except the background), which is then used to pop up the label when the person's cursor is over one of the bars. Best of all, clicking on the bar takes the person to the category page for the specific category.

Example 15-10. Interactive, brightly colored, and dynamic bar chart via SVG

```
<?php      header( "Content-Type: application/xhtml+xml" ); ?>
<!DOCTYPE html PUBLIC
        "-//W3C//DTD XHTML 1.1 plus MathML 2.0 plus SVG 1.1//EN"
        "http://www.w3.org/2002/04/xhtml-math-svg/xhtml-math-svg.dtd">
<html xmlns="http://www.w3.org/1999/xhtml" xmlns:svg="http://www.w3.org/2000/svg"
      xmlns:xlink="http://www.w3.org/1999/xlink" xml:lang="en">
<head>
<title>Bar Chart: inline SVG</title>
<meta http-equiv="Content-Type" content="text/html; charset=utf-8" />
<style type="text/css">
#legend
{
        color: #ffff00;
        position: absolute; top: 10; left: 10px;
        font: italic small-caps 900 16px Georgia;
        padding: 3px; background-color: #000;
        border: 1px solid #fff;
}
</style>
  <script type="text/ecmascript">
    <![CDATA[
```

Example 15-10. Interactive, brightly colored, and dynamic bar chart via SVG (continued)

```
      // add mouse over event handler to each rectangle
      window.onload=function( ) {
        var rects = document.getElementsByTagName('rect');
        for (var i = 0; i < rects.length; i++)
          if (rects[i].id != 'banner')
            rects[i].onmouseover=showLegend;
      }
      // display legends
      function showLegend(evnt) {
        evnt = (evnt) ? evnt : ((window.event) ? window.event : "");
        var rectangle = (evnt.target) ? evnt.target : evnt.srcElement;
        var width = parseInt(document.getElementById('banner').getAttribute('width'));
        var height = parseInt(document.getElementById('banner').getAttribute('height'));
        var x = width  - parseInt(rectangle.getAttribute('x')) - 45;
        var y = height - parseInt(rectangle.getAttribute('height'));
        var legend = document.getElementById('legend');
        legend.style.top = y + "px"; legend.style.left = x + "px";
        legend.innerHTML=rectangle.id;
      }
    ]]>
  </script>

</head>
<body>
<div id="legend">
Move mouse over bars to see category
</div>
<svg:svg baseProfile="full" version="1.1" width="100%" height="1600" >
<svg:defs>
    <svg:linearGradient id="gradient">
      <svg:stop stop-color='rgb(0,0,255)' offset='0%'/>
      <svg:stop stop-color='rgb(127,127,255)' offset='40%' />
      <svg:stop stop-color='rgb(0,0,127)'  offset='100%'/>
    </svg:linearGradient>
    <svg:linearGradient id="gradient2" x1="0%" y1="0%" x2="100%" y2="100%">
      <svg:stop stop-color='rgb(255,255,0)' offset='0%' />
      <svg:stop stop-color='rgb(255,127,0)' offset='100%' />
    </svg:linearGradient>
</svg:defs>
<?php

$handle = fopen("categories.csv", "r");
$maxxx = 0;
$maxy = 0;
while (($category = fgetcsv($handle,1000,',')) != FALSE) {
    $y =  $category[1];
    if ($y > $maxy) $maxy = $y;
    $maxx += 50;
}
```

Example 15-10. Interactive, brightly colored, and dynamic bar chart via SVG (continued)

```
print("<svg:rect id='banner' width='$maxx' height='$maxy' x='0' y='0'
fill='url(#gradient2)' stroke='black' style='z-index: -1' />");
print("<svg:g id='container' transform='translate($maxx $maxy) rotate(180)'>");

rewind($handle);

$x = 0;
$ctr = 0;
$maxy = 0;
while (($category = fgetcsv($handle,1000,',')) != FALSE) {
    $y =  $category[1];
    if ($y > $maxy) $maxy = $y;
    $legend = $category[0];
    print("<svg:a xlink:href='http://burningbird.net/category/$legend/'><svg:rect
id='$legend' width='50' height='$y' x='$x'
            y='0' style='fill:url(#gradient);' stroke='navy' /></a>");
    $x += 50;
    $ctr++;
}
fclose($handle);
echo "</svg:g>";

?>
</svg:svg>
</body>
</html>
```

Notice in the code to assign the legends to the bar chart that the position of the item is adjusted for the fact that the reference for the graph is 180 degrees different from the document: the document's left is the graph's right, and the top is the graph's bottom. Figure 15-8 shows the page just after loading, and Figure 15-9 shows it with the mouse over the Technology category.

Reading the values in twice may seem like overkill, and it wouldn't be necessary if we knew ahead of time the number of categories and the maximum height of a bar. However, with the way the bar chart is created, we can add new categories to the CSV file, and the counts can change. For instance, Figure 15-10 shows the same page, except I've added four new categories to the CSV file. Oh, and I've changed the colors, to get a little variety.

Bar charts are relatively simple to create, but I've always had a problem with creating pie charts. Luckily, others have persevered more than I have, and created reusable libraries that can generate any number of graphs: line, bar charts, scattergrams, and so on. The web site, CSS Juice, has gathered most such libraries into a single page of links at *http://cssjuice.com/22-code-snippets-for-creating-decent-charts/*. The libraries do everything from manipulating div elements into bar charts to creating charts dynamically with SVG or the canvas element.

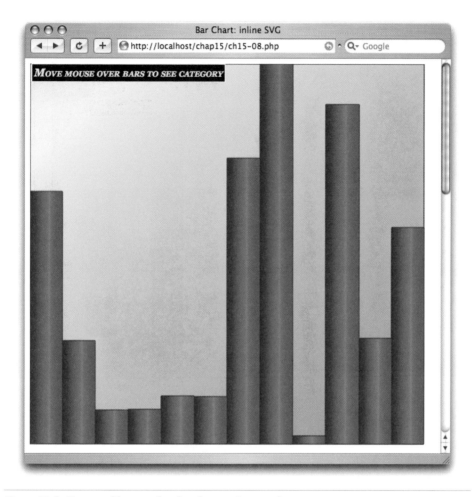

Figure 15-8. Generated bar graph, after the page is opened

Mining Your Photos

In earlier chapters, we peeked beneath the hard surface of our photos. In this chapter, I want to cover mining your photos for information and then using that information effectively.

When you use most of the photo editors I covered in Chapter 3, you're given the option to edit metadata associated with each image. This metadata includes title, description, photographer, keywords, and a whole lot of other information. This is then added to the information that most cameras add to the photo, such as aperture, ISO, and other relevant data. Each photo becomes a miniature filesystem, with data that can be accessed, edited, and restored.

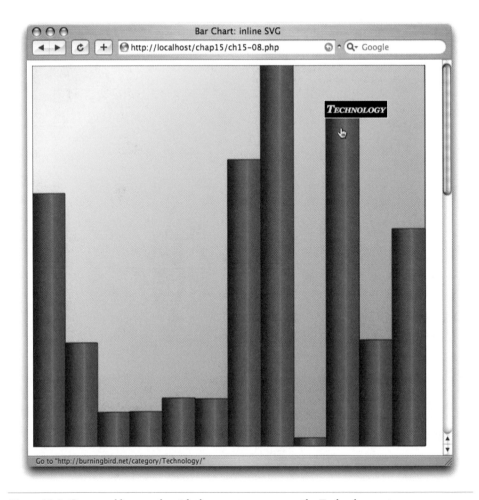

Figure 15-9. Generated bar graph, with the mouse cursor over the Technology category

If you're really interested in what you can store in a photo, check out Stepic, a Python tool that supports steganography: storing information in photos. Stepic is available at *http://domnit.org/2007/02/stepic*.

Most of the online photo sites, such as Flickr, can read this data and do something with it. For instance, the sites will pull out title, keywords, and description, and use this data to annotate the photo at the site so you don't have to. The keywords typically get built into tags for external search, and if present, they'll also list the EXIF camera information, which is really handy for people wondering about the camera settings for a photo.

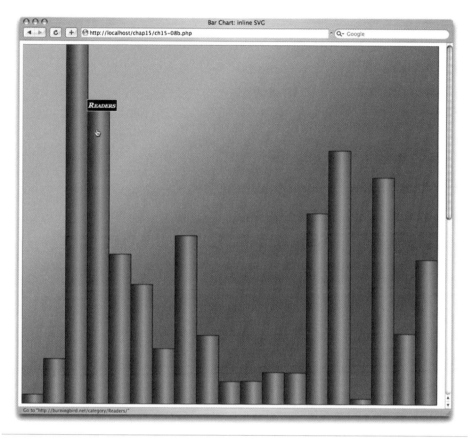

Figure 15-10. Bar chart with new entries and changed gradients

Among the keywords that can be added to a photo, two can be used to record information about where the photo was taken:

- geo:lat=38.48585
- geo:lon=−90.38273

Just as with microformats, covered in Chapter 14, photos can have their geo location recorded. By attaching this information to the photo, any site that provides functionality specific to geotagging, such as displaying a map or grouping by location, can make use of this information without any work on your part. You can also make use of the data in your own web pages, by mining the available metadata for the photo and utilizing it creatively.

To start, you need to add some metadata to your photos, as shown in Figure 15-11, which uses Photoshop. The data you add for use by an application typically has a different format than the one you use for people. Keywords for people are single items, like the following:

- cat
- Sharon
- Seattle
- Mountains

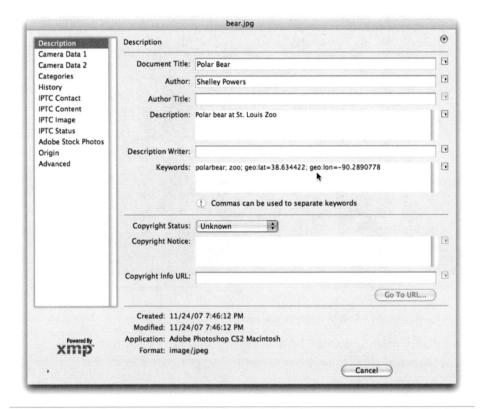

Figure 15-11. Editing metadata with Adobe Photoshop

These can be used for applications, usually to tag the photo for global search. However, other keywords are formatted specifically for use by applications. One way is to use the Dublin Core data set (a specialized set of information) to mark the data for global access:

```
dc:subject=garden
```

The latter technique, including namespace if any (such as dc:) and using equality, is how to *geotag* the photo:

```
geo:lat=(latitude)
geo:lon=(longitude)
```

Most programming languages have some functionality for mining the data out of a photo. PHP has some built-in libraries, and there are also external libraries. One I've used quite a bit in the past is Evan Hunter's PHP JPEG Metadata Toolkit (at *http://www.ozhiker.com/electronics/pjmt/*). It's not been updated for over a year, but it's pretty complete. Included with the library is an example page, which you can pass a photo to and have it display all the metadata present, including the data we've added, as shown in Figure 15-12.

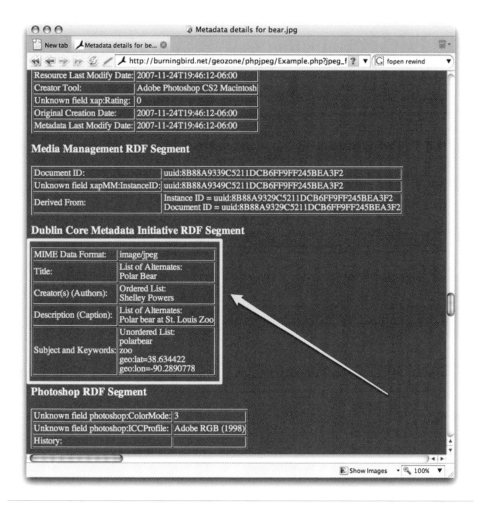

Figure 15-12. Metadata displayed using PHP JPEG Toolkit

There's a lot of data in a picture! It's a wonder there's any room for the actual picture!

Regardless of what you do with the data, I recommend downloading the toolkit to your site and running the *Example.php* application, passing in a photo located in the same directory as the file. This will give you a good idea of what kind of data you can mine from a photo.

 Want an interesting alternative to EXIF printed out as text? The camera type is also part of the metadata. Use it to pull up a picture of the camera, and then attach the EXIF data as an annotation to the image. The examples for this book include a subdirectory, *picturethis*, which demonstrates the various ways of using photographic data, including the suggestion just given, as well as merging maps and photo geo locations.

Rosy Glow of Completion

Years ago I attended a developers conference in Boston. One of the sessions I attended was given by one of the originators of the user interface design for Visual Basic. He was talking about how, in the future, every action a person takes in an application will generate feedback in some format. As an example he mentioned a form that would gradually change color as each field was filled in. He called it the "rosy glow of completion," or something along those lines.

In past years, we could implement a rosy glow of completion for forms using dynamic HTML, but we'd either have to create background images, or lose the gradually increasing effect associated with this technique. Now, with both the canvas element and SVG, implementing the "rosy glow of completion" is a piece of cake.

Example 15-11 shows a web form with a rounded box around the five input fields and div-based button. I used a div element because I didn't want to mess around with having to cancel a form submit, since this example is demonstrating just the visual aspect of the rosy completion effect.

Behind the form is an SVG rounded rectangle. As fields are filled in and the Try It button clicked, depending on how many fields are completed, the background color is gradually filled in with—what else?—a nice misty rose.

Example 15-11. Rosy glow of completion à la SVG

```
<!DOCTYPE html PUBLIC
    "-//W3C//DTD XHTML 1.1 plus MathML 2.0 plus SVG 1.1//EN"
    "http://www.w3.org/2002/04/xhtml-math-svg/xhtml-math-svg.dtd">
<html xmlns="http://www.w3.org/1999/xhtml" xmlns:svg="http://www.w3.org/2000/svg"
    xmlns:xlink="http://www.w3.org/1999/xlink" xml:lang="en">
<head>
<title>Rosy</title>
<meta http-equiv="Content-Type" content="text/html; charset=utf-8" />
<style type="text/css">
form
{
    width:590px;
    margin: 30px 0 0 30px;
}
```

Example 15-11. Rosy glow of completion à la SVG (continued)

```
input
{
    display: block;
    margin: 5px 0;
}
#tryit
{
    padding: 5px; background-color: white;
    border: 1px solid #000;
    width: 60px;
}
</style>
<script type="text/javascript">
//<![CDATA[

window.onload=function() {
    document.getElementById('tryit').onclick=checkFields;
}

function setStopColor(stop) {
        document.getElementById(stop).setAttributeNS(null,'stop-color','mistyrose');
}

function checkFields() {
    var inputs = document.getElementsByTagName("input");
    var ctr = 0;
    for (var i = 0; i < inputs.length; i++) {
        if (inputs[i].value.length > 0)
            ctr++;
    }

    switch(ctr) {
        case 1 :
            setStopColor('last');
            break;
        case 2 :
            setStopColor('last');
            setStopColor('fourth');
            break;
        case 3 :
            setStopColor('last');
            setStopColor('fourth');
            setStopColor('third');
            break;
        case 4 :
            setStopColor('last');
            setStopColor('fourth');
            setStopColor('third');
            setStopColor('second');
            break;
```

Example 15-11. Rosy glow of completion à la SVG (continued)

```
        case 5 :
            setStopColor('last');
            setStopColor('fourth');
            setStopColor('third');
            setStopColor('second');
            setStopColor('first');
        }
    return false;
}
//]]>
</script>
</head>
<body>
  <form action="">
      <p>Rosy Glow</p>
      <label>Field A:</label>
          <input type="text" id="fielda" size="60" />
      <label>Field B:</label>
          <input type="text" id="fieldb" size="60" />
      <label>Field C:</label>
          <input type="text" id="fieldc" size="60" />
      <label>Field D:</label>
          <input type="text" id="fieldd" size="60" />
      <label>Field E:</label>
          <input type="text" id="fielde" size="60" />
    <div id="tryit">Try it!</div>
  </form>
<svg:svg version="1.1"
    width="650" height="600" style="position:absolute; top:10px; left:10px; z-index:-1;">>
    <svg:defs>
    <svg:linearGradient id="gradient" x1="0%" y1="0%" x2="0%" y2="100%">
      <svg:stop id="first" stop-color="rgb(255,255,255)"  offset="0%"/>
      <svg:stop id="second" stop-color="rgb(255,255,255)" offset="25%" />
      <svg:stop id="third" stop-color="rgb(255,255,255)" offset="50%" />
      <svg:stop id="fourth" stop-color="rgb(255,255,255)" offset="75%" />
      <svg:stop id="last" stop-color="rgb(255,255,255)"  offset="100%"/>
    </svg:linearGradient>
    </svg:defs>
    <svg:rect x="0" y="0" rx="30" ry="30" width="600" height="380"
      fill="url(#gradient)" stroke="#ffcccc"/>
  </svg:svg>
</body>
</html>
```

Of course, in a real-world form, you'd also provide textual feedback about missing values, but as Figure 15-13 (one field completed) and Figure 15-14 (three completed) demonstrate, the implementation does provide great feedback.

The rosy glow of completion can also be implemented with the canvas element. All that's required is the ability to place a rectangle in the background and fill it with gradient colors at different stops. However, I do prefer SVG's look, and its finer control over rectangle rounding.

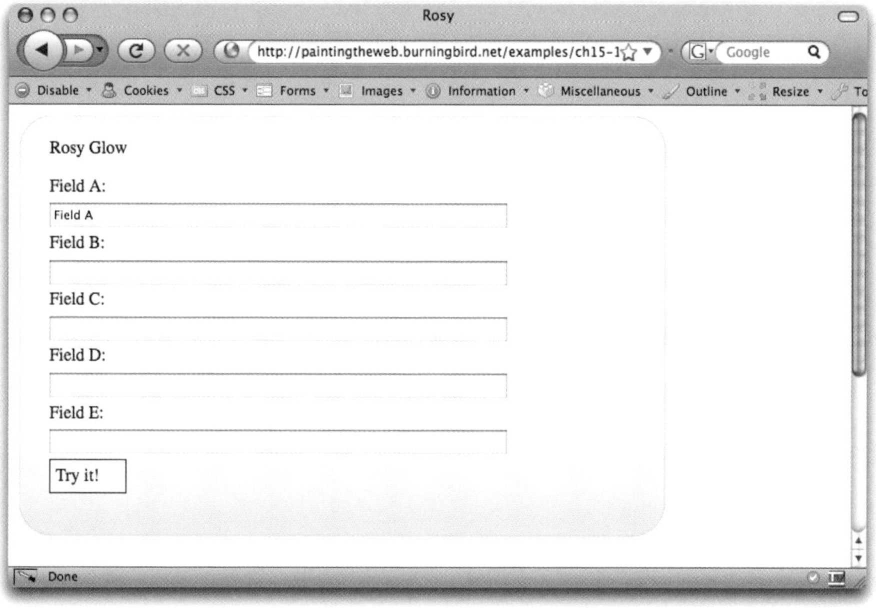

Figure 15-13. After one answer

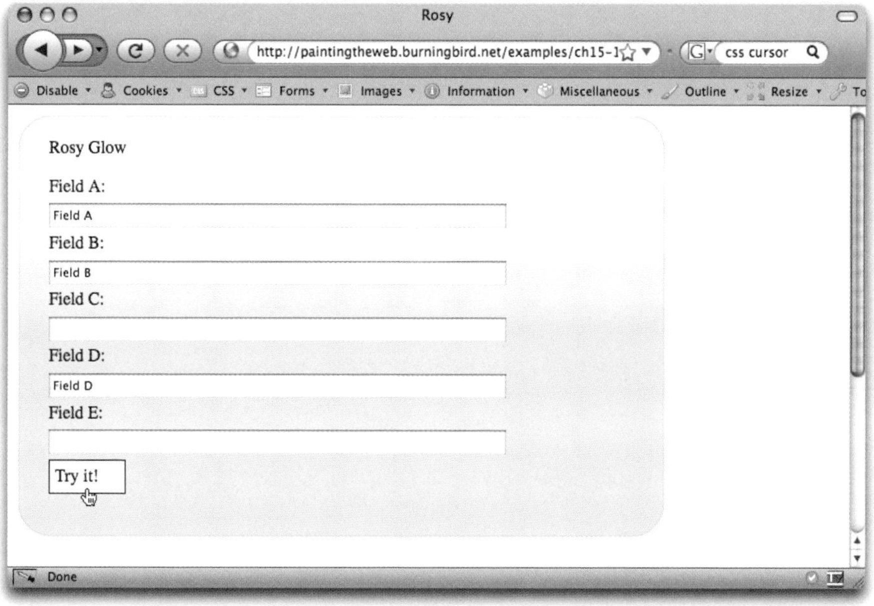

Figure 15-14. After three answers

One Last Look at Data and Visualization

Hopefully you'll come away from this chapter with some ideas of how you can present your data using visual elements. In this last section, I want to briefly mention some other forms of data visualizations you'll come across as you begin your own explorations.

The data: URI

Here's an oddball one for you, the data: URI. The principle behind the data: URI is to include image data inline rather than via an external file. The data can be HTML, script, an image, and, yes, even CSS. Our target browsers of Opera, Safari, and Firefox support the data: URI, but IE does not.

For web page purposes, the data: URI doesn't really buy us much. It is a way to generate an image using JavaScript without having to resort to a Flash-like workaround. However, with wider implement of both the canvas element and SVG, I'm not sure why the data: URI would be useful in the future for our own pages. It is, however, useful for posting images in forums that don't allow images but do allow links, since the data: URI is a link.

I'm including the data: URI mainly because it's an interesting and twisted trick, and the chapter wouldn't be complete without at least one such trick. I'm also including it because Greasemonkey scripts will use the data: URI to insert small graphics into web pages.

To create the URI for use as a data: URI, all you need is a base-64 encoding function, such as that provided by PHP and most other common programming languages. There are also web sites that generate the data: URI for us given a URL, HTML, text, image, or even script.

 Greasemonkey, available at *http://greasepot.net*, is a Firefox extension that modifies web pages in the browser. One data: URI encoder is at *http://www.scalora.org/projects/uriencoder/*. Another is the data: URI kitchen, at *http://software.hixie.ch/utilities/cgi/data/data*.

The format for a data: URI is:

```
data:[<MIME-type>][;base64],<data>
```

The MIME type specifies the type of data, such as image/png; the base64 denotes base-64 encoding. If the base64 is missing, standard URL encoding is used. An example of a very small icon is given in the following data: URI:

```
<img src='data:image/
png;base64,AAABAAEAEBAAAAAAAAABoBQAAFgAAACgAAAAQAAAAIAAAAEACAAAAAAAQAEAAAAAAAAAAAAAA
AAAAAAAAAAAAAA////AM18LACpq6wAUFBQAP/
PgQBzNAAA1tbVAJZOUwDio2IAISIiAIeHhwD+4LMAllQUAEUfBADgwaEA848sAGZmZAD+9t4At39GALJpJQDp
toMAJxMDAGpCGwC8vLwADxARADExMQDt7e4AdXRyAIFPHgDPtZYA/bx1AJSUlAD+z5cAhUYMAEstEQATBQAA/
+fFAE5FQwDuyqQA//zvAN/f3wDAdCcAFRgfAFIlAAD33b8A/+zSAK16RADO8/MA//
XoAPn5+QAQCwcACgQAALe3twBMHgAA4dzYABsdHwAYGBkA/tKRABQTEwD///QAFQOFAP/
24wBIKRAA+969APm6dgADAgAAUVJSAImIhQAPCQYYA19fXADEwLwD+/v4A3t7eALi4uAALAwAAUVFRAAEAAAD/
//4A//
zwABUZHwAxMDAAqqusAAAAAAAAAAAAAAAAAAAAAAAAAAAAAAAAAAAAAAAAAAAAAAAAAAAAAAAAAAAAAAAAAAAA
AAAAAAAAAAAAAAAAAAAAAAAAAAAAAAAAAAAAAAAAAAAAAAAAAAAAAAAAAAAAAAAAAAAAAAAAAAAAAAAAAAAAAA
AAAAAAAAAAAAAAAAAAAAAAAAAAAAAAAAAAAAAAAAAAAAAAAAAAAAAAAAAAAAAAAAAAAAAAAAAAAAAAAAAAAAAA
AAAAAAAAAAAAAAAAAAAAAAAAAAAAAAAAAAAAAAAAAAAAAAAAAAAAAAAAAAAAAAAAAAAAAAAAAAAAAAAAAAAAAA
AAAAAAAAAAAAAAAAAAAAAAAAAAAAAAAAAAAAAAAAAAAAAAAAAAAAAAAAAAAAAAAAAAAAAAAAAAAAAAAAAAAAAA
AAAAAAAAAAAAAAAAAAAAAAAAAAAAAAAAAAAAAAAAAAAAAAAAAAAAAAAAAAAAAAAAAAAAAAAAAAAAAAAAAAAAAA
AAAAAAAAAAAAAAAAAAAAAAAAAAAAAAAAAAAAAAAAAAAAAAAAAAAAAAAAAAAAAAAAAAAAAAAAAAAAAAAAAAAAAA
AAAAAAAAAAAAAAAAAAAAAAAAAAAAAAAAAAAAAAAAAAAAAAAAAAAAAAAAAAAAAAAAAAAAAAAAAAAAAAAAAAAAAA
AAAAAAAAAAAAAAAAAAAAAAAAAAAAAAAAAAAAAAAAAAAAAAAAAAAAAAAAAAAAAAAAAAAAAAAAAAAAAAAAAAAAAA
AAAAAAAAAAAAAAAAAAAAAAAAAAAAAAAAAAAAAAAAAAAAAAAAAAAAAAAAAAAAAAAAAAAAAAAAAAAAAAAAAAAAAA
AAAAAAAQBMmAOgBAQEBAQEBAQEuFEVDSQEBAQEBAQEBAQEBAQwNABoYAQEBAQEBAQEBAQEBQSwAOQsyAQ
EBAQEBAQEBAU8JPwAABAcBAQESNzABAQEBASoIFgAKRB4vFzNHAQEBAQEBAScdTUI9AFBMHAEBAQEBAQE8ECQ
AABlKAQEBAQEBAQEBMRUjNAA7RgEBAQEBAQEBBBTYAADUBAQEBAQEBAToGAAAgAQEBAQEBAQEl
KgAAEQEBAQEBAQEBAQEBTh8OAFEyAQEBAQEBAQE+Aks4KQEBAQEBAQEBASEiKxsBAQEBAQEBAQEBA
QEoD1IBAQAAAAAAAAAAAAAAAAAAAAAAAAAAAAAAAAAAAAAAAAAAAAAAAAAAAAAAAAAAAAAAAAAAAAAAAAAAAAAA
AAAAAAAA='/>
```

Yup, helpful stuff. The encoded image given in this data: URI is of the favorite icon, *favicon.ico*, from my web sites, which features a silhouette of a flying bird.

The encoders for the data: URI can generate CSS, script, or an image like the one just shown. The concept and the encoding are the same, just the surrounding material differs. It's an interesting idea, and a way of incorporating a small image that requires no storage.

Sparklines

Sparklines: the best thing about them is the name. Sparklines were named by Professor Edward Tufte, to describe small, intense, word-sized graphics embedded in documents. In the web world, the concept has been extended to mean small, high-resolution images embedded in content.

 See Professor Tufte's paper on the subject at *http://www.edwardtufte.com/bboard/q-and-a-fetch-msg?msg_id=0001OR&topic_id=1.*

In Chapter 6, where I introduced SVG, I converted larger musical notes into tiny annotations. These could be considered sparklines. However, most sparklines are similar to a line graph, but very, very small. Figure 15-15 shows the page at sparkline.org, which both demonstrates sparklines and provides a PHP library for same.

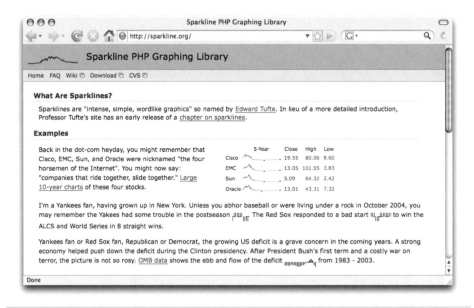

Figure 15-15. Example of sparklines

There are several libraries you can use that implement sparklines , and even a few web services. Joe Gregorio provides a Sparkline generator at *http://bitworking.org/ projects/sparklines/*, and there are dozens of implementations in most common programming languages, including PHP, Ruby, Python, and JavaScript. Most use the canvas element or generate a static image. Some even use the data: URI I just covered.

At the End of This Rainbow

I don't consider myself to be a great artist, photographer, or web designer. There are probably few people who can be considered "great," though many do a decent enough job. If the world of web graphics were restricted to those who are "great," though, what a colorless Web we'd create.

What I, and probably many of you, have isn't so much oodles of talent, or a degree or two in fine arts, but a love of graphics—matched with a passion for exploring new uses, new implementations, and new ideas related to visual elements.

In this book, we've explored how to get the most of your photos on the Web; investigated new tricks for image display; tried our hand at building sparkling graphics; tinkered around with all sorts of tools; and used any number of technologies to create imagery on the run. In none of the chapters did I begin with: you must have talent; you must be trained; this is for professionals, don't try this at home. On the contrary: do try all of the ideas introduced in this book at home. Better yet: alter them, improve on them, and generally have a blast.

Thank you for sharing your time with me. Now, go forth: paint the Web.

Index

We'd like to hear your suggestions for improving our indexes. Send email to *index@oreilly.com*.

Ajax web service
    canvas element support, 595
    as function calls, 10
    useful nature, 17
aliases, namespaces and, 232
align attribute (img), 43
alpha transparency, 40
alt attribute (img)
    accessibility support, 43
    embedding photos, 137
    specificity rule, 317
Amazon S3 (Simple Storage Service), 53
ampersand (&), 532
anchor element, 135
animate element (svg), 474, 480, 481
animateColor element (svg), 474
animated GIFs
    ImageMagick support, 543–548
    overview, 38
    Web Graphics Hall of Shame, 17
animateMotion element (svg), 474, 476–477
animateTransform element (svg), 474,
        477–480
animations
    animated clock, 487–501
    Bubblemark test site, 393
    canvas element and, 504–508
    GIF support, 17, 38, 543–548
    SVG support, 234, 252, 473–481,
        493–501
anti-aliasing, 40, 41
Apache Batik toolset, 302
Apple Aperture tool, 57, 113–115, 151–153
Apple iPhone, 125
Apple iWeb, 391
application icons, 181, 182
A-Prompt tool, 391
arc element (vml), 225
arc function (canvas), 439, 440, 444
arcSize attribute (vml), 224
asterisk (*), 311
attributeName attribute (svg), 474
attributeType attribute (svg), 475, 480
Avidan, Shai, 126

B

background attribute, 20
background images
    additional resources, 392
    creating, 346, 347
    shadow effect, 361
backslash (\), 549

badges
    application icons and, 182
    defined, 181
    glowing, 187–191
    rounded rectangles, 169
    shiny irregular, 183–186
Bailey, Bob, 388
bandwidth
    image storage, 50, 51
    mobile sizing, 123
    sizing considerations, 8, 9
bar charts, 600–604
base2 library, 10
base-64 encoding function, 614
baseProfile attribute (svg), 232
batik-rasterizer tool, 302
BBEdit editor, 390
begin attribute (svg), 474
beginPath function (canvas), 443, 445
Berners-Lee, Tim, 16
beveled effect, 142–143
Bézier curves
    canvas element support, 445, 447–452
    cubic, 275, 280–282
    Inkscape support, 298
    quadratic, 275, 277–280
    VML curve element, 224
bezierCurveTo function (canvas), 445
bgcolor attribute, 20
Bicubic algorithm, 122
binary transparency, 40
bindEventListener function, 409
bitmap graphics (see raster graphics)
bitmap images
    tracing, 298
    VectorMagic support, 302–303
bitshifting, PHP, 532
black-and-white conversion
    GIMP, 107, 108
    ImageMagick, 547
    overview, 80–83
    Paint Shop Pro, 103
    Paint.NET, 105
    Photoshop Elements, 100
blink element, 19
Blogger site, 391
Bluefish editor, 390
blueMarine workflow tool, 57, 113
blur attribute (svg), 496
blur effect
    ImageMagick support, 544
    manipulating photos, 84–88

GIF (Graphics Interchange Format)
  additional information, 38
  animation, 17, 38, 543–548
  image optimization, 44, 45
  ImageMagick support, 537
  lossless compression, 37–38, 44
  overview, 22–24, 36
  PHP/GD support, 524
  SVG support, 272
  throbbers, 17, 38
  transparency, 23, 40, 41
GIMP (GNU Image Manipulation Program)
  color matching, 79
  creating shapes, 169
  functionality, 7, 106–109
  layer styles, 170
  shiny buttons, 171–173
  SVG support, 298
  UFRaw support, 60, 62
  wet effect for buttons, 180
GIMP Toolkit, 60
GIMPShop, 298
GLatLng object
  draggable markers, 562
  marking routes on maps, 564
  passing latitude/longitude, 560
glob function (php), 555
global whitespace reset, 311
globalAlpha property (canvas), 455
globalCompositeOperation property
    (canvas), 456, 458–461
GMap2 object, 560
GMarker object, 560
GNU Image Manipulation Program (see
    GIMP)
Google Maps
  API key, 558, 559
  background, 558
  centering/adding controls, 559–561
  draggable markers, 561–564
  marking routes on maps, 564–567
Google search engine
  canvas element alternative, 595–597
  canvas object support, 433
GPolyline object, 564
GPS devices, 577–579
GPS Visualizer site, 576
gradient element (svg), 264–266
gradient fill
  Adobe Photoshop, 184, 198, 203
  canvas object support, 461–464
  GIMP support, 171

SVG support, 264–266
  tool functionality, 169
Gradient Fill tool (Photoshop)
  reflecting screenshots, 203
  shiny irregular badges, 184
  truly reflecting reflections, 198
Graphics Interchange Format (see GIF)
Greasemonkey extension (Firefox), 614
Gregorio, Joe, 616
group effects, 149–151
group element (vml), 228
groups, SVG elements as, 272
GRSites site, 392
Guardian Unlimited site, 355–356

H

H (horizontal) command, 274
hCalendar microformat, 317, 579–580
hCard microformat, 317
HDR (High Definition Resolution), 153
head element (html)
  DOM example, 398
  JavaScript support, 396
  VML support, 223
height attribute (img), 20, 38, 43
height attribute (svg), 252, 253, 284
Hellsing, David, 354, 355
Henderson, Lofton, 216
hexadecimal format
  Opera browser, 402
  SVG support, 241, 253
High Definition Resolution (HDR), 153
high key photographs, 66
Highslide software, 136
histograms, photo, 66, 71
horizontal accordions, 424–432
horizontal lists, 330–332
horizontal pages, 380
hot linking, 49
HotDog Pro editor, 390
href attribute (xlink), 237, 265
hspace attribute (img), 20, 38, 43
HSV color model, 26
.htaccess files, 49, 246
HTML
  animation comparison, 393
  canvas object support, 433, 437, 459, 461
  closing tags, 396
  design considerations, 360
  embedded SVG example, 593–594
  embedding photos, 139–140

International Color Consortium (ICC), 33
Internet Explorer browser
    canvas object support
        example workarounds for IE8, 434,
          502
        lack of support in IE8, 434, 502
    CSS support, 400, 402
    embedded scripting, 483, 484, 492
    embedded SVG example, 593–594
    Media Machines Flux plug-in, 219
    opacity support, 415
        example workarounds for IE8, 416
        lack of support in IE8, 416
    porting data: URI, 614
    Silverlight support, 436
    SVG animation and, 474
    SVG support, 233, 242, 243, 589, 592
    SwirlX3D plug-in, 219
    transparency limitations, 556
    VML support, 222, 223, 227, 229, 564

J

Java language, 393, 537
Java2D API, 302
JavaScript
    animation comparison, 393
    assigning properties dynamically, 415
    canvas element support, 433, 501
    canvas object support, 595–597
    color fade, 406
    data: URI support, 614
    element support, 396
    mobile sizing, 124
    programming with images, 420–423
    stylesheet switchers, 333, 334
    SVG support, 236, 482
JavaScript replace method, 419
JavaScript switch statement, 408, 409
Joint Photographic Experts Group (see JPEG)
JPEG (Joint Photographic Experts Group)
    animated GIFs, 543
    converting to PNG, 540
    digital camera support, 57
    drop shadows, 128
    image optimization, 45
    ImageMagick support, 537
    LCD for color, 35–36
    lossy compression, 23, 31, 32
    managed color, 32–34
    overview, 22–24, 30
    PHP/GD support, 524
    SVG support, 272

JPEG2000 format, 40
JPEGCrops tool, 45
JQuery library, 10, 402, 432
Juicy Studio site, 392

K

KhtmlOpacity attribute, 415
knockouts (see cut-outs)
Koppanen, Mikko, 553, 554

L

L (lineto) command, 274
ladder masks, 142–145
lasso tools, 100, 103, 105
lat method (GLatLng), 562
latitude
    finding, 576–577
    Google Map markers, 560–564
    latitude/longitude converter, 576
    mapping events, 581
    Yahoo! Maps markers, 571–572
layers
    canvas element support, 458–461
    functionality, 169
    reusable ladder mask, 142–145
    shadow effect, 361–365
    shadowed border effect, 365–371
    styling, 170
    truly reflecting reflections, 198–199
LCD (lowest common denominator), 35–36
LCE (Local Contrast Enhancement)
    Inkscape support, 299
    Paint Shop Pro support, 102
    Photoshop support, 63, 87
leukophobia, 383
Levels tool
    Adobe Photoshop, 70–72
    Apple Aperture, 114
    Paint Shop Pro, 101
    Paint.NET, 104
Levine, Matthew, 375
li element (html), 330–332
light manipulation
    consistency in images, 207
    editing photographs, 64–65
    shadows, 363
Lightbox2 application, 135, 136, 419
Lights special effects tool, 101
Lilley, Chris, 215
line element (svg), 236, 256–258

Mozilla browser
	canvas object support, 433, 440, 459, 461
	opacity support, 415
	SVG animation support, 474
	SVG support, 251
	SwirlX3D plug-in, 219
MozOpacity attribute, 415
mozPathText function (canvas), 461
mozTextAlongPath function (canvas), 461
mpath element (svg), 476
music notes SVG, 305, 307
musical notation SVG, 305

N

name attribute (img), 43
namespaces
	aliases and, 232
	defined, 232
	embedded scripting, 485
	SVG support, 232
	VML support, 223, 225, 564
navigation, 349–352, 358
NEF (Nikon Electronic Format), 58
nesting elements, 360–365, 394
.NET Framework, 391
New York Times, 356
Notepad, 389

O

object element (svg), 243–244, 487, 593
objects
	grouping in SVG, 237–239
	sizing, 287
	2D rendering context, 437
	VML support, 223
onclick event, 482, 504
onclick event handler, 412, 427, 483
onload event, 482
onload event handler, 483
opacity
	Google Maps support, 564
	ImageMagick support, 550
	overview, 410–419
opacity attribute, 415
Open Clip Art Library, 305
open loop workflow, 33
open source
	Bluefish editor, 390
	creating graphics, 10
	GD Graphics Library, 519
	photo manipulation tools, 57

photo workflow tools, 113
PNG optimizers, 45
software alternatives, 8
openInfoWindow method (marker), 563
openInfoWindowHtml method
	(marker), 563
openInfoWindowTabs method
	(marker), 563
openInfoWindowTabsHtml method
	(marker), 563
OpenLaszlo, 10
Opera browser
	canvas object support, 433, 504
	CSS support, 323, 400, 402
	embedded scripting, 483, 492
	mobile sizing, 123, 124
	porting data: URI, 614
	Silverlight support, 436
	SVG animation support, 474
	SVG support, 236, 242, 243, 261, 292,
		309, 589, 592
operating systems, 3D effects and, 222
optimization in numbers concept, 66
OptiPNG optimizer, 45
orient attribute (svg), 283
oval element (vml), 223
oval thumbnails, 130–132
Overlay blending mode, 78–80

P

p element (html), 317, 394
Paint Bucket tool, 78
Paint Shop Pro
	affordability, 7
	layer styles, 170
	overview, 100–103
	rounded rectangle tool, 169
	transform tools, 170
Paint.NET, 104–106, 169
palettes
	COLOURlovers site, 383
	defined, 37
Pascal language, 537, 553
path attribute (svg), 272
path attribute (vml), 227
path element (svg)
	creating patterns, 284
	cubic Bézier curves, 275, 280–282
	d attribute, 274
	elliptical arc curves, 276, 276, 284
	quadratic Bézier curves, 277–280

rotate attribute (svg), 261, 477
rotate transformation
    canvas element support, 464, 465, 466
    SVG support, 293–294, 477
rounded rectangles
    canvas element, 440
    purpose, 169
    SVG support, 252
    wet effect for buttons, 180
roundedRect function (canvas), 440, 441
roundrect element (vml), 224
row ordering technique, 45
Ruby language
    graphics support, 10
    ImageMagick support, 537, 552, 553
Ruby, Sam, 5
rx attribute (svg)
    ellipse element, 236, 264
    elliptical arc curve, 275, 276
    rect element, 252–253
ry attribute (svg)
    ellipse element, 236, 264
    elliptical arc curve, 275, 276
    rect element, 252–253

S

Safari browser
    canvas object support, 433
    CSS support, 325, 400
    embedded scripting, 483, 492
    embedded SVG example, 594
    porting data: URI, 614
    RGB support, 402
    Silverlight support, 436
    SVG animation support, 474
    SVG support, 236, 242, 243, 261, 292,
        589, 592
Safari WebKit engine, 492
sans-serif fonts, 384, 387
saturation
    black-and-white conversion, 80–83
    color fade and, 405
    light manipulation, 64
    manipulating RAW format, 58, 62
save method (canvas), 452, 466
Scalable Vector Graphics (see SVG)
scale transformation
    canvas element support, 464, 465
    SVG support, 293, 295–297, 477

Schewe, Jeff, 63
Schiller, Jeff, 235, 240
screen readers, 360
screenshots
    capturing, 208–214
    reflecting, 200–205
Scriptaculous library, 135, 432
scripting
    canvas element support, 501–513
    canvas object support, 433, 434, 437
    cross-document, 485–487
    embedded, 482–487
    SVG support, 234, 473, 482
seam carving, 126
Second Life community forum, 216
Secure Shell (SSH), 515, 539
selectors
    child, 315
    descendant, 314, 315, 316
    universal, 311–313
serif fonts, 384, 387
set element (svg), 474, 480, 481
setInterval attribute (svg), 495
setOpacity function, 422
shadows
    bordered effect, 365–371
    cast, 194–196
    creating with CSS, 324–327
    ImageMagick example, 550
    nesting div elements, 361–365
    (see also drop shadows)
Shamir, Ariel, 126
shape element (vml), 227
shapes
    application icons, 181, 182
    badges, 181–186
    canvas element support, 439–443
    canvas object support, 444–447
    graphics tools support, 169
    Inkscape support, 298
    predefined for SVG, 236
    predefined for VML, 223–226
shapetype element (vml), 227
sharpness
    manipulating, 64, 84–88
    manipulating RAW format, 58, 62
    Smart Sharpening filter, 94, 98
Shea, Dave, 353
shell scripts, 549–552

U

UFRaw workflow tool, 60–62, 106
ul element (html), 330–332
Uniform Resource Identifier (URI), 237, 614
units of measurement
    flexible design and, 372
    font size and, 241, 332
    (see also specific units of measurement)
universal selector, 311–313
University of Minnesota Duluth, 391
unsharp mask technique, 85
URI (Uniform Resource Identifier), 237, 614
usability, design considerations, 358–360
use element (svg), 237, 309
UTF-16 encoding, 263
UTF-8 encoding, 263

V

V (vertical) command, 274
v namespace, 225
validation
    CSS, 344
    design considerations, 360
vector graphics
    advantages, 215
    defined, 22
    SVG support, 230–241
    system requirements, 215
    3D languages overview, 216–221
    VML support, 221–229
    WebCGM, 216
    (see also SVG)
Vector Markup Language (see VML)
VectorMagic tool, 302–303
version attribute (svg), 232
vi editor, 389
viewBox element (svg), 287–293
vim editor, 389
Virtual Reality Modeling Language
        (VRML), 215–221
visualizing data
    bar charts, 600–604
    data: URI, 614–615
    line graphs, 587–599
    mining photos, 605–610
    pie charts, 604
    rosy glow of completion, 610–612
    Sparklines, 615

VML (Vector Markup Language)
    arc element, 225
    background, 221, 223
    canvas element alternative, 595–597
    canvas object support, 433
    curve element, 224
    fill element, 228
    Google Map support, 564
    group element, 228
    line element, 224
    oval element, 223
    polyline element, 224
    roundrect element, 224
    shape element, 227
    shapetype element, 227
    specification, 223
    SVG comparison, 230
    syntax, 223–226
    system requirements, 215
vml namespace, 223, 225
VRML (Virtual Reality Modeling
        Language), 215–221
vspace attribute (img), 20, 38, 43

W

W3 Schools, 122
W3C
    animation example, 476
    canvas specification, 436
    CSS validation, 344
    DOM specification, 397
    RGB color values, 253
    specificity rule, 316
    SVG specification, 243
    transforming SVG, 302
Watt, Jonathan, 232
web authoring tools, 390
Web Content Accessibility Guidelines, 387
web content management tools, 391
web design
    color management, 378–384
    div element consideration, 360–371
    flexible, 372–378
    graphics considerations, 8, 9
    minimizing confusion, 358–360
    purposeful sites, 356–358
    recommended elements, 349

Y

y attribute (svg)
    g element, 273
    gradient element, 265–269
    rect element, 252
    text element, 259
Yahoo Flickr site, 50–51
Yahoo! Maps
    API key, 559, 568
    background, 558
    centering/adding controls, 568–571
    mapping photowalks, 577–579
    markers, 571–572
    marking routes on maps, 573–575

YMarker object, 577
YMax attribute (svg), 289
YMid attribute (svg), 289
YMin attribute (svg), 289

Z

Z (close path) command, 274
zoom functionality
    canvas element, 504–513
    Google Maps, 559–561
    Yahoo! Maps, 568–571

About the Author

Shelley Powers has been writing about technical topics—from the first release of Java to the latest graphics tools—for more than 12 years. Her recent books, all published with O'Reilly, have covered the semantic web, Ajax, JavaScript, Unix, and now the world of web graphics. She's an avid amateur photographer and web graphics aficionado who enjoys applying her latest experiments on her many web sites.

Colophon

The cover font is Adobe ITC Garamond. The text font is Linotype Birka; the heading font is Adobe Myriad Condensed; and the code font is LucasFont's TheSans Mono Condensed.

Try the online edition free for 45 days

*Catching Users' Eyes—
and Keeping Them on Your Site*

Painting the Web

O'REILLY®   *Shelley Powers*

Get the information you need when you need it, with Safari Books Online. Safari Books Online contains the complete version of the print book in your hands plus thousands of titles from the best technical publishers, with sample code ready to cut and paste into your applications.

Safari is designed for people in a hurry to get the answers they need so they can get the job done. You can find what you need in the morning, and put it to work in the afternoon. As simple as cut, paste, and program.

To try out Safari and the online edition of the above title FREE for 45 days, go to www.oreilly.com/go/safarienabled and enter the coupon code WFUJSAA.

To see the complete Safari Library visit:
safari.oreilly.com

70502